Democratic Promise

About the author

Lawrence Goodwyn is Associate Professor of History at Duke University
and Co-Director of the Oral History
Program of the Center for Southern
Studies.

I hope we shall crush in its birth the aristocracy of our monied corporations which dare already to challenge our government to a trial of strength, and bid defiance to the laws of our country.

THOMAS JEFFERSON, 1816

The people need to "see themselves" experimenting in democratic forms.

DEMOCRATIC PROMISE

The Populist Moment in America

LAWRENCE GOODWYN

New York
OXFORD UNIVERSITY PRESS
1976

Photographic credits: *Arena:* pp. 137, 193, 263; Colorado State Archives: pp. 489, 502; W. H. Harvey: pp. 15, 454–55; Kansas State Historical Society: pp. 100, 106, 196, 198, 365, 511; Minnesota State Historical Society: p. 266; Montana State Historical Society: p. 526; Russell G. Pepperell: p. 61; *Puck:* 365; Mrs. Susie Roligan: p. 303; University of North Carolina: pp. 193, 504; University of Texas: p. 235; Wooten Studios: p. 37.

To Nell

Introduction

This book is about the decline of freedom in America, and that thought, culturally out of step as it is, presents a problem. Historians necessarily offer their understanding of an earlier era not only from the perspective of the present, but also within the constraints imposed by the present. In the highly politicized environment of the twentieth century, these constraints are formidable.

In both the capitalist and the socialist worlds, an unconscious presumption has long since settled into place that the present is "better" than the past and that the future will bring still more betterment. Progress, we are admonished in both quarters, is occurring. This reassuring belief rests securely on statistical charts and tables certifying the steady upward tilt of economic production in every "advanced" and "advancing" nation in the world. On this point, good capitalists and socialists agree—with respect to their own countries. However many imperfections may remain, everyone, it seems, is part of a "progressive society."

The assumption of progress extends beyond mere material

considerations to embrace what is now fashionably described as the quality of life. Especially for the millions on this planet who value mankind's experiment in democratic forms over the past three centuries, the quality of life is most crucially measurable by the extent to which open discussion is possible—the simple but profound conviction that serious ideas deserve a broad hearing, however much they might call into question prevailing customs in this or that country. In this realm of ideas, too, the twentieth-century presumption prevails with great authority: the present is generally more open than the past; progress is being made. To the abvocates of each, our sundry societies are safely "progressive."

In the United States the power of this cultural presumption is such that it is unnecessary in most circles to assert it. The thought is so thoroughly internalized within the society that it is part of the democratic culture itself. One result, however, is perhaps not immediately apparent. Our assumption of progress casts across the heritage a heavy shadow of modern condescension, grounded upon a curious kind of circular logic: the democratic strivings of the past must fall short by modern standards if the present is to be seen as constituting a higher pleateau. Both the condescension and the logic are edged with overtones of complacency. Thus, if the failure of Reconstruction consigned most black Americans to four additional generations of peonage, we can point to the legal advances of the Fourteenth and Fifteenth Amendments as concrete evidence of the progress that would someday come. Similarly, if Teddy Roosevelt was not remotely the trust-buster he wished his contemporaries to believe he was, we can pass on his harmless homilies to the younger generation and designate his time of prominence, fittingly enough, as the Progressive era. The idea of progress is thus not only consoling, it gathers additional power because it represents an ideologically essential defense of the culture itself. Historians are both the purveyors and the victims of this idea.

In an era of ideological confrontation on a global scale—an era, let it be acknowledged, of the intense politicization of knowledge throughout the world—there seem to be distinct limits to which good capitalist historians can criticize their own societies, just as there are limits within which good socialist historians can criticize theirs.

It is hardly necessary to add that historians are sometimes unhappy with this state of affairs, not only because they resist, no less than other mortals, the idea of being culturally confined, but because it offends their professional vision of free and untrammeled scholarly inquiry. However, their caution is evident in the circumlocution with which they deliver critical verdicts relative to the common national experience. Their distress is visible also in the release that is evident when they find something to praise. At such moments, the dull monotones of academic prose oftentimes become almost lyrical. In a world that (despite the abundance of progressive societies) is weary, we have no lyrical critics. Such are the constraints of modern culture—on both sides of the ideological curtain. If the historian acts as a cameraman, focusing his own lens on the common heritage, his is a fragile instrument, scarred by the grinding materials of history itself. His search for the symbolic meaning of the national experience, for the crucible of its culture, lures him onward, but both the national experience and the inherited culture are like mists that cloud his range of vision and obscure his quest itself. More often than not, the triumph of the received culture is so subtle it is not apparent to its victims. Content with what they can see, they have lost the capacity to imagine what they can no longer see. Ideas about freedom get obscured in this way.

In the face of such compelling hazards, anyone afflicted with historical curiosity must select his questions prudently, and pick with equal care the particular moment in the past to which they are to be applied. What *are* the central historical moments of the American experience? The Revolution? The Civil War? The Great Depression? And in in our attempt to unlock the secrets of these moments what are we to ask? In truth, are they really the right moments, the revealing moments, for us, in our time?

What of still another era, one falling between the Civil War and the Great Depression—the period that Mark Twain labeled "The Great Barbecue" and others have called the Age of Excess? It is now generally called the Gilded Age—a time of the first great gathering of American wealth, of the consolidation of new forms of power, and of experiments in ostentatious consumption. Is this the place to look? Many have seemed to think so; the era of the 1890's, culminating in the climatic presidential "Battle of the Standards" in 1896, has, over the decades, been the object of exhaustive scrutiny. Most seem to agree it was a time when the nation had critical choices, made them, and thereupon shaped the twentieth-century world we live in.

Even conceding this, there are reasons for passing over the Gilded Age in our quest for symbolic keys to the national experience. The "Battle of the Standards" was, after all, a struggle between one political party led by gold-standard financiers and another led by silver mineowners, a parochial contest within a narrow segment of the nation's emerging capitalist elite. Could a war between gold and silver coin truly be a "crucible of culture?" One that shaped our contemporary world? At first glance, one would be compelled to say no.

Yet some elusive force apparently was at work then, something surely seems to have been happening, for again and again, American political and cultural historians have returned to the 1890's with the persistence of a Diogenes, their lamps flickering in obscure corners in quest of some overlooked artifact, some undefined relationship that, once fathomed, would provide the elusive insight that would bathe modern America in new meaning.

Let it be said at once that this inquiry is a part of that continuing tradition. My lamp is aloft, and in corners that seem certifiably obscure. For though I have sought explanations about political power and cultural authority in modern America, I have not pursued either of the two contending parties in the "Battle of the Standards." Rather, I have probed a third party that distrusted both and had a vision of its own about a very different kind of America. I have operated under the presumption that the story of this third party illuminates the other two and, indeed, lights the culture itself. This third party was, of course, the People's Party.

Self-evidently, the People's Party was a political institution. But it was also "Populism"—a word that connotes something more than a party, something more nearly resembling a mood or, more grandly, perhaps, an ethos. Yet, the third party was also the Farmers Alliance, the least known of the ingredients in the protest movement we now call the "agrarian revolt." The Alliance was more than a party and more than an ethos. It was, in fact, a new way of looking at things—a new culture, if you will, and one that attempted to shelter its participants from sundry indoctrinations emanating from the larger culture that was industrial America itself. This fragile new culture defined American Populism, and Populism, so defined, provides a radically altered perspective on the Gilded Age and on modern America as well. For these reasons, Populism is not an obscure corner after all.

But if, in an intellectual sense, American Populism was more than a passing political creed, it was also less than a fundamental social theory. Indeed, its achievements in the area of social criticism, while interesting and revealing, do not, in my view, comprise the essence of the passionate happening we call the agrarian revolt. This is so for a number of reasons. First of all, before the People's Party was created, the institution known as the Alliance gave to American farmers in the 1880's a compelling new opportunity: it gave them, in their neighborhood suballiances, a place to think in. It also gave them something to think about—a massive cooperative vision of a new way to live. Finally, it gave voice to the vision—40,000 voices, in fact—mobilized from New York to California and marshalled as the "Alliance lecturing system." For seven years, the farmers, grouped together in a few hundred suballiances on the edge of the Great Plains, experimented in democratic forms in an effort to address the causes of the poverty of their lives. Gradually, they learned the strength of what they called "cooperation and organization." With growing confidence they learned a way to address their condition, and they also learned how to explain their way to others. It was a new democratic language, fashioned out of the old heritage, but straining to break free so as to give definition to liberating new conceptions about the social relations of man. This language began to take form in 1886 and the things it inspired came into full view in 1888. The movement, already in motion in a dozen states, then surged across the nation.

The new way of thinking developed by the people of the Alliance was grounded in large-scale cooperation. The edifice they constructed—the Alliance Exchange—was the world's first such working class institution. Its ultimate purpose addressed human needs with such compelling clarity that it generated something more than a mass movement, it generated new possibilities of individual self-respect and mass aspiration. These individual and collective hopes were beyond the range of vision of most Americans, then or later. But the political expression created by these aspirations would acquire a name: Populism.

The capitalist and socialist languages of political description available in the twentieth century cannot easily characterize the human ingredients that were at the core of American Populism. These modern terminologies are ideological, and therefore limited. The agrarian revolt does not yield easily to these languages, for Populism was both more and less than an ideology, as that word has come to be understood in the twentieth century. Consequently, for four generations Americans have not been able to understand that moment in their own history when a certain democratic ethos emerged in this country and then withered. There are reasons for this misunderstanding that go beyond mere limitations in the categories of political description. The industrial cultures that gave birth to and now support and constrain modern interpretive thought are part of the problem too.

It is essential to recognize that Populism appeared at almost the very last moment before the values implicit in the corporate state captured the cultural high ground in American society itself. When considered in their own time, and by their standards of hope rather than our own, the Populists not only come to life, they send a very different message than we have possessed the poise to hear. It is difficult to hear people, however, when we are trapped within our cultural need to condescend to them. To understand people who aspired in the past, we have to give ourselves permission to have significant aspirations in our own time. The Populists spoke clearly enough; the burden of hearing them is ours alone.

It is necessary, therefore, to hold the camera as steady as possible, letting events be recorded as they happen, letting the movement culture of Populism narrate its own flowering. The Alliance lecturers were articulate Americans; they help us to understand the story that our camera records. If we do not condescend too much to them, we can hear what they say rather clearly.

Populists were not capitalist reformers, as we understand that phrase in modern political language; neither were they socialists. Though their mass movement literally grew out of their belief in the power of man as a cooperative being, they also accepted man as a competitive being. They cannot conveniently be compressed into the narrow (theoretically competitive) categories of political description sanctioned in the capitalist creed, nor can they be compressed into the (theoretically cooperative) categories of political description sanctioned in socialist thought. More than this, our modern presumption of progress is at all times a peril. If the Populists were, indeed, more democratic, more "free," than we are, our very presumption of continuous progress fills us in advance with disbelief about the agrarian experience.

But though the evidence is culturally difficult to imagine, it is clear: the Populists did have a greater sense of self as democratic citizens and a more hopeful view of democratic possibility than that which is culturally licensed within the modern progressive societies around the globe, either socialist or capitalist. Indeed, the ideas that surged to life during the brief Populist moment make the fragile hopes of participants in our own twentieth-century American society seem cramped by comparison. Against the widespread modern resignation about the fate of mere humans, psychologically trapped by their own technological inventions and in homage to the seemingly rigid and uncontrollable industrial structures that have generated those inventions, the Populist view of human possibility is a strange and unexpected phenomenon indeed. For Americans, the puzzle is compounded by the fact that Populism appeared just before the world we live in was created, the world of the "progressive society"—a term I shall continue to use with all its implicit irony.

The principal task facing any modern reader bent on discovering what American Populism was all about lies in the fact that Populists dissented against the progressive society itself. Our cultural loyalty to our own world, together with the personal resignation that is a central component of that loyalty, is the underlying cause of our inability to understand the nineteenth-century reformers.

Populists dissented against the progressive society that was emerging in the 1890's because they thought that the mature corporate state would, unless restructured, erode the democratic promise of America. Not illogically, therefore, they sought to redesign certain central components in the edifice of American capitalism. More modest reformers, not bent on structural reform, were regarded by Populists as betrayers of this democratic ideal. At the time, Populists characterized such practitioners as "trimmers." In the political usages that are culturally sanctioned today, these "trimmers" are described as "liberals."

To the distress of its adherents, the popular movement generated by the nineteenth-century agrarian radicals ultimately came to possess, on its fringes, some of these "trimmers." These people generally had not participated in the transforming ethos that made American Populism such a unique popular movement in modern history, and, in this study, I have described their involvement in the context of what they *did* participate in—a superficial shadow movement of the agrarian revolt.

The deepest irony that hovers over the politics of Populism is that today we know almost nothing about its generating sources and the remarkable human story embedded in its growth. So overpowering have been the cultural limitations of our own vision that when we have looked back to the 1890's we have been able to see only those people who most nearly resemble modern participants in the progressive society. "Liberalism" being the outer limit of our understanding of reform in modern American culture, historians of the movement have unconsciously seen the Populists as "liberals." Accordingly, almost all of the literature about Populism concerns the shadow movement.

The latter has had its capitalist defenders and critics and its socialist defenders and critics. Their scholarly contest has now proceeded for half a century and today stands as one of the more elaborate disputes in the literature of American history. In their bearing upon the interior human reality at the core of Populism, these arguments by rival historians are essentially irrelevant. Such is the power of contemporary culture.

Populists sought what they called a "cooperative commonwealth" in order that individual human striving might be fairly respected. The cooperative ethos was the animating spirit of the popular movement they created—it literally gave hundreds of thousands of impoverished people what Martin Luther King would later call a "sense of somebodiness." Yet they articulated their collective creed in the name of winning for themselves control over their own individual lives. In the politicized rigidities of today's world, Populism is seen to have drawn too much, and too little, from both competing traditions to be comforting to either—or even discernible to either.

2

All of which serves as background to a certain problem hovering over the ensuing narrative. While this difficulty will not trouble the general reader (he may skip forthwith to Chapter I), it will concern that numerous band of professional scholars whose research at one time or another has touched upon the agrarian revolt. Those modern historians who have severely criticized the agrarian radicals, and those who have offered high praise, have jointly accepted as their premise the conceptual framework originally laid down in the first broad-gauged study of the movement, written in 1931 by John Hicks and entitled *The Populist Revolt: The Farmers Alliance and the People's Party*. Similarly, the hundreds of regional and state studies that have been written on Populism since 1931 have, with exceedingly rare deviations, polished one or more of the stones first quarried by Professor Hicks. Unfortunately, while John Hicks believed he had interpreted the central meaning of the agrarian revolt, he had not. He had produced instead a detailed chronicle of what was in fact a superficial derivative of the farmers' crusade—the shadow movement. The *Populist Revolt* left Populism itself essentially unexamined. The agrarian reformers have not since been approached in national terms outside the definitions fashioned by John Hicks almost a half-century ago.

This circumstance has yielded a curious result. In its twentieth-century usage, the word "Populism" has come to imply—simply and inaccurately—a mass popular movement unencumbered by serious intellectual content. As one measure of this slippage in language, consider the fact that the very actors on the stage of Gilded Age politics who are most often cited in modern literature as symbols of "Populism"—William Jennings Bryan, W. H. "Coin" Harvey, and "Pitchfork" Ben Tillman—were never at any time members of the People's Party, were opposed to its specific doctrines of reform, and worked with zeal to undermine or deflect its purposes.

It seems necessary at the outset, therefore, to outline briefly what the prevailing conceptual limits of Populism actually embrace. John Hicks saw the Populist revolt as the sequential unfolding of two movements—the years of the Farmers Alliance and the years of the People's Party. His text further tells us that two "alliances" existed, the most influential being the Northwestern Alliance, the other, more conservative group being characterized as the Southern Alliance. In Hicks's narrative, written in the tradition of Frederick Jackson Turner's frontier thesis, the driving energy to create the People's Party emanated from the Northwestern order, which, in 1892, was able to achieve its goal and to induce some members of the Southern Alliance to join in the political phase of the reform movement. The end result, Populism, was seen by Hicks as an expression of the political style and purpose of the Northwestern frontier group and particularly of its leading state organization in Nebraska. The People's Party Senator from Nebraska, William Allen, is characterized as the "genuine Populist" and his role in the third party's stance of 1896 is interpreted as an understandable end product of the long agrarian crusade.

Both in organizational terms and as a body of political doctrine, American Populism bears no resemblance to this portrait. Rather than providing the inspiration for Populism, the Northwestern Alliance opposed the People's Party—though some of its late-arriving recruits were swept along by others into the third party crusade. For his part, Senator Allen joined the reform movement belatedly—in 1891, five years after its fundamental political principles had been initially fashioned and three years after these doctrines had reached their final basic form. Occurring far from Allen's Nebraska homeland, these developments produced a set of political beliefs fundamentally alien to him. He was never able subsequently to come to terms with them. For reasons that grew out of the very formlessness of the shadow movement for which he spoke in Nebraska, Allen experienced no serious difficulty with his constituency as a result of his non-Populistic conduct. Indeed, both the Nebraska Senator and his supporters were so far removed from the sources and purposes of American Populism that they were literally at a loss to account for the anger their actions stirred among those who had generated the reform movement.

The wellspring of Populism emanated neither from the Nebraskans nor from the small, ephemeral Northwestern farm group of which they were a part. Rather, the agrarian reformers attempted to overcome a concentrating system of finance capitalism that was rooted in Eastern commercial banks and which radiated outward through trunk-line railroad networks to link in a number of common purposes much of America's consolidating corporate community. Their aim was structural reform of the American economic system. Most Nebraska farmers did not participate in the cooperative crusade—a circumstance that was unique within the many large Populist state parties in the South and West—and thus they did not understand and cared little about the radical political objectives shaped by that crusade. Though they assumed they were acting and thinking in the same ways as third party people in other states, in fact they were not. Whereas Kansans, Georgians, and Texans, among others, set out to reform organic power relationships within the emerging corporate state, Nebraska farmers, though similarly victimized by the new rules of commerce, were content, within the existing structure, merely to try to elect good men to public office. They simply had not learned the Populistic premise of thinking in structural terms. A clear understanding of the specific goal of overhauling the basis of the American financial system—a lesson learned in the cooperative struggle—remained foreign to the movement in Nebraska throughout the entire life of the agrarian revolt. The state's reformers, including Senator Allen, never developed into Populists. Yet they have been made to stand as symbols of the Populist crusade.

3

The agrarian revolt itself was a richly varied saga that spanned a full generation. The final phase of the reform movement, the volatile years of the People's Party in the 1890's, extended in practical terms only over the last four of these twenty years. The People's Party, though it was certainly the most visible expression of agrarian aspirations, cannot be understood merely through a study of these final years, because the significant limits of Populism were marked off in the period preceding the party's birth. The central element of this experience—the cooperative crusade—was suffering its death throes by 1892, yet the experience itself created the People's Party as a multi-sectional instrument of radical aspiration. To describe the origins of Populism in one sentence, the cooperative movement recruited American farmers, and their subsequent experience within the cooperatives radically altered their political consciousness. The agrarian revolt cannot be understood outside the framework of the economic crusade that not only was its source but also created the culture of the movement itself. The organization that provided the foot soldiers of Populism was a multi-sectional mass movement known as the National Farmers Alliance and Industrial Union. While the origins of this organization were Southern, by 1892 the National Alliance had reached into forty-three states and territories, had developed the specific political platforms of Populism, and had recruited the rank and file members who were to constitute the mass base of the People's Party.

The agrarian revolt had been germinating for thirteen years before its sudden radical flowering caught the attention of a startled nation. Americans first took serious notice of the National Farmers Alliance and Industrial Union in 1890, when delegates representing thirty states convened in Ocala,

Florida. In the preceding years, the South and West had learned about the Alliance as its organizers conquered every state of the Old Confederacy and then energetically invaded the Western plains. The Alliance had come from Texas. There the organization methods of large-scale cooperatives were developed, and those methods in turn led to the democratic culture the nation was to know as Populism. The mass movement created by the Alliance founders constituted a strange democratic interlude within an era of triumphant self-consolidating capitalism that has characterized the mainstream of American politics ever since the Civil War. Though to some observers the political principles they generated would appear to involve a backward look toward a Jeffersonian ethos, they would speak less to the past, or to their contemporaries, than to the future. When the central role of these founders is included within the over-all third party framework, the political movement that emerges is Populism.

Under the circumstances, it is helpful at the outset to underscore the significant political tension which existed between two men whose careers, though central to the evolution of Populism, have not been sufficiently traced, singly or together. Charles W. Macune was an agrarian spokesman who conceived of the multi-sectional cooperative movement as a vast structure of radical economic reform. William Lamb was an insurgent strategist who seized upon that movement and turned it into an instrument of third party political revolt. The two men are important to the story of the agrarian movement because they and the allies they attracted warred for the soul of the National Alliance for six years, and the outcome of their effort largely determined the strength of the third party that materialized. The struggle between the two men has never been recorded: though Macune is familiar to some students of the agrarian revolt, Lamb is virtually unknown. Yet without the presence of William Lamb, a detailed picture of the internal dynamics that produced the People's Party cannot be reconstructed. The non-recording of a number of events emanating from the activities of Lamb and his allies has had the effect of dropping the left wing out of a left wing movement and leaving the evolution of the People's Party almost as a causeless happening—a mass insurgent movement achieved without organizational insurgents. Taken alone, the leadership style of C. W. Macune, a genuine as well as a self-proclaimed political traditionalist, somehow functioning as the energizing force of the Alliance, seems beyond interpretation, and, in truth, no one has attempted to puzzle through the political meaning of his remarkable career. Macune becomes a much more intelligible politician of reform, however, when he is seen as an innovative moderate responding to intense radical pressure from within his own organization. But this perspective on Macune depends upon the presence of Lamb. The tension between the two men was creative: it ended with the formation and consolidation of the People's Party. William Lamb was the tireless tactician of Alliance radicalism. Alliance radicalism *was* Populism. Charles Macune, therefore, was necessarily a casualty of the driving insurgent politics that created the People's Party.

But while it is necessary to identify these two agrarian reformers at the outset, their styles were a function of something larger than either man—the cooperative crusade itself. The dream of the cooperative commonwealth was the core experience of the agrarian revolt because it gave desperately needed hope to millions. That hope fused huge masses of impoverished Americans into an army of cooperating people, and the same hope injected into their songs, mass encampments, mass rallies, and "parades of the people" the Populistic vitality that made the agrarian revolt such a passionate moment in American history. The vision of the cooperative commonwealth also seized and guided the agrarian captains. Banker and merchant opposition to the cooperatives instructed William Lamb politically as to the coercive potential of the emerging corporate state, and when he undertook radical "education" as a means of bestowing his new perceptions upon his fellow Alliancemen, he precipitated an internal crisis that brought Charles Macune to power. Cooperation in turn captured Macune's imagination, galvanized his abundant organizational creativity, and eventually produced a multi-sectional coalition of farmers that reached from Florida to the state of Washington. Lamb thereupon labored to turn the economic coalition into a political one. Each man learned in his own way what the common crusade could teach, but, unfortunately for them both and for the third party that came, the educational capacities of the cooperative movement were not unlimited. Though it offered guidance in how to generate the social energy necessary for a mass people's movement and guidance also in how the movement could create a radical third party, the cooperative crusade provided far less instruction in how to conduct such an institution once it had been created. In one week of intense conflict and confusion in 1896, the Populists lost control of their own movement, and its life ebbed away.

The Alliance founders are central to the evolution of the People's Party, both structurally as a multi-sectional coalition and ideologically as a body of political doctrine. In contrast, the variant of the agrarian crusade—what we have been taught to think of as "Populism"—was not a seminal expression, but rather was derivative from the first. The original mode challenged the existing structures of the American party system and the nation's financial system; the shadow movement provided a mechanism for accommodation to both. In a concrete sense, the issue at stake was the specific form that American capitalism would assume in the twentieth century. But the ultimate issue was even larger and concerned the degree of autonomy to which citizens had a right to aspire as members of an advanced industrial society. It is in this latter sense that the enormous Populist effort speaks most directly to the problems facing mankind in the twentieth century.

4

An understanding of the development of national Populism requires, from time to time, a special emphasis on the evolution of agrarian thought in certain specific states. The role of the cooperative movement being central to the whole of the Populist experience, three early chapters are focused on one state, Texas, because the theory and tactics of cooperation were confined to, and were maturing within, that region. Later, in the Alliance years prior to 1892, though not always in the Populist years, a great deal of agrarian political creativity emanated from the trans-Mississippi West, from the Canadian to the Mexican border. No such thing as Western unity could exist, however, for the political options for reformers were limited by North-South sectional legacies dating from the Civil War. Though the Alliance leaders in the Dakotas, Kansas, Arkansas, and Texas were able to surmount the hazards of sectional prejudice in their personal relations, their constituencies found this task more difficult, so that there were certain radical duties which Kansans could best address and others that Texans had to perform. I have traced these events in Kansas and Texas between 1888 and 1891 with some care, for they brought Populism to America. From the moment the third party materializes in 1892, the scope of this study becomes national, though the chapter on bi-racial Populism necessarily emphasizes the third party's struggle in the South.

So much for procedure. A final prefatory comment concerns method. In leading the People's Party to broad-based reform, radical Alliance organizers were forever enjoining the nation to "remember the industrial millions." As much as narrative clarity permits, this study endeavors to heed that admonition by concentrating rather more on the presence of some of the voiceless members of American society, and on the men and women who came to speak in their name, than on those who retained political power after the wave of the democratic movement had passed. (In so doing, I have reproduced the language of Populism, grammatically correct or otherwise, without recourse to the designation *sic*.) In the 1890's the precipitating cause of the national debate over "concentrated capital" did not come from those who ruled, but from those who suffered. As the instigators of this debate, the agrarian radicals merit sustained attention on their own terms. But as reformers of any era inevitably discover, social energy is a highly perishable ingredient; it burns, if at all, with consuming heat, and then flickers out abruptly. This investigation seeks, in the first instance, the source of the energy that fueled Populism and animated the brooding social introspection that not only created a mass culture of hope and self-respect among the voiceless, but also gave shape to such radically new and unsettling perceptions about the meaning of the American experience.

For the triumph of Populism—its only enduring triumph—was the belief in possibility it injected into American political consciousness. The Alliance and the People's Party made too many mistakes to serve as a model, but the manner of their failures pointed to much that was potential in the democratic spirit. Tactical errors aside, it was the élan of the agrarian crusade, too earnest ever to be decisively ridiculed, too creative to be permanently ignored, that lingers as the Populist residue. The irony of what befell the agrarian radicals was that they would have failed even if they had made no tactical errors of any kind, for their creed centered on concepts of political organization and uses of democratic government that—even though still in a formative stage—were already too advanced to be accepted by the centralizing, culturally complacent nation of the Gilded Age. That more mature concepts can conceivably be attained within the less provincial but even more centralized environment of modern America remains the open question that describes the range of political possibility in our own time. Presumably, the quest for an answer begins with an attempt to understand the failure of this society's sole previous mainstream attempt to bring democratic structural reform to a triumphant industrial system. Such an inquiry would, of course, also seek to discover something about the forces and values that prevailed over Populist objections to shape American social and political relations in the twentieth century. The issues of Populism were large. They dominate our world.

Contents

Contents

PART ONE

THE TIDE RISING

We think it is a good time to help the Knights of Labor in order to secure their help in the near future.

William Lamb, in defense of the boycott proclamation

March 1886

1

Creating an alliance of farmers

He was the largest landholder . . . in one county and Justice
of the Peace in the next and election commissioner in both,
and hence the fountainhead if not of law at least of advice
and suggestion . . . He was a farmer, a usurer, a vet-
erinarian; Judge Benbow of Jefferson once said of him that
a milder-mannered man never bled a mule or stuffed a ballot box. He owned most of the good land in the county and
held mortgages on most of the rest. He owned the store and
the cotton gin and the combined grist mill and blacksmith
shop in the village proper and it was considered, to put it
mildly, bad luck for a man of the neighborhood to do his
trading or gin his cotton or grind his meal or shoe his stock
anywhere else.

The furnishing merchant in The Hamlet, *by William Faulkner*

The suballiance is a schoolroom.
Alliance lecturer

CHAPTER I

Prelude to Populism:
Discovering the Limits of American Politics

"The people are near-sighted. . . ."

To Walt Whitman, writing in 1879, the essence of history, philosophy, art, poetry, and even personal character "for all future America" reposed somewhere in the inexhaustible mine of the American Civil War. So it seemed to many Americans at the time. It did not require a poet's sensibility to perceive that all that began at Fort Sumter had not ended at Appomattox, or to know that the emotional legacies of the war continued to pulse through broad sectors of national life. Indeed, many of Whitman's contemporaries would have gone further and pointed to a most crucial area of human endeavor that was reshaped by the war—the very structure of the national party system itself. The view from a modern perspective merely reinforces such contemporary assessments: whatever the Civil War imposed on the nation's literature, philosophy, or character, it clearly had enormous impact on the structure of American politics.

To a number of thoughtful Americans, the crucial postwar topic for the nation—as important in the long run as the future status of the freedman—concerned the need to reorganize the country's exploitive monetary system to bring a measure of economic fairness to the "plain people," white as well as black. However this idea—like almost any economic idea in post-Civil War America—confronted national political constituencies seemingly impervious to new concepts of any kind. This state of affairs was traceable to a party system which had been so massively altered by the war that the new situation seemed to make Whitman's sweeping description appear to be an understatement.

The old Jacksonian resonances of Whig-Democratic conflict, containing as they did, still older rhythms of the Jeffersonian-Federalist struggle, were all but obliterated by the massive realignment of party constituencies that had accompanied the war and its aftermath. The memories and even some of the slogans of ancestral debates still persisted in the postwar American ethos, but they no longer possessed a secure political home. Sectional, religious, and racial loyalties and prejudices were used to organize the nation's two major parties into vast coalitions that ignored the economic interests of millions.

The post-Civil War nation contained three basic occupational groups. Ranked in order of numbers, they were farmers, urban workers, and the commercial classes. The war had divided the three groups into six constituencies—Northern farmers, workers, and men of commerce, and their counterparts in the South. Two additional groups were defined less by occupation than by caste—free Negroes in the North and ex-slaves in the South—making a total of eight broad classifications. It was a striking feature of post-Civil War politics that a substantial majority of persons within seven of these eight constituencies followed their wartime sympathies, "voting as they shot," into the 1890's.

The sole exception was the urban working class of the North, which fought for the Union but voted in heavy majorities for the rebel-tainted Democratic Party. For the voters in this class, sectional loyalty had given way before religious and racial loyalties as the prime determinants of political affiliation. Uneasily adrift in a sea of Yankee, Protestant Republicanism, the largely immigrant and overwhelmingly Catholic urban workers clustered defensively in makeshift political lifeboats fashioned after the Tammany model. Generally run by Irish bosses, these scattered municipal vessels essentially conveyed patronage and protection. Though nominally Democratic, little in their design reflected Jeffersonian patterns; their chief function, aside from affording their captains a measure of income and status, was to provide the immigrant masses with local security in an alien world. The Catholic Democratic tendency, defensive though it was, encouraged a reaction among Protestants that they themselves considered defensive. By inescapable, if circular logic, it provided many thousands of Protestants one more reason to vote Republican—to protect themselves against "immigrant hordes" who voted Democratic. A quarter of a century after the Civil War, the organization of party constituencies along lines of sectional, racial, and religious loyalty had been confirmed by the remarkable stability and relative balance of the multi-state network of local political institutions each major party came to possess.[1]

2

A review of the allegiances of these Republican and Democratic constituencies reveals the extent and depth of their war-related commitments. By 1868 the white farmers of the North who had filled the ranks of the Grand Army of the Republic found a settled home in the army's political auxiliary, the Grand Old Party. The decision had been made simpler by the convenient fact that both party and army possessed the same commander in chief, Ulysses S. Grant. Throughout the North the politics of army pensions, orchestrated by loyal Republican leagues, contributed additional political adhesive. From New England to Minnesota, hundreds of small towns, as well as broad swaths of rural America became virtual rotten boroughs of Republicanism. The original prewar coalition of free soilers, abolitionists, and Whigs which had carried Lincoln to the White House thus found in postwar sectionalism a common ground that proved far more serviceable than the controversial issue of Negro rights.[2]

Northern blacks voted Republican for war-related reasons also, though they preferred to see the G.O.P. as an egalitarian idea—the party of emancipation—rather than as the political manifestation of a sectional army. But the passing of radical abolitionism proved rapid. The bankers, manufacturers, shippers, and merchants who had provided much of the direction for the G.O.P. from its inception soon wearied of their attempt to build a postwar party in the South based on black suffrage. As election victories in the 1860's and 1870's proved that the G.O.P. could rule with a basically Northern constituency, Negroes, their morale declining and white radical abolitionists, their numbers thinning, lost the intra-party debate over Southern policy. For most white Republicans, the choice was not hard; party professionals, more enamored of election results than theories, found the politics of sectionalism—"waving the bloody shirt," in the contemporary expression—to be far more persuasive to voters than the elaborate defenses of black rights that were necessary to justify Reconstruction policy in the South. As early as 1868 the Freedman's Bureau was, in effect, allowed to lapse, and the G.O.P. thereafter gradually abandoned both the cause of the freedman and the commitment to a "reconstructed" South that it implied. Given the known prejudice toward blacks of a large portion of the party's white adherents in the North, the superiority of the bloody shirt as a campaign appeal was unassailable. As Negro spokesmen grimly noted, blacks were steadily losing their political influence—though their votes were still counted by the reoriented Republican Party.[3]

The orientation, it soon became apparent, belonged to business. Indeed, the decline in abolitionist zeal was more than balanced by the triumphant spirit of business enterprise that suffused the remodeled Northern G.O.P. Though all participants in the world of commerce did not habitually march in perfect political lockstep, particularly on monetary policy, a workable hegemony within commercial ranks was fashioned in the 1870's and 1880's as a precursor to its near total ascendancy in the 1890's. Thus, the many-faceted Republican coalition that had come to power in 1861 became in the postwar years a much narrower business party, closely tied to the politics of sectional division. Only faint echoes of the multi-sectional impulses of prewar business Whiggery remained.[4]

If Northern blacks faced a dilemma as the party of emancipation became an engine of enthusiastic enterprise, Southern white farmers encountered a similar problem of identification in the restructured politics of the shattered Southland. Like blacks, Southern whites had an emotional basis for party loyalty—though, of course, it was to the party of the Confederacy rather than to the party of the Union. But when federal troops marched away at the end of Reconstruction and conservative white rule returned, the reconstituted Democratic party ceased to be recognizable as an institution of "the plain people." Though Southern farmers from Virginia to Texas looked upon their political home as "the party of the fathers," the postwar Democracy no longer responded to such agrarian rhythms as had existed in the times of Jefferson and Jackson. Rather, the Southern Democratic Party responded to the needs of "New South" entrepreneurs—even as the farmers who had fought in the Confederate Army continued to provide their dazed allegiance. Conceived in white supremacy and clothed with the symbolic garments of the Lost Cause, the postwar institution of business was able to attract the allegiance of white southerners of all classes, including the small number of urban workers in the region. Indeed, in the maturing system of nostalgic "Solid South" Democratic politics, tributes to the fallen and the gallant of the Lost Cause became such ritualistic features of public speaking that almost all orations, including those at funerals, were inherently political in form—though they remained essentially nonideological in content.[5]

These developments, of course, left Southern blacks as isolated as their counterparts in the North were. Immediately after Appomattox the war legacies that shaped the voting habits of the ex-slaves had the distinction of merging emotional loyalties with visible self-interest. The black Republican Party of the South might have been a product of the war, but it was also a logical expression of the political presence and needs of Negro people. However, by the late 1880's, with the steady deterioration of Northern Republican commitment to the civil and economic rights of freedmen, the clear political purpose underlying black allegiance to the party of Lincoln made no more sense in terms of self-interest than did the other residual war loyalties operating in the land.[6]

3

Everywhere—North and South, among Republicans and Democrats—business and financial entrepreneurs had achieved effective control of a restructured American party system. To innovative monetary theorists, the fact was central: sectional prejudices in the 1880's and 1890's persisted as an enormous political barrier to anyone bent on creating a multi-sectional party of reform. Indeed, the mature relationship between sectionalism, issueless politics, and the business direction of both major parties not only became the animating political cause of the emergence of Populism, but the almost wholly nonideological climate created by sectional politics was also to prove the third party's principal obstacle.

By the time Benjamin Harrison settled in the White House in 1888, the postwar restructuring of the American party system had seemingly become quite settled. Though each party remained dominant in its own section and possessed lesser or greater pockets of strength in the other's bailiwick—largely for reasons of sectional, racial, or religious loyalty—both responded primarily to the needs of businessmen. Of course, neither always found it convenient to stress the matter with relentless precision.[7]

Not political ideas, but war-related emotions that had intrinsic political meaning became the central element of post-Reconstruction politics in America. While practical politicians might employ ritualistic references to the high or low tariff to dress up their party's principles, they also maintained an inventory of oratorial fire to rekindle the embers of the sectional and racial patriotism that had flamed during the war. The politics of sectionalism contained a reserve of partisan firepower that could be used against any candidate or any party attempting, through an innovative appeal to "issues," to rearrange the nation's basic postwar alignment.[8]

Prior to the outbreak of Populism, the basic constituencies of both major parties thus remained, in terms of party loyalty, substantially unaffected by the social and economic changes

9

occurring in industrial America. The pervasiveness of this reality testified to the marginal impact of political theorizing.

4

It was in such a non-ideological milieu that the nation first encountered the political issue that was to transform public dialogue in the 1890's—the "financial question." The importance of the issue could scarcely be exaggerated. How money was created, and on what basis it circulated, defined in critical ways the relationships of farmers, urban workers, and commercial participants in the emerging industrial state. The answers would go a long way toward determining who controlled the rules of credit and commerce, who shared in the fruits of increasing American production, and, ultimately, how many Americans obtained that minimum of income necessary to ensure that they lived lives of dignity. With the stakes so high, all questions about the currency were clearly not of equal weight. One of the weightiest concerned the origin of money. Whether the government issued money, or whether private bankers did, obviously shaped the precise forms of finance capitalism to a telling degree. The resolution of this issue might well determine which occupational groups had a measure of influence over their own economic future and which did not. How much money circulated also was important—in terms of price and income levels, interest rates, and the relations of creditor and debtor classes. Central to the whole issue, of course, was a clear definition of money itself. Was it gold? Gold exclusively? Silver and gold? Did the currency include paper money? [9]

These matters tended to be discussed by monetary conservatives in rigid, moral terms. Their answers were short and clear, if often, in retrospect, inane. It was an article of faith for them that a proper monetary system had to be based on the gold standard. Yet simple faith was not enough to win the day for hard money; the debate never seemed to go away. The currency question erupted in each decade and often became entangled in levels of contention that soared beyond simple morality into new and surprising realms of social, economic, and political philosophy. The stakes were inherently high because ultimate answers, if ever obtained, would define the basic economic ground rules for American society. But if the "financial question" seemed somehow organic, it arrived upon the stage of national politics with something of a stumble. The origin of the issue, however, was appropriate enough: money arguments stemmed from the war, too. In fact, the controversy over "greenbacks" fitted easily within Walt Whitman's perception of the Civil War as a guide to the American future.[10]

5

In the first year of the war the government had contracted with commercial banks for a number of war loans that had the effect of substantially increasing the currency and thus the pressure on gold reserves. Long before McClellan's army embarked for the first great Richmond campaign, the nation had quietly left the gold standard. In technical language that millions of Americans would try to comprehend over the next two generations, "specie payments" had been "suspended." Two months after the Treasury ceased paying coin for its obligations, Congress, under relentless wartime spending pressure, authorized the issuance of "legal tender treasury notes" to cover obligations. Because of the color of their ink, the notes quickly became known to the public as "greenbacks." By the end of the war some $450 million of these treasury notes were in circulation, having contributed to wartime inflation, greater commercial liquidity, and prosperity.[11]

In orthodox financial circles favoring "gold monometallism" the postwar problem was one of ending "suspension" and achieving "resumption" by retiring the greenbacks and returning to a redeemable currency of hard money. The currency "contraction" that necessarily would follow might be painful for various members of the society, especially debtors, but only as the painful cleaning of a wound was essential to ultimate health. At the heart of the banker's approach was an understanding of gold and silver money not as a medium of exchange, but as a commodity that had "intrinsic value." In the language of orthodox "goldbugs," money "was only as good as the gold which is in it." Gold was orderly and civilized;

11

money not backed by hard metal was "fiat money," which failed the measure of intrinsic value. It was money only because legislators, by arbitrary fiat, said it was. Such currency was essentially corrupt, and its continued use constituted a morally corrupt method of running a society. The view reflected a creditor's perspective generally and a banker's view specifically, but in a cultural sense it rested on moral values rooted in both religion and primitive capitalism and shared by millions of Americans.[12]

However, bankers and other creditor-bondholders had a more specific motive for specie resumption. The currency had depreciated steadily during the war, and, having purchased government bonds then, they, understandably, looked forward to the windfall profits to be made from redeeming their holdings in gold valued at the prewar level. A governmental decision to begin paying coin for its obligations would mean that, though the Civil War had been fought with fifty-cent dollars, the cost would be paid in one-hundred-cent dollars. The nation's taxpayers would pay the difference to the banking community holding the bonds. Bankers marshalled a number of moral imperatives to support their case. They argued that they had supported the war effort—albeit with depreciated money—by buying government securities on the assumption that the postwar dollar would be returned to "par." For the government to take any action to render this assumption invalid would be unethical. Bondholders and the Eastern financial community—the two terms were more or less interchangeable—further argued that resumption would encourage saving, investment, and economic growth by assuring holders of capital that the dollar would have "long-term stability." The country would be placed on a "sound" footing. Finally, the banker's case was patriotic: the nation's honor was at stake.[13]

Some practical difficulties intruded, however. A return to hard money could only be accomplished in one of two ways— both quite harmful to a great number of Americans. The first was to raise taxes and then employ the proceeds to redeem wartime bonds and to retire greenbacks from circulation. This, of course, would contract the currency abruptly, driving prices down, but also depressing business severely and increasing unemployment, perhaps to socially dangerous levels. Such a contraction was not immediately attainable in any case, because United States prices were so high compared to world prices that it would have been quite profitable for Americans to redeem dollars in gold and then buy products overseas. Any immediate attempt to "resume specie payments" would have quickly exhausted the nation's gold supply through an unfavorable balance of trade.

The second method of contracting the currency spread the resulting economic pain over a longer period of time. The government could merely hold the supply of money at existing levels while the population and the economy of the nation expanded, thus forcing general price levels down to a point where it was no longer profitable to redeem paper dollars in gold to finance imports. In due course, this is what happened.[14]

To the nation's farmers, that contraction constituted a mass tragedy which eventually led to the Populist revolt. Although the economic relationships sound quite complex, they can be spelled out in fairly simple terms through an arbitrary numerical example. Letting ten farmers symbolize the entire population, and ten dollars the entire money supply, and ten bushels of wheat the entire production of the economy, it is at once evident that a bushel of wheat would sell for one dollar. Should the population, production, and money supply increase to twenty over a period of, say, two generations, the farmers' return would still be one dollar per bushel. But should population and production double to twenty while the money supply was held at ten—currency contraction—the price of wheat would drop to fifty cents. The farmers of the nation would get no more for twenty bushels of wheat than they had previously received for ten. Moreover, money being more scarce, interest rates would have risen considerably. A person who borrowed $1000 to buy a farm in 1868 would not only have to grow twice as much wheat in 1888 to earn the same mortgage payment he made earlier, he would be repaying his loan in dollars that had twice as much purchasing power as the depreciated currency he had originally borrowed. Thus, while contraction was a blessing to banker-creditors, it placed a cruel and exploitive burden on the nation's producer-debtors.[15]

To summarize the goldbug stake in contraction, while holders of wartime bonds would admittedly reap a harvest in receiving 100 cents for fifty-cent bonds—and at considerable cost to the nation's treasury—"sound money" would be the undeniable result. And while it was also true that deflation depressed business activity in a way that meant a rise in unemployment for urban workers, and inflicted severe hardships upon all debtors, especially the great numbers of farmers caught between rising interest rates and falling farm prices, monetary conservatives consistently put forward the gold standard and the "national honor" as the paramount considerations.

The contrary debtor philosophy offered another way of stabilizing prices. By reducing the content of the dollar to one-half its prewar figure, the nation could have simply accepted the fact that the currency had lost one-half of its purchasing power, frankly and rather painlessly acknowledging that currency devaluation had taken place during the war. Granted that such a solution would remove the windfall profits that bondholders anticipated from the return of the gold standard, it also avoided the multiple hazards to the rest of the society implicit in the objectives of "sound money" bankers.[16]

To greenbackers, the case for a fiat currency was completely persuasive because the nation needed an expanding monetary system to keep up with population growth and commercial expansion. Greenbacks were "the people's currency, elastic, cheap and inexportable, based on the entire wealth of the country." As the ensuing narrative of American Populism seeks to reveal, the greenback cause was a many-faceted phenomenon, sometimes put forward in arguments which were opportunist and ephemeral, but more frequently presented in a coherent analysis that attained a level of advanced social criticism.[17]

Whatever the short-run economic equities, the greenback critique of American finance capitalism—should it ever gain a mass popular following—constituted a political issue of the first magnitude. In this strictly political sense, greenback doctrines can be interpreted in terms of interest-group politics for the simple reason that, at one time or another in the decade following the war, portions of every sector of the American population felt defrauded in their relations with bankers. In its various mutations, the soft-money creed confronted the nation with labor greenbackers, agrarian greenbackers, business greenbackers and Negro greenbackers. However, such a simplistic interest-group approach to what is essentially an intellectual matter is both unwieldy and, almost unavoidably, misleading. Soft-money theory is most easily grasped as a political ideology grounded in a desire of non-bankers to cope with changing commercial power relationships within an industrializing society. As such, the proper place to begin is with the developing ideology itself and then pass to the movement's immediate political phases—the National Labor Union (1871), the Greenback Party (1876–1884), and the Union Labor Party (1888). It is pertinent to do so because the final and most powerful assertion of the greenback critique of the American monetary system came through the mobilization of the multisectional political coalition known as the People's Party.

6

The postwar doctrines of greenbackers went back to the 1840's, to the writings of Edward Kellogg, a self-made merchant who retired to devote himself to a study of international finance after being ruined by the Panic of 1837. In Kellogg's view, the nation's currency was solely a creature of law. Far from viewing money as a commodity of "intrinsic value," Kellogg and his disciples held that "pebbles or any other material would answer the same purpose as gold and silver, if law could make them a tender for debt, and control the quantity." Since government-issue paper promised to be more manageable than stones, Kellogg advocated a fiat currency issued by a central bank. He also proposed government supervision of interest rates, which he saw as "the all-pervading force" which, "by fixing rent and the use of all property, determined the reward of labor." Kellogg's first full-scale work, published in 1849, outlined in its title most of the dimensions of future nineteenth-century monetary struggles: *Labor and Other Capi-*

tal: The Rights Of Each Secured and the Wrongs of Both Eradicated. Or, an exposition of the cause why few are wealthy and many poor, and the delineation of a system, which, without infringing the rights of property, will give to labor its just reward.[18]

Kellogg's book was later described by a Populist editor and labor leader as "the Bible of the early currency reformers." Its impact multiplied as new editions were published in the second half of the century. Kellogg's ideas, elaborated by Alexander Campbell following the war, became the conceptual basis of the labor-greenback cause in the late 1860's. Pennsylvania economist Henry Carey, also building upon Kellogg, developed a romantic and ill-conceived philosophy of "producerism," which was designed to deliver the soft-money message with equal force both to entrepreneurial capitalists and to labor. Reduced to its political essentials, Carey attempted to oppose usurious moneylenders and foresaw a "harmony of interest" between labor and productive entrepreneurs against a common and parasitic foe, the finance capitalist.[19]

These business greenbackers developed a measurable following among western Pennsylvania iron and steel men and others who felt gouged by Eastern commercial bankers. As articulated in the *Workingman's Advocate* of Chicago, the ideas of Campbell and Carey gained some credence within the labor movement as well. Under the circumstances, it is singular that these educational efforts achieved their greatest impact neither upon those who could be influenced by ironmasters nor upon the labor movement, but rather upon a specific section of the nation's farmers! This anomaly, perhaps more than any other evidence, defines the limits of the purely ideological appeal represented by the soft-money creed. One is forced to confront the social fact that hard-money ideas eventually prevailed in business circles even among men who had little to gain and much to lose by the ascendancy of the gold dollar. Indeed, the transformation of soft-money ironmasters into submissive, financially orthodox Republicans casts an interesting light on the social pressure for political conformity operating within affluent Northern society. The failure of the greenback cause among urban workers was more readily predictable, if only because of the fragile condition of the existing labor movement. The scarcity of labor newspapers or other organizational methods of communication within the ranks of labor deprived labor greenbackers of the means of presenting their case. Either because urban workers accepted the moral criticism of greenbacks, or because the entire matter seemed too difficult to grasp, or because they simply never heard of it, or because they developed other priorities, the soft-money creed proved fairly easy for laboring people to resist. Ideologically, the greenback doctrine failed in its effort to penetrate deeply into either the ranks of entrepreneurial capital or those of labor.[20]

Beyond its ideological difficulties, the political failure of the greenback cause is even easier to explain. The doctrine of a fiat currency fell victim, simply and forcefully, to sectionalism. The soft-money creed had nothing to offer in the way of sectional appeal; it offered instead an idea about economic relationships and then tried to prevail by explaining the idea to major party constituencies that still had emotional and cultural needs related to war-rooted loyalties. Against the sectional politics of the bloody shirt and the Lost Cause, the politics of a fiat currency recruited comparatively few regiments. Sectionalism, augmented by the moral values presumably challenged by the idea of a fiat currency, ensured that the emotional resistance to greenback doctrines would be broad, indeed. Ideologically innovative, culturally embattled, and irrelevant in terms of sectional loyalties, the soft-money creed endured a fragile political life within a national party system geared to noneconomic memories.[21]

7

Rather effortlessly, then, Congress was able to defend the nation's honor after the war, resuming the payments of gold for wartime bonds and gradually contracting the currency by consciously declining to increase volume in step with population growth and commercial expansion. After a measure of government hesitancy traceable to agitation by business and labor greenbackers, the amount of currency in circulation was held at a stable level through the decade of the 1870's while expanded population and production reduced price levels and

GOLD UP, AND COMMODITIES DOWN.

spread severe economic hardship throughout the nation's agricultural districts. Hard-hit farmers were brusquely told they were guilty of "overproduction." The economic depression was both protracted and severe. Business was badly hurt, and unemployment rose, but by the end of the decade the goal was reached: the United States went back on the gold standard on January 2, 1879.[22]

8

As if these developments were not enough, still a final irony awaited the nation's currency reformers—and it was one that would cast a shadow forward, all the way into the Populist period. The greenback cause was not only defeated politically by sectionalism in the popular mind, and by "intrinsic value" homilies of sound money moralists, but even the intellectual arguments in behalf of a fiat currency became obscured by another "financial question" that intruded into the nation's politics in the 1870's. This development, which centered around a bizarre topic popularly known as "The Crime of '73" almost destroyed what little public understanding had materialized on American banking practices. To the undying distress of greenbackers, the "Crime of '73" focused popular attention on an extraneous issue—the fancied need for a "remonetization of silver." This development, a part of the general conservative drive to return to a redeemable metallic currency, was rather symbolic of almost all nineteenth-century monetary wars: the "Crime of '73" arrived in the midst of the nation's political dialogue without much comprehension on the part of most of the participants. The silver episode merits brief attention because, as refurbished in the 1890's by silver mine-owners, it provided the rationale for the shadow movement of Populism known as "silver-fusion."

In the early 1870's, a currency bill had been introduced that, in one of its less debated features, quietly dropped the silver dollar from the nation's coinage. As silver was at the time selling at a premium to gold on the international market, the effect of the change was presumed to be negligible. But by the time the bill had proceeded toward enactment late in 1872, new mining methods had vastly increased the production of silver, depressing prices at a rate that indicated to all those who were aware of the meaning of such developments that silver would soon fall below par with gold. Now specie resumption threatened to become a hollow victory for the cause of sound money because the more valuable gold dollars would soon disappear from circulation and silver would necessarily be employed to redeem the wartime bonds. Perhaps more to the point, depreciated silver would remove much of the anticipated profit windfall for wartime bondholders. To knowledgeable advocates of the gold dollar, the new coinage bill to drive silver out of circulation became not merely attractive, but absolutely necessary. Actually, however, the importance of the silver provisions in the multi-purpose bill were not widely grasped, even in Congress, and certainly not in the country at large. Partly as a result of disingenuous explanations by its congressional sponsors, the bill attained final passage in January 1873 without even a roll call vote in the Senate. Though specie payments were not resumed at once, silver was "demonetized" and the country placed on a gold standard. Thus occurred what a generation of Americans would come to know as "The Crime of '73." [23]

It took some time for the crime to be discovered. A gradually deepening economic depression provided the necessary awareness. As the money market noticeably tightened, the first hint of trouble came late in 1873, when farm commodity prices slackened, as did manufacturing and foreign trade. The unexpected collapse of the famed investment banking house of Jay Cooke in the autumn of the year then ignited panic in an already nervous Eastern financial community. Unemployment rose, demand softened, and wage cuts followed. As the depression worsened, prices fell, though neither as swiftly nor as far as wages did. Commodity income for farmers slumped badly. Less visible but more relevant in terms of existing and future currency debates was the fact that Germany shifted from a silver to a gold standard at the same time America demonetized silver. These developments, coupled with slackening silver demand elsewhere, had the effect of raising the worldwide demand, and thus the price, for gold and further devaluating silver.[24]

What all this meant was beyond the ken of orthodox financial thinkers of the day, though a number of erroneous causes and solutions were offered as the depression became worldwide. In America, however, the facts seemed to be relatively simple: silver suddenly was not worth much and the country was gripped by a depression. It was at this point that the alarms sounded on the "Crime of '73." Once its congressional origins were understood, the perpetrators of the coinage bill were condemned by the public in creative language that exposed any number of conspiracies. Counter-legends, hurriedly promulgated by goldbugs, soon earned acceptance among creditors. But both views came well after the fact: the "Crime of '73" went undiscovered for almost three years before the depression had deepened sufficiently to stir inquiries and reappraisals across the land. The outcry for silver that materialized emanated from debtors, farmers, laborers, and others most vulnerable to the hardships of the depression. Yet the groundswell for silver derived less from broad public understanding of currency than from moral outrage at the apparently surreptitious means by which the bill had achieved congressional approval.[25]

To greenback apostles, the entire controversy bordered on madness. The cry for silver was an utter delusion. To fiatmoney men it was elementary that silver, like gold, was but another prop in a hard-money currency. As such, it contributed to a relatively rigid money supply that hurt the economy and, among other maladies, fostered high interest rates that benefited only moneylenders. While a measure of inflation could be achieved by coining silver on the proper terms, such terms were not being debated, were not widely understood, and were not likely to be as long as bankers continued to convince Americans that money had to have "intrinsic value." [26]

Such greenback arguments, baffling and therefore suspect to many, drove the curious to look for corroboration in the nation's press, universities, and pulpits. With a few exceptions, the representatives of all three were rigidly orthodox on the money issue, their attitudes grounded in an unshakable acceptance of the bankers' argument that currency had to have a metallic base. Though greenbackers themselves looked upon "silver Republicans" and "silver Democrats" with equal disdain, the soft-money cause had to swim upstream against the cultural presumptions of the era. As soft-money advocates looked on helplessly, the nation returned to specie payments on terms that brought deep satisfaction to goldbugs and a modest measure of "sound money inflation" to silverites. The resulting mild upturn in the price of agricultural products following resumption further diminished whatever prospects soft-money partisans had of making their case to the nation.[27]

9

Given such a remarkable range of intellectual, political, and cultural constraints, it is understandable that the political institutions created by greenbackers in the 1870's and 1880's fared rather badly. Soft-money doctrines enjoyed a brief period of prominence as a centerpiece of the politics of the National Labor Union in the early 1870's before they acquired something of the dimension of a national political presence when the Greenback Party was formed in 1876. From that point to its effective demise in 1884, the Greenback Party drew little more than ridicule from respectable society. Luhman Weller, Iowa's greenback Congressman, became widely known as "Calamity" Weller, and Texas' George Washington Jones was reduced to "Wash" Jones.

To any currency reformer who could read election returns, it became plain in the 1880's that the Greenback Party could not achieve anything remotely approaching a realignment of the nation's party system. Except for a surprisingly large, though losing, vote for the governorship of Texas, the Greenback Party's success in the 1882 elections was largely limited to a few scattered congressional districts. A perfunctory presidential effort in 1884 netted only 300,000 votes for General James Weaver, the party's standard-bearer from Iowa. "Sound money" seemed a fixture in American culture.[28]

By 1886 virtually the only legacy of a generation of soft-money agitation and party-building was a network of agrarian radicals scattered along the western frontier from Dakota Territory to Texas. The older generation among this radical coterie, husbanding memories that dated back to the first debates on the wartime greenbacks in the 1860's, felt fatally disillusioned. A goodly portion of the incoming mail to ex-Congressman Luhman Weller reflected the desperation of men who had spent years trying to employ economic arguments to overcome the sectional loyalties of the nation's voters. In Kansas and Iowa, overwhelmingly Republican, the farmers preferred the politics of the bloody shirt. In Arkansas and Texas, overwhelmingly Democratic, they preferred the rhetoric of the "party of the fathers." When a final, desperate effort to reconstitute a third party structure collapsed in the abortive bid of the Union Labor Party in 1888, a number of greenbackers simply gave up. They were not of a mood to blame themselves. "The people are near-sighted," an embittered reformer wrote Weller. "The collapse of the Greenback Party and the poor showing made by the Union Labor Party has in my opinion destroyed all hope for a new party during the next decade, if not during a generation." That cryptic judgment (and a singularly misplaced one, considering what was about to happen) merely reinforced the deepening gloom that had been gathering over currency reformers since the middle of the decade. The money question might be central to the ongoing problem of economic inequity and corporate concentration in America, but the nation's political culture, reduced to a primitive level by the emotions of sectionalism, seemed thoroughly in harmony with the needs of "sound-money" bankers. "Calamity" Weller's mailbox filled with the complaints of earnest but battered reformers.[29]

Yet beneath the surface returns of national defeat, the achievements of the greenbackers contained instructive possibilities that scarcely seemed to justify such settled despair. Along the Western farming frontier the third party idea had partly conquered the sectional barrier. The two leading third party states in 1888 were Kansas and Texas—an indication that, at least along a narrow fringe of the Great Plains, radicalism could draw from the ranks of Republicans in the North and Democrats in the South. Moreover, greenbackers had recruited at least the beginnings of a mass constituency among Western farmers without the assistance of a leading agrarian theorist of soft money. Greenbackers had learned their monetary theory from businessmen and economists such as Kellogg, Campbell, and Carey, or from labor intellectuals such as Andrew Cameron of the *Workingman's Advocate* in Chicago. They had not yet developed a spokesman of their own capable of dramatizing soft-money ideas in a context that would appeal with special clarity to farmers. In view of the popular confusion about the nature of money, did not the soft-money cause need some powerful and effective method of communication within its natural constituency among debtor farmers? Either an appropriate organization with its own internal medium of communication or an effective advocate who could mobilize agrarian distress in behalf of monetary reform? Might not prospects for reform soar if such a farmer advocate or institution appeared? Or if both appeared?

It had to be granted, however, that such a possibility hardly constituted a firm basis for optimism concerning independent political action. In the aftermath of the abortive campaign of 1888, radicals in Kansas could scarcely take comfort from the fact that their state had polled the greatest number of third party presidential votes in the nation. The more germane political fact was that the Republican ticket had polled a higher percentage of the total vote in Kansas than in any other state in the Union. No state in the South seemed more solidly Democratic than Kansas was solidly Republican.

Texas, the nation's second-leading incubator of greenback radicalism, offered similarly gloomy prospects. The Democratic presidential ticket of 1888 had swept over Texas radicals with a plurality exceeding the Republican margin in Kansas. Monetary wars had come to the reconstructed nation and might come again, but the central political reality a generation after Appomattox continued to be the fact that ingrained sectional loyalties ruled the lives of American voters. Walt Whitman seemed prophetic: the Civil War might indeed determine matters of substance in the Republic "for all future time."

The surface calm of two party stability, however, concealed a slowly incubating germ of greenback insurgency. In the very years of apparent greenback decline, the virus had infected thousands and was spreading to millions. "Calamity" Weller's mailbox was merely not the place to look for it.

CHAPTER II

The Coming of the Farmers Alliance

"Organization and cooperation is our only hope. . . ."

The agrarian revolt first stirred on the Southern frontier, then swept eastward across Texas and the other states of the Old Confederacy and thence to the Western Plains. The gathering of democratic momentum required almost fifteen years—seven within a tier of counties along the Texas farming frontier, three more to cover the rest of the state, and another five to envelop the South and West. Yet the best way to view this process of mass radicalization of farmers is not by focusing on the farming frontier from which the doctrines of insurgency emanated, but rather by discovering the humiliating conditions of life which penetrated into every farm and hamlet of the South. These conditions really illuminated the potential support for the agrarian revolt because they caused thousands to flee to the frontier and armed those who remained behind with a fervent desire to join the movement when it eventually swept back through their region. Further, these conditions were so pervasive in their impact, shaping in demeaning detail the daily options of millions of Southerners, that they constituted a system that ordered life itself.

2

The "system" was the crop lien system. It defined with brutalizing finality not only the day-to-day existence of most Southerners who worked the land, but also the narrowed possibilities of their entire lives. Both the literal meaning and the ultimate dimension of the crop lien were visible in simple scenes occurring daily, year after year, decade after decade, in every village of every Southern state. Acted out at a thousand merchant counters in the South after the Civil War, these scenes were so ubiquitous that to describe one is to convey a sense of them all. The farmer, his eyes downcast and his hat sometimes literally in his hand, approached the merchant with a list of his needs. The man behind the counter consulted a ledger, and after a mumbled exchange, moved to his shelves to select the goods that would satisfy at least a part of his customer's wants. Rarely did the farmer receive the range of items or even the quantity of one item he had requested. No money changed hands; the merchant merely made brief notations in his ledger. Two weeks or a month later, the farmer would return, the consultation with the ledger would recur, the mumbled exchange and the careful selection of goods would ensue, and new additions would be noted in the ledger. From early spring to late fall, the little ritual would be enacted until, at "settlin'-up" time, the farmer and the merchant would meet at the local cotton gin, where the fruits of a year's toil would be ginned, bagged, tied, weighed, and sold. At that moment, the farmer would learn what his cotton had brought. The merchant, who had possessed title to the crop even before the farmer had planted it, then consulted his ledger for a final time. The accumulated debt for the year, he informed the farmer, exceeded the income received from the cotton crop. The farmer had failed in his effort to "pay out"—he still owed the merchant a remaining balance for the supplies "furnished" on credit during the year. The "furnishing merchant" would then announce his intention to carry the farmer through the winter on a new account, the latter merely having to sign a note mortgaging to the merchant the next year's crop. The lien signed, the farmer, empty-handed, climbed in his wagon and drove home, carrying with him the knowledge that for the second or fifth or fifteenth year in a row he had not paid out.

Such was the crop lien system. It constituted a new and debasing method of economic organization that took its specific form from the devastation of the Civil War and from the collapse of the economic structure of Southern society which had resulted from the war. In the aftermath of Appomattox, the people of the defeated Confederacy had very little either of capital itself or of the institutions dealing in it—banks. Emancipation had erased the slave system's massive investment in human capital, and surrender had not only invalidated all Confederacy currency, it had also engendered a wave of Southern bank failures. In 1869 there were only 26 national banks in the eight states of North Carolina, South Carolina, Georgia, Alabama, Louisiana, Texas, Arkansas, and Mississippi, while there were 829 national banks in the four states of New York, Massachusetts, Pennsylvania, and Ohio. Massachusetts alone had five times as much national bank circulation as the entire South, while Bridgeport, Connecticut, had more than the states of Texas, Alabama, and North and South Carolina combined. The per capita figure for Rhode Island was \$77.16; it was 13 cents for Arkansas. One hundred and twenty-three counties in the state of Georgia had no banking facilities of any kind. The South had become, in the words of one historian, a "giant pawn shop." [1]

The furnishing merchants, who were themselves paying 18 per cent or more for credit extended through Northern banks, bought supplies and "furnished" them on credit to moneyless farmers, taking a lien on the farmer's crop for security. Farmers learned that the interest they were paying on everything they consumed limited their lives in a new and terrible way; the rates that were imposed reached levels that strained credulity—frequently well in excess of 100 per cent annually, sometimes over 200 per cent. The system had subtle ramifications which made this mountain of interest possible. At the heart of the process was a simple two-price system for all items—one price for cash customers and a second and higher price for credit customers. Twenty-five to 50 per cent interest would then be charged on this inflated base. An item carrying a "cash price" of 10 cents would be sold on credit for 14 cents and at the end of the year would bring the merchant, after the addition of, say, 33 per cent interest, a total of 19 cents—almost double the standard purchasing price. Once a farmer had signed his first crop lien he was literally in bondage to his merchant as long as he failed to pay out, because "no competitor would sell the farmer so much as a side of fat back, except for cash, since the only acceptable security, his crop, had been forfeited." The farmer rarely was even aware of the disparity between cash and credit prices, for he usually had no basis for comparison; "many of the merchants did a credit business so exclusively they set no cash prices." The farmer soon learned that the prudent judgment—or whim—of his furnishing merchant was the towering reality of his life. Did his wife want some calico for her single "Sunday dress," or did his family need a slab of bacon? Whether he got them or not depended on the invisible scales on which the merchant across the counter weighed the central question—would the farmer's crop yield enough money to pay off the accumulating furnishing debt? [2]

In ways people outside the South had difficulty perceiving, the crop lien system became for millions of Southerners, white and black, little more than a modified form of slavery. "When one of these mortgages has been recorded against the Southern farmer," wrote an anguished contemporary, "he had usually passed into a state of helpless peonage. . . . With the surrender of this evidence of indebtedness he has also surrendered his freedom of action and his industrial autonomy. From this time until he has paid the last dollar of his indebtedness, he is subject to the constant oversight and direction of the merchant." Food, clothing, farm implements, fertilizers—everything—had to be sought from the merchant holding the crop lien, "and in such amounts as the latter is willing to allow." The man with the ledger became the farmer's sole significant contact with the outside world. Across the South he was known as "the furnishing man" or "the advancing man." To black farmers he became, simply, "the Man." As the furnishing debts accumulated, the merchant imposed ever stricter criteria in measuring what his farmers could have. One student of the system concluded that "literally thousands of bare subsistence accounts were so limited in their purchases that if the customer had twice the money to spend he would in no way have been extravagant." [3]

The account books of Southern furnishing merchants present grim evidence not only of the gradations of privation between blacks and whites, but the near universality of privation itself. In South Carolina low farm prices forced a middle-class white farmer named S. R. Simonton to open a credit account with the furnishing house of T. G. Patrick. While Simonton's first year's expenditures were $916.63, declining prices helped reduce his after-sale "credits" to only $307.31, leaving an unpaid balance of over $600, which he settled by note. The subsequent annual credit extended to him by the furnishing merchant did not exceed $400 per year, showing that he had suffered a drop of well over 100 per cent in his standard of living. Still, he was never able to "pay out." For seven years between 1887 and 1895 Simonton spent a total of $2,681.02, but he produced credit enough to pay only $687.31. The debt was settled by a transfer of land to the furnishing merchant. Simonton had become a landless tenant. [4]

Detailed records of the account of a Mississippi Negro farmer over a seventeen-year period reveal an even grimmer personal degradation. Matt Brown purchased his supplies from the Jones Store at Black Hawk, Mississippi, from 1884 to 1901. Brown was not free of debt at any time in those seventeen years. He began the year 1892 with an indebtedness of $226.84 held over from previous years. At final settlement on January 3, 1893, his obligation had increased to $452.41. His credits during the year came from selling cotton, cutting wood, clearing land, and hauling for the store. They amounted to $171.12. His expenditures for the year were $33.15 for food; $29.45 for clothing; and $173.64 for household and farm supplies such as bagging and ties, mules and land rent, ginning, plow tools, and seeds. He also spent 55 cents for drugs, $4.00 in a cash advance, and $112.81 for miscellaneous supplies. By 1895 his credit standing had diminished to the point that his twelve-month expenditure for food totaled $8.42. In that year he spent $27.25 on clothing, $38.30 on farm and household supplies, 95 cents on drugs, $2.35 for a cash advance, and $12.08 on miscellaneous supplies. Matt Brown's account, it appears, was ultimately settled by a mortgage. In 1905 an entry appears for a coffin and burial supplies. The record was permanently closed by "marking it off." [5]

For millions of farmers of both races throughout the South, those were the realities of life in the last half of the nineteenth century. The Dallas *News* was typical of scores of Southern metropolitan newspapers that told farmers they "bought too much and sold too little," but farmers who spent $10.00 to $50.00 a year for food knew better. They could have cited another statistic: the Southern cotton crop of 8.6 million bales in 1890 brought $429.7 million to the farmers; the next year's crop, 9.0 million bales, brought only $391.5 million—a decrease of $38.2 million despite an increase in production. [6]

New South editorialists said that the Southern farmer should diversify and grow perishable food supplies as well as cotton, but both the farmer and the furnishing merchant knew better. Aside from the compelling fact that an acre of corn produced even less financial return than an acre of cotton did, other factors habitually overlooked by those who advised farmers also precluded extensive departures from the one-crop system. Most perishable farm products could not have taken the abuse of being hauled over the atrocious Southern dirt roads or transported on Southern streams in ill-equipped boats. And corn and other farm products were subject to ruinous damage in the ramshackle warehouses of the rural South. In their innocence, editorialists could convince their readers of the impracticality of Southern farmers, but more informed observers concluded that the "lack of imagination on the part of critics and planners of the agricultural South were as much to blame for the region's one-crop system of agriculture as were the sins of the furnishing merchants." [7]

In any case, conservatives who advised the farmer assumed he possessed a degree of autonomy that he simply did not have. Furnishing merchants demanded that their debtors plant the one certain cash crop, cotton. One phrase, repeated across thousands of counters of supply merchants, defined the options: "No cotton, no credit." Moreover, goldbug newspaper editors rarely focused on the reality that, in an era of tightening money supply, the federal government's reliance on the gold standard meant deflation, which translated into the long, sustained postwar fall of cotton prices. Farmers, caught between high interest rates and low commodity prices, lost almost all hope of ever being able to pay out. Every year more and more of them lost their land to their furnishing merchant and became his tenants. Merchants began to consider a "run" of fifty to one hundred tenants on their lands as normal. They "advanced" supplies to their tenants, sometimes even hiring riders to check on them weekly, and gradually acquired title to steadily increasing portions of the lands of the country. Through the 1870's and 1880's there appeared to be a direct and desperate relation between the South's rising cotton harvest and the region's rising poverty. As thousands, then millions descended into the world of landless tenantry, the annual output expanded, but both the soil and those who worked it gradually became exhausted as a result of the desperate cycle of crop lien, furnish, cotton harvest, failure to pay out, and new crop lien.[8]

3

It is not surprising that men were lured or driven west. Yet even the great migration that began in the 1870's did not alter the guiding principles of the new system. One Southern historian described the bitter logic which had made cotton a new king of poverty: "Let . . . the soil be worn out, let the people move to Texas . . . let almost anything happen provided all possible cotton is produced each year." [9]

For simple, geographical reasons, "Going West" for most Southerners meant, in the familiar phrase of the time, "Gone to Texas." The phrase became so common that often only the initials "G. T. T." scrawled across a nailed-shut door were needed to convey the message that another Southerner had given up on his homeland. White and Negro farmers by the thousands drove down the plank roads and rutted trails of the rural South, westward across the Mississippi River to the Sabine and into the pine forests of East Texas. The quest for new land and a new start drove lengthening caravans of the poor ever deeper into Texas, through and beyond the "piney woods" and into the central prairie blacklands of the state. Through the decade of the 1870's, almost 100,000 beleaguered farmers came each year.[10]

Finally, the tide of migration lapped against the Balcones uplift in the heart of Texas and trickled beyond—into the hill country and the prairie Cross Timbers. There the men and women of the South stepped out into the world of the Great Plains. Having fled the crop lien and the furnishing merchant, they came up against new foes in the strange new environment. The immigrants flattened their Georgia plows against the limestone strata lurking inches beneath the topsoil of the Edwards Plateau, and the bottomland settlers, however deeply they might plow, vainly waited for the rains they had known in the piedmont and deltas of the Old South. The Southern farmers could not know, but anguish had driven them too far. Eventually, scientific meteorological data would show that along the western edge of the Central Texas blacklands, on a line running just west of the cities of Forth Worth and Austin, stretched the crucial limit of annual thirty-inch rainfall. The farmers had reached and, unsuspectingly, had crossed, the practical agricultural boundary of the American South.[11]

Besides the man-made burdens of crop lien and furnishing merchant, and the geographical ones relating to rainfall patterns, the immigrating farmer encountered still other problems. A Tennessean fleeing worn-out land, interest, and the freight rates of the Louisville and Nashville Railroad would arrive in the Cross Timbers of Texas to find that the Texas and Pacific Railroad owned much of the most promising land. He also found that, in the middle 1870's, the separate world of the cattlemen lay perilously close and that feeder cattle trails for the long drives from South Texas to Abilene ran right through the frontier farming districts now filling with land-hungry refugees from the South. An estimated 100,000 horses were stolen in Texas between 1875 and 1878, 750 men were reported regularly engaged in the business, and it was said that not more than one in ten was caught. Corrective efforts had been "discouraging" because "men of wealth and influence were doing a considerable part of the stealing." To the farmer's list of plagues—the inescapable furnishing merchant, the railroad land shark, the discriminatory freight rate—was added the rustler.[12]

Yet the incoming tide from the Old South continued. Farm families unhitched their wagons, dug in on the rim of the Great Plains, and scratched for survival. The frontier jammed up with people; seven counties supporting 11,405 residents in 1870 bulged with 75,918 by 1880. They were desperate years, more desperate than outsiders could know. It was here that the organizational base was created for what historians would later call "the agrarian revolt." [13]

4

Lampasas County, Texas, is nestled in the rugged foothills of the Edwards Plateau, a land streaked with limestone outcrops and located beyond the thirty-inch rainfall line. There, in September 1877, a group of farmers gathered at the Pleasant Valley farm of J. R. Allen and banded together as the "Knights of Reliance." In the words of one of the founders, they all "were comparatively poor" and the farm organization was the "first enterprise of much importance undertaken." The overriding purpose, he later said, was to organize to "more speedily educate ourselves in the science of free government" in preparation for "the day that is rapidly approaching when all the balance of labor's products become concentrated into the hands of a few, there to constitute a power that would enslave posterity." In his view, the farmers needed to construct "a grand social and political palace where liberty may dwell and justice be safely domiciled." [14]

The new organization soon changed its name to "The Farmers Alliance," borrowed freely from the rituals of the older farm organizations, and plunged into Greenback politics. The movement spread to surrounding counties, and in the summer of 1878 a "Grand State Farmers Alliance" was formed. The growing county and state structure was to be a rural organization of self-help, though of precisely what kind no one could be certain. "There were about as many objects in

view for organization as there were men participating," said
one of the members. Some, seeing the farmers' plight in terms
of governmental land, money and transportation policies, advocated independent political action. Loyal Democrats among
the group looked for tangible benefits that could be secured
through less drastic organizational policies. Others thought
that concrete steps to halt cattle rustlers and horse thieves
were sufficient justification for maintaining the order. With
such unfocused aims, an excursion into Greenback politics
proved fatal, and the founding Alliance in Lampasas collapsed
after an abortive third party effort in 1880.[15]

Four years later, as the statewide organization, now led by
men from other sections of Texas, began its period of spectacular growth, the Lampasas Alliance reconstituted itself and
grew far beyond the limits reached in the founding period.
When the third party was formed in the 1890's, Lampasas
County became a Populist stronghold. But the memory of the
perils of political action associated with Lampasas plagued Alliance radicals for the next decade.[16]

Meanwhile, the organizational sprouts in frontier counties
north of Lampasas, unhampered by internal political division,
slowly took root. A new state organization was chartered and
the order selected a frontier weekly as its official journal in
1881. By the summer meeting of 1882 the order could boast
of some 120 suballiances in twelve counties. Despite this organizational energy, the Alliance was still groping haphazardly
for a firm sense of direction and purpose. It had limited its

---

Texas

The base of the early Alliance in the frontier farming counties during the
period 1877–83 is evident from this map. Prior to the organizing campaign
launched in January 1884, the Alliance numbered 120 sub-alliances in
twelve counties, ten along the northwestern frontier. The county containing
Alliance members in central east Texas is Houston County, where the Colored National Farmers Alliance was organized in 1886. The encircled
county is Lampasas, where the original Alliance organizing effort collapsed
after the Greenback campaign of 1880. The other non-contiguous county
identified is Red River County, original home of the Alliance State President
for 1883–84. The Alliance counted 100,000 members by the summer of
1886 and 250,000 by the summer of 1888.

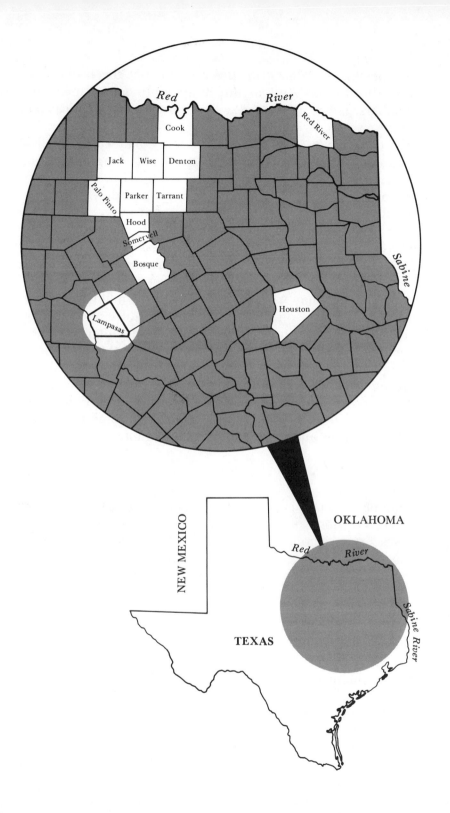

membership to whites, on the ground that the order was a social institution. And to the disappointment of many new members, it had fashioned a firm nonpartisan political position.[17]

The largest tasks lay beyond the immediate capacity of the leadership. Alliancemen wanted to do something to solve the underlying problems of agricultural credit. However, their cooperative efforts at buying and selling were, they discovered, "treated with contempt by tradesmen and others." Efforts to increase the Alliance's bargaining power by achieving a cooperative plan with the Grange for the sale of cotton proved fruitless. In 1883, an off-election year, the Alliance lost its momentum—only thirty suballiances were represented at the state meeting that August. The organizing failure might be blamed, as it was, on the shortage of literature and lecturers, but the inability to generate continuing interest among members already recruited was more ominous. Clearly, something had to be done or the collapse of the first Alliance through political schism would rapidly be followed by the slow death of the second Alliance from sheer apathy. Either some new policy would have to be fashioned or some new leader called forth to inject new life into the organization.[18]

5

The new Alliance president, elected in August 1883, was W. L. Garvin. An original participant in the first post-Lampasas organizational drive, he had performed ably and had learned something of the built-in hazards to effective recruitment. In January 1884, Garvin created a new post, that of "Traveling Lecturer," and gave its occupant broad executive powers to appoint sub-organizers and sub-lecturers for every county in the state of Texas. To this post Garvin named a thirty-six-year-old former Mississippian, S. O. Daws. It proved a decisive choice. A man of good judgment and tact, Daws also had a fluent command of the written language of political exhortation. He also nursed a growing impatience with the refusal of the commercial world to treat with respect the cooper-

Populist Roots

The cabin where the Alliance's first formal meeting was held in 1877 in Pleasant Valley, Lampasas County, Texas. The cabin was uprooted and exhibited at the Chicago Exposition of 1893; later, it was chopped up, and pieces passed out to Populist partisans.

ative buying and selling efforts of the young Alliance. Perhaps most important of all, at least in terms of the short-run needs of the organization, Daws was a compelling speaker. In January 1884 there were only fifteen alliances known to be active out of the 157 that had officially been chartered since 1880, so Daws, determined to activate the membership and promote the most energetic men he could find to positions of influence, went on the road. With the broad powers given him by Garvin, Daws was, in effect, the Traveling President and Executive Committee all in one.[19]

Within a month Daws had energized fifty suballiances into sending delegates to the state meeting. At that meeting the status of the cooperative effort was reviewed. If merchants practiced monopolistic techniques by refusing to deal with the Alliance, perhaps Alliance members could reply in kind. A "trade store" system was agreed upon wherein Alliance members would contract to trade exclusively with one merchant. The range of discussion was broad: it extended to the role of Alliance county business agents and Alliance joint stock companies, to the opposition of cotton buyers and the resistance of manufacturers who refused to sell to the Alliance except through middlemen, and even to the refusal of townsmen to sell farmers land for Alliance-owned cotton yards where they might store their crops while awaiting higher prices. The order formally resolved to "encourage the formation of joint stock companies in sub and County Alliances for the purpose of trade and for the personal benefit of members financially." Even politics was discussed, though an effort to put the Alliance formally on record in favor of political action was rejected. Determined to test the trade store system thoroughly, and armed with what was for the Alliance a new organizing device—the joint stock company—which could appeal to potential members in concrete terms of self-interest, Alliance delegates dispersed from the February meeting with new hope. Daws's efforts had been so impressive that his office and his appointment powers were confirmed by the convention.[20]

The spring of 1884 saw a rebirth of the Alliance. To farmers long at the mercy of furnishing merchants the "Alliance store" struck a spark of hope that seemed to spread with a momentum all its own. Adding to that momentum was the relentless continuation of the long slide in cotton prices. From a year-end level of 18 cents a pound in 1871, cotton fell to 9 cents in 1883 en route to the post-Civil War low of $4\frac{1}{2}$ cents in 1894. The number of suballiances increased as the order spread eastward across Texas from its base along the frontier countries.[21]

But of far greater significance than mere numbers was the new mood of the growing order. The Alliancemen had an evident and surprisingly militant determination to break the hold that furnishing merchants had on the economy of the agricultural districts. Their spirit had political as well as economic

38

implications. The Alliance had reiterated its nonpartisan posture—the specter of the Lampasas disaster still shaped policy—but Daws's speeches were rich in insurgent language. Using phrases that would soon gain almost doctrinal authority inside the Farmers Alliance, Daws denounced credit merchants, railroads, trusts, the money power, and capitalists. Little that he saw on his first excursions into new, unorganized Alliance territory softened the sense of collective urgency. Everywhere the farmers were poor. From the bleak Cross Timbers to the fertile blackland counties of Central Texas, the work-worn men and barefooted women who gathered to hear the Alliance lecturer were not impressive advertisements for the blessings of the crop lien, the furnishing merchant, or the gold standard.[22]

The results of moving west had proved doubly galling, and the reaction that Daws often found, and tried to capitalize upon, was not apathy, but anger. His audiences did not require detailed proof of the evils of the two-price credit system and the other sins of the furnishing merchant. But Daws could climax his recitation of exploitation with a call for a specific act: join the Alliance and form trade stores. Were monopolistic trusts charging exorbitant prices for fertilizers and farm implements? Join the Alliance and form cooperative buying committees. Did buyers underweigh the cotton, overcharge for sampling, inspecting, classifying, and handling? Join the Alliance and form your own cotton yard. Daws was not afraid to draw sweeping political implications from his economic analysis of the farmers' plight, and he studded his speeches with calls for immediate collective action. One measure of the new urgency was mathematical: a steady increase in suballiances in newly organized areas—to a total of over 200 by the summer of 1884. Other indications were the proliferation of seemingly endless variations of cooperative arrangements for the buying and selling of goods and a discernible improvement in the political awareness of the letters dispatched to the order's official state journal, appropriately named the Jacksboro *Rural Citizen*. But even more significant was the brand of local leadership Daws appointed as he organized new suballiances. The changed mood was evident in the style of the men who materialized as presidents and lecturers of the recently organized county structures—men who bore the Daws stamp: articulate, indignant, and capable of speaking a language the farmers understood.[23]

6

Foremost among them was a thirty-four-year-old farmer named William Lamb. Beyond his red hair and ruggedly handsome appearance, there was at first glance little to distinguish Lamb from scores of other men who had come west to escape the post-Civil War blight of the South. A Tennessean, Lamb had arrived on the frontier at the age of sixteen, settling first near what was to become the town of Bowie in Montague County. Like most rural Southern youths, Lamb had had almost no formal education—a total of twenty-five days. After working as a hired man, he married (in 1873), rented land, and began farming in Denton County. In 1876 he "preempted" a farmstead in Montague County, living alone part of the time in a rude log hut until he could clear the land and build a homestead. As children came, he farmed by day and read by night, acquiring the strengths and weaknesses of self-taught men. When he spoke publicly, his sentences were overly formal, the syntax sometimes losing its way; in the early days, when he began to write in behalf of political causes, the strength of his ideas had to overcome impediments of grammar and spelling. To Daws, who was seeking other men of energy, those faults were no liability; the younger man had strength of mind, and this was what Daws realized when the two men met in 1884. Lamb knew the extent of the agrarian disaster in the South as it had affected him personally, and he had an urge to do something about it. He was ripe for the missions Daws was ready to give him. By the time of the 1884 state meeting, Lamb's work in organizing suballiances in his own county had attracted enough attention that a new statewide office was created specifically for him. He was made "state lecturer" while Daws continued in the role of traveling lecturer.[24]

Unquestionably, Daws was instrumental in this elevation of Lamb, for the older man still retained much of the executive authority in the organization. William Lamb fully justified the choice, emerging in 1884–85 as a man of enormous energy and tenacity. As president of the Montague County Alliance he had organized over 100 suballiances by October 1885, a record that eclipsed even Daws's performance in his own county. Lamb soon surpassed his mentor in other ways. As a spokesman for farmers, the red-haired organizer thought in the broadest tactical terms. He early saw the value of a coalition between the Alliance and the Knights of Labor, which was then beginning to organize railroad workers in North Texas. Lamb also pushed cooperative buying and selling, eventually becoming the Alliance's most aggressive advocate of this program. And, after the business community had shown its hostility to Alliance cooperatives, Lamb was the first of the Alliance leaders to react politically—and in the most sweeping terms. From the beginning, William Lamb took station on the extreme left wing of the farmer organization.[25]

The increasing momentum of the idea of the Alliance cooperative inexorably shaped the lives of Daws and Lamb as they, in turn, shaped the lives of other men. They spent their lives in political reform, and in so doing became allies, exorted their comrades, crowded them, sometimes challenged them, and performed the various acts that men in the grip of a moral idea are wont to perform. They influenced each other steadily, the impetus initially coming from Daws, as he introduced Lamb into an environment where the younger man's political horizons could be broadened, then from Lamb, as he tenaciously pressed his views to the point of crisis and carried Daws along with him until the older man could use his influence and creativity to resolve the crisis and preserve the forward momentum of the organization.[26]

We do not know if the personal relationship between William Lamb and S. O. Daws was a close one; we only know that they traveled the long path to the People's Party together. A rhythm, however, is discernible: along the course they set toward independent political action, Daws was always a step or two behind; at the moment of triumph, when the third party was formed in the South, Lamb, not Daws, held the gavel in his hand.

7

The young organizer learned in 1884–85 that cooperative buying and selling was easier to plan at country meetings than to carry out in the society at large. Town merchants opposed cooperative schemes, as did manufacturers and cotton buyers. The initial attempts to establish a trade store system proved something less than an unqualified success. The first few manufacturers approached by Lamb in his capacity as the order's purchasing officer refused to sell their products direct to the Alliance and routinely referred all inquiries to their wholesale and retail agents.[27]

Yet the sheer variety of Alliance efforts at cooperation and the energy with which these efforts were pursued captured the interest of farmers desperately seeking relief from the growing agricultural depression. If "cooperation" did not invariably produce immediate economic gains, it spurred organizing work. The 1885 state meeting of the Alliance, the largest gathering of farmers ever held in Texas to that time, attracted 600 delegates from 555 suballiances. Groping for new ways to make selling cooperatives function, the Alliancemen adopted a resolution calling on members of all suballiances "to act as a unit in the sale of their produce" and, to this end, have each county alliance "set apart a day or days in which to put their produce on the market for sale." Alliancemen called it "bulking." These mass cotton sales were to be widely advertised and cotton buyers contacted in advance, for the Alliance wanted a representative turnout of agents who might engage in competitive bidding. To bolster their buying cooperatives, the state organization urged each county Alliance to "appoint a committee of three discreet members" to examine bills of freight and the charges of merchants with whom the Alliance had made contracts for sale of goods at specified rates. "A refusal to show such bills by said merchants shall terminate and make null and void such contracts with said merchants." Another move proposed at the 1885 convention carried the Alliance nearer to the forbidden area of politics. Probably introduced by William Lamb, the motion called for "unity of action" between the Farmers Alliance and the

Knights of Labor. Just how the two orders might find common ground other than in political coalition was not clear to some of the delegates, and a second resolution, one declaring that "capital and labor should be allies and not enemies," was offered. Thus formulated, the motions passed.[28]

The sense of movement generated by the sheer size of the 1885 convention, as well as the concrete steps toward economic cooperation and, for some at least, the declaration of friendship with the Knights of Labor, added momentum to the Alliance's organizing effort. Having consolidated its hold on the frontier counties, the order spread over North and Central Texas and probed into the eastern "Old South" part of the state. Through the fall and winter of 1885 the Alliance state journal was filled with evidence of the new enthusiasm. Two weeks after the convention the *Citizen* printed a euphoric report, announcing that an "Erath County Alliance Lumber Company," with 2800 Alliance members, had been formed. "We stand united and as closely allied to one another as the delegates that represented us in the Grand State Alliance," declared an Erath Alliance official. There was much enthusiasm for the buying cooperative, he added. "We can purchase anything we want through our agent, dry goods, and groceries, farm implements and machinery. We have a market for all of our wheat, oats and corn." As for selling cooperatives, the official was even more sanguine: "We expect to build a cotton platform, weigh and load our own cotton and ship direct to the factories." In September, a "grand mass meeting and basket picnic," under the joint auspices of the Farmers Alliance and the Knights of Labor, gathered to hear a Knights official lecture on "the Necessity of Organization." The farmers seemed to take him at his word; in the following month the Tarrant County Alliance announced the organization of its forty-sixth suballiance and claimed a total of 2000 members throughout the county.[29]

"The Farmers Alliance is making its power felt in this state now," the Whitesboro *News* reported approvingly. "It is only by such combinations as the Knights of Labor and the Farmers Alliance that the laborers or producers can expect to cope with the organized power of capital, and the measure of their worth will be determined by the thoroughness of their organization." The order seemed determined to heed the paper's advice. On October 18, 1885, the Alliance State Secretary reported that 160 new suballiances had been organized in the preceding thirty days and that the total number for the state stood at 815. Each suballiance had its lecturer; each county had its county Alliance and county lecturer. The message of agrarian self-help now sounded from hundreds of Alliance platforms.[30]

8

But the Alliance did not grow in a vacuum. It had to overcome the opposition of older and better known organizations. On October 29, 1885, an irate Granger in Erath County, Texas, sought advice from the Worthy Grand Master of the Patrons of Husbandry. "We unfortunately have a unruly and objectionable element in our Grange," he wrote. "You may reply that there is a law by which we may rid ourselves of such incubus, but I will state that they have such a number of votes in the Grange as to make futile any effort we can make to get rid of them." He wondered if the county charter could be surrendered and the Grange reorganized, "leaving out the bad element." They were, he said, "discordant." [31]

While the Erath Grange tried to defend itself against restless farmers, the Erath Alliance two weeks later shared with the brethren who read the order's official journal a different attitude toward farmer organizations.

> The time has come in the history of the Farmers Alliance in Erath County that we are respected by the commercial world and our enemies are beginning to recognize us as a power in the land. . . . We can sell anything we have for market and buy anything we want. . . . Organization and cooperation is our only hope from the iron wheel of oppression . . . or we will be trampled under the steel-shod feet of combined monopolistic oppression. Farmers Alliance Awake! Stand forth on the balcony of human rights and assert your independence.[32]

Neither the dull, measured tread of the Grange nor the impassioned trumpeting of the Alliance caused the skies to tremble. Indeed, as the outside world knew little or nothing of Alliance newspapers, few in the power centers of Texas or the nation were remotely aware of the gathering impatience among the members of a rural organization calling itself the Farmers Alliance. Ironically, it was the stolid, purposeful conservatives of the Grange who became the first to sense the new mood in the rural districts of the state. The route to this perception was a painful one. Initially, Grangers had watched with equanimity the early stirrings of the Farmers Alliance, and, courteously, if condescendingly, they had rebuffed suggestions for cooperation. But slowly—the timing depending upon the region of Texas and the speed of the Alliance mobilization—complacency within the Grange leadership gave way to alarm, then to anger, and finally to helpless, private denunciation. Nothing availed. Within the space of thirty-six months, the Grange was all but obliterated in Texas.[33]

The Patrons of Husbandry probably deserved a less ignominious fate. The National Grange, as it was more commonly known, had spread across the Midwestern Plains states in the early 1870's, and the Grangers had helped lay the first fragile foundations of class consciousness in the nation's farming regions. But when the new form of agrarian self-respect manifested itself in political action, the order suffered internal divisions and lost its organizing momentum. By this time the Grange system of cash-only cooperative stores, based on the English Rochdale plan, had already failed to address the real ills of farmers. Because of the appreciating value of the currency—and attendant lower farm prices—most farmers simply could not participate in cash-only cooperatives. They did not have the cash. The simple, unavoidable truth was that a cash store was of little help if one had no money and had to deal with credit merchants. By failing to alleviate the farmer's distress, the Grange soon lost the bulk of its membership. The National Grange movement could not cope with the internal ideological dilemma caused by the political situation it confronted. If the order "went into politics," it would risk the divisions that splintered the Midwestern Granges and later ended the first Texas Alliance at Lampasas. On the other hand, failure to seek political reform placed the full burden on the Grange's social and educational program, augmented by whatever direct benefits could be extracted from the Rochdale Cooperative plan. For most farmers, these services simply were not enough.[34]

Yet the latter course was the one the Patrons decided to pursue. In an official statement of "the Purpose of the Grange," the order's national office announced: "The Grange is not, as some have falsely assumed, a crusade against the moneyed capitalist, or the railroad interest; it is a farmer's organization for self-improvement and self-help." In this fashion the vigor of the Grange expired, and the order became a static repository of agrarian cultural values. In time, the propagation of these values became the central life of the order, and they continued so—with remarkable consistency, considering the temper of the times—throughout the period of the agrarian revolt. Worried about the sagging prestige of farmers, Grange leaders seized upon the inherited myth of the yeoman farmer and expanded the idea. Simplicity, thrift, and industriousness were extolled to men and women whose lives already reflected all three. Farmers who could be satisfied with such peripheral social and educational embellishments as the Grange offered were likely to live above a level of immediate economic crisis. Most Texas Grangers who stayed with the organization came from the relatively small agricultural middle class. By 1879 a Grange newspaper could assert with unconscious irony that "the Grange is essentially *conservative* and furnishes a stable, well-organized, rational and orderly opposition to encroachments upon the liberties of the people, in contrast to the lawless, desperate attempts of communism." In view of the number of communists who were suborning the Southland in 1879, the remark reveals as much about the Grange's capacity for political analysis as it does about its status presumptions.[35]

In its organizational policy, social tradition, and political outlook, the Grange gradually rendered itself incapable of responding to the kind of agrarian desperation that was gathering force in Texas in the middle 1880's. Under the circumstances, its further decline was inevitable. The Farmers Alliance, in contrast, had begun to grow. Its membership total of 10,000 in the summer of 1884 soared to 50,000 by the end of 1885.

9

The rise of the Alliance was a direct result of its determination to go beyond the cash stores of the Grange and make pioneering efforts in cooperative marketing as well as purchasing. Negotiations with town merchants through Alliance county trade committees had marginally improved purchasing conditions for thousands of Texas farmers by 1885, but it was in the field of cotton marketing that the aggressive young order encountered its greatest resistance and scored some of its most notable victories. The Alliance developed a plan for pooling the cotton production of its members, concentrating the bales in a single locality and inviting cotton buyers in to bid on the entire lot. The tactic of "bulking" was implemented over the vocal objections of many cotton buyers. County trade committees amassed 500, 1000, and in some instances as many as 1500 bales of cotton at Alliance warehouses and, in an effort to overcome the resistance of local buyers, issued invitations to cotton brokers from outside the immediate trade area. Because of the convenience to buyers of "bulking," the trade committees asked for premium prices, 5 to 10 cents per 100 pounds above prevailing levels. Though results were mixed, the successful sales gave the farmers a profound sense of accomplishment. After one mass sale at Fort Worth that brought 5 cents per 100 above what individual farmers had received, Alliancemen were ecstatic, and, as one metropolitan daily reported it, their "empty wagons returned homeward bearing blue flags and other evidence of rejoicing." It did not take long for such stories to spread through the farming districts, and each success brought the Alliance thousands of new members.[36]

Though such achievements brought both fame and members, the cooperative movement encountered mounting hostility from merchants. Commenting on the failure of Dallas cotton brokers to purchase cotton from the Alliance cooperative, the strongly pro-Alliance Dallas *Mercury* put the best possible face on events. "The Alliance is growing in a most wonderful way and in a little while the farming community will be united solidly against these few dictatorial speculators and it is plain which side our merchants will be compelled to take." The paper added some gratuitous advice for the merchants: "It certainly would be wise on their part to take some action to protect their patrons from the imposition of the cotton buyers." [37]

Such insurgent innocence was, of course, grandly irrelevant to the continuing privation of farmers. "Bulking" helped, but it did not eliminate the furnishing merchant, nor did it fundamentally alter the two-price credit system. In dealing with purchasing, the Alliance slowly discovered it had to achieve two preliminary goals if farmers were to bargain effectively with the commercial world. It needed to establish an internal method of communication which would arm the Alliance purchasing agent with hard facts so that he could inform manufacturers of the size and value of the Alliance market for their products. In negotiating with a manufacturer on price, an Alliance agent who could rightfully claim to represent 200 prospective purchasers of plows would be in a much stronger position than would an agent who could present no such concrete inducements. It also needed an agent who could deal aggressively with a large number of manufacturers selling to the agricultural market. The more sellers were made aware of the Alliance market, the better the order's chances of negotiating lower prices on the basis of bulk sales should be. With these imperatives clearly demonstrated by the events of 1885, the Alliance moved late in that year to centralize its cooperative procurement effort by naming its own purchasing agent. The Alliance state president appointed William Lamb as the official "Traveling Agent" to represent the order "for sale of farm implements and machinery through the state where the Alliance is organized." [38]

Though the long-term effects of this decision were to change the whole direction of the Farmers Alliance, the results in the short run were disappointing. Despite zealous efforts, Lamb's attempts to establish direct purchasing arrangements with manufacturers failed. Some savings might be made if the Alliance could establish a central store where goods could be shipped, but otherwise, he reported, with ungrammatical clarity, "the local rates of freight is too high" to re-ship to individual purchasers. On specific products, the news was not much better. It was the credit problem again. "I can furnish wagons in car-load lots cheap for cash, but as yet I have no offer on time," he reported to his Alliance brethren. Lamb had learned about the nation's economy through his experiences as the Alliance purchasing agent, and he proposed, in lieu of cooperative buying, a more basic solution: cooperative manufacturing. "Please say to all members of the Alliance of Texas," he wrote the editor of the state journal, "that I have made arrangements to furnish a full line of mill machinery, and can furnish anything from a 14-inch corn mill to a 500-barrel full roller flouring mill on good terms." The young farmer advised every county Alliance to "get up a cooperative mill" and "have cooperative stores in connection with the mill to handle their own produce." Lest the size and complexity of this undertaking intimidate the membership, Lamb added that his own Montague County Alliance had "passed a resolution last Friday to go into the cooperative mill and store business, and elected a committee of seven to draw up a suitable plan." Lamb's plan of cooperative milling, based on his loss of faith in the good will of merchants, did not constitute a serious threat to the commercial world, but it represented the first public hint that his political perspective was shifting. And he was not alone.[39]

10

Something new had stirred to life in the rural areas of Texas. The pace of growth since the spring of 1884 had steadily quickened as Alliance organizers, spurred by the two state lecturers, Daws and Lamb, polished their ability to articulate the grievances of impoverished farmers. As yet the city press was largely unaware of the agricultural ferment. The Knights of Labor had noticed, however, and they had been rewarded with a friendly response from the growing farm organization. Others noticed, too. In Milam County, east of Lampasas, a young country doctor, a man destined to become the most widely read editor of Alliance-Populism, joined the order. His name was Charles W. Macune. And in Lampasas itself the original founders reorganized. A suballiance once again met

49

at J. R. Allen's farmhouse at Pleasant Valley, where the "Knights of Reliance" had been formed in 1877.

Eight years had passed since the fledgling order had plunged into politics and fragmentation. Sobered by the experience, its leaders built anew with greater patience, exploring at length the opportunities for cooperative buying and selling. Though the effort had not yet produced a method of dealing effectively with the farmer's problem of credit, it had instructed large numbers of farmers in the possibilities of joint action. In the course of learning these lessons, the Farmers Alliance had developed an identifiable style, one demonstrably more aggressive than anything seen in a Southern state before. One of its young leaders, William Lamb, had begun nursing the idea of a vast coalition of the rural and urban laboring classes to restructure American politics. The idea was not new, but now it was attached to an organizational framework containing a developing system of internal communication and education. The idea thus had new potential as a source for a mass movement. In response to such initially unobtrusive rhythms along the Southern frontier of the United States, the "agrarian revolt" began.

CHAPTER III

The Emergence of Alliance Radicalism

". . . the morning sunlight of labor's freedom . . ."

The organizational methods and ideological basis of American Populism were fashioned in 1886–87. Through months of turbulent controversy and spectacular growth, a mass movement of anonymous people became highly charged with a breathtaking new hope: they could free themselves of the ancient bonds of the credit system. The thought was transforming; it generated a sweeping new perception of what politics was. As this perception began to permeate the full membership of the Alliance, it became the source of a new, collective experience—a movement culture. This new way of looking at things came into being in 1886–87, though it would not be until 1892 that it acquired a distinctive name—Populism.

A bold new assertiveness on the part of emerging Alliance spokesmen was essential to this development, but so too were the new cooperative experiences within the membership that had the effect of sanctioning radicalism. These dynamics affected conservative agrarians, an embattled labor organization, a unilaterally called and richly controversial boycott, the actions of one of the nation's robber barons, the most violent strike in the history of Texas, the reactions of the metropolitan press, and, ultimately, the structure and purpose of the Farmers Alliance itself. In the light of this variety of influences, the emergence of Alliance radicalism is perhaps most easily perceived as it happened—one step at a time.

The Great Southwest Strike of 1886 was an energizing, though not a central, element in what essentially remained a debate among farmers. However, it merits attention, for it formed the backdrop against which agrarian radicalism came into view. Labor unrest was endemic in the Southwest in the early 1880's, and by 1885 Texas ranked ninth among the states in the number of workers involved in strikes. Twelve-hour and even sixteen-hour days were common on the railroads, and wages ranged from approximately $1.00 a day for track laborers to slightly over $2.00 a day for the most skilled engineers. Working conditions were particularly bad on the Gould railroads, where wages were sometimes withheld for two to three months.[1]

Despite a partially successful strike in 1885 over long-standing grievances on the Gould lines, the leaders of the Knights of Labor were unable to achieve clear recognition of their union as the representative of the railroad's employees. In February 1886 Gould's general manager, H. M. Hoxie, an implacable opponent of labor organization, fired an employee for attending a meeting of the Knights District Assembly in Marshall, Texas. The dismissal was a direct challenge to the Knights' continued existence, since the employee, a Master Workman of a local assembly, was attending an official meeting after having secured permission to do so. According to the historian of the strike, the workers felt that if the Knights could not protect their own leader, "they were weak as well as disloyal." Within three hours of the notice of the employee's discharge, the local Knights assembly asked the union's hierarchy to support their demand to the railroad for his reinstatement. When the company refused to consider the matter, the strike began from below, with individual locals walking off the job at various points along the railroad lines from Marshall across North Texas to Fort Worth. The Knights' national leaders, unable to find anyone in company authority who would listen to their grievances, reluctantly acquiesced in the walkout on March 6. By that time most of the locals of the Texas and Pacific were already on strike, and by March 10 many of the locals of the Missouri Pacific, also owned by Gould, had joined the walkout.[2]

The governors of Missouri and Kansas offered their services for arbitration, but General Manager Hoxie took the position he would meet only "employees," not "men who are out." Gould's position had been strengthened because in December 1885 he had thrown his Texas-Pacific holding into receivership for defaulting on bonds owed to its parent company, the Gould-owned Missouri-Pacific. Through the receivership, all railroad workers on the Texas-Pacific became employees of the federal government and thus subject to court control. Both state and federal courts "gave freely of their services with bench warrants and writs of assistance," while cooperative judges deputized scores of strike-breakers.[3]

The workers were not in a mood to accept this state of affairs quietly. From beginning to end, the Great Southwest Strike was a series of minor and major battles between armed strikers and armed deputies and militiamen, interspersed with commando-like raids on company equipment by bands of workers. Thousands were indicted, hundreds were jailed, and many were killed. Most of the violence occurred in Texas, though two sensational pitched battles that resulted in ten deaths occurred in the Louisville and Nashville Railroad yards in East St. Louis.[4]

In Texas, the most publicized incident occurred in Fort Worth. As one reporter described the scene, by the end of the first month of the strike the city "had all the appearances of a town during the civil war." Over 100 special deputies patrolled the streets and they were augmented by no less than eight companies of state guard troops and an additional company of Texas Rangers—400 men in all. However, the "Fort Worth Massacre" was not attributable to any of these units, but rather to one Jim Courtwright, a "top-ranking gunman of the disappearing frontier." Courtwright had been hired by the Missouri-Pacific Railroad after the strike began, and he was installed as city marshal of Fort Worth. Though a "notorious desperado and outlaw but recently a fugitive from justice," Courtwright was given leadership of a group of deputies charged with escorting trains into Fort Worth. He soon became involved in a wild gun battle which left one deputy dead, two more wounded; and three or four strikers killed or wounded.[5]

There was lawlessness on both sides. Workers "killed engines" by displacing various connections, in the words of one indictment, "in such a manner as to unfit said engine for use by said company and its agents." Such acts were sometimes condoned by Texas juries sympathetic to the strikers. One jury in Waco found two strikers guilty of "injuring a locomotive engine"; it fined them each $1.00. The railroads utilized friendly courts and newspapers too. Nine workmen from New Orleans were brought by the railroad to Marshall on the assurance that "everything was quiet and no strike was in progress." After being sworn in as deputies, they learned the truth and walked off the job, issuing a denunciation of the company for deceiving them. The strikers were jubilant. The United States Marshal for East Texas, however, arrested the workmen under a charge of contempt for defrauding the company by accepting transportation from New Orleans. All were given sentences of three or four months in the Galveston County jail.[6]

Major Texas dailies denounced the strikers,[7] suggested that their grievances were imaginary,[8] praised Hoxie's "singularly evidenced magnanimity,"[9] and repeatedly predicted the imminent return of the strikers to their jobs.[10] It was within the shifting emotional currents of this maelstrom that Alliance radicalism emerged.

2

In the Spring of 1886, against the background of the Great Southwest Strike, a curious drama of political controversy among Alliancemen was played out in the columns of the official Alliance journal. William Lamb did not instigate this debate, but his actions brought it to crisis, and the crisis in turn galvanized the Alliance into new paths of organizational effort. The question of how best to achieve effective cooperative buying and selling frequently fed the controversy, though this issue was soon overwhelmed by even more threatening concerns. The debate eventually involved the Alliance president, the relationship of the Alliance to the labor movement, the editorial policy of the Alliance journal, most of the order's leaders, and eventually all of the membership. There was, however, one constant. Throughout the months of controversy, William Lamb acted as a catalyst as the debate surged into ever-widening realms.

At the heart of the affair was a deceptively simple question: Was the Alliance "in politics" or not? The initial premise, derived from Alliance doctrine dating from the Lampasas collapse, assumed that the answer was a firm "No." But as alternative modes of organizational conduct failed to change the conditions under which farmers lived, increasing numbers of Alliancemen began to look for ways to turn "No" into something less passive—something that sounded increasingly like "Yes." This change, which took place during the spring and summer of 1886, forced the Alliance to confront the central dilemma that the Grange had pretended did not exist.

As is frequently the case with arguments in reform-minded institutions, the ideological debate occurred publicly, in the presence of the membership, and principally in the pages of the order's journal. In fact, the *Rural Citizen*'s editor, J. N. Rogers, became a central object of the debate. In the earliest days of the Alliance, Rogers had attracted attention with his earnest attacks on monopoly and the "money power." But after 1882, when the *Citizen* was named the Alliance's official journal, he gradually grew more cautious in his approach to political questions. By the summer of 1885 he was bluntly writing that "the Farmers Alliance is not a political organization and was not organized for that purpose." While this disclaimer faithfully tracked the traditional Alliance posture on politics, by the mid-1880's it had worn rather thin. Independent political action outside the framework of either major party was by no means unknown in Texas, as the fleeting success of the Greenback Party illustrates. In addition, a number of articulate advocates who were attracted to the Alliance during the upsurge of 1884–85 brought with them an inclination to think in terms of political party realignment. An Alliance editor named Thomas Gaines laid bold plans to lead Comanche County farmers to a complete independent party sweep over local Democrats in 1886, and the same thing was in the process of happening in Erath County under another farmer-radical named Evan Jones.[11]

The Alliance editor began to receive letters taking issue with his nonpolitical stance. Rogers printed the letters, but he developed the habit of editorializing against their contents in the same issue. Soon the "Alliance in politics" argument dominated the letters column. The president of one county Alliance asked,

> How much longer will we sleep on our interest and rights? Rather, than submit to those unjust oppressions, let us come out like men and claim our rights and if we starve in the struggle, let us starve by manly resistance, rather than submit to a pauperized suicide. . . . We propose to cooperate with trade unions, and such other associations as may be organized by the working masses to improve their condition and protect their rights.[12]

3

As the "Alliance in politics" matter gathered force in the pages of the *Citizen,* regional events outside the order began to raise other questions about Alliance policy. Late in 1885 even before the Great Southwest Strike, Knights of Labor longshoremen had struck the Mallory Steam Ship Line in Galveston, Texas. When the company refused to negotiate, the Knights declared a boycott against products shipped over the line and asked all friendly labor organizations to join the boycott. William Lamb appealed to the Alliance's state president, Andrew Dunlap, to issue a statewide boycott order in support of the Knights. In conjunction with this move, Lamb's Montague County Alliance, in January 1886, authorized Lamb to call a boycott. Dunlap replied to Lamb that he did not have the authority to order a statewide boycott. The Alliance state secretary followed with an official denial that the Alliance had "anything to do with the boycott." [13]

Both state officers seriously underestimated the sense of

comradeship many rank and file Alliancemen felt toward the members of the Knights of Labor. Most of all, the Alliance leadership underestimated Lamb's feeling. In a resolution passed by the Montague Alliance and issued over his signature as president, Lamb challenged the state secretary in language edged with anger and impatience: "Whereas we do not understand that it is his business to fully decide this matter for us as members of the Farmers Alliance, [we] ask his honor the President . . . to order all County Alliances to enter said boycott with the Knights of Labor. . . ." [14]

Meanwhile the Dallas County Alliance joined in a local boycott by the Dallas Knights of Labor in a labor dispute with a prominent Dallas merchandising house. Apparently certain of support from the Alliance president and secretary, the *Citizen's* editor took the side of the company against the Dallas Alliancemen. Rogers's tone was scarcely calculated to smooth matters. The officers of the company, he announced, were "certainly right in continuing the management of their own business." He added that advocates of boycotts were "busy bodies in other men's business. When inexperienced men take the management of commerce into their hands, then woe to the commerce and business interests of our land . . . continue the strikes and we will continue the hard times." [15]

It was evident from Rogers's reference to "strike" that he was reacting to more than just the boycott. The same issue of the *Citizen*—and virtually every other newspaper in Texas as well—carried news of the outbreak of "The Great Southwest Strike." To many, the stakes were enormous. The day the strike began, March 1, 1886, the Fort Worth *Gazette* printed an interview with one of the strikers. He announced: "You will see in this country something never seen before—a revolution: it has come, there will be a great change before this strike is over, and many powerful organizations beside the Knights of Labor will engage in the struggle." A somewhat awed *Gazette* reporter added that the striker "is a good citizen, a prudent man, he is sober, he is intelligent, and the manner of speaking showed how deeply in earnest he was. Is the great contest upon us?" [16]

It was in the heat of such events—including news stories

about "powerful organizations besides the Knights of Labor"—that Rogers wrote his inflammatory denunciation of Alliance support of Knights of Labor boycotts. It is possible that
he did not realize how his choice of words created an all but
unbridgeable chasm between himself and thousands of
farmers who had made a clear choice between the Knights of
Labor and men like Jay Gould. To refer to the Knights—or to
Alliancemen who supported the Knights—as "inexperienced
men" and "busy bodies" was to misread the temper of the
order. In the same issue, the *Citizen*'s editor also criticized the
boycott authorization of the Montague Alliance as "unwise." [17]

5

The Farmers Alliance now embarked upon a course that was
to give definition to the agrarian revolt. In an open letter to
the Alliance membership, Lamb set out to clarify Rogers's
thinking on the issues at stake. In the process, he directly
challenged Alliance President Andrew Dunlap and, indeed,
brought all the issues confronting the Alliance into as sharp a
focus as his skill as a writer permitted him. These issues included the failure of the cooperative buying program, the
resulting need for political action, the advisability of political
coalition with the Knights of Labor, and the relationship of
the Alliance rank and file to its leadership. His letter was nothing less than a review of the animating purpose of the farmers
movement.

He began with a blunt appraisal of the politics of the *Citizen:*
"We did not expect to please all members of the Alliance and
especially the Ed. of our official journal, as we have never yet
seen where he has come out and shown his true colors editorially on the labor question." And he redefined the relationship between members of the order and the state president:

> we think all members should show the world which side they
> are on . . . and if our State President don't wish to do so, we
> know that it will not kill him to say so, and do it in a kind
> manner, and not tell us that we are unwise or fools. . . . We
> also know that it is the duty of the President to preside with
> impartiality. . . .

Then Lamb analyzed the immediate policy question: "If what we have done is a sample of haste and foolishness and it can be thus proved to our satisfaction, we will retract our action in the matter and make apologies. . . . Otherwise we will stand firm by our action and insist on Boycott." Lamb's experience as the order's central purchasing agent shaped his attitude. "The writer of this article has many letters from factories today, to the effect that they will not trade with the Farmers Alliance except through their [own] agents." He was anxious for Alliancemen to ponder the implications of this reality and to set a new course in response. In one long breathless sentence he indicated that he himself had made his own decision:

> Knowing that the day is not far distant when the Farmers Alliance will have to use Boycott on manufacturers in order to get goods direct, we think it is a good time to help the Knights of Labor in order to secure their help in the near future, knowing as we do that the Farmers Alliance can't get a plow today except it come through two or three agents, and feeling assured that the only way we can break this chain is to let them alone, and let them make their plows and wear them out themselves.

Having explained the situation as he saw it, Lamb addressed what he regarded as the leadership's inadequate response. "We have worked hard to get plows direct and can't do it, and I feel satisfied that I know more about what is going on against us than the State President of the Alliance or our Ed., either. . . . Would say that one Sub-Alliance in our county killed a weekly paper some time ago, and we are looking forward for men that will advocate our interests, those who are working against us are no good for us."

Lamb's cutting criticism was grounded in moral outrage, and in closing he made this underlying attitude explicit:

> we know of a certainty that manufacturers have organized against us, and that is to say if we don't do as they say, we can't get their goods. . . . Then for it to be said that we are unwise to let them alone, we can't hold our pens still until we

have exposed the matter and let it be known what it is we are working for.

[Signed] W. R. Lamb.[18]

Alliance radicalism—Populism—began with this letter. The phrases, directed at so many different yet related targets, formed a manifesto of insurgent thought, summarized in the conclusion that "those who are working against us are no good for us." The obstacles that had to be overcome were clearly, if not always grammatically, delineated: editors who failed to show their "true colors on the labor question," presidents who did not know "what is going on against us," and people who failed to realize that it was "a good time to help the Knights of Labor in order to secure their help in the near future."

But Lamb's open letter to the Alliance journal was more than a political statement. His argument reflected a new conception about the farmers' place in American society. The farmer as producer-entrepreneur and small capitalist—the "hardy yeoman" of a thousand pastoral descriptions—is nowhere visible in Lamb's view. This traditional portrait, dating from a simpler Jeffersonian era and still lingering in the social tradition of the Grange, was patently out of place to a man who saw society dominated by manufacturers and their "agents." To Lamb, the farmer of the new industrial age was a worker, and the "labor question" was the central issue on which editors, presidents, and others were expected to show their "true colors." Once such a perspective was attained, it was axiomatic that the organized farmers of the Alliance should join forces with the organized workers of the Knights of Labor. In the new era of business centralization, farmers who continued to aspire to friendship and parity with the commercial world were simply failing to comprehend "what is going on against us." Alliancemen had to put aside such naïveté: "all members should show the world which side they are on." Lamb was asking the farmers of Texas to achieve a new evaluation of what they were so that they might manage a fresh assessment of their relationship with other participants in industrial American society. His sense of moral authority— "we can't hold our pens still"—ensured that he would carry the struggle over Alliance tactics to a conclusion.

William Lamb
Lamb emerged as a leader of the Alliance radicals in 1886 when his boycott proclamation in support of the Knights of Labor produced the internal revolution in agrarian politics that led to the Cleburne Demands. This photograph was taken around 1910.

Once joined, the battle was fought with considerable vigor. Both sides approached the contest with confidence. To the order's president and its journal editor, it was inconceivable that the average Alliance farmer would gamble the future of the organization on such risky action as public coalition with the controversial Knights of Labor. As Lamb and Dunlap exchanged letters, the majority of the daily newspapers of Texas took an increasingly hostile view toward the strikers. Dunlap was convinced that, under the circumstances, placing the Farmers Alliance in such a line of fire would destroy all the organization had gained over nine difficult years.[19]

Lamb, on the other hand, felt he was much closer to the mood of the suballiances than either the order's president or the editor of its journal was. Both as state lecturer and as the chief agent of the cooperative buying program, Lamb had been in intimate contact with thousands of Texas farmers for two years. Dunlap might be sensitive to public opinion as reflected in the daily metropolitan press, but Lamb could claim to be equally sensitive to the discontents coursing through the suballiances.

In the course of the ensuing six-month struggle over organizational policy, Alliancemen defined themselves politically, were defined by others, and began to ponder the differences between the two. In the process, what was still a regional organization of farmers developed a new sense of mission and self-confidence. Alliances in Robertson, Palo Pinto, Erath, and Dallas counties passed resolutions favoring the boycott. Other alliances in Rockwell and Hopkins counties resolved against it. On March 18 Rogers asserted in the *Rural Citizen* that the boycott was "striking at the fundamental principles of American liberty. It is putting burdens on the farmers that they are not able to bear. It is tyranny." But he received plenty of evidence that his stand was heartily opposed by many Alliancemen. The same issue of the *Citizen* carried the admonition of a farmer that "we have to combat with a strong opposition and we have simply got to put brains and numbers against capital or we are going to be switched off by those who are our pretended friends." Lamb's boycott in support of the Knights was the central issue in the Alliance, and everyone knew it.[20]

On March 22 Alliance President Dunlap assembled parts of his correspondence with Lamb into one long account and dispatched his own summary to the *Citizen* and to other papers in North Texas. His attack was a personal one. He sardonically referred to Lamb as a "distinguished historian" of recent events who "claims to be a dealer in agricultural implements solely for the direct benefit and economical working of members of the Farmers Alliance." Dunlap "individually and officially" declared the boycott order by "this man, W. R. Lamb," to be null and void. He called Lamb's unauthorized proclamation of the boycott an act of "unblushing impudence."[21]

But support for the workers was growing in dozens of Alliances and went beyond boycotting to include joint political meetings with Knights of Labor assemblies and direct aid to strikers. Alliances in an East Texas county contributed farm produce and even money to strikers, and the practice soon spread to other Alliances along the trackage of the railroad. While outside observers pondered the implications of organized farmers bringing food to organized strikers, Alliancemen and Knights joined in a "Laboring Men's Convention" in President Dunlap's home county, where they laid the groundwork for an independent political ticket.[22]

The state's press drew various conclusions from these evidences of Alliance solidarity with the strikers. The Waco *Examiner* blamed the Alliance for the strike's continuation: "But for the aid strikers are receiving from farmers alliances in the state and contributions outside, the Knights would have gone back to work long ago." The Dallas *Mercury,* strongly pro-labor, was pleased: "The Farmers Alliances of Texas are generally regarded as the spinal column of this great railroad war." The Austin *Statesman* worried about the political implications. "Unless some eruption occurs between the Knights of Labor and the Farmers Alliance," reasoned the paper, "the affairs of Texas stand a good chance of falling into the hands of those organizations at the state elections next fall." The Galveston *News* was less alarmed. "It is inevitable that the association of the Farmers Alliance and the Knights of Labor will cause a good deal of embarrassment to farmers," the paper said, adding that it was "very likely" that reports of farmer-labor cooperation were "exaggerated" and "put forth by some unofficial and over enthusiastic Knight of Labor." [23]

On the same day this last analysis was offered, however, H. F. Broiles, running as an "Independent Party" candidate and supported by Knights and the Alliance, was elected mayor of Fort Worth. The Galveston *News,* taken aback, promptly interviewed a leader of the Knights, W. E. Farmer, who had worked for the winning radical candidate. The paper printed his startling assessment without comment.

> Labor societies must be organized [and] have a legal status. . . . It is not right to treat those who band together to buy labor as somebody and those who band together to sell it as nobody. . . . It is nothing less than a revolution which now has begun. Don't misreport me on this. By revolution, I don't mean violence, necessarily. The greatest revolution may be peaceful, but a radical change must take place in government and society, and that is revolution. . . . The ballot box is our battlefield. We are done allowing ourselves to be divided into hostile camps to vote against ourselves and neutralize our strength.[24]

If the Galveston *News* was trying to achieve a better focus on events, it was hardly alone. Every issue of the Alliance's own journal offered new and changing interpretations. Late in March an outspoken Alliance leader in Central Texas attacked the *Rural Citizen*'s anti-politics position with heavy-handed irony: "Thanks to Providence for sending us so many good lawyers, honest bankers, and unsophisticated editors who are so good and kind to bestow all their efforts to guide and direct us in the ways of prosperity." He added, in some anger, "Show us wherein either of the great political parties reflect any of the features of the honest face of toil. . . . Shame on your boasted institutions of liberty." Another Allianceman had given up on the *Citizen*. He wrote instead to the pro-labor Dallas *Mercury* to complain about journalists who wanted legislation enacted against boycotting. "How their sympathies run out for the bloated monopolists, the men who have robbed the producer of his labor and the day laborer of his living." [25]

As Lamb and others criticized the *Citizen*'s editor and Dunlap attempted to nullify the boycott, S. O. Daws tried to bridge the growing gaps within the Alliance. Writing as "Goose Quill" in the same issue of the *Citizen* that contained Dunlap's rebuke of Lamb, the Alliance's senior statesman pointed out that "capital as a rule is thoroughly organized against the interest of the laboring class we must admit. But when the laboring class begins to organize, they . . . call it communism and other hard names, which is unjust. We have the undoubted right to organize." Cautiously, Daws defined the options, "I am proud that the morning sunlight of labor's freedom is shining in the political horizon of the east. We should never resort to the Boycott unless it becomes absolutely necessary, then we should enforce it to the letter. The Alliance and Knights of Labor should unite in setting down on those who first set down on us." This ambivalent statement on the boycott could please either Lamb or Dunlap, depending on which part of it one chose to emphasize, but the general tone of the article reflected the growing militance of the order. As the strike entered its second month, Rogers attempted to find a new middle ground in his editorials. "Our people have two extremes to watch," the *Citizen*'s editor said, "the arrogance and greed of capitalists and the tyranny of leaders among labor organizations. One is as dangerous as the other." [26]

His views failed to impress growing numbers of Alliancemen. Late in April, as railroad traffic, protected by armed guards, returned to normal and defeat loomed before the Knights of Labor, a North Texas Alliance attacked Rogers for trying "to arouse the Farmers Alliance against the Knights of Labor." In a resolution that expressed the mid-strike mood of the order's emerging left wing, the farmers concluded: "We know if the Knights of Labor could receive all they deserve [of] the support of all the laboring classes, they would in the near future bring down the great monopolists and capitalists and emancipate the toilers of the earth from the heavy burdens which they now have to bear on account of organized capital." An East Texas Alliance added further evidence that agrarian radicalism had moved well beyond the frontier counties. It resolved to "unite with the Knights of Labor" to secure passage of such laws to achieve a "tribunal for the adjustment of their grievances against chartered corporations." [27]

5

As tempers worsened, Alliancemen could agree on one thing—the order was growing. In February, state officials placed the membership at "about 55,000," and in March, as controversy over the boycott heightened, the *Citizen* reported that Alliances were "on the increase very fast in the whole state." But the growing membership of the Alliance was balanced by the losses in the ranks of the Knights of Labor. In May, the Great Southwest Strike came to an end. No formal settlement was necessary. The members of the union were utterly destitute, and the union itself had been crushed. Most of the leaders and hundreds of members were in jail. Those of the survivors who were acceptable to the Gould management went back to work on company terms. The Knights of Labor never recovered from its defeat at the hands of Jay Gould and H. M. Hoxie. In four years its 700,000 national membership, which had reached its peak in 1886, dwindled to 100,000.[28]

Within the Alliance, however, the organizing of farmers accelerated. New leaders emerged, some of them possessed of an activism that should have given Editor Rogers pause. These men, and the Alliances they led, were in the process of achieving a new outlook as the Knights of Labor went under. In Erath County, on the farming frontier, the cooperative movement was led by Evan Jones, an articulate spokesman destined for national fame in the agrarian revolt. One of their resolutions, written by Jones and passed unanimously, fairly bristled:

> Whereas combined capital by their unjust oppression of labor are casting a gloom over our country and . . . Whereas we see the unjust encroachments that the capitalists are making upon all the different departments of labor . . . we extend to the Knights of Labor our hearty sympathy in their manly struggle against monopolistic oppression and . . . we propose to stand by the Knights.[29]

Throughout May the virus of political independence spread through the North Texas Alliances. The Austin *Statesman* was puzzled by their growing hostility to the Democratic Party. Overlooking the fact that Democratic state officials and the Gould railroads had cooperated closely throughout the Great Southwest Strike, the paper asked, "Why should the Knights of Labor or the Alliance seek to oppose or destroy a party which is essentially fighting for their interests as citizens of Texas?" [30]

The Dallas *News*, perhaps more than any other paper in Texas, was offended by the changing structure of politics in the state. In an effort to slow the pace of Alliance cooperation with the Knights, the paper declared that "the Knights of Labor caused the strike . . . millions of dollars have been lost and the farmers will have to make it good." The Dallas County Alliance thereupon resolved to "use its best effort to suppress the circulation of the Dallas *News*," and it was seconded by a neighboring Alliance, which said, "The hour demands that each Alliance let its colors be seen and its voice heard in unmistakable terms." The Alliance leadership tried various methods of coping with this restless energy. Late in May, President Dunlap was reduced to issuing public pleas to the Alliance membership to abandon the boycott he had tried to halt since January. He got nowhere.[31]

6

The organizational father of the Texas Alliance, S. O. Daws, took an entirely different approach. Having stirred new life into a handful of frontier Alliances and shepherded the order through its first rocky days of cooperation, Daws knew, perhaps better than any other Alliance official, the temper of the membership. He decided that they had to have greater freedom of action if the order was not to tear itself to pieces in partisan argument. Daws's solution, printed in the *Citizen* on May 20, 1886, was sufficiently conservative in its appearance and sufficiently radical in its specific uses as to constitute an entirely new definition of the order's relationship to the political process. It became the tactical foundation upon which third party radicals always thereafter rested their case.

Daws began with a traditional appeal to Alliance conservatives: "To degrade the Alliance to a political machine will subvert its purposes, ruin the order, and fail to accomplish anything in politics. It will only divide the order into factions, one against the other, and all outsiders against the order." The words were not as traditional as they appeared to be. The Alliance would not be degraded by "politics" *per se,* but rather by making itself over into a "political machine." No Alliance radical could take offense at this, for a course of action that turned the order into something that could be characterized to voters as a "machine" was obviously not good politics. Such a patently clumsy course would, as Daws himself put it, "fail to accomplish anything in politics."

In two sentences, Daws then presented his solution: "There is a way to take part in politics without having it in the order. Call each neighborhood together and organize anti-monopoly leagues . . . and nominate candidates for office." The economy of the message did not lessen the heavy ideological load it carried. At first glance the advice seemed not unlike the traditional "nonpartisan" position which, since Lampasas, had consisted of instructing Alliancemen to vote as they pleased as individuals but to keep the order out of politics. But the phrase "each neighborhood" not only neatly defined the basic political subdivision of state politics, the precinct convention, but also the order's basic organizational unit, the suballiance. And the phrase "anti-monopoly leagues" imparted a distinct ideological definition to the kind of political effort Alliancemen should fashion in their "neighborhoods." Democratic conservatives would hardly flock to anti-monopoly leagues.

Indeed, if the political environment of 1886 had any bearing on how one looked at issues—as Daws hoped it did—anti-monopoly leagues should prove especially attractive to those who participated in Alliance cooperatives as well as to members of the Knights of Labor. Common action against railroad capitalists had welded the Knights together; cooperative buying and selling efforts against furnishing merchants, cotton buyers, and wholesalers should certainly help create a unifying cohesion in the suballiances.

The phrase "anti-monopoly league" thus not only provided a locus for political action, it also built on the internal educational program around which the increasingly successful Alliance recruiting effort was organized. In promoting the cooperative movement, Alliancemen habitually used anti-monopoly arguments; the same arguments could also provide the foundation for political action. That this political action would be decidedly independent was underscored by Daws's advice about what the anti-monopoly leagues in each neighborhood should do: nominate candidates for office. This was radical. Traditionally, the Alliance had accepted the existing political structure in the nation, the "two old parties," or, in Texas, the one-party domination of the Democratic "party of the fathers." To a radical anti-monopolist like Daws, simple political action within such a framework was useless; the farmers needed to make their political choices in their own organization, free of the lobbying influences of "trusts," "combinations," and other capitalist inventions. Presumably, the farmers had learned something about the politics of Democrats in the Great Southwest Strike. If, during that struggle, the strikers had been able to discover any comradeship with the state police—who were Democrats all, of course—any testimony of such affection had been hard to hear above the gunfire. Democrats could not be the friends of railroad workers because the old party was dominated by the railroad corporations. Democrats, like Republicans, served the likes of Jay Gould, not the Knights of Labor or the Farmers Alliance. In his new description of "neighborhood anti-monopoly leagues," Daws, the man who had said that "the Alliance and the Knights of Labor should unite in setting down on those who first set down on us," was rendering his settled conviction that it was futile for farmers to vote as "individuals" in Democratic primaries.

The practical political effect of the three phrases—"call each neighborhood together . . . organize anti-monopoly leagues . . . and nominate candidates for office"—added up to a one-sentence mandate for insurgent political action. It pointed to a new political institution—a third party.

But S. O. Daws was not merely a radical activist, he was an organizational leader. From the standpoint of the immediate needs of an organization threatened with a massive split, the conservative merit of Daws's solution was that the order would not appear to be "in politics." The buying and selling cooperatives would function in the Alliance; the political preferences of Alliancemen would be expressed through a separate institution, the third party. The economic arguments that served to justify the first course of action found political expression in the second.

In summarizing his interpretation of what the order's stance should be, Daws provided additional protection for the newly defined momentum toward insurgent political action. Once again he used what seemed to be familiar Alliance terminology; indeed, he was driven to do so by the nature of the organizational problem he faced:

> We believe in the farmer voting himself, and not being voted by demagogues. . . . Beward of men who are trying to get politics into this non-political organization, instead of trying to devise means by which the farmers may have the opportunity to emancipate themselves from the grasp of political tricksters, without pulling down the only organization they have for their mutual benefit.

This interpretation radically redefined the evils threatening the order. The Alliance was to avoid demagogic politicians—but not farmers who were "trying to devise means . . . to emancipate themselves." "Political tricksters" were to be feared—but farmers who voted their own minds were not. It was but a short step from this interpretation to one that defined a trickster as a major party politician who used spurious arguments about nonpartisanship to keep farmers loyal to a party that defended monopoly. This analysis turned on the same perception of the role of farmers in an industrial society that William Lamb had articulated in his defense of his boycott proclamation. Daws was recommending to the farmers a course of political action that corresponded with the new definition of their class position.

The new course represented a fundamental alteration in the Alliance's public posture. Custom warned the order against "politics"; Daws warned it against "demagogues." President Dunlap contended that Alliancemen should vote "as individuals"; Daws counseled them to meet in their neighborhoods and nominate anti-monopoly candidates for office. Editor Rogers called the boycott a "tyranny"; Daws asserted that the Alliance "should never resort to the boycott unless it becomes absolutely necessary, then we should enforce it to the letter." Dunlap denounced Lamb for his "unblushing impudence" in pressing the boycott; Daws praised Alliancemen who were "trying to devise means by which the farmers may have the opportunity to emancipate themselves."

Yet Daws did not ignore the underlying anxiety that drove the Alliance's right wing to rhetorical excess in denouncing the order's activists. On the contrary, he respected their fear that political action would destroy the order itself. Having provided a chart to convey the membership toward political action, Daws cautioned that the farmers must reach this goal "without pulling down the only organization they have for their mutual benefit." [32]

7

In 1886, Daws's ideological achievement was internally consistent, politically artful, and highly germane to the immediate

S. O. Daws
The "father" of the Alliance movement and the order's Traveling Lecturer. Daws breathed new life into
the struggling movement in 1883
and carried it beyond the counties of
the farming frontier. In 1886, the
Daws formula for politics liberated
the order's emerging left wing from
the inherited constraints of its "nonpartisan" tradition and set the stage
for the triumph of alliance
radicalism within the movement.

demands of the agrarian movement. Its relevance was
promptly demonstrated. President Dunlap was sufficiently impressed with Daws's description of the perils of precipitate action that he decided to overlook the long-term political implications of anti-monopoly leagues. He endorsed the speech in
the *Citizen.* Rogers, loyal organizational man that he was, also
commended it to his readers.[33]

But Daws had done more than extract a personal endorsement from the Alliance leadership. With a directness and a
diplomacy no Grange leader was ever able to achieve, he had
confronted the central dilemma of a "reform" organization
saddled with a "nonpolitical" tradition. In so doing, he redefined politics in a way that provided necessary breathing room
for the rival factions at a time when the order was beginning
its greatest period of growth. The change was achieved in ten
months: Rogers had articulated the Grange inheritance; Daws
now charted the future course of the Alliance.[34]

The shift in ideology did not originate with S. O. Daws, of
course. The causative agent was William Lamb's unilateral
proclamation of the boycott in support of the Knights of
Labor. Lamb wanted political action and Dunlap feared it.
Daws stood between the two men. It was not political action he
feared, but premature political action. His pace toward insurgency was measured in steps that did not threaten the carefully constructed edifice of the Alliance. Daws's conduct to-

ward the boycott issue reflected the inherent concern of the organizer to protect the cohesion of the organization he had built. Daws did not oppose the boycott as a logical policy, but he would not have risked alienating the Alliance president by calling one unilaterally, as William Lamb did. Proof of this lies in a series of negatives: Daws did not attack Lamb, nor did he defend Dunlap, nor did he call the boycott himself.

Both an organizer and a political radical, the Alliance's senior statesman was driven by the insurgent energy on his left to try to find some method of holding his organization together without at the same time impeding a growing political sensibility which he himself endorsed. Daws's achievement was that he not only defended the idea of innovation as applied to inherited Alliance policy, but he also vastly extended its immediate possibilities. The fact that he was able to do so in language that retained the flavor of the organization's early doctrines helped make his argument persuasive to the order's conservatives and thus validated its legitimacy as the new working policy of the Alliance. Once this was assured, his redefinition of what Alliancemen could and should do politically took on enormous potential meaning, for it created considerable maneuvering room for the order's activists. The speed with which the Alliance moved to exploit this opportunity was dramatic: less than three months later the Alliance, in convention assembled, promulgated an aggressive seventeen-point political program that soon became famous in the agrarian movement as the "Cleburne Demands."

The ideological momentum toward the explosion at Cleburne came from two events: William Lamb's boycott of January, which threatened the unity of the Alliance, and S. O. Daws's political redefinition of May, which preserved it on new grounds. And yet Lamb's agitation on the boycott would have had far less meaning to either Daws or Dunlap had it not found strong support among the anonymous men who farmed the North Texas prairies. The resolutions supporting the boycott, the joint political meetings with the Knights of Labor, the anguish and impatience surfacing in the letters column of the official Alliance newspaper—these were the realities that spurred S. O. Daws to his redefinition. And it was this visible energy, asserting itself in so many diverse ways, that the Alliance president acknowledged when he endorsed Daws's new policy. Dunlap really had no choice—unless he wanted to risk losing so many restless members to some more activist cause.

Thus, the most significant development within the Farmers Alliance in the spring of 1886 was not that William Lamb initiated certain events or that S. O. Daws responded to them, but rather that thousands of farmers began evolving the desire to express their discontent through tangible political acts.

8

The emergence of William Lamb's radical leadership and the development of the Daws formula for political action gave direction to the organizational consolidation by the Alliance of its farmer constituency in Texas in 1886. In the bitter aftermath of the Great Southwest Strike, in the face of rising newspaper awareness and concern, and in the midst of worsening drought, the order's growing corps of lecturers combed rural Texas and recruited farmers by the tens of thousands. After nine years of trial and error, the Alliance organizers had a story to tell. Their organizational framework had evolved since the founding days of 1877. Their message of economic cooperation drew from experiences dating back to the early 1880's. The order's relationship to politics had become increasingly focused since 1884. By 1886, Alliance lecturers were speaking in behalf of a maturing idea. As the summer began, the order counted 2000 suballiances and over 100,000 members.[35]

As the Alliance came to envelop whole regions of the state, its leaders reacted in new ways to the new facts of organizational maturity. The men of the order's state leadership evolved their political attitudes in response to the specific pressures of their professional duties. The Alliance administrators—the president, the state secretary, and the state treasurer—acquired the coloration of centrists. Their attempts to slow down the gathering political momentum inside the order no longer took the form of harsh personal attacks on Alliance radicals. Intent on holding their restless organization together, most of them adopted a cautiously moderate posture.

Some among the state leadership, however, were becoming even more activist. The two officials whose jobs kept them in frequent contact with the mass of farmers in the suballiances, the Traveling Lecturer and the State Chaplain, raised political questions in increasingly aggressive terms. The Chaplain, J. H. Jackson, pilloried the Democratic Party in speech after speech, while the Lecturer, Daws, maintained a steady anti-monopoly fire. Alliancemen and Knights of Labor partisans in a number of counties responded with local level third party political tickets. In such ways the order began to apply the Daws formula—"meeting in neighborhoods" and "nominating candidates for office." [36]

Closest of all the order's officials to the economic anguish at the bottom of Texas society were the Alliance county lecturers. Like the state leadership, they, too, were evolving new attitudes in response to their Alliance duties. Day after day the lecturers traveled through the poverty-stained backwaters of rural Texas and met with farmers in country churches or crossroads schoolhouses. The small stories of personal tragedy they heard at such meetings were repeated at the next gathering, where, in an atmosphere of genuine shared experience, they drew nods of understanding. The most astute organizers soon learned that farmers were more likely to link their own cause to another, larger one whose spokesmen knew and understood their grievances. The difficulty was that the lecturers themselves were altered by these experiences. They were, in effect, seeing too much. Hierarchical human societies organize themselves in ways that render their victims less visible; for a variety of reasons, including pride, the poor cooperate in this process. But the very duties of an Alliance lecturer exposed him to the grim realities of agricultural poverty with a directness that drove home the manifest need to "do something." Repeated often enough, the experience had an inexorable political effect: slowly, one by one—and in many instances unknown as yet to each other—local Alliance lecturers came to form a nucleus of radicalism inside the Texas Alli-

74

ance. Among them were men like J. M. Perdue, who was soon destined to be the principal author of the first radical political document of the agrarian revolt.[37]

Perhaps nothing illustrated the deepening alienation of Texas farmers better than the response one of them made to an editorial in a North Texas weekly newspaper. The Weatherford *Times,* formerly a vitriolic foe of the early Alliance, had mellowed in the presence of the order's enormous growth and had actually praised the increasing evidence of joint action by the Alliance and Knights of Labor. The paper added nervously: "There is great fear displayed in some quarters that they should unite" in opposition to the Democratic Party. A Parker County farmer angrily replied that he had

> . . . no doubt that the old political bosses have fears of that sort, but I do not see that such a result would be fraught with a great deal of danger to the country. . . . The Farmers Alliance and Knights of Labor . . . will oppose being gagged and muzzled or being whipped into supporting false men or false principles by a party lash, in the hands of party bosses, of any party. I think they have determined to be free men and vote their own honest convictions, independent of party bossism. . . . Who will be hurt, except the party bosses? Monopolies will still pay them to use the party lash the same as ever. . . . You see, Congress had to legislate for capitalists or they would have been compelled to take all the toils and risk of business like other men. . . . They cannot make anything by legislating for us poor devils.[38]

This was sobering language indeed. The Dallas *News* was hard put to explain such alienation. "The discontented classes are told, and are only too ready for the most part to believe, that the remedy is more class legislation, more government, more paternalism, more State socialism," the paper asserted. "The current gospel of discontent as a rule is sordid and groveling. Its talk is too much about regulating capital and labor . . . and too little about freeing capital and industry from all needless restraints and so promoting the development and diffusion of a high order of hardy manhood." [39]

The *News* was not alone in its formula for hardy manhood.

The editor of the Alliance journal, J. N. Rogers, though accepting S. O. Daws's political redefinition of Alliance involvement in politics in May, decided in July to oppose any further loosening of the reins. Rogers not only reprinted the July 16 editorial of the Dallas *News* in his *Rural Citizen,* he endorsed it as "sensible." The chasm between the Alliance editor and the activists was now unbridgeable, as the latter soon made abundantly clear.[40]

9

The summer turned into one of searing drought, bringing crop failures not only to the old frontier counties, but to other areas of Texas as well. Despite prospects for a smaller harvest, cotton prices did not rise. More and more farmers questioned the universal application and beneficence of the law of supply and demand. It seemed only to work to the benefit of capitalists. Evidence of political insurgency was no longer restricted to the frontier Alliances, for the Alliance as an organization and Alliance radicalism as a genre had by 1886 completely overwhelmed the Grange in that organization's old stronghold in the central part of the state. An Alliance gathering drew thousands to a day-long Central Texas political outing at which Knights of Labor leader W. E. Farmer enunciated the new radicalism to an enthusiatic audience. The emerging style was enough to give pause to any party regular:

> The laboring classes must either take charge of the ballot box and purify the government or witness one of the most gigantic revolutions known for ages. . . . Lay aside all political parties. Class legislation is robbing you. Sectional strife and hatred has downed the people. . . . The Republicans stole the goods and the Democrats concealed them. . . . We have labored two years and now have an enthusiasm infused among the people that all hell cannot crush out. We acknowledge no leader. Party has led the country to financial ruin. . . . You may crush out the Alliance, the Knights of Labor, and other organizations for the laboring man but you cannot stamp out the principles they have sent throughout the land. . . . We have an overproduction of poverty, barefooted women, political thieves and many liars. There is no

76

difference between legalized robbery and highway robbery. . . . If you listen to other classes you will only have three rights . . . to work, to starve, and to die."

That same evening, after dinner and more speeches, "a huge call was sent up for Farmer," and he responded with a second address which lasted for another hour and a half. A startled metropolitan reporter commented that "A great majority of the people seemed to endorse all he said." [41]

In county after county, Alliance meetings begun in prayer and ritual ended in political speeches, many of them delivered by the suballiance chaplain, who frequently doubled as lecturer and organizer in spreading the new social gospel. Voices repeating the familiar doctrine of nonpartisanship became difficult to hear above the mounting din of insurgent political language. To the dismay of the order's old guard, Alliancemen by the thousands had gone "in politics" on the eve of the Alliance state convention in Cleburne. In the final days of pre-convention maneuvering, Rogers of the *Rural Citizen,* now a much embattled editor, launched a frontal attack on the Knights in an effort to weaken the political coalition of farmers and workers. The *Citizen* roundly assaulted the Knights and characterized any suggestion that the Alliance and the union might have a "correlative position" as "slobbering gibberish." On this note the months of internal controversy initiated by William Lamb's boycott ended. Whatever the majority of organized farmers now thought, the state would soon know, for the years of Alliance anonymity were over. [42]

10

In August 1886 metropolitan reporters descended on the little farming community of Cleburne, near Dallas, to learn what they could of the large and strangely aggressive organization that called itself the Farmers Alliance. Newsmen quickly discovered that the order had little to offer in sartorial elegance. Alliancemen, they reported, looked "grangy." The appearance of the delegates, however, did not diminish their obvious seriousness. Rather, it provided visible evidence that the Alliance had traveled widely over the back roads in recruiting both its members and leaders.[43]

A welcoming speech by the mayor of Cleburne was the only break in a relentless four-day round of delegate caucuses, committee meetings, and lengthy executive sessions of the convention itself. One fact was immediately clear: the order had spread far beyond its 1884 base along the old farming frontier, as the presence of delegates from eighty-four county Alliances demonstrated. Beyond the ken of observers, however, was the political mood of the delegates.

The fashioning of a proposed political program became the work of the general "ways and means" committee, traditionally known in Alliance circles as "The Committee for the Good of the Order." Like other committees, this group was composed of men from the county Alliances, where leadership rested on organizing and lecturing abilities. In consequence, the committee members had first-hand knowledge of widespread agricultural proverty, and their report reflected a strongly activist sentiment. The committee first announced that it had changed its name to the "Committee for the Good of the Order and Demands." The meaning of the additional two words was lodged in the committee's report itself. That lengthy document went beyond a mere catalogue of agrarian grievances on land, money, transportation, and marketing issues: it proposed that the Alliance offer specific legislative remedies. These proposals were not like the "petitions" which had historically characterized Grange resolutions touching on legislative matters. Rather, each of the committee's proposals was preceded by two words: "We Demand." [44]

The committee presented its report to the convention, and a long debate followed. It was intermittently interrupted for other business, including the election of officers. The order's activists, perhaps aware that they had put enough before their colleagues for one convention, did not contest the official slate, with its nice balance of centrists and radicals. Andrew Dunlap was quietly reelected in the midst of the very internal debate over politics he had tried unsuccessfully to forestall.[45]

But though the schism did not extend to personalities, the Alliance made a fundamental shift on another matter more directly related to the political question. The delegates, in executive session, voted to dispense with J. N. Rogers and to reject his *Rural Citizen* as their journal. They then placed the imprimatur of the Alliance on the most outspoken anti-monopoly newspaper in Texas, the Dallas *Mercury*.[46]

With these matters decided, the delegates focused on the committee's "demands," which listed an accumulation of post-Civil War grievances. Seventeen in number, they were addressed to the governments of Texas, the United States, and, in the case of the seventeenth, to President Dunlap himself. The demands sought "such legislation as shall secure to our people freedom from the onerous and shameful abuses that the industrial classes are now suffering at the hands of arrogant capitalists and powerful corporations." Five of them dealt with labor issues, three with the power of railroads, and two with the financial problem. Of six demands relating to agricultural matters, five focused on land policy and the sixth on commodity dealings in agricultural futures. The final demand, directed to Dunlap, could be classified as "educational."[47]

The committee placed first on its list a demand for the recognition of trade unions, cooperative stores, "and such other associations as may be organized by the industrial classes to improve their financial condition." Other labor planks called for the establishment of a national bureau of labor statistics, headed by a commissioner of cabinet rank, "that we may arrive at a correct knowledge of the educational, moral, and financial condition of the laboring masses," the passage of an improved mechanics lien law "to compel corporations to pay their employees according to contract, in lawful money," and the abolition of the practice of leasing state convicts to private employers. The final labor plank recommended a national conference of all labor organizations "to discuss such measures as may be of interest to the laboring classes."

The railroad planks betrayed agrarian anxiety over the power of railroad lobbyists to manipulate state legislatures and law enforcement agencies, as well as the ability of railroad financiers to profit from watered stock. Railroad property should be assessed at "full nominal value of the stock on which the railroad seeks to declare dividends" and the state attorney general should "rigidly enforce" corporation taxes. The farmers also demanded an interstate commerce law "to secure the same rates of freight to all persons for the same kind of commodities" and to prevent rebates and pooling arrangements designed "to shut off competition."

The most explosive portion of the committee report concerned the financial question. It revealed the extent to which Alliance farmers were being radicalized by the Texas financial community's opposition to the Alliance cooperative movement. The proposal called for a federally administered national banking system embracing a flexible currency, to be achieved through the substitution of legal tender treasury notes for existing issues of private national banks. The sums involved should be issued by the federal treasury and regulated by the Congress to provide "per capita circulation that shall increase as the population and business interests of the country expand." In short, the plank advanced the doctrines of the Greenback Party. To address the immediate problem of a severely contracted money supply, the committee proposed, as a consciously inflationist measure, the "rapid extinguishment of the public debt through immediate unlimited coinage of gold and silver" and "the tendering of same without discrimination to the public creditors of the nation."

Though most Texas Alliancemen were Democrats, the experience of their cooperative movement had persuaded a number of them to make a fundamental shift in their political outlook. The greenback critique of American finance capitalism was not a doctrine one learned in "the party of the fathers." For the farmers, the plank was, in fact, a direct product of their new awareness of the power of the commercial world that opposed the cooperatives of the Alliance.

The five land planks addressed agrarian grievances that stemmed from the activities, state and national, of Scottish and English cattle syndicates and domestic railroad land syndicates. By 1886 both groups had seriously diminished the remaining public domain available for settlers. The committee demanded that all land held for speculative purposes should be taxed and, in a brusque reference to usurious interest rates, urged that they should be taxed "at such rates as they are offered to purchasers." Also recommended were measures to prevent aliens from speculating in American land and "to force titles already acquired to be relinquished by sale to actual settlers." The farmers were also asked to demand that forfeited railroad lands "immediately revert to the government and be declared open for purchase by actual settlers" and that fences be removed, "by force if necessary," from public school lands unlawfully fenced by "cattle companies, syndicates, and every other form or name of corporation." The lone agricultural demand not relating to land policy was one designed to end a capitalist activity that had never found favor with American farmers—"the dealing in futures of all agricultural products." [48]

The seventeenth and final plank was a resolution rather than a "demand," but its wording reflected the same concept of the power relationships existing between Alliance members and their state president as had characterized William Lamb's unilateral boycott proclamation six months earlier: "Resolved that the President of the Grand State Alliance be, and he is hereby, directed to appoint a committee of three to press these demands upon the attention of the legislators of the State and Nation" and that he "report progress at the next meeting." The resolution also specified that Texas newspapers be furnished copies of the demands and that 50,000 copies be distributed through the suballiances.

The committee report was the first major document of the agrarian revolt. It isolated the land, transportation, and financial issues that were to become the focus of Populist agitation in the 1890's, as well as labor issues, which the People's Party later tended to neglect. The presentation of the report to the farmers at Cleburne was both electrifying and divisive, and the resulting debate consumed the final two days of the convention. Proceeding behind closed doors, the discussion grew acrimonious as it became clear that a majority of the delegates supported all seventeen demands and were determined to press the committee report to a formal vote. The minority conservative faction, deeply concerned over the greenback demand that seemingly arrayed the Alliance against the Democratic Party, took refuge in a series of parliamentary maneuvers that extended into the evening hours of the last day of the convention. One-third of the delegates had given up and departed for home when, around 11 p.m., the order's activists brought the committee report to a formal vote of the convention. The count revealed that though many of the three-man county delegations were divided on the issue, the twelve "old" Alliance counties on the frontier, including President Dunlap's own Parker County, supported the demands almost solidly. The final tally was 92 delegates in favor of the demands and 75 opposed. By this margin the Alliance had launched a program of political "education"—the necessary foundation for eventual agrarian insurgency. William Lamb's radicalism of January had become, by a narrow margin, the radicalism of the Alliance in August.[49]

11

The "Cleburne Demands" were front page news across Texas on August 8, 1886. The first newspaper reports were restricted to lengthy and precise descriptions of the demands, but as the implications of the Alliance action became clear, newspaper reactions turned hostile. "The Democratic Party is in perilous position," warned the Galveston *News.* The Dallas *News* thought about the matter for a week and then pronounced its judgment: the Cleburne Demands were "essentially repugnant to the spirit, the traditions, and the fundamental ideas of Democracy." The Alliance had become "dominated by the spirit of class legislation, class aggrandizement, class exclusiveness, and class proscription." The *News* told Democrats that it was "scarcely less than treason to be indifferent to such a danger." [50]

Though Alliance conservatives did not attempt to match the condemnatory spirit of the Dallas *News,* they too were profoundly disturbed by the Cleburne Demands. Their attitude marked the first surfacing of deeply held cultural presumptions that stood as forbidding barriers to the long-term goals of the People's Party. While Alliance conservatives shared with the radicals an abiding concern over the plight of the farmer, they felt, or at least hoped, that they would not have to break with their received political heritage to express that concern effectively. But the eleventh demand of the Cleburne document, the greenback plank, was unacceptable to the Democratic Party, and that fact created an agonizing dilemma for conservative farmers. For some among them, loyalty to the Democrats was a matter of habit and social conformity; for others, it was a pragmatic evaluation of what they took to be the invulnerability of the "party of the fathers" to effective attack from without; for still others, the stance of "nonpartisanship" was simple evidence that their commitment to reform was a step lower on their personal scale of political priorities than other commitments were. Among those priorities, in some cases, was an emotional dedication to white supremacy and to its institutional expression in the South, the Democratic Party. Some farmers, finally, simply could not conceive of a Southern farm organization prospering outside the Democratic Party; their loyalty to the party was a function of their loyalty to the Alliance. Whatever the individual variants, the Cleburne conservatives expressed traditional attitudes that Alliance activists and Populists would have to cope with throughout the years of the agrarian revolt. For, as events were to show, the political ideology of both the parent Alliance and its organizational offspring, the People's Party, was grounded in the greenback monetary interpretation of post-Civil War American finance capitalism.

After midnight on the evening of the final vote on the Cleburne Demands, a group of conservative "nonpartisans" met and drafted a public statement of dissociation. Supporters of the demands thereupon drafted a counter-statement, providing details of the tactical maneuvering and upbraiding the minority for publicly revealing divisions within the order. The conservatives then formed a rival "Grand State Farmers Alliance" of an avowedly nonpartisan character. Among other assets, Dunlap's group held all the funds of the regular Alliance, which were safely in the possession of the decamping treasurer. The destructive Lampasas experience of 1879–80 seemed to be repeating itself.[51]

12

Into this sensitive situation stepped one of the most talented and enigmatic men brought forward by the agrarian revolt. In August 1886 Dr. Charles W. Macune was on the verge of an extraordinary career. Born in Wisconsin, and orphaned at ten, he had roamed the West and arrived on the Texas frontier in 1870 at the age of nineteen. He "read" for the professions and in time came to practice both medicine and law. But Macune also possessed untapped talents as an organizer. A strikingly handsome man, he was both a lucid writer and a sonorous, authoritative public speaker. Above all, he was a creative economic theorist. He had joined the order in the winter of 1885–86 and had risen quickly to local prominence in the Milam County Alliance, which elected him as one of its three delegates to the Cleburne convention. Though the 1886 meeting marked Macune's first statewide convention, his farmer associates, impressed with his diplomatic performance during the tense debate over the demands, elected him chairman of the executive committee. He stepped quickly into the vacuum left by Dunlap's resignation and immediately sought to placate the disgruntled conservatives while not incurring the displeasure of the radicals. Aware of the delicacy of the situation, Macune called the order's leadership together at a special meeting even as their differing interpretations of the Cleburne meeting were being debated by Alliancemen around the state. Macune concentrated on two men—Dunlap, spokesman for the "nonpartisan" position, and Evan Jones, spokesman for the radicals. Jones, like Macune, had come into prominence at Cleburne. President of the Erath County Alliance, Jones was typical of the new brand of local leadership that had emerged in the Alliance since 1883. A "political Allianceman"—that is to say, a greenbacker—he led the Erath County farmers into independent political action with a full county ticket against the Democrats in 1886. A firm proponent of the Cleburne Demands, Jones, like Macune, had been elected by the Cleburne convention to the state executive committee. Dunlap on the "nonpartisan" right and Jones on the "political" left represented the divergent tendencies in the order—with Macune trying to find tenable ground in between.[52]

Neatly balancing his words, Macune persuaded Dunlap of the "importance and danger" of the conservatives' action. For the moment, the very demonstration of such concern by Macune seemed enough to immobilize Dunlap. He acquiesced in a passive course. To Jones, the advocate of aggressive action, Macune talked of the need for the Texas Alliance to broaden its base by seeking mergers with whatever progressive farm organizations could be found in other states. As Macune doubtless expected, Jones was quite responsive to the suggestion. Only after getting both sides to agree to a special statewide meeting at Waco did Macune finally accept the resignations of Dunlap and the conservative executive committeemen that had been tendered at Cleburne. It can be safely assumed that Macune was able to keep the nonpartisans—and the order's treasury—within the Alliance "family" while shearing them of their power primarily because of the remarkable response of Texas farmers to the Cleburne Demands. The tactical position and the self-confidence of the conservatives had been eroded by the sheer fame of the Cleburne document.[53]

The two Alliance factions were talking to Macune, if not yet to each other. Indeed, Macune had no sooner disposed of the immediate menace on his right than he moved into closer coalition with his left. He agreed that Evan Jones should journey to Louisiana to sound out the leaders of the struggling Louisiana Farmers Union on the possibility of merger.[54]

Temporarily, at least, the Alliance was intact—and under leadership that now excluded the order's older traditionalists. In the new officialdom composed of Alliance radicals and Charles Macune, Macune represented the right wing. Yet Macune was much more an activist than Andrew Dunlap. Indeed, if the Alliance somehow remained unified, the Cleburne Demands could be seen to have produced an internal political revolution. An impulse toward aggressive action, greenback in implication but as yet not wholly internalized, had come to power within the Texas Alliance.

As Macune labored behind the scenes, the Alliance grew spectacularly. Farmers by the thousands heard about the Cleburne Demands and decided that the Alliance meant what it said about helping "the industrial classes." Hundreds of charters for new suballiances were issued, and older local groups took on new members until whole farming areas were enrolled. New members were added at a rate of up to 20,000 per month through the autumn and winter of 1886. Alliance lecturers were "sweeping everything before them." [55]

The incoming mail to the Texas Grange measured the fury of the Alliance organizing drive. "Please try to send me a lecturer down here soon," wrote one local Grange leader. "The Alliance man had passed this way and played havoc. . . ." The reference to "the Alliance man" reveals an interesting difference in scale of thought. The Grange often had but one organizer at work, "the Grange man." In the fall and winter of 1886, the Alliance had literally scores of organizers in the field. By the time Macune convened the special Alliance meeting at Waco in January 1887, the statistics were overwhelming: the Grange numbered less than 9000, while the Alliance claimed 200,000 members in over 3000 chartered suballiances. As spokesmen for the order's radical wing had hoped, the aggressive young farm organization had become "a power in the land." [56]

CHAPTER IV

The Rise of Western Insurgency

"Extensive movements are on foot."

To all appearances, the agrarian revolt developed in the South and West in a fashion that merged separate currents of reforming energy. The National Farmers Alliance seemed a powerful tributary of insurgency that conveyed sluggish Southerners toward the People's Party. There the mobilized reform energies of the South flowed into a raging Western torrent. That torrent had no apparent source; it seemed to have materialized from an unknown well-spring concealed somewhere in the Great Plains. The revolt in the West had simply "happened"—times were hard. So the movement of the farmers appeared to the puzzled nation in 1892. Appearances, however, were misleading. The "tributaries" of the People's Party were not divergent; indeed, they were not even tributaries; the radical currents merely needed to be traced to their common headwaters.

The ideological course to the 1892 Omaha Platform of the People's Party ran back through the Ocala Demands of 1890, the St. Louis Platform of 1889, the Dallas Demands of 1888, and the Cleburne Demands of August 1886. For in 1886 the organizational impulses generated by farmer cooperatives, impulses that were to lead to the People's Party, identified themselves. Shaped by the tensions of expansion across the nation, the new kind of a people's politics that had materialized in Texas in 1886 became known to the nation in 1892 as "Populism."

The spectacle of earnest farmer-lecturers setting off on continent-spanning journeys in the late 1880's to organize the folk, and, furthermore, doing it, appears now to have had a kind of rustic grandeur. It was, in fact, the most massive organizing drive by any citizen institution of nineteenth-century America. The broader outlines had a similar sweep: the Alliance's five-year campaign carried lecturers into forty-three states and territories and touched two million American farm families; it brought a program and a sense of purpose to Southern farmers who had neither, and provided an organizational medium for Westerners who had radical goals but lacked a mass constituency.

Yet none of these achievements described, in themselves, what Populism was. At bottom, what spread through the South and then through the West was a popular movement that developed its own supportive "movement culture." Populism is the story of how a large number of people, through a gradual process of self-education that grew out of their cooperative efforts, developed a new interpretation of their society and new political institutions to give expression to these interpretations. Their new ideas grew out of their new self-respect.

Despite the ultimate long-term effects, the massive recruiting campaign of 1887–91 nevertheless also dramatized the impending tension within the ranks of the new movement that was beginning to form. The immediate results were far too divisive to produce any portrait of grandeur, however rustic.

As matters developed late in 1886, the remarkable growth of the Texas Alliance was a direct product of the accelerating political momentum within the order. Earnest radicals soon discovered, however, that this very momentum had produced an acute internal crisis. After some anxious months the organization preserved its cohesion, but only by a new burst of creativity keyed to further expansion. More than anything else, the surge of the Farmers Alliance across the South and then the West developed out of the order's attempt to save itself from fratricidal destruction in Texas. This ideological tension had had its origin in a tense internal struggle that took place on the eve of the campaign to organize the South.

2

Many of the delegates who gathered for Charles Macune's specially called conference in Waco in January 1887 carried militant instructions from their home Alliances. The continued growth of the order since Cleburne had confirmed for the activists the practicality of aggressive advocacy. From a radical perspective, the demands had not been divisive, but rather had attracted thousands of farmers to the Alliance. The activists saw no need to turn back, and their cause had a number of articulate spokesmen. Besides William Lamb, the new radicalism found willing advocates in J. M. Perdue, co-author of the Cleburne Demands, Evan Jones of Erath, H. S. P. Ashby of Fort Worth, and scores of lecturers from county Alliances and suballiances. The lean harvests and low prices of 1886 lent strength to their repeated injunctions for action. Balancing this thrust was the psychological hold the Democratic Party had on Southerners. Those who opposed the Cleburne Demands did so not so much because of their specific content—which faithfully expressed grievances most farmers regarded as legitimate—but because of their implicit repudiation of the Democractic Party of the South.[1]

Amid such contradictory influences, the Waco conference deteriorated into partisan discord over the precise relationship of the Alliance to the political process. Macune was kept in the chair throughout the opening day, hearing motions and ruling on parliamentary questions. The next morning he refused to recognize anyone until the delegates named a chairman. After Macune made a short speech, he was unanimously elected. He then moved to the podium with what turned out to be a transforming proposal. Ignoring the delegates' internal divisions, he oriented them toward a more elementary purpose—combating the farmer's traditional problem of credit. As Alliancemen of all factions listened attentively, Macune proposed a central, statewide "Farmers Alliance Exchange," as a giant cooperative to oversee the marketing of the cotton crops of Alliance members and to serve as the central purchasing medium for Texas farmers. Then, reviewing the spectacular growth of the order, Macune told the delegates that the men who had developed the Alliance cooperative and had organized Texas could "organize the cotton belt of the nation." He outlined his recently conceived plans for projected merger of the Alliance with the small Louisiana farm organization and offered an inspiring vision of a South-wide monopoly of organized agriculture to combat the marketing and financial monopolies of the nation. "Whatever other objects an organization may have . . . I hold that cooperation, properly understood and properly applied, will place a limit to the encroachments of organized monopoly, and will be the means by which the mortgage-burdened farmers can assert their freedom from the tyranny of organized capital, and obtain the reward for honesty, industry, and frugality, which they so richly deserve, and which they are now so unjustly denied." [2]

The delegates were, to say the least, responsive. There had been talk in Texas in 1886 of carrying the Alliance to other states, but only tentative steps had been taken. Macune brought an individual capacity to act, and a specific plan, at the precise moment when the Alliance had completed its basic organizing job in Texas and was ready—structurally and psychologically—to move to larger tasks. In addressing the government of the United States as well as that of Texas, the Cleburne Demands themselves had explicitly acknowledged that the ultimate objectives of the Alliance could not be achieved on a regional basis. Macune's proposal to organize the nation's cotton belt was a step toward a national presence that every Allianceman could appreciate regardless of his political inclinations. Conservative objections to the Cleburne Demands receded in importance in the face of this larger objective. Partisan wrangling was put aside. All seemed relieved that the Alliance, so obviously healthy in other respects, had not been shattered. In a wave of good feeling, the Cleburne Demands were reaffirmed—this time without dissent—and the merger with the Louisiana Farmers Union was approved. A new organization, "The National Farmers Alliance and Cooperative Union," was established. C. W. Macune was unanimously elected president, and the Louisiana representative who was present was elected vice-president.[3]

The return of the conservative treasurer, and the order's treasury, removed a possible obstacle to the massive organizing campaign needed to carry the Alliance message to the South. Travel funds were allocated, organizers were selected and briefed at a specially called statewide meeting of lecturers, and the campaign was launched—all within five weeks of Macune's Waco speech.

3

Six lecturers were initially dispatched to Mississippi, six to Alabama, seven to Tennessee, five to the border state of Missouri, and three to Arkansas. Others moved into the Carolinas, Georgia, Florida, Kentucky, and Kansas. Tested in the process of organizing 200,000 farmers in Texas, they took with them detailed plans for state charters, county organizations, and suballiances, and the aggressive anti-monopoly oratory of the Alliance movement. With cotton down to eight cents a pound, the Texans went forth with large expectations. The Macune formula for a centralized buying and selling cooperative was outlined to gatherings at hundreds of Southern crossroads from the Gulf to the Ohio River. Farmers were told how to establish the trade store system on a county level and members of suballiances were instructed in the advantages of electing one of their own number as a business agent. All of the experiences of the founders were drawn upon, as organizers also explained the value of Alliance cotton yards, Alliance trade committees, and Alliance county warehouses.[4]

The results were spectacular. Alliances sprouted not only in every state, but in almost every county of the Old Confederacy. Dazzled by his success, lecturer J. B. Barry sent in a rhapsodic report from North Carolina. "In spite of all opposing influences that could be brought to bear in Wake County,

I met the farmers in public meetings twenty-seven times, and twenty-seven times they organized. . . . The farmers seem like unto ripe fruit—you can gather them by a gentle shake of the bush." [5]

The first organizer to leave Texas for the Deep South was the order's Traveling Lecturer, S. O. Daws. He departed in February and organized the first Mississippi Alliance on March 3, 1887. Within six months thirty Mississippi counties had been organized and a State Alliance had been chartered. Throughout the South, Texas organizers followed the precedent set by Daws in his 1884 Texas campaign: the most aggressive local farmers were named as organizers and briefed in the techniques of conveying the Alliance doctrine. According to a Mississippi historian, "deputies swept to every part of the state," and one even took to announcing his itinerary in the public press! By the end of 1887, twenty-one North Carolinians were at work as Alliance organizers, and the new state spokesman, L. L. Polk, declared he needed "five times that number" to meet the demand. Alliances had multiplied at such a rate in one North Carolina county that there was "hardly an interval of five miles . . . that does not have an organization." [6]

The pattern was much the same everywhere. The word spread, as it had earlier in Texas, that the Alliance meant what it said about "doing something for the dirt farmer." A. T. Jacobson organized the first Alliance in Alabama at Beech Grove, Madison County, in March, and W. C. Griffith planted the order throughout the sixth and seventh congressional districts of the state. By late summer, Griffith had organized over 1300 farmers in a single county. Another Texan stayed an entire year and later claimed to have organized 1500 suballiances in Alabama and Tennessee. But not all farmers were like "ripe fruit." J. M. Perdue, the author of the Cleburne Demands, wrote back from Opelika, Alabama, that many farmers were "so crushed under the crop mortgage system that they have lost almost all hope of bettering their condition." In a comment that revealed the depth of agrarian animosity toward furnishing merchants and the crop lien system, Perdue added that "the threats of the grab-all family have been given out, and many of the poor are afraid to join the Alliance, fearing the major or the colonel will quit issuing rations to them at 50 percent over cash price." In spite of all hazards, however, the organizing momentum of the Alliance gradually conquered whole farming districts, the hesitant tenants joining a bit late, but joining. In Alabama, as in North Carolina and other states, the demand for lecturers became so great that not enough could be supplied. In one county the farmers organized themselves at a mass meeting and formally requested an organizer to visit the county and show them how to establish an Alliance.[7]

Nothing could reveal the pent-up frustrations and long-repressed aspirations of Southern farmers more than the speed with which they responded to the hope represented by the Alliance. Within three years of the arrival of the first Texas organizers, the Georgia Alliance had enrolled more than 100,000 members and had penetrated into 134 of the state's 137 counties. In Tennessee, where the Agricultural Wheel had pioneered in organizing, membership rose to 125,000 in 3600 suballiances covering 92 of the state's 96 counties. Elsewhere across the South the idea of farmers working together to throw off the fetters of the furnishing merchant spread with the power of a biblical prophesy. A Virginia patrician attributed the phenomenon to "almost a universal conviction that financial salvation was come." [8]

As fast as farmers mastered the legal niceties—and sometimes before—state exchanges were chartered, purchasing agents selected, and trade stores established across the Old Confederacy. To baffled Southern Grangers, only metaphors drawn from nature could explain the organizational phenomenon that had engulfed them. The Alliance had "swept across Mississippi like a cyclone." A North Carolinian added that "a great movement, called the Farmers Alliance, has about ruined the Grange." [9]

By the time the National Farmers Alliance and Cooperation Union of America held its inaugural convention at Shreveport, Louisiana, in October 1887, the cooperative campaign had invaded ten states—all in eight months. The organizational scaffolding erected by the founders had proved to be a stimulus, several states putting the final touches on their state organizations shortly before the Shreveport conclave so that they would have a legal means of sending delegates to the national convention. President Macune announced that the Texas organizers had brought some $2,866.50 in dues money to the national treasurer, more than enough to repay a $500 loan advanced by the Texas Alliance. After a generation of unrelenting poverty, the farmers of the South were desperate for a message of economic salvation. The Southern yeomanry had indeed become "like ripe fruit." But the memories of political and social orthodoxy were deeply imbedded. The question posed itself: ripe for what? [10]

4

Throughout the Western plains, the question posing itself was of a different order at first. The succession of third party defeats throughout the 1880's in the West seemed, to many radicals, to doom any possibility of broad-based reform. The swift death of the Union Labor Party in 1888 so disillusioned one young radical in Kansas that he retreated to a self-conscious display of bravado in the face of what he clearly regarded as a hopeless situation:

> I know that for the man who sees the evils of the time—the want, ignorance and misery caused by unjust laws—who sets himself so far as he has strength to right them, there is nothing in store but ridicule and abuse. The bitterest thought, and the hardest to bear, is the hopelessness of the struggle, "the futility of the sacrifice." But for us who have taken up the crusade, there shall be no halting; and as our ranks grow thin by death and desertion, we should close up, shoulder to shoulder, and show an unbroken battle line to the enemy.[11]

The author of these somber words was Jeremiah Simpson, a man destined within a very short time to achieve national notoriety as "Sockless Jerry" Simpson, the very symbol of fiery prairie Populism. Indeed, a mere eleven months after he brooded over ranks grown "thin by death and desertion," Simpson offered a remarkably different appraisal of the

94

health of the reform movement: "Our meetings are growing; at first they were held in country school houses while the other parties held theirs in the open air; now ours are outside, and the other parties are never heard of at all." [12]

To reform candidates who saw politics solely in terms of the size of crowds at summer speech festivals, a marvelous change had indeed come over the people of Kansas sometime between 1889 and 1890. But if the gulf between Simpson's exaggerated despair one year and his romantic optimism the next had the merit of pointing to anything at all of substance, it was that essential forms of social change are rarely those most easily seen from the rostrums of meeting halls.

There was, in truth, much more to the agrarian revolt than could be inferred from the size of crowds listening to reform politicians in Kansas. New forms of political insurgency came to the West in the late 1880's and appeared sufficiently visible by 1890 for Jerry Simpson to see, but the process itself worked unevenly across the prairies and developed variation in different states that were to have decisive ramifications. If Populism was a river of discontent and aspiration, it seemed to be fed by many currents, and their confluence sometimes produced temporary eddies and whirlpools that made forward motion difficult for many to see. The source of them all, however, was the same. Some of these currents were flowing with accelerating speed at the very moment in 1889 when Jerry Simpson assumed that the reform cause was bleakest.

5

If economic instability was a necessary precursor to political unrest, the Kansas which stirred such despair in Simpson in 1889 should have generated precisely the opposite response. The economy of Kansas, more than that of any other state in the nation in the 1880's, had rested on financial quicksand. By 1887 a runaway speculative boom had given way to a calamitous bust which had thrown thousands back from the frontier and plunged the entire state into sudden shock. All of the states of the Northwestern plains participated in the vigorous boom of the 1880's, but the magnitude of the speculative fever in Kansas was unmatched elsewhere. Immigration, the frantic building of railroads, and a sensational increase in land values were simultaneous and mutually supporting events. In the central third of the state, near the thirty-inch rainfall line, more than 220,000 immigrants poured in between 1881 and 1887. Almost half of them arrived in the three-year period between 1885 to 1887. Railroad trackage soared—from 3104 miles in 1880 to 8797 miles in 1890.[13]

The orgy of railroad building was financed by every level of governmental authority—national, state, and local. One student of the period has computed that Kansas railroads harvested from all sources about $85 million, or approximately $10,000 per mile, "which should have satisfied a significant portion of the real costs of building the rickety roads on the Kansas prairie." Some measure of the ascendancy of the railroads may be gained from statistics of the time, which show that fully one-fifth of the total acreage of Kansas had come into the possession of railroad companies.[14]

Predictably, land values soared, partly as a result of a massive railroad promotion effort and partly as a natural function of the huge injection of capital into a relatively sparsely populated area. The boom in Wichita, which lasted from January to June 1887, brought 30,000 people to the city, and real-estate transfers for the five months totaled over $34 million. Immense fortunes were made. The feeling of well-being extended to thousands of ordinary Kansans who, though mortgaging themselves deeply to buy into the boom, counted sizable paper profits as land values soared everywhere. Virtually the entire population of the state was mortgaged, there being one note for every two adults, or as one writer has put it, "more than one for every family." [15]

But the boom rested heavily on the largesse of nature. The early 1880's experienced a pattern of bountiful rainfall throughout the plains, extending even into Colorado, far beyond the 100th meridian. To the happy participants the rain was not an unusual freak of nature, but rather a permanent feature of Western life. Scientists said that rain was "following the plow," and the populace was duly informed that "these vast extents of plowed land not only create a rainfall by their evaporation, but invite rains by their contrasts of temperature." [16]

Scientists and railroad boomers notwithstanding, the rains stopped in 1887—not only in Kansas, but throughout the Great Plains, from the Dakotas west to Colorado. In western Kansas, Nebraska, the Dakotas, and all of newly settled Colorado a pronounced economic jolt was felt almost immediately. Kansas, where the boom psychology had been most pronounced, felt by far the sharpest retrenchment. Corn production plummeted from 126 million bushels in 1886 to 76 million bushels the next year. Wheat production fell by half. Mortgage foreclosures increased sharply and land values crumbled. Good Republicans in Kansas immediately discovered that their tax burden, raised to pay for inflated bond issues for railroad building and improvements of all kinds, did not diminish merely because prices fell. The favored tax status enjoyed by railroads suddenly appeared outrageous. Interest rates on land mortgages were so high that the possibilities of repayment under the new conditions seemed almost hopeless. The depression appeared all the more severe because of the exaggerated hopes that had preceded it.[17]

Under the circumstances, it might have appeared reasonable to expect the ancient political slogans of the long-dominant Kansas Republican Party to have suddenly become ineffective. Could stories of "bloody shirts" and "rebel Democrats" continue to attract an electorate reeling from good times suddenly turned sour? Would the G.O.P.'s vintage pronouncements on the tariff seem relevant to farmers who owed $2500 at 18 per cent interest on land now valued at $1500? Perhaps not. But deep-seated political habits do not vanish easily at the first hint of economic distress. It took a while for Kansas farmers to ponder the implications of the new economic conditions ruling their lives. The collapse of the land boom in 1887 did not produce immediate changes in the structure of state politics. The Union Labor Party's maiden third party venture in the presidential election year of 1888 attracted only 12 per cent of the Kansas vote. The Democrats also failed to benefit from a depression psychology; the Republicans swept to a complete statewide victory with a plurality of over 80,000.[18]

6

Yet beneath the surface of election returns, a potentially volatile movement had begun in the farming districts of the West—not only in Kansas, but also in scattered regions of the Northern plains reaching to the Canadian border. The origins of this movement, in fact, had predated the events of 1887–88 and its first signs had become visible in the Dakota Territory as early as 1884–85. An energetic farmer named Henry Loucks began mobilizing wheat growers into rural clubs in 1884 to protest the monopolistic practices of grain elevator companies and the high freight rates of Northern railroads. The movement "caught fire" in the central counties of the Territory, and by the spring of the following year delegates from eleven counties had formed a state organization. In the same months that the early Texas Alliance began experimenting in bulking cotton as part of its cooperative marketing program, Loucks led his Dakota farmers into a series of tentative efforts toward cooperation. Some thirty-five cooperative warehouses were erected in the Territory. These attempts were not crowned with marked success, but Dakota farmers learned a great deal both about the wholesale and retail practices of the commercial world and about what they themselves had to do to create an effective purchasing program. They also pressed the territorial legislature for reforms to curb the abuses of railroads and grain elevator companies. Though legislative victories initially eluded them, the Dakotans pushed forward their organizing efforts and, by early 1888, they had formed a territory-wide cooperative exchange. It proved a great boon to farmer recruitment. In that year, Dakota farmers made significant membership gains, developed an internal lecturing system, created their own organizational newspaper—*The Ruralist*—under Loucks's editorship, and, perhaps most important, reached southward to make contact with the spreading National Farmers Alliance. To anyone who cared to look, it was clear that the Dakotans had begun to work toward a specific program of action.[19]

In Iowa, Illinois, Nebraska, and other states of the Northern plains, however, the farmers lagged quite a bit behind their cooperatively inclined brethren in the Dakotas. Northwestern farmers urgently needed both strong regional leadership and a program of action, but neither seemed to materialize through the middle 1880's.

In the same years, however, organizers for Macune's National Farmers Alliance began to probe northward, and they encountered some willing local assistance. Some months before the Texas Alliance deployed its lecturers through the South, the town of Winfield, Kansas, in Cowley County near the Oklahoma border, discovered that it had suddenly acquired a young radical named Henry Vincent, who had descended upon the quiet hamlet with the intention of opening a newspaper. He was to prove one of the most energetic Populists of them all.

Henry Vincent was one of five sons of James Vincent, a rather unusual man in his own right. A radical egalitarian, abolitionist, and free thinker, the senior Vincent put himself through Oberlin College as a youth, married, and moved to a farm near Tabor, Iowa. He became western correspondent for Greeley's *New-York Tribune* and Garrison's *Liberator,* worked for the American Anti-Slavery Society, and operated an underground railroad and school at Tabor. He seems to have rather thoroughly transmitted his humanist views and a measure of his tenacity to all of his children—especially to young Henry. At the age of seventeen, Henry began a journal called the *American Nonconformist,* which he printed on a thirty-five-dollar hand press in Tabor. Seven years later, he, along with two of his brothers, thirty-year-old Cuthbert and twenty-three-year-old Leopold, migrated to Cowley County in Kansas. The brothers selected Winfield for the site of their journalistic effort after a careful inspection of other locales in what seems to have been a search for a climate conducive to social change. Grandly entitling the venture *The American Nonconformist and Kansas Industrial Liberator,* Henry and his brothers unleashed among their boom-conscious Kansas neighbors a startling brand of journalism. The inaugural issue of October 7, 1886, declared:

> This journal will aim to publish such matter as will tend to the education of the laboring classes, the farmers and the producer, and in every struggle it will endeavor to take the side of the oppressed as against the oppressor, provided the "underdog" has concern for his own hide to defend himself when he is given the opportunity, and not turn and bite the hand of him who has labored for his freedom, by voting both into a worse condition than before.[20]

The Vincents established a far-flung system of exchanges with other agrarian and labor newspapers and kept a careful nationwide watch on political activities in behalf of the "underdog." They soon became remarkably well-informed on the activities of both the Knights of Labor, then at its national peak of influence, and the Farmers Alliance, then still confined to its Texas origins. The *Nonconformist* praised the racial liberalism demonstrated by the Knights at their integrated 1886 convention in Richmond, Virginia, and similarly applauded the aggressive spirit of the Cleburne Demands, which emerged from the little-known farm order in Texas in the same year. It duly noted the spread of the Alliance across the South, and when the Texas organizers ranged over Missouri and edged into neighboring Kansas in the summer of 1887, they quite naturally found a welcome first and foremost in Cowley County. One Texan organized a number of suballiances in the county and a second arrived later in the year to extend the Alliance message to surrounding counties. The Vincents meanwhile were busy applauding the efforts of Western radicals to reconstitute a new national third party as a home for displaced greenbackers. The Vincents were joined in these sympathies by an impressive assortment of veteran Kansas greenbackers, including still another Vincent, William, who was not related to the newspaper brothers. In the course of these third party efforts, the Vincents established relations with the radicals in the Texas Alliance who had engendered the Cleburne Demands.[21]

By the time the third party men were ready to hold a nominating convention for the new national Union Labor Party in Cincinnati in the spring of 1888, a coterie of politically insurgent Westerners had established contact and had begun

Henry Vincent
Founder of the *American Non-conformist*, organizer of the newspaper alliance of the Union Labor Party, and trustee of the first Kansas cooperative organized by the Alliance. Vincent's peripatetic career was to make him a leading figure in the Populist movement in three states.

working together. The network, which was primarily composed of Kansans and Texans, also included greenback veterans from Arkansas, Alabama, and a half-dozen Midwestern states. The Vincents got no ideological guidance from the Texans, nor did they need any, but they urgently required an understanding of the cooperative structure of the Alliance, which had already demonstrated its unprecedented capacity as an instrument of mass organization. While they were at it, the Vincents apparently also took the opportunity to join a radical group that set itself up as a vanguard adjunct to the new third party movement. This self-appointed elite group, the "Videttes," seemed to be highly influential in the Union Labor convention. William Vincent represented Kansas and William Lamb represented Texas on the party's national executive committee. Lamb also served as ex-officio chairman of the convention's credentials committee. Captain Sam Evans of Forth Worth, one of Lamb's closest associates, and a fellow Vidette, was offered the Union Labor Party's vice presidential nomination, but he declined, and the honor went to C. E. Cunningham of Arkansas, still another Vidette and a man closely associated with another rising agrarian institution, known as the Arkansas Agricultural Wheel.[22]

The "Union Labor" name was selected for the new party in an obvious attempt to cope with the repeatedly demonstrated weakness of the Greenback Party—its inability to appeal to urban workers in the East. This crucial deficiency had restricted the influence of the Greenback Party to a handful of states in the trans-Mississippi West throughout the 1880's. The 1888 organizational meeting in Cincinnati brought Western soft-money radicals together with Eastern labor delegates, including socialists and single-taxers, who had formed "the United Labor" party. Despite strenuous organizational efforts, the attempt to merge agrarian "Union Labor" with urban "United Labor" failed. Evans headed a special conference committee on permanent organization which attempted to achieve a compromise on the platform, but the New Yorkers were devoted to Henry George's Single Tax on land, and a compromise proved unattainable. Soft-money agrarians utterly dominated the convention as well as the Evans committee; discovering this, the laborites, after failing notably to affect the platform, denounced the new party's leadership as being controlled by "wealthy land barons" and cited "Evans of Texas" as one of the examples of this capitalistic infiltration. Apparently, William Lamb did not qualify as a "land baron" even by the relaxed standards of urban single-taxers. The Vincents did not either.[23]

7

While the subsequent poor showing of the Union Labor Party in the fall elections of 1888 helped plunge radical politicians such as Jerry Simpson into despair, there was a more germane development—the spread of the Kansas Farmers Alliance from its base in Cowley County. The enormous growth of the order in Texas in 1885–86 came only after the founders had earlier consolidated a strong geographical base in a nucleus of counties, in the process perfecting their organizational doctrines and an accompanying rhetoric of recruitment. In 1888, the Kansas Alliance consolidated a similar base in south-central Kansas. The effort to familiarize Kansas farmers with Alliance doctrines received help not only from Henry Vincent and the *Nonconformist,* but also from the state's leading farm journal, the *Kansas Farmer,* which was edited by William Peffer, a bearded oracle destined for wide Populist fame. The

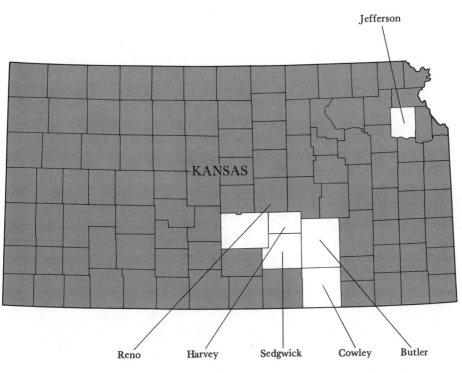

Kansas

The pattern of Alliance organizing in Kansas followed the Texas precedent—consolidation of the order's strength in a handful of contiguous counties before a rapid organizing burst across the entire state. Prior to the fashioning of coordinated statewide organizing plans late in 1888, the Alliance had sunk roots in six Kansas counties: Cowley, Butler, Harvey, Reno, Sedgewick, and the non-contiguous county of Jefferson, home of organizer J. F. Willits, the 1890 Alliance candidate for governor.

Kansas Farmer printed long letters from prominent Texas Alliancemen, describing the order's program. Though this incoming mail emphasized the significance of the cooperative movement in fashioning the order's internal structure and external purpose, Peffer, who was at that time a political moderate, did not immediately grasp its centrality, so his paper played no galvanizing role beyond providing intermittent publicity. But some of the third party partisans who had gathered around the *Nonconformist* did perceive the meaning of the Alliance cooperative. Late in 1888, following the diastrous third party showing in the November elections, a group of Kansas radicals made a pilgrimage to Dallas, Texas, for further briefings on the structure of the Alliance movement at the organization's national offices. Though precisely who made the trip remains a matter of some debate among Kansas historians, all accounts name one or more of the Vincent brothers as participants. Of greater importance, W. P. Brush, in the course of his official duties as state organizer for the Kansas Alliance, attended the 1888 convention of the National Farmers Alliance at Meridian, Mississippi. There he acquired further details of the cooperative movement and was appointed one of twelve "national lecturers" designated by the Macune-led Southerners.[24]

In December 1888 the Farmers State Alliance of Kansas was organized. Lecturers armed with charters and equipped with the new lecturing methods spread over the state. They met with an immediate response, just as their counterparts in the South had earlier. Kansas farmers listened to the outline of the cooperative program and promptly joined the Alliance in droves. Suballiances elected business agents and county Alliances formed trade committees. As evidence of the success of the organizing campaign mounted, the *Nonconformist* interviewed Ben Clover, the new Kansas Alliance president on the progress of the order. He announced that "extensive movements are on foot." It was not an idle remark. A new culture of politics was being born. As the cooperative banner went up in central and eastern Kansas, a new and surprisingly radical energy began to surface in ways that newspapers, friendly and

otherwise, could scarcely ignore. In February 1889 the Harper
County Alliance, in obvious response to proliferating land
foreclosures, petitioned the Kansas legislature for stricter
usury laws. Two months later Brown County farmers met in a
mass meeting to protest against the newest arbitrary price rise
in agricultural supplies, characterized by the group as "the ex-
tortions of the binding twine trust." A month later the county
Alliance decided "to proceed at once to the erection of a cooperative manufactory for binding twine." Elsewhere, alliance
county trade committees met with merchants, wholesalers, and
manufacturers. Where the farmers were rewarded with small
successes, their self-confidence, and their respect for their Alliance, grew. Where they encountered rebuffs, they talked
about it together and debated the meaning of existing commercial relationships in American society. Some of them got
pretty angry and all of them wanted to do something about it.
The suballiance in Kansas, like its predecessors in Texas and
the South, became a schoolroom.[25]

Some regions of Kansas were not yet ready. In August
farmers in Fulton failed in an attempt to organize an Alliance
and postponed the matter "indefinitely." But in the same
month the state secretary of the Kansas Alliance announced
that the order numbered 25,000. The word was spreading:
the Alliance was "doing something" for farmers. The rate of
recruitment accelerated with the passage of each week, and by
the time Jerry Simpson made his gloomy assessment of reform
prospects late in 1889 the Kansas Alliance counted in the
neighborhood of 50,000 members.[26]

Before the potential scope of the new movement began to
make itself felt in 1889, however, the intensity of the order's
capacity to generate a new kind of political activism had been
confirmed by activities in the handful of "old" Alliance counties near the Kansas-Oklahoma border. Off-year elections in
Cowley County brought a hint of the storms soon to come.
Area farmers, already organized as an Alliance cooperative,
further organized themselves in a mass meeting and nominated a complete independent ticket against the Republican
incumbents. Affiliating with neither major party, the ticket

Ben Clover
The president of the original county Alliance in Kansas (Winfield County), first president of the Kansas State Alliance, first non-Southern officer of the National Alliance, and Populist congressman.

was elected by a surprisingly large margin. The political culture of the agrarian movement had literally reached a majority of the people in the county.[27]

In steadfastly Republican Kansas, this result was a bit startling in itself. A glance behind the returns, however, yielded even more instructive insights. Whatever had happened in Cowley County over the preceding twelve months, it had clearly not happened countywide. For example, the townsfolk of Winfield had voted Republican in 1888 by a comfortable eight to five margin and had even added slightly to the party's plurality the following year. But a phenomenal change had come over the rural districts of the county. The farmers who voted at Rock Creek precinct were typical. In 1888 they had cast 96 votes for the Republican party, 23 for the Union Labor Party, and 60 for the Democrats. In the following year, however, the Republican vote plummeted to 45 while the new independent ticket swept the precinct with 117 votes. Clearly, something was happening at the forks of the creek.[28]

8

As the coming agrarian whirlwind kicked up its first particles of dust in Kansas in 1889, not everyone found the pace of events easy to follow. The somewhat puzzled perspective of one of the Cowley County newspapers that competed against Henry Vincent's *Nonconformist* provides a fascinating window into the dynamics that soon were to be at work throughout the state. The paper, *The Daily Visitor* of Winfield, had none of the aggressively radical proclivities that characterized its rival. But as the strange new stirrings in Kansas materialized literally before the startled eyes of the *Visitor*'s editor—and among his own subscribers—he could hardly avoid comment. The striking fact is that the editor provided his readers with the telling information in January 1889—many months *before* the unexpected political overthrow of county Republicans. And though he reported that "the farmers of Kansas have caught up in the spirit of the times," the information he conveyed was economic rather than political. After announcing that the activity extended "to every part of the state," he added that, "at present, it looks as if the Farmers Alliance is getting more sway than any other farmers organization." By way of confirmation, the *Visitor* reported that the local Cowley County Alliance contained no less than 1500 farmers organized in thirty suballiances. "The Farmers Alliance of Kansas," the paper concluded, "is already a formidable body." Three days later, the *Daily Visitor* undertook to account for the phenomenon more fully. Under the headline "A New Enterprise," the paper reported to townspeople on the curious energy emanating from the Cowley County countryside:

> For some time there has been talk in this city of a cooperative association, the intention of which was to establish a sort of general store in this city and sell goods on a plan by which the members of the association expect to save money in their purchase. A charter was granted by the state this week to the company, the capital stock of which is $10,000. The name of the association will be "The Winfield Co-operative Mercantile and Manufacturing Association."[29]

Listed among the directors of the "new enterprise" was the editor's rival, one Henry Vincent. In such apparently mundane, if purposeful ways, so seemingly unrelated to the flamboyant Populist oratory that would later startle the nation, the agrarian revolt surfaced in Kansas in January 1889.[30]

2

To Build the Cooperative Commonwealth

In their attack on the national banking system, the agrarian economists were on solid ground in contending that private privilege was exercising a sovereign power, the power of regulating national currency, for private gain rather than for meeting the needs of the country.

C. Vann Woodward, Origins of the New South

It is time for each brother to realize that faltering now means unconditional surrender.

Evan Jones, in defense of large-scale cooperation, May 1888

CHAPTER V

The Cooperative Crusade

". . . the foundation that underlies the whole superstructure . . ."

The agrarian revolt cannot be understood outside the framework of the cooperative crusade that was its source. Amidst a national political system in which the mass constituencies of both major parties were fashioned out of the sectional loyalties of the Civil War, the cooperative movement became the recruiting vehicle through which huge numbers of farmers in the South and West were brought into an interest-group institution geared to a new kind of internal "political education." The central educational tool of the Farmers Alliance was the cooperative experiment itself. The massive effort at agrarian self-help, and the opposition it stimulated from furnishing merchants, wholesale houses, cotton buyers, and bankers in the South and from grain elevator companies, railroads, land companies, livestock commission agencies, and bankers in the West, brought home to hundreds of thousands of American farmers new insights into their relationship with the commercial elements of American society. Reduced to its essentials, the cooperative movement recruited the farmers to the Alliance in the period 1887–91, and the resulting cooperative experience radicalized enough of them to make independent political action a potential reality. While other developments were also necessary, those developments, when they materialized, built directly upon the cooperative experience in ways that confirmed its centrality to the evolution of the People's Party. That the chief oracle of cooperation, Charles Macune, consistently opposed Alliance political radicalism and feared the emergence of the third party added a paradoxical dimension to the internal politics of the agrarian revolt.

2

Irony dogged Charles Macune throughout his years as national spokesman of the Farmers Alliance. The scores of Alliance organizers who fanned out across the South and Midwest in 1887–89 and who sallied north of the Ohio River and across both the Rockies and the Appalachians in 1890–91 had been defined by their previous experience not only as "lecturers," but also as incipient political radicals. Their duties as lecturers carried them to the remotest backwaters of the rural countryside and into the very maw of the crop lien system of the South. Upon the lecturers fell the burden of explaining the function of the suballiance business agent, the county trade committee, and the visionary state exchange that, in the South, might free them all from the furnishing merchant. Upon the same lecturers also fell the burden of explaining the delays, the opposition of merchants, bankers, commission agents, and sundry other functionaries who came to represent "the town clique." Whether in Alabama or South Dakota, a cooperative encountering difficulty constituted an implied rebuke to the Alliance leaders who had praised the idea in the first place. At such a time of difficulty—and it came, eventually, to every Alliance cooperative in every state, from Florida to Oregon—the farmers, so recently brought to a new level of hope by the promise of their movement, looked to the messengers of cooperation both for explanation and guidance. The latter responded in one of two ways. They could blame the difficulties on the farmers, assert that rank and file members did not understand cooperation well enough, and insist that they expected too much, too soon. In the course of this response they could counsel patience and devote much time to thorough explanations of the theory and practice of cooperation. Many Alliance leaders followed such a course, none with more grace than Macune himself. But the mass program of agrarian cooperation that Macune had visualized also set in motion another and rather different response. In this view, cooperative difficulties were not inherently the fault of the idea itself, nor were they traceable to deficiencies in farmers generally; rather, cooperatives encountered trouble because of the implacable hostility of the financial and commercial world. Alliance leaders holding such views could explain that town merchants selectively cut prices to make the Alliance trade store look bad and that bankers refused to take the notes of the Alliance state exchange because the bank's mercantile clients wanted the exchange to go under. They could add that the Alliance store or warehouse often performed its duty even if it sold not a dollar of goods—if, simply by its presence, it introduced genuine wholesale and retail competition into rural America. Macune was also capable of this analysis, and sometimes with a passion that rivaled the anti-monopoly intensity of spokesmen for the Alliance's left wing.

But however individual leaders responded initially, the cooperative crusade and the experiences it generated set in motion an intense dialogue within the Alliance, one that reached realms of radical political analysis that Macune had not foreseen and from which he instinctively recoiled. Yet the cooperative experience increasingly set the terms of the debate in ways neither the order's moderates nor its radicals could conveniently ignore. The mass of farmers themselves saw to this. They wanted freedom from what they regarded as intolerable conditions, and the delays they experienced in their local and state cooperative efforts brought forth questions to which lecturers had to respond, whatever their politics. Indeed, a raw irritant persisted at the core of this internal Alliance dialogue between the farmers and their spokesmen, a criticism by the rank and file that, however respectfully implied, ate at the very heart of the lecturers' sense of justice. It was not the lecturers' fault! They felt, more tellingly than some of them could explain, the totality of banker and merchant opposition, the calumny of news stories about the Alliance in the metropolitan press, the deceptive style of traditional politicians who voted for the commercial classes while pretending to be friends of the farmer. In ways that Macune both understood and resisted, Alliance leaders came to have such thoughts in the late 1880's, and their knowledge constituted an organizational imperative for a new political party free of the control of bankers and their allies. The men who believed in cooperation the most, the Alliancemen who became trustees of local trade stores, county warehouses, and state exchanges, who counseled against politics as a divisive influence at a time when the cooperative needed the support of a united farming class, who then saw the cooperatives stagger under financial burdens born of lack of credit—it was some of these very men, Macune's lecturers, who eventually carried the Farmers Alliance to the People's Party. Indeed, they were the only ones who could have done so. Strong third parties failed to materialize in some states precisely because the order's most influential leaders in those states, for a variety of personal, political and cultural reasons, chose not to lead the Alliance membership in that direction. But the interior logic of the cooperative crusade, both in the hopeful early days of recruitment and in the more difficult days of implementation, drove Alliance leaders toward such ultimate political choices.

3

The cooperative crusade was not the product of individual creativeness: considering the enormous number of farmers eventually involved, it could not have been. Even Macune's persistently inventive role cannot be regarded as having been wholly decisive. Macune had told the Alliance lecturers in January 1887 to "organize the cotton belt of the nation," and they had, to a remarkable degree. But the reality that explained this organizational feat rested in the substance of the daily lives of millions of farmers.

In the late nineteenth century a national pattern of emerging banker-debtor relationships and corporation-citizen relationships began to shape the lives of millions of Americans.

Throughout the western granary the increasing centralization of economic life fastened upon prairie farmers new modes of degradation that, if not as abjectly humiliating as Southern forms, were scarcely less pervasive.

Of the many ingredients in the new way of life, most easily understood is the simple fact that farm prices continued to fall year after year, decade after decade. The dollar-a-bushel wheat of 1870 brought 80 cents in 1885 and 60 cents in the 1890's. These were official government figures, computed at year's end when prices were measurably higher than those received by the farmer at harvest. Actually, most Dakota farmers received closer to 35 cents a bushel for their wheat in the days of Populism, though the figures cited by government economists were far higher. Similarly, the 1870 corn crop averaged 45 cents a bushel; thereafter it fell steadily, plunging below 30 cents in the 1890's, according to official figures. But as early as 1889 corn in Kansas sold at 10 cents a bushel, the U.S. Agriculture Department's figures to the contrary notwithstanding.[1]

Moreover, the grain that made the nation's bread was a demanding crop; it had to be harvested at breakneck speed each fall before it became too dry and brittle to bind well. The farmer with fifty acres of field grain had to have a $235 binder to cut it. Though he used his binder only five days a year, that time fell in the same five days when his neighbors had to use their own binders. So he went into debt to buy the needed equipment. He made chattel mortgage payments on such machines at rates of annual interest that ranged from 18 to 36 per cent and in currency that appreciated in value every year. Under these circumstances, the steady decline of commodity prices further reduced his margin of economic maneuver.[2]

But this was only a part of the problem facing western agriculturalists. Like most nineteenth-century Americans, farmers were enthusiastic about the arrival of each new railroad that promised to further "open up the country" to new towns and new markets. But the farmers' euphoria at the appearance of a new rail line inevitably turned to bitter resentment. Alliance leaders learned the rationalizations of the railroads for their "discriminatory freight rates" while their rural members complained less elegantly of simply being "robbed" and "gypped." Whatever the terminology he employed, the farmer in the West felt that something was wrong with a system that made him pay a bushel of corn in freight costs for every bushel he shipped—especially since the system somehow also made it possible for large elevator companies to transport grain from Chicago all the way to England for less money than it cost a Dakota farmer to send his wheat to the grain mills in near-by Minneapolis. A number of railroads also forced shippers— grain dealers as well as individual farmers—to pay freight costs equal to the rail line's most distant terminal, even should they wish to ship only over a lesser portion of the line. (The extra fee was called "transit.") In many locales, the farmer had the option of paying or seeing his crop rot.[3]

Underlying the entire new structure of commerce was the national banking system, rooted in the gold standard and dominated by Eastern commercial banks, most prominently, the House of Morgan. The most apparent result of the system was a sharply contracted currency that failed to keep pace with population growth and economic expansion. It produced an annual harvest of steadily diminishing farm prices and a routine condition of "tight" credit that kept interest rates high. The gold-based money supply was so constricted, in fact, that virtually every year the calls on the Eastern money market by Western banks at harvest brought the nation dangerously close to financial panics. The sheer burden of providing the necessary short-term credit to finance the purchasing and shipping of the nation's annual agricultural production was more than the monetary structure could stand. The prevailing system, however, did have the effect of administering a strong downward pressure upon commodity prices at harvest time.[4]

On the "sod-house frontier" of the West, the human costs were enormous. Poverty was a "badge of honor which decorated all." Men and children "habitually" went barefoot in summer and in winter wore rags wrapped around their feet. A sod house was a home literally constructed out of prairie sod that was cut, sun-dried, and used as a kind of brick. Out of such materials, the very "civic culture" of the agrarian revolt was constructed—for "leaders" as well as "rank and filers": the occupant of one such abode ran for office on the "Alliance ticket" of 1890 and thereafter became the speaker of the Kansas House of Representatives. The first wave of agrarian protest, made a generation earlier, in the 1870's, had produced what were popularly called "granger legislatures" because of the large number of farmers elected. But the efforts of these legislatures to curb railroad and elevator abuses failed to alter the emerging patterns of trade. A social historian reports that farmers in the 1870's and 1880's reserved their "deepest enmity" for grain and stock buyers and for the railroads that served farmers and middlemen alike.[5]

Occasionally an agrarian spokesman would probe to deeper levels of analysis than was common in nineteenth-century politics by treating railroad pooling arrangements and other monopolies as part of a specific system of large-scale capital concentration anchored in the "money trust." Such theorists called for a new national money, issued by the government rather than national banks. Such "legel tender" was to be based not on gold, but on the "entire wealth of the country." These advocates of a fiat currency were dismissed by bankers, businessmen, newspaper editors, and educators—everyone of substance—as "cranks" and "calamity howlers." Needless to say, these "greenbackers" had something less than a commanding status. Meanwhile, through the years of the rise and fall of the Greenback Party, continuing hardship was a constant of rural life through wide swaths of the Western granary. In a system in which the new rules of commerce seemed to be fashioned by giants, the farmers appeared to be pygmies.

Everywhere the farmer turned, he seemed to be the victim of strange new rules that somehow always worked to the advantage of the biggest business and financial concerns that touched his world. To be efficient, the farmer had to have tools and livestock that cost him forbidding rates of interest. When he sold, he got the price offered by terminal grain elevator companies. To get his produce there, he paid high rates of freight. If he tried to sell to different grain dealers, or elevator companies, or livestock commission agents, he often encountered the practical evidence of secret agreements between agricultural middlemen and trunk line railroads. The Northern Pacific named specific grain terminals to which farmers should ship, the trunk line simply refusing to provide railroad cars for the uncooperative.[6]

Pool agreements extended beyond commission houses to include rival railroads so that the rules of competition appeared to have been suspended. Among the large new business combinations that were engaged in creating trusts in virtually every major branch of American commerce, the watering of stock became so routine that it is not too much to say that the custom provided the operating basis for the entire industrial system that was emerging. To pay even nominal dividends on watered stock, companies needed high rates of profit—in effect, they converted their customers into real sources of direct capital. Railroad networks that cost $250,000 in public money to build were owned by companies that capitalized themselves at $500,000 and then sold construction bonds on $500,000 more. Agrarian spokesmen wondered out loud why the citizenry should be paying interest on public indebtedness of one million dollars, 75 per cent of which was watered stock. Railroad magnates rarely bothered to reply to such critics beyond offering an occasional opinion that popular concern about the interior affairs of business corporations was "officious." [7]

But widespread as suffering was throughout the West, nowhere in America did the burdens of poverty fall more heavily than upon the farm families of the rural South. The achievement of Macune's lecturers emanated not so much from their rhetorical skill as it did from the grim realities in the lives of those who heard the lecturers. It was here that the fuel of Populism had come to be stored, waiting to be ignited. While the invisible restraints of a contracted currency affected farmers everywhere, they became unbearable when tied to the crop lien system. The raw mathematics of the situation simply offered farmers no escape from peonage.[8]

The extremely narrow sources of agricultural credit—the continuing reality that armed furnishing merchants with their ubiquitous power—worried Southerners of all classes from time to time. New South optimists like Henry Grady hailed moves, such as occurred in Georgia in the 1880's, to bring to the South new loan agencies that would lend to farmers on real estate security for periods of up to five years at announced interest rates of 7 to 8 per cent. "Closer investigation," one scholar reported, "revealed the fact that the agent would deduct at the outset some twenty dollars on the hundred as a commission for negotiating the loan; leaving the victim eighty dollars cash in return for a note of one hundred plus interest. . . . They did a thriving business." A contemporary concluded that "Nothing shows more clearly the need of better credit facilities in the South than the willingness on the part of the more thrifty and industrious farmers to borrow money on such terms rather than to submit to the high prices and dictation of the advancing merchant." [9]

The crop lien system had driven millions west in the 1870's; by the late 1880's the system had graduated to new plateaus of exploitation: as every passing year forced additional thousands of Southern farmers into foreclosure and thence into the world of landless tenantry, the furnishing merchants came to acquire title to increasing portions of the Southern countryside. Furnishing men had so many farms, and so many tenants to work them, that it became psychologically convenient to depersonalize the language of agricultural production. Advancing merchants spoke to one another about "running 100 plows this year," a crisp phrase that not only referred to thousands of acres of land but also to hundreds of men, women, and children who lived in peonage. Prosaically, the Tenth Census officially described the lien as "a bond for the payment of a specific amount—usually about $100—given to the storekeeper by the farmer, and pledging the growing crop as collateral security." Ominous acreage and production statistics accounted for the small annual sums of "about $100" that cotton croppers received. The Southern tenant farm of the 1890's averaged seventeen acres, and with an average cotton yield per acre of about one-third of a bale, a five- or six-bale crop was all a family could reasonably expect for its year's labor. Cotton was priced at eight cents a pound, and the $200 gross return allowed the farmer's family roughly $100 credit for the year's living expenses after deductions for fertilizer and other production costs. This sum translated into less than $10.00 per family per month for food, clothing, medicines, and all other essentials. Any tenant showing enough independence to dare to check his merchant's bookkeeping ledger ran the risk of being branded a troublemaker and dispatched from the county by a local deputy sheriff. If he was black—and sometimes if he was white—he could easily find himself exchanging his participation in the crop lien system for a role in the convict lease system. Layers of legal safeguards to protect lien-holders were built into the structure of Southern law. Statutes were so drafted that a tenant "had little chance lawfully to leave his landlord and move elsewhere." If a farmer tried to escape the clutches of his merchant by growing corn and hogs, which would make him less a customer for high-priced pork and meal, he was, in the words of one observer, "notified that reducing his cotton acreage was reducing his line of credit." The universal rule continued to be "no cotton, no credit." [10]

As the degradation of the crop lien spread over the South, middle-class farmers lived in terror of the one bad crop that would put them in the hands of the furnishing merchant. "Never mortgage," children of such families were told, in language they could recall years later; "no matter what happens, don't mortgage . . . and if you haven't cash, don't buy." But regional scholars reported that up to 90 per cent of the farmers in Mississippi, Alabama, and Georgia were living on credit.[11]

Two generations after the days of the Farmers Alliance, James Agee described the unchanged world of landless Southern farmers:

> They learn the work they will spend their lives doing, chiefly out of their parents, and from their parents and from the immediate world they take their conduct, their morality, and their mental and emotional and spiritual key. One could hardly say that any further knowledge or consciousness is at all to their use or advantage, since there is nothing to read, no reason to write, and no recourse against being cheated even if one's able to do sums.[12]

The simple, degrading elements of the lien system so defied the possibility of bland description that even the usually pale jargon of the government bureaucracy took on faint overtones of a muckracking tract:

> The system of advances, or credit, so prevalent throughout the State [Alabama], is not without its evil influence for the laborer and too often the owners of the land are obliged to get advances of provisions from their merchants, for the payment of which the crop is mortgaged; and as cotton is the only crop which will always bring ready money, its planting is usually insisted on by the merchants making the advance. In this way cotton comes to be the paramount crop, and there is little chance for rotation with other things. The system of credits in the large cotton-producing regions prevails to such an extent that the whole cotton crop is usually mortgaged before it is gathered.[13]

Through a 1500-mile swath of the Southland, from Virginia to Texas, such absence of choices came to characterize the monotonous lives of millions, tenants and "landowners" alike.[14]

4

It was into this vast domain of silent suffering that the lecturers of the Farmers Alliance deployed in 1887–88. The results were difficult to describe, though a South Carolina Granger made an effort by reporting to his national offices that the Alliance had "swept over our state like a wave." Southern farmers had been poor for years and had listened and had largely been unresponsive to any number of suggested panaceas. The spark that lit the fuse of agrarian discontent was the message offered by the latest visitors: join the Alliance, build a cooperative, and get free of the credit merchant. A fully organized county Alliance could form its own cotton yard, its own trade committee, and, if need be, its own store.[15]

Taken in all its parts, it was the organizing message first enunciated by S. O. Daws in 1884 and polished by his lieutenants in Texas in 1885–86. By 1887 the doctrine was relatively mature, could be delivered with settled confidence, and verified with persuasive stories. It had to be conceded, of course, that one needed to be free of the merchant's crop lien to participate in such Alliance ideas as "bulking" cotton, for only farmers who held title to their own crop could sell it. There were, the lecturers were forced to explain, two stages in the process of economic cooperation—the first designed to redress the power balance with the local merchant in order to get lower prices so the farmer could "pay out," the second focusing on the Alliance selling cooperative that could hold part of the crop off the market at harvest time, when prices were lowest. The farmers of the South thus learned that the Alliance offered two forms of organization—"buying" cooperatives and marketing cooperatives. On whatever level of verbal elegance it was offered them, Southerners learned that the plan of the Farmers Alliance would take a bit of time. But, they could ask themselves, had not the plan worked in Texas?

The message of the lecturers was persuasive because the core of the Alliance program was Macune's central state exchange, which could provide credit at bearable rates for great numbers of moneyless farmers. The established goal—to change the way most Southerners lived—was one the Grange had never dared to attempt. This, quite simply, explains why the Grange could not reach the farmers and the Alliance could. The larger dream contained in the new and untested Texas plan—the formation of a central state exchange to market the entire state's cotton crop and free everyone from the credit system in one dramatic marketing season—added the final galvanizing ingredient to the formula of hope that was the Farmers Alliance. "It is not an organization" reported one participant happily, "it is a growth." [16]

5

But the new recruits did not wait idly for the arrival of a state-wide marketing system. Across the South, farmers in a dozen states competed with one another in pioneering new varieties of purchasing cooperatives that could be constructed to defeat money-lenders and wholesale and retail merchants. The leader of a local Georgia Alliance wrote the order's national journal in Texas that "we are going to get out of debt and be free and independent people once more. Mr. Editor, we Georgia people are in earnest about this thing." The sheer variety of the efforts "to be a free and independent people" pointed to the fact that the crusade for cooperation took the form of thousands of initiatives within tiny sub-alliances scattered across the South. In North Carolina, a prominent agricultural spokesman, L. L. Polk, moved into the forefront of the cooperative effort because "There is a limit to silence even in the submissiveness of farmers." As the order grew in the state, the circulation of Polk's newspaper, the *Progressive Farmer,* soared, from 1200 when the Alliance arrived in 1887 to over 11,760 by the end of 1889. Meanwhile, farmers in the Virginia-Carolina tobacco belt discussed plans for a large-scale marketing cooperative.[17]

In Florida, Oswald Wilson, one of the Texas organizers, liked what he found so much that he stayed to direct the Florida movement. Wilson pushed cooperation aggressively, and within nine months of his arrival he had Florida Alliancemen making serious plans for a central state exchange. Some 300 alliances had been organized by the spring of 1888, when a statewide cooperative exchange was chartered. A "respectable amount of business was transacted," and the Floridians went forward with their organizing work in high spirits.[18]

Alabama farmers, a bit more experienced than their neighbors, moved into cooperation on a variety of fronts. The state's farmers had received earlier lessons, largely political, from lecturers of the Agricultural Wheel, an energetic organization based in Arkansas which began expanding late in 1886. The Wheelers had a pronounced radical streak, though they had by no means mastered the intricacies of cooperation even to the extent the Texans had. The Alabama Wheels, numbering perhaps 15,000 members at its peak, soon converted to the Alliance, as the Arkansas founders themselves did later. The cooperative movement grew with great speed in Alabama. In one hamlet the Alliance warehouse in one day loaded 150 wagons with fertilizer purchased in bulk at lower prices than Alabama farmers had ever had to pay. Commercial animosity toward such tactics led to violence in Dothan, where merchants, bankers, and warehousemen succeeded in obtaining a $50 tax on the Alliance warehouse. Alliancemen responded by moving their warehouse outside the city limits, whereupon the town council attempted to make the farmers pay for draying their cotton into and out of town. A gunfight resulted, and two men were killed and another wounded. As the depth of commercial opposition began to be perceived by Alabama Alliancemen, a movement developed for an Alliance state bank, though the means were never found to carry out the proposal. Nevertheless, as an Alabama historian reported, "the magic of the Alliance label had wide appeal" and businessmen soon appropriated the name for its commercial value. Alliance hotels appeared at Montgomery and Monroeville, and a Negro cafe called the "Alliance Restaurant" opened in Union Springs. Many warehouses adopted the name, "whether they were sponsored by a local Alliance or not." The order finally drew the line in Dale County, where the local suballiance passed resolutions condemning an "Alliance Bar." [19]

Both Alabama and neighboring Georgia followed earlier Texas and Florida precedents in moving to establish statewide marketing exchanges. The Alliance swept through Georgia with such organizing energy that the Alliance warehouse became a ubiquitous local landmark throughout the state, particularly in the "wire grass" regions of South Georgia. The Georgia Exchange capitalized itself—optimistically—at $500,000. The subordinate units handled marketing procedures through their warehouses and operated on a cash-only basis for purchasing through the state exchange.[20]

In Virginia, some of the most respected names of the Old Dominion—Beverley, Page, Venable, Ruffin, Cocke—moved into the orbit of the Farmers Alliance. Virginia farm spokesmen saw their existing "Farmers Assembly" overwhelmed by the Alliance, but they accepted the development in good grace and moved into the leadership of the Virginia Alliance. Mann Page became State Alliance president and A. R. Venable became state business agent. Another somewhat unusual Alliance recruit was Charles H. Pierson, an Englishman turned Virginian who had been educated at both Oxford and Cambridge. An ordained Anglican priest, he founded an Alliance newspaper and christened it *Necessity*. These Virginia patricians moved ahead in an organizing manner several cuts removed from the radical style of the Texans, but they were destined to encounter problems spared Alliance advocates elsewhere in the South.[21]

In Tennessee, South Carolina, and Mississippi the order spread with the same fury that characterized its growth elsewhere. A Mississippi historian placed Alliance membership in that state at 50,000 in 1888 and at 75,000 by the summer of 1890. Tennessee Alliancemen, under the leadership of John P. Buchanan and John McDowell, adopted the agency system of neighboring North Carolina, while South Carolina and Mississippi, in common with the cotton belt states of Georgia, Alabama, and Texas, opted for the state exchange system. In organizing their cooperatives South Carolina Alliancemen began a long and abrasive relationship with a rising agrarian spokesman who had ideas of his own—"Pitchfork Ben" Tillman.[22]

Yet for all the hope that it stirred the Alliance movement remained just that—a hope. Indeed, the seeming simplicity and sweep of the Alliance cooperative goal shone through almost any attempt at description, however wooden, ornate, or romantic. The Alliance, said a rural Alabama weekly, "has gone before the public with its principles clearly defined, its mission being to free the farmers from the oppression of debt, restore the county to a cash basis, to bring prosperity to the farming interest and happiness to the farmers' homes." But though the farmers came by the thousands, the Alliance found it difficult to implement an effective cooperative program. While local stores or local arrangements for marketing might produce marginal improvements, a statewide undertaking was needed to cope with the lien system. As Southern Alliances grew, and as both farmers and their spokesmen learned more about the intricacies of cooperation, they increasingly tended to keep one eye cocked on Macune's Texas Exchange, where the mass marketing concept was undergoing its first major test in the South. In 1887–88 the Texas effort entered its crucial stage—and Alliance leaders throughout the South watched in hope and apprehension as the idea of a cooperative commonwealth endeavored to coexist with banker-centered American capitalism.[23]

6

The original plan of a central state exchange which Macune had outlined in his speech of January 1887 had been consummated in stages. Macune had been appointed business agent in March and had immediately made a trip to Boston and Fall River, Massachusetts, in an effort to arrange for sale of the 1887 Texas cotton crop. He learned on the trip that a central exchange in Texas could sell directly to Eastern factories if it possessed sufficient capital to underwrite its contracts properly. He reported this to his Texas colleagues, and the Alliance, after taking competing bids from several cities, selected Dallas as the site for the exchange. The Dallas offer, though it amounted to about $100,000 in cash, deferred rentals, and real estate, was contingent upon a number of specifications that reduced the immediate cash bonus to $3500.[24]

On this shred of capital the "Farmers Alliance Exchange of Texas" opened for business in Dallas in September 1887. The intervening months had confirmed that the uncentralized trade store system could not function effectively within the existing American system. As one student of the Alliance put it, "The local bourgeoisie became very artful in devising and circulating false reports" to complicate life for local Alliance stores. The hostility of merchants increased as the sheer size of the farmer organization dramatized the threat posed by Alliance cooperatives. But even where local Alliancemen became sophisticated enough to cope with false rumors and selective price cutting by merchants, a marginally successful effort merely increased their longing for the statewide marketing cooperative. No sooner had Macune settled into the new exchange in Dallas than he found his directors awash in petitions from suballiances calling for the implementation of some plan so they could "make a crop independent of the merchant." [25]

The infant exchange was seriously undercapitalized for such a venture. Though the capital stock of $500,000 was to be subscribed through $2.00 assessments on the members, the exchange had little more than the bonus money from the city of Dallas to begin operations. Nevertheless, Macune used the internal organizational structure of the Alliance to bring the individual farmer closer to the prevailing prices being paid on the world cotton market. Each county business agent, working through the Alliance cotton yard established by the county trade committee, was instructed to weigh, sample, and number the bales of cotton in his local yard. The local agents, following detailed instructions contained in circular letters distributed throughout the state by Macune, wrapped samples from each bale, placed tickets on them giving weight, grade of cotton, and yard number, then expressed them in sacks to the Dallas exchange. There they were placed on display in a sample room where cotton buyers could examine them. Each local Alliance agent had been provided with a cipher code so that the latest cotton quotations could be telegraphed to him in a manner that would permit the farmers, rather than local cotton buyers, to benefit from marginal price increases. The Macune system thus brought the world market into direct competition with local cotton buyers. The exchange charged only twenty-five cents for each bale sold, plus telegraphic expenses. Export buyers were sufficiently impressed; they came to the Texas Exchange. And in one massive transaction, 1500 bales of cotton were selected from samples in Dallas and sold for shipment to England, France, and Germany. The cotton was shipped from twenty-two different stations in Texas.[26]

Impressive as all this activity was as a demonstration of agrarian self-help, the Texas Exchange leadership soon realized it was not nearly enough. Macune could claim, as he subsequently did, that the technique of bulking cotton to export buyers had a discernible effect toward raising prices for all farmers, but while this was true it did not free the small farmer or the tenant farmer from all the personal and financial indignities involved in the crop lien. In hundreds of suballiance resolutions the farmers repeated the agonizing truths about life in the rural South. Significantly, the fact that Alliance leaders felt pressure from tenants and crop-mortgaged land owners followed directly from their own efforts; the leaders had created the internal lecturing network of communication that made possible this expression of pain from below. The message from the Alliance rank and file was clear:

"You said we could get free of the merchant if we joined the Alliance and formed a cooperative. We have done it. Now you do your part." Late in 1887 the directors of the Texas Exchange faced the challenge squarely. The plan they embarked upon was one of the most creative in the annals of American farm organizations, and it led directly to the one enduring new political concept of the agrarian revolt, the sub-treasury plan of 1889. At a meeting of its directors, held in Dallas in November 1887, the Texas Exchange advanced an imaginative plan to provide the poorest Alliance members with the credit necessary to enable them to harvest their 1888 crop and sell it themselves through the exchange.[27]

The exchange announced a "joint-note" plan. Each Alliance county business agent was to acquire from each suballiance member who wanted supplies on credit a schedule of his probable individual needs for the coming year, together with a showing of "full financial responsibility" and a pledge of cotton worth at least "three times as much" as the amount of credit requested. The farmers were then to execute a collective joint note for the estimated amount of supplies for all of them. The plan was "cooperation" in the purest sense. The note was to draw interest after May 31 and was to be paid November 15, after the 1888 crop had been harvested. The notes were also to be signed by financially responsible local Alliance farmers who would secure themselves against loss by taking mortgages on the growing crops. The exchange attempted to fortify itself with additional information. Each signer of the joint note was required to specify the number of acres of land he owned, its value, outstanding indebtedness, the number of acres cultivated both in cotton and grain, and the value of his livestock. He also agreed to allow his co-signers to harvest his crop in the event he became incapacitated. Such joint notes from suballiances were then to be screened by the county business agent and the county trade committee before being passed on—along with the collective supply order of all participating suballiance members—to the state exchange in Dallas. The exchange did not warrant itself to fulfill the request until a "committee of acceptance," consisting of the secretary of the exchange and two directors, accepted the note and authorized the manager, Macune, to deal with the suballiance.[28]

The third part of the plan was, of course, that the exchange would use the notes as collateral to borrow money to purchase the supplies. The supplies were to be shipped on a monthly basis, one-sixth of the order for each of the months between May and November. The notes would draw 1 percent per month from date of shipment until the individual farmer repaid his debt. In addition to making substantial savings in credit costs, farmers might expect much cheaper prices on supplies as a result of the exchange's bulk purchasing power. Finally, by producing a way for farmers to live while they worked their crop the joint-note plan permitted the individual farmer to retain title to his cotton so that he might sell it "independent of the merchant" through the exchange's central selling system.[29]

To explain this elaborate plan the Texas Alliance mobilized its lecturing system once again, utilizing many of the men who had been seasoned in the organizing campaign in the South the year before. The procedure and all its complicated components were outlined to every county Alliance in Texas and eventually to every participating suballiance. The Alliance journal, the Dallas *Mercury,* now renamed the *Southern Mercury,* printed explanations of the plan. Meanwhile, the exchange initiated semi-monthly circulars, written by Macune, containing relevant administrative instructions as well as the latest price quotations. The Alliance marshalled all of its educational resources in a gigantic effort to overcome the crop lien system and all of the furnishing merchants of Texas.[30]

As the joint notes flooded into the Dallas nerve center, efforts to induce the membership to pay the $2.00 per capita assessed for the capital stock of the exchange were intensified. When the exchange directors met in March 1888 to review the situation they found that, while paid-up stock had climbed from its September value—virtually nothing—to $17,000, this "blood money" from the farmers of Texas had to be balanced against the steadily rising amounts contained in the joint notes approved by the "committee of acceptance." The committee, anticipating brokering the joint notes through bank loans, began buying supplies to fulfill the orders from the suballiances. By April, when the paid-in capital stock had climbed above $20,000, the joint notes approved by the exchange totaled no less than $200,974.88 on local collateral of over $600,000 in the land and stock of Texas farmers. On this foundation, the exchange had ordered goods in the amount of $108,371.06.[31]

Macune had meanwhile begun the quest for outside banking capital in March, using the joint notes as collateral. After repeated conferences in Dallas, bankers there refused to advance loans. Macune then went to Houston, Fort Worth, Galveston and New Orleans. In Houston he acquired one loan of $6000 by pledging $20,000 in joint notes as collateral, and some mercantile houses advanced supplies, taking the notes as security, but with few exceptions the answer elsewhere was "no." Macune's regular report to the exchange directors sounded an ominous note:

> The business manager spent the whole of the month of March in trying to negotiate banking arrangements whereby a loan could be affected at a reasonable rate of interest, to provide funds to purchase goods with which to supply the contracts accepted by the committee of acceptance; but all the efforts made were unsuccessful, and tended to produce the conviction that those who controlled the moneyed institutions of the state either did not choose to do business with us, or they feared the ill will of a certain class of business men who considered their interests antagonistic to those of our order and corporation. At any rate, be the causes what they may, the effort to borrow money in a sufficient quantity failed.[32]

The Texas exchange was suddenly in serious trouble. Obligations assumed by the exchange for supplies shipped to suballiances fell due in May, and the agency was unable to meet them. The Alliance leadership rallied to the exchange. Late that month, Evan Jones, the Erath County radical now elevated to state president, presided over a joint meeting of the order's executive committee and the exchange's directors. Finding the exchange's books in order, Jones confirmed to his members their hope that "the entire business is and has been

Evan Jones
A leader, with William Lamb, of the
Cleburne radicals. Jones subsequently served as a member of the
post-Cleburne Alliance executive
committee, president of the Texas
Alliance during the cooperative
struggle of 1888 and second national president of the Alliance in
1889.

conducted upon sound, conservative, practical business principles." He added grimly: "It is time for each brother to realize
that faltering now means unconditional surrender." Jones and
the exchange directors then announced that "grave and important issues confront us. . . . Unjust combinations seek to
throttle our lawful and legitimate efforts to introduce a business system." In order that "proof of the existence of this combination" could be submitted to the membership, the Alliance
leaders "most earnestly recommended" that a mass meeting be
held at the courthouse in each county of the state on the second Saturday in June. At these meetings documentary evidence "disclosing facts of vast importance" would be submitted along with a plan to meet the crisis.[33]

A confidential circular to the order's leadership in each
county added the information that Dallas bankers, wholesale
merchants, implement dealers, and manufacturers had "entered into a combination to crush the exchange," that bankers
had tried to force the exchange to buy through jobbers and
had refused to lend the exchange money "upon any terms of
any security," and that they had "kept the mails full and the
wires red hot" to prevent the exchange from getting money

from Fort Worth, Houston, Galveston, and New Orleans. This final bit of confidential information completed the preparation of the Alliance county leaders for the more than 175 simultaneous county meetings scheduled to act on the exchange crisis.[34]

7
"The day to save the exchange . . ."

That "second Saturday in June" fell on June 9. It was a day men remembered for the rest of their lives. The response to the call made one fact dramatically clear: the central reality in the lives of most Southern farmers in the late nineteenth century was the desire to escape the crop lien. True, there were farmers in Texas in 1888 who had known a sense of failure in their dealings with merchants for so long that they thought first of the $2.00 they had invested in the exchange. And there were others whose anxieties, honed by the same sense of failure, led them to condemn Macune and believe rumors he had taken the exchange money and headed for Canada. For such men, June 9, 1888, had little significance. But many thousands of Alliancemen had too great an emotional investment in the exchange to view its threatened demise with such precipitous pessimism.[35]

The farmers came by the hundreds, and in some cases, by the thousands, to almost 200 Texas courthouses on June 9, 1888. Townspeople in the far reaches of the state who were not privy to the Alliance internal communication network of circulars, lecturers, or the columns of the *Southern Mercury* knew little of the "Farmers Exchange" and its financial troubles in Dallas. They watched with puzzlement the masses "of rugged honest faces" that materialized out of the countryside and appeared at the courthouses of the state. In scores of county seats, the crush of farm wagons extended for blocks in every direction, some beyond the town limits. Reporters remarked about the "earnestness" of the effort to save the exchange and the "grim determined farmers" who were making pledges of support to some far-off mercantile house. The correspondent of the Austin *Weekly Statesman* recorded that observers were "completely astonished by the mammoth proportions" of the turnout. In the far north of Texas, 2000 farmers from over 100 suballiances in Fannin County marched impassively down the main street of Bonham behind banners that proclaimed "The Southern Exchange Shall Stand." A brass band led the procession to the meeting place where Alliancemen stood for hours in the summer heat to learn about the plight of their exchange.[36]

Little in the farmers' experience led them to doubt the interpretation of recent events made by their state officers. They reported soberly in their county Alliance journals that "we found the trouble was that a number if not all of the banks and wholesale merchants in Texas had turned against the exchange." In farmhouses all over Texas women dug into domestic hideaways for the coins that represented a family's investment in the hope of escaping the crop lien. At a mass meeting in southeast Texas frugal German farmers collected $637.70 and one of their number respectfully tendered a five-year lease on some property to the state exchange for use as it saw fit. In Parker County in northwest Texas, the crowd of farmers was so large the hall could not accommodate it and the mass meeting moved in a body to another location. In the county seat of Rockwall, near Dallas, a "large and enthusiastic mass meeting" lasted from 9:00 a.m. to 6:00 p.m., and, though the reporter was hazy about the specifics, it was clear, he said, that they "intend to stand by the exchange." The Hays County Alliance wired that it "loves Dr. Macune for the enemies he has made," and the radical president of the Lamar County Alliance dispatched a lengthy telegram declaring, among other things, that "we have the right to buy where we please and to sell to whom we please." The Lamar Alliancemen paid their respects to newspaper rumors about Macune's malfeasance by tending their "thanks and appreciation to the manager of the state exchange." County presidents sent wires to each other as if the sense of solidarity thus engendered might produce greater contributions from a membership notoriously low in capital assets. An East Texas Alliance received telegrams from seven County Alliances, some halfway across the state. A North Texas County contributed $4000 to the exchange, while Gulf Coast Alliancemen pledged

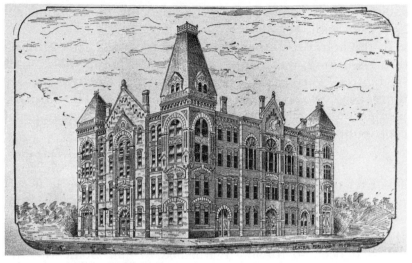

The Big Store of the Alliance
The statewide marketing and purchasing warehouse of the Texas Alliance Exchange, in Dallas.

"several thousand" more before adjourning to a joint meeting with the Knights of Labor to plan a local political ticket. On the old frontier, other gatherings, including a well-attended mass meeting in drought-wracked Young County, pledged smaller amounts, and in the center of the state Bell County farmers announced that their pledges constituted "a success in every respect." [37]

Following this remarkable demonstration from the grass roots, Macune announced that results "had exceeded expectations" and that the exchange was on solid footing. But though pledges seemed to have totaled well over $200,000, the central truth of the Texas Alliance was that it represented precisely those it said it did—the agricultural poor. A letter to the *Southern Mercury* earlier in the year portended the outcome of the June 9 effort: "We voted the $2.00 assessment for the exchange, and as soon as we are able, will pay it, [but] we are not able to do so at present." The dignity with which the admission was made, and the willingness of the *Mercury* to eschew proper "promotional" techniques by printing it without comment, is indicative of the commonplace recognition of prevailing poverty among great numbers of those intimately associated with the Alliance movement.[38]

In the light of existing economic conditions in the farming districts, June 9 was indeed a success, but not in the scale of six figures. The Texas Exchange eventually received something over $80,000 from its feverish effort. The farmers' pledges represented their hope for the exchange; their actual contributions measured the reality of their means.[39]

8

The exchange survived the season, though manifestly it was not well. Credit—the farmer's age-old problem—was the exchange's problem too. In Dallas, during the summer of 1888, Macune put his fertile mind to work on this old truth that had been so forcibly reaffirmed to him. Somehow, the farmer's crop that the advancing merchants took as collateral had to be utilized by the farmer to obtain credit directly. Precisely how this could be done obviously required something less ephemeral than joint notes that bankers would not honor. But what?

The August 1888 convention of the Texas Alliance provided a tentative answer. Though the Texans were now at the peak of their organizational strength and political influence in the national agrarian movement, the delegates, representing some 250,000 Texas Alliancemen, were absorbed in only one issue, the future of their cooperative exchange. Macune faced an anxious gathering of Alliance county presidents and lecturers on the convention's first day. As always, he was well prepared for his public presentation. His exhaustive report, running to sixty-six typewritten pages, presented in minutest detail the record of his stewardship. Reporters noted that the address, "though tedious and exceedingly complex," was listened to throughout with "the most intense interest." The stakes were high and all knew it. "Not a few there were," said the Dallas *News,* "who had come many a mile to hear this report and who believed that on this document depended in a large degree the rise or fall, the success or destruction of this experiment." Macune interpolated as he went, interjecting extemporaneous summaries "which never failed to be met with the most encouraging applause." He needed all his persuasive wiles, for his address went beyond a mere defense of his direction of the exchange. It included an entirely new approach to the central management of agricultural credit. His months of intensive brooding about the causes of his own and the exchange's crisis had produced a bold new stratagem: he intended to escape the need for bank credit by generating the necessary liquid capital from the farmers themselves.[40]

Macune proposed the creation of a treasury within the exchange to issue its own currency—exchange treasury notes—in payment of up to 90 per cent of the current market value of commodities. Farmers would circulate these notes within the order by using them to purchase their supplies at the Alliance stores. The latter were to be strengthened by having each county Alliance charter a store of $10,000 capital, half paid in by the local farmers and the other half by the central exchange. As outlined by Macune, the plan actually cost the central exchange nothing in capital, for it acquired the use of the $10,000 capital of each of the county Alliances for half that amount—in effect, using the credit of the local stores. The plan, while certainly strengthening the local operation, had as its principal intent the strengthening of the central exchange; indeed, each county Alliance was to be coerced into subscribing for its proportionate per-capita share, based on paid-up membership roles, of the over-all $500,000 capital of the central exchange—on pain of being excluded from the benefits of the treasury note plan. This in turn provided the central exchange with the funds needed to underwrite its half of the capitalization of each county Alliance store. The practical effect of establishing a treasury department in the state exchange, one empowered to issue its own currency to Alliance members upon deposit of warehouse receipts of their commodities, was to expand the money supply circulating within the order in a way that strengthened the capitalization of both the central exchange and its local branches.[41]

The plan permitted the farmer to hold his harvested crop off the market until prices rose, rather than having to dump it when prices were lowest. It also created a combination of legal money and Alliance treasury notes negotiable at Alliance stores which he could live on in the meantime; thus he could escape the advancing man. As for the cost of his supplies, the plan ensured that the lower retail prices achieved through the first year's operation of the existing exchange would be continued. With a more stable capital base, these accomplishments might even be improved upon.

The treasury note plan attempted to do for farmers what decades of cooperative experiments, including, apparently, the joint-note plan, had failed to do—end the reign of the furnishing merchant by providing the farmer with the non-usurious credit he needed to break the chain of the crop lien. Macune, speaking before the Texas Alliance in August 1888, argued for his treasury-note idea with customary sweep, dismissing the "cash-only" Rochdale inheritance of the Grange as wholly inadequate to the task at hand:

> We have been talking co-operation for twenty years. Now we have made an aggressive movement. It has thrown the whole community into the wildest confusion. . . . It saved us last year from one to five million dollars on our cotton; it saved us forty percent on our plows; thirty percent on our engines and gins; sixty percent on sewing machines; thirty percent on wagons. . . . In spite of all this the question today is: shall we endorse the aggressive movement, or shall we go back home and say to the people, we stirred up the bees in the bee tree and made them make the biggest fuss you ever heard; we saw barrels of honey in there, more than we could number, but we declined the fight and have come back home to starve and let our children grow up to be slaves. In a nut-shell then, the question is: will you cease an aggressive effort that promises certain relief, simply because the opposition howl and curse? [42]

Macune's words underscored the fact that he was fighting for his life as exchange manager and national spokesman for the Alliance. Even as a specially appointed convention committee reviewed the entire operation of the exchange, the Dallas *News* threw a bombshell into the convention by publishing a report that, though "not generally known," the state exchange "has been in receivership for six weeks." The story named a Major Hugh Ewings as being in charge of all monies

Charles Macune
Founder of the National Alliance, business manager of the Texas Alliance Exchange, and originator of large-scale cooperation, the basic organizing tool of the agrarian revolt.

going in or out of the exchange operation. The "receiver" appeared before the investigating committee, reported he had been hired merely as an auditor by the exchange, and denied the *News* report. The *News* retracted the story on the following day, and the convention accepted a judgment of its investigating committee that no "lack of honesty" on the part of Macune had been found. Macune, if not yet the exchange, had passed through the Texas crisis.[43]

But the experience had shaken the farmers. Alliancemen stood loyally by Macune, their "past, present, and future business manager," but they clearly felt they did not have the immediate means to implement the treasury-note plan. In essence, both Macune and the farmers were forced to acknowledge that the treasury-note plan, however ingenious, was beyond the means of the penniless farmers of Texas. The exchange drew up new by-laws relinquishing, at least for the present, the basic struggle against the credit system: "all purchases made from branch exchanges must be for cash, and notice is hereby given that the books of the exchange are closed against any further debit entries." This was a bitter retreat; it reflected the belief that if the cooperative effort were ever to make a second attempt, the exchange had to be placed on a sound footing. The exchange president, J. D. Fields, who was one of the more moderate members of the Texas leadership, issued a public statement showing how thoroughly all participants understood the issues at stake:

> Do not remain in a dependent position any longer. We can, we must succeed. All is at stake with us. It is success and freedom, or failure and servitude, doomed to drudge for the moneyed classes until despair will drive the poor to rebellion and then God defend us. . . . We will send out a plan in the next circular letter for the management of the business in the coming year. We expect cooperation from every Alliance member in the state. Patronize your business and stand firm, and we cannot fail to make a grand success of our movement.[44]

The officers betrayed their anxiety by exhorting the membership to pay up the joint notes: "settlements are at once required, and must be made as soon as possible." Yet neither Macune nor his principal advisers in the Texas leadership appeared to be intimidated by the experience or inclined to shrink from the complexity of managing large-scale farmer cooperatives. At the Alliance's second national convention in Meridian, Mississippi, late in 1888, Macune reluctantly approved the Georgia modification of the Texas Exchange, which emphasized purchasing over the more burdensome credit demands of cooperative marketing. While the Georgia approach, modeled after the Rochdale plan inherited from the Grange, clearly involved less risk, it was only at the price of forgoing the goal of freeing all farmers from the crop lien system. Macune and another cooperative theorist from Texas, Harry Tracy, argued earnestly with state Alliance leaders that the Rochdale system helped only the thin layer of the agricultural middle class in the South, that it ignored the crushing needs of the great mass of tenant farmers and the hundreds of thousands of declining landowners caught in the cycle of debt to merchants. Macune insisted at Meridian that the Alliance cooperative had to go beyond the joint-stock Rochdale plans of the past. The central state exchange, he said:

is pure and simple cooperation, with no joint-stock features whatever, and differs from similar plans before introduced in several important particulars. It is calculated to benefit *the whole class,* and not simply those who have surplus money to invest in capital stock; it does not aspire to, and is not calculated to be a business for profit in itself. . . . Another distinctive feature of the exchange plan is that, instead of encouraging a number of independent stores scattered over the country, each in turn to fall a prey to the opposition, whenever they shall think it of sufficient importance to concentrate a few forces against it—this plan provides for a strong central State head, and places sufficient capital stock there to make that the field for concentrating the fight of the opposition, and a bulwark of strength and refuge for the local store efforts.[45]

Alliance delegates could not with consistency argue against an attempt "to benefit the whole class," as the Alliance itself was predicated upon that approach. And they did not. Tracy, Macune's colleague, elaborately spelled out the central state exchange concept and informed North Carolina's L. L. Polk that cooperative stores in every Southern hamlet would accomplish little in the way of "financial liberty" as long as "they buy, ship, and sell independent of each other." In terms of the mass of Alliance farmers, Tracy saw no "utility" in lesser cooperative attempts. Such ideas were inherently radical, of course, though men like Tracy who were allied with Macune still voted Democratic and did not regard themselves as political insurgents.[46]

But to farmer advocates who sought to benefit "the whole class," the dynamics of the cooperative movement had also brought a breathtaking new perspective on the larger American society. The discovered truth was a simple one, but its political import was radical: the Alliance cooperative stood little chance of working unless fundamental changes were made in the American monetary system. This understanding was the germ of the Omaha Platform of the People's Party.* In August 1888 it materialized in the organization that would carry it to millions of Americans.

* See Appendix D: "The Ideological Origins of the Omaha Platform."

9

At the 1888 convention of the Texas Alliance, the intense intellectual discussion of the future of the exchange—and the
cooperative crusade that had generated the climate for such
discussions—brought the agrarian movement to a critical ideological threshold. In the very months that Macune and the Alliance leadership labored frantically to anchor in place the cornerstone of the cooperative commonwealth—indeed, in the
very weeks the dirt farmers of the Alliance met, marched, and
contributed in an effort to save their exchange—Alliance radicals quietly and almost imperceptibly achieved a decisive ideological breakthrough: they conveyed the greenback political
heritage to the spreading agrarian movement as the centerpiece of Alliance doctrine.

This seminal development, one that hammered into place
the ideological framework of the famed Omaha Platform of
the People's Party, was an achievement suffused with irony,
for it was accomplished over the objections of the most inventive greenbacker among them—Charles Macune. That it happened at all, conclusively verified the ascendency of radicalism
within the ranks of the Alliance founders.

In April 1888, as Macune searched in vain for bankers who
would honor the collateral of the Alliance Exchange, H. S. P.
Ashby, one of S. O. Daws's original radical organizers, issued a
"waking up circular" calling for a statewide meeting "for the
purpose of considering what steps, if any, should be taken in
the approaching campaign." As the most effective stump
speaker in the Alliance movement, Harrison Sterling Price
Ashby had acquired a somewhat handier name—he became
known as "Stump" Ashby. A leader of the earlier independent
political movement which had elected a radical mayor of Forth
Worth in the midst of the Great Southwest Strike of 1886,
Ashby had become a key participant in a loose coalition of
like-minded farmer spokesmen that included Evan Jones,
president of the Texas Alliance; J. R. Bennett, editor of the
Southern Mercury, the order's national journal; A. L. Kessler,
president of the Texas Manufacturing Cooperative; J. M. Perdue, author of the Cleburne Demands; Samuel Evans, a

prominent Texas greenbacker; and, perhaps not surprisingly, William Lamb. Along with other radicals in the nation in 1888, these men wanted to construct a third-party political institution to replace the defunct Greenback Party. Ashby's meeting, convened in Waco in May 1888 as the "Convention of Farmers, Laborers, and Stock Raisers," promulgated a six-point platform that featured the abolition of the national banking system, the replacement of national bank notes with legal tender treasury notes issued on land security, prohibition of alien land ownership, and "government ownership or control of the means of transportation and communication." [47]

Macune took time out from his Exchange wars to write a lengthy letter to the *Southern Mercury* warning the 250,000 Alliance members in Texas against independent political action. But while Ashby, Kessler, and others held their Waco meeting, Lamb and Evans were in Cincinnati assisting in the formal creation of the new national "Union Labor Party." In Fort Worth on July 3, 1888, Lamb chaired a statewide "Non-Partisan Convention" which accepted Ashby's Waco platform. It added additional planks calling for a federal income tax, free coinage of silver, and the enactment of compulsory arbitration laws. With respect to the railroads, the phrase "government ownership or control" was altered to read "government ownership *and* control." No sooner had Lamb's "non-partisans" finished their work in Fort Worth on July 4 than the "Texas Union Labor Party" held its inaugural convention in the same city on July 5. In an amusing—and revealing—overlapping of delegates from the two conventions, Samuel Evans became chairman of the Union Laborites, J. M. Perdue and William Lamb materialized as members of the state executive committee, and the new party adopted—without so much as changing a comma—the platform of the "non-partisans" written two days earlier. The new third party's nominee for the governorship of Texas was no less than Evan Jones, president of the Texas Alliance. As the struggle to save the Exchange reached its climax in the summer of 1888, Jones reluctantly decided that a divisive political campaign would weaken the Alliance at the moment it needed maximum solidarity to preserve the forward thrust of the cooperative movement. Therefore, shortly before the annual convention of the Texas Alliance at Dallas in August 1888, he declined the nomination "of this noble body of men." [48]

But at the convention itself—even as Macune made his lengthy report on the exchange to the attentive delegates— J. M. Perdue chaired an Alliance committee that delivered a radical "report on the industrial depression" that placed greenback monetary theory at the heart of Alliance politics. This document, which concluded with the "Dallas Demands," conveyed to the agrarian movement the radical greenback heritage; the three documents written at Waco, Fort Worth, and Dallas between May and August 1888 provided the entire substance of the St. Louis Platform adopted by the National Alliance the following year.[49]

These developments set in place the central political definition of Populism and revealed clearly the dynamics that produced the multi-sectional People's Party: the cooperative crusade not only recruited the farmers to the Alliance; opposition to the cooperatives by bankers, wholesalers, and manufacturers generated a climate that was sufficiently radical to permit the acceptance by farmers of the greenback interpretation of the prevailing forms of American finance capitalism. Greenback doctrines thus provided the ideology and the cooperative crusade provided the mass dynamics for the creation of the People's Party. Both reached their peak of intensity in the Texas Alliance in the tumultuous summer of 1888, and the emotional heat from that experience welded radical greenbackism onto the farmers' movement. After 1888, only one step—a rather sizable one—remained to bring to fruition the creation of a multi-sectional radical party—the conversion of the bulk of the national Alliance membership to the greenback doctrines which had become the central political statement of the agrarian movement. Two men, Charles Macune and William Lamb, working toward opposite purposes, were to provide the tactics that produced the mass conversion.

10

But in 1888 radical politics was not yet the uppermost thought in the minds of the growing army of farmers who met in thousands of suballiances scattered from Florida to Kansas. Their attention of the Alliance was focused on the cooperative crusade. The Texans offered the agrarian movement a bold blueprint of large-scale cooperation, and the very promise of this blueprint recruited farmers by the hundreds of thousands. Large-scale cooperatives were dangerous, it seemed, but men like Macune and Tracy, as well as the more radical leadership among the Alliance founders, argued that only broadly gauged cooperatives could acquire the capital strength to combat the array of weapons available to forces of monopoly. Indeed, the more one learned of the variety of options open to commercial opponents of farmer cooperatives, the more imperative centralized exchanges seemed.

One new state Alliance that agreed was Kansas. As the order moved into its greatest period of growth in 1889, the "Kansas Alliance Exchange Company" was chartered as a centralized marketing and purchasing agency. It later began to publish its own newspaper, the *Kansas Farmers Alliance and Industrial Union*.[50]

The Farmers Alliance apread across the Western plains in 1889, through Missouri as well as Kansas, and moved on into the Dakotas. The Rochdale cooperative plan that Henry Loucks had introduced in the Dakota Alliance was abandoned in the face of banker-merchant hostility and the shortage of farmer capital, and a broader system was instituted that borrowed freely from Texas experiments. The Dakotans, after reorganizing their cooperative approach, stepped up the order's political activities as the Dakota Territory neared statehood. Meanwhile, Alliance organizers moved through Kentucky, crossed the Ohio River into Indiana, and established enclaves in Oklahoma Territory and Colorado in the West and Maryland in the East.[51]

As a decade of Alliance organizing came to an end, cooperation had begun to acquire a record of accomplishment that was both highly visible and highly mixed. The Mississippi Alliance adopted bulking and, lest the suballiances be defrauded by false quotations from cotton buyers, set up a system whereby the state purchasing agent kept local suballiances informed on latest price quotations. The Florida state exchange began the cooperative marketing of citrus, and it was successful. The Georgia exchange became heavily involved in bulk purchases of fertilizers, and farmers in both bright and dark-leaf tobacco belts of Tennessee, Kentucky, North Carolina, and Virginia cautiously moved forward with plans for cooperative marketing through Alliance-owned tobacco warehouses. As early as 1888, the North Carolina Alliance began to lead in this effort when one of its county Alliances established a factory to manufacture its own tobacco. Alliance tobacco warehouses were constructed in half a dozen towns in North Carolina and Virginia.[52]

The Alliance's most striking achievement involved victory over its announced enemy, a bona fide national "trust." Cotton bagging had traditionally been made from jute, and in 1888 a combine of jute manufacturers suddenly announced that henceforth jute bagging would be raised from seven cents a yard to eleven, twelve and, in some regions, fourteen cents a yard. The action laid a "tribute of some $2,000,000" on the nation's cotton farmers. Alliance leaders in Georgia, Alabama, Mississippi, South Carolina, Louisiana, and Florida reacted with vigor. Evan Jones of Texas, Macune's successor as the order's national president, convened a southwide convention in Birmingham in the spring of 1889 to fashion final plans for a boycott throughout the cotton belt. The state Alliances agreed on common plans for action and entered into arrangements with scores of mills across the South for the manufacture of cotton bagging. Some buyers, particularly in England, complained about the inferior cotton bagging, a problem Florida farmers ingeniously solved by arranging to import cheaper jute bagging from Europe and paying for it with farm produce consigned to the Florida Alliance Exchange. In Georgia, a rising agrarian advocate named Tom Watson helped fortify Alliancemen for the struggle by delineating the larger implications: "It is useless to ask Congress to help us, just as it was folly for our forefathers to ask for relief from the tea tax; and they revolted . . . so should we." He added, with an eye to future struggles, "The Standard of Revolt is up. Let us keep it up and speed it on." Georgia Alliancemen apparently took him at his word. When North Carolina's Polk appeared at a

Georgia Alliance convention in the middle of the jute war, he encountered an up-country farmer dressed out in cotton bagging who told him that 360 Alliancemen in his county had uniform suits of it and "they are literally the cotton bagging brigade." A double wedding at an Alliance Exposition in Atlanta found 20,000 Alliancemen looking on approvingly as "both brides and both grooms were attired in cotton bagging costumes." Such innovations testified to the fervor with which state and local Alliances threw themselves into the battle with the jute trust, but its ultimate outcome depended on less colorful but more demanding organizational arrangements to substitute cotton bagging for jute at thousands of local suballiances across half a continent. The farmers of the Alliance met this test in 1888–89, and the manufacturing combine, suddenly awash in its own jute, conceded that the price-rigging scheme had collapsed. In 1890, Southern farmers were buying fourteen-cent jute bagging for as low as five cents a yard.[53]

This triumph for cooperative purchasing was matched in quality, if not in scope, by innovations in cooperative marketing that emanated from Kansas. At the local level, county alliances formed a variety of marketing and purchasing cooperatives with an élan born of their new sense of collective powers. But cooperation in Kansas soon moved beyond the stage of local efforts. In 1889, the Kansas Alliance entered into joint agreements with the Kansas Grange and the Missouri Alliance and, in 1890, with the Nebraska Alliance, to establish the American Livestock Commission Company. The experiment in multi-state marketing of livestock opened in May 1889 with paid-up capital from farmer members totaling $25,000. The effort proved successful from the start. Within six months the commission company had over $40,000 in profits to distribute to its members. The animosity toward the cooperative among commission companies scarcely promised a serene future, however.[54]

These successes were balanced by a crucial failure. In the late summer of 1889, after twenty months of operation, the Texas Exchange, unable to market its joint notes in banking circles and therefore unable to respond to insistent demands from its creditors, went under. The Texas effort, the first to be chartered, was thus the first to fail. The news sent a wave of anxiety through the entire South: was the Alliance dream unattainable? Were the Texas lecturers wrong? As the Alliance grew, so did the burdens of explaining and proving its program of self-help. With increasing frequency the Alliance founders, driven by the difficulties of cooperation, had to explain to farmers that the opposition to their movement derived from the self-interest of gold-standard financiers who administered and profited by the existing national banking system. Greenback doctrines were thus increasingly marshalled to defend the Macunite dream of large-scale farmer cooperatives. By this process radical monetary theory began to be conveyed to the suballiances by growing numbers of Alliance lecturers. The farmers had joined the Alliance cooperative to escape the crop lien in the South and the chattel mortgage in the West, and the failure of cooperatives, particularly the huge model experiment in Texas, spread deep concern through the ranks of the Farmers Alliance. Wherever a cooperative failed for lack of credit, greenbackism surged like a radical virus through the organizational structure of the agrarian movement. Slowly, the Omaha Platform of the People's Party was germinating.[55]

Charles Macune was not present in Dallas for the death of the exchange, for the ubiquitous Alliance leader now operated out of Washington, where, in addition to serving as national president, he edited the new Alliance national newspaper. The *National Economist,* underwritten by Texas Alliancemen, became, under Macune's tutelage, easily the best edited journal of agricultural economics in the nation. Circulation soon passed 100,000. As the Alliance organization completed its second year as a national institution, the enigma that was Dr. Charles W. Macune rivaled that of the cooperative crusade itself as a case study in complexity. Macune's belief that cooperation must serve landless tenants and others bound to the crop lien system stamped him as an economic radical, yet he remained firmly traditional on political issues and adamantly opposed to all talk of a third party. In his presidential address, given at Shreveport in 1887, he outlined his political creed:

> Under our system of government, we should not resort to a new political movement to carry out every reform necessary. . . . We have the two great principles and conceptions . . . contended for by John Adams and Thomas Jefferson, as a basis for division into two great political parties; that should suffice. . . . [A]s the agriculturists comprise a large majority of all the voters, they will necessarily comprise a majority in each party . . . but in partisan politics, the members of our order should participate, not as Alliancemen, but as citizens, because politics is for the citizen.[56]

If this homily betrayed a certain innocence, Macune was at the time still experiencing his executive apprenticeship. Indeed, the evolution of his thought toward a more complex analysis of American political institutions constitutes one of the more reliable guides to the dynamics within the Alliance that led to the People's Party. The growing tangle of political beliefs that represented his public position became more apparent the following year in his presidential address in Meridian. On economic issues he was as aggressive as ever: "Ours is no common struggle; upon it depends in a great measure the future prosperity of agriculture and the liberty and independence of those engaged in that pursuit." On political issues he revealed that his opposition to independent political action might emanate from a marked partiality toward the Democratic Party, and that his loyalty might be based on an allegiance to white supremacy. The Alliance was not only a "business organization" and a "nonpartisan" one, it was also "strictly a white man's organization." Macune was able to summarize all of these beliefs in a single sentence: "The people we seek to relieve from the oppression of unjust conditions are the largest and most conservative class of citizens in this country." [57]

Yet in organizational terms that carried inherent political implications Macune was even more aggressively expansionist than he was in his regional cooperative programs. At Shreveport in 1887 he had acquired approval of plans for exploratory talks toward merger with the Arkansas Agricultural Wheel, the Illinois-based Farmers Mutual Benefit Association (FMBA), the Northwestern Alliance, and the Knights of

Labor. At Meridian in 1888 he largely completed union with the largest of these groups, the seven-state Agricultural Wheel.[58]

The membership of the Wheel far exceeded the combined totals of the FMBA and the Northwestern Alliance and perhaps reached 150,000. Some 85 per cent of these members resided in Arkansas, Tennessee, and Missouri. Though the Wheel borrowed freely from Alliance experience in cooperatives, organizational structure, and methodology, the Arkansas leadership needed little spurring in the area of political action. The Wheel, headed by successive Union Laborite presidents, early became politically active. The racial liberalism of its state secretary, R. H. Morehead, and its chief propagandist, W. Scott Morgan, was another unusual folkway, one not broadly emulated in the Alliance or the nation as a whole. Indeed, when joint committees of the Wheel and Alliance agreed on union in Meridian, it was a close question whether Macune had improved his own position in behalf of an eventual national farmer cooperative more than he had improved the position of Alliance radicals who sought to carry the movement into independent political action. The Wheel provided numbers, certainly; it also provided a political militancy beyond Macune's.[59]

Some organizational gymnastics necessary to achieve merger with the Wheel at Meridian indirectly added to the political pressure on the Alliance national president. Pending ratification of the merger by subordinate state units of both orders, Macune created a new organizational superstructure. In a transparent move to pave the way for amalgamation with the Knights of Labor, the Alliance was renamed "The Farmers and Laborer's Union of America." The Wheel moved into confederation. Macune stepped down as president and Evan Jones, the Texas radical, became his successor, but Macune immediately stepped up as national president of a new parent institution, presiding over the two organizations headed by Isaac McCracken, the Wheel president, and Jones. To this organization Macune affixed the old name: The National Farmers Alliance and Cooperative Union. Though the new structure, headed by three presidents, represented a melange of rank-and-file urges and ideologies, Macune, the vocal partisan of nonpartisanship, could not even win a vote among his fellow presidents on the issue of third-party activity. Neither McCracken nor Jones considered independent political action beyond the limits of agrarian policy. And, judging by the political allies with whom each traveled, neither agreed with Macune on the white eligibility clause. These sundry developments must have seemed all the more ominous to Macune, particularly in view of the heightened political activity that accompanied—and seemed to threaten—the cooperative crusade.[60]

11

Precisely what the Alliance movement was in the process of becoming could scarcely have been predicted by the farmers themselves from the contradictory events of 1888–89. Only one thing was certain: the Alliance was attempting to construct, within the framework of American capitalism, some variety of cooperative commonwealth. Precisely where that would lead was unclear. More than any other Allianceman, Charles Macune had felt the power of the corporate system arrayed alongside the power of a self-help farmer cooperative. He had gone to the bankers and they had replied in the negative. Though his own farmer associates had said "yes," they could not marshall enough resources to defeat the crop lien system. Macune knew that an exchange of considerably reduced scope could be constructed on a sound basis within the means available to organized farmers. One could avoid the credit problem simply by operating cash stores for affluent farmers. But while he was an orthodox, even a reactionary social philosopher, and still a political traditionalist, C. W. Macune was an economic radical. The collapse of the Texas exchange threatened his personal prestige, but he knew the essential problem was not unsound business stewardship, but absence of sufficient capital. The pressure of the multiple experiences that had propelled him to leadership amid the Cleburne schism, to fame as an organizer and national leader during the Southern expansion, to crisis and potential loss of political power over the exchange, and to constant maneuvering against his driving, exasperating, creative left wing—all, taken together, conjoined to carry Macune to a conception of the uses of democratic government that was beyond the reach of orthodox political theorists of the Gilded Age. Out of his need for personal exoneration, out of his ambition, and out of his exposure to the realities in the daily lives of the nation's farmers, Macune in 1889 came to the sub-treasury plan. Politically, his proposal was a theoretical and psychological breakthrough of considerable implication: he proposed to mobilize the monetary authority of the nation and put it to work in behalf of a sector of its poorest citizens through the creation of a system of currency designed to benefit everyone in the "producing classes," including urban workers.[61]

The main outlines of the sub-treasury plan gradually unfolded in the pages of the *National Economist* during the summer and fall of 1889. There can be no question that Macune saved his proposal for dramatic use in achieving, finally, a national merger of all the nation's major farm and labor organizations. He now planned that event for St. Louis in December 1889, when a great "confederation of labor organizations," convened by the Alliance, would attempt to achieve a workable coalition of the rural and urban working classes, both North and South.

At that meeting, the two contending streams of Alliance thought—political radicalism and economic radicalism—materialized with considerable clarity. Evan Jones, in his presidential address to the Farmers and Laborers Union, endorsed both approaches. He saw the cooperative effort as central. "The advancement of civilization . . . depends, largely if not wholly, upon the intelligent application of the true principles of cooperation. . . . Most if not every failure of all the various business efforts of our order is due to a want of a proper understanding and a strict adherence to the business principles of cooperation. It is the foundation that underlies the whole superstructure of our noble order." Yet cooperation was tied to the entire problem of the national currency. "It is impossible to have an equitable adjustment of capital and labor so long as money is contracted below that which is adequate to the demands of commerce." To Jones, the only way to "correct the abuses and powers" that had "now paralyzed an almost ruined agricultural and laboring people" was through full-scale greenbackism: "the coinage of silver [must] be as free as gold" and both must "be supplemented with treasury notes (which shall be a full legal tender for all contracts), in a sufficient amount to furnish a circulating medium commensurate to the business necessities of the people." [62]

In clarifying these relationships, Jones drew class lines with sharp definition. While the cooperative effort has achieved "a salutary influence upon commerce," he told the Alliance delegates, "it has aroused the hostility of the greedy and avaricious trusts, rings, and monopolistic combinations to such an extent that great and persistent efforts are put forth by them to thwart us in every attempt at reform." The political implications were, he felt, quite clear. While conceding that "our order, as an order, is strictly non-partisan in politics," he added, significantly:

> We have reached a period in our history when confidence in our political leaders and great political organizations is almost destroyed, and the estrangement between them and the people is becoming more manifest every day. The common people are beginning to see that there is not just cause for the now almost universal depression that pervades the laboring classes of every section of our country and are disposed to attribute the same to the corrupting influence [of] these great combines and corporations.

And in his closing political injunction he said that "So long as our people neglect to inform themselves . . . and continue to follow blindly machine politicians to the neglect of their own interest, they will continue to lose their individuality, influence, and power in our political institutions, and be wholly at the mercy of the soulless corporations." [63]

Faced with a rising tide on his left, symbolized by his radical presidential colleague from Texas, Macune responded with a tactical plan that resembled his solution to the political schism that had threatened the Texas Alliance in 1886. He had thwarted William Lamb, Evan Jones, and the other Cleburne radicals by harnessing sweeping organizational expansion to a new concept of cooperation, one in behalf of "the whole class" of farmers. Now, three years later, he readied plans to respond to the same radical pressure by marrying a new national structure of working-class institutions to the idea of the sub-treasury plan.

But the latter was more than a tactical adjunct to organizational expansion. Macune's sub-treasury concept was the intellectual culmination of the cooperative crusade and directly addressed its most compelling liability—inadequate credit. Through his sub-treasury, Macune proposed to mobilize the currency-issuing power of the government in behalf of the agricultural poor: the federal government would underwrite the cooperatives by issuing greenbacks to provide credit for the farmer's crops, creating the basis of a more flexible national currency in the process; the necessary marketing and purchasing facilities would be achieved through government-owned warehouses, or "sub-treasuries," and through federal sub-treasury certificates paid to the farmer for his produce—credit which would remove furnishing merchants, commercial banks, and chattel mortgage companies from American agriculture. The sub-treasury "certificates" would be government-issued greenbacks, "full legal tender for all debts, public and private," in the words of the Alliance platform. As outlined at St. Louis in 1889, the sub-treasury system was a slight but decisive modification of the treasury-note plan Macune presented to the Texas Alliance the year before. Intellectually, the plan was profoundly innovative. It was to prove far too much so for Gilded Age America.[64]

In its own time, the sub-treasury represented the political equivalent of full-scale greenbackism for farmers. This was the plan's immediate import: it defined the doctrine of fiat money in clear terms of self-interest that had unmistakable appeal to farmers desperately overburdened with debt. As the cooperative crusade made abundantly clear, the appeal extended to both West and South, to Kansas and the Dakotas as well as to Georgia and Alabama. Macune's concept went beyond the generalized greenbackism of radicals such as Evan Jones to a specific practical solution that appealed directly to farmers in a context they could grasp. But more than this, the sub-treasury plan directly benefited all of the nation's "producing classes," including urban workers. Its benefits extended, in fact, to the nation's economy itself. For the greenback dollars for the farmers created a workable basis for a new and flexible national currency originating outside the exclusive control of Eastern commercial bankers. Beyond the benefits to the economy as a whole, Macune's system provided broad new options to the United States Treasury in giving private citizens and business entrepreneurs access to reasonable credit. As Macune fully understood, the revolutionary implications of the sub-treasury system went far beyond its immediate value to farmers.

The line of nineteenth-century theorists of an irredeemable currency—one that included such businessmen as Kellogg and Campbell and extended to such labor partisans as Andrew Cameron—culminated in the farmer advocate, Charles Macune. As Macune argued, the agrarian-greenbackism underlying his sub-treasury system provided organizational cohesion between Southern and Western farmers. As he did not foresee, it also provided political cohesion for a radical third party. The People's Party was to wage a frantic campaign to wrest effective operating control of the American monetary system from the nation's commercial bankers and restore it, "in the name of the whole people," to the United States Treasury. It was a campaign that was never to be waged again.

CHAPTER VI

Toward the Sub-Treasury System and a National Farmer-Labor Coalition

". . . the one most essential thing . . ."

The twin phenomena of organized farm cooperatives and radical political ideas began to surface across America's western granary as the decade of the 1880's came to a close. Not only in Kansas and the Dakotas, but also in Illinois and Minnesota, the small victories, the larger frustrations, and the resulting political lessons generated by the cooperative crusade came to be a part of the lives of increasing thousands of Western farmers. Yet, in some parts of the West, this new form of cooperative-insurgency did not immediately take hold, a circumstance that led to an uneven growth of agrarian organization in the Western plains.

The Illinois example flowed from an accidental happening that reflected existing power relationships among farmers and grain dealers. After the 1883 grain harvest, five farmers in a small town in southern Illinois were told by a buyer that unsettled market conditions prevented him from purchasing their wheat. Suspecting he was trying to panic them into selling at distressed prices, they telegraphed the St. Louis market and received a favorable reply and a good price. They then located a boxcar and shipped their wheat directly to the wholesale purchaser, bypassing the local middleman in the process. Word of this event spread rapidly through the county, and the "Farmers Mutual Benefit Association" was born. The order grew slowly but steadily through a half-dozen counties in the Illinois wheat belt as farmer members attempted to fashion new methods of dealing with grain commission dealers, railroads, and farm implement wholesalers. As Illinois farmers learned by doing, the marketing cooperative became a purchasing cooperative as well. By 1887, the FMBA had 2000 members who met in subordinate lodges. These groups elected representatives to a county lodge which met quarterly and exercised the kind of direct coordinating guidance over the locals required for cooperative buying and selling. The FMBA was structurally sound. The locals were supported by twenty-five-cent quarterly fees, the county and state groups by $1.00 annual dues.

Delegates to meetings were to receive per diem pay and lecturers to carry the details of cooperative planning were to be paid, as were the state officers who supervised the cooperative program. In 1888 came the founding of a newspaper and the proliferation of circulars, instructions, and rituals; growth became rapid. Having achieved a membership of 40,000, the FMBA met with leaders of the Alliance and the Agricultural Wheel at Meridian, Mississippi, in December 1888. Since the three institutions were unique among the nation's new agricultural organizations in that they rested on a cooperative foundation that was structurally integrated into their organizational hierarchy, it was perhaps not unexpected that they cooperated quite well. The Wheel approved plans for merger with the Alliance and the FMBA worked out plans for immediate cooperation and eventual amalgamation.[1]

Another clear indication of agrarian energy in the Western plains emanated from Dakota, where Henry Loucks's determined efforts at cooperation were augmented by a strict reporting system that spread upward from local lodges to state headquarters. The central effort of the Dakotans was a territorial exchange system chartered in 1887. The "Dakota Farmers Alliance Company" was capitalized at $200,000, with the planners seeking $10 from each of the 20,000 members. Essentially a joint stock company which employed Rochdale "cash-only" methods, the Dakota cooperative opened in 1888 and immediately encountered resistance from implement dealers who refused to do business with the cooperative. Though such roadblocks had a discernible radicalizing effect on the Dakota leadership, particularly on Loucks himself, the exchange did manage to do $350,000 in business in 1888, primarily as a purchasing cooperative. The Dakotans were unable to fashion a workable marketing cooperative despite strenuous efforts that included the introduction of secrecy into the order. The problems of mass marketing heightened Loucks's interest in the marketing procedures of Macune's National Farmers Alliance. The two orders moved into closer relationship in 1888.[2]

The most important contribution that the Dakotans made to the gathering agrarian movement was a unique cooperative insurance plan. Administered under the leadership of Loucks's close associate, Alonzo Wardall, the plan not only saved farmers something above 200 per cent over previous rates, but also proved to be an unusually effective organizing tool. The "Alliance Hail Association" met with "violent opposition" from insurance companies after it announced plans to offer protection for 21 to 25 cents an acre to farmers who were used to paying anywhere from 50 to 75 cents an acre. The Association insured 2000 farmers and 150,000 acres in 1887 and, as the good news spread, 8000 farmers and 600,000 acres in 1888. In the four years between 1886 and 1890 the Dakotans amassed a remarkable record: 30,000 policies covering two million acres were issued at a rate of 20 cents per acre. Three thousand claims were made against the cooperative, all were adjusted and paid, and the officers were able to assert with pride that "not a single loss had been contested or law suit grown out of any insurance work." The order pioneered in cooperative life insurance also, and converted its small army of 273 local insurance agents into suballiance organizers who sold policies, collected dues, and lectured on the latest refinements of the state cooperative.[3]

Flushed with success, Loucks and Wardall personally ex-

Alonzo Wardall of South Dakota. With Henry Loucks, Wardall organized the cooperative movement in the Northern plains. Wardall joined the National Alliance in 1888 and the Dakota Alliance followed suit the next year.

ported their cooperative insurance plan to neighboring Minnesota, resurrecting in the process a moribund organization known as the Minnesota Farmers Alliance. The feat constitutes one of the more interesting vignettes of the agrarian revolt, for they achieved it through the unlikely organizational auspices of a writer-lecturer, social critic, and part-time politician named Ignatius Donnelly.

Though the small and loosely formed Minnesota Alliance dated from 1880, it had always been more or less a plaything of politicians, and the twists and turns in its political maneuvers had scarcely augmented the legislative influence of its membership, which was less than robust in any case. By 1888 the Minnesota Alliance, after eight years of membership in the Northwestern Alliance, had but eighty active chapters, something less than 2000 members, and no internal program of any kind. It was mostly a forum that politicians visited in season. Donnelly, almost by default, came to have influence in the organization. Indeed, in 1886 he had, at the request of its leaders, written the Alliance platform. An irascible and loquacious raconteur, utopian novelist, gentleman-farmer, and reform politician, Donnelly enjoyed a reputation as an anti-monopoly warrior and was locally known as "the Sage of

Nininger." Serving as legislative spokesman for the farmers, Donnelly had little success in securing passage of reforms, but he did provide the Minnesota Alliance with much of what political ideology it possessed.[4]

In the spring of 1889, the order, casting about for any straw, asked Donnelly to become its official state lecturer. Having just completed a sensational anticlerical, anticapitalist novel entitled *Caesar's Column,* and doubtless seeking a new outlet for his restless energies, Donnelly accepted the offer. Though he had played little role in bringing the Loucks-Wardall insurance plan to Minnesota, he formed a workable partnership with the newcomers, and the triumvirate of two cooperative advocates from Dakota Territory and an aging writer-politician gradually generated the makings of a genuine agrarian movement in Minnesota. Donnelly's deputy state lecturer wrote from the field excitedly that the Alliance was "catching on" because of the appeal of the Loucks-Wardall insurance program. Donnelly immediately began a persuasive promotional correspondence with his huge array of personal acquaintances in the state and soon had fashioned several platoons of mutual insurance salesmen to double as Alliance organizers.[5]

In common with many dissident politicians, Donnelly believed that reform politics was grounded in the art of stump oratory, and his dalliance with organization-building could easily have ended disastrously. But Loucks and Wardall supervised the campaign, Loucks taking temporary leave from his Dakota duties to move in as manager of the Minnesota Alliance business office while Wardall directed the insurance program. In 1889, through Donnelly's ability to recruit agents and Loucks's and Wardall's experience as agrarian organizers, the Minnesota Alliance became a functioning, though embryonic, cooperative. It therefore acquired new members and, for the first time, the beginnings of organizational cohesion. Zealously, Donnelly went about recruiting lecturer-agents. "If we can build up the Alliance," he wrote one unsuspecting target, "we can have a machinery to do some good." He promised to keep the man busy "all winter." Donnelly did not appoint lecturers by counties, but rather grandiloquently named each one a "deputy state lecturer." In the last six months of 1889 the Minnesota Alliance acquired a somewhat uncertain lecturing apparatus, a functioning state office, an official newspaper named *The Great West,* a bank balance, and something approaching 15,000 members. Donnelly was so impressed he asked Loucks for material on insurance so he could learn why the farmers were joining the Alliance. Once he discovered the rate structure of private companies, he became more fascinated by the program than ever—though he continued to think of the Minnesota Alliance primarily as a local political pressure group. Minnesota farmers did not undertake to form a purchasing or marketing cooperative, either at the state or the local level.[6]

While the evidence from Illinois, Dakota, and Minnesota seemed to offer at least some promise for Midwestern farmers, the evidence from Kansas was even more instructive. The South might have seemed energetically responsive to the Alliance message, but Kansas set a new standard in organizational consolidation. The cooperative movement surged across the state with astonishing speed. In nine months between the spring of 1889 and the winter of 1889–90 more than 75,000 Kansans joined the Farmers Alliance as the order created local, county, and statewide cooperatives. The new movement quickly drew the support of a network of radical newspaper editors whom Henry Vincent had earlier brought together in behalf of the Union Labor party. John Rogers's *Kansas Commoner,* Stephen McLallin's *Advocate,* and, after a pause reflecting years of Republican orthodoxy, even William Peffer's *Kansas Farmer* all joined the *Nonconformist* in defending the cooperative crusade and exhorting farmers to stand firm in trade. By the end of 1889 the cooperative movement had reached west to Jerry Simpson's part of the state, and the gloom that had punctuated his earlier appraisals began to disappear. When he spoke now as lecturer of the Barber County Farmers Alliance, new faces appeared in the crowd—farmers who had joined the cooperative movement and for the first time were hearing new, radical political interpretations expressed in a setting congenial to their acceptance.[7]

2

Yet beyond the statewide movements in Kansas and the Dakotas and the pockets of cooperation building in Illinois and Minnesota, prospects for anything that future historians might describe as an "agrarian revolt" were simply not visible in the Northwest. In most of Illinois, as yet untouched by the FMBA, as well as the whole of Nebraska, Iowa, and Wisconsin, farmer discontent, if it existed, had clearly not found significant institutional expression.

The explanation lay not in some strange Midwestern acquiescence in the routine of hardship, but in the peculiar history of an organization known as the Northwestern Farmers Alliance. Actually, the group, like the organization Macune headed, called itself the "National Farmers Alliance," but in the interests of clarity it seems best to refer to it simply as the Northwestern Alliance—especially as that term more accurately describes its narrow range of influence.

The Northwestern group, which dated from 1880, was certainly the most curious institution that came to be associated, however incidentally, with the agrarian revolt. After eight years, for example, its Kansas affiliate, numbering something less than 500 members in the entire state, still found it necessary to hold an organizational meeting to try to create a state body. The 1889 state meeting of the neighboring Nebraska Alliance mustered delegates from only 14 of the state's 91 counties. Though the Nebraskans also dated their Alliance history back to 1880, their membership did not exceed 2000. It is a measure of the vitality of the Northwestern Alliance that Nebraska and Kansas enjoyed a reputation as being among the strongest states in the order.[8]

The weakness of the organization could be traced to the personality and political style of its founder, promoter, and guiding spirit, Milton George, the owner and editor of a Chicago-based farm magazine, *The Western Rural*. It is not too much to say, in fact, that the alliance served the needs of the magazine better than it did those of Midwestern farmers.

George had a penchant for agrarian homilies characteristic

of the Grange tradition, and his group never developed an internal or external program of any kind, so the few farmers who joined soon departed after discovering they had nothing to do. Meetings were abandoned after 1883, and the editor himself seems to have lost interest in the effort. The principal result of the George regime was to siphon agrarian creativity in the Western plains into an organizational cul de sac and leave the Northwestern Alliance a skimpy repository of few and transitory members.[9]

Apparently emboldened by stories of Alliance growth in Texas and the Dakotas, George attempted to hold "national meetings" in 1886 and 1887 with desultory results. Nevertheless, he published such extravagant membership claims that Macune was induced to invite the Northwesterners to join in the 1888 Meridian meeting of the National Alliance. However, it was perhaps just as well that the George group did not put in an appearance, as the comparative membership totals would have proved quite embarrassing, especially given the sensational claims that periodically appeared in *The Western Rural*. With the National Farmers Alliance at that time numbering something in the vicinity of 400,000 members, the Arkansas-based Agricultural Wheel in excess of 150,000, and the Farmers Mutual Benefit Association counting roughly 40,000, the organized membership that the Northwestern Alliance could have legitimately claimed—less than 10,000—would have exposed the emptiness of George's previous posturing. The 10,000 figure, of course, did not include the 20,000 members of the Dakota Alliance because, though George did not know it yet, the Loucks-Wardall team had already broadened its base to the south: after an abortive effort in 1888 to energize their colleagues in Nebraska, Illinois, and Iowa, Loucks and Wardall decided that merger with Macune's organization was a prerequisite to aggressive agrarian policy-making in the Western plains. Wardall shaped the Dakota insurance plan into a multi-state program under the auspices of the National Alliance and, for good measure, formally joined the order in Kansas. The Dakotans merely awaited the 1889 St. Louis meeting to make their full intentions known.[10]

3

Amid such developments, the attempted merger of the two Alliances in St. Louis in 1889 was considerably less crucial to the future of the agrarian movement than it has since been painted. By the end of the decade the ephemeral nature of the Northwestern order was well known to officials of the National Farmers Alliance. Having no reason to believe that their own cooperative movement could not prevail in other Western states as speedily as it had been in Kansas, the National Alliance officers went to the 1889 "coalition meeting" in St. Louis with higher priorities than amalgamation with the Northwestern order. Macune hoped to consummate the preliminary accord with the Farmers Mutual Benefit Association that had been worked out a year earlier at Meridian, and he also sought some sort of amalgamation with the Knights of Labor, perhaps one leading to merger. While the Knights were in severe decline, they provided a much-needed urban foothold for the agrarian coalition. As for the FMBA, it had pushed its grain cooperatives aggressively across Illinois and Indiana and even beyond in 1889 and now numbered some 75,000 or so farmers. The FMBA had long since earned the solid respect of the Alliance leaders. Merger was earnestly sought, for FMBA lecturers had a credibility with Northern farmers that Southern organizers could not match.

As matters turned out, the attempt at federation failed at St. Louis. The Northwestern group submitted three conditions for merger: that the new institution be called "The National Farmers Alliance and Industrial Union," that the white eligibility clause be abandoned, and the provisions for secrecy be discarded. The Southerners accepted the name change, a concession rather more evident in appearance than in fact since no one in the South, Missouri, Kansas, Indiana, or Oklahoma had ever called the order anything but "the Alliance." They also agreed to drop the white eligibility clause from the constitution. That concession also had little meaning, for the Southerners negotiated an option permitting individual states to set their own terms. (It is perhaps a fair measure of the general ascendancy, North and South, of white supremacist modes of thought that this gesture, patently evasive as it was in real terms, proved an acceptable means of bridging this organizational difficulty.) However, the third condition—abandonment of secrecy—was not negotiable from the Southern standpoint. Indeed, the reasons underlying the final Northern demand are difficult to deduce, as the Alliances in the Dakotas and Nebraska were then utilizing secrecy, as was the shaky new Kansas affiliate of the Northwestern group. As the National Grange had demonstrated a generation earlier and the FMBA was proving once again, one could not organize effectively outside the framework of cooperation, and confidentiality was essential to a number of cooperative decisions—from choosing among competing bids of trade stores to the developing of tactics suitable for effective battle with supply manufacturers, jute combines, or, should it come to that, binder twine manufacturers in the Western plains. The final demand must have seemed incomprehensible to the National Alliance delegates; in any case, they proposed as a compromise a one-year delay to all states not ready to "receive the secret work." Though Henry Loucks lobbied earnestly for merger, the other officials, led by the delegates representing the small state organization in Iowa, drew back. Neither August Post nor N. B. Ashby, the two most enduring agrarian spokesmen for the Iowans, had a clear grasp of the benefits of the cooperative movement or the institutional lessons that might be gained from such a program. Both were, above all, loyal Republicans and thus thoroughly unresponsive to the kind of radical imperatives contained in Evan Jones's presidential address or, for that matter, to the sweeping anti-monopoly sallies of Charles Macune. It may fairly be assumed that they did not join because they did not wish to join. Those who did understand—the cooperatively inclined farmers of the Dakotas—promptly did join.[11]

But perhaps the biggest causes of the merger failure were simply the enormous size of the Alliance itself and the style of its leaders. By the end of 1889, Macune, Jones of Texas, L. L. Polk of North Carolina, Isaac McCracken of Arkansas, W. L. Peek of Georgia, and Oswald Wilson of Florida had all acquired a considerable amount of on-going cooperative experience and a number of ideas about their immediate organizational goals. The Northwestern leadership circle had only a vague sense of either. Despite the leavening from Kansas, Colorado, Missouri, and Indiana—and Dakota—the Southerners in the Alliance leadership must have appeared to outsiders as a cohesive and formidable clan, perhaps even an exclusive one. So, apparently, felt President John Stelle of the FMBA, as well as the Iowans. Stelle pledged cooperation, but he declined to take his order into the National Alliance on the ground that to do so would involve the "loss of our name and all we hold dear." Sectional feelings evidently were a subverting force in St. Louis. In any case, it was clear that if the National Alliance wanted trained organizers to carry its cooperative message to the Northwest it would simply have to find its own. Perhaps the Kansans and Dakotans could perform that mission.[12]

The Alliance did move into closer association with the Knights of Labor at St. Louis, however. The two orders issued a joint declaration of considerable scope and assertiveness. Written and approved by the Alliance at its own session, and later accepted by the Knights, the "St. Louis Platform" codified the three platforms written in Texas during the cooperative struggle the year before. The seven-plank St. Louis Platform was, in effect, the substance of the 1892 Omaha Platform of the People's Party and, in 1889, it moved the agrarian crusade a large step nearer an insurgent posture nationally. After the fashion established at Cleburne three years earlier, all the planks were presented as "demands." The first, which represented a full restatement of the greenback heritage, testified to the "educational" impact of the cooperative movement on the organized farmers.

> We demand the abolition of national banks and the substitution of legal tender treasury notes in lieu of national bank notes, issued in sufficient volume to do the business of the country on a cash system; regulating the amount needed on a per capita basis as the business interest of the country expand; and that all money issued by the Government shall be legal tender in payment of all debts, both public and private.[13]

Terence Powderly
Grand Master Workman of the Knights of Labor, Powderly led the labor order into close association with the Alliance at the 1889 St. Louis meeting, styled as the "Confederation of Labor Organizations," which brought together under Alliance leadership a half-dozen farmer and labor organizations.

The other six planks, reflecting the evolution of agrarian thought since Cleburne, called for government ownership of the means of communication and transportation, prohibition of alien land ownership, free and unlimited coinage of silver, equitable taxation as between classes in society, a fractional paper currency, and government economy. The preamble also indicated a discernible lessening of inherited party loyalties. To "carry out these objects," the two organizations announced, they would support for office "only such men as can be depended upon to enact these principles uninfluenced by party caucus." Excepting only the formal addition of the sub-treasury system, the People's Party platform was in place.

However, the grievances of organized labor did not receive prominent mention in the St. Louis document. Indeed, by demonstrating the willingness of the Knights to take their cues from the National Farmers Alliance, the St. Louis Platform revealed the conclusive psychological and ideological dependency that had come to characterize the labor order in its association with the agrarian movement. While the relationship of Knights leader, Terence Powderly, with the Farmers Alliance at times gave a gloss of aggressive advocacy to his conservative regime, Powderly was determined that the fraternal relationships of farmers and laborers should not lead to third party action. However, his national lecturer, Ralph Beaumont, was a socialist, and Beaumont made common cause in St. Louis with the radicals in the Alliance who shared his goals. After the conference Powderly quietly returned to Washington and settled down to play a steadily declining role in any projected national agrarian-labor coalition and, indeed, within the dying Knights of Labor itself. Beaumont, meanwhile, began to take an increasingly active hand in the politics leading to the People's Party.[14]

4

The most important long-term product of the St. Louis conference, beyond the greenback doctrines embedded in the new "Alliance demands," was the unveiling of Macune's sub-treasury system. Actually, the plan's substance presented Macune with a delicate tactical problem, for the sub-treasury was implicitly derived from the realization that the Alliance dream of self-help farmer cooperatives could not be achieved without outside assistance.

Macune was thoroughly awake to the fact that his proposal constituted a candid comment on past agrarian policy, including his own. In his lengthy address at St. Louis, Macune gently pointed out the limitations of the cooperative crusade: "If we admit all that is claimed in this direction, we must still realize that there is a limit to the power that can be enforced by these methods." Farmers had three choices, he asserted. They could put their hopes on "more efficient farming"—the orthodox view offered by non-farmers, especially those of the metropolitan press. Or they could concentrate their total energies on cooperation—the alternative then being attempted on a massive scale by the Alliance. Or, finally, they could adopt a new approach: "by organization, a united effort can be brought to bear upon the authorities that will secure such changes in the regulations that govern the relations between different classes of citizens." In arguing for changed relations between "different classes," Macune suggested a conscious raising of the stakes above those being gambled in the cooperative movement. The sub-treasury plan was predicated upon the "maxim of political economists" that "a general rise in prices always attends an increase in the volume of the circulating medium of the country and a general fall in prices always attends a decrease in its volume." To Macune, this state of affairs simply gave bankers too much control over the lives of their fellow citizens.[15]

Macune's presentation was sufficiently circumspect that the sub-treasury plan was approved by the Alliance delegates at St. Louis, though it was not pushed forward as part of the joint declaration with the Knights. Macune's plan called for federal warehouses to be erected in every county in the nation that annually yielded over $500,000 worth of agricultural produce. In these "sub-treasuries," farmers could store their crops to await higher prices before selling. They were to be permitted to borrow up to 80 per cent of the local market price upon storage, and could sell their sub-treasury "certificates of deposit" at the prevailing market price at any time during the year. As the plan was framed for congressional presentation, farmers were to pay interest at the rate of 2 per cent per annum, plus small charges for grading, storage, and insurance. Wheat, corn, oats, barley, rye, rice, tobacco, cotton, wool, and sugar were included under the marketing program.[16]

Conceptually, the sub-treasury plan carried far-reaching ramifications for the farmer, the nation's monetary system, the government, and for the citizenry as a whole. It shattered the existing system of agricultural credit in the South, and returned to the crop-mortgaged farmer some direct control over the sale of his produce by giving him the means to participate in what was, for all practical purposes, a crop withholding program. By paying him 80 per cent in advance of final sale, the sub-treasury promised to permit him to avoid both the two-price system of the furnishing merchants on all that he bought and the rock-bottom prices prevailing at harvest on all that he sold. It also, for the first time, gave him flexibility in the selling of his certificates. Perhaps the most realistic feature of the plan was that it clearly confronted the fact that Southern farmers had nothing of value to mortgage except their crops. Because the prevailing crop lien system had helped to drive land values down to a point where real-estate mortgages simply were not feasible, the farmer's crop was, as furnishing merchants and bankers alike knew, his only tangible asset. In effect, Macune had replaced the high-interest crop-mortgage of the furnishing merchant with a plan that mortgaged the crop to the federal government at low interest. It thus provided the farmer with the means to escape, at long last, the clutches of the advancing man and recover a measure of control over his own life. For the downtrodden farmers of the South, both black and white, the sub-treasury plan was revolutionary.[17]

Its manner of presentation at St. Louis, however, was the first clear sign that, as national spokesman for a farmer-labor coalition, Charles Macune possessed serious provincial limitations. Technically, the sub-treasury plan had been placed before the Alliance delegates at St. Louis in the form of a report from a "Committee on the Monetary System" composed entirely of Southerners. Any chance that creative amendments to Macune's idea might be forthcoming suffered from precisely those geographical limitations. As soon as the Kansans heard about it—in public session—they quickly pointed out that it was their farms, not their crops, that were mortgaged. The provision for low-interest loans on farmlands was easily incorporated into the sub-treasury system without seriously disturbing its basic monetary implications for the larger society. Once their cooperatives began encountering strong banker and merchant opposition—soon after the St. Louis meeting—the Kansas leadership quickly became quite taken with the potential of the sub-treasury as an organizational appeal to farmers.[18]

As amended, the sub-treasury had potential appeal to a multi-sectional coalition of farmers, but it clearly faced stout opposition from other quarters. It was soon estimated by opponents that the plan, if implemented, would inject as much as several billion dollars in sub-treasury greenbacks into the nation's economy at harvest time. In the America of the Gilded Age, neither politicians nor businessmen had yet become used to thinking on such a scale. After all, only $400 million or so in greenbacks had been printed in the course of the entire Civil War. Also, the sub-treasury seemed to be "class legislation," and thus could be opposed, somewhat spuriously, as unconstitutional. Such an argument conveniently over-looked an array of government subsidies to business, from whiskey warehouses to trans-continental railroads, but it was a viewpoint that was to be expressed repeatedly as the sub-treasury came to be discussed nationally.

5

But the most explosive implication of Macune's monetary theory was also an ironic one: he had fatally undermined his own traditional "nonpartisan" position by introducing the flexible currency system. How could it become law without ag-itation, followed by legislation? How could it be passed with-out overt Alliance political support? And if neither major party supported the sub-treasury, what could the creative young spokesman say to third party advocates then? Whether Macune realized it or not, the sub-treasury represented a clear admission that his own dream of a farmer-led nationwide co-operative commonwealth had failed—that is to say, it had failed on its own terms both as an unaided instrument of agrarian self-help and as a purely economic solution to the farmer's woes. The farmers simply lacked the capital to make large-scale cooperatives workable. And large-scale coopera-tives were the only kind that could address the needs of the sharecropper, the rent-tenant, the marginal smallholder, and anyone else unfortunate enough to fall into the clutches of the lien system. Similarly, only a large-scale cooperative could save Western farmers from either exploitive interest rates or mo-nopolistic marketing practices at both the manufacturing and wholesale levels.[19]

But since the central state exchange was simply beyond the means of farmers, the sub-treasury had become absolutely necessary. Across the South and West in 1889, neither the leaders nor the members of the Farmers Alliance yet per-ceived this unpleasant truth about the vulnerability of the co-operative movement. But the Texans had been forced to learn it, and Macune knew it best of all. Underlying the negotiations at St. Louis was a new and desperate reality that had surfaced in 1889: the "mother alliance" in Texas had suffered a shuddering organizational trauma in the aftermath of the collapse of the Texas Exchange. The vast agrarian army of 250,000 that had rallied on "the day to save the exchange" in June of 1888 had lost many soldiers from the cooperative struggle. Though those who persevered in their loyalty to the Alliance were undoubtedly wiser in the ways of wholesale houses, bankers, and party politicians, the incontestable fact was that only 150,000 did so persevere through 1889. One hundred thousand other Texas farmers had tested the heralded "big store of the Alliance," had found it wanting, and had, temporarily at least, crept back into the silent world of landless tenantry from which they had so briefly emerged. Many would not soon reappear. When the nation next noticed them, a generation or so later, they would come not with an identity, as the "earnest, determined farmers" of the Alliance, but as a stereotype: the apathetic "Southern poor white." [20]

At St. Louis in 1889, the inevitability of this social type had by no means been established. Rather, the Farmers Alliance remained a veritable symbol of salvation across the South and had begun to be so regarded in its outposts in the West. But to Macune and Jones, the very leaders who spoke at St. Louis in the order's name, the first signs of dry rot underneath the entire superstructure of the Alliance cooperative were visible. In the case of Charles Macune, the collapse of the cooperative had confirmed the danger to the Alliance of broad-scale advocacy, which generated too many enemies at the same moment. For him, the sub-treasury was not only the logical culmination of the cooperative experience, it represented a reopening of the exchange conflict on new and stronger grounds. It was on the sub-treasury, not on third party agitation, that the Alliance needed to put its emphasis. He wrote in the *Economist* that the Alliance "scattered too much and tried to cover too much ground" and therefore needed to concentrate upon the "one most essential thing and force it through as an entering wedge to secure our rights." The government's capital would put a firm foundation underneath the cooperative crusade—and nothing else could.[21]

For Charles Macune, emphasis on the advocacy of the sub-treasury was an acknowledgment of how desperate the farmer's struggle against the existing American financial system had become. On the eve of the Alliance's growth to national status, the economic options for farmers had begun to narrow, and none was more aware of that fact than Charles Macune. As the next three years were to demonstrate, he was destined to live the Alliance cooperative experience more fully than any man, but beginning in St. Louis in 1889, he no longer functioned in a position of uncontested national authority. Though he continued as chairman of the executive committee and editor of the order's national journal, he now had a co-partner in leadership. The new national president of the Alliance, elected at St. Louis, was the eloquent leader of the North Carolina Alliance, L. L. Polk. Henceforth Macune's role, while extensive and at times pivotal, would begin to diminish as more and more new spokesmen for the agrarian cause emerged in both the South and West.

Even in advance of the massive evidence soon to come out of Kansas, Macune knew that third party radicals like Evan Jones and William Lamb spoke for growing numbers of Alliancemen. As more cooperatives failed the Alliance might have fewer members, but it would also have more radicals. In response, Macune dedicated himself to persuading the Alliance that the sub-treasury was imperative—because he saw it to be the only way the idea of agrarian self-help could be preserved and radical political adventures avoided. It would take time, of course; the farmer-leaders of functioning cooperatives would scarcely want to hear the topic framed in such a forbidding context of desperate options. But as the cooperatives lost their battle with the American banking system, the sub-treasury philosophy promised to become more comprehensible. Indeed, to one such as Macune, who had no faith in a radical third party, his plan was the last real hope for economic justice for the great mass of American farmers. They merely needed to understand it.[22]

He turned to the task with considerable energy. In 1890–91 the *National Economist* became a virtual schoolroom of currency theory. The details of the plan and the relative importance of each of its features were outlined again and again in the thirty months during which the National Farmers Alliance slowly transformed itself into the People's party.

6

While the sub-treasury dominated Macune's thoughts from St. Louis on, its importance was, for a time, overshadowed by two other concepts which jointly controlled immediate Alliance policy. One, naturally enough, was the cooperative crusade itself. In a number of forms—purchasing, marketing, and even manufacturing cooperatives—and in a number of sizes—local, county, state, and regional—the idea of cooperation consolidated its grip on the imagination of farmers throughout the South and West. Indeed, the days of highest hopes and most ambitious planning were still ahead. From Florida to North Dakota, the cooperative crusade moved into its most intensive period of experimentation. It became, quite simply, the consuming day-to-day life of the Alliance. As a by-product, it generated an enormous amount of political "education," as farmers encountered the opposition of retailers, wholesalers, railroads, commission houses, and bankers.

The second animating influence on Alliance policy, one that fit in rather neatly with the political impulse, was the idea of a national institution of the "producing classes." This, too, had great potential in terms of policy. Drawing from both anti-monopoly and greenback inheritances, the goal sprang easily from eighteenth- and nineteenth-century egalitarian thought and drew sustenance from both individualist and socialist traditions. Though it had not gained the status of doctrinal authority in any significant American institution, the concept of a radical farmer-labor coalition embodied visions of attainable human societies that had transforming impact on those who fell under its sway.

It perhaps does not require an excessive leap of the imagination to conclude that Alliance national presidents literally meant what they said when they spoke of "centralized capital, allied to irresponsible corporate power" and pronounced it a "menace to individual rights and popular government." State Alliance presidents described causes and effects in ways that cast the American idea of progress in new and ominous terms. "While railroad corporations are penetrating almost every locality with their iron rails, they are binding the people in iron chains." Ostensibly, these corporations were "creatures of law," but in fact they were "unrestrained save by their own sense of shame," and shame was "a virtue rarely if ever found among the attributes of monopolistic corporations." In the face of such invulnerable adversaries, county alliance leaders believed, quietly, if passionately, that "cooperation means to us more than any other word in the English language." Radical Alliance editors summarized the movement as a struggle for freedom by "the agricultural masses" who had been "robbed by an infamous system of finance." From where these men viewed the nation's developing economic system, the American population did, indeed, consist of "the masses" and "the classes." The latter were already in harmony with themselves, manipulating both of the old parties and consistently "downing the people." They were, in short, "organized capital." The Alliance, then, was called upon to organize the masses. The burden fell on the Alliance alone, since the Knights of Labor had lost its momentum and the tiny Northwestern farm group had never acquired any.[23]

7

The national organizing campaign of the Farmers Alliance began in the spring of 1890. Alliance lecturers moved across the West to California and up the Pacific coast to Oregon and Washington. Whether in confidence or with a controlled sense of trepidation, they moved through West Virginia and across the Alleghenies into Pennsylvania, Delaware, New Jersey, and New York. In mingled Southern and Midwestern accents, they told the veterans of the Grand Army of the Potomac about their new vision of cooperative agriculture in the modern state, and about an idea for land loans and deferred commodity marketing known as the sub-treasury plan. The anti-monopoly oratory of the Alliance movement was sent across the Ohio River into Indiana, Illinois, and Ohio and beyond to Michigan and Wisconsin. In the mining and cattle regions of the mountain West—Montana, Idaho, Wyoming, Colorado,

New Mexico, and Arizona—farmers in scattered valleys heard traveling lecturers and christened their first local Alliances. Even in faraway Boston a "New England Industrial Alliance" appeared on the scene, for a brief moment at least. "We are trampling sectionalism under our feet," L. L. Polk told Michigan Alliancemen. They gave him "cheers for the speaker and the Alliance." Polk came home to tell North Carolina farmers about it and wrote happily in the *Progressive Farmer,* "when a Southern orator can address a Michigan meeting, and receive three rousing cheers, it begins to look like the 'bloody shirt' war was about at its end." The old radical dream was happening, they told themselves. The producing classes of the North and South were no longer going to vote against each other and keep monopoly in power.[24]

They were heady days, indeed—the organizing months of 1890–91. The Farmers Alliance itself would be the great national coalition of the masses. The lecturing system expanded in stride with the new élan, drawing willing believers who set out to convey the Alliance message to the millions who needed it. Confidently engaging in well-attended public debates in town halls and at outdoor rallies across the nation, they even acquired some nicknames in the process. In the course of demolishing an urbane Republican dandy named "Prince Hal" Hallowell, one Kansas Alliance orator, somewhat less regally attired, conceded that "princes wear silk socks" and confessed that he himself had none. From that day forward he was "Sockless Jerry" Simpson—a sobriquet pinned on him by a hostile Kansas press, but one that carried him to the United States Congress. In the first of a well-advertised series of debates in Kentucky, a rangy Southern apostle mobilized the more radical speeches of Thomas Jefferson, stirred in selected social gospels in behalf of the new faith, and overwhelmed a staid city Democrat. The regional press dubbed the intruder the "Cyclone from Texas" and the nation learned that it henceforth would have to cope with a political evangelist known as "Cyclone" Davis. Alliance national headquarters sent him travel money, and "Cyclone" was soon bringing the New Testament, a jacobinized Thomas Jefferson, and the subtreasury plan to farmers from Colorado to Oregon.[25]

As the lecturing system acquired some stars, Macune pressed state alliances to establish official newspapers as a prelude to something more fundamental in the way of truth-bringing—an alliance of country newspaper editors. Macune's newspaper alliance met an obvious need, and the structure of the "National Reform Press Association" was readied for submission to the Alliance membership at the 1890 meeting. The idea was destined to take hold: the reform press association, uniting over 1000 newspapers across the nation, in due course became the propaganda arm of the People's Party. The agrarian leaders moved to correct other structural weaknesses uncovered by the sheer scope of their organizing effort. They would need an "Alliance Lecture Bureau" to coordinate what had become a national circuit and volumes of literature to explain and justify the cause. The National Economist Publishing Company in Washington began to pour forth a veritable torrent of pamphlets, broadsides, and books on "the financial question," on "concentrated capital," and on the sub-treasury system. The movement had many—and growing—forums. Polk's *Progressive Farmer* went to 12,000 farmsteads in North Carolina and the rest of the Southeast, the *Southern Mercury* to 30,000 readers throughout the South, and the *National Economist* to over 100,000 throughout the nation. A dozen well-written and rapidly expanding journals in Kansas, led by the official Alliance journal, *The Advocate,* and including *The American Nonconformist,* the *Kansas Commoner,* and the *Kansas Farmer,* spread the good news, the indignant and sometimes angry news, that had become the message of the Farmers Alliance. The *Advocate*'s circulation soared toward an eventual peak of 80,000. The teachings of the Alliance, fully grounded in the greenback heritage, began to reach millions of Americans.[26]

8

The St. Louis Platform was first and last a political document. Beginning in the spring of 1890, an astonishing percentage of the agrarian leadership—Polk and Macune in Washington, hundreds of country editors, and literally tens of thousands of lecturers across the nation—began to talk movingly about something new on the immediate horizon, something vague but portentous, which they characterized variously as "the great contest" and "the coming struggle." They talked about this looming event in different ways because they had different levels of faith in existing American political institutions. Polk and Macune talked of the "sweeping reforms" that were needed and that were coming. Editors like Henry Vincent in Kansas, W. Scott Morgan in Arkansas, Henry Loucks in South Dakota, William Lamb in Texas, and spokesmen like Evan Jones, Jerry Simpson, and a new ally in Georgia named Thomas Watson all talked more frequently of "the coming revolution."

But each group thought in terms of ballots, not bullets. For them, "reform" meant change through the existing two-party system. "Revolution" meant the overthrow of that system by the creation of a "third party of the industrial millions." Perhaps only the leaders themselves knew the importance of these subtle distinctions; to the rest of the nation all of the Alliance spokesmen sounded alarmingly radical. To many, Macune, with his startling theory of the uses of money, sounded wildest of all.[27]

In the promising springtime of 1890 the National Farmers Alliance and Industrial Union pushed its organizational tentacles to the Canadian border and to both coasts. If Alliancemen and their leaders were asking perhaps a bit too much of their farmer organization with respect to the "coming great contest," they did not seem to think so. Grand political dreams are seldom fashioned by cautious men. To many of the agrarian leaders, in any case, there was no time for caution. The farmers of the nation were in trouble, serious and seemingly permanent trouble, and the Alliance had sprung up out of their needs and given voice and meaning to their desperation. Together, in the Alliance, then, they would jointly decide whether to strive for "reform" or for "revolution."

In 1890 the farmers of the Alliance, now well over a million strong, tried both.

The First Political Breakthrough

The Alliance calls "the convention of the people"

In the summer and fall of 1890 the National Farmers Alliance found itself in politics. This development was scarcely a model of organizational planning. It represented no consensus among Alliance leaders, reflected no coordination within the emerging national apparatus of state, county, and local alliances, demonstrated no common ideological assertion of agrarian purpose. The emerging forms of political activity signaled instead a very old reality suddenly linked to a new one—the continuing hardship confronting many millions of American farmers and the new collective means they possessed to assert themselves politically. Precisely what they wished to assert, however, varied considerably.

As the St. Louis Platform indicated, they sought some specific remedies and had some concrete ideas about how those remedies should be applied. But agreement ended at that fairly preliminary stage of analysis. Though many of the leaders of the Alliance had brooded about strategies of implementation for some years, the great majority of farmers had not. To some—notably in the South and in Nebraska—it merely seemed necessary to elect good men to public office. A smaller number of Alliancemen felt that both old parties had long since become agents of corporate America, that the two-party system had ceased to function on behalf of most American citizens. Since they believed that "concentrated capital" would never acquiesce in greenback restructuring of the American monetary system, these men looked upon independent political action as the only possible remedy. The two views existed in every stratum of the Alliance structure, all the way up to the presidential level. At St. Louis Charles Macune had represented one view and Evan Jones the other. No one could yet be certain of the position of the new president, L. L. Polk of North Carolina.

In practical political terms, of course, the two positions were fundamentally incompatible. Yet a kind of first step was available which gave the appearance of harmonizing both, and it was this expedient which ruled agrarian politics in 1890. For the moment the nation's party system was basically left untouched and the Alliance asserted itself politically by endorsing "Alliance candidates" for office. The tactic, though national in scope, evolved as a series of local- and state-level decisions, reached through a variety of processes that reflected the realities of regional and local politics and were without coordination at the national level among the order's leaders.

In the South the process of finding and endorsing "Alliance candidates" took place fairly consistently within the framework of the one-party system. Overwhelmingly, the "Alliance candidates" tended to be Democrats. In the Western plains the process was much more complex, producing not only a breathtakingly radical triumph in Kansas but the beginnings of an agrarian shadow movement in Nebraska. But to most farmers, South and West, and to most national political observers, the varied portions of the whole process seemed to constitute a single development: the farmers of the country had "gone into politics."

Yet it is perhaps more instructive to view the workings of the agrarian revolt from the perspective of those who did not look upon the politics of 1890 as a unified whole, but perceived instead the deep-seated tensions it really contained. For the significant politics of 1890 represented a tortured groping by farmers toward workable forms within a national political environment that, since the Civil War, had proven essentially impervious to new economic ideas. Though not everyone realized it—or wanted it—this groping carried the Alliance toward a new national political institution of "the plain people." At the time this perspective was confined to Alliance radicals, the men who wished to lead a new third party onto the stage of national politics sometime in the early 1890's—in 1892, perhaps, and certainly by 1896. Though these greenbackers were indeed able to create their third party in 1892, their viewpoint, while fervently held, was by no means a self-confident one during the volatile months of 1890. Greenbackers had, after all, been third party men for a long time; many had presided over the birth and death of both the Greenback and the Union Labor parties. More than most Americans they knew the difficulty of attracting large numbers of voters to the idea of independent political action or, for that matter, to sustained thought about basic monetary reform itself. The mass constituencies of the two major parties had been organized by the sectional politics that grew out of the Civil War, and both continued to contain millions of loyal followers whose political memories were grounded not in economic ideas but in war-related emotions. Radicals, viewing the political task they confronted after twenty-five years of neo-Confederate electioneering in the South and the politics of the "bloody shirt" in the North, considered the American voter to be culturally incapable of thinking about politics in terms of ideas that reformers would regard as serious. Too many Americans, including Alliancemen, were, as Evan Jones put it, "still wedded to the 'good old party.'" Though monetary reformers had taken renewed hope from the huge growth of the Farmers Alliance and generally held a more sanguine view in 1890 than they had at any time in previous years, they still felt that their immediate prospects were uncertain. From their standpoint, a number of questions still had to be addressed. Could the educational program of the Alliance overcome the inherited political innocence of the American people? Could the cooperative movement be counted on to spell out the power relationships between bankers and non-bankers that were imbedded in the American monetary system? Could a broad enough lecturing apparatus be constructed to support such a burden of political interpretation? Could the politics of greenback reform under the sub-treasury system be made understandable to Republican farmers in the North and Democratic farmers in the South, both caught in the grip of sectional politics? And by what means could political bridges be built to the largely immigrant, largely Catholic, factory workers of the North, who so often followed the lead of Tammany-style Democratic politicians? How could these urban voters be made to understand enough about currency to grasp the fact that greenback doctrines could help them as much as they could help farmers? And, finally, could political bridges be built to black Americans, most of them landless tenants in the South? As devotees of the "party of Lincoln," they were just as much victims of sectional politics as all the other members of "the industrial millions," North and South. Could the message of reform be shaped to reach them? Such questions were not easily answered, as the Greenback and Union Labor experiences had proven.[1]

Beyond such ideological and tactical hazards, a nagging structural problem persisted within the farmer movement. The immediate task in the West centered on finding some way to initiate a genuine agrarian movement in Iowa, Nebraska, Illinois, and Wisconsin, one that would complement those incubating in Kansas, the Dakotas, and Minnesota. In addressing this latter task, Alliancemen encountered still more evidence of the sectional barrier to a national coalition of the "producing classes."

The results of the St. Louis meeting of December 1889 partially concealed the organizing problem. To Alliancemen, the task of energizing their passive brethren in the Northwestern group did not seem especially difficult. The National Alliance appeared to be in a decisive position, for the simple reason that one of its own greenback leaders, Henry Loucks of South Dakota, had become president of the Northwestern group. The Dakotas, which had the only mature farmer organization in the Northwest, had far more delegates at the St. Louis meeting than all the other Northwestern states, and they promptly elected Loucks to the presidency. Following the merger failure, Loucks decided to remain as president even while leading the Dakota farmers into the National Alliance. He stayed on in the hope that, as president, he could activate and energize the stagnant state chapters in Illinois, Wisconsin, Iowa, and Nebraska.[2]

Loucks appeared before the Nebraska Alliance early in 1890 to plead for union, but he ran afoul of the opposition of Jay Burrows, chairman of the order's state executive committee and editor of its embryonic state journal. Though Burrows had publicly favored merger before the St. Louis meeting, he seems to have been intimidated by the sheer size of the National Alliance, and it was J. H. Powers, the state president, who gave Loucks the only encouragement he received from the Nebraska leadership. Powers was slow to grasp the essentials of the cooperative movement but he demonstrated no hostility to the idea of union; he merely proved unable to lead his organization in that direction in any systematic way. Though a man of good heart, he apparently was immobilized by the influence of Burrows. At the beginning of 1890, the nub of the problem remained what it had always been in Nebraska—the relative narrowness of the order's organizational base. After almost ten years in the Northwestern group the Nebraska Alliance still counted less than 15,000 members in the entire state. Four-fifths of them were brand new recruits, products of the continuing hard times of 1889 who were clearly in search of some forum for their grievances. The principal difficulty was that the Nebraskans had no program, a fact that did not augur well for holding the relatively few members who had been attracted.[3]

The most telling influence on the Nebraska leadership proved not to be the presidential prodding of Henry Loucks but rather the sheer fury of the agrarian movement in neighboring Kansas and the Dakotas. The blizzard of their neighbors' activities eventually caught the attention of Nebraska farmers, and the latter—after considerable difficulty, and with help from other Nebraskans unconnected to the Alliance—

finally caught the attention of their spokesmen. This revolution from below and from without added a certain impromptu style to the stormy politics that shook the South and West in 1890. It created a shadow movement of Populism. A number of Nebraskans dutifully trailed their neighbors in Kansas to the People's Party, but they did so with no understanding of the cooperative crusade of the Alliance or of the greenback doctrines that the cooperative struggle had raised to preeminence in the agrarian movement. In essence, the Nebraskans remained outside the "movement culture" of Populism. To trace the evolution of the Nebraska shadow movement, it is necessary to begin where the culture of Populism *was* developing—in Kansas.

2

By the spring of the year the Kansas Alliance had initiated widespread cooperative programs and the momentum of the effort had begun to produce a noticeable increase in the political awareness of the state's farmers. The Cowley County cooperative chartered by Henry Vincent and others in 1889 had been followed not only by a successful independent Alliance ticket, but also by the organization of a statewide Kansas State Exchange and a multi-state cooperative livestock marketing plan. Even more ambitious projects were on the drawing board. The Kansans had improved their internal lecturing structure at their second state Alliance convention late in 1889 and soon thereafter had placed over fifty organizers in the field. By the new year suballiances were appearing at the rate of twenty-five to fifty per week. One lecturer reported that he alone had organized seventy-four suballiances in two months. By March of 1890 one of the order's growing corps of supporters among country newspapers placed the statewide membership at 100,000. Meanwhile, throughout the state Alliancemen who had gone forward with considerable resolve to establish local trade committees had begun to encounter firm merchant opposition. This first stage of cooperation by farmers and its predictable response by merchants also had a predictable educational effect: members of many Alliances became so upset with their merchants that they began organizing their own cooperative stores. The movement produced some passionate voices in behalf of the merits of cooperation, perhaps none more stentorian than the Kansas county president who proclaimed that cooperation among wheat farmers could raise prices throughout America and, further, throughout "the markets of the world." [4]

Kansas lecturers also brought a ringing idealism to the Alliance movement, while retaining the anti-corporate flavor that characterized its style in more Southern climes. "The conscienceless rule of the privileged classes cannot be curtailed a day too soon," one lecturer asserted. "Fully realizing that our past lives have been too much influenced by prejudice and superstition, the fruits of which have divided the community and prevented united efforts for the general welfare, let us in the language of the Alliance (work) till . . . bigotry and prejudice shall disappear as despoiling forces forever from our midst." Profound economic hardship infused such rhetoric with meaning beyond the flavor of the words themselves, and helps explain the phenomenal appeal of the cooperative movement. A dairy farmer named John Otis who was destined to become a future Populist Congressman declared in January 1890 that the farmers of western Kansas were "burning corn for fuel, while coal miners and their families in another section of our land are famishing for food." Alliance President Ben Clover drew attention to a single law firm in his region of the state that had a contract to foreclose 1800 mortgages! An observant Kansas Republican caught the proliferating signs of farmer restlessness and decided "the air is full of lightning." [5]

It was indeed. Kansas farmers no longer suffered in isolation, but collectively sought remedies in Alliance meetings. The sheer momentum of the process, one that was central to the developing political movement, became evident in a sequence of events that took place in two county alliances early in March 1890. On Saturday, the farmers' day in town, the members of the Douglas County Alliance gathered at the courthouse at Lawrence to consider a cooperative crop-withholding program designed to achieve better prices. The farmers elected a committee to pursue the matter. An Alliance county officer then rendered a gloomy report to the effect

A Sod House on the Great Plains
Some of the raw materials of Western Populism. In 1890, one Kansas farmer moved directly from a house similar to this one to the state capital where he served as Speaker of the Kansas House of Representatives.

that prices received by local farmers for corn and cattle had fallen below the cost of production. This information produced a series of corroborating stories of personal hardship from the assembled farmers, and a general discussion of prevailing injustices followed. It succeeded only in convincing all present that something had to be done. They resolved "to find out and apply the remedy." Three days later, farmers in Shawnee County, entrapped in the same economic realities, moved beyond resolutions of inquiry to a discussion of political solutions. The unanimous decision of the group, according to one writer, "was that the farmer was being slighted by the legislator, who used him only as a voting tool so that he, the politician, could serve the interests of other classes." Annie Diggs, an Alliance reporter in training for future service as a leading Populist propagandist, wrote in the Lawrence *Daily Journal* that such Alliance gatherings were proving that "there will be little cause in the future to complain of the over trustfulness or gullibility of the farmer. He is awake." [6]

In actuality, this judgment was an understatement. The farmers of Kansas had created in their suballiances an environment to think in. As a result, their self-respect and self-confidence as individual citizens grew. Taking root in the Kansas plains was a democratic culture of ideas emerging in oppostion to the received culture of democratic hierarchy and commercial privilege. In sundry rural forums of democracy, the farmers discussed the difficulties their cooperatives were encountering. They moved, variously, to "apply the remedy." This political evolution—literally the development of a movement culture of cooperative hope and mass aspiration—described the essence of American Populism.

These various examples of political "lightning" observed by alarmed Republicans were also fully visible to state Alliance leaders, a group that included a number of veteran third-party advocates. These activists clearly felt that the movement toward independent political action needed only a small boost. At Topeka, they convened a gathering of the "State Reform Association" which advertised itself as being in search of a "union platform" upon which the Kansas affiliates of the Farmers Alliance, Knights of Labor, Grange, and Farmers Mutual Benefit Association could agree. It may be safely assumed that the old greenback elite group, the Videttes, were fully as well represented as any of the above named organizations, if for no other reason than that many participated fully in the statewide Alliance organizing campaign. The "union platform" duly materialized with the full panoply of Alliance reforms, including the sub-treasury plan. A week later Alliance state president Clover convened a statewide meeting of county Alliance presidents. As a beneficiary of the independent movement in his native Cowley County, Clover saw little reason to fear insurgent political action. Virtually every farmer in Cowley County was in the Alliance and had participated with equal fervor in the county cooperative exchange, the Winfield cooperative store, and the 1889 election that had swept the Alliance independent ticket into county office.[7]

The Kansas Alliance conference produced a large turnout of county Alliance leaders who undertook an aggressive move that surprised the state's political observers. By all odds the most prestigious Kansan in Washington, and perhaps the best known politician in the West, was a venerable patriarch named John J. Ingalls, the state's senior United States Senator. The Alliance county presidents resolved that after eighteen years of Ingalls "it is a difficult matter for his constituents to point to a single measure he has ever championed in the interests of the great agricultural and laboring element of Kansas; and we will not support by our votes or influence any candidate for the legislature who favors his reelection to the United States Senate." Kansas Alliancemen reinforced this pronouncement with a series of political demands for state legislative reforms that culminated in a provocative disclaimer: "we will no longer divide on party lines, and will only cast our votes for candidates of the people, for the people, and by the people." [8]

Dismayed by this development, The Topeka *Daily Capital* noted that most delegates seemed "strongly anti-Republican." The paper observed, hopefully, that "a large majority of the farmers of Kansas are republicans, and while they are ready to join cooperative organizations for the mutual benefit of producers, they will not consent to being led [by] wild theorists who expect to cure all the ills of financial depression by defeating the republican party." The rebuke did not draw the desired response. An emerging editorial spokesman for the Alliance, Dr. Stephen McLallin of *The Advocate,* announced new political criteria: "We have ends we mean to secure . . . if the same men or the same class of men that have been in office in the state and national governments heretofore are still supported by the old parties, there will be a great big bolt." McLallin added, "To the re-election of John J. Ingalls, for instance, we will never consent. He has been in office eighteen years, but he has got to go." [9]

Precisely how the Alliance intended to elect proper candidates while "no longer dividing on party lines," as the Topeka meeting specified, posed a problem in a statewide organization filled with farmers of Democratic and Union Laborite backgrounds, as well as loyal Republicans. It was decided an "Alliance ticket" should be fielded, but—lest such an action be construed as placing "the Alliance in politics"—plans were implemented to hold a June convention inviting all "interested citizens." It was the old Daws formula of pre-Cleburne days.

Events now proceeded with accelerating momentum. Though some county Alliances disassociated themselves from the anti-Ingalls resolution in April and May, many others came to its support. Some, such as the radical Harper County Alliance—one of the "old" Alliance counties near the Oklahoma border—not only nominated an entire independent county ticket but also required a pledge from its legislative nominees publicly affirming their intention to vote against Ingalls.[10]

In the early summer of 1890 much of the state's metropolitan press and the leadership of the Republican Party remained sublimely oblivious to the "signs of lightning." A generation of uncontested rule had bred a mood of invulnerability so pervasive that the only response most orthodox journalists could muster toward the reform movement consisted of patronizing advice. The Fort Scott *Daily Monitor,* for example, avuncularly assured its farmer readers of the paper's support as long as the Alliance was "content" to restrict itself to "the best methods of raising cabbage" and "how many rows of corn should be on a cob."

> But when the farmer transcends that sphere of action and undertakes to discuss economic questions (e.g.) the causes that lead to the price of farm products which are now below the cost of production . . . then the *Monitor* will denounce the farmers' organization as breeding discontent and treason to the republican party.[11]

Complacency was general; it extended to almost the entire Republican hierarchy. The party was a closely held institution largely managed by railroad lawyers who made little attempt to conceal their control of Republican state conventions. The latter routinely rubber-stamped slates of nominees previously determined by the party's corporate elite. As a party loyalist later admitted, "It was for a long time too plain that Republican Legislatures of Kansas simply obeyed the orders of railroad companies. . . . The Railroad Commissioner Law, that is supposed to be for the purpose of maintaining justice between the people and railroads, was really got up by the attorneys of railroad companies, in order to ward off the enactment of laws regulating freight rates." While the Grand Old

Party in Kansas had become a more or less wholly-owned sub-
sidiary of business corporations, the rather ruthless tactics it
sometimes employed against political opponents received a remarkable public defense in the very months of Alliance agitation—and by no less a figure than John J. Ingalls himself.
Seemingly undisturbed by the rumblings against him back in
Kansas, the state's senior Senator gave a startling interview to
a New York newspaper in April of 1890. Asked if "political
ends justified the means," he replied:

> The purification of politics is an irridescent dream. Govern-
> ment is force. Politics is a battle for supremacy. Parties are
> the armies. The decalogue and the golden rule have no
> place in a political campaign. The object is success. To defeat
> the antagonist and expel the party in power is the purpose.
> The republicans and democrats are as irreconcilably opposed
> to each other as were Grant and Lee in the Wilderness. They
> use ballots instead of guns, but the struggle is the same. In
> war, it is lawful to deceive the adversary, to hire hessians, to
> purchase mercenaries, to mutilate, to destroy. The com-
> mander who lost a battle through the activity of his moral
> nature would be the derision and jest of history. This mod-
> ern cant about the corruption of politics is fatiguing in the
> extreme. . . .[12]

3

The Senator's comments suddenly gave new dimension to an
eighteen-month-long controversy that stemmed from the single most dramatic event of the 1888 Kansas election—the "anarchistic bomb plot" of the "Coffeyville Conspirators." This
knotty little affair had occurred in the closing weeks of the
Union Labor Party campaign of 1888 and had demolished
whatever prospects the third party had enjoyed. It seems that
a package addressed to the editors of the *Nonconformist* in
Winfield had arrived at the post office in Coffeyville. As it was
marked for special handling, the postmaster took the package
home with him overnight before forwarding it on the morning train. That evening the package exploded, seriously injuring his wife and daughter. The Kansas press, and particularly
the Topeka *Daily Capital,* promptly responded with frighten-

ing stories of conspiracy on the part of the Vincent brothers and other "anarchists" in the Union Labor Party. The *Daily Capital* ran a series of front-page stories linking the Videttes, the Union Labor Party, and bombs into a tightly woven case of anarchy. Indeed, the response was so immediate and the details were so precise that suspicions were quickly aroused in radical circles that the Republican Party and certain of its journalistic organs had been privy to the "plot." Matters got quite complicated as the ensuing inquiry proceeded. Though rather languidly pushed by Republican prosecutors, the investigation was relentlessly pursued by the *Nonconformist,* which hired its own investigatory staff. As some interesting transfers of money were uncovered and traced to Republican sources the whole affair eventually placed the G.O.P. thoroughly on the defensive. But these developments took place well after the 1888 election, which saw the Union Labor Party decisively defeated. The topic was sufficiently fresh in everyone's mind in the spring of 1890, however, that Senator Ingall's view of politics tended to cast the Coffeyville affair in a distinctly new light. As political contentions visibly accelerated in the early summer of 1890, Henry Vincent, for one, saw to it that Ingall's remarks received immediate and wide dissemination through country newspapers friendly to the Alliance.[13]

4

But if anarchy had worn a bit thin as an issue useful to the Grand Old Party, the "bloody shirt" remained the serviceable, all-weather foundation of Republican electioneering. In 1890, in Kansas, the brunt of this assault fell not on state Democrats, who were not a threat, but on Alliancemen, who were. As the Topeka *Daily Capital* never wearied of pointing out, the Alliance was, after all, a Southern-based institution; language usually reserved for Democrats could therefore be applied with equal force to the farm organization. Respectable Republican farmers, the *Capital* charged, were being duped into doing the work of the Democratic Party at the behest of an organization "officered by rebel brigadiers." The *Weekly Kansas Chief* added that "In Democratic communities, the Alliance is flourishing . . . the most nauseating sight is the course of a lot

of Republican papers that are pandering to this organization.
. . . Clover is a shyster, a fraud, and an anarchist." The
Kansas Alliance thus found what Southern Alliancemen were
soon to discover in their own part of the nation—that the
agrarian reform program ran headlong into the politics of sectionalism.[14]

In this setting, the much-publicized appearance before the
Kansas Alliance convention of the order's national president,
L. L. Polk of North Carolina, was watched with anticipation by
the state's Republican press. Leaders of the new political
movement also watched, but their interest was edged with
anxiety. If the reform cause were truly to have a multi-sectional base, it would be crucial that their Southern colleague
prove politically acceptable in Kansas.[15]

As it happened, no man in the South was better equipped to
cope with this kind of challenge than the wiry, fifty-four-year-
old North Carolinian. Polk's family heritage and personal political life had instilled in him a driving determination to
preach against sectionalism. He had been a Whig as a young
man, and had first been elected to the North Carolina legislature as a Unionist in August 1860. That circumstance had
profound impact on his life. He opposed secession through
the firing on Fort Sumter, through Lincoln's call for troops,
and even through the period in April 1861 when Virginia
seceded. He then "went with his state" into the Confederacy,
only to suffer from repeated discrimination because he was
marked as a "Union man." Declining a captain's commission to
serve as a private soldier, he became sergeant major of a
North Carolina regiment, was wounded at Gettysburg as a
lieutenant, and returned to duty for the difficult campaigns of
1864. His letters home during the war, while reflecting his essential optimism, occasionally grew bitter over the constant
hostility directed toward him by Confederate firebrands.
Charges that he "skulked" in battle were circulated against
him by political opponents at home, though he remained high
in the esteem of his North Carolina troops. While still on duty
with the Army of Northern Virginia, he became an Army candidate for the legislature and was elected in August 1864. One
month following his election, Polk was arrested and charged

with "misbehavior before the enemy" and "absence without leave" for having taken his wounded captain to a hospital during a skirmish. Polk proved at his formal court-martial that he had "fought a good fight that day" before his captain was hit. He was acquitted and serenaded by his regiment before his triumphant return home to legislative service, but the affair was grist for demagogues and it haunted Polk the remainder of his public life.[16]

In the postwar years Polk played an active role as a spokesman for agrarian interests in North Carolina—as an ardent Granger, as founder of the State Agriculture Department, and as first Agricultural Commissioner. In 1886 he founded the *Progressive Farmer,* and he led in the formation of Farmers Clubs and a state agricultural college. When Alliance organizers came to North Carolina in 1887 he watched closely and quietly, and then threw his support to the cooperative movement. He became a member of Oak Ridge Alliance No. 24, one of the "ripe fruit" shaken by Texas organizer J. B. Barry. Polk became an immediate Southwide spokesman for the Alliance movement, was elected vice president of the National Alliance in 1887, and became chairman of the national executive committee in 1888. By the time of his election to the Alliance presidency in St. Louis in December 1889 he had made the *Progressive Farmer* the largest and most influential newspaper in his state and had established himself as an outspoken reform Democrat.[17]

Thus, by heritage and temperament, as well as through the experiences of his personal life, the Alliance president was ideally suited to cope with the sectional imperatives of national agrarian politics. He roamed the nation literally from coast to coast in 1890 and habitually culminated his declarations for reform by an attack on the sectionalism that still guided the voting habits of millions of Americans.[18]

Polk's performance in Kansas in the summer of 1890 demonstrates clearly the extent to which the order's leaders were caught up in a rolling momentum which they themselves had helped to generate but which seemed to have acquired a life of its own. His tour came after a June convention in which the Kansas Alliance leadership had decided to field an independent Alliance ticket but before an August convention that was to select the actual nominees. Though Polk was still not personally committed to a third-party course for the Alliance his appearance in Kansas had the effect of committing both his personal prestige and, to some extent, the order itself to public support for independent political action.[19]

A crowd of 6000 gathered in Winfield on "Alliance Day"— the Fourth of July—to hear the Alliance president. His address focused on the need for economic reform, but his argument was carefully constructed to attack frontally the politics of sectionalism.

> I tell you this afternoon that from New York to the Golden Gate, the farmers have risen up and have inaugurated a movement such as the world has never seen. It is a revolution of thought. A revolution which I pray God may be peaceful and bloodless. . . . The farmer of North Carolina, Georgia, Texas, South Carolina is your brother. . . . Some people have stirred up sectional feeling and have kept us apart for twenty-five years . . . and tried to work upon our passions. The man who has waved the bloody shirt. The man who has taught his children the poisonous doctrines of hate. . . . They know that if we get together and shake hands and look each other in the face and feel the touch of kinship, their doom is sealed. I stand here today, commissioned by hundreds of thousands of Southern farmers, to bid the farmers of Kansas to stand by them.[20]

To those who had heard Polk's platform eloquence before— Ralph Beaumont of the Knights of Labor, who traveled with him on this Western trip, and Ben Clover of the Kansas Alliance—it not only was the right speech at the right moment, but one they knew Polk would make as a consequence of his own political past. Polk handled the delicate question of "the Alliance in politics" with the poise and confidence that augmented his personal style of radicalism:

> Will you tell me who has a better right in America to go into politics than the farmers? . . . I will tell you what you are going to see. . . . You will see arrayed on the one side the great magnates of the country, and Wall Street brokers, and the plutocratic power; and on the other you will see the peo-

Leonidas Lafayette Polk
A Southern Unionist of Whig antecedents and North Carolina's leading agrarian spokesman. Polk was
ideally equipped to cope with the
politics of sectionalism during the
movement's first trial of political insurgency in Kansas in 1890.

ple . . . there shall be no Mason and Dixon line on the Alliance maps of the future.[21]

To Polk, the "masses" and the "classes" were separated by a
fundamental difference of economic philosophy, one which
measured the selective vision of the wealthy. Sobered by the
arguments advanced in Washington against the sub-treasury
plan, he shared with Kansas farmers his sense of indignation
at the inability of Congressmen to see the conditions of life
around them.

When I went up to Washington City and showed them statistics from all over the country, they said it was overproduction that had caused our trouble. Mr. Morrill declared from
his seat that it was overproduction. . . . If Mr. Morrill had
come out onto the streets of Washington on a cold November morning he would have seen the children picking
bits of coal out of the ash piles to warm themselves by, and
morsels of food out of the heaps of garbage to satisfy their
hunger. . . . As long as a single cry for bread is heard, it is
underproduction and underconsumption. And in that great
and final Day, when all the crime and misery shall be revealed, some one will have to answer for this lack of food.
There is something besides over-production that has caused
it. Congress could give us a bill in forty-eight hours that

would relieve us, but Wall Street says nay. . . . I believe that both of the parties are afraid of Wall Street. They are not afraid of the people.[22]

Reduced to its essentials, the language of the Alliance was the same, North and South—and it was a language not often heard in mainstream American politics. On the Western plains in 1890, L. L. Polk proved "acceptable." He was invited back for the fall campaign, and he came. The bloody shirt was met with economic radicalism and Polk was hailed by Jerry Simpson as "the conductor" of the "through train" of the Alliance that was "going through to Washington." Polk's appearances provided, in the words of W. F. Rightmire, another Kansas leader, "the quasi-endorsement of the National Alliance to the political movement." [23]

5

But while indignation and sometimes bristling radical anger was a part of the message of reform, there was another and far more elusive ingredient at work in Kansas in 1890. Comprised of many diverse elements, it can perhaps best be described—in counterpoint to the politics of reform—as the pageantry of reform. Poring through the newspapers, scrapbooks, pamphlets, and speeches of the agrarian revolt, one comes away with the certain knowledge that something decidedly distinctive for nineteenth-century America materialized out of the Kansas countryside during the summer and fall of 1890. It has been called a "pentecost of politics," a "religious revival," a "crusade," and it was surely all of those things. But it was also mile-long parades of hundreds of farm wagons and floats decorated with evergreen to symbolize "the living issues" of the Alliance that contrasted with dead tariffs and bloody shirts of the old parties. It offered brass bands and crowds "so large that much of the time it was necessary to have four orators in operation at one time in order for all to hear." It was 2000 bushels of wheat being donated by hard-pressed farmers to help finance their political movement. And it was parades composed simply of the Alliance itself. Some industrious soul counted, or said he counted, 7886 persons and 1500 vehicles in one six-mile-long procession through the city of Wichita. One wonders how the townsfolk of Wichita regarded this vast tide of people. Were they intrigued? attracted? frightened? [24]

The sources of such a mass folk movement obviously cannot be isolated in a single phrase or a single happening. But surely the immediate background of the harsh winter and the low prices of 1889–90 informed the events of the following summer and fall with a certain urgency. It was a winter when corn was so valueless it was used as fuel, a winter Kansas farm boys could recall years later, as Vernon Parrington once did: "Many a time have I warmed myself by the kitchen stove in which ears were burning briskly, popping and crackling in the jolliest fashion. And if, as we sat around such a fire watching the year's crop go up the chimney, the talk sometimes became bitter . . . who will wonder?" As a Kansas historian later wrote: "This was the era when a wintry schoolhouse debate on the proposition that Kansas was remarkably prosperous was won by the negative speaker when, without saying a word, he rose and threw a few more corncobs into the potbellied stove." If, at such a time, it proved helpful to have pretty girls on floats knitting socks for "Sockless Jerry" (and no Populist parade in Kansas was complete without girls with knitting needles performing that particular task), it was also necessary to have spokesmen like Jerry Simpson to give voice to their hopes and to place in downhome Kansas venacular the complex monetary ideas of the greenback heritage. [25]

Perhaps the street parades of rustic humanity, the sprigs of evergreen, the wagons of donated wheat were what they appeared to be, the spirit of a movement; and perhaps that spirit derived from the possibility of cooperative action itself, from the fact that no longer did farm families have to suffer in isolation but labored together in the Alliance to try to do something about their debasement. Perhaps this, at root, was what Populism was. In sundry pieces—a parade, a speech, a schoolhouse debate, a brass band, an Alliance picnic—the politics of Populism took form in Kansas in the months of 1890. If Texans led the farmers to the Alliance, Kansans led the Alliance to the People's Party.

Yet, in its deepest meaning, Populism was much more than

Going to the Meeting
Perhaps the most evocative single photograph of the agrarian movement is
this picture of Kansas farmers on their way to a gathering of the Populist
faithful in the 1890's.

the tactical contributions of Kansans or Texans. It was, first
and most centrally, a cooperative movement that imparted a
sense of self-worth to individual people and provided them
with the instruments of self-education about the world they
lived in. The movement gave them hope—a shared hope—
that they were not impersonal victims of a gigantic industrial
engine ruled by others but that they were, instead, people who
could perform specific political acts of self-determination. The
movement taught its participants who they were and what
their rights were and the people of the movement thereupon
created its program and its strategy. The Alliance demands
seemed bold to many other Americans who had been culturally intimidated as to their proper status in the society and
the same demands sounded downright presumptuous to the
cultural elites engaged in the process of intimidation. But to
the men and women of the agrarian movement, encouraged
and enhanced by the sheer drama and power of their massive
parades, their huge summer encampments, their far-flung lecturing system, their suballiance rituals, their dreams of the

196

new day of the cooperative commonwealth, it was all possible because America was a democratic society and people in a democracy had a right to do whatever they had the ethical courage and self-respect to try to do. Populism was, at bottom, a movement of ordinary Americans to gain control over their own lives and futures, a massive democratic effort to gain that most central component of human freedom—dignity.

In Kansas, in the summer of 1890, the August convention to nominate the candidates who would carry the Alliance banner statewide was called "the convention of the people." It was an adequate description. The men chosen came up out of the ranks of the Alliance—county lecturers, county presidents, some with a long greenback past, others only recently recruited to the Alliance cooperative and to insurgent politics. The gubernatorial candidate was John Willits, the county Alliance leader who had pronounced cooperation "the most important word in the English language." An earnest, sometimes passionate advocate, he was an authentic if not always smoothly articulate spokesman for the farmers he represented. The third district's congressional candidate was the Alliance state president, Ben Clover. He looked forward to a statewide reprise on the victorious theme first sounded in Cowley County the preceding year. The fourth district's congressional candidate was a socialist named John Otis who had earlier written Clover an open letter in which he stated, with appropriate capital letters: "When the American people shall introduce cooperation into the field of PRODUCTION as well as into the field of DISTRIBUTION, and shall organize for 'work' as we organize for 'war'! then shall we behold PROSPERITY. . . ." Otis amplified this theme in the ensuing campaign: "We are emerging from an age of intense individualism, supreme selfishness, and ungodly greed to a period of co-operative effort." Otis provided "perhaps as intense and sober a personality as Kansas Populism counted among its leaders." An abolitionist in his youth, he attended Williams College and, later, Harvard Law School. During the Civil War Otis organized and commanded Negro troops, but after Reconstruction he turned his back on the party of Lincoln and became a greenbacker.[26]

"Sockless" Jerry Simpson
Characterized by one Republican as
a "rabid fiat greenbacker with communistic proclivities," Simpson was
one of the most flambouyant orators
of the agrarian revolt.

In the western part of the state William Baker brought a
different style to Alliance doctrines, but his definition of the
issues was no less radical in specific content and, as his successful congressional career proved, no less convincing to the voters. Even so, his style scarcely added up to a "pentecost of politics." William Baker was the most deadly serious and,
perhaps, the dullest Populist of them all. A fifty-nine-year-old
ex-Republican, he also proved to be one of the third party's
most formidable local campaigners.[27]

The pedestrian speeches of Baker and the sustained intensity of Otis were balanced—perhaps more than balanced—by
the flamboyant, idiosyncratic, and vividly effective oratory of
Jeremiah Simpson. "Sockless Jerry" was an endless source of
debate. There was, first of all, the matter of his intelligence.
Some years after the third-party threat had been safely repelled, William Allen White, an arch-enemy of Kansas Populism, confessed that Simpson had persuaded him to read
Carlyle and added, in explanation, that Simpson was the
better read of the two. Be that as it may, there were others
who pointed out that self-taught Jerry Simpson was easily one
of the most atrocious spellers ever to grace the halls of Con-

gress. There was also the matter of his appearance. He was described by one contemporary admirer as a "rough-looking farmer," though his photographs reveal an attractive and neatly dressed man who could easily have passed as a small-town minister. Perhaps the Washington environment affected his sartorial style, if not his radical politics. Both his friends and his enemies, in any case, agreed that the mere act of placing Simpson on a rostrum transformed him—but whether into a "good talker" or into "a rabid fiat greenbacker with communistic tendencies" seems to have depended rather more on the observer. To novelist Hamlin Garland, who heard Simpson in Washington, he was "a clear thinker . . . a remarkable speaker [with] a naturally philosophical mind." He was also, as events were to show, a decidedly pragmatic fellow.[28]

6

When L. L. Polk returned to the Kansas hustings for the autumn campaign, he entered a political tempest that had been gathering in intensity for months. By October the doctrines of the Alliance had become no more convincing to the state's Republican press than they had appeared in March, but the size of the Alliance crowds had destroyed the Republican complacency of the spring. The old order seemed clearly imperiled, and Republican journals responded to the danger.

As one of the journalistic participants conceded after the election, the Republican attack on the Alliance ticket was based on "abuse and vituperation." The Topeka *Capital* thought that Kansans should reject the new political movement because of the war record of the chief Allianceman, North Carolina's Polk. From July through election day the *Capital* kept up a running bloody shirt attack on Polk, and it renewed the theme when he returned to the state the following year. He was described as an "ultra-secession Democrat" who had shot down federal prisoners in cold blood at Gettysburg and had practiced barbarous cruelties on Union soldiers while commandant of Salisbury prison—a post, it might be noted in passing, that he had never held. The *Capital* also circulated the story that the "old soldiers of Wichita" were threatening to tar and feather "The Escaped Prison-Hell

Keeper." Sectionalism took other forms, too. The idea that Polk should come "calamity howling" from North Carolina, "where your illiteracy is the biggest thing you have," to prosperous Kansas ranked as "one of the most sublime exhibitions of gall of which there is any record in ancient or modern history." To augment the portraits of sadism and effrontery with one of incompetence, Polk's *Progressive Farmer* was described as a "small paper at Winston" which had "soon collapsed." [29]

The Republicans unlimbered other vintage artillery to counter the reform cannonading on "living issues." Simpson was variously described as "unpatriotic" and a "swindler." For the religious-minded, he was "an infidel" and an "atheist." As a politician, he was an "anarchist," and as a human being, he had "simian" characteristics. Vituperation proved to be general. When Ralph Beaumont of the Knights of Labor traveled with Polk through Kansas, they were described as "designing wicked mountebanks," "tramps," "worthless schemers," "enemies of God and man," and "would-be revolutionists." Perhaps worse of all, they had "hellish influence." [30]

On election day, Willits was narrowly defeated for the governorship, but hardly any other Alliance candidate lost. Simpson, Baker, Otis, Clover, and a fifth Alliance candidate, John Davis, all were elected to Congress. The returns carried an especially ominous portent for John J. Ingalls. In an era before the popular election of Senators, his future in the Senate would depend on a Kansas legislature in which 96 of the 125 seats were to be occupied by Alliance-elected candidates.[31]

Actually, in terms of over-all party strength, the gubernatorial vote was more indicative, for the 1890 election at least, than the combined legislative totals. The Republicans managed to get about a 5000 vote advantage statewide, though G.O.P. strength was heavily concentrated in cities and thus was not effectively reflected in the legislative races. But to Alliance partisans, such facts could be taken as mere quibbles. On the morning after the election, it was abundantly clear that some sort of earthquake had occurred. By any standard, the Republican Party was a shaken institution. The tremors reached all the way to Washington, where President Harrison was moved to describe the Republican performance in the

West as "our election disaster." "If the Alliance can pull one-half of our Republican voters," he said, "our future is not cheerful." It was not necessary, of course, for agrarian insurgents actually to win elections to directly affect Republican fortunes. Every Alliance or independent vote cast in the West, whether it helped elect radicals or not, weakened the G.O.P. The startling news in states other than Kansas was that the decrease in the Republican vote was enough to send a flood of Democrats to Washington.

The totals were sobering. While in 1888 the House of Representatives had had 166 Republicans and 159 Democrats, the new House would contain 88 Republicans and 235 Democrats.[32]

Yet it was precisely this last statistic that sent a wave of anxiety rolling over the newly victorious Kansas Alliancemen. The effect of the revolt in Kansas had been to give convincing meaning to the Republican claim that the agrarian movement was a Democratic plot and that Republican farmers were being duped by the Southern leaders of the Alliance. If the bloody shirt had waved in Kansas in 1890, Alliancemen shuddered to think of the convincing arguments newly available to Republicans for the Kansas municipal elections of 1891 and, most important of all, for the presidential year of 1892. In the aftermath of victory, the Kansas reformers suddenly found themselves face to face with an immediate crisis: they absolutely had to persuade the Alliance in the South to abandon "reform through the Democrats," and create, with the Western Alliances, a national third party. In the West, it was the only defense against the sectional argument that the Alliance was a "front" for the Democratic Party. The convention of the National Alliance, scheduled for Ocala, Florida, in December 1890, thus became of decisive importance to the Westerners.

7

The Kansans soon realized, however, that they had precious few allies in the West to assist them in their earnest internal discussions with their Southern brethren. The movement toward independent political action in Nebraska provided stark evidence of the price the agrarian movement had begun to pay for the years of programmatic drift by the Northwestern Alliance. For if Kansas had achieved a veritable revolution, at times flamboyant but politically coherent, Nebraska had engaged in an ad hoc brand of politics comprised of about equal portions of indecisive leadership and organizational anarchy. Indeed, it is perhaps a fitting testament to the extreme severity of economic conditions and the sheer naked appeal of the cooperative movement that Nebraska farmers were able to generate any sort of political movement—however fragile—in the face of the disarray of their own spokesmen.

It was not that Jay Burrows and his Nebraska associates lacked for significant guideposts to help point them in the direction of agrarian self-help. As early as 1886 farmers in Custer County, Nebraska, had organized themselves into a local-level cooperative movement, and they soon boasted some fifty-seven suballiances—more than half of the entire state membership of the Nebraska group. In the absence of any coordinated state program, their local effort achieved only marginal success, but even that was sufficient to maintain an on-going farmer organization. Finally, in 1889, a year of severely declining prices for Nebraska corn, oats, and wheat, Custer farmers moved boldly into politics in an effort to gain relief. The revolt was centered in the town of Westerville, where each participant in a relatively new cooperative store owned a $10 share and "almost every man in the community belonged to the organization." As it had elsewhere, the movement toward cooperative buying and selling generated outright hostility from Custer County merchants, causing Alliancemen under the leadership of a relatively unknown but articulate farmer named Omar Kem to put a county ticket in the field for the fall elections. They followed this move by holding primaries and selecting nominees for county offices. When Burrows belatedly heard details of this revolt from below in the name of the Alliance, he asserted in his newspaper that it was "to say the least, a breach of faith." In November, the Custer independent ticket nearly swept the field, all but one of its candidates being elected.[33]

The startling local victory provided one of three influences that were to propel the Nebraskans into independent politics in 1890. The second was the larger cooperative crusade of which the Custer County movement was but a local expression. Through the actions of the leadership of the National Farmers Alliance and the regional cooperative efforts of the Kansas and Dakota Alliances, the idea of cooperation gradually, if imperfectly, seeped into Nebraska. Kansans had attempted to provide the earliest guidance in 1889, when Henry Vincent hailed the inaugural issue of Jay Burrows's newspaper, the *Farmers Alliance,* with an open letter: "Good for Nebraska. Your farmers are getting on the right track at last." After spelling out some relevant details of the cooperative movement in Cowley County, Kansas ("4,000 members" and a "cash business of $300 to $1,400 per day" in the exchange store), Vincent added, "It is tee-totally revolutionizing everything and politicians are, as never before, wholly at sea." But though Burrows had printed a notice of the chartering of the new Custer County cooperative store in his own state a week earlier, the subsequent political relationship of this event to the further organization and education of that county's farmers escaped him, as, indeed, did Vincent's admonitions.[34]

As a result, the cooperative education of the Nebraska state leadership was delayed until the St. Louis merger meeting in December 1889, a month following the Custer County victory. At St. Louis, the Nebraskans were exposed to the full array of Alliance business agents, exchange managers, and delegates from local units who had served on county trade committees. Here was something tangible for Alliance lecturers in Nebraska to talk about—something upon which they could build a movement. The Nebraskans also discovered that the National Alliance contained a satellite institution known as the Association of State Business Agents. Upon their return, Burrows and his colleague, John Powers, hesitantly began exploring ways to create a business agency. Unfortunately, when this institution was finally established in the summer of 1890, no means was provided for it to acquire capital to carry out significant assignments in behalf of organized farmers. Nevertheless, even talk about cooperation helped. The Nebraska Alliance took on the trappings of a cooperative movement and, as Custer County had shown, acquired an organizing tool.[35]

An important additional pressure toward cooperation came from the Kansas and Dakota Alliances. The multi-state Kansas cooperative to market livestock, chartered in 1889, had promptly reached a $2.5 million level of business in 1890—to the considerable profit of all participants. As might have been expected, the success of the venture aroused intense opposition from commission houses, but this development merely furthered the educational influence the cooperative movement had on Midwestern farmers, including Jay Burrows's own members in Nebraska, some of whom benefited from the marketing effort. Meanwhile, through Alonzo Wardall, the Dakota Alliance introduced the particulars of the Alliance Aid Society, as the successful Dakota mutual insurance program had come to be known. By this means Nebraska's leaders learned they could talk about cooperation in terms of insurance, too.[36]

Collectively, these outside cooperative influences affixed upon the structureless Nebraska Alliance the appearance of a program and the reality of a promise. And promise, for the time being, was enough. As had previously been the case in Texas, the South, Kansas, and the Dakotas, in Nebraska the farmers now had a reason to join the Alliance—to help organize "the Alliance store." In the spring of 1890, after ten years of sleepy existence, the Nebraska Alliance began to stir.

The third and final influence on the Nebraska leadership came from outside the ranks of the Alliance, from a number of active political figures, labor leaders, and Republican professionals who had become disillusioned by railroad domination of the Republican Party in the state. Especially exasperating was the presence of "oil rooms" in Lincoln when the state legislature was in session. Run by lawyers and other lobbyists for railroads, these rooms were for the purpose of "oiling" legislators to vote correctly on pending legislation in which railroads were interested. Apparently, "oiling" at times extended beyond mere alcoholic lubrication to include matters of finance. The political climate was visibly corrupt, and thousands of Nebraskans knew it.[37]

The single most popular political figure in the state in the 1880's was Nebraska Senator Charles Van Wyck, an active anti-monopolist. The legislature, under visible lobbying pressure from railroad attorneys, had retired Van Wyck in 1886 in favor of a less troublesome party regular, and the experience caused the ex-Senator to brood deeply about the deteriorated moral tone of his party. By 1890, Charles Van Wyck had become an angry politician looking for a constituency.[38]

In the five-month period between November 1889 and April 1890, the three influences of Custer County, the Alliance cooperative movement, and the Nebraska reformers led by Charles Van Wyck worked to ignite a galvanizing fire under Jay Burrows and J. H. Powers. The growth of the Nebraska Alliance, lackluster through the first ten months of 1889, suddenly accelerated in November and December, following the Custer County breakthrough, and was particularly noticeable in areas contiguous to Custer County. In the spring of 1890, as the word "cooperation" began to filter more frequently into Jay Burrows's newspaper, the gathering of new recruits carried membership totals above 20,000. Though Burrows lacked the understanding to answer the multiple queries of new members about how to initiate marketing and purchasing cooperatives, he gave generalized support to cooperation in his paper, augmented as frequently as possible by references to the success of the cooperative movement of the National Alliance in other states.[39]

For their part, Custer County farmers kept up a steady political pressure from the grass roots. Without seeking the approval of their state officers, Custer Alliancemen expanded their caucuses from their home county to include the surrounding congressional district. The Custer leader, Omar Kem, described one such gathering:

> There were two unique features about this convention. It was made up of delegates by invitation and there was not a delegate in it that had ever been heard of out of his county and many of them not outside their immediate neighborhood and no member of any delegation had ever heard of any other delegation.[40]

To whatever extent Kem's report exposed the organizational vacuum between the leadership caucus at the top of the

Nebraska Alliance and the proliferating local lodges below, it spelled out rather clearly the self-organizing capacities of co-operating farmers.

In March the watchful Charles Van Wyck decided that Nebraska needed to cross the same political Rubicon that the Kansas Alliance had already navigated. Three weeks after the county presidents of the Kansas Alliance had signaled the movement of the order into independent political action, Van Wyck decided to show Nebraska leaders how to lead. In a well-publicized address he announced his support for the Alliance, demanded "the abolition of party lines," and otherwise made it clear that the proper business of the Alliance was independent political action. A startling pronouncement coming from a man of his prestige and previous Republican constancy, Van Wyck's address was immediately countered by Jay Burrows. After years of organizational passivity, Burrows suddenly found himself a much embattled spokesman experiencing pressure both from below and from his political left.[41]

Omar Kem added weight to the pressure applied by Van Wyck. Indeed, Kem's role was crucial, for while the ex-Republican politician might lure the Nebraska Alliance into insurgency, someone first had to recruit the farmers into the Alliance. After one abortive conference with Burrows, Kem wrote in some disgust that he had "terminated the gabberfest by telling him frankly that we proposed to make the fight and that we would take the Alliances of the West and North part of the state with us whether the State Alliance went with us or not." [42]

Amidst this controversy, the Alliance continued to grow—the Custer cooperative store providing the inspirational model—as the long pent-up grievances of Nebraska farmers at last found a forum for expression. Through April and May, as Kansas moved in measured strides toward independent political action, Jay Burrows was forced to maneuver frantically to keep control of a farmer movement suddenly alive after ten years of passivity.

Finally, in May, Burrows acquiesced to a conference of local Alliance representatives where he agreed to a test of popular sentiment through the circulation of petitions calling for independent political action—though admittedly, the specific goals of such a movement had yet to be fashioned in the state.

Nevertheless, some 5000 signatures were obtained in Custer County, matching an additional 5000 collected across the remainder of the state. Veteran greenbackers and anti-monopolists added their voices, and the resultant din pushed Burrows to call an official convention. In July an assemblage of delegates from seventy-nine counties nominated an independent ticket on a platform that emphasized railroad regulation. In a move that Burrows must have found galling, Omar Kem received the congressional nomination from the third district. But Burrows was able to deny to the new movement its most formidable statewide spokesman, Charles Van Wyck. Burrows settled this factional rivalry by throwing his support to his associate in the Alliance, John Powers, and Powers narrowly defeated Van Wyck for the gubernatorial nomination. In the eyes of Nebraska historians, the maneuver placed the weaker man at the head of the ticket.[43]

During the upsurge from the grass roots that characterized Nebraska farmer politics from November 1889 through July 1890, the Nebraska organization enjoyed all of the growth it was ever to attain in the state. Membership totals peaked somewhere in the vicinity of 35,000 to 45,000. The addition of suballiances fell off sharply after mid-summer and—in the absence of organizational structure—membership quickly began to dwindle away. Local cooperative efforts, undirected and uncoordinated by the state organization, either never actually got started or met some sort of early difficulty and quietly expired even as the political movement gathered momentum with the addition of radicals who had up to then been bystanders. Within the Alliance itself, many new members found they had nothing to do—or nothing anyone showed them how to do—and they shifted their attention to the political movement. In 1890, the Nebraska Alliance thus served primarily as a sort of revolving door to some unspecified kind of insurgent political activity. The decline in Alliance membership continued through 1891.[44]

The ultimate problem in Nebraska was the absence of the kind of statewide cooperative infrastructure that elsewhere provided the agrarian movement with its vehicle of organization, its schoolroom of ideology, and its culture of self-respect. The principal meaning of the haphazard events of the spring and summer of 1890, however, went beyond mere organizational considerations to the substance of politics itself. Missing from the Nebraska Alliance from 1880 to 1890 was the animating essence of American Populism: the simple, radical fact that the cooperative movement led to political education in terms of farmer-merchant, farmer-creditor, and farmer-shipper relations and that such education in turn led to the kind of energizing self-perception of the farmer's subordinate place in industrial society which had first moved William Lamb to action back in 1886 in Texas. Cooperation, sometimes merely the promise of cooperation, could attract farmers to the Alliance and, under other additional influences, could propel them toward an insurgent political stance; but only the cooperative *experience* over a period of time provided the kind of education that imparted to the political movement the specific form and substance of the greenback heritage. It was banker opposition to large-scale cooperatives that made farmers want to do something about private banking control over the nation's currency and credit. The cooperative experience itself made persuasive the greenback critique of the power relationships prevailing within the American version of finance capitalism. This organic Populist insight into the structure of American society and American politics simply was not present in Nebraska in the years after 1890 because it had not been part of the internal organizational program developed in the Northwestern Alliance in the years before 1890.

In 1892, after Nebraska radicals finally succeeded in displacing Jay Burrows from the leadership of the independent movement, J. H. Powers was able to lead the remnants of his organization into the National Alliance, as he had wanted to do two years earlier. But by the time the National Alliance was in a position to institute a cooperative structure in Nebraska, most of the state's farmers had departed into the independent movement, where they were trying to achieve political solutions within a framework of farmer-creditor relationships they had only barely begun to analyze. Thus, from beginning to end, the agrarian movement in Nebraska stamped itself as organizationally shallow and ideologically fragile.[45]

In the short run, the absence of clear definition seemed to help the independent political movement, for it induced thousands of voters to support its vaguely defined non-greenback position in November 1890. The "independents" elected Omar Kem to Congress, joined with Democrats to elect a "fusionist" Congressman, and took consolation in the fact that the state's other Congressman would be a Democrat rather than a traditional regular Republican. The newly elected Democrat—also a respecter of the political uses of imprecision—took "the farmer's side" on the tariff, and he was a crowd-pleasing speaker; in the vague climate of 1890 Nebraska politics, the combination proved sufficient to send him to Washington. In such a manner the nation's politics acquired a new personality—William Jennings Bryan. The young Congressman was able to work easily with the Nebraska independents, for they all shared a common political heritage almost entirely extraneous to the Alliance movement and the doctrines of greenbackism.

The state level independent ticket headed by Powers lost narrowly, but in the three-party split the independents elected a majority to both houses of the state legislature. The fragility of the Nebraska reform movement quickly became apparent when the legislature convened in 1891. Despite their numerical majorities, the independents were able to advance only a truncated reform program centered around a weak railroad regulatory agency. The watered down legislation, known as the Newberry bill, finally passed, but it was vetoed by the Republican governor.[46]

In the final analysis, the decade-long legacy of the Northwestern Alliance proved too much for the cooperative movement of the Alliance to overcome. The result in Nebraska was a fragile shadow movement unrelated to the doctrines of Populism that elsewhere had materialized within the cooperative movement to bring the greenback analysis of the banking system to masses of American farmers.

But in the deepest meaning of mass citizen politics—in the Populistic sense of public life as a shared *experience* of people—

it is really too much to say that Nebraska had only a fragile shadow movement. It really had no "movement," and Populism cannot be said to have existed there at all. The agrarian cause in Nebraska had no institutional base, no collective identity, and no movement culture to counter the constant intimidation of the prevailing corporate culture. It possessed no mechanisms for self-education, no real lecturing system, no methods for developing individual self-respect among impoverished people. In this same sense, it is not so much that the Nebraskans did not understand the money question—that they were "ideologically uninformed." Rather their truncated movement was too exclusively "ideological": it concerned *only* policies and "politics"—expressed essentially in the desire to win the next election. In human terms of shared experience and shared hope, the twin legacies of the cooperative crusade, the farmer movement in Nebraska had no purpose. It only appeared to have one, because of its external resemblance to the real movement which did.[47]

Whatever the Populist future was to hold, one thing was clear in Nebraska in 1890: the Nebraskans would not be on hand at the National Alliance convention in Ocala with the organization credentials to assist their fellow Westerners from Kansas and the Dakotas in their self-assigned but politically decisive task of persuading the Southern Alliances to abandon the party of the Confederacy. In breaching the sectional barrier to achieve a multi-sectional third party, the Nebraskans were to prove of no value to the national reform cause.

The events of 1890 demonstrated that old Republican loyalties on the Western plains could be dislodged for a time— given enough organizational skill, drought, low farm prices, timely outside influences, or a combination of these elements. But the sectional barrier to broad-based reform nudged uneasily to the fore in the first year of what promised to be a tumultous political decade. The reach of the Civil War could be seen to be even longer than reformers had feared. It was all too apparent that the bloody shirt still waved. Republican taunts of "rebel brigadiers" followed Western alliancemen across the plains as relentlessly as the continuing agricultural depression dogged their constituents. When the root causes of

agrarian poverty were uncontested by the Alliance cooperative, the resulting political aimlessness affected local agrarian
spokesmen in ways that raised serious obstacles to reform.

8

The high hopes of the spring had by no means been extin-
guished, however. From many points of the compass came
signs of lightning in the political sky. The spectacular Kansas
victories brought a surge of hope to old Alliancemen from
Dakota to Florida and to new Alliancemen from Colorado to
Oregon. In 1890, as L. L. Polk interpreted the agrarian victories in the South, highlighted by the triumph of Tom Watson in Georgia, "the coming revolution" had truly begun.
"Congress will contain thirty-eight straight-out Alliancemen,"
Polk said enthusiastically after the November elections. "We
are here to stay. . . . The people of this country are desperately in earnest. They will no longer put up with nonsense.
Old Party fossils have lost their grip. The people want men;
they want live issues; they are going to have them." [48]

Polk's confidence was typical. Traveling lecturers from
Pennsylvania to California felt in their bones that a new political day was coming. Indeed, the strongest weapon of Alliance
organizers was their faith in the movement they were creating,
the movement that had created them as spokesmen for a new
America. It was a faith that had produced an organizational
sweep through the backwoods of the South in 1887 and had
brought forth wagonloads of wheat to help finance a political
campaign in Kansas in 1890. It had erected literally thousands
of cooperative warehouses across rural America and, on a
river in Tennessee, it had even produced plans for a cooperative steamboat! In the midst of such an outpouring of energy
and hope, a great many believed that a new mass democratic
politics was coming to America. An Alliance partisan in
Florida expressed the élan as well as the sense of broadening
horizons of the millions who had been touched by the aspirations of the agrarian movement: "We shall knock sectionalism
in the head, wrap the bloody shirt about it for a winding-
sheet, and bury it so deep that it will never hear the call on
resurrection day." [49]

The Floridian gave voice to the new political consciousness, but among his co-regionists across the South, no less than among his newly acquired allies in the West, the sectional legacy of the Civil War lingered. Though the evidence was barely visible to outsiders, sectional influences had already contributed to the emergence of an ephemeral shadow movement. And in the South, sectionalism meant more than mere loyalty to a party, even to "the party of the fathers." It meant loyalty to the party of white supremacy.

For Alliance radicals dreaming of a multi-sectional third party of the "industrial millions," the biggest task loomed ahead.

CHAPTER VIII

Severing the Bonds of The Fathers: The Politics of the Sub-Treasury

". . . in the heyday of power and popularity . . ."

The political culmination of Alliance radicalism was the creation of the People's Party as a multi-sectional institution of reform. Given the immense practical obstacles that had to be overcome, the mere fashioning of a Southern-Western third-party coalition a generation after the Civil War was a political achievement of some magnitude. In view of the previous failure of the Greenback and Union Labor parties, the significant achievement of the People's Party—one that permits the phrase "agrarian revolt" to be applied to the Populist era—was the addition of the South to the trans-Mississippi West. This accomplishment, which provided the basis for the political threat posed by the People's Party to the established order of Gilded Age America, was set in motion largely through the tactical creativity of one agrarian spokesman, William Lamb. Yet the degree to which the goal was achieved across one-fourth of a continent ultimately depended on choices made by hundreds of thousands of individual people.

The organized drive by the Western Alliances for a national third party was the product of a political moment that occurred late in 1890—the strong initial showing made by the Alliance tickets in the November elections from Kansas to the Canadian border. Prior to that moment the Western Alliances were too preoccupied with attempting to mobilize their own rank and file to have time to worry about the vast membership of the Southern Alliances.

Yet the underlying political processes at work in the West pressed the Southern Alliances toward conflict with the established political institutions of their region also. While Kansans busied themselves with their "Alliance ticket" in 1890, Southerners applied the "Alliance yardstick" of the St. Louis platform and ran their candidates in the only political home that a great majority of white Southerners had considered since the war—the Democratic Party. They did so, as a matter of fact, with a certain confidence. So enormous had the Alliance become and so pervasive was it in its very presence that the order did not have to "capture" the Democratic Party: as the *Atlantic Constitution* put it, "The Farmers Alliance *is* the Democratic Party." [1]

2

"Reform" was definitely in the air across the South in 1890, extending even into citadels of conservatism within the Democratic Party. As one student of the period described the phenomenon, "it was surprising how many of the old leaders had long been convinced of much that Alliancemen now demanded." Like the *Atlanta Constitution,* established politicians could endorse the Alliance and its platform, as long as both functioned through the Democratic Party. In such a manner, the organized farmers of the Alliance achieved what appeared to be a "party revolution" across the South in 1890. In Tennessee the Alliance state president, John P. Buchanan, won the Democratic nomination and was speedily elected governor. In Georgia the Democratic convention simply adopted the Alliance platform and nominated Allianceman William Northen for governor. The ensuing elections appeared decisive. Besides taking the Georgia governorship, Alliance-supported candidates won three-fourths of the seats in the State Senate, four-fifths of the state House of Representatives, and six of the state's ten congressional seats. "Being Democrats and in the majority," explained one Allianceman, "we took possession of the Democratic Party." Another exclaimed, "As in the day of Jackson, the people have come to power." [2]

In Virginia, where no state elections were held in 1890, five Congressmen hastened to pledge support to the party's state platform, which was strongly influenced by Alliance doctrines. The president of the Florida Alliance felt the battle was won when the order "secured our cardinal principles in the Democratic platform." The Alliance "insisted," he said, that the Democratic Party furnish the candidates to run on the platform, and the farmers proposed to "stand by them." "Should we be deceived," he added, "we have a speedy remedy at hand and shall exercise it." [3]

Amid the general euphoria there were some disturbing signs. In Alabama, where the Alliance claimed more than 75 of the 133 members of the state assembly, Democratic conservatives were able to prevail in the party's gubernatorial nominating convention, narrowly selecting the Bourbon leader, Thomas Jones, over the Alliance candidate, Reuben Kolb. In Tennessee the order's state president and new governor, in order to please what he regarded as his entire Alliance and non-Alliance constituency, decided it would be politically expedient to remain silent about most of the Alliance demands. [4]

Apparently while agricultural poverty might, under some conditions, lead to reform, it might also lead merely to personal political machines that traded on the language of reform. In South Carolina a ranting, one-eyed orator named Ben Tillman launched a campaign for power based on upland hostility to the tidewater gentry. Tillman's organizational efforts had already stirred up South Carolina farmers before the first Alliance organizers arrived in the state from Texas. He regarded the Alliance warily at first but eventually decided to join it, gain control, and use it for his own political ends. Though his hate-filled oratory terrified conservatives, the Tillman regime proved surprisingly amenable to the established order of things. Tillman's determined opposition to a political coalition of the South and West against the industrial East proved so galling to the Alliance that he was denounced by the

National Economist, the *Southern Mercury,* and even the South Carolina Alliance. The latter formally repudiated Tillman by a unanimous vote in 1891 "in spite of the protests of the Governor, who was present." The *Economist* charged that Tillman was "scattering seeds of discord and discontent for the sole purpose of injuring the Alliance," and the *Mercury* asserted he had "consorted with the most violent and vicious enemies of the Alliance." But these were later conclusions, available only after a good deal of evidence had been amassed. In 1890 Tillman avoided trouble with the Alliance and used his oratorical skills to gain the votes of most of its members. Meanwhile in Georgia the victory of Governor Northen came to be seen more as a triumph for continuity than a breakthrough for the Alliance. Georgia newspapers regarded the new Governor as "progressive but safe." Northen, it further developed, worked easily with that symbol of New South industrialism in Georgia, the railroad executive and ex-Confederate general, John B. Gordon.[5]

A close analysis of the 1890 elections might well have given the agrarian reformers reason to pause in their exultation. The party of the Confederacy, with its pliant relationship with corporations, had several well-fortified lines of defense. Only one had apparently been breached. In many states the party machinery remained in the hands of old-line regulars, and almost everywhere the controlling mechanisms of the parliamentary process—the chairmanships of powerful committees—as well as the continuing leverage available through corporate lobbying influences, were retained by politicians oriented toward business rather than toward the Alliance. However much the election results of 1890 appeared to constitute a veritable revolution by the Alliance, it was assuredly an elusive revolution and, most of all, one that could not be measured until the newly elected Alliance governors and legislatures met in 1891. Whatever the reading as of the end of 1890, however, one development seemed unarguable: by educating the farmers, the Alliance had brought the idea of reform into the dialogue of the Democratic Party of the South for the first time since the Civil War.

Such, at any rate, was the way Alliance victories of 1890 appeared to the nation. But from the viewpoint of Alliance radicals—and particularly from the viewpoint of the radical Alliance founders in Texas—the cooperative movement had, ironically, accomplished precisely the opposite result. Far from being an energizing force, the cooperative crusade seemed to have sidetracked reform in Texas in 1888 and kept it there through the elections of 1890. As the old Cleburne radicals analyzed matters, the politics of 1890 in the South constituted a total sham, suggesting the mere appearance of reform without the slightest shred of its substance.

This interpretation, of course, differed markedly from that of other Southern Alliance leaders, and from that of National President L. L. Polk as well. Nevertheless, the origin of this analysis demands brief attention, for its subsequent development charted the path that brought the Southern Alliances to the People's Party.

3

The intellectual and tactical nucleus of Alliance radicalism consisted of six men who first came to prominence in the year of the Cleburne Demands of 1886. All six had subsequently acquired a measure of prominence among the leadership of the national agrarian movement. Most visible, of course, was Evan Jones, the homespun, loquacious radical who successively served from 1884 to 1890 as chief spokesman for the Alliance movement in his home county, in his home state of Texas and, in 1889, as president of the National Alliance. He had voted a third-party ticket since 1884 and, as his presidential address in St. Louis in 1889 revealed, he was dedicated to using his full powers to bring the National Alliance to that political perspective.[6]

A second insurgent tactician was H. S. P. Ashby, one of the most effective "stump" speakers in the reform movement. He was known, appropriately enough, as "Stump" Ashby. A "good natured man said to be very popular among the ladies," Ashby was a devout but most unusual kind of Methodist preacher. By turns a cowboy, schoolteacher, actor, and farmer as well as minister of the gospel, Ashby also had a fondness for whiskey that gave him some difficulty with prohibitionists in his mature days as state chairman of the People's Party in Texas. But by then his oratorical skills, if not also his rich fund of humor, represented a demonstrably marketable asset for the agrarian cause. Ashby, too, was well known outside his home state, having served on the blue ribbon panel at St. Louis that had brought forth the sub-treasury plan. He possessed one other attribute—a rare ability to earn and hold the confidence of political colleagues who were black.[7]

A third prominent activist was J. M. Perdue, principal author of the Cleburne Demands. A greenback theoretician, Perdue was one of the group of Kansas and Texas radicals who had played a prominent role in the creation of the national Union Labor Party in 1888. Perdue had a lucid intelligence and a biting prose style, and he normally found his niche on the platform-writing committees of Alliance and third-party gatherings from 1884 on. As a vice president and one of the original national trustees of the Alliance, and as state lecturer during the Jones regime, he was strategically placed to bring respectability to radical doctrines inside both the state and the national Alliance organizations. Above all, Perdue brought a driving determination to the internal "educational" program of the Alliance. He brought one additional credential to radicalism: like Ashby, he was a Methodist minister.[8]

The fourth leading member of the Texas coterie was Colonel R. M. Humphrey, white founder of the Colored Farmers National Alliance.* Like Perdue a native of the eastern "Old South" part of Texas, Humphrey was a former Confederate officer and a Baptist missionary. An early devotee of independent political action, Humphrey's years of association with the Colored Farmers Alliance gave him fresh insights into "the Negro problem" in a way that had an interesting affect on his racial views. While his colleagues among the Texas radicals took racial stances that were regarded as quite "liberal" for the 1890's, either in the South or the nation, Humphrey's posture

---

* Humphrey's career is discussed in more detail in Chapter X, "The Populist Approach to Black America."

of racial liberalism came in time to be the most pronounced of all. A huge man with a decided flair for self-promotion, Humphrey was also the most diplomatic of the Alliance radicals. Though all of them, in the interest of their tactical struggle with Charles Macune, handled the *National Economist* editor with considerable care, Humphrey was the only one Macune publicly singled out for praise. Given Macune's racial views, Humphrey's personal diplomacy may be taken as no small achievement.[9]

Another member of the strategically important Texas group was Harry Tracy of Dallas. Urbane and, by Texas standards, courtly, Tracy was a man of the middle class. He possessed advanced views on labor, women's rights, and the necessity for cooperation with the Colored Farmers Alliance, but it was the cooperative crusade to free the mass of Southern farmers from the crop lien system which captured his attention in the 1880's and converted him to greenback doctrines. As deputy national lecturer of the Alliance and publisher of the *Southern Mercury,* Tracy was a close associate of Macune, from whom he apparently received his initial introduction into greenback monetary theory. Thoughtful and articulate, Tracy, along with Macune and Cuthbert Vincent of Kansas, eventually became one of the most sophisticated greenback theoreticians in the People's Party and one of the very few men in Gilded Age America who understood the function of currency velocity—as distinct from currency volume—in assessing the merits of various monetary systems. A Macunite through 1890, Tracy's disenchantment with the "reform wing" of the Democratic Party and his conversion to political radicalism in 1891 came at a tactically decisive moment.[10]

The final member of the radical leadership in Texas was, of course, William Lamb. The red-headed apostle of cooperation and farmer-labor coalitions had scarcely mellowed since his 1886 boycott proclamation had led to the internal revolution that produced the Cleburne Demands. Lamb had risen to leadership of the Texas third party men, coordinating their efforts with the Vincent brothers in Kansas during the national planning for the Union Labor Party in 1888 as well as orchestrating the third-party drive in his home state. He maintained close ties with the Knights of Labor and—a testament to his growing mastery of the English language—opened a radical newspaper in his home town of Bowie in Montague County. He read widely on the money question and came to have a number of creative innovations to suggest in other areas of national policy as well.[11]

In 1890 these radicals were a frustrated group. They were, perhaps, not as gloomy as Jerry Simpson of Kansas had been in 1889 after the Union Labor debacle of the preceding year, but they approached his despair and for the same reason: the failure of the third-party effort both nationally and in their own state. And the height of the irony lay in the fact that the central cause of their difficulty was the cooperative movement itself.

The Texas radicals had made a massive effort in 1888 to assist in the creation of a new national third party and to rally the entire Alliance to its support in Texas. In the spring of that year "Stump" Ashby had led the early organizational effort in Texas while Lamb and others were busy in Cincinnati organizing the national Union Labor party. That summer, upon his return to Texas, Lamb, aided by Perdue, Humphrey, and Ashby, shepherded the new party to organizational life, culminating the effort by awarding the gubernatorial nomination to Evan Jones, the Alliance state president. While the Austin *Statesman* described the Union Labor platform as the "most startling document that has been given to the public in the last decade," the unpleasant reality for radicals was that their 1888 political plans collided with the desperate struggle of the Texas Alliance to save its central state exchange. The effort consumed the energies of President Jones from May through August, and he finally decided that his personal involvement in the much-needed political contest would dangerously weaken the Alliance at the very moment it needed its maximum unity for the cooperative struggle. However necessary, Jones's decision to decline the third-party gubernatorial nomination postponed for at least two years what he and his principal colleagues considered to be their central political mission—beginning the process of weaning rank-and-file Alliance farmers from their inherited loyalty to the "party of the fathers." [12]

It became apparent in 1890 that the postponement might be for four years rather than two. As the emergence of Tillman in South Carolina and Northen in Georgia revealed, a new variety of Southern politician had materialized in response to the arrival of the Alliance in politics. In Texas the new aspirant's name was James Hogg, a 300-pound, railroad-baiting Democratic loyalist who asserted himself as a man of the people. Hogg had a colorful platform style that tended to obscure the lack of specifics in his reform program. While campaigning, he often took off his coat, threw his suspenders from his shoulders, letting them dangle about his knees, and drank "lik a horse" from a water pitcher. William Lamb, for one, was not impressed, particularly after reading the 1890 Democratic platform tailored by the Hoggites. Moreover, the old Cleburne radical had a weapon to employ in 1890 that had been unavailable in 1888. Ironically, he could thank his old rival, the "nonpartisan" Charles Macune, for the weapon was Macune's sub-treasury plan. The sweeping soft-money proposal was unlikely to please Democratic regulars, even when they displayed the trappings of reform in support of James Hogg. Unfortunately for the radicals, in a juxtaposition of scheduling they must have found maddening in the "reform summer" of 1890, the Alliance state convention began two days after the Democratic convention ended; the timing thus precluded the possibility that the Alliance could adopt a reform platform that would put the Democrats to a genuine test of their sincerity. The Hoggites assisted in clarifying any ideological confusion, however, by taking the initiative and resolving against the sub-treasury. At the time, few political observers gave the matter any thought, for the topic of the sub-treasury appeared to be only a minor element in the politics of 1890; with no rival for the support of the farmers, Hogg was safely "in" as the next governor of Texas. [13]

However, it was precisely at this point—August 1890—that William Lamb consciously set in motion the elaborate campaign of radical education that was destined to carry the National Farmers Alliance to the People's Party. First, he publicly defined his opposition to the Southern Democracy. The Democratic platform had "sidetracked" the farmers, he said. "The declaration against banks without proposing a substitute is a piece of trickery," he added. But most outrageous of all was the pronouncement against the sub-treasury. "I have offered to wager a ginger cake and a jug of buttermilk," said Lamb, "that not one of the committees on resolutions in the Democratic primary of my precinct has even read it." To Lamb, the Alliance had been far less effective in capturing the Democratic Party, as some conservative newspapers had suggested, than Hogg had been in captivating Alliancemen. In the aftermath of the 1890 Democratic convention, Lamb readied his plan to drive home this analysis to the annual Alliance state meeting. The daylight between the Alliance on the one hand and the Democratic Party on the other had finally appeared in a way that farmers should be able to see—for the sub-treasury was the one issue that addressed the enduring realities in the lives of most Southern farmers, the furnishing merchant and his crop lien. William Lamb proposed to draw a radical distinction on the sub-treasury issue.[14]

The arguments easily presented themselves. If the Alliance was not willing to take a stand for the sub-treasury, then it mocked its own claim that it represented the true interest of farmers. Thirteen years of devoted experimentation with cooperative buying and selling had failed to alter the basic injustices traceable to the crop lien and the furnishing merchant. Not only was this reality obvious to men like Lamb and Macune, it was also apparent to everyone intimately associated with the multiple efforts at self-help through farmer cooperatives. The sub-treasury plan faced this harsh fact squarely. Collectively, these arguments added up to a radical ultimatum: if the farmers were unwilling to take on all comers on the basis of the sub-treasury, they might as well abandon the Alliance. "Cooperation" having failed to dislodge the furnishing merchant, what other course was left? The Alliance had to stand on the issue of the sub-treasury or concede its own irrelevance on the fundamental question of agricultural credit.

Four months before the Ocala convention of the National Alliance Lamb pressed the choice on the Texas Alliance in the order's state convention at Dallas. Lamb enjoined the Alliance formally to endorse the issue that the Democratic Party had formally opposed. If the sub-treasury issue drew a line between the Alliance and the party of the fathers, it also pressed the delegates toward a realization of the implications of their own commitment, as Alliance leaders, to farmers generally. The pull of conflicting loyalties was evident, but awkward. Must one choose between the Democratic Party and the farmers?

The supporting arguments for both sides—destined to be heard throughout the South in 1891–92—began to resound through Texas in 1890. Was not the Alliance strong enough to insist that the Democrats support the sub-treasury? The Democrats had already pronounced against it. Was not the Democratic Party the party of the people? If the party was not willing to try to cope with the furnishing merchant and the crop lien, it did not care about the people. What about the Democratic argument that the sub-treasury was class legislation, or unconstitutional, or both? Opposition to the sub-treasury was admission that the farmers could not be helped.

The arguments were stark and the choice painful. William Lamb did not win friends among some of his Alliance associates by insisting that the choice be made. After a debate extending over two days, the roll call of counties was ordered on the question of a formal endorsement of the sub-treasury plan as official Alliance policy. Sixteen counties abstained. Twenty-three voted "no." Seventy-five voted "yes." On a fundamental issue, the Texas Alliance had declared itself in opposition to the Texas Democratic Party.[15]

But since the Alliance had met a week after the Democrats had decided for Hogg and against the sub-treasury, the new Alliance stand could not have immediate political effect. Only on the leadership level had the Alliance vote on the sub-treasury drawn a line between the order and the Democratic Party. To the thousands of farmers in the suballiances, the relationships of candidates, political parties, and the sub-treasury issue was not remotely so clear as it loomed to the Alliance leaders who debated Lamb's motion in August. The painful decision thrust on the Alliance leadership therefore had to be recapitulated at all levels of the order in a manner that would bring home to hundreds of thousands of farmers the choices that had to be made. To this course Lamb persuaded the agrarian leaders in Texas to dedicate themselves. Let the sub-treasury be explained by the lecturers. Let the farmers in the suballiances debate the plan. Let them see its implications in terms of their daily relationships with the furnishing merchant. Let the line be drawn.

To this end Lamb moved to mobilize the Alliance's internal organizational machinery to address an enormous lecturing task. The job was huge, but something of a precedent existed—the Alliance lecturing system had successfully explained the complicated "joint-note" plan to the Texas farmers in 1888. Yet the challenge of explaining the sub-treasury to thousands of suballiances was even more intricate. The sub-treasury not only contained monetary theory, a subject with which few Americans felt comfortable, it encompassed new marketing procedures based on the theory. Moreover, both its theoretical base and its specific provisions were under attack in the daily press and by Democratic politicians, whereas the joint-note plan had not been.

Clearly, the order's lecturers not only had to be increased in number, but they also had to be thoroughly briefed on the workings of the sub-treasury system and armed with intelligent defenses of its provisions. Following the state meeting Lamb and Perdue implemented a plan to add an additional layer of executive structure to the Alliance organization in order to meet the lecturing challenge. With the full cooperation of Evan Jones, a multi-county lecturing school on the sub-treasury was established in each congressional district of Texas. County Alliance presidents, lecturers, and assistant lecturers were convened and briefed, and speaking assignments were integrated into a systematic plan to cover the hundreds of suballiances in each district. In the fall and winter of 1890, one congressional district after another organized its "lecturing school." Lamb presided over the most elaborate—and the best publicized—in November. It resulted in the instruction and appointment of seven special "district lecturers" to work alongside the regular county lecturers throughout the fifth congressional district of Texas. Perdue presided over another two-day training program in the third district. By the end of the winter the sub-treasury test that had been put to the Alliance county leadership in August 1890 was being recapitulated in hundreds of suballiances across the state. The farmers were being asked to choose between the Farmers Alliance and the Democratic Party. The politics of Populism had arrived in the rural districts of Texas.[16]

4

While Hogg, Northen, Tillman, and other "Alliance Democrats" were sweeping to victory in the fall of 1890, the Alliance ticket won its stunning victory in Kansas. If not all Southerners shared the anxieties about "reform through the Democrats" that animated the Texas radicals, the Kansans certainly did. While the great mass of Southern delegates to the Alliance national convention in Ocala might be committed to observation of their newly elected "Alliance legislatures" in 1891, the Western Alliances were equally committed to pushing the order directly into independent political action. And, indeed, the Ocala meeting and its famous "Ocala Demands" became one of the memorable events of the agrarian revolt.

The year since the merger attempt at St. Louis had seen the harnessed energy of the Alliance organizing technique applied over a large part of the continent. Though still youthful, the order had become a truly national institution and could look back over a surprisingly rich history. A little less than seven years had elapsed since an articulate farmer named S. O. Daws had reinvigorated the sagging Alliance movement. Four years had passed since the Cleburne Demands, three since the organizing sweep through the South, two since the cooperative movement had taken root on the Kansas plains, one since the propagation of the sub-treasury plan. The Ocala gathering bore witness to another year of earnest organizing. Alliance state organizations had been established in four states of the old Northwestern group—Michigan, Indiana, Illinois and Ohio. Other new jurisdictions on the Alliance roll included Idaho, Montana, Oregon, California, New Mexico, and Arizona in the West and New York, New Jersey, and Pennsylvania in the East. Representatives were even present from Jay Burrows's Nebraska, while August Post, the troubled Iowa conservative, arrived to take part in the deliberations of the Association of State Business Agents. Together, the delegates represented thirty states and well over one million farmers, and the nation had at last taken notice. The presence of correspondents from the Associated Press, the *Times,* the *World,* the *Herald,* and the *Sun,* all of New York, and a dozen other well-known newsgathering agencies testified to the political arrival of the Farmers Alliance. Beyond all question, the November elections in the South and West had proven that the Alliance was "in politics." [17]

But while liberal journalists might be in the act of writing optimistic interpretive stories about "the Alliance Wedge in Congress," the Kansans knew the wedge could easily be dislodged. They would be extremely vulnerable in the state elections of 1892 unless agrarian insurgency had by that time acquired a national presence. The virulent bloody shirt attack on L. L. Polk in the 1890 campaign in Kansas had been an omen of what they might expect in 1892 unless a political identity clearly separate from the party of the Confederacy had been created to insulate the reform movement from the ravages of sectional politics. A party that seriously hoped to challenge the dominant Republicans of the North simply could not be tainted with the stain of rebellion.[18]

Sharing this general perspective were the Alliance radicals of the South. Except for two states of the trans-Mississippi South—Texas and Arkansas—their numbers were still small as long as "reform through the Democrats" appeared to be a possibility. Until that verdict was in, the majority of Southern Alliancemen could—and did—insist that they would appear foolish to make any move toward a new party. This position of the Southerners was logically unassailable. They had created an "Alliance yardstick" composed of the national demands formulated in the St. Louis Platform plus a variety of local issues applicable in each state. They had done this even before the Western Alliances had moved into independent political action in the summer and fall of 1890. Having announced their Alliance yardstick, the Southerners had then measured candidates by it. So great was the Alliance sweep that literally hundreds of legislators who had "measured up" had been elected, and six Georgia Congressmen who had not, had been defeated. Indeed, the order promised to be in numerical control of a number of "Alliance legislatures." To abandon the Alliance representatives even before their legislatures convened not only would make the order appear irresponsible before the world, it also would constitute an abandonment of the Alliance platform. How could the order go back to the voters as a third party with the same program without having given the men it had already elected a chance to act upon it? The question was unanswerable.

A sectional deadlock threatening the national dimensions of the Alliance thus loomed at Ocala. L. L. Polk endeavored to meet the problem squarely in his presidential address. After condemning both old parties, he warned of "political or monopolistic combinations" from without as well as "treachery of foes within." The "foes within" were "wicked sectional agitators" who were working to divert the masses from reform. "It is as needless as it would be criminal to disguise the fact that as an organization, we have reached a critical period in our existence," he said. The foe materialized in the form of W. S. McAlister, an anti-third party, anti-Macune, anti-subtreasurite segregationist from the Mississippi Alliance. McAlister introduced a resolution condemning the Lodge election bill, or, as it was known in white supremacist quarters of the South, the "Force Bill." Sponsored by Henry Cabot Lodge of Massachusetts, the 1890 bill was one of the last Republican assertions of the G.O.P.'s old abolitionist commitment to voting rights for Black Americans. Alonzo Wardall of South Dakota moved to table the Mississippi resolution and, after considerable and at times impassioned debate that carried intermittent overtones of a referendum on independent political action as well as Negro rights, the vote was called by states. The Northern and Western delegates voted in support of Wardall, 18 to 13, while the Southern Alliances voted against, 35 to 11. The four-man delegations from Alabama and Texas voted unani-

Alliance Supreme Council at Ocala
The movement's senior statesmen gathered at Ocala, Florida, in 1890 in the
first Alliance meeting to attract national attention.

mously with their Western and Northern brethren, and the
Arkansas Alliance divided 2 to 2. The other Southern vote for
a protected franchise was cast by a Floridian. The remaining
seven states of the Old Confederacy voted unanimously
against the Lodge bill. With the National Alliance going on
record against the election measure by a margin of 48 to 29,
third-party men were discouraged. Ben Clover, speaking for
the Kansans, concluded that "agitation over the Lodge bill
precludes the possibility of an independent political movement at this time." [19]

Still the exigencies of the situation demanded that an effort
be made, and the Kansans pressed hard. Actually, when reduced to its essentials, the substance of the dispute proved to
be surmountable, in an organizational sense at least. As was
his custom, Charles Macune provided a compromise. A third
party could service no one, neither the Westerners nor the
Southerners, in 1891. The operative question was what the
posture of the agrarian movement would be in the presidential election year of 1892. "Reform through the Democrats"
(of which there was no more fervent supporter than Macune)
could be tested in the legislatures which would convene across

the South in 1891. If that solution were found wanting, other alternatives, including a third party, could be considered early in 1892 in ample time to organize for the fall campaign. Let the matter be postponed, said Macune. Agree at Ocala to convene a great confederation of all the industrial organizations on Washington's birthday in 1892. That date, only fourteen months away, would provide a much better perspective from which to view the progress of the reform movement. As Macune put it, "If the people by delegates coming direct from them agree that a third party move is necessary, it need not be feared." [20]

Yet while the radicals were forced to accept these imperatives as they applied directly to the Alliance, there were compelling reasons why at least some basic organizational steps toward a third party had to be achieved in 1891. To be successful, the third party must be larger than the Alliance and therefore could not be guided solely by the internal considerations of the farm organization. Radical strategists were convinced that the failures of the old parties and the remedies the new one would bring needed to be explained throughout the land, and not just within the confines of labor organizations, however impressive their membership claims might be. Quite obviously, millions of the voters they hoped to reach did not belong to any labor organization. For this reason, the radicals accepted the Macune compromise and then promptly went beyond it—technically outside the structure of the Alliance. A call for an immediate reform convention was drawn up by the Vincent brothers of the *Nonconformist*. Reformers throughout the nation were called to a "mass meeting of the industrial classes" to be held in Cincinnati in 1891.[21]

In ways that were not directly traceable to pressure from its left wing, however, the Alliance, inexorably, moved closer to third party action at the Ocala convention. The six-day conference revealed the growing confidence of the farmer delegates in their own organization and their heightening impatience with the two major parties. President Polk's incipiently radical address and a new joint plan of cooperation between the Alliance, the Knights of Labor, the Colored National Alliance, and the Farmers Mutual Benefit Association both pointed to a consolidating mood of insurgency. Above all, the national platform of the Alliance outlined a political agenda that seemed to place the order well beyond the reach of the two major parties. The "Ocala Demands" focused on the financial, land, and transportation issues that had come to represent the political objectives of the agrarian movement. In addition to the radical demands adopted at St. Louis the year previously, these now officially included the sub-treasury plan. The Alliance platform demanded the abolition of the national banking system, the substitution of legal tender treasury notes, an increase in circulating currency to a level of "not less than $50 per capita," * establishment of the sub-treasury plan, free and unlimited coinage of silver, a graduated income tax, removal of the protective tariff "from the necessities of life that the poor of our land must have," and direct election of United States Senators. The Alliance also called for rigid regulation of public communication and transportation and, should that prove insufficient to "remove the abuse now existing," government ownership. It was not to be imagined that either of the two major parties would soon move in step with such sentiments. The Alliance movement had, in fact, achieved something the Union Labor and Greenback parties had never been able to accomplish: a national political presence for the greenback interpretation of the financial structure of American capitalism.[22]

As the distance between the Alliance and the third party narrowed, the emotional commitment of individuals both for and against the final step intensified. While Macune maneuvered desperately to prevent that step, Southern radicals like Lamb, Perdue, and W. Scott Morgan of Arkansas worked closely with the Kansans on the call for the Cincinnati convention. Yet, though Lamb and Macune were now clearly divided over Alliance tactics, the ironic outgrowth of still another Macune innovation was their move into even closer organizational proximity. That was the creation at Ocala of the Na-

* This ratio of currency volume to population was not achieved until 1947. See Appendix B.

tional Reform Press Association. Macune, as editor of the
order's national weekly, was appointed chairman, while Lamb
was named as one of the three national directors. The other
two were Cuthbert Vincent of Kansas and Ralph Beaumont,
the socialist national lecturer of the Knights of Labor. The
secretary-treasurer was W. Scott Morgan of Arkansas, editor
of the radical *National Reformer*. Clearly, the reform press
would be far more responsive to Lamb's politics than to Macune's; in fact, the network of reform editors served as one of
the primary organizational bases of Populism throughout the
era of the People's Party; in 1891–92 it provided the basic internal communication agency through which greenbackers labored for the third party.[23]

However convoluted the developing leadership relationships might have appeared, no one endeavored more earnestly to remain attuned to the mood of the National Farmers
Alliance than its founder. The spreading sense of insurgency
among the delegates so evident at Ocala had forced Charles
Macune to give tacit approval to the possibility of a third
party. His compromise plan calling for an 1892 convocation of
reformers reflected his awareness of the political location of
the new center of gravity within the Alliance. After Ocala,
Macune, like Lamb, felt the need for a broader organizational
base than existed solely within the Alliance. At Macune's
suggestion, representatives of the Alliance, the Knights of
Labor, the Colored Alliance, the Farmers Mutual Benefit Association, and the radical new National Citizens Alliance met
in Washington in January 1891. There, under Macune's guidance, a new "Confederation of Industrial Organizations" was
formed, with Ben Terrell of Texas, Macune's close associate,
as chairman. Terrell had been National Lecturer of the Alliance since its inception in 1887. He was a reliable Democrat,
an energetic advocate of the sub-treasury, and a devoted follower of Macune. The "Confederation" constituted a tactical
holding operation by Macune. As the sounding board of the
major reform organizations of the nation it might, under
proper leadership, ward off the third party. If the third party
came anyway, nothing would be more natural, Macune hoped,

231

than for the Confederation to provide its basic structure. In either event, the *Economist* editor gained the broader organizational base that was essential to the formulation of policy.[24]

Yet the "Confederation" was scarcely a bastion of party regularity. At least two of its five affiliates, the National Citizens Alliance and the Colored Farmers National Alliance, were already openly committed to the third party. The Knights of Labor was barely being held in line through a combination of Macune's personal friendship with Knights' leader Terence Powderly and Powderly's innate conservatism. Finally, the signs of growing restlessness in the two other units of confederation, the Illinois-based Farmers Mutual Benefit Association and Macune's own National Farmers Alliance, were only too evident at Ocala. The "Confederation of Industrial Organizations" thus represented a distinct shift to the left for Macune, though he only made the move in order to attain the conservative objective of gaining an additional pulpit from which to resist the third party.[25]

5

The decisive battleground—as Macune, Lamb, and Western radicals all knew—was the South. Sectional legacies from the Civil War ensured that a third party could gain no lasting foothold in the West unless it quickly acquired a national presence. The fears of the Westerners were publicly expressed in the spring of 1891: they did "not intend to be used to elect a Democratic president," and unless the South responded to the call for the Cincinnati conference, "many of the Republican farmers in Kansas and the West will return to their old party allegiance." It was also apparent that if Southern farmers were to be persuaded to break with the party of the fathers, the Alliance founders would have to chart the route. Far more than the Kansans, the Texans possessed the essential sectional credentials to talk to other Southerners about abandoning the Democratic Party—credentials that were augmented by the fact the Texas lecturers had conducted the organizing sweep through the South in the first place. They could share with their Southern brethren the sense of joint accomplishment they had won in their successful war against the jute trust in

1888–90, and they alone could speak with shared sectional urgency about the need to overcome the furnishing merchant through the sub-treasury plan. It seemed apparent to the radicals in both regions that if the Southern Alliances were to join the third party, the Texas Alliance would have to lead the way.[26]

William Lamb proposed to do just that. To some thoughtful Democrats within the Alliance the radical political uses of the sub-treasury, as exploited by Lamb, were no idle threat. In the spring of 1892, after the third-party banner had been successfully raised in the South, a prominent Alliance Democrat publicly stated he had "feared" Lamb for six years and never more so than when the red-headed tactician had made the sub-treasury the fundamental test of Alliance loyalty. But this interpretation, augmented by a hindsight connecting the sub-treasury issue with the formation of the third party, was by no means immediately clear to many ardent Democrats.

It certainly was not clear to Charles Macune. His devotion to the sub-treasury was still dictated by economic considerations, not political ones. Four months after Lamb had forced a declaration on the sub-treasury in Texas, Macune and all other national Alliance leaders expressed approval of the Ocala convention's endorsement of the plan. They went beyond that: they institutionalized the district lecturing system throughout the nation.[27]

An Allianceman's interpretation of the politics of the sub-treasury depended upon his perspective. He could view the Ocala endorsement as the latest expression of a long and consistent Alliance policy aimed at the crop lien, the furnishing merchant, the chattel mortgage—and the national banking system that underlay them all. On the other hand, he could consider endorsement of the sub-treasury as a dramatization, in practical political terms, of the differences between the Alliance and the Southern Democracy. If this relationship was not yet evident at Ocala, not even to Macune, the momentum of political events soon made it so. For under Lamb's projected formula, every·farmer in the National Alliance was to be asked to stand up and be counted on the sub-treasury issue!

The speed with which such a breathtaking assignment could

be achieved depended on the depth of the Alliance organizational structure in each Southern state as well as on the energy and political flexibility of its leadership. Needless to say, these varied from state to state at the beginning of 1891. The one existing certainty was that the winning over of more than a million Southern farmers to the sub-treasury plan constituted a formidable organizational task, one that would require many months of internal discussion and debate.

In the spring of 1891, radical Alliancemen in Texas moved to their task with considerable energy, and the district lecturing schools on the sub-treasury pioneered by Lamb and Perdue were speedily expanded across the state. Additionally, a legislative watchdog committee was established in the state capital under the direction of Harry Tracy. It was to render careful reports of the promised reform program of the incoming Hogg regime. The Tracy committee achieved surprising results in a matter of weeks. In a legislative atmosphere that they found to be crowded with railroad lobbyists, Tracy and the other Alliance committeemen soon lost their respect for "Hogg Democrats." The farmers got one of their state-level demands, a railroad regulatory commission, but little else. Almost all of the anticipated reforms had been bungled, withdrawn, or postponed under relentless corporate lobbying pressure, and Hogg's continued public insistence that his legislative program was succeeding scarcely eased Harry Tracy's doubts about the governor's reforming zeal. Until that moment a loyal Democrat, Tracy broke with the party on the ground that Hogg's reform movement was devoid of substance. Selected Alliance legislators close to Hogg felt the squeeze most tellingly. The Alliance wanted too much—free textbooks in the public schools, a mechanic's lien law, a public usury law, an elective railroad commission, and, in the interim, at least one Alliance farmer named by Hogg to the appointive commission. As the major elements of the farmers' demands were shunted aside and the Hogg administration's counter-program became increasingly watered down or devoted to minor matters, the chorus of anti-Hogg voices in the Alliance grew louder.[28]

Governor Hogg, now deeply concerned, moved to discredit

James Hogg
Hogg's effort to destroy the Alliance movement failed in Texas in the spring of 1891.

the Farmers Alliance. A "manifesto" attacking the Tracy legislative committee as well as the sub-treasury, signed by a half-dozen "Alliance legislators" allied with Hogg, received wide circulation in the state press. The manifesto asserted that Alliance insistence on the sub-treasury foreshadowed a third party, an unnecessary result since the Alliance was strong enough to purify "the leading party, if purity is needed." Though couched in partisan invective and badly garbled in its interpretation of internal Alliance politics, the manifesto was correct in its tactical essentials. Thanks to Lamb's efforts, the line between the Alliance and the Democracy was being blacked in by the sub-treasury issue. But Hogg had blundered: the attack on Tracy, the sub-treasury, and the Alliance came as the internal lecturing program on the sub-treasury was in full swing in suballiances across the state. The close relationship that Harry Tracy had long enjoyed with Macune imparted special significance to Tracy's alienation from the Democratic Party of James Hogg. If, for reasons of geography, Texas had become the tactical centerpiece in the struggle to form a Southern-Western third-party coalition, the diminishing reputation of Hogg in Alliance circles not only upset the Governor, it narrowed the maneuvering room for Macune as well.[29]

Amid mounting evidence that Lamb and the Alliance radicals were winning the Texas battlefield, Macune dropped matters in Washington and went home. He found himself more and more isolated in the polarizing Texas political environment. He had become a political rarity—a Democrat and a sub-treasury advocate. Approached by reporters in Dallas, Macune was asked whether he favored the Democratic side or the sub-treasury side. With some difficulty, he explained to the reporter—who was necessarily not too well informed on the increasing complexity of internal Alliance politics—that he was for the sub-treasury but against a third party, joining the Democrats in the latter sentiment. The contradictions implicit in this stance became more sharply clarified for Macune the longer he stayed in Texas. The crop-mortgaged farmers in the suballiances were discussing his plan with an intensity given no public question in the South since secession, but he could scarcely take comfort in the obvious ramifications of such discussions. Everywhere he went in Alliance circles the sub-treasury had found increasing favor, but more often than not in the context of the need for a third party. After all, Jim Hogg was against the farmers on the sub-treasury![30]

Meanwhile, in a tactically decisive move, the Alliance leadership vastly expanded the already enlarged district lecturing system on the sub-treasury. Evan Jones issued a proclamation calling the "first annual Alliance Conference"—a special four-day statewide "educational" meeting in Waco on April 21, 1891, for the express purpose of "perfecting the lecturing system." Macune could hardly oppose such a program, but he had read enough signs to take some precautions. He arranged to have three well-known national Alliance Democrats—Lon Livingston, Democratic Congressman and state president of the Georgia Alliance, E. T. Stackhouse, Democratic Congressman from South Carolina, and Alonzo Wardall, Macune's co-operative associate from the South Dakota Alliance—invited to the April conference.[31]

Yet the spread of third-party sentiment within the highest echelons of the Texas Alliance was evidenced by other guest speakers invited to Waco, all recruited from the membership roles of the National Reform Press Association: Henry Vincent and M. L. Wilkins of the *American Nonconformist* and Ralph Beaumont of the *National Citizens Alliance* of Washington. The tactical importance of the Texas Alliance was now well understood by both factions of reformers throughout the nation. Both had used their national bases in reform organizations to mobilize their forces.[32]

The *Economist* editor could throw his own prestige and oratorical persuasiveness into the battle, but even this could almost be balanced by the popularity and verbal skill of the Alliance state president, Evan Jones. By any standard, the preparations by both sides indicated general agreement that the Waco meeting had assumed crucial importance for the political future of the National Alliance and the third party as well. As for the sub-treasury, both Alliance factions were, of course, fully committed: on the eve of the Waco meeting, that was the one certainty accruing from thirteen years of Alliance experience with the furnishing merchants of Texas.

This latter circumstance was lost on the metropolitan press as well as on the leaders of the Hogg Democracy. Both were far removed from the economic travail of American farmers that undergirded the agrarian revolt. From the relatively prosperous perspective of Democratic politicians and the major Texas dailies, a battle was expected at the Alliance meeting—but the internal schism in the farm organization was presumed to concern Alliancemen dedicated to Hogg and Alliancemen loyal to Macune and the sub-treasury plan. The Texas press had reported that the Farmers Alliance was "splitting" on the issue of Hogg and the sub-treasury, and the Waco meeting was expected to illustrate its dimensions.[33]

It was with some dismay, then, that reporters discovered during the first two days of the Waco meeting that the Texas Alliance was "united" behind its "official family." To the eyes of the press, this included Macune, Evan Jones, Lamb, Perdue, Tracy, and Ashby and extended to such visitors as Ralph Beaumont, Henry Vincent, and E. T. Stackhouse.

In general, the Waco meeting seemed to border on a mass celebration. "Stump" Ashby was "the favorite," the "famous agitator and humorist," while Evan Jones, "sadly needing a patch on his pants," was "by odds the most popular leader." Taken together, the Alliance "official family" was "now in the heyday of power and popularity," while the half-dozen or so Hoggites among the 400 Alliance county leaders were "discouraged." [34]

But this solidarity existed only when the Alliance leadership was described in terms of personalities rather than policies. The truth was that esteem and policy making had, in the case of Charles Macune, ceased to be mutually supporting elements. Though the "nonpartisan" *Economist* editor was the best known Allianceman in America, he publicly revealed his inability to enunciate a clear policy for the order. In the name of the sub-treasury, he stood for legislative political action, though not for the only method through which it could be obtained, namely independent political action. Because both major parties had rejected the sub-treasury, the politics of the issue left Alliance "nonpartisans" such as Macune defenseless against the simple political logic of the order's radicals. This situation became clear in Texas in April 1891, as it was to become clear in Georgia in the spring of 1892 and in other parts of the South later in the same year. Macune's words at Waco revealed both the extreme delicacy of his position and his uncertainty about his own future course:

> I remember that five years ago, the Alliance was afraid of politics, but the order has got bravely over that . . . and if it is necessary as a method of accomplishing their aims to enter the ranks of politics and dislodge some of the leaders hereabouts, they are equal to the emergency. . . . I have learned a great deal since joining the order and expect to learn more. I felt when I first joined I could give a better description of its objects than I can today. . . . I am not afraid of politics. . . . But . . . let us use it as a method, never as an object.[35]

Those were no longer the words of a man who was leading. Nor were they the most applauded parts of his speech. On April 22, 1891, a day he described "as the proudest of my life," the *Economist* editor reached the pinnacle of his personal standing in the agrarian movement. The next day, the passage of the Southern Alliances into independent political action began with the Texas Alliance's decision to send delegates to the Cincinnati convention.

In sudden increments of discovery, the four-day Waco meeting materialized before observing reporters as a series of shocks, each more startling than its predecessor: unanimity of support for the anti-Hogg legislative committee; an emotional outpouring of affection and loyalty for Macune, rising to "deafening" ovations each time he made guarded allusions to the possibility of independent political action; the formation of radical new institutions headed by Lamb, Ashby, and a third radical named W. E. Farmer; and, finally, evidence of the emergence of "the third party movement" as the dominant political influence in the Texas Alliance. By the week's end, interest among reporters in "Democratic Alliancemen" had dissolved and was replaced by inquiries concerning "the new party crusade." The immediate business, the mobilization of a statewide lecturing system on the sub-treasury, was obscured by the heavy ideological cannonading that seemed to be emanating from every Alliance rostrum throughout the meeting.[36]

The pace of events was rapid. On the first day Lamb attempted to engender leadership agreement to dispatch a delegation to Cincinnati; it ran afoul of Macune's contention that the Alliance, as an organization, could not commit itself officially to a specific party. On the second day a compromise was reached to permit the decision to be made by individual caucuses in the congressional districts. The shifting center of gravity became still clearer on the third day of the conference when the Alliance radicals narrowly lost a series of indirect test votes on the third party issue by margins of 85 to 83 and 82 to 81. Debate was not heated, as the radicals, and perhaps most of the delegates, were intent on appraising the political pulse of the order. Another compromise was quietly achieved. The radicals agreed to confine further third party exhortation to separate meetings already scheduled in Waco; in exchange, the Texas Alliance would send delegates to Cincinnati. The same day, before "large and enthusiastic" crowds of third-party advocates in the Waco courthouse, two new institutions were created—the Texas Citizens Alliance and the Texas Reform Press Association. The press association's new president was William Lamb and its vice president was to be the editor of the *Southern Mercury,* the official journal of the State Alliance. The Texas Citizens Alliance was organized as an affiliate of the overtly third-party National Citizens Alliance. Its secretary-treasurer was William Lamb.[37]

Taken together, these events produced a new view of the meaning of the "first annual Farmers Alliance conference." The Waco *News* confessed it had found the conference truly "educational" and, in reporting on the Alliance county presidents and lecturers, said that "one is forced to suspect that they have been to school before." "Enough has been learned," the paper added, to conclude that the meeting "has a political significance of no mean importance" and that "the third party is in fact, a probability." The editor attached special significance to the election of Lamb both as president of the Texas Reform Press Association and as the secretary-treasurer of the Texas Citizens Alliance. He surmised that since membership in the Citizens Alliance "requires every member to renounce his allegiance to both old parties . . . the work of 'reforming' the press will go hand in hand with the work of educating the people." [38]

When the newspaper editor singled out William Lamb as a causative agent, he was closer to the mark than he knew. In conceiving the political tactics of the sub-treasury, Lamb had integrated the lecturing system and the reform press into an effective instrument of political democracy. As events were soon to show, the "politics of the sub-treasury" was the critical tactical instrument needed in the South to "draw the line" between the farmers' loyalty to their Alliance and their inherited sectional loyalty to the party of the fathers. It made them confront the reality of the credit system in ways that had tangible political meaning. In this manner, William Lamb provided the South with a model through which the Alliance could be brought to Populism.

Yet there was a much deeper meaning to the events at Waco in the spring of 1891. The "first annual Farmers Alliance Conference" revealed how William Lamb, Charles Macune, and Alliancemen generally had been lifted by their collective cooperative efforts to a new plateau of democratic possibility. In strictly ideological terms, it may be said that Alliance radicalism—the greenback interpretation of American finance capitalism—*was* Populism. Though asserted as a theoretical interpretation of the meaning and uses of currency, the greenback creed reflected a certain kind of democratic understanding of a just society. But beyond the ideology of democracy rests its human component and it was in this realm that Populism demonstrated something new—something that went beyond the subject of money: greenback doctrines had spread to the great host of Alliance farmers through, and because of, the vivid movement culture generated by the cooperative crusade itself. This democratic ethos armed individual Alliance farmers to perform a most difficult act—to break with one's political heritage. Whether in the South or West, the process of turning on one's old party required a new kind of individual autonomy and self-respect, as well as the knowledge that one was not alone, that one was participating in a new kind of collective self-confidence. Both the individual self-respect and the collective self-confidence were grounded in the democratic environment of the suballiances and were nourished by the many ingredients that comprised the Alliance cooperative effort: the election of suballiance business agents and county trade committees, the erection of cooperative warehouses, the give and take of explanations and understandings between Alliance lecturers and the members of the brotherhood, and, of course, the visionary state exchange that embodied the deepest hopes of everyone for freedom from the American credit system. All of these acts were "practical" demonstrations of democratic striving; but there was something else, something that might be called the ritual celebration of success: cloth flags flying from wagons heading home after a successful "bulking" sale of one's crop, a private celebration; or the collective one, with the whole brotherhood and sisterhood in long wagon trains leading to massive rallies and encampments · and culminating in twilight meals for thousands. And if, as inevitably happened, there came speeches about the "new day for the industrial millions," followed by "cheers for the Speaker and for the Alliance," these were also cheers for oneself, for one's new vision of hope and for one's new self-confidence that had come to life in the democratic environment of the Alliance. Taken in all its parts, Populism was something more than the greenback interpretation of American capitalism, it was what the gifted greenback theoretician, Harry Tracy, called "the spirit that permeates this great reform movement." Simply enough, that "spirit" was the expression of pride—an individual pride that had been encouraged to flourish by the appearance of the collective pride of the Alliance itself.

The link that connected the people of the Alliance, that carried the hopes of the many forward to their elected leaders and carried the response of the same leaders back to the brotherhood, was the far-flung Alliance lecturing system. Here lay the essential democratic communications network within the movement and it was this ingredient that William Lamb mobilized in the spring of 1891 for yet one more post-Civil War attempt to bring a democratic "new day" to America. Through the politics of the sub-treasury, with its vividly direct connection to the crop lien system of the South, Lamb put the movement culture that had grown up out of the cooperative crusade to its ultimate test against the received culture of inherited sectional loyalty to the "party of the fathers." [39]

Ironically, the behind-the-scenes struggle of William Lamb and Charles Macune over Alliance policy at Waco marked the intersection of their influence in the agrarian crusade. For the time thereafter available to both, Lamb's impact on policy increased while Macune's declined, as the radicalism Lamb had engendered at Cleburne in 1886 continued to transform the national organization Macune had envisioned at Waco in 1887. Though their long ideological conflict did not finally culminate for another nineteen months, their debts to each other were already plain at Waco in April 1891 and could be summarized in three facts: Lamb's radicalism, splitting the Alliance founders in 1886, brought Macune to power; Macune's organizational creativity constructed a national constituency of farmers that made possible Lamb's dream of a third party of the laboring classes; and their shared objective, economic parity for farmers in an industrial society, was symbolized in the sub-treasury plan, which Macune conceived as an instrument of economic reform and Lamb converted into one of political revolt. In the process, the stakes were substantially raised. The struggle to free the Southern farmer from the furnishing merchant was subsumed in the struggle to bring economic redress to "the industrial millions." It was a contest Macune felt could not be won, and one Lamb felt had to be waged. The respective successes of William Lamb and Charles Macune and the partisan attacks these successes inspired against each, plus their own actions, eventually used up the political credit of both. A third casualty was the sub-treasury plan. The achievement was the creation of a multi-sectional institution of reform: the People's Party.

6

In the state conventions of the Alliance across the South in the summer and fall of 1891, Alliance leaders were asked to stand up and be counted on the sub-treasury. In Democratic defections from Alliance membership the cost was sometimes substantial, but at whatever cost, the line was drawn. As Lamb had demonstrated in Texas, it marked out the starting point for the People's Party in the South. However painfully—and it was quite painful in some states—the politics of the sub-treasury, fashioned some twenty-six years after Appomattox, became the sword that cut the ancestral bonds to the party of the fathers. Macune's sub-treasury, in Lamb's hands, defeated Macune and created Southern Populism.

CHAPTER IX

The High Tide of Alliance Radicalism: Formation of the People's Party

"They're Here! The Great Industrial Army!"

In the opening campaign of 1892, the strength of the People's Party across the West and South essentially measured whether or not the organized farmers of the Alliance in each state had managed to break with their political past and make the full trek to the new party. Where they did, the third party was an immediate political factor; where they did not, it was not. In general, the depth and duration of the cooperative experience in a state, culminating in the lecturing campaign on the sub-treasury, was the single most significant element in this politics of transition, though such other factors as the dexterity of the opposition and the personality of individual agrarian spokesmen also affected events in important ways. The personal determination and platform eloquence of Thomas Watson was a prominent element in bringing Populism to Georgia, while the cunning and deceit of Ben Tillman destroyed the Alliance and the third party in South Carolina. Outside influences in 1890 helped bring a form of insurgency to Nebraska despite the hesitancy of the state's agrarian spokesmen, while in Tennessee a huge agrarian organization became immobilized by the indecisive tactics of its leaders. The planter-industrialist conservatives of Alabama saddled the reform cause with unforeseen problems of fraudulent elections, while simple violence helped to intimidate a large Mississippi Alliance into submissiveness. Finally, those state Alliances in the West and South that had failed for whatever reason to recruit the bulk of their farmers into the cooperative movement by 1891,—Iowa, Illinois, Louisiana, Virginia and Wisconsin among them—simply possessed no opportunity to engage seriously in the politics of reform.

These are retrospective conclusions, available after the successes and failures of the agrarian revolt could be subjected to the insights of time. In 1891–92, the needs of the third party cause were visible in simpler ways. First, radicals were desperately anxious to raise the flag of revolt, to serve as a lure for the hesitant and to add confidence to the already converted. The third party's organic structure had to be created. Additionally, if the People's Party were not to go the way of its Greenback and Union Labor predecessors, the Southern Alliances somehow had to be rallied to radicalism. And, finally, momentum for reform had constantly to be accelerated—from as many podiums and with as many voices as earnest radicals could find. It was against this background of priorities that the nation's agrarian spokesmen gathered in Cincinnati in 1891 in yet another post-Civil War attempt to fashion a multi-sectional political solution to the stifling two-party politics of sectionalism.

2

"THEY'RE HERE! THE GREAT INDUSTRIAL ARMY!" proclaimed the headlines of the Cincinnati *Enquirer* of May 18, 1891. Many agrarian "generals" were, indeed, present—Jerry Simpson from Kansas, Ignatius Donnelly from Minnesota, and James B. Weaver, the old Greenback presidential candidate, from Iowa. But after one day to assess the ranks, it was apparent that the "army," as well as its leadership, was geographically unbalanced. The Eastern states were unrepresented and "cut no figure." Third-party men were also deeply disappointed in the delegations from the South. Except for

Arkansas and Texas, only one or two delegates appeared from most of the Southern states. Moreover, as in the case of Lon Livingston of Georgia, some of the Southern men arrived to oppose a third party. Also on hand, not as a delegate but in his journalistic capacity as president of the National Reform Press Association, was C. W. Macune.[1]

Among the 1400 reformers in Cincinnati were large delegations from the Western plains states, over 400 from Kansas alone. They were divided over tactics, some favoring the immediate formation of the third party, others wishing to wait until the scheduled February 1892 meeting called under the Macune compromise by the National Alliance at Ocala. The latter group, including such radicals as Weaver of Iowa and Simpson of Kansas, thought it expedient to let the South finish its experiment in reform through the Democrats. Others, notably the loquacious Ignatius Donnelly of Minnesota and Illinois state legislator H. E. Taubeneck, believed that organizational work on the third-party structure had to begin immediately.[2]

All, however, were deeply worried about the absent South. The Texas delegates, headed by William Lamb, R. M. Humphrey of the Colored Alliance, and the rising agrarian orator, James H. "Cyclone" Davis, were questioned closely about the development of the third-party movement in their state. Radical editors in the Reform Press Association who had attended the Waco conference, including Vincent, Wilkins, and Beaumont, were in a good position to join Lamb in assuring the anxious Western delegates that Texas was ready. W. Scott Morgan was able to provide evidence that the Arkansas Alliance was ready, too. But a national third-party movement could not be built solely upon the votes of the trans-Mississippi West, even if it did extend from Canada to the Gulf. The Union Labor Party experience had proved that. Where was most of the South?[3]

Even before Cincinnati, Westerners had been quoted as suspecting that Southern Alliance leaders were only "pretending to favor a new party" while actually being committed to the Democratic Party "at all times and at all circumstances." The Southerners were reported to be stalling on the third party until the February 1892 meeting, when it would be "too late" to form a new party, thus giving them "an excuse to stick to their own party" and encouraging Republican agrarians in the West to vote an independent ticket. In short, Western radicals were afraid they were being used to elect a Democratic president in 1892. Sectionalism, the bane of the Alliance movement since 1888, clearly exerted a visible presence in 1891. Conservatives, North and South, contented themselves with the thought that "the prospect of uniting the North and South in a third party movement appears almost hopeless." [4]

Political observers everywhere had watched the stance of the Alliance national president, L. L. Polk of North Carolina, ever since the Alliance election sweep of 1890 and the subsequent Ocala convention had first made the third party movement a national conversation piece. Polk did not sound like a traditional Southern Democrat. In the aftermath of Ocala he had warned Democrats that the Alliance would insist upon the sub-treasury, the abolition of national banks and government ownership of railroads. The order would not accept such pap as "free silver" or other minor reforms as addressing the real needs of the farmer. In February, Polk described Grover Cleveland as a "true and consistent friend of the money power," unacceptable to Alliancemen. Shortly thereafter, another influence was brought to bear on Polk—that of Charles Macune. The radicalism of the Waco meeting of the Texas Alliance had achieved a notable impact on the *Economist* editor, and once back in Washington he seemed for the first time to be publicly welcoming independent political action.[5]

But at the time of the Cincinnati meeting, Polk did not yet feel it expedient to declare in favor of the third party. He sent a message to the convention, asking them to address a "manly declaration" to the country and wait until February 1892 before proceeding further. An Arkansas delegate drew applause when he suggested that the convention "sit down on that communication in no uncertain terms." The fact remained, however, that excepting the state Alliances of Texas and Arkansas, neither the order in the South nor its national leadership provided any evidence that the decisive third-party step was near. Nothing had happened since the Ocala meeting to alter the fact that Southerners were going to spend 1891 testing "reform through the Democrats." The Cincinnati convention had to accept the reality that the "great industrial army" could not march without its Southern regiments. A provisional national committee of the People's Party, headed by H. E. Taubeneck of Illinois, was established, but little else could be done except to hope that the Southern Alliances would find a way to forsake the party of the fathers.[6]

3

Third party partisans got some help from the business interests of the South. Throughout 1891, as southern state legislatures were put to the test on the "Alliance yardstick" of legislative reform, the business orientation of the party of the fathers revealed itself. One by one, the legislatures of the Southern states did not produce "reform through the Democrats." Whether Democratic officeholders styled themselves as traditional "states' rights" conservatives or as "Alliance Democrats," the intellectual and political distance between themselves and the farmers became all too evident. To Alliance radicals, of course, this denouement was predictable. Given the close railroad connections and the resulting political support enjoyed by both varieties of Democrats, neither could be expected to press for the kind of serious government regulation that farmers regarded as their only safeguard against continued railroad abuses. As for the one obvious political anomaly among the Democratic governors, South Carolina's Ben Tillman, Southern radicals regarded the "Pitchfork Man" as a transparent charlatan who was far more dedicated to the building of a personal political career than to leading a party revolution.[7]

In general, the Southern situation provided promising soil for tillers of the sub-treasury. Sometimes orchestrated through specially constituted lecturing systems organized by congressional districts, and sometimes not, the politics of the sub-treasury began to penetrate downward to the thousands of suballiances across the South in 1891. Beginning in the summer and extending into the following spring, state alliances formally declared for the sub-treasury as the essential element of the "full Ocala Platform." The battle for the political allegiance of the Southern yeomanry was on.

4

Nowhere did the radical imperative to break the loyalty of Southern farmers to the party of the fathers produce a more tense and vivid political struggle than in Georgia. In this heartland of the Old Confederacy, the sprawling Georgia Alliance became a dramatic and bitter battleground, as the state's press and politicians watched anxiously and, wherever possible, added their influence on the side of orthodoxy. To many observers, the struggle for the soul of the Georgia Alliance appeared to be a war between two rival captains—Lon Livingston, Alliance state president, and Tom Watson, radical agitator. Though a measure of truth graces this assessment, Livingston and Watson were symbols of a decision-making process that ultimately had to find its resolution through the individual choices of thousands of Georgia farmers.

The Georgia struggle came to embrace almost all of the nineteenth-century political realities that had been called into question by the growth of the cooperative movement in the South. Watson threw the "living issues" of the Alliance into a new political dialogue where they immediately encountered all the old shibboleths through which business-oriented "New South Democrats" had come to exercise political dominance in the state. Foremost was the matter of loyalty to the Democrats as the party of white supremacy. To Watson, loyalty to the principles of the Alliance was the central issue. The third party was necessary because it provided the only avenue through which those principles could be expressed. The platform of the Alliance, said Watson, "is sacred to us because it gives hope to our despair; gives expression to our troubles; gives voice to our wants. Our wives have knelt and prayed for it. Our children have learned to love it. [There is] not a church in all the land, where God's blessing has not been invoked upon it." As early as the summer of 1889, Watson had sensed the long-term implications of the Alliance organizing message. "A new era had dawned in Georgia politics," he said. "The old order of things is passing away. The masses are be-

ginning to arouse themselves, reading for themselves, thinking for themselves. The great currents of thought quicken
new impulses. At the bar of public opinion the people are
pressing their demands and insisting that they be heard." [8]

Near the end of his life Watson fondly recalled the "radiant
visions" of the years of struggle in the 1890's: "I did not lead
the Alliance; I followed the Alliance, and I am proud that I
did follow it." The remark may well have been over-generous.
Given the forces of traditionalism arrayed against the third
party movement in the state, it is doubtful if nearly as many
Georgia Alliancemen would have become Populists had it not
been for the dramatic and tireless leadership provided by
Tom Watson. Yet the relationship of the movement to the
movement's spokesman was necessarily a mutually supportive
one. Watson's audiences in Georgia were responsive because,
in the words of his biographer, they had been "saturated by
their lecturers, by debates, and by Alliance reform literature,
with facts and figures and queer ideas and heresies of all descriptions, shouting their slogans and singing Alliance songs."
For his part, Watson knew that the crop lien, and the systems
of politics and justice that supported it, was the source both of
the despair of the Georgia countryside and of the hope represented by the Alliance. "Here is a tenant—I do not know, or
care, whether he is white or black, I know his story. . . . He
knows what an order to the store means. He knows perfectly
well that he cannot get goods as cheap as for cash. . . . The
contrast between the status of the southern farmer before the
war and at the present time is indeed discouraging. . . . Like
victims of some horrid nightmare, we have moved ever
since—powerless—oppressed—shackled." The system "tears a
tenant from his family and puts him in chains and stripes
because he sells cotton for something to eat and leaves his rent
unpaid." When such a system cannot punish its "railroad
kings," it was "weak unto rottenness." [9]

Yet beyond the language of reform, Watson understood—a
good deal earlier than most of the thousands of his followers
in the suballiances—that reform movements require tactics
and strategy. He knew the Alliance dream had to take the political form of a coalition of the South and West, in direct op-

Watson versus Livingston

The sprawling Georgia Alliance became a "dramatic and bitter battle-ground" in 1891–92 as the agrarian crusade moved into its political phase. Congressman Tom Watson, left, emerged as the spokesman of the radicals, while Congressman Lon Livingston, right, tried to hold the farmers within the "party of the fathers." Populists wrote a campaign song about their conflict. (See page 275.)

position to the other alternative of a Southern-Eastern coalition of industrialists. The ascendancy of the latter since the Civil War had skewered popular democracy and left captains of industry and finance in firm control, whichever party temporarily exercised national leadership. With special urgency, Watson pushed the idea of a Southern-Western reform coalition: "Today, there stands waiting in the South and West as grand an army as ever brought pride to a warrior. It only needs leaders bold and true. . . . We know what we want; let us take nothing else." [10]

But though the issues were clear, the political path to their implementation was far less so. Even as Livingston signaled clearly his intention of staying with the party of the fathers, Watson began to maneuver for tactical ground with broader options. Addressing the Georgia Assembly two months after the Cincinnati convention, Watson indicated—in words that only seemed elliptical—his steady progression toward third party rebellion.

> We are in the midst of a great crisis. . . . We have before us three or four platforms, the republican platform, the democratic platform, and the Ocala platform. I say here and now that the Ocala platform is the best of all three. It is the only one that breathes the breath of life. . . . Let third party talk take care of itself. I have none of it to do, but . . . let the democratic party take warning. We have borne your ridicule long enough, we will bear it no longer. I am going to bear the Ocala platform wherever my voice can be heard.[11]

The words were those of a committed politician who knows he must move one step at a time in league with his supporters. In emphasizing the distinctions between the Ocala Platform and the Georgia Democracy, Watson consciously moved to foment properly radical preconditions for the decisive choices yet to be made in 2000 Georgia suballiances. Yet it took a while for such a process to work. A short time after his legislative address, Watson challenged Livingston's control over the Georgia Alliance at the order's August state convention. Though the sub-treasury plan was approved, Watson's radical candidate for state Alliance president met defeat at the hands of Livingston. Even more ominously, a resolution instructing Georgia Congressmen to vote for no man for Speaker of the United States House unless he endorsed Alliance principles was also defeated because of Livingston's influence. Throughout Georgia, Livingston's position within the Alliance appeared invulnerable. He knew the rhetoric of revolt and could hurl thunderbolts at railroad barons with every bit of the fervor of a Tillman in South Carolina or a Hogg in Texas. He could avoid the taint of conservative party leaders by questioning their actions, as he did Governor Northen's, meanwhile following a conservative strategy of Democratic party loyalty. Above all, Livingston had the command posts within the Alliance. He was not only state president, but also the guiding political influence over the Alliance official state newspaper, the *Southern Alliance Farmer*.[12]

It was from this position of relative isolation that Tom Watson renewed his struggle to define the political issues in language the farmers of Georgia could grasp. Beginning in October 1891 Watson made two alterations in his argument—he began to put renewed emphasis on the sub-treasury plan and he got himself a newspaper to carry the message. Watson's journal unfurled itself on October 1, 1891, as *The People's Party Paper* even as the politics of the sub-treasury became the center of attention in the Georgia suballiances. The following month the Supreme Council of the National Alliance held its 1891 meeting in Indianapolis in a setting that illustrated the impact a year of lackluster "reform through the Democrats" had had on a number of Southern Alliance spokesmen. With Livingston and Watson watching carefully, the National Alliance provided Watson with his first significant victory in the struggle to lead Georgia's farmers. On the same issue on which he had met defeat in the Georgia Alliance convention—the loyalty of congressional Alliancemen to the Ocala Platform—the National Alliance solemnly implored all Congressmen elected "by the aid of Alliance constituencies" not to participate "in any party caucus called to designate a candidate for speaker, unless adherence to the principles of the Ocala platform are made a test of admission to said caucus." The vote was heavy with third party overtones for the National Alliance, and for Georgia, too.[13]

Like the *People's Party Paper* in Georgia, L. L. Polk's *Progressive Farmer* in North Carolina focused increasingly on the sub-treasury. The Macune plan was "the one real living issue . . . the other demands are subordinate to this one." Polk and his editor broke over the issue and the latter left the newspaper in June 1891. Smaller Alliance journals joined the chorus. "The sub-treasury is the most essential demand in the Alliance platform," asserted the *Farmers Advocate* of Tarboro, North Carolina.[14]

Alabama reform editors, supported by the state Alliance president, flocked to the sub-treasury standard. "The people are learning that the sub-treasury means more money, more liberty and final freedom from serfdom," said one. "They believe it and all Hades cannot prevail against it." Another re-

form paper added that the sub-treasury was "the main piller
. . . if this plank is knocked out, the whole structure is
ruined." A farmer punctuated the judgment: "Hurrah for
Ocala, first, last, and forever! Amen." The Alabama state president, S. M. Adams, declared the Ocala Platform to be official
policy in the spring of 1891 and by the summer he had decided the financial question had come to the front and that it,
in turn, was headed by the sub-treasury plan. The national
banks, he said, were "conceived in sin and born in diabolical
inequity." In South Carolina, too, embattled Alliance radicals
seized upon the sub-treasury in a desperate effort to "draw
the line" between the South Carolina Alliance and Pitchfork
Ben Tillman.[15]

To outsiders the full implications of these furious controversies were not always much better understood than when
the Texas Alliance took the same step in the summer of 1890.
But the same internal dynamics were at work. To all who
looked, the politics of the sub-treasury measured the strength,
reform instinct, and internal cohesion of the Alliance movement in each of the Southern states. The votes varied from
near unanimity among the county leaders of the Florida and
Arkansas Alliances to an ominous postponement in Tennessee, where the issue came at an awkward moment in the political life of John Buchanan, the Alliance state president. The
difficulty in Tennessee centered on the fact that Democrat
Buchanan also occupied the gubernatorial chair, a circumstance that made him pause before launching a tactical campaign to draw a line between the Alliance on the one hand
and the Democratic Party on the other. After much behind-
the-scenes maneuvering, the Tennessee Alliance trimmed its
sails on the Ocala Platform and postponed any and all tests of
sentiment until 1892. The decision effectivively destroyed the
third-party movement in the state.[16]

In Mississippi the politics of the sub-treasury erupted amid
the 1891 state elections. Alliance leader Frank Burkitt was
forced to throw the sub-treasury into battle against the state's
planter Democrats even as a district lecturing system was mobilized for internal "Alliance education" on the same issue. As
a result, the importance of the time factor in completing the

organizational sequence to insurgency was clearly revealed. The Bourbon Democracy, led by Senator James Z. George, opposed Macune's plan. In George the anti-subtreasurites had the advantage of incumbency, but the Alliance forces had a prestigious spokesman also. George's opponent was a man with a name to be reckoned with in Mississippi, Ethelbert Barksdale. The pace of events, however, did not permit the Mississippi Alliance to utilize properly its internal lecturing system, so that the intricacies of the sub-treasury were brought home to Mississippi farmer as a part of the campaign itself. Though stump oratory was hardly the best medium for dissecting an issue as unusual and controversial as the sub-treasury, "immense crowds" attended both George and Barksdale wherever they spoke. The same constituencies tended to show up at rallies for both men. The farmers of Mississippi, wracked by racial phobias but wracked also by a generation of living under the crop lien, were plainly in a volatile state. Alliance leaders were encouraged while Democratic regulars privately expressed deep concern.[17]

The public press of Mississippi became stridently engaged. Bourbon newspapers established a steady drumfire against the sub-treasury. The reform press, led by Burkitt's *Choctaw County Messenger,* replied with earnest justifications of the plan and blunt reminders of the facts of life under the crop lien system. Burkitt, the state lecturer of the Mississippi Alliance, took to the campaign trail and by example showed the order's county lecturers how to put the politics of the sub-treasury to work in the reform cause. In bone-poor Mississippi, Burkitt clearly scored telling points. By the early fall observers privately agreed that the Mississippi electorate, centered in the huge (60,000-member) state Alliance, could not be counted in anyone's camp. A new kind of Southern politics had come to Mississippi.[18]

In October an older politics reasserted itself. Night riders descended on Frank Burkitt's *Choctaw County Messenger.* They set the building afire and destroyed the printing press. The courthouse at Pontotoc was broken into and all the voter registration books were "stolen or concealed or probably burnt." The mood of the campaign altered. The canvass became "one of the meanest ever conducted in the state," and the audiences became quieter. Mississippians were thinking things over, but since they no longer talked as freely no one could be certain of the situation. On election day, Senator George and the regular Mississippi Democracy won a clear-cut victory.

Party regulars, aware that the returns were misleading, privately conceded that the election had been a near thing. The old order had repelled the first attack, but the margin of victory—and perhaps even more—had been a product of the final stages of the campaign. Aside from a ramshackle political appparatus that involved state and county officeholders, local judges, and sheriffs, and the numerically small business community that existed in agricultural Mississippi, the Democratic Party's hard-core support had come from the furnishing merchants, many of whom had become large landowners over the years. The great mass of Mississippi people remained poor farmers, a fact the Democracy belatedly focused upon. The party's public appearance, so long neglected, definitely required face-lifting for any future engagements with its impoverished electorate—perhaps something along the lines Hogg had followed in Texas, or perhaps something resembling the Tillman regime in South Carolina. Whatever route was to be taken, the farmers clearly needed to be diverted from wild schemes like the sub-treasury. The plan itself, in all events, needed to be discredited. Such were the post-election imperatives facing Mississippi's Democratic chieftains. From the perspective of Alliance leaders, the postmortem conclusion was much simpler: it had all happened too quickly. They had not had enough time.[19]

In the Arkansas Alliance the near unanimity of support for the sub-treasury was misleading. The explanation for that lies in the history of Arkansas radicalism. The early militance of the Agricultural Wheel in Arkansas had carried the order to an internal political controversy in 1886 that was remarkably similar to the Texas experience at Cleburne in the same year. The Arkansas radicals, however, made a fundamental error that the Texans might well have committed had it not been for the diplomatic skills of Macune. The numerically dominant left wing of the Arkansas Wheel forced its political demands upon the order and literally drove their "nonpartisan" Democratic colleagues into the wilderness. "Education" could scarcely take place when the would-be pupils were no longer in the classroom. Reduced in size, but in the full swing of political revolt against the established conservative Democracy, Wheelers in 1888 formed a covert coalition with Republicans under the label of the Union Labor Party and ran a strong race against the old regime. The Democrats thereupon juggled thousands of votes and stole the election. The official returns showed 99,214 votes for the Democratic gubernatorial candidate and 84,213 votes for the Union Labor standard-bearer. In the aftermath, as a careful perusal of the election returns revealed the pattern of Wheel-Republican cooperation, the Arkansas press lectured the state's voters both on their narrow escape and the future perils of "Negro domination." When a Wheel leader provided New York newspapers with the grisly details of vote frauds by Democrats, the metropolitan press denounced the order for bringing the state's honor into disrepute among Yankees.[20]

The press campaign was effective, but since the Wheel had already dispatched its Democratically inclined members in 1886, the remaining stalwarts were able to hold their lines substantially intact. In 1890 Wheel candidates ran a strong race principally because of a large Negro vote. By that time it was clear that the agrarian movement in Arkansas could not rally more than about a fourth of the state's white farmers. The order's endorsement of the sub-treasury plan by a 69 to 1 vote in the state convention of 1891 thus did not have the meaning it carried in other Southern states, where farmer-Democrats had remained in the Alliance environment long enough to measure the possibilities of independent political action. In 1892 the agrarian movement in Arkansas was, as it had always been, convincingly dedicated to reform; along the way, it had ceased to be the organizational gathering place for most of the state's farmers.[21]

5

By the end of 1891, the politics of the sub-treasury across the South had clearly forced thousands of Alliancemen to make individual political decisions. The year-end Indianapolis gathering of the National Alliance revealed clearly that the Kansans and Texans had required a number of third party allies in the ranks of the Southern Alliance leadership. Foremost among them was the order's national president, Leonidas Polk of North Carolina.

As his performance in the Kansas campaign of 1890 revealed, Polk's pace toward independent political action had quickened almost from the moment of his election as National Alliance president. His speeches against partisan exploitation of sectionalism by both major parties defined the meaning of Alliance "nonpartisanship" in broad new strokes. Though Polk's refusal to commit himself openly to the third party at the time of the Cincinnati meeting in May 1891 had not been well received by Alliance radicals, he privately conveyed a revealing personal decision to his son-in-law: "Let 'em rage. I will come in on the home stretch." [22]

After corporate lobbyists had stifled the central feature of the Alliance program of "reform through the Democrats" in state after state across the South in 1891, Polk became more precise in his condemnations of the Southern Democracy. By the time of the Indianapolis meeting, Polk had found his "home stretch." His presidential address to the delegates was a clear and emphatic assault on the old parties. He advised the farmer leaders "to be deceived no longer" by "arrogant party dictation" and provided a demonstration of how a united third party might parry the blows of sectional agitators in both parties.

> To the charge that we selfishly seek the promotion of only class interest, we have only to point to our legislative records of a quarter of a century—every page of which is burdened with legislation glaringly partial and in favor of other classes.
>
> To the charge that our policy tends to centralization of government power, we have only to point to the fearful encroachments of irresponsible corporate power upon the functions of government. . . . To the charge that our organization is dominated by Southern influence, we have only to call the roll of this body to find that of the thirty-four states comprising it, twenty-three of them are denominated Northern states.

Not the war of twenty-five years ago . . . but the gigantic
struggle of today between the classes and the masses . . . is
the supreme incentive and object of this great political revolution. In the appalling presence of such an issue, buried
and forgotten forever be the prejudices, animosities, and
estrangements of that unfornate war.[23]

Polk's address, which drew "thunderous ovations" from the
Alliance leadership gathered from across the nation, uniquely
symbolized much of what the agrarian revolt had been since
the days of the Cleburne Demands in 1886—Southern in origin,
national in purpose, radical in ideology. As one newspaper reporter put it after Polk finished, the election of anyone else as
Alliance president for the coming year of struggle "would
have been regarded as a blow to the People's Party." [24]

Yet Polk's reelection was not the only indication of the ascendancy of third party sentiment among Alliance leaders.
Named as vice president was Henry Loucks of South Dakota—
a provocative choice since at Cincinnati Loucks had been
named to the provisional national executive committee of the
new People's Party. The thrust of the Indianapolis meeting
thus was strongly in the direction of independent political action. Press accounts said that the People's Party representatives, led by the provisional national chairman H. E. Taubeneck, were "happy as clams." So was Tom Watson. *The
People's Party Paper* declared that "Georgia is ready for a third
party and will sweep the state with the movement." [25]

6

All across the Northwest in 1890–91, however, the ill-starred
Northwestern Alliance slowly disappeared from the agrarian
revolt. In Minnesota the sheer momentum of the Loucks-War-
dall-Donnelly cooperative campaign had seemed to carry the
order to new heights of membership in the early months of
1890. Ignatius Donnelly had been euphoric at the prospect of
waging a full-fledged reform campaign at the head of organized legions of farmers. Unfortunately, the departure of
Loucks back to South Dakota and of Wardall to a new role in
Macune's Washington office removed from the Minnesota
leadership the only people who understood the organizational
principles of the cooperative movement. Donnelly himself

clearly did not and made no pretense that he did. At heart, the aging advocate did not believe in the cooperative movement; he regarded it as being based on the same ill-conceived profit motive that animated its capitalist opposition. Moreover, Donnelly continued to believe that "the masses" could be organized by stump speeches and policy formulated by parliamentary dexterity in the nation's legislatures. Through simple neglect, organizational innocence, and ideological preference, the fragile framework of a mass movement set loosely in place by Loucks and Wardall was allowed to go untended. In this manner, the Minnesota Alliance gradually, almost gracefully, fell apart in 1891. Though the "Alliance Party" had won a balance-of-power position in the Minnesota legislature as a result of the 1890 election, its organizational grass roots withered and maladroit parliamentary leadership by Donnelly vitiated its strength there. For his part, Donnelly continued to see politics from the top down as his role in platform-writing for the national People's Party brought him a modicum of national attention. He remained optimistic, unaware that he led a movement in his home state that possessed a steadily decreasing number of followers. "The sky is luminous with promise," he said in 1891. The inevitable electoral shocks of November 1892 in Minnesota were to leave him baffled and embittered.[26]

Elsewhere in the territory of the Northwestern group, the Iowa Alliance, under the conservative direction of loyal Republican state presidents, never developed an internal program of interest to the state's farmers. The agrarian movement in Iowa shaped a course of action that steered well clear of the state's most widely known reformer, General James B. Weaver, former Greenback Congressman and the third party's 1884 Greenback presidential nominee. Another well-known old Greenbacker, L. L. "Calamity" Weller, had associated his newspaper with the order when it was the sole bearer of the Alliance banner in the state, but he became increasingly restless as Post, Ashby, and state lecturer Will Sargent repeatedly asked him to fill his paper with earnest, pious, but empty pleas to the state's farmers. Weller truly lived in two worlds; the leading soft-money radicals in the West fired off messages to him filled with plans for the "coming great contest," while the same mail brought homilies from the embattled hierarchy of the Northwestern Alliance protesting against the actions of the same men! [27]

The cooperative career of the Iowa Alliance was compressed into a five-month period during 1891 after the sheer fame of the National Alliance and its cooperative programs had begun to have some effect in the state. August Post of Iowa attended the Ocala meeting of the National Alliance in December 1890, and there he met a score of experienced state agents and exchange officials. Upon his return Post, as a newly installed "state business agent," was able to induce a scattering of Iowa lodges to go so far as to form committees to talk to local merchants. Though the doctrines of the subtreasury system remained alien to them, the Iowans had begun to learn in 1891 the more elementary truths about cooperation. As one nonplussed local officer put it, "In our section the feeling of merchants against the Alliance is so strong that they will not advertise in the Alliance paper." The Iowa state lecturer discovered that merchant hostility interferred with his effort to activate dormant lodges. A city marshal locked him out of a town hall because, as the lecturer explained, "the businessmen of Monticello are not friendly to the Alliance." [28]

These activities, however innocent for such a late stage of the agrarian movement, did not take place within an organizational environment well populated with farmers. During eleven years of association in the Northwestern Alliance, the Iowans never achieved a membership much in excess of 15,000 farmers. The incoming state president of 1891 was so surprised to learn of the weakness of the order that he promptly called for a "special effort" from local leaders "to get some representation from alliances that have gone down." Unfortunately, he did not spell out a program that might aid such a special effort. "The Farmers Alliance is in the worst shape imaginable," wrote one member just before he decamped to the National Alliance. In the same months of 1891, South Dakota's Henry Loucks also became disillusioned. "I regret the Alliance in Iowa is so backward in taking hold of our economic measures," he wrote "Calamity" Weller. Alliance National President L. L. Polk was equally dismayed. He ordered a frontal organizing assault by the National Alliance on the Iowa territory of the Northwestern group. Loucks asked Weller to throw his influence behind the drive and Polk personally traveled to Iowa to install the new president and his organizing team.[29]

But in the case of Iowa, the National Alliance had waited too long before moving. There, on the eve of the Populist revolt, simply too little foundation existed upon which to build a statewide cooperative movement. Though the old Iowa Alliance continued in its normal condition of passive disarray, and its state lecturer conceded that the National Alliance was making "slow progress" in the state, the truth was that the agrarian crusade was over in Iowa before it had much chance to begin. The state's farmers, who were only a bit less debt-ridden than they had been in their Greenback days of a decade earlier, might not have generated the kind of flaming insurgent spirit that emanated from neighboring Kansas, but the tiny vote (5 per cent) that native son James B. Weaver polled in 1892 pointed to additional causes for the routine party loyalty of the state's Republican farmers. The agrarian revolt in Iowa, as elsewhere in states occupied initially by the Northwestern Alliance, had been sidetracked. Though the farmers of Iowa suffered from the same financial and marketing practices that plagued farmers elsewhere, the doctrines of cooperative-greenbackism remained alien to them. Politically, therefore, they did not know what to do about their plight.

The months of 1891 saw the slow decline of Jay Burrows's political status in Nebraska and a corresponding rise in the influence of Nebraska anti-monopolists associated with ex-Senator Charles Van Wyck, such cooperative advocates as Omar Ken, as well as a small group of labor greenbackers. Alliancemen such as John Powers who endeavored to work congenially with incoming third party men also gained in stature. After wholesale membership losses in the Alliance in 1891, Powers had finally grasped the relationship of the cooperative movement to organizational continuity. He moved to put some flesh on the ramshackle Nebraska lecturing system,

Henry Loucks of South Dakota
A determined advocate of large-scale cooperation, Loucks failed in his efforts to induce the Northwestern Alliance to "take hold of our economic measures" and watched helplessly as the Milton George organization backed away from the new third party.

noting rather sadly at the state convention that "there seems to be a disposition in some of our subordinate Alliances to turn their meetings into mere literary entertainments or debates." The National Alliance, through its vice president, Henry Loucks of South Dakota, made one final effort to activate the Nebraska Alliance in January 1892, and this time, with Powers's help, he succeeded. Under Powers's leadership and over Burrows's objections, the Nebraska Alliance resolved to try to induce the remaining Northwestern states to merge with the National Farmers Alliance.[30]

In another sharp departure from preceding years, Powers also stressed the sub-treasury plan in his presidential address. The Nebraskans dutifully tracked the platform of the National Alliance, except for some resolutions on the money question written by Burrows that tended to emphasize "free silver" rather than the central aspects of the greenback heritage.[31]

Coming as late as they did, these moves had only marginal impact on the disorganized structure both of the Alliance and the third party in Nebraska. They had even less effect on the organizational residue of the Milton George group still clinging to life in other states of the Northwest. The "national" meeting of the Northwestern Alliance, held in Chicago late in January 1892, bared the terminal illness of the order. Though Ignatius Donnelly and a number of Nebraska delegates arrived to argue in behalf of independent political action, the Northwesterners flatly refused to participate in the 1892 Populist national conventions and formally dissociated themselves from any connection with the third party movement. The Northwestern order at this juncture had no genuinely active state organization other than the Republican-oriented chapter in Iowa. The only visible reform activity in that state emanated from counties affiliated with the National Alliance. Thus, a month before the agrarian revolt formally entered its political phase in 1892, the Northwestern group completed its decade-long definition of itself as a conservative and narrowly based "social" institution. Its members shared a penchant for meeting in congenial rural settings and little else; they numbered less than 25,000 members in its entire jurisdiction. After the Chicago meeting, the Northwestern Farmers Alliance was—almost literally—never heard from again.[32]

On the eve of the long awaited general conference of reformers due to convene in St. Louis in February 1892 under the Macune formula at Ocala fourteen months earlier, the politics of the sub-treasury had left the plan's original proponent with only one remaining political option. At St. Louis Macune maintained an extremely low public silhouette and worked through his surrogate "Confederation of Industrial Organizations" headed by Ben Terrell, his lieutenant. Terrell labored to convince his many influential friends among the Southern leadership that the fashioning of a "broad statement of principles" would constitute an adequate political achievement for the convention; "moral reforms," went his argument, could wait until the delegates had "more time." But it was not to be.[33]

Leonidas Lafayette Polk, having entered the "home stretch" at Indianapolis two months earlier, was driving toward the finish. In an address of welcome at St. Louis that drew rising ovations, Polk said:

> The time has arrived for the great West, the great South, and the great Northwest, to link their hands and hearts

together and march to the ballot box and take possession of
the government, restore it to the principles of our fathers,
and run it in the interest of the people.[34]

Amid the enthusiastic response to this declaration, a St.
Louis reporter noted that "Some of the delegates rose to their
feet, and at the top of their voices announced their intention
of carrying out Mr. Polk's suggestion." Polk's election over
Terrell as the convention's chairman ensured the immediate
formation of the People's Party.[35]

But the emotional peak at St. Louis was provided by Ignatius Donnelly, the "Sage of Nininger." Donnelly's famous preamble was an expression of the deepest drives of the agrarian
radicals who filled the hall and who had worked so many years
to gain the allies who joined them there. If Donnelly's words
seemed harsh and excessive to the comfortable, the delegates
at St. Louis felt he described the American reality:

> We meet in the midst of a nation brought to the verge of
> moral, political and material ruin. Corruption dominates the
> ballot box, the legislatures, the Congress, and touches even
> the ermine of the bench. The people are demoralized. Many
> of the States have been compelled to isolate the voters at the
> polling places in order to prevent universal intimidation or
> bribery. The newspapers are subsidized or muzzled; public
> opinion silenced; business prostrate, our homes covered with
> mortgages, labor impoverished, and the land concentrating
> in the hands of capitalists. The urban workmen are denied
> the right of organization for self-protection; imported pau-
> perized labor beats down their wages; a hireling standing
> army, unrecognized by our laws, is established to shoot them
> down, and they are rapidly disintegrating to European con-
> ditions. The fruits of the toil of millions are boldly stolen to
> build up colossal fortunes, unprecedented in the history of
> the world, while their possessors despise the republic and
> endanger liberty. From the same prolific womb of govern-
> mental injustice we breed two great classes—paupers and
> millionaires. . . .
>   We charge that the controlling influences dominating the
> old political parties have allowed the existing dreadful condi-
> tions to develop without serious effort to restrain or prevent
> them. They have agreed together to ignore in the coming
> campaign every issue but one. They propose to drown the

The "Sage of Nininger" Ignatius Donnelly of Minnesota, author of the ringing preamble of the Omaha Platform. An indefatigable orator, writer, and reconteur, Donnelly was not at his best as an organizer of mass movements. He was, however, one of Populism's most colorful personalities.

cries of a plundered people with the uproar of a sham battle over the tariff, so that corporations, national banks, rings, trusts, "watered stocks," the demonetization of silver, and the oppression of usurers, may all be lost sight of. . . .[36]

Men and women surged forward to surround Donnelly on the platform and grasp his hand. Waves of enthusiasm greeted the presentation of the Populist platform itself, which, being shorter than Donnelly's preamble, was quickly read. Georgia's Lon Livingston, aware of the practical political import of Donnelly's preface, moved the adoption of the platform. A Watsonian immediately rose to move the adoption of the platform and the preamble. The convention, in the full thrust of its radical momentum, adopted the substitute motion. A date for the party's first presidential nominating convention was set: July 4, 1892.[37]

As the convention raced toward adjournment, a defeated but thoughtful Charles W. Macune silently decided to follow his National Alliance into the third party. He was not one to remain a follower for long. As the gavel signaling adjournment fell, Macune leaped to the stage and shouted to the delegates to halt in place and return to their seats. Startled, they obeyed. Carefully, Macune explained that the Ocala convention had established machinery, through the "Confederation of Industrial Organizations," to plan the meeting they had just attended, in conjunction with others of like mind who also desired a grand amalgamation of the laboring classes. Now that the convention was ending, new machinery had to be established to merge the two groups so that orderly planning might ensue. With the delegates responding attentively to his admonitions from the speaker's podium, Macune had become once again—for a moment, at least—the presiding captain of the reform movement. As the officials of the People's Party listened with what can be surmised were mixed emotions at best—the provisional national committee included, among others, William Lamb—Macune suggested that the convention reassemble immediately as a committee of the whole to establish its third party administrative apparatus. The delegates agreed and one of the fifteen named to this committee—in the nick of time—was Macune. His ambivalence on the third party issue forfeited any possible claims to popular leadership of the movement. The new party's presidential nomination would go to L. L. Polk, not to Macune. But Macune was still editor of the movement's national journal, and his considerable organizing talents and diplomatic skills might enable him to become a successful and, perhaps, honored party chairman. But the convention's committee of fifteen soon found itself absorbed by the national committee and no one in either group rose to suggest that Macune, rather than the newly appointed Taubeneck, should head the crusade into its political phase. So much work loomed for everyone, in any case, that questions of leadership fell by the wayside to await future consideration. These ad hoc arrangements were to have large consequences for the future of Populism, for Herman Taubeneck was to become a central character in the "free silver" controversy in 1895–96.[38]

In truth, the third party's enlarged executive committee faced a monumental task. From the "top down," as it were, it had to create a complete national party machinery, from the states down through county, township, and precinct levels; the new apparatus thereupon was expected immediately to begin functioning from the "bottom up" by initiating in the precincts the process of selecting delegates to the national nominating convention of the People's Party. The plan unfolded: precinct and local groups were to form People's Party clubs in March and meet no later than April 16 at the county level to arrange each county's precinct convention. The latter gatherings would be held in May, the state conventions in the various states in June—the whole process to be completed in time for the party's national nominating convention on July 4 at Omaha.

The chief anxiety among third-party strategists in the four months between the two inaugural Populist conventions concerned the progress of the campaign by Southern radicals to wean the Southern Alliances from the party of the fathers. Given the fate of other third party efforts as recent as 1888, the concern about the South outweighed all other considerations. Would the Southerners come to Omaha, or were they to leave the Western Alliances in isolation?

As the Southern Alliances continued to employ their internal lecturing systems on the sub-treasury after St. Louis—with varying success in different states—L. L. Polk called a South-wide conference for Birmingham in May. His specific purposes were not understood in the West, and Stephen McLallin, editor of the official Alliance newspaper in Kansas, wrote Polk a pleading letter that starkly revealed the continuing impact of sectional politics on radical hopes.

> The call for meeting at Birmingham of state presidents and executive boards of [Southern] states, as it appears in the daily papers, is causing considerable anxiety here. Your signature to the call alone allays suspicion with regard to the purpose of the meeting. . . . You know our people are extremely nervous at this time, and while they are beginning to believe that the south is with them, they are trembling lest something may happen to disappoint them. I cannot tell you how anxious they are or how they are hoping almost against hope that this momentous year will show them "the way out." You know these things better than I can tell them to you. I give you the fact that this call is causing much discussion and anxiety here and you will exercise your own judgment as to what it is best to say, if anything, in regard to it.[39]

The Kansans had done all they could to help. Whenever they could spare the time from their own political movement in Kansas, Henry and Cuthbert Vincent, Jerry Simpson, Mary Lease, William Peffer, and others toured the South to provide visible evidence that non-Southerners had made the break with political tradition, too. Indeed, the willingness of the Kansans to expend such energies provided a measure both of their concern and their need.

Polk's concern matched those of his Western allies. In Birmingham the Alliance president engaged in the delicate business of holding together a "nonpartisan" order as it moved into independent political action. The two-day conference of thirty-seven top Alliance officials from eleven Southern states endured intermittent tension, but ended on a relatively amicable note addressed specifically to "the brotherhood in the North and great Northwest." The Southerners announced their intention to work "in unison," to "stand by them in all laudable efforts to redeem this country from the clutches of organized capital," and, finally, to "stand with them at the ballot box for the enforcement of our demands." Though the Alliance statement was signed by all thirty-seven participants, the delicacy of the situation was underscored by an additional fact not included in the press announcement: despite Polk's importunings, the Southern Alliance leaders declined, by a vote of 21 to 16, publicly to express an outright endorsement of the People's Party. Tennessee and Florida, both with prominent "Alliance Democrats" high in their counsels, were balking and Ben Tillman was working zealously to clamp a lid on insurgency in South Carolina. Even in Polk's own North Carolina, young Marion Butler, who had replaced Polk as state leader when the latter assumed the order's national presidency, had fashioned an elaborate scheme that involved cooperation with North Carolina Democrats in state races while charting a third party course in national politics. Clearly, the radical agrarian leadership in the South had much work still to perform. The cause of independent political action in the states of the Old Confederacy still rested on shaky grounds. Polk's energies, skill and prestige obviously confronted an ultimate test.[40]

Meanwhile, throughout the nation, radicals held their precinct, county, and state conventions to select the delegates who would go to Omaha to convene the new People's Party of the United States. The selection procedures worked unevenly, needless to say, but by one method or another, through democratic processes or through self-selection, some 1400 certified Populists appeared in Omaha on July 4, 1892, to nominate the national standard-bearer of the "new party of the industrial millions."

7

L. L. Polk was not among them, however. Three weeks before the convention, on June 11 in Washington, the fifty-five year old Alliance chieftain died suddenly, after a brief illness. His loss altered the thrust of Populism—how much will never be known—but enough, certainly, to camouflage for many subsequent students of Populism the movement's strength across the South. At least one Boston observer of the national political scene, H. H. Boyce of the liberal journal *Arena,* had told Polk just before his death that he was "the one man in the country who can break the Solid South." The judgment was well-considered. Through his personal standing and inherent appeal in the South, Polk's candidacy might have done much to make up for the extremely late start the third party attained in 1892 through most of the Old Confederacy.[41]

Beyond this, it is difficult to imagine a third party leader more uniquely armed to counter the politics of sectionalism than Polk, the old Southern Unionist from North Carolina. His performance, from New York to California, on his exhaustive speaking tours of 1890–91 forcefully demonstrated that his ability to transcend the sectional barrier was as highly developed as that of any other politician in the nation. His untimely death was a heavy and unexpected blow to Populism in the South and, conceivably, elsewhere.[42]

The new party was fated to encounter sectional prejudice whomever it nominated. With Polk heading the ticket, the West would have had to bear the first shock of sectionalism as Republicans pressed bloody shirt attacks against the third party's "ex-Rebel" leader. As it was, the nomination at Omaha of James Baird Weaver elevated a former Union general from Iowa to the head of the new party's ticket. This decision ensured that the new leaders in the South would be the ones fated to receive the first wave of sectional attacks. The Weaver ticket was balanced with Virginia's James G. Field, giving the new party both an ex-Unionist and an ex-Confederate at the head of its ticket. The party they sought to lead had a platform that addressed the "living issues," a preamble that excited its true believers, and a structure of state leadership at the top, but the most direct initial appeal the new party could make to masses of people was in the form of a memory—the emotional and recent memory of the Farmers Alliance.

The cooperative crusade had brought hope to millions, a victory over the jute trust, and a provocative political upset in Kansas. Had it done more than that? What was the true significance of the long trains of Alliance wagons in Kansas, the huge encampments in Texas, the growing adoration that farmers, their wives, and their children bestowed on a fiery young Congressman named Tom Watson? What did it all mean? In Omaha 4000 delegates and spectators had erupted in sustained cheering, clapping, yelling and crying after hearing, one by one, the political planks of the Alliance "demands" they would come to revere as "the Omaha Platform." To one observer who saw in it the frightening specter of socialism, the sounds of the convention "rose like a tornado" and "raged without cessation for thirty-four minutes" while "men embraced and kissed their neighbors, locked arms, marched back and forth, and leaped about tables and chairs." To the right of the stage hung large bunting bearing the words: "We do not ask for sympathy or pity. We ask for justice." The dignified statement blended awkwardly with the emotional scene on the convention floor. Was the People's Party a hope or a threat? To *The New York Times* the sub-treasury plan appeared as "one of the wildest and most fantastic projects ever seriously proposed by sober man," yet alongside the rolling thunder of Ignatius Donnelly's preamble Macune's formula seemed as thoughtful and attainable as its author had always insisted it was. Could such seeming variety have materialized solely from the Alliance experience, so recent and yet so impassioned? [43]

The men and women of the Omaha convention were asking their new party to overcome deeply ingrained sectional and racial loyalties in the name of their vision of reform. Conceivably, the biggest obstacle facing the People's Party might be the culture of America itself. But such a thought would not have traveled far among the ranks of the Populist faithful: the one current that merged the Alliance with the People's Party, and Northerners with Southerners, was their shared faith. It was an emotion that went beyond their belief in the reasonableness of their reforms to include a faith in the civility and openness of the larger society to which they would submit those reforms. The Populist faith was grounded in a democratic conception of the potential responsiveness of the American electorate. It is true that Populists were demonstrably worried that the nation had been brought to "the verge of moral and political ruin" and that the "cries of a plundered people" were being ridiculed by a "subsidized" press in spiritual thrall to corporate power. And it is also true that they were desperately concerned that the aggressions of "concentrated corporate capital" might be lost sight of by a numbed and beguiled citizenry. But it was the Populist faith that, though the hour was late, the people could be rallied to defend the democratic idea. They could, in Polk's words, "link their hands and hearts together and march to the ballot box and take possession of the government, restore it to the principles of our fathers, and run it in the interest of the people." Here, perhaps, was the heart of the Populist belief: though the democratic heritage was imperiled by the demands of the industrial culture, the people were not yet helpless victims. The "coming great contest" had finally arrived, and the people would prevail.

PART TWO

THE TIDE
RECEDING

There never was, nor can there be, a more brutal, utterly selfish, and despicable doctrine than the Darwinian 'struggle for existence' when applied to the social relations of man.

Kansas farmer

The Populist editors will do their whole duty in the mighty conflict that lies so near before us.

Indiana editor

3

The tasks of a party of the people . . .

When Watson led the people out,
They marched through flood and flame;
Old Livingston tried to turn them back
But they got there all the same.

Georgia Populist Song

CHAPTER X

The Populist Approach to Black America

"They are in the ditch just like we are."

The People's Party materialized in a nineteenth-century American environment suffused by the cultural values of white supremacy.* No sector of American society and no region of the country was insulated from a slowly consolidating national attitude that was overtly anti-black. Perhaps the most conclusive evidence was provided by the rapidly deteriorating residue of abolitionism. In 1891, on the eve of the Populist revolt, a Northern Republican, writing in the liberal magazine *Arena,* confessed to the extent of white disenchantment with the concept of a genuine interracial society, even among former advocates. In an article entitled "Qualification of the Electoral Franchise, The Need of the South in Solving the Negro Question," Robert Williams wrote:

> The drift of Northern sentiment for a number of years has
> been in the direction of a more unimpassioned view of the

---

* Two points should be stressed at the outset. First, it is as misleading to segregate within one chapter the approaches of white Populist farmers to their black neighbors as it is to segregate "race relations" from other elements of American life which surround, define, and are defined by racial tension. To say this is merely to assert that

subject, until the opinion has come to be pretty generally acquiesced in that where hostility to the Negro as a voter still exists, it is to be attributed to a dread of misrule rather than to the less defensible motive of prejudice. When Southern men of intelligence and integrity stand up and solemnly assert that it is self-preservation and not prejudice that leads them to participate in or connive at the suppression of the Negro vote in certain sections, these men are only asserting in effect that it is not the Negro vote as such but the ignorant and vicious vote they are seeking to protect themselves against.

The author insisted that "the Negro as Negro has nothing to do with the question," only the Negro "as illiterate." [1]

It took a rather highly developed complacency to overlook a generation of planter-industrialist intimidation and terrorism and accept unskeptically the words of "Southern men of intelligence and integrity" as the true state of affairs in the South. In view of the number of vote frauds in the 1870's and 1880's that had been directed against white candidates who received black votes, it would also seem that the equanim-

---

"race" is central to the American experience and, therefore, to the Populist experience. However, placing chronologically through the entire narrative of the agrarian revolt the events of Populist interracial life when they occur would seriously diminish both their internal relationship and their overall cultural meaning. The recoverable evidence is simply too thin to permit such a treatment.

Second, as to the title of this chapter itself, what follows is essentially a study of white views of race relations in the Populist era. The relatively small number of black perspectives historically recoverable tend to be restricted to those black newspaper editors who, as orthodox Republicans, stoutly opposed the agrarian revolt. Black Populist views, preserved in archival sources, are limited, to say the least. Oral history investigations came too late; except in rare instances, these sources are now ten to fifteen years beyond recovery for the Populist years—because the participants are dead. (A black perspective on one event at the very end of the Populist era—black disfranchisement—has been recovered in a local study of a single county. See Lawrence C. Goodwyn, "Populist Dreams and Negro Rights: East Texas as a Case Study," *American Historical Review* (Dec. 1971), 1135–71. Since this study, made only five years ago, four of the six principal sources have died and the study itself could no longer be duplicated, even though the event described occurred at the very end of the Populist period. Earlier events, occurring in the 1890's, are now effectively beyond reach through oral research techniques.) For these reasons, a perspective that would merit the title, "The Black Response to Populist Approaches" must be inferred; it cannot be documented. Where possible, I have attempted to draw such inferences, but the bulk of the source material is unavoidably derived from white participants. Thus the emphasis in the title.

ity with which Northerners accepted traditional Southern concern about "misrule" revealed rather more about the deepening climate of white supremacy throughout the nation than it did about the fine points of black capabilities. In truth, white Southerners defined "corruption" as the mere presence of blacks in the structure of government or, increasingly, as participants in the democratic process at all. This was done so unconsciously—as an assertion of the deepest form of white cultural presumptions—that white Southerners not only *sounded* sincere, but in fact *were* sincere when they offered stories of black "corruption" to their Northern countrymen. More ominously—if possible—this traditional Southern white view of Reconstruction and its aftermath became the nation's view with an ease and rapidity that offered striking evidence of the depth of white supremacy permeating the whole society. Louis Agassiz, a member of the American School of Anthropology, offered the observation that Africans had always "groped in barbarism and never originated a regular organization among themselves." The dean of the faculty of Political Science at Columbia added his judgment that "a black skin means membership in a race of men which . . . has never created any 'civilization' of any kind." As historian Sterling Stuckey has pointed out, such was the "going thesis" of highly influential members of the American academic community. Small wonder that a ritualistic offer made by Henry Cabot Lodge in defense of Negro voting rights—the "Force Bill" of 1890—stirred such little interest among Republicans that the bill was allowed to lapse. On the eve of Populism, the Southern way of white supremacy had become the American way.[2]

2

Like other aspects of the agrarian revolt, the Populist approach to black voters grew out of the Alliance experience and included both organizational and practical lessons learned from that experience. It was also, at times, a manifestation of lessons never learned at all.

The Colored Farmers' National Alliance and Cooperative Union was an outgrowth of the political analysis of committed greenback radicals among the Alliance founders in Texas.

278

Though the cooperative struggle to preserve the Texas Exchange eventually brought almost the entire leadership of the founding Alliance to a firm third party position, so that all Texas Alliancemen tended to appear "radical" to the nation, degrees of difference always persisted in their ideological participation in the most radical dream of all—an intersectional, interracial, farmer-labor coalition of the "plain people." A half-dozen years before the formation of the People's Party, the necessary political formulas for constructing such an adventuresome coalition had become fairly settled doctrine among what might be loosely described as the "Lamb wing" of the Texas Alliance. The politics of sectionalism that had defeated the Greenback Party was to be overcome through the Alliance cooperative; the white farmers would join the cooperative movement, learn their radical lessons, and then cross the Alliance "bridge" from the Democratic "party of the fathers" to the new "third party of the industrial millions." But the politics of sectionalism quite obviously worked its will on blacks as well. Their dedication to the party of Lincoln represented an equally effective barrier to any participation in independent political action. Was not a similar institutional "bridge" needed to convey the black "plain people" from the Republican Party into third party coalition with the white "plain people"?

The massive organizing drive of the Texas Alliance that followed the promulgation of the Cleburne Demands in 1886 generated a self-confidence and enthusiasm among Alliance lecturers about "the coming new day for the plain people" that made organization of black farmers a distinct possibility. In the months following the Cleburne meeting, as Alliance lecturers enrolled whole farming districts in the "Old South" part of East Texas, several black Alliances came into being. One, organized at a farm near Lovelady in Houston County, became the institutional base of the Colored Farmers' National Alliance. Sixteen participants in the meeting were black, and one of them, J. J. Shuffer, was elected president. However, the seventeenth person present, the man on whose farm the meeting took place, was R. M. Humphrey, a white Baptist minister, ex-South Carolinian and ex-Confederate officer. Humphrey was named "general superintendent" of the order and always thereafter served as its chief national spokesman.[3]

It seems clear, both from his personal associations within this Alliance at the time and from his subsequent conduct as an avowed third-party advocate, that Humphrey visualized the organization of black farmers as part of a larger commitment to national radical politics. But it seems equally clear that he had a short-run personal objective as well—a desire to be elected to Congress from his East Texas district, which was heavily populated by blacks. After a measure of organizing success in Texas in 1887, the "Colored Alliance" came into being as a national organization in the spring of 1888—in time for Humphrey's congressional effort. His rather conclusive lack of success in the subsequent campaign seems to have permanently ended his pursuit for higher office. Thereafter, Humphrey's interest in the organization he headed became almost the entire focus of his subsequent life as an Allianceman and Populist. The black organizers who deployed through the South carried the basic cooperative message of the Alliance, and Humphrey later wrote publicly about the state cooperative exchanges established by the order in New Orleans, Mobile, Charleston, Norfolk, and Houston. By the time of the Ocala meeting in 1890 the portly minister, who had a decided talent for press relations as well as self-promotion, claimed no less than 1,200,000 members in sixteen states.[4]

Organizers of the Colored Alliance were both black and white, the latter tending to serve in the cooperative exchanges. The black president of the Alliance in Alabama, Frank Davis, was characterized in an Alabama newspaper as "a solvent and successful Negro farmer." Other black Alliancemen who grew to prominence in the movement included E. S. Richardson and J. W. Carter of Georgia, J. S. Jackson and J. F. Wassengton of Alabama, J. L. Moore of Florida, W. A. Patillo of North Carolina, William Warwick of Virginia, H. J. Spenser of Texas, Joseph H. Powell of Mississippi, and L. D. Laurent of Louisiana. The political world in which these men lived was not simple. To the extent that black Alliancemen led their members into political coalition with white agrarians under the banner of Populism, they threatened a number of existing political arrangements in both races.[5]

3

The political problem facing Southern blacks was enormously complex, even though it contained few genuinely palatable options. The economic imperatives were quite real—blacks suffered as much from the ravages of the crop lien and the furnishing merchant as white farmers—and more. The black man, too, wanted to find a way to finance his own crop without putting his economic life in the hands of the man with credit. He, too, wanted a more flexible currency, higher commodity prices, an end to discriminatory freight rates, and all the rest of the Populist goals. But in an era of transcendent white prejudice, the curbing of "vicious corporate monopoly" did not carry for black farmers the ring of salvation it had for white agrarians. It was the *whiteness* of corporate monopoly—and the whiteness of those who wanted to trim the power of the monopolists—that worried Negroes. Both sets of white antagonists lived by the cultural values and presumptions implicit in the American caste system. The rare black farmer with enough capital to stay out of the clutches of the furnishing merchant knew quite well that he was just as vulnerable to the whims of Southern justice, just as unprotected against lynch law, as the most downtrodden tenant farmer. In this fundamental sense, economic improvement gave him not the slightest guarantee of protection. For black Americans there was no purely "economic" way out. Though every black person in the nation over the age of ten knew this, neither white conservatives who prided themselves on their "tolerance" nor white radicals in the grip of ideological visions of "a new day for the plain people" were aware of their own participation in a caste system that lay at the heart of this crucial question for blacks. The self-serving capacity of different—and competing—groups of whites to disassociate themselves from "the race problem" was a fact that was abundantly clear to black leaders, both North and South. Blacks therefore approached the whole issue of politics from a much more sophisticated—and cautious—perspective than either white conservatives or white insurgents. They, unlike the whites on both sides, did not enjoy the instinctive presumption that elections had to do with economic and political power. As historian William Chafe has pointed out, the two races came to Populism for different reasons: "the white man was concerned with economics, the Negro with prejudice and protection from violence." Before the black man could worry about economic injustice, he had to worry about survival.[6]

Black community leaders needed to find ways to develop safeguards both for themselves and for blacks generally. These leaders knew that no Southern farmer needed to escape from the crop lien more than the black tenant, but they also knew that the economic appeal of Alliance-Populism raised a number of other possibilities, few of them good. First and foremost, black Alliancemen incurred the wrath of Southern white conservatives who exercised the power of governmental authority, including the police authority. The staunchly Bourbon Montgomery *Advertiser,* for example, became extremely offended by signs of fraternization between the black and white Alliances and reminded the members of both that "the white people don't want any more Negro influence in their affairs than they have already had, and they won't have it." [7]

Black Alliance organizers not only had to keep an eye out for white Bourbons; they also had to cope with Negro Republicans. Populism threatened the power bases of both groups. In Virginia, North Carolina, South Carolina, Alabama, and Texas, entrenched black Republican leaders systematically undercut the efforts of organizers for the Negro Alliance. Their reasons were not difficult to understand. Negro Republicans had to ponder carefully the long-range gamble implicit in public identification with the cause of Alliance-Populism. If these black leaders relinquished their power base within the Republican Party—and it was the sole political base black men had remaining to them in the South—only to discover that the third-party movement failed politically, they faced the probability of being left with no personal foothold at all in the electoral process. Many black Republicans decided—correctly, as it turned out—that the People's Party was going to lose its battle with the party of white supremacy. Accordingly, they held aloof. Populism thus divided both races, whites along economic lines and blacks according to decisions based on cold and necessary calculations of political and physical survival.[8]

Because of the prevailing white racial attitudes, those blacks who led the Alliance in their states frequently functioned covertly. Black lecturers who ranged over the South organizing state and local Alliances did not enter Southern towns behind fluttering flags and brass bands. They attempted to organize slowly and patiently, seeking out the natural leaders in rural black communities and building from there. For this reason, even though the Colored Farmers Alliance was an institution of great range and political significance, its development is shrouded in mystery. Hints of its activities have cropped up in reports of cooperative efforts around Norfolk, Virginia, and in South Carolina, and also in such incidents as the one involving a black newspaper in Vaiden, Mississippi, which was forced to suspend publication during organizing activities in and near the Mississippi delta. Even more public evidence appeared in the form of letters in the *Southern Mercury* and the *National Economist* from newly appointed business agents, occasional press statements by R. M. Humphrey, and the public political activities of the Colored Alliance both at the Ocala convention of 1890 and at the founding meeting of the People's Party in St. Louis in February 1892. All attested to the order's continuing political presence across the South. But it is through local reports of scattered county weeklies that the halting agrarian experiment in race relations produces some of its more tantalizing glimpses of cooperation, contradiction, and paternalism.[9]

The agrarian dream of a new era for farmers struck a responsive chord in quite a few white rural Southern editors who put their pens to work for the cause, and an Alabama newspaper even dared speak publicly of racial solidarity. "The white and colored Alliance are united in their war against trusts, and in the promotion of the doctrine that farmers should establish cooperative stores, and manufactures, and publish their own newspapers, conduct their own schools, and have a hand in everything else that concerns them as citizens or affects them personally or collectively." Sometimes, however, progressive Southern editors expressed their advanced ideas in ways that smacked of old-time paternalism. Thus the official newspaper of the Alabama Knights of Labor, the Alabama *Sentinel,* could fortify the union's progressive racial stance by proclaiming support of the Farmers Alliance in broad terms: "The Bourbon Democracy are trying to down the Alliance with the old cry 'nigger.' It won't work though." The next sentence of the paper's editorial, however, revealed just how difficult it was for whites to shake off the cumulative effects of the caste system: "The Bourbon Democracy have used the Negro very successfully in keeping their supremacy over us and by—our lady! we propose to use him in turn to down them for the good of whites and blacks alike." In such ways agrarian and labor spokesmen for the poorer classes in the South grouped for new formulations of interracial political alliances throughout the years of the Populist revolt. In the process they sought new definitions of race relations that would make such coalitions workable. Black agrarians also groped for new language. "We are aware of the fact that the laboring colored man's interests and the laboring white man's interest are one and the same," said a leader of the Florida Colored Alliance. "Especially is this true in the South. Anything that can be brought about to benefit the workingman will also benefit the Negro more than any other legislation that can be enacted." The same idea was advanced, with measurably different emphasis, by another Allianceman. "What we desire," said white organizer Andrew Carothers, "is that the Farmers Alliance men everywhere will take hold and organize or aid in organizing the colored farmer, and placing in him an attitude to cooperate intelligently and systematically." [10]

If the language was sometimes halting, the stakes were high, bearing not only on the long-range economic goals of both white and black farmers, but also on the overall political climate of the South. In its finer moments, the language of Populism from black and white alike stressed cooperation between the races, not hostility. As such, it challenged the time-honored electioneering technique of the industrialist-planter South, the formula that the Alabama *Sentinel* properly characterized as "the cry of 'nigger.' " In its focus on what was "good for whites and blacks alike," the slowly evolving rhetorical appeal of the Farmers Alliance and the People's Party represented a politics of hope, not one of hate, and thus appealed to the best instincts of the voter rather than the worst. But evidence of this is sketchy at best. Throughout the operative life of the Colored Farmers Alliance, which extended essentially from the spring of 1887 through 1892, only two events occurred which produced an historical record of sufficient detail to provide a measure of genuine insight into the internal life of radical black agrarianism in the Gilded Age. One concerned what turned out to be a violent strike by black cotton pickers; the other grew out of the first convention of the People's Party in the South, a meeting that triggered an intimate and revealing exchange between black and white Alliancemen. Both events occurred during the summer of 1891, as the agrarian movement edged toward independent political action amid a worsening agricultural depression that placed ever greater strains on black laborers in the South.

4

The political event occurred first, in Dallas, on August 17, 1891, when Alliancemen convened the founding meeting of the Texas People's Party. The interracial public session developed such a combination of radicalism and candor that it received meticulous coverage in the North Texas metropolitan press. When William Lamb gaveled the meeting to order—one day before the Texas Alliance was to meet in the same working-class hotel in the same city—he faced a room of Alliance veterans who had labored with him for seven years for the institutional moment that was finally at hand. Joining Lamb was J. M. Perdue, "Stump" Ashby, and Samuel Evans, all greenback warriors of considerable experience, as well as R. M. Humphrey of the Colored Farmers Alliance. Among the other men in the hall were R. H. Hayes of Fort Worth, H. J. Jennings of McKinney, and Melvin Wade of Dallas. Like the others, these three were subtly attuned to the nuances of 1890 Southern politics and all were politically radical. Unlike the others, Hayes, Jennings, and Wade were black.

R. H. Hayes had teamed with Ashby and Evans in an "Independent Party" movement in Fort Worth that dated back to 1886. In five years of political insurgency, the Independents had known moments of success—as when they elected an "anti-monopoly" Mayor of Fort Worth—and moments of defeat. In the process, they had learned something of the tactics of their white conservative opponents and a great deal about the racial attitudes of each other. If they were not entirely free of American racial folkways, they were considerably more knowledgeable about the implications of the caste system than were most Americans of the 1890's. The second member of the black contingent, H. J. Jennings, was an old man. In 1891 he could look back to Reconstruction, the Civil War, and antebellum slavery. He had seen the high hopes of emancipation wrecked in the collapse of Reconstruction, had endured the reaction of white "redemption" government in Texas, had participated in the remaining political bastion—a black-controlled Texas Republican Party—and had seen the rise of the "Lily White" Republicans across the South. If he thought the new third party was a risky undertaking, he kept his own counsel; he well knew that the political options for Negroes had become steadily narrower. Jennings had been disappointed before and might be again; meanwhile, he tested the new party and awaited developments. Melvin Wade was a young trade unionist, a member of North Texas District 78 of the Knights of Labor. The Knights, aided by the Alliance, had conducted their tumultuous strike against Jay Gould's railroad in 1886, and the traumatic defeat they had suffered had induced them to seek new tools for the working class. They had turned from strikes to politics. In the period 1887–90 the Knights had reached out to other sectors of the labor movement: they had helped to form the Texas Federation of Labor, had strengthened their ties to the Alliance, and had admitted hundreds of blacks to their North Texas locals. By 1891, Melvin Wade, a politically active Knight, had acquired an intimate knowledge of the political methods of railroad employers, white trade unionists, the farmers of the Alliance, and traditional black Republican leaders. He did not like many of the things he saw in all of these sectors of Texas political life. And, unlike Jennings, he was given to speaking his mind.[11]

The founding meeting of the People's Party in the South

was one of those rare historical moments that not only explain much that has happened previously, but also illuminate the pattern of events yet to occur. The shared experiences that the Texas Populists brought to the meeting in Dallas ensured that the environment in which they labored would be sufficiently relaxed to encourage a measure of free exchange. But the differences in the options available to black Southerners and to white Southerners also underscored the fact that the experiences these reformers had shared had been sharply circumscribed. They might be able to speak their minds to one another, but whether each understood the full meaning of the other's words was another matter. Within minutes after William Lamb gaveled the People's Party organizers to order, the racial tension that would haunt the movement throughout its life in the South surfaced in open public debate. With unsympathetic reporters from metropolitan newspapers present and taking notes, the Populist leaders debated the new party's stance on the race issue. A good deal of what Populism represented, and aspired to represent, became clear.[12]

As William Lamb opened the meeting, he noticed Melvin Wade, whom he knew well, enter the hall. Lamb inquired if Wade was "in sympathy with the People's Party." Wade replied that he did not know there was a People's Party and he added, noncommittally, "I have read what this body is here for and I am in sympathy with the objects of the meeting."

Lamb's keynote address which followed involved a recitation of the ills of American capitalism, the corruption of both old parties, the destitution of both farmers and workers, and the specific Populist remedies that needed to be enacted. He called for the appointment of a platform committee that would write a "brief but comprehensive" statement of Populist principles. "Submitting these suggestions for your careful consideration," Lamb concluded, "I assure you that the People's Party of Texas is gaining ground rapidly, and that many of the colored people are asking admission, promising that they will put their speakers in the field and battle for the cause. I ask that you give their claims consideration."

Melvin Wade promptly sought further clarification: "I would like to know what you mean by considering the colored man's claims in contradistinction to the claims of any other citizen of the United States?"

"The chair disclaims drawing distinctions," said Lamb. "I had been asked who was entitled to work in the organization. The [platform] committee will proclaim the answer to the world."

Sam Evans, the old greenbacker, no stranger to such verbal jousts within the vanguard of the Southern reform movement, interjected, "Every colored citizen in these United States has the same privileges that any white citizen has, and that is what is meant."

Wade was not impressed. "When it comes down to the practice," he said, "such is not the fact. If we are equal, why does not the sheriff summon Negroes on juries? And why hang up the sign, 'Negro,' in passenger cars? I want to tell my people what the People's Party is going to do. I want to tell them if it is going to work a black and white horse in the same field."

"That is what I meant in bringing it before the committee," said Lamb, "so that they should know our action."

Invoking the memory of Lincoln and Republican assistance to the Negro cause in America, Wade pressed on to ask the third party spokesmen what Populists proposed to do about the predominantly Republican Negro vote in Texas. All the complicated political legacies of the Civil War—black loyalty to Lincoln, Southern white loyalty to the party of white supremacy—reinforced the pointedness of the question.

The black Independent Party leader from Fort Worth, R. H. Hayes, apparently saw Wade's inquiries as part of a Republican plot hatched by N. Wright Cuney of Galveston, the black leader of Texas Republicanism. "It is well known that Wright Cuney of Galveston and Melvin Wade of Dallas would not affiliate with the third party," said Hayes. "The colored people in the rural districts will affiliate with any party against monopolies in the interest of the poor man."

This counterthrust in behalf of the third party brought the discussion of race to a temporary standstill. The People's Party representatives moved on to the work of permanent organization, appointing committees—all white in composition—and then named "Stump" Ashby the party's permanent chairman.

In his initial remarks from the podium Ashby attempted to put the race issue in a larger perspective. "We are not looking to men of the past," he said, "but to men of the present. The time has passed when an American citizen, especially among the working classes, will, before he give the hand of fellowship, ask whether the man wore the blue or the gray or whether he came from Maine or Florida. Our swords are rusted and we are not preparing for war again. We feel that we have been sadly neglected by both parties. The colored man said that the Negroes are naturally Republicans. I do not blame them. I was a natural Democrat. The attention of the colored brother has been called to what that grand old Moses, Abraham Lincoln, said in announcing their freedom, but they are not told that the labor of this country is in slavery." Ashby thus rested his case on the standard radical agrarian analysis of American politics—that both black Republicans and white Democrats had been exploited by the capitalists who managed both major parties.

However, Hayes, addressing his old Fort Worth associate now presiding as the party's chairman, approached the question from a more down-to-earth perspective. Hayes had opposed what he regarded as a traditional black Republican view; now he pressed the white agrarians. "If you are going to win, you will have to take the Negro with you. . . . The Negro vote will be the balancing vote in Texas. Cuney of Galveston is going to oppose this movement." Then, in a reference to the all-white composition of the party's committees, Hayes said, "When [Cuney] reads of the report of your proceedings in the [Dallas] *News,* he will say there were a few niggers in the convention bobtailing to the whites and they were not recognized and amounted to nothing."

Hayes's speech drew applause, and Ashby became more specific. Discussing the makeup of the party's executive committee, Ashby asserted, "I believe that the colored people should have representation in the committee." He further suggested that local committees, particularly in the "Southern districts" comprising the Old South part of Texas in the eastern half of the state, should also have black representation.

Evans expanded on this theme: "We should have one [black

representative] in each district of the state. The colored man would have gone with the Democrats years ago if they had been recognized. They are in the ditch just like we are."

Well aware that the People's Party was groping in a promising manner toward a workable base for interracial coalition, Ashby counseled the delegates: "you are approaching a battlefield in which many errors have been made in the past. The Democrats have never given these people representation; they would say they would buy enough of their votes with liquor and money. The Republicans have left the Negroes without a party. If he has a friend, it is we, and he can be our friend. If the committee is large, we do not propose to be governed by party regulations in the past. I am in favor of giving the colored man full representation." This last remark drew applause from the radical assemblage, and Ashby went on to conclude: "We want to do good to every citizen of the country, and he is a citizen just as much as we are and the party that acts on that fact will gain the colored vote of the South."

Some white delegates, notably from the predominantly black sections of East Texas, attempted to soften the thrust of Ashby's words. One suggested that separate white and black Populist clubs be formed and "let them confer together." Another white delegate moved that each congressional district, through its committee chairman, appoint one black spokesman to cooperate with the white district committee.

The paternalism implicit in this arrangement drew a blunt response from R. M. Humphrey. That veteran of years of organizing work in the Colored Farmers Alliance interrupted to say, "This will not do. The colored people are part of the people and they must be recognized as such."

If the words of this white Populist left room for doubt, Negro leader Hayes rose again to make the issue clear beyond doubt: "If you cannot take us and elect us in this convention, we will not thank you. We do not propose to be appointed by chairmen. You must appoint us by the convention and make us feel we are men."

Sam Evans thereupon nominated Hayes to the statewide executive committee of the Texas People's Party. A second delegate moved that two Negroes be appointed, and a third nominated H. J. Jennings of McKinney. The motions were put to a vote and unanimously adopted. The People's Party would go before the electorate of Texas with two blacks prominent in its leadership.

A sense that they had lived through an historic moment seized the delegates. Jennings, said: "The time I have craved for has come. The people's eyes are open and farewell to the political lash. The lion and lamb would now lie down together."

William Lamb also joined in the moment of euphoria. Surveying the gathering of farmer and labor delegates from both races—a coalition he had labored seven years to bring into being—Lamb turned to the delegate who had recalled the biblical injunction about the lion and the lamb. Speaking in his capacity as chairman of the fifth congressional district for the third party, Lamb expressed his sense of accomplishment in personal terms, but also with an awareness of the meaning of black participation in the People's Party. He said to Jennings, "The fifth district has furnished the lamb and the gentleman has furnished the lion."

The debate on race policy ended on this note. The encounter had generated a definite advance in the new party's posture on the subject of race, but it had also demonstrated the limits of that advance—though apparently none of the white radicals in the room were aware of the fact. In selecting Hayes and Jennings as executive committeemen, the People's Party organizers had unconsciously revealed their attitude toward the racial militancy of Melvin Wade. The white agrarians wanted Wade as an ally, but they were not yet sure they wanted him as an ally in leadership. If the debate in Dallas was any indication, Populism was to be something new in the South, perhaps even something innovative, but it seemed destined to stop short of sweeping the caste system totally into discard. If no one else in Dallas knew this in 1891, Melvin Wade certainly did.

5

Three weeks after the Dallas meeting, R. M. Humphrey, speaking from the Houston headquarters of the Colored National Alliance, issued a strike order, to become effective September 6, 1891: the black field hands of the South were going to demand higher wages. Though Humphrey acted like any typical strike leader—issuing confident press claims that over a million cotton pickers would leave Southern cotton fields the day the strike began—there is reason to believe that the action was forced upon him by his members. The strike effectively pitted the membership of the two Alliances against each other, for the cotton pickers were seeking to increase their wages from the average of 50¢ per day prevailing in most of the South to $1.00. Leonidas Polk of North Carolina, president of the white Alliance, promptly denounced the strike as "a great mistake on the part of our colored friends at this time. With cotton selling at 7 and 8 cents, there is not profit in it." Polk's newspaper, the *Progressive Farmer*, advised Alliancemen to leave their cotton in the field rather than meet the wage demands announced in the strike order.[13]

Whatever the sources of the strike, it is clear that a number of prominent spokesmen of the Colored Alliance opposed it. In any event, it did not immediately materialize. The entire affair brought Humphrey much advice and abuse in the public prints. According to a careful student of the cotton pickers' strike, two local suballiances in East Texas voted for it. One of them retreated in the face of the combined opposition of all the other black suballiances in the county. However, the second, near the town of Palestine, did go on strike. The planter whose fields were affected discharged all the strikers and announced that the matter was "immediately settled." The event demonstrated rather vividly the almost nonexistent resources at the disposal of the strikers and the overwhelming forces arrayed against them. Nevertheless, in at least one isolated pocket of the South the strike of 1891 did belatedly materialize. Two weeks after the original strike deadline, black laborers in the Arkansas delta near Memphis went on strike. Their leader was a thirty-year-old black man named Ben Patterson, a member of the "Cotton Pickers League," an organization formed by Humphrey to carry on the strike. Working quietly, Patterson won the loyalty of some twenty-five black laborers. The strike began on one plantation and the strikers

R. M. Humphrey
A Baptist missionary and a radical
third party Allianceman, Humphrey
became the Superintendent of the
Colored Farmers National Alliance
after it was formed at a meeting on
his farm in Lovelady, Texas, in
1886.

were immediately ordered off the place. They soon returned,
however, and urged other pickers to join them, which some
did. For a tense week, Patterson and others traveled throughout the county, attempting to persuade laborers to walk out of
the fields. A fight apparently developed between strikers and
non-strikers on one plantation and, according to reports circulated in the decidedly pro-planter newspapers in the area, the
strikers killed two of the workers. A large posse was immediately formed to seek out Patterson's band. Tension was further heightened when the manager of a plantation was killed.
The posse grew in size, and some blacks joined it. But trouble
developed in another quarter when a second group of strikers
rode onto a nearby plantation and burned a cotton gin. They
were almost ambushed by whites but were warned by a black
preacher and fled into dense canebreak. Patterson and his followers were eventually caught, some after pitched battles. Fifteen strikers, including Patterson, were killed in what the historian of the affair, William Holmes, has described as "mass
lynchings." The strike permanently disrupted what had been
fairly cordial relations between the Arkansas state branches of

the two Alliances, and Humphrey, who had been rather well regarded, was vigorously denounced.[14]

Across the South, the passage of prominent men of both Alliances into independent political action in 1891–92—a move which coincided in time with the spreading collapse of the cooperative effort in both organizations—shifted the entire focus of the agrarian revolt into its political phase. Both the black and white Alliance organizations, already in advanced decline in some states and in partial decline in all of them, were, in fact, artificially kept alive for a number of months in 1892 by the fervor of the debate over independent political action. After the St. Louis and Omaha conventions of 1892, however, the end of the economic phase had clearly come, for the cooperative dream had been its sustaining force and the hopes of cooperation now lay entirely with the political movement which alone could achieve the enactment of the subtreasury system. Coupled with these factors, the abortive cotton pickers strike of 1891 effectively ended the career of the Colored Farmers Alliance.[15]

6

Black Populism, however, had just begun. The Colored Farmers Alliance made its principal impact on the agrarian movement through pressure as a third party force. The strong stance of the black Alliance in behalf of a new party of reform added momentum to Alliance radicalism during the decisive period leading to the creation of the third party in 1892.[16]

In several forms and in literally hundreds of individual contexts, black-white cooperation materialized gradually in the People's Party. The very act of negotiation itself, of course, disfigured traditional patterns of racial relationships; indeed, such bartering, repeated often enough, threatened the whole structure of the caste system itself. One Alabama Populist in thrall to the culture of white supremacy found the emotional burden of interracial cooperation almost more than he could bear. After negotiating with black spokesmen far into the night, he sighed, "God forbid that I shall stay up another night until 1 o'clock to ask a Negro what we shall do." The style of interracial association varied widely, and it would be incorrect to read revolutionary implications into most of them. Apart from the social realities, however, the political stakes for black voting rights carried fundamental and long-term implications. In 1892 Reuben Kolb's "Jeffersonians" came under vicious assault for what the Alabama metropolitan press called its "Negro plank." The offending article read: "We favor the protection of the colored race in their political rights, and should afford them encouragement and aid in the attainment of a higher civilization and citizenship, so that through the means of kindness, a better understanding and more satisfactory condition may exist between the races." Despite the paternalism and the implicit social caution—not to mention the psychological distance evident in the reference to black Alabamians as "them"—the statement served to confirm all that Democrats professed to see as subversive in the reform movement. The plank was nothing less than a "slap in the face of every white Democrat in the State," said one paper. To another it represented the "nigger rights section" of Kolb's platform. Because of the climate of white supremacy which has informed American culture throughout the nation's history, it is necessary to evaluate the Populist racial stance in Alabama in the relative contexts provided by the various participants, and by the folkways of the period. Convinced that their own cause authentically represented the best interests of "the plain people," black and white, a considerable number of white reformers in Alabama viewed black voting in extremely positive terms. One white farmer wrote to the Union Springs *Herald* in May, 1892, "I wish to God that Uncle Sam could put bayonets around the ballot box in the black belt on the first Monday in August so that the Negro could get a fair vote." As an Alabama historian has said, "if this sounded like an endorsement of the Force Bill, he intended it to." [17]

The Democratic counterpart to the Kolbite pronouncement on the race issue was the thirteenth plank in the Democratic state platform: "We favor the passage of such election laws as will better secure the government of the State in the hands of the intelligent and the virtuous, and will enable every elector to cast his ballot secretly and without fear of restraint." The Ozark *Banner* pondered the standards employed to define "the intelligent and the virtuous" in the state. "If college graduates alone are permitted to vote, it will keep the aristocratic and plutocratic Jonesocrats in power world without end." The paper concluded that the plank was sufficiently vague that "under it, every poor man, white and colored, in Alabama could be disfranchised."[18]

In North Carolina, Populist-Republican fusion in 1894, and the electoral reforms that the same two parties cooperated to achieve in the 1895 legislature, ensured a protected franchise unmatched elsewhere in the South. The prompt election of numerous local black officials in North Carolina in 1896 tested the racial commitment of white Populists most tellingly. Out of the tumultuous struggle that ensued one fact became evident: the North Carolina Populists did not possess the vindictive, disfranchising temperament that was characteristic of the North Carolina Democrats. The record of the third party in North Carolina can be described as unimpressive by modern standards, but it was rather hopeful in the climate of the 1890's. The public outcry against black officeholders came almost wholly from staunchly Democratic newspapers, led by Josephus Daniel's Raleigh *News and Observer*. While many Populists worried about the eventual political consequences for the third party of an interracial reform movement, and still other Populists did not even like the short-run presence of black officials, the interracial political record of the third party was measurably superior to its Democratic rival and compared well with that of whites in the Republican Party. It is necessary to emphasize, however, that all these judgments are quite relative; after all, these were public actions within a three-party political environment that was inherently white supremacist.[19]

In Georgia Tom Watson's successive defeats through the Democratic custom of fraudulent voting of blacks altered the thrust of his public calls for political and economic rights for Negroes. Watson had held rather traditional Southern views before the coming of the Farmers Alliance, and he was to revert to them with a vengeance years after the collapse of Populism, but, as in the case of the North Carolinians, the internal dynamics of Populism had a measurable impact on him. During the epic Populist-Democratic wars of the 1890's Watson was clearly more open-minded than his rivals were. Among Southern politicians of the Gilded Age, Watson was the most persistent and vocal critic of lynching and of the convict lease system. The Georgia party as a whole did not seem wildly out of step with such sentiments. Black representation at third party conventions rose from two delegates in 1892 to twenty-four at the state conclave in 1894. The underlying idea of a party of the "plain people" pushed Southern Populists (the cultural heritage of many of them still intact) toward adventurous innovations in interracial politics. In the South, the Populist era was one of those moments in American history when things could have changed somewhat.[20]

But internal dynamics aside, the People's Party had diverse spokesmen. The *Southern Mercury,* for example, was in the hands of five different editors during the era of Alliance-Populism, and the paper's stance on race swerved to conform to the personal views of each. Two writers, E. G. Rust and J. R. Bennett, had rather advanced views on black rights, while Clarence Ousley and J. H. Dixon, the two Hoggites briefly associated with the *Mercury* during the nadir of the radicals in 1889–90, were at times overtly white supremacist. Milton Park, the paper's guiding spirit during the Populist years, was quite radical on economic issues but demonstrably less so when it came to blacks. Under Park, the *Mercury* had a marked tendency to voice its concern for blacks just prior to elections. It did the same with organized labor. Neither group performed on election day in a manner calculated to measure up to the *Mercury's* preferences. Interestingly enough, the *Mercury's* inevitable post-election disillusionment, while rather righteously delivered to both groups, seems to have focused a bit more on the labor movement than on the black community. Depending upon one's perspective, this reaction might serve as well to verify Park's Southern traditionalism as it does to contradict it.[21]

The 1894 Populist state platform in Texas offered a nineteenth-century·version of "black power": it proposed a revision of the prevailing practice of permitting the white-controlled commissioners' court in each county to apportion the public school budgets, a practice which uniformly resulted in blacks receiving a greatly reduced share of per capita education appropriations. "We favor an effective system of public free schools for six months in the year for all children between the ages of six and eighteen years, and that each race shall have its own trustees and control its own schools." Either in nineteenth-century or twentieth-century terms, this stance contrasted markedly with the overtly anti-black position on education contained in the Texas Democratic platform.[22]

Arkansas Populism, both politically and personally, demonstrated the clearest record of racial liberalism of any of the Southern third parties. In 1889, when Arkansas editor W. Scott Morgan first began laboring for a third party, he called for "a party that will make it fashionable to be honest, to pay an equal labor, regardless of color, creed, country or sex." Third party men in Arkansas seem to have lived up to this aim with more consistency than any other group of Southern Populist leaders. In its state platform the Arkansas People's party took an official stand in behalf of the "downtrodden, regardless of race."[23]

The extent of an effective black political presence in each Southern state had a marked effect on the behavior of white reformers. The organizing effort of the Colored Farmers Alliance seems to have been most effective in the states of Alabama and Texas, while in Mississippi blacks had been effectively disfranchised in 1890 before the People's Party was even formed. Prior to the arrival of the third party in South Carolina, spokesmen for rival Democratic factions, Wade Hampton and "Pitchfork" Ben Tillman, publicly and repeatedly competed in racism in the 1890's. Tillman successfully employed deception and demagogy on the sub-treasury issue to co-opt agrarian discontent in 1892. During the Populist era, Tillman held the loyalty of the Democratic faithful by a race-baiting and class-baiting assault on blacks and the tidewater gentry. The conservatives matched him with attacks on blacks and "Tillmanism."[24]

The Colored Alliance was never so successful in organizing black farmers in Tennessee or Florida as it was in the adjoining state of Alabama, though Humphrey made extravagant membership claims in both states. To the extent that black as-

pirations in Tennessee could be effectively asserted at all politically, they continued to find voice through the Republican
Party.[25]

7

What was the Populist approach to Black America? In a general sense, the aspirations of both black and white Populists in
the South were thwarted by three mutually supportive political facts. First, the received cultural inheritance of white supremacy continued to hold a greater sway over Southern
whites than issues of economic reform did, however ably such
issues were articulated by Populist spokesmen. The educational triumph of the cooperative movement lay in its success
in persuading hundreds of thousands of poor Southern white
farmers to forsake the party of white supremacy for a politics
of economic self-interest in the People's Party. But Populism's
failure ultimately was traceable to its inability to persuade still
more thousands to the same conversion. Second, the Democratic Party's principal campaign technique was the cry of
"Negro domination." Race demagogy, along with the received
cultural tradition, drove thousands of Populist-leaning white
Southerners back to the party of the fathers. Such Southern
Democrats as Oates and Jones of Alabama, Northen of
Georgia, Hogg of Texas, and Tillman of South Carolina all
profited by race demagogy or vote-stealing—or both—in the
course of keeping the farmers in the Democratic Party and
themselves in office. Third, when all else failed, the party of
white supremacy was willing to use violence to maintain Democratic Party control. Murder, intimidation, fraud, bribery—
all were employed. The ominous truth was that such tactics
were condoned and often explicitly sanctioned by influential
Southern businessmen, politicians, and editorialists. In essence, the race issue was used by those who ruled in the South
to divert attention from issues of economic reform upon
which the agrarian challenge was based. Some white Populists,
in order to blunt this tactic, retreated from the third party's
innovative approach to interracial political action. By denying
they were "nigger-lovers," they attempted to keep the issue between the parties focused on economic reform. Other Popu-

299

lists did not retreat. But in either case, there was not much the
third party could do, short of armed warfare, to defeat an ad-
versary determined to retain power by any means necessary.
For their part, the Populists did not resort to armed insurgency. Thus, the Southern Democrats who employed terrorism were the true "revolutionaries" of the Populist era.* It
was only one of many ironies attached to the agrarian revolt.[26]

Under this enormous extra-legal pressure of physical and
psychological intimidation, Populists behaved in various ways.
One student of the Texas movement wrote that John Rayner,
a black state executive committeeman of the third party, "took
his life in his hands" every time he ventured forth to preach
the gospel of Populism in East Texas. The white speakers of
the party in Texas were also molested more than once. In
Georgia, the Reverend H. S. Doyle braved hostile mobs and
sniper fire to speak for Tom Watson. At the height of Watson's bitterly contested congressional campaigns, both he and
Doyle adopted the policy of speaking from platforms surrounded by armed Populist guards. And in Alabama, Negro
leader L. W. McManaway was prevented from speaking by
hostile bands of Democrats.[27]

Some Negro leaders who originally had questioned the Populists' motives ultimately became convinced of the third party's
importance and joined its ranks. One such man was
W. A. Patillo of North Carolina. Another was Melvin Wade of
Texas. Others, among them Wade's associate, Norris Wright
Cuney, held back and remained closely affiliated with the Republican Party. Still others, such as Alabama Republican
leader William Stevens, vacillated between cooperation and
opposition. Some black leaders may possibly have pulled back
from the third party because of a lack of convincing proof by
local white Populists that the agrarian movement promised
any meaningful change in race relations. Certainly the stance
of a number of local third party leaders in every Southern
state provided black leaders with good reason for making such
a decision. In every state there were some white Populists who
were definitely more interested in appearances than in sub-

---

* See Chapter XI, pp. 324–337.

stance. Indeed, even when taking what they felt to be advanced positions on race questions, many white Populists were sufficiently influenced by prevailing customs that they joined with Democrats in frowning on most forms of social integration. Finally, it should be noted that some white Populists were willing to advance the claim that the People's Party was more an institution of white supremacy than the Democratic Party was—though comparative evidence does not support such a notion.[28]

The Populist with the longest involvement in interracial politics, R. M. Humphrey, demonstrated on occasion that he was capable of the judgment that a good Negro was a radical Negro. And, given his perspective, a Negro who opposed Humphrey could not be radical. In such ways the cultural legacy of the caste system worked its will on white reformers as well as their more traditional opponents. Yet Humphrey's position was not paternalistic, in the sense that he was judging blacks by their politics rather than their color. Orthodox white Southerners had a simpler view. Indeed, a more subtle distinction existed: Humphrey attempted to associate politically with the most racially assertive blacks, orthodox Southerners with the least assertive. This fragile opening in the cloistered world of white supremacy was undoubtedly one of the more important long-term opportunities for the larger American society that was created through Populist interracial hopes. The fact that Humphrey was willing to suffer the irritation of some of his white farmer allies, not to mention the wrath of metropolitan newspapers, by supporting black farm laborers in strikes for higher wages seems worthy of note. He sometimes found himself standing between the two races—and between the two groups of radicals—and doubtless he knew moments of severe personal isolation. He must have learned a great deal about his own and the nation's racism in the course of his years of intimate association with black farmers. The details of this experience seem to be beyond the possibilities of documentation but not beyond imagining. Humphrey generally worked with the most disadvantaged people of Southern society—along the forks of the creek where newspaper reporters and historians rarely travel. Though a fragile outline of his political life can be reconstructed from the fragmentary evidence available, the rich texture of his experience, along with that of the black organizers with whom he worked, is lost forever—an unfortunate archival legacy of nineteenth-century racial values.

8

The private papers of one black leader have survived, however; because of the prominence of his career, they provide a chilling glimpse of the emotional price white Americans have exacted over the generations from their black countrymen. The most famous black orator in all of Populism was the third party's state committeeman from Texas, John Rayner. A schoolteacher from Calvert in East Texas, Rayner organized a corps of assistants to work for Populism in black districts of the state in the nineties. As signs of progress appeared and Rayner's reputation grew among third party men, he began delivering addresses before mixed audiences, and, on occasion, all-white audiences. The Populist state chairman, "Stump" Ashby, joined Rayner on the organizing circuit, and Ashby repeatedly issued public appeals through the *Southern Mercury* for funds to keep Rayner at work in the cause of Populism. Rayner was an unquestioned leader of the Texas People's Party and ranked as an orator only behind two nationally known Texas third party men, "Cyclone" Davis and "Stump" Ashby.[29]

With the collapse of the third party in 1896, and the advent of black disfranchisement after the turn of the century, Rayner faced long years of humiliation as a well-known "public man" whose personal politics had become untenable in the changed world of the new century. An organizer who had braved sniper fire as well as physical assaults, Rayner relinquished one by one the goals of the program of interracial political action that he had carried throughout East Texas in the 1890's. By 1904, after repeated rebuffs, he had been reduced to one goal, the cause of private Negro education, which could only be supported by wealthy white people in Texas. Gradually, desperately, Rayner learned the language that would open this channel of communication. It was a language of submission that at times neared, if it did not breach, the bounda-

John B. Rayner
One of Populism's most effective
stump speakers, Rayner served as
state executive committeeman for
the third party in his native state of
Texas.

ries of personal abasement. With these credentials, he raised
funds for the "Farmers Improvement Society" and its agricultural school to keep Negroes down on the farm. By 1910
Rayner could draw what satisfaction was possible from the
knowledge that he represented "the right kind of Negro
thought" in the opinion of those who shared in power in
Texas.[30]

He returned to the Republican Party, and his old-time fire
occasionally reappeared in angry letters about the racism of
the "Lily Whites." In 1912, the ground for a free-thinking
black to stand upon in the South had narrowed to the vanish-
ing point, and Rayner accepted private humiliation rather
than endure the psychic cost of further ritual servility. He
went to work for John Kirby, a famous Texas lumber king,
and spent the remaining years of his life as a labor agent
recruiting Mexican peasants and transporting them to East
Texas to work in Kirby's lumber mills. Rayner, a man who had
spent his youth learning the art of spoken and written persuasion, employing both in political radicalism, and who in his
middle years had acquired the new art of spoken and written
dissimulation, became in his old age an instrument of exploita-

tion of those having even narrower options than himself. According to his descendants, he died "very bitter." Rayner's private papers, which extend over the period 1904 to 1916, provide a harsh insight into the years following slavery in which an aggressive white supremacy triumphed politically in the United States and gave rise to the settled caste system of the first half of the twentieth century. Before his death in 1918, Rayner pronounced a one-sentence judgment on the political system that had defeated him throughout his life. "The South," he said, "loves the Democratic Party more than it does God." However, it was not just the Democratic Party that defeated him, it was the culture itself.[31]

9

The rise and fall of the People's Party occurred during the same period that Northern Republicans ceased altogether to look upon their institution as the party of emancipation. Across much of the Northern half of the country, from Illinois to New England, farmers, relatively less downtrodden than their counterparts of the South and West, overwhelmingly remained loyal to the Republican Party of the Gilded Age. The resulting impotence of the third party throughout the East and Midwest precluded Northern blacks from taking more than passing interest in the reform movement. This did not hold true for Kansas, where Populist interracial efforts were in keeping with the abolitionist sympathies of many of the old-time greenbackers who had helped organize the Alliance and the third party movement in the state.[32]

As Republicans in the North stopped pressing for legal measures that would guarantee even a minimum of Negro political rights in the South, the Democratic Party in the states of the Old Confederacy moved toward outright disfranchisement. By 1906 Negroes had been systematically excluded from voting in Democratic primaries in every Southern state. If the collapse of Populism left hundreds of thousands of poor whites disenchanted with politics, black disfranchisement forced other hundreds of thousands out of the electoral process altogether. As a result, the elections across the South in the first decade of the twentieth century saw a precipitate decline in the voting electorate. The Democratic Party, free at last from the rumblings of Populist agitation, reaffirmed its suzerainty over the South with strengthened and almost unchallengeable power. The political presence of blacks having finally been eliminated through wholesale disfranchisement, the political experiments of the post-Civil War years faded from Southern life. A settled caste system again descended upon the region. Politically, the South was "solid" again. Orthodoxy in behavior begat orthodoxy in ideas. The interchange of political possibility that punctuated the years of the agrarian revolt ceased between the races. Indigenous Southern white opposition to segregation was left powerless as reformers on the race issue became stigmatized. Most fell silent and left critical comment on the South's social order to the region's brooding and often brilliant novelists of both races. After the passing of the People's Party, more than a half century elapsed before more than a handful of politically active white Southerners could be found who would publicly reaffirm the language of racial cooperation that had been spoken by white and black Populists in the 1890's.[33]

For Southern blacks, the silencing of their last white political allies, coupled with black disfranchisement, created a desperate situation. The politics of reform gave way to a politics of survival. It was an art which all blacks, not just the political leadership of the race, had to master. The anguish of the post-Populist years created new ideological tensions, manifested in the divergent paths chosen by Booker T. Washington, W. E. B. DuBois, Marcus Garvey, and the National Association for the Advancement of Colored People. In the South, articulate black spokesmen were forced to shift their public stance in the face of the harsh imperatives of resurgent white supremacy. The tactic produced few tangible results for the race, as the politicians of a triumphant Democratic party found it safe to ignore the spokesmen for people who could not vote. In 1903 a resurgent Democratic legislature in Georgia passed a sweeping new crop lien law to the effect that the failure of a tenant to fulfill his obligations was to be regarded as prima facie evidence of fraudulent intent. In the words of an historian of these years, "farmers in debt to lienholders could not lawfully move away without satisfying all their obligations, and therefore many thousands were in effect bound to the land in an oppressive system that resembled slavery." [34]

Following the defeat of the Alliance cooperatives and the political challenge of the People's Party, the crop lien system, undergirded by the caste system, again became the uncontested way of life. Since the reigning culture permitted landowning furnishing merchants to exploit black tenants more totally than they could whites, a new custom emerged at the beginning of the new century: the debt accounts of many white tenants were wiped out and they were evicted, to be replaced by black tenants. In some states, the white yeomanry, driven to desperation, tried to recover its rights to peonage by staging night-riding raids in an effort to drive the replacements off the land. The custom acquired a name. It was called "whitecapping." It soon passed. The crop lien did not.[35]

As conditions for millions of black and white farmers remained unchanged year after year, decade after decade in the twentieth century, many observers decided that the white South had lost the capacity to reform itself. And, in fact, when the banner of reform was again raised in the South in the 1960's, the hands holding it aloft were black.

CHAPTER XI

An Unresolved Strategy: The People's Party as a National Institution

"Welcome honorable allies and go forth to victory."

In the absence of such highly charged stimuli as a revolution or a civil war—events that create massive political constituencies overnight—new institutions such as the People's Party necessarily face the prospect of building out of the material at hand. The National Farmers Alliance was to convey masses of rural people to the new party—enough, surely, to carry the party quite a bit beyond the Western frontier limitation that had strangled the Greenback and Union Labor efforts. Beyond that, the question remained: how was Populism to become the institutional voice of the "industrial millions?"

In 1886 William Lamb had implemented a boycott in support of the Knights of Labor "in order to secure their help in the near future." Obviously, the task of reaching urban workers was central to any reform movement seeking, as the Populists did, to speak in behalf of the "producing classes." Terence Powderly, the Grand Master Workman of the Knights, like his friend Charles Macune, had been swept reluctantly into the third party. But the Knights' leader had brought few members with him. The union's membership had fallen from its peak of

700,000 in 1886 to less than 100,000 by the autumn of 1892. A new organization, the American Federation of Labor, had materialized out of the wreckage of the labor struggles of the 1880's, but its chief spokesman, Samuel Gompers, made it clear he proposed to avoid distracting political adventures. Under the circumstances, the A. F. of L. chieftain seemed to offer even less assistance than Powderly did. To Populists, the only promising labor spokesman was a railroad union man named Eugene Debs. But while Debs had caught the attention of such Populist journals as the *Nonconformist* and the *Southern Mercury,* he had not yet placed himself in position to lead masses of American workers into independent political action.[1]

In a fundamental cultural sense, the American labor movement was simply not yet ready for mass insurgent politics. As of 1892, it had not developed, through its own institutions, a working-class culture of economic and political consciousness essential to the maintenance of an insurgent posture in the presence of the continuing cultural influences of the corporate state.

To hopeful Populists, of course, the possibility existed that urban workers could be reached outside of labor organizations. Henry George, for example, had mobilized Irish workers in New York behind his "single tax," and had engineered a surprisingly strong campaign for the mayoralty of New York City in the middle 1880's. His subsequent efforts, however, had failed to generate either a structure of reform or an incoming tide of new working-class recruits. The single tax movement, loosely attached to some socialist trade unions in New York, seemed little more than a piece of radical flotsam drifting insecurely just beyond the clutches of the Democratic ward organizations of Tammany Hall. After George himself broke with the socialists, his affinity for Democrats increased. In 1892, he decided to cast his lot with the Democratic hard money advocate, Grover Cleveland. By that time the largest institution in America that espoused the philosophy of the single tax was the Colored Farmers National Alliance.[2]

Edward Bellamy's humanistic novel, *Looking Backward,* published in 1887, had been widely read in reform circles and had led to the creation of a new political group called the Nationalists. The organ of the Nationalists, *The New Nation,* had enthusiastically hailed the formation of the People's Party, as had Bellamy himself, but, as of 1892, the Nationalists could rally little more than scattered groups of middle-class liberals across the nation.[3]

However one looked at urban America—as masses of incipiently class-conscious workers or as democratic citizens who could be politically activated through such appeals as Henry George's single tax or Edward Bellamy's Nationalism—it is clear that the agrarian organizers who had created Alliance-Populism had not, by 1892, thought through the dimensions of the task they faced. At its most elemental political level, that task turned on the need to create among urban workers a culture of cooperation, self-respect, and economic analysis that matched the political achievement of the Alliance cooperative crusade. While the sub-treasury plan might have represented the ideological culmination of both the greenback heritage and the impassioned cooperative movement—and thus constituted a living symbol of the cause of reform for farmers—Macune's innovative conception had no such symbolic meaning for the nation's urban workers. And though Populist monetary theorists could argue that the doctrines of greenbackism would benefit urban workers, as, indeed, would all the other third party goals aimed at coping with "concentrated capital," neither the Alliance nor the affiliated Knights of Labor had ever been able to create an ongoing environment of economic education that extended to the masses of urban workers. While the suballiance had been a "schoolroom," the local lodges of the Knights of Labor had not been. The internal program of the Knights never created an educational equivalent of the far-flung cooperative structure of the Alliance. As of 1892, neither the Knights of Labor nor any other American working-class institution had been able to create in its own ranks the culture of a people's movement that had animated the Farmers Alliance since 1886.

Reduced to its essentials, the organizing problem facing the People's Party in its maiden campaign of 1892 grew out of the cultural limitations of the Alliance movement itself. What could a Protestant, Anglo-Saxon Alliance organizer say to the largely Catholic, largely immigrant urban working classes of the North? Indeed, since urban workers were largely insulated within the Northern Democratic Party, and further insulated within Tammany-style Democratic ward organizations, how could third party partisans even gain access to the teeming masses in the nation's great industrial centers? The lessons learned in the cooperative crusade simply did not supply answers to such questions.

In 1892, what Alliance-Populism lacked was a social theory of sufficient breadth to appeal to all those who had not received an education in the Alliance cooperative. The most creative theoretician produced by the agrarian revolt was Charles Macune: he alone had combined economic analysis with the needs of organizational expansion; he alone had achieved not one, but two creative breakthroughs: the large-scale credit cooperative and the land, loan, and monetary system known as the sub-treasury plan. What the cause of the third party urgently needed in 1892 was for Macune or someone else to go beyond the social conceptions embedded in the sub-treasury system to develop a broader theoretical analysis that could be shaped to speak with special power to the millions of the "plain people" in the nation's cities. Admittedly, this assignment constituted a cultural challenge of enormous dimension; indeed, it was a challenge that was to confront—and, in a great many ways defeat—succeeding generations of democratic theorists in America down to the present.

In 1892, the prospects of urban Populism could be summarized in one sentence: the Alliance organizers looked at urban workers and simply did not know what to say to them—other than to repeat the language of the Omaha Platform. While that document could be quite persuasive in intellectual terms, few Americans understood better than veteran Alliance lecturers that organizers could not create mass institutions of reform by winning, one at a time, intellectual debates with individual citizens over the fine points of a political platform. In order for great numbers of hard-pressed people to achieve the self-confidence, the self-respect, and the psychological autonomy essential to a movement aiming at significant changes in the culture of a society, it was obvious that something more than the Omaha Platform was needed.

At root, what the People's Party lacked in the nation's cities in 1892 was the essence of Populism itself—the "movement culture" that the Alliance had created in over 40,000 suballiances across rural America in the course of building its far-flung structure of economic cooperation. This culture was, in the most fundamental meaning of the word, "ideological": it encouraged individuals to have significant aspirations in their own lives, it generated a plan of purpose and a method of mass recruitment, it created its own symbols of politics and democracy, and it armed its participants against being intimidated by the larger corporate culture. Perhaps most important of all in human terms, the movement culture of Populism generated the visible evidence of community that gave meaning and substance to all of the lesser individual and collective hopes unlocked by the movement itself. The community of Populism had verified itself in the successful struggle against the jute trust in the South, in the ambitious multi-state livestock marketing cooperative in the West, in the long Alliance wagon trains, and in the "joint notes" of the landed and the landless. The people's movement gained in self-confidence with each new torchlight "parade of the people," with each impassioned "convention of the people," and with the addition of each new oracle who found a way to open a weekly newspaper and add it to the growing ranks of the National Reform Press Association.

In the cities of America, in vivid contrast, the People's Party of 1892 was an institution still searching for a way to reach and talk to the "plain people."

2

Thus, outside the ranks of the Farmers Alliance, the People's Party possessed few institutional means to attract the "industrial millions." This fact led to a vital—though apparently unconscious—shift in the tactics of the organizers who had generated the agrarian revolt in America. In effect, the Alliance founders gave away their cultural claims within the new party they had worked so hard to create.

This alteration within the reform movement began in 1892 and proceeded essentially from the successive stages of the Alliance organizing process itself. On the eve of the great lecturing campaign that carried the cooperative movement to much of the nation in 1890–92, the Alliance had been centered in eleven Southern states plus Kentucky and the Midwestern states of Kansas, Missouri, and the two Dakotas. In most of these sixteen states the cooperative program of the Alliance had organized the bulk of the farmers. But the twenty-odd states added to the Nationl Alliance after 1889 still had relatively small memberships in 1892. When the agrarian revolt moved into its political phase at Omaha, the Alliance spokesmen in the new states generally represented small pressure groups rather than mass insurgent constitutencies. The organizational weakness surrounding such spokesmen presaged a kind of brokerage approach to the political process. Unable to elect candidates on their own, they tended to be drawn toward accommodation with one or the other major parties. Should such moments of "fusion" actually occur, of course, the Omaha Platform of the People's Party would constitute a hindrance, as it contained radical planks offensive to both major parties. In consequence, organizational fragility often led to a brand of politics organically unrelated to the greenback doctrines bequeathed to the third party by the Farmers Alliance. Indeed, such modes of brokerage politics contrasted sharply with the long-term objectives of radical Alliance organizers who were dedicated to their Omaha Platform as an essential prerequisite to the restructuring of both the American party system and the American banking system.

The immediate result of these dynamics was the unusual makeup of the party's national committee, where the men who had created Alliance-Populism were clearly outnumbered by aspiring Populist political brokers. Even the party's new national chairman, Herman Taubeneck of Illinois, came from a state containing a relatively small agrarian movement. Though the Farmers Mutual Benefit Association had achieved some organizing success in Southern Illinois, the possibility of a genuine statewide agrarian presence had been crippled by the unsuccessful policies of Milton George and the Northwestern Alliance. Taubeneck himself, was therefore an incipient political broker.

Interestingly enough, there is no record that the Alliance

organizers voiced any objection to the leadership arrangements in their new third party. Most of the incoming representatives seemed thoroughly at home with the purposes of Populism. Many were good speakers, and that seemed to make them well-equipped for the task at hand. Were they not Populists all, whether politicians or organizers? Was not their very presence proof of their reform intentions? Jerry Simpson was a politician, for example, and no stouter defender of Alliance principles could be found. So matters seemed in 1892.[4]

Though the national strategy of the new party remained to be fashioned, third party men moved to put what repairs they could on obvious structural defects. Even before the Omaha convention Alliance radicals had created a second organizational shelter, the National Citizens Alliance, to spread Populist doctrines to the nation's cities. The Citizens Alliance organized a newspaper, edited by Ralph Beaumont, the Knights of Labor lecturer, and made ready to assault the urban bastions of the two major parties. With such fragile organizational patches and adjustments, the People's Party made ready to enter its maiden campaign in 1892.[5]

In the midst of these frantic months of party-building and institutional arrangements, certain underlying components of the reform movement were not focused upon—perhaps because it was not reassuring for Alliance radicals to do so. The principal component was a theoretical one. In conception, the sub-treasury system obliterated the "intrinsic value" theory of money, swept the gold standard into discard, and freed millions from some of the more exploitive features of the nation's banking system. But while farmers obviously learned a great deal about bankers, chattel mortgage companies, furnishing merchants, and "concentrated capital" generally, during the course of their struggle to make their cooperatives work, they absorbed these experiences with widely varying degrees of understanding.

In ways that very few of the participants fully grasped, the fate of the individual third parties across the nation in 1892 revealed the intimate relationship between the Alliance cooperative movement and the People's Party. Where the Alliance organizers had performed their task in great depth, the third party appeared with an immediate mass base of support. On the other hand, where the organizers had reached the farmers but had failed to follow through with the organized lecturing campaign that constituted the "politics of the sub-treasury" in 1891–92, great numbers of potential Populists failed to cross the "Alliance bridge" from their old political allegiance to the new party of reform. Finally, where the Alliance lecturers, for whatever reason, had failed to recruit the bulk of a state's farmers, the third party movement in such areas was fatally undermined from the outset.

Relative degrees of agricultural poverty did not play a decisive role in this process. Rather, third party performance was a simple matter of the presence or the absence of mass political consciousness. A critical weapon available to the defenders of the received culture was, obviously, the politics of sectionalism. Whether in peonage or not, farmers might be kept loyal to "the grand old party" or to "the party of the fathers" by the politics of the bloody shirt, or by the politics of white supremacy. Individuals could find a source of resistance to these inherited tribal appeals only through their identification with the democratic culture of their own movement. This was why the sub-treasury plan of Charles Macune, while symbolically and practically useful in providing Alliancemen with a flag to follow, had to be augmented by the "politics of the sub-treasury," as conceived by William Lamb. The latter was necessary to draw clear democratic lines between the Alliance on the one hand and both old parties on the other; in states where Alliance leaders, for whatever reason, did not implement a massive lecturing campaign on the sub-treasury in 1891–92, the People's Party had only a shadow presence. Thus, while the cooperative movement was central, the style and political posture of individual Alliance leaders was quite germane to the development or non-development of strong third parties. The fate of Populism across the nation in 1892 turned on these relationships.[6]

In the South the politics of the sub-treasury had been brought home, with varying degrees of organizational thoroughness, to the farmers of Georgia, Alabama, and Texas; less so in North Carolina; and not at all in Tennessee and Florida. Ben Tillman succeeded in destroying the South Carolina Alliance in 1892, while the order's lecturers had never built a statewide mass movement in Virginia and Louisiana. In all these states, the third party cause was heavily burdened in 1892 with a national ticket headed by a former Union general. Sectional loyalties, therefore, concealed the depth of the Alliance organizing achievement; in 1894, with no national ticket, state third parties with strong cooperative bases in the South grew surprisingly.

The same dynamics described the third party's fate in the West. The mass cooperative movements in Kansas and the Dakotas implemented coordinated lecturing campaigns on the sub-treasury in 1891–92 and succeeded in transferring sizable proportions of their Alliance memberships to the new third party. The relative thoroughness with which the doctrines of greenbackism had been absorbed by thousands of farmers in Kansas and the Dakotas ensured a Populistic dedication to the Omaha Platform, even in those instances where temporary alliances with Democrats were affected. But in Nebraska, the absence of a cooperative structure, and the absence of the cooperative experience itself, left a political movement wholly unrelated—and unresponsive—to the greenback doctrines of the Omaha Platform. The extremely shallow base for the third party in Illinois, Wisconsin, Iowa, and Minnesota left by the Northwestern Alliance had only been partially augmented by the belated organizing campaign of the National Alliance in 1891–92. Similarly, Alliance organizers had raised the banner of cooperation from the mountain states to California in the national lecturing campaigns of 1890–92. Where the shoots had taken root—especially in parts of Washington, Oregon, California, and eastern Colorado, impressive numbers of farmers became Populists. In mining states, the agrarian base was augmented by miners who liked the free silver plank of the Omaha Platform. In such instances, of course, the miners were no more imbued with the greenback principles underlying the cooperative crusade than their agrarian neighbors in Nebraska were. Throughout both the South and the West, therefore, the strength and sense of purpose of Populism was directly related to the strength and sense of purpose of the co-

315

operative crusade that had created the reform movement. The National Alliance and the People's Party were institutional expressions of the same movement and the same movement culture.

3

Nevertheless, a national political institution in a country of continental dimensions is necessarily a complex entity. For this reason, the variety and vitality of Populist creativity can only be grasped by observing the reform movement as it labored in thousands of locales across America.

In the heartland of the Western granary, along the farming frontier from Dakota to Kansas, the new third party had a complicated inaugural campaign in 1892. Nebraska Populism, somewhat ill-defined as a movement of "Independents" in 1890, underwent a partial re-organization before the 1892 elections. In the summer of 1892, in the very week that the advance guard of the National Alliance began arriving in St. Louis to form the People's Party, Jay Burrows retired— somewhat reluctantly—from the agrarian revolt. Having failed of nomination by his fellow Nebraska Alliancemen as a delegate to the St. Louis meeting, and having been rebuffed also on his stand against merger with the National Alliance, Burrows sold his interest in the Lincoln newspaper, the *Farmers Alliance*. He resigned with a strange parting salvo at the subtreasury plan: in it, among other things, he conceded the value of the plan "to the destitute farmers of the North and South." He left behind an organizational shell whose members had been kept securely outside the mainstream of the agrarian revolt ever since the cooperative movement had begun to sweep the South and West in 1887–88. A fitting comment on the termination of his divisive tenure in Nebraska came in the first post-Burrows issue of his old newspaper. The new editors endorsed L. L. Polk for the People's Party presidential nomination and ran a front-page article explaining the sub-treasury system. It was virtually the first time Nebraska farmers had heard of either—other than in denunciatory terms in the metropolitan Republican press.[7]

In the fall of 1892 the shadow movement of Populism in

Nebraska immersed itself in Democratic fusion—and on Democratic terms. A modicum of success resulted. The fusionists re-elected Omar Kem and William Jennings Bryan to Congress, giving each party a man of its choice, and supported a third "straight-out" fusionist who won. The Republicans swept the state offices from the governorship on down and won the other three congressional seats and the state's electoral votes for Harrison. The ideological disarray in these proceedings caused surprisingly few internal tremors—a clear indication that the third party in Nebraska, having failed to generate a culture of reform, possessed few reform principles it considered important enough to defend.[8]

Despite their remarkable showing in 1890, the Kansas Populists entered the 1892 campaign with a certain anxiety. Local municipal elections across the state in 1891 seemed to indicate that the "People's" ticket was considerably more difficult to put across to voters than had been the "Alliance" ticket of 1890. In 1891 the Republicans had won 277 local offices to the Populists' 127, a shocking change from the previous year, when Alliancemen had won 324 to only 71 for the G.O.P. This setback caused a shift in policy. Officeholders, who were rather prominent in the Kansas third party leadership, responded to the election returns by sounding out Democrats on the idea of possible cooperation. For the governorship the Populists nominated L. D. Lewelling, a Wichita merchant and ardent egalitarian who had advised the nominating convention to "welcome honorable allies" and "go forth to victory." Advocates of fusion, though heavily outnumbered in the Kansas People's Party, were hard at work in the state. Except for two congressional districts where bona fide three-cornered races were in prospect, the Republicans faced a united Populist-Democracy running on the basis of the Omaha Platform. The third party's adroit, pragmatic state chairman, John Breidenthal, soon converted both races into two-sided affairs by persuading the Democrat to withdraw in one district and the Populist to do so in the other.[9]

The resulting victory of the People's Party was, or appeared to be, something of a sweep. Lewelling and the entire Populist state ticket won, though by a narrow margin of 5000 votes out of 320,000 cast. The People's Party had gained control of the state senate, but on the face of the Republican-certified returns, the Populists had unaccountably lost their huge margin in the House. A comparison with the 1890 returns reveals that the total of Populist and Democratic votes had declined, from 178,000 to 163,000, while the Republican total had climbed dramatically, from 115,000 to 158,000. Cooperation with Democrats on the basis of the Omaha Platform had staved off defeat, but the great flood of votes in 1890 that seemed to presage a new kind of democratic politics emanating from the American heartland had not been augmented; instead, the rude warning of the municipal elections of 1891 had been confirmed. Though the Republicans had tacked into the wind—their platform appeared to some to be "every bit as radical" as the Populist platform—the violence of the Republican press attack on the third party presumably removed any uncertainty among the voters as to who represented the old order. The statewide Populist vote was the ominous portent. It seemed to contradict the realities of severe economic hardship that persisted among the great majority of the Kansas population. Could it be that the message of radicalism had not been understood by thousands of potential recruits? The rest of the nation interpreted the election as a Populist triumph, but the most astute agrarians in the state might well have anticipated William Allen White and asked, "What's the Matter with Kansas?" The "party of plutocracy" had absorbed the full shock of the land depression, yet it still was able to poll within 1 per cent of its combined opposition. Such resiliency was sobering. Sectional loyalty to the old party was remarkably enduring. Was the "coming revolution" but a fragile illusion? [10]

But this perhaps was an overly pessimistic view. The years of Alliance organizing had clearly created a new climate of politics in the West. The Greenback and Union Labor parties had never achieved the kind of organic presence across the region that the new People's Party attained in 1892. Even in the Dakotas, where Republican partisans frantically waved the bloody shirt in an effort to keep the citizenry from focusing too closely on economic issues, the People's Party emerged in a far stronger position than had any previous reform institution. Though sectionalism was manifestly alive and well in the hearts of hundreds of thousands of voters, the new ideas of the Omaha Platform had reached many other hundreds of thousands.[11]

Evidence to support this reality appeared in Western states all the way to the Pacific coast. Indeed, it was apparent that nowhere in America was sectionalism less of an issue than in the new states of the mountain West. Through the 1880's, the politics of the mountain states had become increasingly centered around the issue of free coinage of silver, particularly in the mining regions of Colorado, Nevada, and Idaho. A kind of one-issue Populism immediately flourished there as soon as the third party was formed. Indeed, both the Democratic and Republican parties developed obstreperous silver factions. Since the Populists possessed the only party free of conservative inhibitions on the silver question, under third party sponsorship fusion became the order of the day.

In Colorado a radical Aspen editor named Davis H. Waite was nominated for the governorship by the Populists, endorsed by the Democrats, and elected in November. After an 1893 speech in which he said "It is better, infinitely better, that blood should flow to the horses' bridles rather than our national liberties should be destroyed," he became widely known as "Bloody Bridles" Waite. Plagued with a Republican-controlled House, Waite could achieve little in the way of lasting reform. The state legislature not only refused to pass the strict railroad regulation bill he proposed, but also repealed the existing law. Waite's subsequent conduct in a complex and bitter strike in the gold-mining district near Cripple Creek averted probable bloodshed, but won him no plaudits from Republicans. In any event, though Waite's broadly democratic ideas have been called "those of a fanatic," ideas as such were not the organizing element in Populism in Colorado. The emotional pull of "free silver" was.[12]

The same single-mindedness characterized the third party in Nevada, where, in fact, it was known as the "Silver Party." Both the national Republican and Democratic parties nominated hard-money champions in 1892, and the newly organized Nevada Silver Party soon acquired a virtual monopoly on presidential electors. Majority "pro-silver" factions of the other two parties in Nevada simply refused to place presidential electors on their ballots. The Nevada third party men were a motley collection of special interest representatives, and the party itself was dominated, interestingly enough, by railroad interests allied with silver mineowners. The victorious Silverites nevertheless gave their three votes in the electoral college to Weaver. In Idaho the free-silver Populists were less successful as a state party, but hardly less so in the presidential contest. The triumphant silver Democrats bypassed Grover Cleveland and cast all their electoral votes for Weaver.[13]

In stock-raising Wyoming it was not free silver, but the Johnson County War of the spring of 1892 that wildly disfigured the state's politics, endangering the Republican edifice that had been painstakingly constructed by patronage-minded Francis E. Warren. An unusual Populist-Democratic fusion that placed the entire Democratic state ticket on the same ballot with Populist presidential electors yielded victory through what was easily one of the most broad-based coalitions of the 1890's. The Wyoming winners, composed of unequal portions of conservative Democrats, Populists, cattle rustlers, and settlers, were variously indignant over the invasion of Johnson County by cattlemen and their hired gunmen. Unfortunately for all parties, their votes placed in power a lemming-like coterie of Democratic politicians who muddled through the ensuing 1893 legislative session with an incompetence that gave the state's citizenry something besides its cattle kings to worry about—leaving the Populists still coalition-minded but shorn of power in 1894.[14]

The third party had a broader thrust in Montana, where it primarily represented a movement of the urban working class, augmented by farmers mobilized by the newly arrived National Alliance. These groups formed the backbone of the Montana People's Party, which ran a fairly strong third to the two major parties in 1892. The strongest Populist vote-getter in Montana was the candidate for Attorney General, a woman's rights advocate named Ella Knowles.[15]

Effective farmer-labor coalitions were also achieved in the Pacific Northwest, where the agrarian element played a larger role than it did in the mining states. Polk's organizers had arrived in Washington in July of 1890 and had established some 200 suballiances by the following year. An Alliance Implement Company was capitalized at $100,000 and a state journal, the *Alliance Manifesto,* inaugurated at Spokane. In 1892, the third party nominated a Whitman County farmer named C. W. Young for the governorship, and he ran particularly well in the Alliance strongholds of eastern Washington. The victorious Republican received 33,000 votes to 29,000 for the Democrat and 23,000 for the Populist aspirant. The agrarian-based third party's maiden performance in state politics both surprised and impressed Washingtonians.[16]

The Alliance, with the oratorical assistance of "Cyclone" Davis, arrived in Oregon in 1890 and came under the aggressive influence of what proved to be one of Populism's hardest working couples, Seth and Sophronia Lewelling. The Oregon People's Party was formed in the spring of 1892, on the day following the state Alliance convention. The new party, strongest in the farming districts, ran third in 1892, as did a somewhat out-manned but militant third party in California. Following the election, the California party immediately began putting out feelers to working-class elements in San Francisco and other cities as a step toward a workable farmer-labor coalition. Signs of cooperation appeared that augured well for the third party's future.[17]

Nevertheless, not all the indicators in the West were positive. Some of the biggest disappointments of the 1892 campaign came in what had been counted on as potentially fruitful third party territory in the Old Northwest. The People's Party did unexpectedly poorly in the entire Great Lakes region extending through Minnesota, Wisconsin, Michigan, Iowa, Illinois, Indiana, and Ohio. In these states, which comprised much of the original territory of the Northwestern Alliance, what little agrarian strength that materialized in 1892 largely stemmed from the efforts of the National Farmers Alliance. This organizing work, while encountering very little counter-organizing by the Northwestern group, did meet with a fair volume of rhetorical resistance. The Republican secretary of the moribund Wisconsin affiliate of the Northwestern group issued a frantic announcement in 1892 that employed the language of bloody-shirt politics. Addressed to the "loyal Alliances of Wisconsin," the missive deplored the latest defection from the ranks, Ignatius Donnelly, characterizing the event as a "sell-out" to the Southern-based order. While such strictures could have small effect on the Wisconsin membership—it being virtually nonexistent—the latent sectional issue produced confusion, and confused farmers proved hard to organize. The People's Party thus had to build upon a very shallow base in much of the Old Northwest in 1892, and the election returns indicate that very little work had been completed prior to the November elections.[18]

Even in Minnesota, where matters were under the management of the author of the ringing preamble to the Omaha Platform, Populism failed to capture the expected following. Engaged in constant internal wrangling within his faction-ridden Minnesota Alliance, Donnelly employed the sub-treasury plan to "draw a line" of a somewhat more subtle variety than was carved in the South. The Sage of Nininger used the subtreasury as a device to outwit rivals among the various labor and farm factions inside the Alliance and thus gain control of the newly formed Minnesota People's Party. He subsequently labored strenuously to heal all wounds while carrying the third party's standard for the governorship. Though Donnelly was enthusiastic and confident, the Alliance had always been so loosely conceived in Minnesota that most potential recruits to the cause of reform still remained securely outside the organization. In 1892, Populism's foremost novelist learned the limits of rhetorical display as an instrument of social change. Despite an exhausting speaking campaign, he led the People's Party to a convincing defeat. In the race for the governorship, the Republican received 109,000 votes to 94,000 for the Democratic candidate and 40,000 for Donnelly. In the presidential race, Minnesota gave Weaver 11 per cent of its vote. Utterly disconsolate, Donnelly wrote in his diary: "Beaten! Whipped! Smashed! . . . Our followers scattered like dew before the rising sun." [19]

Elsewhere the third party showing was even more feeble. Weaver received less than 5 per cent of the vote from

Michigan across to Ohio. Most humiliating of all, he did equally poorly in his native state of Iowa. The Old Northwest still had plenty of agrarians, but no hope of an agrarian movement. The organizing prerequisites that were essential if the heritage of sectionalism were to be overcome had simply never been fulfilled.[20]

4

But whatever happened in the upper Midwest in 1892, Populism's greatest test, as all radicals understood, lay in the American South. The idea of a great multi-sectional party of "the industrial millions" had always shattered on the rock of the solid Democratic South. Indeed, the one enduring lesson of post-Civil War politics in America was the simple, continuing reality that all third party efforts in the 1870's and 1880's had been confined to a narrow tier of states in the frontier West and had never been able to penetrate the South. If Populism was to overcome the sectional bonds that had strangled the Greenback and Union Labor parties, the South had to be one of the principal ingredients of the new mass coalition.

For an answer, radical strategists did not have long to wait; the new party's very first test came a month after the Omaha convention—in the Alabama state elections of 1892. The contest revealed the stresses and strains awaiting Populist candidates across the South during the life of the agrarian revolt. The state's chief agrarian spokesman, a former state agricultural commissioner named Reuben Kolb, had been denied the Democratic party's gubernatorial nomination in 1890 through what both he and his Alliance followers regarded as shameful stacking of the convention delegations. But while Alabama Alliancemen learned the futility of "reform through the Democrats" in 1890–91, and numbers of Alabama farmers moved toward an outright break with the old party, Kolb lagged considerably behind them. In the time available to it in 1891–92, the large Alabama Alliance tried manfully to employ the sub-treasury issue as the driving wedge. But one Alabama writer reported that "many Alliance members did not understand the sub-treasury plan." Nevertheless, the Macune plan found many willing advocates in the state, and the sub-treasury message was brought home, if not to all farmers, certainly to many thousands. As one reform editor hopefully summarized matters, "The people are learning that the sub-treasury means more money, more liberty and final freedom from serfdom." As Alliancemen became more and more alientated from Democratic conservatives in 1891–92, Democratic chicanery in county conventions became brazen. In counties where they were outnumbered, even heavily outnumbered, the regulars simply withdrew and held separate rump conventions, secure in the knowledge that their own state committee would seat them. Kolb thereupon announced his intention to oppose the "machine Democrats" by organizing the "simon-pure Jeffersonian Democrats." And he and his supporters did exactly that. Kolb was chosen as the nominee of the "Jeffersonian Democrats" at a statewide convention dominated by the Alliance, and incumbent Governor Thomas Jones was renominated by the conservatives. The farmers declared that they wanted Kolb for Governor and Weaver for President. The first political battle of the agrarian revolt in Alabama thus took place both inside and outside the Democratic Party, a circumstance that scarcely diminished the calumny and vituperation against the Kolbites.[21]

The resulting election was as fraudulent as the nominating process had been earlier in the year. On the face of the returns, Jones received 126,959 votes to Kolb's 115,524. But, as an unusually candid Democratic paper conceded, "the truth is that Kolb carried the state, but was swindled out of his victory by the Jones faction, which had control of the election machinery and used it with unblushing trickery and corruption." It developed that a largely fictitious black vote had been decisive. In the "black belt" counties, which ranged up to 80 per cent Negro in population but had long been dominated by the planter faction, huge majorities for Jones offset Kolb's margins in the poor-land counties, where white farmers constituted the majority. Twelve black belt counties returned majorities of 26,000 for Jones—more than double his statewide margin. As a later congressional investigation showed, "Negroes who had been dead for years and others who had long since left the county" somehow voted Democratic. Also added to the poll list and counted as voters were "hundreds of ficti- tious names." In the upland counties, many of which had seen the growth of an active Colored Farmers Alliance and a period of cooperation between farmers of both races, the ma- jority of black farmers voted for Kolb along with their white compatriots. Indeed, even in one black belt county, Choctaw, the Colored Farmers Alliance was well enough organized that a majority of blacks voted for Kolb despite all the outside pres- sures that were brought to bear.[22]

Violence was an ever-present dimension of the Alabama campaigns of the 1890's. Reform editors lived a perilous exis- tence. They became involved in shooting affrays, and one, Joseph C. Manning, a white man, narrowly escaped death when he was beaten and driven from the town of Florence by a frenzied Democratic mob. The *Ozark Banner,* the voice of the Colored Farmers Alliance in Alabama, announced its inten- tion to "eschew politics from its columns." Colonel James Whitehead, editor of the *Greenville Living Truth,* spoke for most Alabama Populists when he declared that Jones was not governor of the whole people, but only of "a lot of ballot-box thieves, and this is the whole of it." [23]

Despite the state-level disappointment, the third party elected hundreds of local officials. The agrarian revolt thus acquired a measure of political structure in Alabama, and Populist spokesmen there became determined to push "the revolution" to its proper conclusion. Clearly, the new political movement threatened the inherited ways.

In Georgia the third party sought to lead with its strongest candidate by awarding its gubernatorial nomination to Thomas Watson. But when Watson decided to run for re-elec- tion in his tenth congressional district instead, the Georgia Al- liance turned to the guiding spirit of its statewide cooperative exchange, "a real dirt farmer" named W. L. Peek. A man of considerable ability, Peek was not at his best on the campaign trail, but he did symbolize the commitment of Georgia Al- liancemen to their order, to the cooperative crusade, and to the sub-treasury plan. The final defeat of the views of Lon Livingston inside the Georgia Alliance had been clear since March 1892, by which time no less than 1600 of the 2200

Georgia suballiances had explicitly endorsed the full Ocala Platform in an impressive display of farmer solidarity. Nevertheless, in the fall elections national attention focused not on the governor's race, but on Tom Watson's tenth district. The pro-Alliance Congressman's outspoken attacks on the two old parties in Washington had earned him national attention—and symbolic status as a barometer of the third party's future in the deep South. Watson's statements in *The People's Party Paper,* and the press accounts of his opinions and behavior "were read, reread and vehemently discussed." His Democratic opponent, Major James Black, invoked the familiar appeals of Southern sectionalism, stressing his own Civil War service and the need for white Southerners to stay with the old party to avoid the possibility of Negro "domination." The Democratic press, solidly behind him, raised the specter of Reconstruction and the "revival of bayonet rule." [24]

Watson's ability to overcome such Democratic tactics seemed so symbolically linked with the Southern future of the third party that though the ensuing campaign was waged in a single congressional district no less a personage than Grover Cleveland confided that "he was almost as much interested in Major Black's campaign in the Tenth District of Georgia as he was in his own election." Businessmen in Augusta, the district's principal city, made special appeals to their financial connections in New York City on the grounds that Watson was "a sworn enemy of capital, and that his defeat was a matter of importance to every investor in the country." The *New-York Tribune* reported that railroad and insurance interests responded "liberally" to this appeal, augmenting local Georgia money with $40,000.[25]

The intensity of the campaign was unparalleled. The Atlanta *Constitution* felt that the threat of "anarchy and communism" extended to the entire South because of "the direful teachings of Thomas E. Watson." At one point Watson's supporters rode all night to rally to a black Populist who had been threatened with lynching; the Augusta *Chronicle* was too outraged to feel the need for a bill of particulars. "Watson has gone mad," the paper decided. The conduct of Democratic managers on election day was so openly fraudulent that one historian specified "intimidation, bribery, ballot-box stuffing, and manipulation of the count," as applicable adjectives, while another settled for "terror, fraud, corruption, and trickery." Imposing Populist majorities in rural districts were reduced when Democratic judges threw out whole precincts on technicalities, while in Major Black's sole bastion of support, Richmond County, containing the city of Augusta, Democratic majorities soared to 80 per cent. The total vote solemnly returned by election judges in Richmond exceeded double the number of legal voters. On the face of the returns, Richmond County provided Black with over 60 per cent of the vote he received in the entire district—enough to offset heavy Watson majorities in the surrounding rural counties and provide the margin for a Democratic "victory." [26]

But not even wholesale thefts could conceal the remarkable growth of the new party. In the state elections held in October, a bare three months after the formation of the third party in Georgia, the Democratic plurality had been 71,000, a margin of two to one. Over the next month the Populists organized and campaigned, and the state saw Watson and Black fight it out. When the national election was held in November, the Democrats' statewide total—even on the face of obviously manipulated returns—had been reduced to 31,000. Other, less precise statistics added another dimension to the new Southern politics. Whether the white vote had been counted fairly or not, it was clear to all that blacks now held the balance of power in Georgia. A number of murders occurred—no one knows how many. At Dalton, a Negro man who had spoken for Populism was killed in his home, and a black minister who repeatedly spoke for Watson was fired upon at a rally, the errant bullet striking a near-by white man and killing him. Election day murders took place elsewhere, particularly in Watson's tenth district. Black plantation hands were hauled to the polls in droves by Democratic managers— some from South Carolina, across the Savannah River—and voted "repeatedly." Only by such fraud—one might even say "strenuous fraud," considering the transportation costs involved—did the Democratic Party hold its lines intact in Georgia in 1892.[27]

Populists who took a longer view found much that was encouraging. For white farmers, the prospect of leaving the party of the fathers involved far more than a political choice; it called into question the deepest cultural presumptions of their heritage. Even so, at the first opportunity thousands of Georgia's farmers had successfully made the transition, and thousands more had followed a short four weeks later. Populism had become an immediate and formidable force in Georgia politics.

In Alabama and Georgia, men like Kolb and Watson contested orthodox leaders of the conservative "New South." In Texas in 1892, the third party faced a more complicated political opposition. The Texas Democracy was split into two factions—a dominant "reform" wing, largely based on Alliance voters and headed by Governor Hogg, and a "goldbug" faction, led by railroad lawyer George Clark. While the Democratic division seemed to augur well for the third party, Hogg's platform style and his apparent dissociation from the railroad wing of the party cut heavily into the Alliance vote. The hostility toward Hogg demonstrated by the Alliance leadership in 1891 by no means extended to all the members, particularly those most conscious of their Southern heritage. In 1891 the Hoggites had presided over the enactment of the state's first Jim Crow statute—for separate railroad accommodations—and the Governor was not above augmenting this appeal with patriotic embraces of the party of the fathers.[28]

The Republican Party, which numbered some 75,000 to 90,000 black voters among its constituency, played a decisive but enormously complicated role in the 1892 campaign. The three contending parties competed fiercely for the black vote, the Populists through the structure of the Colored Farmers Alliance and the newly forming Populist clubs across the state, the "Railroad Democrats" through a "top-down" arrangement with Negro Republican leader Norris Wright Cuney, and the Hoggites through the time-tested Democratic methods of bribery, intimidation, and overt violence.[29]

The third party nominated as its gubernatorial standard-bearer Judge Thomas Nugent. He was easily one of Populism's most striking contributions to American politics. A soft-spoken man, Nugent possessed qualifications not normally seen on Southern political hustings. Widely read in both economics and religion, his speeches were studded with quotations from Immanuel Kant, William James, John Stuart Mill, David Ricardo, and Herbert Spencer, in addition to such Populist favorites as Thomas Jefferson, Thomas Paine, and Edward Bellamy. Despite a deep, personal radicalism, Nugent articulated the Populist creed without rhetorical flourish. He addressed himself to the "labor question" and the "problem of the distribution of wealth," which he considered paramount among the nation's political issues, but he also stressed the socio-theological values he felt the Republic and its citizens needed to achieve. A Swedenborgian in religion, Nugent was essentially a radical humanist. His bald head, flowing beard, and quiet but confident manner gave him the aura of a prophet. In ways not common among the Texas electorate, Nugent's followers reacted to him with a strange intensity that sometimes bordered on reverence. Even Populism's most implacable foes were impressed by him. After 1000 delegates—many of whom the Dallas *News* had followed with growing alarm for years—nominated Nugent and then wildly cheered his thoughtful summation of the Populist vision, the *News* pondered the speech and then described the third party's standard-bearer as "a quiet, self-contained, intellectual and scholarly man, and an accomplished lawyer." His presence would lend "dignity and moral elevation to the campaign." As for Nugent's supporters, the *News* decided that "their earnestness, bordering on religious fanaticism, has a touch of the kind of metal that made Cromwell's round heads so terrible a force." Concluded the *News,* "It would be supreme folly to despise and belittle a movement that is leavened with such moral stuff as this." [30]

But in Texas, as elsewhere in the nation, ridicule had an irresistible appeal to politicians who preferred not to discuss the causes of poverty on Populist terms. Nugent calmly turned aside such thrusts by accepting the charge of unorthodoxy—and then linking unorthodox ideas to the teachings of Jesus, one who "did not hesitate to denounce wrong, even though [it was] hedged about and protected by social power and influence." In Nugent's hands, Populism was inextricably linked both to socialism and to a very carefully defined Prince of Peace:

> Jesus . . . saw the fatal tendency of men to think in customary and institutional lines and He apparently sought to lift His fellows into the upper realms, where truth, absolute truth, may be viewed in freedom. . . . Whatever may be said of Christ, whether man only or God-man, His presence in the world strangely and wonderfully moved the common people and the influence which He left in the natural sphere of life aroused an intense sentiment of fraternity in an age and among a people immersed in dead formalities and blindly devoted to ease and priestly rule. Here was the beginning of Christian socialism. A new force was liberated into the world—vital, fundamental truths thrown upon the currents of public thought, and thus sent drifting down the ages. Was Christ the consummate product of divine evolution . . . led forth into the human world to transform and uplift and glorify the social Man? [31]

Texans were not used to hearing their politicians conclude lofty passages with question marks; it took a while for the "Nugent tradition," as it came to be known, to catch on. The three-way 1892 campaign saw the contenders divide the white vote fairly evenly, but both Clark and Nugent were snowed under by black votes for Hogg. The returns gave Hogg 190,000, Clark 133,000, and Nugent 108,000. In the score of Texas counties containing heavy concentrations of black voters, Nugent ran a poor third, sometimes receiving less than 1 per cent of the vote. The same was true in predominantly Mexican-American portions of South Texas, where the neo-feudalistic bosses, the *patrones,* lined up about equally behind the railroad candidate and the incumbent Governor. Intimidation and terrorism proved as effective in Texas as they had in Alabama and Georgia.[32]

If something on the order of half the Alliance membership in Texas had opted for the People's Party at the first opportunity, reformers there seemed merely to increase their efforts to win the remainder in the off-season. Their achievements provide an interesting footnote to the agrarian revolt and to the history of democratic reform movements in America. Veteran Alliance lecturers, augmented by a steadily expanding reform press, carried the radical doctrines of the Omaha Platform to the farthest reaches of the state. Elaborate summer encampments—a Populist folkway that hugely discomfited Democrats in Texas—began to reach alarming proportions in 1893–94. Defections from the Democracy went beyond the remaining moderate Alliance leaders, who were late joining the third party, to include thousands of rank-and-file farmers. With the People's Party beginning to enroll whole farming districts, the growth of the ranks of reform became obvious to everyone in Texas. In the spring of 1894 the Hoggites lost their poise. The Texas Democracy hurriedly closed ranks, the "reform" forces of Jim Hogg making sweeping concessions to the railroad wing of the party in exchange for party unity.[33]

Though Democrats unified in the face of the Populist threat, their fears were scarcely allayed. In the 1894 elections the Texas People's Party set the stars of the Alliance lecturing system upon the party of the fathers. Evan Jones, J. M. Perdue, and "Cyclone" Davis, along with Jerome Kearby, a gifted Dallas lawyer who had defended the Knights of Labor leaders in the Great Southwest Strike of 1886, ran for Congress. William Lamb's Reform Press Association of 1891 mobilized over a hundred editors by 1894, and "Stump" Ashby, the state party's chairman, presided over a corps of orators that included John B. Rayner, the huge, three-hundred-pound black apostle of Populism, and Melvin Wade, the radical black trade unionist. While Wade worked in the cities, Rayner, a tireless organizer, trained scores of local lieutenants to carry the doctrines of reform into the rural underside of the Republican Party apparatus even as Democratic leaders sought to make financial and patronage bargains at the top with black Republican managers. The Populists also printed German-language newspapers and dispatched German-speaking Populists through the hill country of Central Texas. The third party more or less wrote off congressional districts in the southern one-fourth of the state, as the instruments of social control in the Mexican-American districts simply proved too formidable

Populist Gubernatorial Aspirants

Thomas Nugent   Reuben Kolb

for the reformers to overcome. On election day, the third party carried vast sections of North and West Texas and dominated in parts of the central and eastern regions of the state—seven congressional districts in all. The Populists were counted out in every one of them. The methods were the same as in Georgia and Alabama—wholesale ballot-box stuffing, open bribery, various forms of intimidation, and massive voting by dead or fictitious Negroes.[34]

The Richmond County methods of Georgia were almost precisely duplicated in the "Harrison County methods" used in East Texas to defeat "Cyclone" Davis. The same tactics were employed elsewhere to repel the remainder of the Populist ticket. Indeed, in Texas the phrase "Harrison County methods" became the standard term defining the most effective Democratic campaign technique of the Populist era. Even on the face of the returns, and including in the total the controlled vote of South Texas, the Populist vote jumped from the 23 per cent of 1892 to almost 40 per cent in 1894. The "official" statewide total showed Nugent had been defeated for the governorship by 230,000 to 160,000, though a number of steps were taken to ensure that the real outcome would be forever beyond recovery. The Populist candidates went to court—unsuccessfully—and the *Southern Mercury* led a chorus of indignation in the Texas reform press.[35]

Meanwhile, the third party faithful shrugged their shoulders and renewed their off-year "educational" campaign. The trains of farm wagons grew ever longer, and the Populist encampments of 1895 were the largest the state had ever seen. In the eighteenth year of the agrarian movement in Texas, a grim determination settled over the Alliance founders. In a desperate effort to cope with Democratic intimidation and terrorism, the old Vidette organization recreated itself as "Gideon's Band," a paramilitary unit dedicated to ensuring a "free ballot and a fair count." The language of Texas Populism, flowing up out of the greenback-Alliance heritage, had a constancy and passion that few outside of Kansas—or the tenth district of Georgia—could match.[36]

Nowhere else in the South, however, was the Alliance able immediately to transfer its constituency to the third party on the scale achieved in Georgia, Alabama, and Texas. The reasons varied, and they sometimes seemed to stem from contradictory causes. The fate of Populism in Louisiana, however, was scarcely puzzling; indeed, given the interrelated character of that state's fraud and violence, the story of Populism there is most coherently told as a single piece. The rather slow Populist entry in Louisiana politics in 1892 was followed by unmistakable signs of growth in 1894 and then by an impassioned struggle in 1896 that ended in anarchy by conservatives and a threat of civil insurrection. The fledgling People's Party had to compensate for an incomplete Alliance organizing effort in the 1880's that was at least partly traceable to the lack of skill of its founding leader, J. A. Tetts. Even after the minuscule Farmers Union formed by Tetts merged with the Alliance at Waco in 1887 the Louisiana agrarian spokesman proved unable to fashion a broad lecturing system of the kind that spread Alliance growth across most of the South. The agrarian cause was further hampered in 1892 by byzantine factional maneuvering growing out of a campaign to end Louisiana's infamous state lottery. The political arena was crowded with urban politicians and reformers from New Orleans, upcountry Protestants, French Catholics from South Louisiana, lottery and anti-lottery forces, a divided Republican Party, and a fearsome breed of intermittently violent planters from the delta parishes; in all the confusion such issues as the Omaha Platform and the sub-treasury plan never gained much clarity in Louisiana. Nevertheless, periodic visits as early as 1890 by Cuthbert Vincent and other Kansans set some agrarian sparks aglow in the hill parishes of the northern part of the state. One of the Louisiana agrarian spokesmen who emerged from these early organizing efforts showed up at the Cincinnati convention in 1891 with third party credentials signed by 1200 of his constituents—only 131 shy of the total adult population of the parish. It is clear that Populist doctrines had strong roots in at least one region of the state. The name of the parish was Winn, and its thoroughly documented representative at Cincinnati, a minister's son named Hardy Brian, went on to become a third party legislator and the leader of Louisiana Populism. Brian thus antedated a somewhat better known agrarian whom Winn Parish would offer the nation in the twentieth century—Huey Long. The storied career of the Kingfish, in fact, is rendered partly understandable by the prior experiences of Brian in the Populist era.[37]

Well-organized Populist congressional campaigns in two hill-country districts in 1894 were defeated through varieties of ballot box thievery that in sheer arrogance and venality surpassed similar depredations in the rest of the South. Beginning with its founding meeting, which brought together members of both the white and the black Alliances, the Louisiana third party had developed a most un-Southern proclivity for interracial cooperation; after the 1894 campaign, alarmed Democrats concocted an elaborate "election reform" law to disfranchise thousands of impoverished farmers of both races. Populist resistance to this proposal, led by Brian, was of a character that inevitably prepared the way for a Populist-Republican coalition in 1895–96. This combination, though somewhat vague and sometimes even contradictory in the political principles enunciated by its variegated spokesmen, posed a clear threat to the state's ruling oligarchy for the first time since Reconstruction. The conservative press promptly christened it the "Populist-negro social equality ticket," but others saw economic conditions as the underlying threat to the structure of state politics. "I fear if there is nothing done to alleviate the suffering among the people," wrote one farmer, "we will have a revolution. . . . The people are restless." The party of white supremacy readied some revolutionary tactics of its own—and did so in public print. The Shreveport *Evening Judge* announced that "it is the religious duty of Democrats to rob Populists and Republicans of their votes whenever and wherever the opportunity presents itself and any failure to do so will be a violation of true Louisiana Democratic teaching. The Populists and Republicans are our legitimate political prey. Rob them! You bet! What are we here for?" Sometimes, however, conservative repression became too much even for its own agents to bear. A state trooper dispatched to one troubled registration precinct completed his investigation and then indiscreetly told a reporter that Democratic partisans had "unmercifully whipped" a Negro woman with barbed wire in order to discourage Populist-Republican activities.[38]

The gubernatorial candidate of the coalition, John Pharr, might best be described in modern terms as a liberal Republican planter. He had a habit of ignoring prevailing mores. The anti-lynching plank in his platform convinced the New Orleans *Daily States* that he "inferentially approved" of white women being raped. The campaign style of the mild-mannered Pharr, though admittedly a violation of form, fell somewhat short of a call for rape. In one of his campaign speeches, he said: "I was reared with the negro and worked side by side with him for twenty odd years. I have never found him other than a good laborer and as honest as most other men. If he has cut a bad figure in politics, we are to blame for it." Despite the paternalism implicit in Pharr's remarks, the New Orleans *Times-Democrat* derided him for traveling through the state "preaching the good qualities of Negroes," while the Baton Rouge *Daily Advocate* characterized the eminently respectable candidate as an "ignorant and low bred boor" who "proceeds from place to place scattering his fire-brands among the rabble and inciting the baser passions of the populace." Another Democratic newspaper tried to bring Negro political activity to a halt by printing the names of all black leaders who were "brewing up trouble," but the next issue of the paper revealed that the effort had been unsuccessful. "You might as well talk to a brick wall as to try to make the nigger believe who his best friend is," the paper complained. The "baser passions" that the Baton Rouge paper had warned against did, indeed, surface in Louisiana in 1896, though the source of the emotions seems to have been more readily fixed among the paper's subscribers than its political opponents. A multifaceted terrorism prevailed. Twenty-one lynchings occurred in Louisiana that year, one-fifth of the total for the entire nation.[39]

Physical intimidation having failed to achieve the desired end completely, Democrats were forced to steal the governorship through massive and transparent ballot box frauds. One Democrat, not bothering to deny the obvious, justified the action in the name of the political prerogatives of "a vast majority of the very best people" over the pretensions of what another party regular described as the "corrupt mass." The victorious Democratic governor was pleased to have retained "control of affairs" in the hands of what he described as "the intelligence and virtue of the State" over "the force of brute numbers." Neither white nor black farmers, however, submitted quietly. In Natchitoches "hundreds of armed and furious white Populists" threatened to assault the parish seat of government, "where Democratic election supervisors had refused to count the ballots from Negro Populist precincts." The farmers were dispersed by troops sent by the Governor. In St. John black voters seized a ballot box which they believed had been stuffed by white Democrats. After two white men were killed the Governor sent in a field artillery unit of state militia and, though "many Negroes organized for an attack upon the troops," the group ultimately dispersed. The legislature convened three weeks after the election in a state capital rife with threats and omens of Populist insurrection. But, as one chronicler of these events put it, the leaders of the farmers realized that they "did not have the guns or the organization to seize the State House by force of arms." The legislature, narrowly

Democratic, certified the "official" returns, and the campaign of 1896 became history. Though the massive frauds demoralized most Populists, Hardy Brian kept up the struggle until 1899, when he published the final issue of his Populist newspaper. In it the minister's son wrote, "We refused to take up the gun [and] so we lost. . . . The fight will be won some day, but by [unchristian] methods." In an historical sense, the remark was merely the penultimate commentary on possible methods of achieving democracy in Louisiana. The year after Brian gave up, another Winn County candidate running on a Populistic platform was defeated for the state legislature. It was to be this candidate's son, a young boy at the time, who three decades later would write the final apocalyptic paragraph to the rule of Louisiana's lawless oligarchy. Under the circumstances, it is not too much to say that Louisiana's "better element" received from Huey Long an even milder regime than they had earned through their own actions during the earlier decades of Reconstruction and Populism.[40]

The fate of Populism in South Carolina, Tennessee, Florida, Virginia and Arkansas revealed the variety of ways a reform movement could be sidetracked, or could sidetrack itself. In South Carolina, "Pitchfork Ben" Tillman, "the farmer's friend," destroyed Populism after a tense and demagogic campaign in 1891–92. Tillman endeavored to keep his maneuverings against the Alliance obscured by riveting public attention on his "war" with South Carolina's planter Democracy. However, his confidence in his own oratorical skill led him to a near-fatal blunder in 1891, when he accepted a debate on the sub-treasury plan with the national lecturer of the Alliance, Ben Terrell. The scale of the risk lay in the site of the debate: it was held before the South Carolina Alliance at its annual meeting. Though Tillman tried to use friends inside the Alliance to set a proper climate for the debate, the order's state president declared that South Carolina farmers could be "counted on to stand squarely by all the demands of the Alliance, Governor Tillman to the contrary, notwithstanding." The Alliance leader added, ominously, that "the temper of the people is such that they will repudiate any man, however trusted, who cannot support the Alliance demands."[41]

Tillman versus Terrell

"Pitchfork" Ben Tillman, Governor of South Carolina, left, and Ben Terrell, national lecturer of the Farmers Alliance, right, debated the Sub-Treasury plan before the South Carolina Alliance in 1891. Despite the Governor's characterization of Macune's monetary system as "socialistic," the Alliance farmers rebuked him publicly. The setback was temporary, however.

In this unusual struggle between an agrarian organization and a self-appointed agrarian spokesman, the Alliance lecturing system became crucial. On the eve of the debate county Alliances one after another endorsed the sub-treasury plan by lopsided majorities. The Tillman-Terrell debate itself took place on July 24, 1891. Tillman culminated his attack on the sub-treasury by calling it "socialistic." Alliancemen, for once, were not beguiled by their elusive Governor. They promptly endorsed the Ocala Platform, sub-treasury and all. The pro-Bourbon Columbia *Daily Register* gloated that Tillman had been made "to eat a good, large slice of humble pie." Shaken, Tillman confided a new strategy to a close associate: "I cannot speak now without saying something which may be tortured into an attack on the Alliance and its platform, hence my determination to remain absolutely silent and let things drift." [42]

In this immobilized position, Tillman found himself unable

to lead South Carolina's farmers away from their Alliance demands. So, in the spring of 1892, he made a great show of ca-
pitulating on the sub-treasury issue in a speech to an Alliance
assembly. He would stand by "all of the Alliance demands," he
announced. The move was successful. South Carolina farmers
rejoiced and carried Tillman from the platform. "Well, 'I went
and done it,'" Tillman exulted to a friend, "My Alliance
brethern are happy as the father of the prodigal son." The
wily Governor followed with a *coup de grâce*—the Tillman-
dominated Democratic Party endorsed the full Ocala Platform
in its state convention! The state's Bourbon press was outraged, of course, but Tillman had other game in mind: the
political isolation of the Farmers Alliance. By this process the
third party movement in South Carolina became immobilized.
After Cleveland's nomination party loyalist Tillman supported
the hard money candidate of the national Democratic Party.
Talking fast, "the Pitchfork man" said that he and his supporters would "eat Cleveland crow," but only after making the
state's conservatives "eat Tillman crow first." And they did.
Cleveland and Tillman won by overwhelming margins, while
the Populist presidential ticket received only 2410 votes in the
entire state. Dazed by it all, the leaders of the agrarian movement found themselves either outmaneuvered and cornered
or forced to go along with Tillman—even as their organization
lost its internal cohesion and political identity. In the course of
the fall campaign of 1892, the huge South Carolina State
Farmers Alliance, which housed one of the most impoverished
constituencies in the South, collapsed. The politics of the sub-
treasury had worked, but Tillman had co-opted the Alliance
platform and through effective demagoguery, had destroyed
the coherence of the reform movement.[43]

The Tennessee and Florida Alliances, on the other hand,
destroyed themselves. The 1890 Alliance successes in both
states installed in office prominent Alliancemen who subsequently proved quite reluctant to risk alienating part of their
support by breaking with the Democrats. In Tennessee Governor Buchanan and his successor as Alliance state president,
John McDowell, vacillated so long on the sub-treasury issue
that by the time McDowell committed himself to the third

party, a week before the Omaha convention, it was much too late to begin a lecturing program to educate the farmers on Populist issues. The bloody shirt waved long and lustily in Tennessee. McDowell was accused of being a member of the Loyal League during the Civil War and the Alliance leadership was charged with being too friendly to Negroes. McDowell, nearer to third party insurgency than Buchanan throughout 1891–92, was unable to win over his colleague until August 1892. After a hastily organized campaign, the embryonic Tennessee third party, with Buchanan at its head, suffered an overwhelming defeat. The depression of 1893, however, was compounded by riotous labor troubles among Tennessee miners, and the indifference of Democratic leaders to widespread hardship brought renewed determination to the slowly organizing third party forces. They hoped that in 1894 sheer poverty in the farming districts and degrading working conditions in the mines would accomplish what their own belated tactics on the sub-treasury in 1891–92 had failed to do—draw a clear distinction between the "plain people" and the Tennessee Democracy. Florida Alliancemen, influential in the councils of the Democratic Party, persuaded old party regulars to take a leaf from Tillman's book and endorse the Ocala Platform, a development that left the order's radicals with no opportunity to employ the politics of the sub-treasury. With Alliance farmers remaining loyal to the party of the fathers, Florida Populism was stillborn.[44]

The cooperative movement in Virginia, cautiously modeled along the Rochdale lines of the Grange, failed either to recruit or to instruct large numbers of the state's farmers about the underlying relationships between debtors, creditors, and a contracting currency. A belated push on the sub-treasury by the agrarian leadership in Virginia was not successful at the state level until October 1891, too late for the suballiances to achieve any widespread education on the issue prior to the election season of 1892. The slow pace of such necessary developments in Virginia betrayed a loosely organized state structure, a thin lecturing system, and an absence of activist thrust among the leadership. The story of Populism in the Old Dominion may be fairly summarized in a single sentence.

Lacking a strong Alliance organizational base among the state's farmers, the third party simply failed to achieve a genuine statewide political presence. In the one congressional district containing strong Alliance organizations, the Populist candidate won his race in 1892, but was counted out through fraudulent returns.[45]

In Arkansas, by contrast, the new party clearly suffered from the abrasive militancy of the early years of the state Agricultural Wheel, when radicals bypassed thousands of "nonpartisan" Democrats. The close elections of 1888 and 1890 were revealed in 1892 to have been based on a sizable proportion of Negro support. The 1892 campaign, which involved separate Republican, Democratic, and Populist tickets, saw the People's Party run a poor third.[46]

The North Carolina People's Party was unique in the nation. A bizarre juxtaposition of agrarian numerical strength and leadership hesitancy resulted in 1892 in huge defections from the Alliance, a development that was immediately translated into a crushing defeat for the third party in what had been regarded as one of the strongholds of the Southern Alliance. The sudden death of Polk, a decision by the Democrats to nominate the Alliance state president, Elias Carr, for the governorship, and a confused sequence of maneuvers by Marion Butler, Polk's reluctant successor as third party spokesman, all contributed to the massive split in the Alliance organization. But these happenings were essentially a manifestation of a deeper malady. While Polk had led strongly on political issues, he proved quite cautious within the cooperative movement. Under his tutelage the North Carolina Alliance had never implemented a statewide marketing and purchasing cooperative. Indeed, the caution that characterized the Alliance economic program in North Carolina generated an impatience among the state's farmers that weakened the organizational loyalty so necessary to insurgent political adventures. Had Polk lived to head the national ticket of the People's Party, his personal magnetism might well have bridged these institutional fissures in his home state and completed the political tasks left undone by the narrowly focused North Carolina cooperative movement. But in the absence of such a unifying force the conflicting loyalties affecting all Southerners proved sufficient to leave many thousands of North Carolina Alliancemen still poor—and still Democratic.[47]

It soon became apparent that the sundering of the North Carolina Alliance was permanent, and in 1894, Polk's somewhat conservative and pragmatic successor, Marion Butler, boldly decided on a policy of overt Populist-Republican fusion. The tactic was implemented through a wondrous blend of "practical politics," Populist racism, fear of Democratic racism, and—occasionally—a genuine effort to build an interracial political coalition on a cornerstone of election reform to protect the freedom of the ballot. To the consternation of the Democrats, the two-party cooperation produced a Populist-Republican majority in the 1894 North Carolina legislature. When that body convened to elect two United States Senators—one for a regular term and one to fill an unexpired term—the managers of the coalition were able to hold their forces together long enough to send Populist Butler to Washington for the full term and a Republican for the unexpired term. Out of schism and desperation, North Carolina Alliancemen had buttressed their sagging organizational structure with new Republican support and had achieved, momentarily at least, a stunning victory on what appeared to be socially radical terms.[48]

Across the Old Confederacy, the campaigns of 1892 and 1894 revealed both the reforming energy of Southern Populism and the power of the received culture. Both were shaken by the fury of the encounter. The struggle in 1892 showed how a strong inter-regional political movement based on economic ideas could become disfigured by local, sectional, and cultural influences—and by massive fraud. Generally speaking, only the strongest kind of leadership linked with cohesive organizations seemed to be able to challenge the emotional power of the inherited forms that shaped the way Southerners acted politically. As the full impact of sectional attacks fell upon Southern Populists in 1892, the farmers of the region found the pull of the old party harder to resist than did their counterparts in the West. The absence of L. L. Polk at the head of the national ticket was sorely felt by Southern Populists; it may have diminished the third party vote by as much as one-third to one-half in many areas.

But in 1894, to the dismay of Democrats, Southern third parties—with no Union general yoked to their state tickets—grew alarmingly. The longer the third party survived, the more it weakened the political habits of the one-party heritage. By 1895 Democrats from one end of the Old Confederacy to the other had been forced to acknowledge the remarkable zeal and continued growth of the reform movement. To all who could read the signs—and Democratic Congressmen read them with growing fear—Southern Populism had become a power to be reckoned with. Though sectional politics had been employed along with steadily increasing demagoguery and terror in Georgia, Alabama, Mississippi, Louisiana, Texas, and Arkansas, the fact was nevertheless indisputable: in political terms, the "Solid South" had become a contested region.

But this was only in political terms; the underlying culture of white supremacy in the South remained very much intact. This apparent anomaly hovered over the South of the mid-1890's: the party of white supremacy was in trouble, but white supremacy was not, either in the South or in the nation.

5

As a national enterprise by a new third party, the politics of reform clearly involved great organizational and tactical complexities. To ensure voter loyalty a new party could not rely on memories, sectional or otherwise; it had to provide reasons—and the reasons had to include some kind of proof that the party had come to stay. Still, Populists were by no means disheartened. They could remind one another, and with complete accuracy, that the infant prewar Republican Party had leaped from obscurity in 1854 to national power in 1860, largely as a result of the hopelessly anachronistic character of the old Whig Party. Why should reformers feel discouraged? In 1892, *both* major parties appeared anachronistic! Both were hopelessly in thrall to the whims of the money power, and "concentrated capital." The "Gold Democrats" had narrowly defeated the "Gold Republicans" and given the nation President Grover Cleveland. Both old parties were continuing to turn their backs on economic realities and were working in a harmonious "sound money" partnership to "down the people." Despite all the hazards of a maiden campaign, third party leaders found reason for optimism. Their presidential candidate, General James Weaver, had received over one million votes, and five states had cast one or more electoral votes for the Populist nominee, giving him a total of twenty-two in the electoral college. Weaver himself publicly characterized the showing as "a surprising success." Moreover, the thin Western base of the Greenback Party years had been vastly expanded; in parts of the South the voice of protest was remarkably loud, even when temporarily muted by illegal means. Clearly, the arrival of the People's Party had come with sufficient force to attract the rapt attention of political observers throughout the nation.

Yet the sectional barrier to independent political action had shaken the organization of the National Farmers Alliance at every level—including, it turned out, its highest. Indeed, immediately following the November election it became starkly apparent that the new party desperately needed whatever stiffening it could get from Alliance organizers and reform editors—for the final days of the campaign had uncovered an unanticipated organizational crisis of the first magnitude.

6

If the third party had drawn its most promising strength from those states in which the National Alliance had enlisted the most farmers, it was also demonstrably clear in November 1892 that the one man who had done so much to build that membership, the editor of the order's national journal and its founding president, Charles Macune, had slipped out of the fold: in the final days before the election Macune had decided he was not a Populist after all! At the order's national convention—held in Memphis shortly following the November election—the extraordinary details of Macune's defection exploded to the surface.

It turned out that the *Economist* editor's reluctant conversion to the third party cause at the Omaha convention in July had not survived the early fall state election in Georgia. To Macune that election seemed to indicate that the party of the fathers was destined to hold the loyalty of most of its Alliancemen in the South. Macune apparently saw this development as a fatal threat to his power base in the Southern Alliances and a possible curtailment of his prominent—and salaried—role in the agrarian movement. Late in October, just before the national election, Macune acquiesced in the shipment of pro-Democratic campaign literature from Alliance national headquarters in Washington. The mass mailing, which, predictably, created a furor among third party men throughout the nation, bore the signature of J. F. Tillman, the Alliance national secretary, who was a loyal Macune functionary. At the Memphis convention of the Alliance, held immediately following the election, a bitter fight erupted between Macune and Henry Loucks in the course of their contest for the national Alliance presidency. The decision turned not on personalities, but on a single and decisive political question: could an Allianceman in good standing oppose the People's Party? Macune soon discovered the answer was "No." [49]

In an intricate series of maneuvers, the Texan—perhaps with memories of his dazzling speech at Waco in 1887—nominally withdrew from the race and then spelled out a new vision for a national cotton marketing program. He made no mention of his own sub-treasury plan, which, as orchestrated by William Lamb, had helped bring on the unwanted third party movement, and he ended by calling for farmer alignment with the Democratic Party in what he described as a "knockdown" blow at the forces of monopoly capitalism. Unfortunately for Macune, the Alliance "demands" and the Omaha Platform of the People's Party were identical; the delegates at Memphis knew well enough that the Democratic Party opposed the Alliance demands with consummate clarity. When a Macune partisan from Mississippi formally withdrew the Texan's name (was the plan to precipitate an emotional stampede to recall the founder to leadership?), a "red-headed delegate from Texas" jumped to his feet and quickly moved that nominations for president cease, leaving Henry Loucks of South Dakota as the sole candidate. The motion, promptly

345

approved by the delegates, effectively ended Macune's career in the Alliance.[50]

At the moment of the movement's most extreme vulnerability, the central figure of the agrarian revolt suddenly and permanently disappeared from the ranks, even as the crusade of the farmers moved into its climactic political phase. As if that were not bizarre enough, related to the sudden departure of the founder was another sequence of events that cast an ironic shadow over the abrupt culmination of the long tactical struggle between Charles Macune and the radicals of the Alliance.

William Lamb's personal political career—though not his organizational career—also had come to an end by the time of the Memphis meeting. The public standing of the red-headed organizer had, in fact, suffered a dramatic blow in the very week it reached its zenith with the formation of the Texas People's Party in August 1891. Absorbed in rallying the Alliance's growing left wing for the long-sought amalgamation with organized labor and the Colored Farmers Alliance in the new third party, Lamb had spent much of 1891 away from home, leaving the management of his farm to his sons and the operation of his newspaper, *The Texas Independent,* to his printing foreman. While Lamb was presiding over a meeting of the Texas Reform Press Association in early summer in East Texas, his foreman accepted a paid ad from an Alliance partisan that included a written attack on a local Montague County Democrat. Lamb's long years of Alliance activism had earned him the enmity of the hierarchy of the Hogg Democracy in Texas, and he arrived home to learn he had been sued for libel. The plaintiff sought punitive as well as actual damages. As Lamb completed final preparations for the founding meeting of the People's Party in Dallas, the suit against him came to trial. The charge to the jury by the presiding Democratic judge defined the issues with such legal finality that Lamb angrily printed it in full in his own newspaper. The judge explained that neither actual nor punitive liability against Lamb could be diminished by the fact that he was not a party to the acceptance or publication of the ad. Neither were Lamb's public retraction and his offer to open his columns to the offended party to be considered by the jury as mitigating circumstances, again, either for actual or punitive damages. After deliberating, the jury did not award punitive damages, but it found Lamb guilty of libel and fined him $200.[51]

The issue, of course, was not the size of the fine, but the political uses to which the conviction could be put. Lamb learned almost immediately how damaging the conviction was to his political life. At the founding meeting of the People's Party, comprised of Lamb's most intimate colleagues in radicalism, the delegates accepted his role as temporary chairman, but elected "Stump" Ashby as permanent chairman. The new party could not go before the electorate of Texas with an organizational posture that would permit its opponents to label it as a "party of slander." The libel case effectively removed Lamb, the red-headed apostle of farmer boycotts, from the leadership of the party he had been so instrumental in creating; it also prevented him from running for public office under its sponsorship. His personal standing in the Populist community was not affected, and he represented the fifth district in most of the party's internal functions throughout the Populist years. He was present in St. Louis in 1892 as Ignatius Donnelly read the platform preamble of Populism and watched quietly and perhaps with a touch of triumph as his old rival, C. W. Macune, was swept along into the third party by the forces Lamb had done so much to assemble.[52]

But whether he was present in Memphis for Macune's demise later in the year is not certain. That William Lamb understood the tactical uses of political issues was never more thoroughly demonstrated than when he adroitly employed Macune's sub-treasury plan to draw the line between the Alliance and the Democratic Party of the South. Whether he was the delegate at Memphis who made the quick parliamentary motion that ensured Macune's exclusion from the contest for the Alliance presidency remains an interesting question. There is only the intriguing reference by a Memphis newspaper reporter to the motion by "a red-headed delegate from Texas." It is not clear how many red-haired radicals were in the higher councils of the Texas Alliance. In any case, it is clear that the long struggle of the two greenbackers—the economic radical Charles Macune and the political radical William Lamb—ended at the Memphis convention with victory for the third party men and the election of one of their own, Henry Loucks of South Dakota, as the order's new national president. It is also clear that both Macune and Lamb were casualties of their long political rivalry—one that culminated in the organizational consolidation of the National Alliance and the People's Party. Their duel, dating from the Cleburne Demands of 1886, had lasted six years. It personified one of the central ideological tensions at the heart of the agrarian revolt—the power of an idea versus the power of inherited cultural loyalties.

7

The cooperative movement had built the Alliance to national stature, but in state after state in 1892, the cooperatives were strangling from lack of access to credit. The decline of the cooperatives presaged the collapse of the Alliance, for the dream of reform for farmers could now be given life only by the new People's Party. Only if the third party came to power and legislated the principles of the sub-treasury system into law could the farmers of the West and South escape the chattel mortgage companies and the furnishing merchants whose oppressive practices had generated the cooperative crusade in the first place.

The allegiance to the party of the fathers and to the party of white supremacy of such a central figure as Charles Macune underscored the deep-seated sectional and racial emotions brought into the open by the appearance of the new party of reform. The agony of Macune had its counterpart in every state Alliance and in every suballiance. This was true in the West as well as the South, for Populism challenged the bloody shirt as well as the party of the fathers.

In the Populist strategy, the stultifying and self-defeating sectional memories of the American people were to be overcome by the power of an economic idea: the reform movement issued its challenge to the past in the modern language of the Omaha Platform. After the 1892 campaign, it appeared certain that neither major party would ever satisfactorily come to terms with that document. To assert its purpose as a national instrument of reform, therefore, the spokesmen of Populism believed the third party had to avoid both old parties of the North and South and chart a clear non-sectional path between them—in the "middle of the road," to employ the widely used Populist slogan of 1892. Indeed, by definition, all Populists were "mid-roaders," since the idea of navigating between both sectional parties and enlisting the "plain people" in each was the underlying concept of the People's Party. As third party strategists analyzed matters, the doctrines of the Omaha Platform had won the devotion of the host of the Alliance to an extent that imperiled the very foundation of national party loyalties—even in the face of the politics of sectionalism. The painful lessons of the massive cooperative effort had taught hundreds of thousands of farmers that their economic salvation depended upon a fundamental alteration of the way banks and currency related to the independence of people.

Yet reform required victories at the polls, and an unaided third party had fallen short of the necessary majority in 1892 in most of the South and West. Properly handled, cooperation with voters in other political parties might provide the crucial margin to translate defeat for reform into genuine political power. Proponents of temporary fusion arrangements insisted that they were just as sincere in their ultimate purpose as other Populists were; the issue was not a matter of proper dedication to the Omaha Platform, but rather one of finding the political means to enact its provisions. The latter objective could not, of course, be claimed as the purpose of the independent movement in Nebraska, as cooperation with Democrats in that state involved the immediate avoidance of the Omaha Platform.

The mere existence of these different emphases revealed the unresolved strategy and the incomplete ideological development that accompanied the arrival of Populism in American politics. In the aftermath of the first round of the "great contest" it had become quite clear that the People's Party had yet to define precisely how it proposed to bring the greenback critique of the monetary system to the settled attention of the

American people. The stakes, of course, were as high as ever—ending private banking control of the currency and, therefore, ending the immense influence of bankers over the lives of all Americans. Indeed, economic independence from the usurious demands of land and chattel mortgage companies of the West and the furnishing merchants of the South depended ultimately in dealing with the commercial bankers; for it was a contracted national currency and inflated bank interest rates, as well as the cultural ethos legitimizing such practices, that placed pressure on the lesser financial forces such as furnishing merchants to grind the nation's farmers into abject humiliation. As Populists viewed matters, the grievances of "the plain people" had to be listened to by somebody, or the American idea of progress would simply come to describe the economic exploitation and cultural regimentation of millions. How to overcome the inherited sectional loyalties and political deference of an adequate number of Democratic and Republican voters remained the problem. At the end of 1892, the task of the reform movement was clear: it had to fully mobilize its own institutions in a concerted effort to teach the politics of Populism to the American people.

CHAPTER XII

The Reform Editors and the Language of Populism

". . . to educate the people . . ."

In 1893 the American nation plunged into a severe economic depression. The narrow organization of capital markets that derived from the doctrines of an inflexible gold currency precipitated the panic, which occurred during the annual financial squeeze caused by the autumn agricultural harvest; the panic in turn placed intense pressure on what all orthodox goldbugs regarded as the nation's "essential monetary reserves." To the utter dismay of greenbackers, the sins of goldbugs seemed to multiply even as the reform movement gathered momentum. Aside from the obvious social costs, the sheer administrative expense of maintaining the gold standard proved back-breaking to the nation's Treasury Department.

Grover Cleveland's Secretary of the Treasury was forced to sell massive gold bond issues through a syndicate organized by the J. P. Morgan Company in an effort to maintain the government's gold reserves. The effort unnecessarily saddled the country with a debt of over a quarter of a billion dollars, from which only bankers profited. Indeed, the government gained nothing from its frantic efforts, since bankers paid for the bonds with gold they had withdrawn from the Treasury! As one historian later put it, the Morgan syndicate "measured the emergency of the government with little mercy." To opinion leaders in business, banking, the universities, and the metropolitan press—accepting, as they habitually did, the prevailing political culture of their age—reformers in the South and West sounded raucous when they complained that "Wall Streeters and their gold roam through the administration like panthers through their native jungles." The metaphor, however, provided a fairly accurate description of what was actually taking place. Nevertheless, all was obscured behind a luxuriant hedge of language about "sound money." [1] The system the goldbugs sought to preserve was so lucrative to the members of the New York Banking Association that subsequent generations of historians have found it difficult to describe gracefully. It seemed clear to greenbackers at the time, however, that if intelligence were to intrude into the system of American capitalism, someone other than bankers would have to prevail on a theoretical level of currency analysis. Hard-money silverites were, in any case, of no help; they were no better informed than goldbugs.[2]

The depression inflicted great hardship upon those rural and urban Americans the Populists called "the producing classes." Slackened consumer demand created new unemployment and further weakened commodity prices. Cotton fell to eight and then to five cents, far below the cost of production, and corn and wheat prices also plummeted. Millions knew genuine and prolonged privation. In both the South and West there were increasing reports of starvation, both on the farms and in the cities. The depression spread such massive industrial unemployment that "tramps" became a familiar sight in every section of the nation. Marches on Washington by the unemployed gained increasing notoriety, especially since some of them originated in the mountain states and on the West Coast and involved "borrowed" freight trains as a primary source of transportation. The multitude became known as "Coxey's Army," after an Ohio currency reformer and Populist spokesman named General Jacob Coxey, who organized the first such demonstration. The peripatetic Henry Vincent of the *American Nonconformist* wrote a brooding account of this epic of industrial despair; he turned it into a book-length assertion of the need for the immediate rise to power of the People's Party. He called his book *The Story of the Commonweal.*[3]

The doctrines of the Omaha Platform, however, made little impression on the Eastern seaboard. The immigrant masses in the industrial cities suffered terribly as the depression lengthened, and their desperation for work at any wage further heightened the suffering of the working poor generally. Yet the Populist cause appeared hopeless from Indiana eastward to New England. Republican hegemony, rooted in wartime sectionalism, Protestantism, and "progress," sheltered a socially conservative hard-money creed that prevailed throughout the Northeast. The Democratic Party of the region was also well insulated from the winds of insurgency. Buttressed by the loyalty of embattled urban Catholics, the patronage of a number of municipal political machines, a thin but influential layer of capitalists, and the checkbook of an occasional Mugwump, the Eastern Democracy similarly reflected an orthodox, hard-money orientation. The major parties seemed to contain differentiating shades of ideological meaning only when viewed from an extremely narrow perspective, with great attention focused on small differences. The self-interest of rival politicians was the most visible distinction. Indeed, the two parties were so ideologically in step that in 1887, when Grover Cleveland declared for lowered tariffs, he was praised for injecting a "live issue" to supplement the "decaying controversies" of the past. But as Ignatius Donnelly made resoundingly clear in the platform preamble of 1892, Populists believed that a "sham battle" over the tariff between different groups of hard-money businessmen could not command the attention of millions of Americans rendered increasingly impoverished and voiceless by the financial and political realities of the emerging corporate state.[4]

In this climate of rigid orthodoxy and increasing suffering, Populists brooded about the irrelevance of the inherited political dialogue of the nation. Their questions went beyond what capitalists were doing to farmers to include what the new ethos of corporate privilege was doing to the soul of America. It was, in the words of Kansas Populist William Peffer, "a gigantic scheme of spoliation." While the demonstrated ability of private capital to buy state legislatures engaged in electing United States Senators constituted a sobering commentary on the health of parliamentary democracy, both in the states dispatching the Senators and in the national Congress that received them, the ability of the same wealth to encourage a pliant public opinion through metropolitan newspapers supported by the advertising of the business community seemed to Populists to threaten the very substance of the democratic idea itself. If the political application of money to the legislative process fostered a permanent climate of privilege and corruption, its application to the nation's press forestalled the possibility of achieving a democratic remedy for corruption. Thus, Populists asserted, the assumed terms of the social contract were being undone. This intimation of moral finality gave Populism its special quality of urgency. The People's Party was a reflection of the intuition that the rules of the Republic were being permanently altered before everyone's eyes. The people of America had to be alerted, lest they be seduced into accepting rule by a two-party capitalist elite and calling it democracy. Both the language of Populism and the Omaha Platform itself were grounded on this belief.[5]

2

Very close to the heart of the matter was the relationship of corporate wealth and the public press. It was a crucial imbalance, and Populists made massive allocations of time, energy, and sheer physical and financial effort to correct it. Out of this effort came the foremost internal achievement of the People's Party: the National Reform Press Association.

Had Populism been nothing else, the Reform Press Association could stand as a monument to the moral intensity of the agrarian crusade. The thunder of its great journals—*The Advocate, The American Nonconformist, The Appeal to Reason, The Southern Mercury, The People's Party Paper* and *The Progressive Farmer*—was echoed in literally thousands of tiny, struggling weeklies across the nation. The famous journals struggled too;

the common point of unity among the journalists of Populism was their shared poverty. Bereft of advertising support, the reform editors ran ads for books, frequently written by each other, and tried to survive on revenue from circulation. For the great majority of reform papers, circulation rarely exceeded 1000 subscribers—by no means all of them paid up—who lived in the immediate county where the paper was published. Given the economic condition of their customers, it is perhaps understandable that Populist journals were filled with appeals to delinquent subscribers. Usually they got the paper whether they paid or not, for the very reason for existence of the reform press was to "educate the people."

The most extreme case was provided by Tom Watson in Georgia. *The People's Party Paper,* which sometimes had press runs up to 20,000, never at any time acquired over 474 paid subscribers! But Watson was better capitalized than virtually anyone else in the People's Party. The *Southern Alliance* in Alabama was able to last a year because the editor mortgaged both the paper and his own home. After the crops were gathered, the delinquent subscribers still did not pay, and the paper went under. In the depression of the 1890's, many farmers literally could not afford to pay $1.00 or $1.50 a year for the good word of Populism. Many reform papers hung on for a year, or two, or three, and then expired, the editor generally reappearing in another town with a new paper and the same doctrines. The economic imperatives being what they were, most reform papers were one-man operations. As the physical requirements of setting type by hand for a new edition every week were frequently beyond the capacity of an editor who also had to scratch for job printing to survive, the Reform Press Association provided its members with a weekly two-page "ready print," filled with the latest verses of the third party gospel. The two-page inserts, written under the guidance of W. Scott Morgan of Arkansas, became the interior of many four-page Populist weeklies across the nation.[6]

The number of Populist journals that materialized in the 1890's will never be known. The figure was well in excess of 1000. Kansas, Texas, Alabama, and Georgia seem to have had taken the lead in journalistic insurgency, Kansas counting over

150 papers and Texas some 125. Alabama had approximately
100 reform papers and Georgia perhaps as many. Even the
embattled third party cause in Louisiana counted about fifty
journalistic supporters. Some Populist editors developed a talent for satirizing the local establishment, to the outrage of
their targets. It sometimes proved dangerous, especially in the
South. In Alabama, James M. Whitehead's use of ridicule in
his Greenville *Living Truth* was "devastating"; his shop was
broken into and the type scattered in 1892. The following
year fire broke out, destroying the furniture in his rooms
above the plant, though the press was saved. Whitehead continued his barbs without missing an issue. Another gifted sat-
irist, Thomas Gaines of the Comanche *Pioneer Exponent* in
Texas, was a recipient of attacks and threats of attacks, as was
his family. The co-editor of "Cyclone" Davis's *Alliance Vindica-
tor* was shot and killed in Texas. In North Carolina, Marion
Butler's printing plant was burned, and sporadic violence
flared elsewhere across the South. One doughty editor, I. L.
Brock of the Cherokee *Sentinel* in Alabama, eschewed praise
for his own efforts, feeling it should be reserved for people
like the editor of the Selma *Populist,* in the black belt. In that
region of the state, said Brock, people "passed through the
days of reconstruction before they ever learned the war was
over and that slavery was no more." [7]

In the heat of their battle, the reform editors shared a common experience that gave them a distinctive cast within the
Populist mold. As it neared its peak in numbers and influence
in 1895–96, the Reform Press Association was regarded by its
members as the very center of the third party crusade. The
editors' remarkable personal experiences in coping with sudden violence engendered a sense of driving moral purpose
that sometimes gave rise to lofty flights of description. Francis
X. Matthews of the *American Nonconformist,* after returning
from a crucial policy debate at the NRPA convention of 1895
at Kansas City, described his colleagues:

> This band of Populist editors, representing papers from all
> parts of the union, was a study for one inclined to look for
> the causes that produce great effects. . . . They were com-
> pelled to face such a storm of ridicule and vindictive hatred

as seldom falls to the lot of men. They struggled against poverty in its most humiliating form, against ostracism and persecution and all uncharitableness. . . . The quality, tone, and contents of their papers steadily improved until today some of the most ably edited journals of the country are found in their ranks. . . . The note [they] strike is essentially national. It is the same everywhere. Its appeal is to all people . . . regardless of creed, nationality, location, calling, or previous condition of servitude. . . . Nor could anyone look into the earnest faces at Kansas City, and hear the ringing tone of the talk and speeches, without going away convinced that whoever else might waver, the Populist editors and the Populist newspapers will do their whole duty in the mighty conflict that lies so near before us.[8]

In the aggregate, the editors represented a singular local level culmination of the American reforming instinct of the nineteenth century. The one historian who has studied the Populist editors has described them as fostering an "aura of democratic morality" and a "sensitivity toward humanity." [9]

3

The sense of personal involvement so evident in the description by the *Noncomformist* editor was typical. Indeed, to most Populists—greenback theoreticians and dirt farmers as well as reform editors—the entire shape of American democracy seemed to have changed in the space of their own lifetimes. Virtually every line of the Omaha Platform reflected the belief that the very precepts of the schoolroom and the church had been made to count for nothing. What was democracy when aggressive "captains of industry" could buy whole legislatures and keep the United States Congress in a perpetual state of genteel servitude? What was honest labor when ruthless structuring of the currency drove the price of farm products below the cost of production? What was thrift when high interest rates gobbled up farmland or when railroads made more money shipping corn than farmers did in growing it? Where was community virtue when bankers, commission houses, and grain elevator companies wantonly destroyed self-help farmer cooperatives? Where was dignity when farm women were

357

forced to go barefoot and the furnishing man determined
what a farmer's family could or could not eat? Where was
freedom when the crop lien system was enforced by the convict lease system? What did the old virtues mean, in such a setting?

In its underlying emotional impulses, Populism was a revolt
against the narrowing limits of political debate within capitalism as much as it was a protest against specific economic injustices. The abundant evidence that "great aggregations of capital" could cloak self-interested policies in high moral
purposes—and have such interpretations disseminated widely
and persuasively through the nation's press—outraged and
frightened the agrarian reformers, convincing them of the
need for a new political party free of corporate control. To
Populists the ruthless labor practices of Jay Gould seemed bad
enough; when coupled with the power of the Gould-owned
Associated Press to glorify industrial captains in the public
press, it seemed that industrial America had no ethical moor-
ings at all. What value did democratic "public opinion" have
when good reformers were consistently ridiculed as "cranks,"
"calamity howlers," and "anarchists" by well-dressed editors
who thrived on the advertising support of self-interested businessmen? In the broad application favored by Populists, the
"money power" symbolized much more than the gold standard, private national banks, or the "lordly capitalists" of
Lombard and Wall streets. The money power was corrosive
because it was changing the rules under which Americans
acted politically. The new politics of centralized capital not
only seemed to advance through thresholds of privilege unknown to Alexander Hamilton, but the specific procedures
were so destructive of representative government that they
were undermining the institutional basis of a free society.
Nothing less than the democratic heritage was at stake. The
plain people, therefore, had to be aroused quickly. Farmers
had been reached through the internal communications apparatus of the Alliance lecturing system; the rest of the "industrial millions" would have to be reached through the National
Reform Press Association. These ingredients—the organized
farmers, their platform, and their editors—formed the inte-

rior structure of the People's Party and symbolized the culture of reform that Populism represented. They presented to the rest of the nation the creed, its organic constituency, and its advocates. All else—the books on reform, the spokesmen, the candidates, the occasional officeholders—merely added to the surface features of the third party crusade. The Farmers Alliance, the Omaha Platform, and the reform press collectively represented the "movement culture" that constituted the very essence and passion of the people's movement that was American Populism.[10]

4

But the emerging corporate society that Populism challenged possessed defenses beyond those imbedded in economic influence. Many of these defenses were cultural. Gilded Age America was suffused with the mystique of social Darwinism, Calvinism, and a generalized presumption that hard work provided just rewards. Horatio Alger served as a popular model. The emerging national ethos contained a number of contradictions; it was visionary, complacent, energetic, and romantic—above all, it was the ethos of a society self-consciously insulated from serious introspection. It was a time when great fortunes were being amassed by a few, admired enviously by the many, and exalted as a testament both to individual worth and to the merit of the Republic. Though numbers of people besides Populists privately grumbled about the tactics of aggressive capitalists, a simple nod from a great captain could mean a new factory or a grand new railroad venture that might well transform a hamlet into a town or a town into a city. Provincial newspapers, accordingly, rarely if ever reflected private discontents; they provided instead a generally undifferentiated celebration of visiting millionaires. A rapacious Jay Gould could expect as much editorial deference as the somewhat less notorious Andrew Carnegie. The new creed of progress issued forth from public platforms, pulpits, and editorial offices throughout the land.[11]

Populists, of course, were in no way insulated from this massive outpouring of internal propaganda. Though the economic realities of their own daily lives made them question the

359

universal beneficence of the new era, so thoroughly had the cult of forward motion infused itself into the very structure of the American idiom that Populists sometimes encountered great difficulty finding language that could convey their individual disenchantment. Indeed, to the extent that the reformers were able to develop new modes of political expression, they were engaging in an attempt at cultural redefinition of what constituted genuine democracy. The extent to which they succeeded in enlarging prevailing frames of reference measured the meaning of Populism. Similarly, the fact that they were frequently unaware of the larger issues raised by their political creed measured the limitations of their horizons.

The substance of the Populist message was, of course, economic reform—an appeal buttressed by hard times. And that message went not only from reform editors to their readers, but emanated from the poor themselves. The Populist farmers wrote both to their papers and to their spokesmen. Ignatius Donnelly received this letter:

> I am . . . one of those which have settled upon the socalled Indemnity Land . . . now the great Northern. I settled on this land in good Faith Built House and Barn Broken up Part of the Land. Spent years of hard Labor in grubing fencing and Improving are they going to drive us out like trespassers wife and children and give us away to the Corporations how can we support them. When we are robed of our means. they will shurely not stand this we must Decay and Die from Woe and Sorow We are Loyal Citicens and do Not Intend to Intrude on any R. R. Corporation we Beleived and still do Believe that the R. R. Co. has got No Legal title to this Land in question. We Love our wife and children just as Dearly as any of you But how can we protect them give them education as they should wen we are driven from sea to sea.[12]

An Alliance leader explained to a Southern reform paper why his members could not pay dues: "Hundreds of good, hard-working men, true to the Alliance . . . are staying at home, depriving themselves and their households of attending church, for want of decent clothing to appear in public. These people paid all they made to their merchant on their indebtedness, and are now, and have been, practically without a dollar. How can they pay dues?" In a letter edged with desperation, a farm woman living near Mendota, Kansas, wrote to Populist Governor Lewelling in 1894: "I take my pen in hand to let you know we are starving . . . My husband went away to find work and came home last night and told me that he would have to starve. He has been in 10 counties and did not get no work. . . . I haven't had nothing to eat today and it is 3 o'clock." [13]

More fortunate allies of the farmers expressed the language of Populism with greater grammatical precision, but scarcely less urgency. An Alabama physician decried a system that reduced the yeomanry to "menials and paupers, to be driven by monopolies . . . like cattle and swine." The causes, he said, were to be found not only in Wall Street, but "hiding behind railway embankments, or lurking in the vaults of national banks." A sympathetic journalist focused on the human tragedy: "Every year the plunge into debt is deeper; each year the burden is heavier. . . . Independence! It is gone." Whether the instrument of high interest was the crop lien of the South or the chattel mortgage of the West, the effect of debt oppression was the same. In Colorado, where chattel mortgages cost homesteaders 24 to 36 per cent annually, people slipped away in the middle of the night to avoid creditors, and more than one "left his cattle and farm machinery that were mortgaged on the prairie." [14]

Since 1886 the Alliance heritage had provided an explanation of events. In the words of an early Texas radical, "The case as it stands is plainly understood to be an issue between capital and labor and the present leaders in both the old parties are indisputably in sympathy and support of the capitalists." By the time of the arrival of the People's Party such Alliance doctrines had been absorbed by many, and the farmers could augment their chronicle of personal suffering with their own political analysis of the causes: "few Reading, thinking men in America, Deny the Slavery of the Masses, to the Money Power of our Country . . . the `Masses have literally slept, the Sleep that brings on Tenantry and Serfdom, and the Partizan Hireling Press have depended upon our Ignorance."

The sometimes angry, sometimes despairing dialogue between farm families and their Populist spokesmen provided the interior language of the agrarian revolt, a sharing of mutual anguish and hope that described their loyalty to the third party crusade.[15]

5

Far from the agricultural districts of the South and West more contented voices participated in the political debates of the 1890's. Reflecting the settled judgments of the forces of respectability, they provided a language of ridicule rather than despair and specialized rather more in delivering advice than in showing concern. Generally offended by the very idea of a third party in Nebraska, the Republican press of the state reserved its most outraged tone for the men who presumed to speak for the new movement. The Populist slate was a "mongrel ticket" populated by "lightweights." John Powers was a "garrulous old man," and Omar Kem was the farmers' "mortgage candidate" (the latter appellation was perhaps of dubious political utility to Republicans, considering the extent of indebtedness on the Western plains). To the *Nebraska State Journal,* the editorial voice of the Burlington Railroad, third party leaders represented "the shiftless, lazy and improvident" among the homesteaders, "whose sole object in availing themselves of Uncle Sam's gift of farms . . . appears to be to mortgage the property and live off the loans until they are foreclosed." The *Journal* was especially offended by the possible effect in the East of the "slander" that Nebraska was not a land of prosperity. "It is a sin and a shame that these pests are permitted to beslime the state. . . . Something must be done to check the avalanche of lies rolling eastward, or the state will greatly suffer for want of capital." [16]

In Texas, Jim Hogg made essentially the same response to the Populist challenge:

> For the pinks of innocence, for know-alls, for word-slingers, for hat-smashers and smart alecks, who swing around political circles, idling their time away, leaving their wives and children at home to cultivate patches while they are off galli-

vanting in politics, or stay on street corners loafing . . . and cussing out the country, I have the profoundest contempt. If they would exercise a little more muscle, perspire a little more over the brow in honest efforts to make bread, and work their jaws less and exercise their reason more, their condition would be decidedly elevated.[17]

Another of the interested observers of Populism was New York's prestigious editor, E. L. Godkin. *The Nation*'s editor followed the farmers' movement with interest and commented on it frequently. Though *The Nation* under Godkin's stewardship had come to be hailed as "the best weekly not only in America but in the world," the journal augmented its abusive comments on Populism with a considerable amount of misrepresentation and sophistry. After Kansas Senator William Peffer wrote an explanation of the sub-treasury plan in 1891, Godkin blandly ignored the specifics of the proposal to charge that Peffer's "particular craze" centered on government loans "to all comers at low rates of interest—presumably without security." The "only hope" for Kansas, Godkin decided, was for the sensible people of the state to "make their disgust so manifest" that Populists would be "frightened." A resolution by a local Alliance in Nebraska calling for an increase in the currency to $50 per capita led Godkin to probe for the underlying cause of such a baffling and unexpected suggestion. "A very large body of farmers of that region," he found, "are now really peasants fresh from Europe, with all the prejudices and all the liability to deception of their class." The protesting tenor of the founding convention of the People's Party could be explained, said Godkin, by "the vague dissatisfaction which is always felt by the incompetent and lazy and 'shiftless' when they contemplate those who have got on better in the world." [18]

More than he would have cared to discover, Godkin was a man of his time. Passively accepting traditional notions about the function of the monetary system, he, along with the other adherents of the major parties, might argue a bit over the tariff, but the principal difference among them seemed to be the longing of intellectuals for honest men in public life. That alone seemed to fulfill the requirements of modern politics. Men like Godkin had simply been bypassed by the pace of events. From the evidence of their respective writings it is clear that as a social critic E. L. Godkin possessed a range of vision considerably narrower than that regularly exhibited by any one of a half-dozen Populist Congressmen, while the capacity of *The Nation*'s editor to interpret emerging economic relationships within industrial society was scarcely comparable to analyses attained by any number of greenback editors in the reform press. Godkin carried the authority of a classical education, but he could not transcend the provincial inheritance of a complacent culture.[19]

In its essentials, *The Nation*'s editorial stance toward the agrarian reformers mirrored opinions common in metropolitan dailies that more eagerly served the enterpriser ethos. With only moderately subtle distinctions in emphasis, the "abuse and vituperation" that flourished in Kansas in 1890 furnished the recurring staple of major party politics throughout the agrarian revolt. Occasionally, of course, metropolitan newspapers focused on issues. When they did, nothing seemed to generate more journalistic hyperbole than Macune's sub-treasury plan. The New York *Sun* thought the sub-treasury the chief "specimen of absurdities" offered by the Farmers Alliance and trusted neither major party would "bid for the support of these Hayseed Socialists." The Minneapolis *Tribune* regarded the Macune plan as a piece of "imbecility" and went on to explain helpfully that "there is plenty of money to be borrowed upon good land mortgage security." The Philadelphia *North American* decided that "the Farmers Alliance does not want money. It wants due bills. It wants pawn tickets; and though its chiefs do not know a mowing machine from a mully grub, they want the earth." After the Ocala Demands got wide publicity in the East, the Philadelphia paper wondered at it: why do "the new lights want to abolish the national banks?" "But for the national banks," the editor explained, "most of them would have been in the poor house twenty years ago." To the New York *Commercial Advertiser* the problem was not only to defend the banks, but to cope with other planks in the agrarian platform. The paper could not

Kansas Populist Senator William Peffer's long beard made him fair game for Republican cartoon attacks (below).

From bleeding Kansas's wind-swept plains,
Where whiskers take the place of brains,
You come with all your verbose strength
Of speeches of unending length.
Here, take the hint PUCK gives—resign!
Let Mary be your Valentine.

decide which was a larger threat, the sub-treasury plan or government ownership of the railroads.[20]

By and large, however, the nation's metropolitan dailies did not press discussions of economic issues as defined by Populists, especially during the heat of election campaigns. The patented all-season remedy for the third party was the politics of sectionalism. It had its uses, North and South, East and West. "A third party vote in Virginia," the Richmond *State* was certain, "is a vote for high tariffs and the Force Bill. Let our farmer friends make no mistake." While the Populist vice presidential candidate, Virginia's James Field, had to contend with the Richmond press in his native state, he encountered another brand of sectional politics on the Western plains. Commenting on Field's war service to the Confederacy, the influential Omaha *Bee* summarized the relevant issue: "Doubtless like most of his associates in that enterprise, he feels no regret at what he did, but being now a loyal citizen he wants to overturn the politics of the party which preserved the Union and substitute some of those which were promised in the event of the success of the Confederacy." Precisely which features of the Omaha Platform would have enthralled the leaders of the wartime Confederacy the paper neglected to specify. In any event, the music of sectionalism could be played in a number of keys. Eastern goldbugs, for example, appropriated to themselves the mystique of the G.O.P. as the party that saved the Union and used it subtly against Western Populists who could not otherwise be accused of sectional disloyalty. Eastern Republicans decided the only rational explanation for Western discontent was that the plains states were laying a proper groundwork for seceding from the Union! The Eastern conservatives called on the Western radicals to be more "patriotic." However bizarre it now appears, these tactics were politically useful in the 1890's and became sufficiently widespread that spokesmen of Western Populism felt it necessary to take time out to reply in articles in Eastern journals explicitly denying that Westerners were subversive. Such discussions served to shift the political focus away from economic issues and back to less threatening topics.[21]

In the South, of course, sectionalism always carried its

biggest wallop when linked with racial issues. When the Arkansas Alliance overwhelmingly voted in favor of the subtreasury plan, the Dallas *Herald,* a staunch supporter of Governor Hogg, congratulated the Alliance for standing "shoulder to shoulder" with "the niggers of Arkansas." The specter of "bayonet rule" as in the days of Reconstruction was held aloft in Georgia as the predictable outcome of third party politics. The Atlanta *Constitution,* among many others, rallied to the defense of "white rule." As the Populist presidential candidate in 1892, General Weaver was "howled down at Albany, threatened with personal indignity at Waycross, and rotten-egged at Macon." He abandoned his campaign in Georgia after learning that "worse might happen in Atlanta." Meanwhile, in North Dakota, the state lecturer of the Farmers Alliance, campaigning as the gubernatorial candidate of the People's Party, was charged with being a "southern sympathizer." While rumors were circulated that he had been a "guerilla in Missouri" during the Civil War, the Republican candidate was widely billed through the state's press as a "loyal Union man." What all this had to do with government's response to the depression of the 1890's was far less clear than the emotional relationship of such memories to party regularity. Democrats and Republicans alike invoked the past to avoid the present.[22]

6

In both regions of the country, Populists threw the Omaha Platform into battle against sectionalism. Populist monetary theory had as its capstone, of course, the sub-treasury system proposed by Charles Macune. After Macune's disappearance from the ranks of reform, the third party's foremost currency theorist was Harry Tracy of Texas. Tracy had been a member of the original executive board of the Texas Exchange and had played at least some role—possibly even a key role—in the development of Macune's "joint-note" plan of 1888 that preceded the emergence of the sub-treasury system in 1889. Like Macune, Tracy was an advocate of large-scale credit cooperatives on the tenable ground that only such a system of organization possessed the twin potentialities so central to genuine economic change for farmers—large-scale cooperatives alone could free the landless from peonage, and large-scale cooperatives alone possessed the possibility of withstanding the inevitable attacks of the banking community. The most elaborate theoretical defense of greenback doctrines generally and of the sub-treasury system specifically was written by Tracy and published in 1894. In his extensive treatise published as part of James H. Davis's Populist book, *A Political Revelation,* Tracy dealt with the central issues of monetary theory that trouble and divide modern economists: the impact upon the economy, and upon each other, of currency volume, currency velocity, deflation, inflation, underconsumption, overproduction, and the distribution of the gross national product among the members of the whole society.

Tracy also addressed—in a forthright manner not always emulated by modern economists—a number of issues relating to the prerogatives and obligations of bankers, the government, and the citizenry as a whole, including an analysis of how these power relationships affect the long-term health of the national economy itself.

In response to those who said the sub-treasury system was "wild" and "impractical," Tracy quietly spelled out the specific features of the warehouse and elevator marketing system:

> It is plain that this plan changes no system now in vogue for handling [staple agricultural] products, for every bale of cotton or pound of tobacco that goes into commerce goes through the warehouse now; advances are made on it pretty much the same as proposed in this plan. Each bushel of wheat, corn and oats that enters into commerce now goes through the elevator. The only changes made in the system is in the place of storage, and in the name of the man who stores it, and in the rate of interest paid on advances, and the amount for charges. Under this plan, the farmer stores his own product, delivers it to the manufacturer or consumer himself through his elected agent, instead of the speculator doing it.[23]

Tracy defended the flexible currency system by detailing the ruinous effect of the prevailing inflexible system:

The products dumped upon the market by the agricul-
turalist averages over $3,000,000 annually, at the present
low prices. This great demand comes upon the country without any preparation in the way of an increased volume of
money and runs the price of these products rapidly down to
below cost of production, which impoverishes the farmer.
The speculator . . . withdraws the money that has been sup-
plying the demand of the merchant, manufacturer and the
contractor, and invests it in these staple products, places
them in an elevator or warehouse, there to remain while the
manufacturer and merchant is driven to the brink of ruin
because he cannot obtain loans. The result is, the appearance of these crops on the market creates anarchy in every
other branch of business, till they go into the hands of the
manufacturer and consumer.[24]

The government's response to the Panic of 1893—a crisis
precipitated by the contracted currency in the first place—
outraged Tracy. When U.S. Treasury officials in the Cleveland administration bailed out the commercial banks of the
New York Clearing House Association by making $47,000,000
available at 1 percent interest, Tracy could scarcely control his
indignation:

The strongest object lesson that could be presented in favor
of the principles of the sub-treasury plan was that of the associated banks issuing clearing-house certificates that saved
every one of them from bankruptcy. . . . Nice Democratic
government indeed, when it goes into copartnership with a
lot of plutocrats who live in as royal splendor as crowned
heads . . . who use the government offices as their servants
. . . and who make the people pay the officers out of what is
left after they get through spoliating them. Not satisfied with
all the prerogatives . . . they say to Uncle Sam, sign this
check for $47,000,000, we need it for our business, we are
loaning the money we borrowed from you, at one per cent
per annum, to our bondmen and bondwomen, at from 12 to
60 per cent per annum, and find though that we need
$47,000,000 more so as not to cramp us til we get through
cleaning them out of this year's crop . . . Now if the government can loan these bankers money at one per cent on col-

laterals, why can't the government loan it to the people on their collaterals? If the government can bridge the bankers over a close money market and keep them from having to sacrifice their collaterals, why can't the government do the same by the people? What a burlesque on democratic government for 4000 men, because they are rich, to enjoy privileges that are denied 65,000,000 people.[25]

Tracy's work, an intricate, 100-page interpretation that illustrated his understanding of currency velocity as well as currency volume as important ingredients of a sound system of finance, merits his inclusion, along with Kellogg, Campbell, and Macune, among the most important currency reformers of nineteenth-century America. His intellectual achievements placed him considerably above the nation's leading academic defender of the gold standard, J. Laurence Laughlin, a prominent University of Chicago economist.*

However essential elaborate theoretical defenses might be to the self-confidence of the reform movement, Populist monetary advocacy obviously had to be presented to mass audiences in somewhat simpler form. The stifling effect of low farm prices and high interest rates, both severely augmented by the contracted currency, was the centerpiece of most explanations of the financial issue in Populist speeches, newspapers and books. In language that put the money issue in down-to-earth terms, Kansas Senator William Peffer made his case for *The Farmer's Side:*

> Where a person took up a homestead claim and raised one good crop of wheat, he was considerably ahead in the world; but where he had to pay from two and a half to three dollars an acre, borrow the money, and pay 50 per cent interest upon it, renewed every year he had a hard road to travel. . . It required twice as many bushels of wheat or of corn or of oats, twice as many pounds of cotton or tobacco or wool to pay a debt in 1887 as it did to pay a debt of the same amount in 1867. . .[26]

In illustrating how a contracted currency vastly increased the commodity value of debts, Peffer repeated a familiar, and

* See Chapter XVII and Appendix B.

decidedly relevant, third party argument. Populists never wearied of dissecting the oppressiveness of the American monetary system or delineating the logic of the greenback remedy. The first task, obviously, was to define money itself. "We recognize money as a creation of law," explained a newly elected third party Congressman, "a simple representation of value, an instrument of exchange and not in any true sense a commodity." The reform press of South Dakota put the same cardinal greenback principle this way: "Gold is no more money than is paper. Nothing is money in any full legal sense until it will pay a debt without possibility of refusal. You cannot compel a creditor to accept uncoined gold, and ninety-nine hundredths of them would refuse to do so. It is not intrinsic value but the government fiat that makes gold coin good for all debts both public and private." [27]

Such earnestness was endemic. Yet the irrationality of gold-bug dogmas sometimes drove even the most subtle greenback theorists to visible efforts to curb their own exasperation. Dr. Stephen McLallin, the thoughtful editor of *The Advocate* in Topeka, was one of those who struggled throughout the 1890's to control his sense of outrage. "We cannot conceive of any proposition that is more absurd than the assumption that money should possess an intrinsic value equal to the value of the products, the exchange of which it is designed to facilitate," a typical McLallin editorial read. A practicing physician for seventeen years before becoming absorbed in reform journalism, McLallin was described by a co-worker as a "compound of Greek philosopher . . . undemonstrative Scotchman, and the modern socialist." A Kansas historian has characterized him as "above all a genuine humanist." However he was portrayed, McLallin was unrelenting in his editorial assaults on the mystique of the "sound dollar." "There is no more reason that the material in a dollar should have an intrinsic value equal to a dollar than that the yardstick should possess an intrinsic value equal to the value of the cloth that it measures. Money as such possesses neither length, nor thickness, and its only value consists in the fact that by law and custom it is the medium by which debts are paid and wealth exchanged." [28]

In league with scores of Populist editors—and twentieth century economists—McLallin asserted that the true value of the currency rested upon the wealth of the country as defined by its productivity rather than on some presumed "intrinsic value" of a metal. McLallin's distinctiveness lay in the fact that of all the offerings by third party journalists, his prose had the greatest educational potential in behalf of greenback doctrines. As the official newspaper of the Kansas Alliance, McLallin's *Advocate* became the most widely read journal of reform on the Western plains, its circulation reaching 80,000.

Essentially, Populist monetary arguments embodied three elements: an attempt to wrestle away from goldbugs the cultural credentials to define what money was and was not; an analysis of power in terms of bankers, non-bankers, and the currency that connected the two; and an exposure of the prima facie immorality of the prevailing system. While Populists everywhere employed all three arguments, Kansas reformers of the McLallin mold tended to emphasize logical exercises in monetary analysis, agrarians in Texas seemed to focus upon the injustices of existing power relationships, and Populists of the Deep South concentrated on dramatizing the immorality of it all.

When bankers gain control over the nation's money, asserted the editor of the influential Texas *Advance,* "the government conveys to the banks the power to . . . hold up interest to confiscation rates and force the people to pay it, put up or put down prices when they choose." The practical effect, said the paper, was that bankers were able to "transfer the people's earnings and property to themselves at will." The *Southern Mercury* attacked the idea that capital owned labor as part of its investment. When labor tried to assert its rights, said the *Mercury,* "capital then calls on the courts to declare labor in contempt and if labor does not freely consent to be a machine, capital asks the government to call out the standing army and shoot labor down. . . . Then labor wakes up and finds that it is really not flesh and blood but only a machine owned and run by capital." [29]

The moral weakness of the existing economic and political system received due emphasis in the Deep South. A North

Carolina reform journal proclaimed that in a system "where every man is for himself, the devil will get most of them." The *Jeffersonian* of Alabama added that "any nation that holds property rights above human rights" is practicing "barbarism." Another North Carolinian regarded the very definitions of contemporary politics to be immoral: "When plutocracy defrauds the people of this nation out of a billion dollars of value a year through any law, it is business, and when they establish soup houses and extend a helping hand in organized charity working by scientific system, it is charity. When wealth blooms under the law," the paper concluded "manhood and human rights wither." [30]

It would be imprudent to press too far a characterization of Populist exhortation in purely regional terms. Populists in all sections presented, in turn, reasoned arguments, indignant denunciations, and moral injunctions. This reality is perhaps best demonstrated by the fact that the one Populist orator who possessed a facile ability to employ all three techniques—"Cyclone" Davis—was found to be equally useful to embattled third parties in Kansas, Virginia, Alabama, Missouri, Iowa, and Oregon. Though certainly not at his best as an original political theorist, Davis could, on occasion, put his finger on one or more of the raw nerves of life in the industrializing state: "The individual is merged in the money-machine of which he is an integral part, and the morality of its action is the morality of the company, not his; nor is he unhappy over it so long as it produces a gain. Thus its reacting influence on the man corrupts and degrades until at last a sort of financial self-respect will constrain him first to excuse and then to defend all the means, no matter how corrupt, which were used to bring him a fortune." For the cause of democratic values, the hour was late, Davis felt. "I believe that civil liberty is in jeopardy when the aspirations of men are suppressed or exercised by the suffrance of these artificial creations . . . whose influence is vast enough to shape the law of the government which created them." [31]

Populists like Davis were fully aware that they were not only challenging old ideas which they found wholly obsolete in the new age of machines, but that in so doing they were engaged in a kind of cultural pioneering that made their proposals sound radical to the uninformed. A product of the agricultural districts himself, Davis was especially sensitive to the hold that traditional habits of thought had upon potential Populistic constituencies. Indeed, he was by no means entirely free of cultural barnacles himself, particularly with respect to black Americans. Nor did he ever contribute a single new refinement to Populist arguments on the three issues of land, money, and transportation. He was, simply and effectively, one of Populism's foremost rough and tumble debaters, uniquely capable of exposing his opponent's weaknesses in language that never quite read as persuasively in print as it sounded from the speaker's platform. Years after Populism, when partisan emotions had mellowed a bit, Davis was described by a somewhat bruised but magnanimous Democrat: "There are other men fully as logical and rhetorical, but no man is so completely master of the little arts of turning the laughs on his antagonist and making him feel like six pewter nickels." [32]

In an era when the principal means of public persuasion, the press, was in step with the hard-money doctrines of both major parties, the People's Party was forced to reply through its reform editors, augmented as massively as possible by the oratorical powers of its stump speakers. If showmanship could be added to radicalism, so much the better, as Jerry Simpson and Mary Elizabeth Lease proved rather fully in Kansas. The great value of "Cyclone" Davis to the cause of reform—and the reason he became the most widely traveled orator of the agrarian revolt—was his ability to counter the charge of radicalism by invoking the past in behalf of the future. His instrument for accomplishing this feat was that symbol of agrarian and republican virtue, Thomas Jefferson. Few in the ranks of any party could rival the theatrical qualities of "Cyclone" Davis and his gospel of Jeffersonianism. His biographer paints the picture vividly enough:

> Holding in his hand a huge, black sombrero, he was attired in a black Prince Albert coat, a vest to match, and trousers which were far too short to cover up much of the alligator

boots on his over-sized feet. Near his chair stood a stack of books entitled *The Works of Jefferson.*

Davis augmented this persona with a debating style that featured a grim review of corporate, banking, and legislative abuses, summarized by the statement: "Jefferson opposed; so do the Populists." "Cyclone" acquired his nickname in a public debate in Kentucky on the same night that the Democratic attorney general of that state, Watt Hardin, had outshone the somewhat phlegmatic Populist Senator from Kansas, William Peffer. The Hardin-Davis debate that followed, however, turned out to be a disaster for the Democratic cause. Referring frequently to Jefferson and "on occasion picking up a volume and reading an entire paragraph," Davis "wrecked" his opponent. An Associated Press reporter who clearly had no affinity for Populist doctrines nevertheless was apparently taken by Davis's "words of eloquence," his "pithy anecdotes," and his "rousing rejoinders," all of which brought forth—the phrase was fatal—a "cyclone of applause." [33]

Like all showmen, Davis was somewhat larger than life and, by at least a microscopically measurable margin, somewhat more sound than substance. His use of the Sage of Monticello was not always historically or intellectually precise, though apparently unfailingly persuasive in the provinces. Yet, according to a scholar who studied his career with some thoroughness, Davis did not call for a "return to the eighteenth-century world." He sought "Jeffersonian sanction" in order "to achieve Populist ends." [34]

Self-evidently, the cultural burden Davis and other Populists felt—and faced in the course of asserting the Omaha Platform—derived from the American habits of laissez faire in economics and sectional loyalty in politics. To the partisans of the third party, the doctrines of laissez faire were ludicrous at a time when the Treasury itself was being intermittently depleted by the nation's prevailing banking syndicate. Similarly, traditional invocations that Populist remedies required unconstitutional "class legislation" such as the sub-treasury plan also sounded inappropriate in an era when railroads were buying state legislatures in order to acquire massive legislative land

S. F. Norton,
editor of the Chicago Express

Ralph Beaumont,
National Lecturer
of the Knights of Labor

Populist Propagandists

James H. Davis,
"the cyclone from Texas"

grants or to elect railroad lawyers to the United States Senate. To Populists, "class legislation" seemed a major governmental preoccupation of post-Civil War America—from the Exemption Clause of the Legal Tender Act of 1862 to the Supreme Court interpretation of the Fourteenth Amendment that bestowed upon corporations the privileges of "persons." In attempting to contest the presumptions of the emerging corporate state, the ideas of the Omaha Platform constituted a distinct cultural burden, and Populists knew it. The great value of speakers like Davis, Simpson, Lease, Tom Watson, and "Stump" Ashby was that each had a force of style—be it power of logic, humor, an instinct for the impromptu riposte, theatrical flair, or a mastery of the rhetorical embroidery the age loved so well. The value to radicalism of such speakers was that they imparted to plausible but culturally embattled ideas the possibility of immediate use. Populists have received from historians praise—perhaps somewhat sanguinary praise, if the record be read closely enough—for having conceived remedies that came to be applied ten, twenty, or fifty years later. Aside from problems in this familiar homily that flow from comparing what Populists really wanted to the actual legislation enacted in later generations, there is the matter of timing to weigh in the equation: the contemporary Populist liked his ideas well enough to want them to become fact in his own lifetime. Accordingly, the language of the agrarian revolt reflected the urgent economic imperatives of the moment, while the structure of Populist argument attempted to frame innovative concepts in a language that sounded both persuasive and traditional.

This rather fundamental matter of political strategy can easily be passed over too lightly. Given the nature of American politics, there were not many honored theorists of the past who could be invoked in the name of the Populist vision of the future. The radical Jefferson was certainly the most useful, and Davis was his most useful third party interpreter. But Lincoln, Henry George, Edward Bellamy, Wendell Phillips, and Jesus Christ could also be cut to the theoretical and moral cloth of Populism, and were. The irony of the Populist dilemma was that the third party had so few saints to invoke, and none possessing the emotional power (in political terms) of other symbols readily available to their major party opponents. The deepest irony, perhaps, was that Populists employed historical images in support of new political ideas, while the major parties employed the past to escape from ideas entirely. Neither the "bloody shirt" nor "the party of the fathers" could be dragged into Gilded Age political debate in ways that had genuine intellectual meaning. Indeed, the effort to do so almost never was found to be necessary by major party strategists. The symbols were invoked purely for symbolic effect. The purpose was not to hold the loyalty of marginal increments of voters, but to retain the basic organic mass of the party's faithful.[35]

Here was the dilemma of the People's Party, writ large. To survive, Populism needed to create massive defections from one or both of the major parties. It needed nothing less than the kind of wholesale apostasy that occurred during the reform summer of 1890 in Kansas. But though the doctrines of Populism could make deep inroads among Republican farmers in the West and Democratic farmers in the South, the emotional symbols available to both old parties held in thrall to inherited customs many millions of potential third party recruits.

American nostalgia thus became the devastating opponent of Populism. The fact explained the persistence—indeed, the augmentation—of sectional politics through the Populist era. Laissez faire could scarcely speak to mortgage-ridden farmers, any more than could the doctrines of the high protective tariff. But the injunction to "vote as you shot, boys" or to "stand by the party of the fathers, boys" not only served to fill the breech, it became the most effective single campaign tactic—fraud excepted—that could be employed against the third party. In a dramatically changing society, neither major party proved capable of responding in any coherent way to the shifting realities in the daily lives of its own constituents. "Coherence," of course, has rarely been applied by historians as a test of the American party system—and understandably so. Indeed, in the Gilded Age the victorious Republican Party convinced the nation that emerging forms of industrial dislocation did not call for coordinating changes in the processes of American democracy. Above all else, the politics of the Gilded Age constituted a triumph both for traditional ways and for the nostalgia that lent strength to tradition.

Though harnessed in behalf of conservative and commercial purposes in the 1890's, Gilded Age nostalgia was interestingly Jacksonian in its moral simplicities, in its obeisance to laissez faire, and in its reliance on quaint fixations about what constituted "sound money." The Jacksonian persuasion, however, carried a deeper, saving impulse—the feeling that a just republic served the needs of its just and hard-working "plain people." And, of course, this Jackonsian premise found its most committed Gilded Age disciples not in the major parties, but in the ranks of Populism. The point is not so much that Jacksonian memories were inordinately multiple and complex, but that the *Realpolitik* of the industrializing state had fashioned new political norms which few Americans seemed intellectually willing to face.[36]

As Populists knew from their own experience, not only did the old ways not work so well any more, but new ways could effectively be offered to millions of voters only if their proponents exhibited a certain selectivity concerning the heritage. The Omaha Platform required its defenders to be both judicious and culturally innovative—in order to overcome the sectional and cultural symbols available to the two major parties. In defense of government ownership of the railroads or of the sub-treasury plan, Populists did not find it helpful to invoke Jeffersonian injunctions about "the government that governs least." Nor was Jacksonian preoccupation with hard money a notable aid in advancing greenback monetary analysis. Nostalgia for lost agrarian Edens, Jacksonian or otherwise, was therefore in short supply on third party hustings. Rather, the politics of the industrial age received the focus of attention. The rules of commerce had changed, and Populists knew it: indeed, the thought was at the very center of the Populist premise.

In the grip of this belief, Populists tested the intellectual flexibility of Gilded Age America. The substance of the third party's experiment in a new political language for an indus-

379

trial society was the belief that government had fallen disastrously behind the sweeping changes of industrial society, leaving the mass of the people as helpless victims of outmoded rules. The idea was expressed in a variety of ways. In North Carolina a thirty-year-old Populist Senator, Marion Butler, wondered how the nation could hide from the fact that "more than 4,000,000 of our countrymen are without sufficient food, raiment and shelter." The causes, felt Butler, were clearly traceable to new forms of hierarchy: "The power to tax production along the lines of more than 8,000 miles of transcontinental railroads is possessed by less than twenty men." James Murdock of the *Progressive Farmer* also located the cause of widespread hardship in the political backwardness of the nation's leaders and party system. "We are in the era of steam, railroad, telegraph and mammoth machinery. The financial system that answered to the age of the slow coach, sickle and spinning wheel will not respond to this. We have had a revolution in manufactures and transportation, and we must have a radical change in our financial system." Murdock believed that "until this is done, there can be no permanent prosperity." The Lampasas, Texas, *People's Journal* agreed that outmoded "sound-money" arguments between goldbugs and silverites only confused the people and prevented the whole society from grappling with its real problems. A completely greenback currency, the paper asserted, "would avoid confusion and deception regarding the true status of our currency and make it unnecessary to further discuss the question of a single or a double standard of payments. It would entirely eliminate the little understood question of a ratio between the two metals, and give us a currency that could not be increased or decreased in value only by limitation in quantity." A fiat currency, the paper concluded, would place monetary matters in a realm "which legislation could regulate." [37]

In the liberal magazine *Arena*, a Populist writer decided that the claims made on behalf of gold's "traditional consistency" were little short of absurd, and, like McLallin in Kansas, he invoked the image of the yardstick to make his case: "What a wonderfully perfect standard of value gold is, to be sure! Think of a yardstick three feet long in 1789, shrunk to nineteen and one-half inches in 1809, stretched again to four feet in 1849, reduced in 1872 to thirty-eight and one-half inches, and now four feet three and nine-tenths inches long, and growing every day! Would not that be a remarkably safe thing to measure cloth with? And yet we are today measuring our debts and credits by a standard no less perfect." The Populist advocate summarized his analogy with assaults on all non-greenback positions. "Selfish creditors will strenuously insist on maintaining the single gold standard, for by that means they are rapidly growing richer. Foolish debtors will clamor for free [silver] coinage, hoping thereby to get cheaper money with which to pay their debts." [38]

The Populist attack on outmoded shibboleths took many forms. The intellectual accoutrements surrounding capitalism were so behind the times, said Georgia's Tom Watson, that America had gone "forward" to feudalism, bypassing the democratic precepts of the founding fathers in the process. "For the first time it is boldly declared, by judicial decision, that organized Capital can coerce Labor and that organized Labor is forbidden to make effective protest. The old baronial right to 'bind a laborer to the soil' finds its twin-brother in this modern corporation right to bind the laborer to his Engine." Watson concluded that "in all essential respects, the Republic of our fathers is dead. The remnants of its form, its outward semblance, may be left but its animating spirit is gone." The Populist effort at reform was central, he felt, because "day by day the power of the individual sinks (while) day by day, the power of the classes, of the corporations, rises." [39]

In Kansas, reform editors, third party office-seekers, and rank-and-file Populists found common cause in the belief that the American economic system had become encrusted with outdated and inhumane habits of thought. Frank Doster, a Populist who later became the Chief Justice of the Kansas Supreme Court, decried in an 1894 Labor Day speech the "fatal mental inability in both Democratic and Republican parties to comprehend the new and strange conditions of our modern industrial and social life, an utter inability to cope with the new and vexing problems which have arisen out of the vacillation of this latter day." The purpose of Populism, he said, was "to bring the power of the social mass to bear upon the rebellious individuals who thus menace the peace and safety of the state." A farmer supporter of Doster's found the root of the problem in the doctrines of Herbert Spencer. He asserted "there never was, nor can there be, a more brutal, utterly selfish and despicable doctrine than the Darwinian 'struggle for existence' when applied to the social relations of man. It justified oppression, the aggregation of wealth in the hands of those able to grasp it, the occupation of everything the 'fittest' are able to gain and keep." The "modern condition," Stephen McLallin summarized in an editorial in *The Advocate*, "is the monopoly of machinery and other means of production and distribution by which the few are benefited and the many are deprived of fair opportunities in life." [40]

Populists accepted the fact that organized capital was capable of random creativity, but they believed that too many innovations were socially destructive. Foremost among them, of course, were the transparent inequities of the national banking system and the corporate corruption of the democratic process. But agrarian radicals were also outraged by the demonstrated power of corporations to harness the military might of the state to defeat impoverished workers fighting to preserve fragile new unions. In this aspect of national life, the collusion between capital and government, implemented by pliant politicians, seemed to combine political and corporate power in an especially ominous way. During the tumultuous struggle of ragged Alabama miners against the Tennessee Coal and Iron Company in 1894, Populists were quick to spot the Bourbon regime's efforts to promote violence as an excuse to bring in state troops to break the strike. Third party leaders in Alabama refused to recognize the legitimacy of Thomas Jones on the ground that he had stolen the gubernatorial election from Kolb, and they developed the habit of referring to the incumbent as "Governor de facto." In the midst of the 1894 struggle of the miners, the Columbia *People's Advocate* announced that the "Governor de facto" was "doing everything in his power to bring a collision between the striking miners and the military." For a time the paper was pleased to report that the plot had been foiled by the disciplined ranks of labor.

Nevertheless, the Alabama strike was broken by troops, as was the more widely publicized Pullman strike in Chicago in the same year. Kansas Governor Lewelling denounced President Cleveland for "throwing an armed force across the border into Illinois, and other states, without so much as inquiring whether or not it will be agreeable to the authorities of the state itself." Lewelling singled out the "close alliance" of capitalists, judges, and major party politicians and emphasized that the methods of the Illinois and Alabama capitalists were rampant in Kansas, too. "A friend of mine who is nominated for Senator on the Populist ticket had the audacity, my friends, to contribute to the striking laborers of [Arkansas City]. Today, he is arraigned by the United States court and summoned to Topeka and placed on trial for aiding and abetting the strikers against the government of the United States. Think of it!" [41]

In the South the debasement of labor was underscored by the convict lease system. At the onset of the Populist revolt in 1891 the Tennessee Coal and Iron Company discharged free labor from its mines in Tennessee and hired state convicts to replace them. Desperate miners overcame prison guards, burned down company-built stockades, and shipped the convicts away on commandeered outbound trains. Armed troops paid jointly by the company and the state succeeded in reinstalling the convicts in the Anderson County mines. To Populists, the "anarchism" of the Tennessee labor war was all on the side of "arrogant and insolent" owners and their eager supporters among the metropolitan press. Milford Howard, Alabama's Populist Congressman, made no attempt to conceal his concern about the long-term implications of the emerging power relationships within American society. "It is quite the fad among certain large daily papers representing the money power to say there is no plutocracy, that it is all a mere hallucination. They scoff at the idea that this question is to enter into the politics of the future." In such varied ways, the "politics of the future" was the connecting theme of Populist advocacy. Its presence as moral indignation in the Omaha preamble merely fortified with a certain flourish the practical remedies proposed in the platform itself.[42]

Yet there was one final, colorful, and deeply human ingredient in the language of American Populism. It came not from reform editors bent on "educating the people" but from the people themselves. From the movement itself came songs, literally hundreds of songs, that expressed the hopes and despair of the men and women of the agrarian revolt. Collectively, these ballads and ditties, joyful, ironic, or pungent, imparted to the culture of Populism a distinctively American flavor.

The "pentecost of politics" often came across in rhyme:

> It was hardly more than a year ago,
> Good-bye, my party, good-bye,
> That I was in love with my party so,
> Good-bye, my party, good-bye.
>
> I was raised up in the kind of school,
> Good-bye, my party, good-bye,
> That taught me to bow to money rule,
> Good-bye, my party, good-bye . . .[43]

The farmer-poets even wrote a tune against sectionalism. "Clasped Hand In Hand Like Brothers" was written by a Kansan and dedicated to the wife of the Alliance national lecturer, Ben Terrell of Texas. The earnest gentlemen of the Alliance Supreme Council thought so much of the lyrics, they suggested all suballiance meetings be opened and closed with the song.[44]

"The Farmer Is The Man" was a popular favorite:

> When the farmer comes to town
> With his wagon broken down
> The farmer is the man that feeds them all
> If you'll only look and see
> I think you will agree
> That the farmer is the man that feeds them all.
>
> The farmer is the man
> The farmer is the man
> Lives on credit till the fall
> With the interest rates so high
> It's a wonder he don't die
> And the mortgage man's the one that gets it all.

The farmer is the man
The farmer is the man
Lives on credit till the fall
And his pants are wearing thin
His condition it's a sin
He's forgot that he's the man that feeds them all.

Leo Vincent's "Alliance Songster" and, later, the "Alliance and Labor Songster" were literary staples of the agrarian revolt, compendiums of political folk wisdom. But scores of songs, regional favorites as varied as the crops farmers raised, were never "collected" at all. They were sung, nevertheless, at summer encampments, at autumn rallies, and at reform meetings the year 'round. Their titles delineated friends and foes alike: "The Thomas E. Watson Ballad," "The Farmer And The Banker," "Hands Across The Mason-Dixon Line."

The songs, like the "parades of the people," the wagon trains, and the encampments were, in their ways, as authentic examples of the "language of Populism" as the speeches and editorials of third party candidates and reform editors. Collectively, the rustic ballads portrayed the "pageantry of Populism" as individual and collective human striving. In Kansas Populists had a tune for just about every reform in the Omaha Platform and the Kansas Populist glee club carried most of them to each county of the state. The Kansas Singers were often led by the third party's most renowned female orator, Mary Elizabeth Lease. Mrs. Lease, known as Mary Ellen to her friends and as "Mary Yellin' " to her Republican opponents, ensured a place for herself in the chronicles as the agrarian revolt with her famous injunction to Kansas farmers to "raise less corn and more hell." But a talent that only her contemporaries knew was the quality of her singing voice. William Allen White, the prim Kansas newspaperman, rarely had a good word for Populists, but he was willing to concede the effectiveness of Mrs. Lease's songs in establishing a proper kinship between speaker and audience.[45]

Indeed the range of ideas and aspirations conveyed through the politics of Populism, whether in song, in print, or on the stump, was a striking feature of the third party's contribution to American political dialogue. Populists had read enough history to know that neither Jefferson nor Jackson had been forced to deal with an economic system based on corporate centralization, rebates, pools, oil rooms, crop liens, furnishing merchants, or working conditions enforced by armed troops and rural sheriffs. These were latter-day hazards, and Populists proposed latter-day remedies. Rather than Jefferson's limited government, they proposed an expanded government, believing that only a new civic polity—augmented by a clear sense of its own mission to secure equity for the many—could cope with the demonstrated financial power of the few. Rather than Jackson's metallic currency to cope with private banks, the Populists proposed a treasury-based greenback currency that would curb the special privileges embedded in a private national banking system. Populists did, indeed, share with both Jefferson and Jackson the fear that a financial and corporate elite would diminish and even destroy the effective voice of the citizenry in shaping democratic alternatives to inherited public policies. But in proposing the abolition of the national banking system and the establishment of a new national currency based on the nation's productivity and centered in the national treasury, all three innovations to be augmented by basic land reform, government ownership of the railroads, a federal income tax, and direct elections of Senators, it seems rather clear that Populists were responding to contemporary financial and corporate abuses with contemporary remedies. That roughly half the American population refused even to make an effort to understand such remedies testified to the complacency of the cultural values against which Populists rebelled. That another large sector of the population listened to the Populists but responded to sectional memories further revealed the narrow horizons of life and thought in the Gilded Age.

As for the advocates of the People's Party, it seems enough to credit them with the explicit goals of their own doctrines: rather better than their rivals, they endeavored to address the needs of the present in the name of a democratic vision of the future.

CHAPTER XIII

A Shadow Movement Finds Its Spokesmen

"A political party has no charms for me. . . ."

During the years 1892–95 the strongholds of the agrarian revolt gradually identified themselves through the cold statistics of municipal, county, congressional, and statewide returns from polling boxes scattered from Virginia to Oregon. The "coming revolution," codified in the Omaha Platform after years of cooperative struggle and organizational development, had developed its strongest electoral base in three states— Georgia, Kansas, and Texas. But elsewhere across the nation during the same years the political style of the agrarian revolt underwent a variety of alterations that had very little to do with the doctrines so laboriously formulated at Cleburne, Dallas, St. Louis, Ocala, and Omaha.

Most easily identifiable of the new species was an effervescent "single-shot" Populism that had emerged in the Western mining states. Though sometimes producing victories for candidates who called themselves Populists, the Western mutation yielded a variety of reformer who proved difficult to distinguish from more familiar types calling themselves Democrats and Republicans. Indeed, in places like Nevada, where the cause of reform went by the name of the "Silver Party," a mention of the Omaha Platform was likely to extract little more from voters than blank stares. The doctrine of free silver was the overriding thought in the mining states of the West. Silver Republicans, silver Democrats, and silver Populists "fused" in a wondrous variety of ways to contest major party traditionalists on the only matter of interest to any of the participants—the increased coinage of the white metal.[1]

Nevada was not unique. As Populists across the nation discovered in the course of surveying the election returns of 1894, the party of reform had begun to develop a dual personality. Not only in the mining states of the plateau region, but in a number of places through the old cotton belt and the newer Western granary third party organizational difficulties had led to what Alliancemen regarded as ideological "trimming" of the Omaha Platform. The political alternative that emerged as "Populism," particularly in some locales, bore little resemblance to the reform doctrines developed by the agrarian revolt.

Nebraska provided the most striking example of what had begun to happen to the agrarian dream of broad-based reform of the American monetary and political system. In somewhat less telling ways, the reform cause in Alabama also came to be affected by previously concealed weaknesses. By 1894, in both states, it was clear that a number of third party partisans were unable to express themselves in terms of the transforming vision elaborated at Omaha two years earlier. As a matter of fact, with powerful help from outside the ranks of Populism, a shadow movement began taking form.

2

The phenomenon was clearest in Nebraska. Populism there had very little to do either with the Omaha Platform or with the years of cooperative aspiration and political evolution that had produced the third party's basic political statement. The movement that materialized in Nebraska was less a new body of ideas than a loosely floating faction of the familiar low-tariff Democratic Party. Indeed, the so-called "Independent" movement that came into being in the midst of "fusion" politics in

1890 had subsequently ritualized the practice of Populist-Democratic cooperation into a predictable habit of thought. Nebraska independents could not even claim to be the initiating force in this amalgamating process; Democrats not only were most effectively the active agents, but they had a knack of formulating the terms of the compact in ways that reflected their own self-interest.

The most zealous Democrat was William Jennings Bryan, the young Congressman elected in 1890. Though Bryan had rather traditionally stressed the Democratic issue of low tariffs in his 1890 campaign, the proliferation of agrarian demands on the "financial question" induced him, during his extremely close re-election campaign of 1892, to begin calling for "free and unlimited coinage of silver at the ratio of sixteen to one"—a slogan that harkened back to the days of "The Crime of '73," some twenty years earlier. Though Bryan had at best only a shaky grasp of the intricacies of the monetary system, he knew that silver coinage avoided awkward moral questions about a "fiat currency" and an "honest" dollar. Bryan conceded in 1892 that he did not "know anything about free silver," and he added, cheerfully, "the people of Nebraska are for free silver and I am for free silver. I will look up the arguments later." For a major party politician in search of an issue through which to survive in an era of reform agitation and hard times, silver coinage seemed ideal. The silver issue offered the young Nebraskan still another benefit: it gave him entrée to the funds of Western silver mineowners. As one writer put it, Bryan "looked up the arguments" and made a fiery free silver speech in the Congress in 1893. He immediately acquired new friends among the silver mineowners and they promptly printed almost a million copies of the speech for distribution. The action signaled the forceful arrival of a new element in Gilded Age politics—the American Bimetallic League.[2]

Because of its enormous impact in giving genuine political meaning to the Nebraska shadow movement, the story of the well-financed silver drive constitutes the essential background to the unfolding of the changed national politics of 1895–96. While it was eventually to affect the cause of reform in a

389

decisive way, the true center of gravity within the shadow movement rested outside the People's Party.

Though the American Bimetallic League had been formed by silver mineowners as early as 1889 and held its first nonpartisan convention in St. Louis that year, it was not until the depression of 1893 had placed severe pressure on the nation's gold reserves that silver coinage began to have serious possibilities as a national issue. As the depression deepened, President Cleveland's orthodox monetary beliefs induced him to take extraordinary measures to preserve the gold standard, including the expensive, unpopular, and widely publicized gold bond issues and the equally unpopular repeal of the Sherman Silver Purchase Act. That Act, originally passed in 1890, called for a mild expansion of the currency through the purchase of four million dollars in silver coin per month. In an economy suffering obvious economic ills from a contracted currency, the repeal of the Act represented a triumph of gold orthodoxy over practical political reality. But while this development spread despair among Democrats in 1894–95, it also opened a whole new field of lobbying potential for silver interests. Clearly, the best way for an embattled Democratic politician to dissociate himself from the goldbug policies of Cleveland lay in becoming a public advocate of the white metal. In 1893 the silverites hired a publicist named William H. Harvey to supervise their anti-repeal lobbying activities in the Midwest, and while he promptly staged a handsome conference in Chicago, the subsequent repeal of the Act revealed the relative weakness of the silver effort compared to the lobbying influence of the Eastern financial community. Silver interests thereupon stepped up their campaign to recruit unhappy Democrats. The skeletal Harvey operation in Chicago was augmented and Harvey himself put to work writing inexpensive silver tracts aimed at a mass audience and marketed through advertisements in the Democratic and third-party press. The first one, "Coin's Handbook," enjoyed a modest sale.[3]

But while refurbishing the machinery of their Chicago operation, the silver interests broadened their geographical base. The Omaha *World-Herald* was purchased in 1894 and young pro-silver Congressman Williams Jennings Bryan installed as its editor. The silver men put in their own managment, leaving Bryan free to campaign for silver while contributing an editorial or two each week. Other connections were also forged. Such newspapers as Edward Carmack's Memphis *Commercial-Appeal* began to demonstrate an astonishing preoccupation with the silver issue. So did the Washington *Evening Star,* thus providing a base issue of support in the nation's capital to augment the outposts in the South and West. The American Bimetallic League was reinforced by the "National Bimetallic Union" and the "Pan-American Bimetallic Association," and by the emergence of scores of local and regional silver "clubs," silver "unions," and silver "leagues." In the summer of 1894, the Omaha *World-Herald* announced Bryan's candidacy for the Senate at the "request" of the executive committee of a new group called the "Nebraska Democratic Free Coinage League." [4]

Silver influence popped up in a number of places. Scarcely had the Omaha Platform been unveiled in 1892, in fact, than Herman Taubeneck, the national Populist chairman, began writing a select group of third party politicians of his interest in procuring some campaign contributions from Western mining interests. Meanwhile, Charles Macune's long-time editorial assistant, Nelson Dunning, inaugurated *The National Watchman* as an organ for the new third party. Coordinate with silver lobbying inside the Democratic Party in 1894–96, the *National Watchman* began to prosper. For a Macunite Dunning seems to have found it surprisingly easy to dispense with the greenback doctrines woven through the Omaha Platform. Dunning, in fact, became as dedicated to the new cause of silver coinage as Carmack's *Commercial-Appeal* or such robust new journals as the Chicago-based *National Bimetallist* and the Washington *Silver Knight.* The latter journal was edited, nominally at least, by Nevada's silver Senator, William Stewart, a Republican.[5]

Though such diverse support was important to William Jennings Bryan in his new role as one of the nation's spokesmen for silver, his political success at home in Nebraska was directly traceable to the ease with which he was able to work with the representatives of the so-called "Independent," or

Populist movement in the state. Indeed, Bryan had a close friend at the very apex of the new party movement. By a curious and revealing twist of circumstance, the titular leader and acknowledged spokesman of Populism, Nebraska-style, came to be neither Charles Van Wyck, the disenchanted Republican anti-monopolist, nor John Powers, the well-meaning Alliance chieftain, but a friendly, apolitical, and previously unknown small-town lawyer named William V. Allen. As a United States Senator from Nebraska, Allen became the archetype of a strange new breed of third party politician who was a Populist in name only.

William Allen actually had been a typical Republican until 1891. Indeed, his passage into the ranks of the third party provided a rather appropriate example of the kind of formless and free-floating politics that materialized in Nebraska at the onset of Populism. For one thing, even following his late arrival in the reform cause, Allen was never able to piece together in any coherent fashion either the rationale behind the Omaha Platform or an explanation of how such tenets came to find their way onto the Nebraska political scene in the first place. Not only the doctrines, but the very origins of Populism seemed to baffle him. Confusing the 1888 and 1889 Alliance platforms of Meridian and St. Louis with the document drafted at Ocala in 1890, he cheerfully described the Ocala gathering to a New York editor as "the convention of political and agricultural reform elements" that "met a year or two before" his own conversion "in 1890." Allen's innocence of the agrarian movement for which he spoke was not without its immediate political meaning: whatever others might say of Populism, the Nebraskan made it clear he was not a "radical party man." He consistently avoided not only greenback monetary analysis, but also such other doctrines organic to the Populist platform as government ownership of the railroads. As Allen's public statements made clear, the entire subject of the Populist platform tended to fill him with caution. He would not "start off with fiat money," he explained, because paper money should have "its interchangeability maintained" and "kept as good as gold and silver." As firmly as any gold monometallist, Nebraska's Populist Senator thus endorsed a currency of ultimate redemption. He was able to see through the Republican pose for "international bimetallism," which he described as a "farce," but beyond such political levels of monetary interpretation he could rarely proceed.[6]

Equally beyond his purview were such Alliance concepts as the radical vision of basic realignment of the American party system. Far from seeing the People's Party as a new political institution to bring representation to the "industrial millions," Allen had more prosaic intuitions about the proper role of parties. "I have always looked upon a political party simply as a means to an end. I think a party should be held no more sacred than a man's shoes or garments, and that whenever it fails to serve the purposes of good government, a man should abandon it as cheerfully as he dispenses with his worn-out clothes." Confessing that he had taken "very little part in politics" in the past, Allen summarized his credo with the thought that "a political party has no charms for me outside of what it can accomplish conducive to good government." A bit more specifically, he said that he was "not a radical" on the tariff and "in no sense a socialist" on the labor question. Amid the flurry of disclaimers, it was not always easy to isolate precisely what the Nebraska lawyer did endorse. Gradually, however, his politics became clear. By 1894 he could state that he wanted laboring men to "receive the full benefit of their labor," and he wanted the currency regulated "so as to make it of approximately equal value at all times." While the decline in the price of wheat "may not be due to the scarcity of money and the appreciation of gold," Allen said, "yet we Western people believe that the money question has a great deal to do with it." If it was all a big vague, no one questioned his sincerity. In essence, William V. Allen stood for honest, conservative government. He said as much in a summary statement for the *Review of Reviews:*

If my views could be enforced in this country I would purify state and national legislation. I would not suffer a man to become a member of either branch of Congress or of any state lawmaking body who had pecuniary interests which

393

might be materially affected by legislation. If he wanted to become a member of Congress he would have to put aside his own pecuniary interests for the time, so that he might be said to stand as an impartial judge in the determination of any case that came before him. This is foreshadowed, you see, by the bill I introduced the other day entitled "A Bill to Preserve the Purity of National Legislation, and for other Purposes." The bill is imperfectly drawn, but I shall hereafter redraft it with more care. I do not suppose it will get through this Congress, and perhaps it will never get through. . . .[7]

Manifestly, William Allen was cut from different cloth than such platform stemwinders as "Cyclone" Davis and Mary Lease. More to the point in terms of underlying Populist beliefs on the labor, financial, and transportation issues, he was a revolution or two removed from such equally amiable Populist greenbackers as William Peffer of Kansas and Thomas Nugent of Texas. Besides stretching the imagination a bit, a comparison of Allen to the deadly serious Tom Watson of Georgia merely dramatizes how tangential the shadow-movement really was. Yet Allen authentically represented the style of Nebraska Populism, both in his beliefs and in the very manner in which he came to be the state's third party Senator.

Allen gained his Washington office as a result of a confused bit of fusion in the Nebraska legislature in 1893. The Nebraska reform party had polled some 35 per cent of the vote in 1892, a figure that measured closely the voting strength of Populism in the state throughout the 1890's. In the absence of clearly defined Populist doctrines, the vote essentially reflected the extent of farmer discontent, though, in concrete political terms, this discontent was necessarily expressed rather form-lessly in Nebraska. The Republican sweep of state offices in 1892 in Nebraska did not extend to the congressional races, where three fusion candidates headed by Democrat William Jennings Bryan had emerged victorious, or to the state legislature, which had an interesting assortment of Republicans, Democrats, and "Independents." The Republicans had slightly less than a legislative majority over their combined opposition, and balloting for the United States Senate seat was lengthy, confused, and threaded with rumors about back-room deals. At one point the slavishness of Republican legislators to railroad lobbyists became so apparent that the Omaha *Bee* defected from the ranks in general disgust. The *Bee* denounced a "treasonable plot on the part of the confederated corporations to dominate the state." After twelve ballots the Republican senatorial candidate, John Thurston, the general solicitor for the Union Pacific Railroad, almost gained a majority, but the anticipated support of five Gold Democrats failed to materialize at the last moment. Holding the balance of power, the Gold Democrats sought bigger game. They hoped to force the Republicans to support a Democratic conservative, and they threatened to throw their votes to a reform candidate if the Republicans failed to cooperate. For their part, the Nebraska Independents attempted to win the same conservative Democratic support, and to that end they organized coalitions behind three successive candidates—each a bit more acceptable to conservatives than his predecessor. The third political specimen offered to the Democrats was William V. Allen.[8]

After mobilizing all possible Democratic and Populist support for their man, the fusion strategists discovered that they were still one vote short of a majority. The five Gold Democrats then confronted the Republicans with a narrow choice: either the G.O.P. would support a conservative Democrat— such as that great and good friend of the railroads and the sound dollar, J. Sterling Morton—or the Democrats would vote for Allen. The conservative *Nebraska State Journal* reported that the Republicans were buckling to this pressure, but at the last moment they decided to give one of their own a final chance at the senatorial laurel wreath. With that, the Democratic conservatives made good their threat, voted for Allen, and, in this manner, gave Nebraska a spokesman for reform in the United States Senate. In addition to the support of the five Gold Democrats, Allen received eleven other Democratic votes in amassing his winning legislative coalition. The Republican Omaha *Bee* expressed its surprise and pleasure at the final result, particularly in light of the rather low form of knavery that had characterized the balloting. The paper, which had authored a sprightly series of bloody-shirt attacks on Populists throughout the campaigns of 1890 and 1892, judged Allen to be "well balanced, broadminded and conservative." He stood, said the paper, "head and shoulders above any other man proposed by the Populists in point of ability and honesty of purpose." [9]

The easy harmony between such hard-money, low-tariff Democrats as William Jennings Bryan, such committed Republican papers as the Omaha *Bee,* and such moderates as William Allen adequately defined the nature of Nebraska Populism. Virtually issueless, the third party in Nebraska was simply, decently, and solely dedicated to "honest government." To the Omaha *Bee,* which editorialized against the reigning Republican "boodle gang," the circumspect Allen was eminently preferable to debauched railroad candidates, even more so than "Windy Jay" Bryan, whom the paper regarded as a "joke." For their part, Allen and Bryan worked well together. Both avoided the Omaha Platform like the plague and specialized instead in talking in generalities—Bryan about silver and the tariff and Allen about silver and good government. [10]

The off-year elections of 1893 had established, in the words of a Nebraska historian, "even more definitely, if that could be, that the Populists could not defeat the Republicans." While both major parties in a dozen Southern and Western states were frantically tacking into the Populist storm by running "reform" candidates on increasingly radical-appearing platforms, Nebraska Republicans paid their compliments to their rivals by deposing a Republican supreme court judge named Samuel Maxwell, the one state official in a position of power who had refused to align himself with railroad interests. Though railroad regulation was the one "living issue" in state politics, the Republicans moved to augment the railroad majority on the high bench by replacing Maxwell with a "safe" candidate. Predictably, the Omaha *Bee* was outraged, and thereupon pledged its support to the reform candidate for judge during the 1893 campaign. The Nebraska Independents made prompt overtures to the Democrats and even took time out in their state platform to praise William Jennings

Bryan for his congressional vote against the repeal of the Sherman Silver Purchase Act—legislation dear to the hearts of advocates of the silver cause. In an atmosphere of moderate Populist-Democratic-Republican conviviality, undisturbed by references to the greenback doctrines of the Omaha Platform, the 1893 coalition of three-party fusionists selected as its judicial candidate a nominal Populist and political moderate named Silas A. Holcomb. A recent convert from Democratic Party regularity, Holcomb could be relied upon to join both Allen and Bryan in a public posture well clear of the Omaha Platform. Despite the apparent range of the moderate coalition, the Republicans soundly thrashed the fusionists at the polls in 1893. Whatever the outcome said about Republican taste in candidates or about the party's respect for the Nebraska electorate, the victory convincingly verified the G.O.P.'s appraisal of the weakness of its floundering rivals.[11]

By 1894 Nebraska fusionists had picked up the support of a Democratic counterpart to the Republican Omaha *Bee.* The Omaha *World-Herald,* a prominent Democratic newspaper, finally washed its hands of its party's dominant railroad-gold-bug wing, which was led by J. Sterling Morton, one of the Midwest's more implacable conservative Democrats. Morton, though outpolled by Republicans and Populists in the gubernatorial race of 1892, had subsequently found succor as Grover Cleveland's Secretary of Agriculture. From that bastion he continued to direct the Nebraska Democratic Party in support of the gold standard and railroad enterprise. As the depression of the 1890's worsened neither Cleveland's policies nor Morton's endeared themselves to the *World-Herald.* In 1894 the paper endorsed the idea of fusion between Populists, Bryan Democrats, and moderate Republicans. Chastened by repeated defeats, Nebraska Populists continued to prove amenable to the idea of broad-based coalition, as did the rather small number of reform-minded Republicans who materialized in the state. Coalition became a way of life among Nebraska Populists, extending even to the local level. But the most zealous fusionist of all was William Jennings Bryan. According to one authority, fusion "offered a fighting chance to Bryan to avoid retirement." Despite Populist-Democratic cooperation in Bryan's second congressional district, the young orator had barely won re-election in 1892 by a margin of 140 votes over his orthodox Republican opponent. The unpopularity of the Gold Democracy of Grover Cleveland in the depression year of 1894 persuaded Bryan not to run again in his marginal district. Rather, with additional funding from the same sources, Bryan moved in 1894 to challenge goldbug control of the Nebraska Democratic Party and to prepare his followers for top-to-bottom fusion with the willing Nebraska Populists. His objective was to become the choice of the 1895 legislature for Nebraska's available United States Senate seat.[12]

The moderate coalition ran Silas Holcomb for the governorship in 1894, and worked out elaborate fusion arrangements in congressional districts and even at the local level. The supremely confident Republicans increased the stakes by naming a gubernatorial candidate who was not only clearly identified with the railroads, but was also tainted by some unsavory financial dealings. Even the weather cooperated to stir discontent. The drought of 1894 was the worst on record, destroying crops over a wide area. As fodder to feed livestock disappeared, desperate farmers rushed their lean cattle and hogs to market. According to one witness there was "hardly enough moisture in the soil to germinate the seed," and a State Relief Commission Report referred to the "utter destitution of the industrious thousands." The problem of high interest worsened in the midst of this natural disaster. During the period 1890–1895, well over half a million chattel mortgages carrying upwards of 50 per cent in annual interest were recorded on Nebraska farmers, who, because of the contracted currency, had no other means of obtaining money.[13]

Despite the pressure from the financial system and from nature, as well as advantages accruing from the variety of fusion arrangements and the rare benefit of a divided metropolitan press, the moderate coalition again met clear-cut defeat at the hands of the Republicans in 1894. Only one Republican statewide candidate, the scandal-marred gubernatorial aspirant, failed of election. Republicans won 75 per cent of the seats in the state Senate and over 70 per cent of the House. Bryan escaped defeat because he had declined another re-election attempt in his vulnerable district in order to make his bid for a United States Senate seat. The overwhelmingly conservative makeup of the new legislature caused him to withdraw his senatorial candidacy, however. It was at this point in his career that Bryan's friends among the silver magnates purchased the Omaha *World-Herald,* which, with Bryan as its editor, promptly became an even more active advocate of free silver. Bryan's seat in the United States House went to a Republican, along with all the other Nebraska congressional seats except Omar Kem's. Of the House delegation of six Nebraskans, Kem was the lone congressional fusionist to survive. In the wake of the sweeping election trend, Silas Holcomb's capture of the governorship was generally acknowledged, even by fusionists, to represent less a vote of confidence in the cause of reform than a rejection of his tainted opponent. Republican Party loyalty clearly remained sufficiently strong among Nebraska voters to ensure the continuance of a state government in harmony with the self-interest of the Burlington and Union Pacific Railroads.[14]

"Railroad candidates" were safe in Nebraska; the mild lesson for the Republican hierarchy produced by the campaigns of 1893 and 1894 was that only "scandal-tainted railroad candidates" carried a measure of vulnerability. Of the total party vote in the state, the People's Party received but 34 per cent in 1894. By every conceivable criteria that bore on the task of "educating" voters on reform issues, the third party leadership in Nebraska had proved remarkably incapable of reaching its natural constituency. The Nebraska People's Party languished in complete ideological homage to the Democratic Party. The monetary and transportation planks of the Omaha Platform represented no impediment to fusion, for they had never been central to the Nebraska third party and their disappearance from the environment of reform did not call for a single specific political act. In the expedient style of electioneering that characterized the emerging shadow movement in Nebraska, the Omaha Platform was clearly an irrelevant piece of paper. Indeed, at campaign time its existence only created awkward problems for the cause of harmony and fusion. The fate of greenback doctrines in Nebraska was wholly unique in the tier of states from North Dakota to Texas along the farming frontier of the Great Plains.

The provincial legacy of the Burrows-George years had found its practical fulfillment in the political perspective of William Allen. If, in the words of the genial Senator, Populism in Nebraska sought to "purify state and national legislation," that worthy if vague objective was also open to claim by any political party in sudden need of additional votes. Appropriately enough, the Bryan wing of the Democratic Party, increasingly focusing on silver coinage, won organizational control in 1894 from the Gold Democrats of J. Sterling Morton. The Bryanites offered to provide "purity" too. In the South, where the combination of burgeoning Populism and deepening depression had thrown Democratic regulars into a virtual panic, the lure of "free silver" offered pragmatic traditionalists the same route to political salvation that it provided Bryan in Nebraska. Silver coinage might save any number of political chestnuts. If the People's Party had no more to distinguish itself from such maneuverings than a plaintive appeal for "purification," its defenses as a separate institution were shaky indeed. Yet in the kind of reform ethos that materialized in Nebraska, the political meaning of parties seemed to generate little more than passing interest. To Senator William Allen, who compared political ideas to "shoes and garments," such matters as structural change of the banking system, the party system, or the deep-rooted system of corporate influence over the democratic process itself had no relationship to the purpose of the People's Party. The shadow moment that was Nebraska Populism represented little more than a quest for honorable men who would pledge themselves to forsake corrupt practices.

In the environment of the agrarian movement, Nebraska's William Allen gave representation to the same part of the political spectrum that Andrew Dunlap, the early Alliance conservative, had occupied in Texas in 1886, or that Lon Livingston, the Democratic party loyalist, had endeavored to defend in Georgia in 1891. Though possessed of less ambition than Livingston and more polish than Dunlap, Allen shared their allegiance to existing political forms. Contrary to the dynamics at work in Texas and Georgia, however, the aimless political environment lingering inside the Nebraska Alliance through the 1880's produced no William Lambs to argue the farmers' case for political revolt, nor any Tom Watsons to rally the Alliance faithful to a defense of their own platform.

The most telling ideological distinction between Populism and its shadow movement lay in the history of the agrarian experience itself during the turbulent years between 1886 and 1892. William Lamb, and the momentum he and other Alliance radicals helped create within the agrarian movement, succeeded in conveying all the way to the People's Party most of the Andrew Dunlaps of Texas and a good many others of similar persuasion in the rest of the South. Such relatively conservative third party men rarely occupied positions of leadership, but most of them thoroughly understood the issues imbedded in the Omaha Platform and they added their weight to the cause of reform. In Georgia, Watson had been forced to wage and win a furious struggle with Livingston even to create the Georgia third party. The defeated Livingston, his allegiance to "reform through the Democrats" still intact, thereupon disappeared completely from the agrarian movement. Yet the Nebraska counterpart of Dunlap and Livingston, William V. Allen, became Populism's leading spokesman in his native state. Like Livingston, Allen found reform through existing (and unreformed) institutions a perfectly reasonable expectation. And, like Livingston, Allen easily became a supporter of silver and the Democratic Party of William Jennings Bryan. Ironically, while a thoughtful student of the Gilded Age would later remark that Livingston had "occupied a dubious and shifty position" in the agrarian movement in the South, Nebraska's Allen would be perceived by still other historians as the essential Populist, and his policy of fusion as the essence of American "Populism." Be that as it may, the shadow movement of silver-fusion had found not one spokesman, but two—Populist Allen and Democrat Bryan. They shared identical political perspectives.[15]

3

In less fundamental ways, the reform cause in Alabama also encountered problems that kept the state's third party men in a state of perpetual anxiety lest the new movement lose its way. The path to insurgency in Alabama was a tortured one that revealed the difficulties of reform movements within the post-Civil War American political environment of sectionalism.

As embattled Bourbons saw it, Alabama reformers had performed their duty all too well in getting the "plain people" ready for a new politics of economic issues to replace the inherited politics of the Lost Cause. The cooperative crusade had been serious business in Alabama and the victory over the jute trust had verified the usefulness of Alliance doctrines of self-help. But the Alabama Alliance never produced a consummate organizational spokesman on the order of Leonidas Polk, or a tenacious people's advocate in the style of Thomas Watson. With no such models to emulate, the lecturing system of the organization never quite acquired the drive or skill to complete its task of conveying to some 125,000 Alabama Alliancemen the politics of the sub-treasury plan. As a consequence, the hard, divisive, and liberating line that had to be drawn between the Alabama Alliance and the Alabama Democratic Party was never fully penciled in by the farmer-lecturers or their foremost spokesman, Reuben Kolb.

Kolb was a hesitant politician. Despite the verbal abuse he received, and the grotesque vote frauds that characterized conservative Alabama politics in the 1890's, never at any time was he able to make the ultimate psychological break from the party of the Confederacy. His acquiescence in inherited forms went beyond mere political considerations to include a curious loyalty—sometimes almost approaching deference—to the self-styled respectable elements in Alabama that profited from conservative, "Big Mule" one-party politics. The sheer radicalism of Alliance demands had, in fact, kept Kolb a bit off balance ever since the St. Louis meeting of 1889. Macune's sub-treasury plan, greenback doctrines generally, and such issues as government ownership of the railroads appeared almost (though not quite) as unnerving to Kolb as they did to William Allen and William Jennings Bryan in Nebraska. The difference was the enormous pressure organized Alliancemen could place on an Alabama "leader," a force not present in Nebraska. The spring day in 1892 when Clay County farmers in Alabama greeted with dead silence Kolb's declaration of loyalty to the Democratic Party was symptomatic of the intensity of the problem confronting him in that year of ultimate political decision. Though such radicalism from below eventually pushed Kolb into an insurgent campaign, his reluctance to make a final break with his Democratic past produced what one unimpressed Alabama reform editor sardonically described as a "second fiddle faction party." Kolb's "Jeffersonian Democrats" achieved the straddle-legged posture of supporting Populist candidates in congressional and national campaigns in the November general elections while challenging the ruling conservative regime for state control as "Democrats" in the August state elections.[16]

After the convention frauds of 1890 and the vote frauds of 1892 had established the pattern of Alabama politics for the 1890's, Kolb had a new way to avoid the radical clarity of the Omaha Platform. His campaigns now centered around a call for "a free ballot and a fair count." Granted that this objective (like the goal of "purification" in Nebraska) had a certain relevance if the idea of democracy was to gain credibility in Alabama, the extreme emphasis that Kolb personally placed on the issue in the federal elections of November 1892 diverted attention from basic third party goals. Though he belatedly endorsed Weaver, his own speeches were hardly calculated to clarify the monetary program of the People's Party, and his caution stirred considerable discontent among Alliancemen. For these reasons Reuben Kolb did not generate the kind of affection among Alabama reformers that Watson and Nugent attracted in other strong Alliance states of the South.[17]

But if the politics of Alabama Populism as shaped by Reuben Kolb sometimes dulled the cutting edge of the Omaha Platform, the divisions that materialized in the electorate were real enough. The sheer magnitude of the bitterness, abuse, and violence that attended the third party's struggle in Alabama verified that growing power of the challenge to orthodox conservative rule. The alarming fact that explained the conservative reign of terror in Alabama was a simple one: the party of the fathers had lost the struggle to hold the loyalty of the state's white farmers. The Alliance movement had been built on twelve-cent cotton that left farmers no hope of escape from the crop lien system; ten-cent cotton heightened the meaning of the Ocala Demands of 1890 and eight-cent cotton coincided with the arrival of the third party in 1892. In 1894 the price sank to five cents. A great deal was being asked in the name of party loyalty: did the farmers seriously have to accept the possibility of starving in order to protect white supremacy? [18]

In 1894 Alabama's all-Democratic congressional delegation came to the conclusion that too many of their constituents were not measuring up to this new test. Indeed, a discernible panic came over orthodox Democrats representing over fifty vulnerable districts from Virginia to Texas. But in no state delegation in Washington did morale plunge quite to the depths reached by the Alabama contingent. The first to break was William Denson, Congressman from the impoverished seventh district. In 1894, he announced a personal decision to go off the Cleveland standard. He informed his colleagues that he would seek re-election as a Populist. Denson had gradually signaled his change of heart in a series of speeches on the Alabama hustings, so his move came as no sudden shock to his Washington associates. As a matter of fact, it developed that the same option was being seriously considered by a number of them! A mass defection was, in fact, seriously discussed. Such a dramatic course not only promised to ease the pain of transition; it might have a certain political selling power among their restless and depression-ridden constituencies at home. That Populism had been denounced by each of them as a threat to every sacred tenet in the Southern creed admittedly posed a certain problem; on the other hand, there was the increasing certainty of defeat to consider. The Alabama Congressmen agreed to put their proposal to John T. Morgan, the state's influential senator. A stout Democratic regular who could launch eulogies to the Southern heritage with the best of the silver-haired colonels, Morgan had loyally supported Grover Cleveland, in the process repeating all the familiar litanies of railroad enterprise, white supremacy, and honest money—in approximately that order. His advice to his congressional colleagues, however, indicated the nadir to which the Southern Democracy had sunk. Turn Populist? "If I were younger, I would do it myself," he said equably. But, he sighed, he was too old to become an insurgent. He was now a free silver man himself, he added, and he would tell the Alabama electorate so in no uncertain terms. The people needed relief—he was certain of it! He showed his anxious guests to the door and left them to ponder their own course in the quiet of their own consciences.[19]

The organized defection of the Alabama delegation collapsed with this pledge of non-support, though the subsequent elections confirmed how badly matters had deteriorated. Of the nine Democrats in the delegation, only three legally survived the cataclysm of 1894. Two more were "counted in," but the remaining four could not be saved—not even by fraud. The whole mess produced a flurry of contested election cases in the United States House of Representatives. As the white vote not only "divided," but swung decisively against the conservative Democracy in 1894, two Populist congressional aspirants were ultimately conceded by Democrats to have survived fraud.[20]

They were joined in Congress by two Republicans elected by North Alabama districts. In many areas, Democrats who ran second or even third behind Populist and Republican candidates were declared victorious on the basis of transparently doctored returns. The presence or absence of exclusively Democratic election judges in given areas seemed to be the deciding factor in who won or lost. The party of white supremacy again demonstrated its remarkable electoral appeal to black voters, amassing margins of forty to one and even fifty to one in the black belt. By this happy circumstance, a single black belt county proved able to offset sizable Populist majorities in a dozen counties that contained both a majority of white voters and election judges who represented all contending parties. It was, of course, from the black belt districts that the three genuinely elected Democratic Congressmen hailed. Not only was almost all of the rest of the state convincingly Populist or Republican, but a truly "free ballot and a fair count" in the black belt undoubtedly would have produced Democratic defeat and Republican victory in that region also. As shaped by the striking "official" results from the black belt, however, statewide totals solemnly confirmed that Reuben Kolb had again suffered defeat in his effort to become the Governor of Alabama.[21]

The farmers of Alabama had been duly educated on the issue of a free ballot and a fair count; only their conservative opponents failed to grasp the merit of this plank in the platform of Reuben Kolb and the Populists. Clear to all, however, was the certainty that the gold standard no longer provided adequate support for serious Democratic politicians. In the aftermath of the 1894 campaign, Democratic office-seekers rapidly moved toward a consensus on this conclusion. The outcome of contested elections decided in the United States House of Representatives proved that even with firm control of the Alabama election machinery there were practical limits to how many votes could be stolen. Alabama Democrats decided, therefore, that open support for "free silver" was necessary to redress their tarnished image and prevent the total collapse of the party. As Democratic Senator Morgan had forecast, the white metal offered the last handhold on the cliff. If the Democrats did not grasp it, the entire state of Alabama would plunge into the murky waters of Populism.

The salability of the "free silver" tactic obviously depended on the electorate's understanding of the money issue. In Alabama, Reuben Kolb's stewardship had left some promising openings for Democratic regulars. While a goodly number of Alliance lecturers and Alabama reform editors had hammered away in behalf of greenback themes, and while incoming Populist Congressman Milford Howard had a considerably clearer perception of the matter than William Allen and his Nebraska allies did, precisely how thoroughly these doctrines had overcome Kolb's vague pronouncements and reached the farmers themselves was another question. The proposition, in any case, would be tested in 1896. For the time being, and depending upon which third party orator one used as a guide, Alabama Populism emphasized radical greenbackism, honest elections, or both.[22]

4

As the Populist experience in Nebraska and Alabama indicated, the task of rearranging the American party system presented immense difficulties. In 1894 Populists in Kansas, North Carolina, and Illinois tried three different stratagems in an effort to achieve an enduring political presence for the cause of reform. One of these propelled the party toward an urban socialist coalition, another represented a "mid-road" defense of the Omaha Platform, and the third involved departures that appeared transcendently radical in social terms, though its long-term political implications were unmistakably conservative. The fate of these experiments suggests the complexity of the challenge the third party faced in its effort to become a permanently energizing ingredient in the political life of the American nation.

The Kansas effort is the simplest to recount, for it involved nothing more than a formal rededication to the original agrarian objective of national party realignment. The agrarian crusade in Kansas had materialized in 1890 as an extraordinarily passionate happening, and the political hopes of the huge Kansas Alliance had been given broadly radical definition by the hundreds of greenbackers who had helped carry the movement to the four corners of the state. The heady outlook of 1890, diminished by the defeats of the third party in municipal elections in 1891, indicated that the transition from Alliance politics to Populist politics had apparently jolted a number of temporary recruits back to their ancestral homes in the major parties. The chastened third party in Kansas accepted fusion with Democrats in 1892, though the procedure was for the most part carefully formulated on the basis of the Omaha Platform. The third party's constituency in Kansas insisted on this precaution, which was overwhelmingly confirmed in the Populist state convention in 1892. The fusion candidates won that November, which pleased the Populists mightily, but it became obvious that fusion carried dangers beyond the matter of ideology. Democratic participants in the coalition expected patronage as their reward for sacrificing their principles, and the political wing of the third party—Populist officeholders—moved to accommodate them. Both Populist Governor Lewelling and third party legislators were aware that the margin of votes brought to the coalition by Democrats, while small, had been decisive. Without the Democratic votes the Populist ticket would have been defeated. The patronage policy decided upon by the Populist political leadership culminated in the election by the Kansas legislature of a new United States Senator—a Democrat. The move deeply troubled a substantial number of Alliance leaders and others among the third party faithful. An organized uprising from below soon materialized that made fusion all but impossible to consummate in 1894, however eagerly the party's politicians might have desired it. Accordingly, by the time all of the political parties had completed their arrangements for 1894, fusion had virtually disappeared from the Kansas scene.[23]

Analysis of the succeeding campaign was rendered a bit obscure by the issue of woman suffrage—which the Populists supported and the Republicans opposed—but the result was abundantly clear: Lewelling, Simpson, and the other Populist luminaries all went down to sharp defeat in 1894. The Republican Party elected its entire state ticket, seven of eight Congressmen, and 91 of 125 state legislators. The third party's share of the total vote provided the most sobering statistic of all, however, for it revealed institutional stagnation. The reform ticket had received 108,000 votes out of 290,000 cast in the great three-party campaign of 1890; after four more years of gospel spreading, the People's Party won 118,000 votes out of 300,000 in another three-way contest. Despite all the advantages of visibility that incumbency gave to politicians, the third party had won few additional converts. The maximum allegiance of Kansans to the Populist cause stood at 39 per cent of the electorate. Meanwhile, the Democratic Party, with less than 30,000 adherents, had seemingly been all but destroyed in Kansas. The Republican Party, on the other hand, had emerged as the dominant political institution of the state; it possessed an absolute majority over its combined Populist and

Democratic opposition. As 1895 approached, it was apparent the third party had reached some sort of crossroads in Kansas.[24]

5

If the divergent varieties of Populism that developed in Kansas and Nebraska are not enough to demonstrate the complexities of reform, the People's Party of North Carolina provides still another dimension of third party strategy. In North Carolina the line between the Alliance and the Democratic Party had still been in the process of being defined when national Populism came into being at Omaha, and the death of L. L. Polk in June 1892 had been a devastating blow. Though twenty-eight-year-old Marion Butler belatedly stepped into the breach for the new party, North Carolina Democrats won the hearts of most farmers by nominating Elias Carr, the Alliance state president, for the governorship. Carr's decisive victory in November 1892 propelled Butler into an immediate and bold change of front. As third party chairman, Butler opened correspondence with Thomas Settle, the North Carolina Republican Congressman and party leader, on prospects for a Populist-Republican coalition for the 1894 campaign.[25]

The energizing circumstance that made a coalition of the outs possible in North Carolina was an 1889 Democratic election "reform" that gave enormous power to polling judges and vote canvassers. Provisions of the law encouraged the denial of registration rights to blacks. It also provided broad new opportunities to manipulate election returns, a possibility that rather abruptly became a reality in the early 1890's. Though various Republican factions had differing views on the subject of fusion with the new party of radicalism, the national Republican Party maintained a hands off attitude. Eventually, Butler was able to achieve a workable relationship with the Republicans and the two-party coalition of Populists and Republicans promptly made up an elaborately conceived joint state ticket and won a majority of the legislature in the 1894 elections. The two non-Democratic elements immediately joined in passing a sweeping election reform law by which the rights of voters, including black voters, attained an unprecedented level of state legal protection. The Republicans also lent assistance to the agrarians in the repeal of a repressive Democratic statute that had crippled the Alliance cooperative effort in the state. Additionally, a pioneering "School History of the Negro Race in the United States" was authorized for use in the fourth grade of the public schools and the whole tone of civil liberties was improved. The political high point of the legislative coalition, however, was the election of Butler to a full six-year term in the United States Senate and the election of a Republican to a second Senate vacancy, caused by the death of the incumbent Democrat.[26]

By 1895 the short-term implications of fusion politics in North Carolina had become quite plain. That the coalition produced socially radical results was apparent. Indeed, under the election law guarantees the state bid fair to have a record number of black officeholders at the local and county level after the very next election. This new development was particularly predictable for the eastern part of the state, where blacks predominated. But beyond this central social change, the political meaning of fusion was less certain, even with respect to the guaranteed rights of black citizens. Viewing the matter strictly in Populist terms, fusion had imposed one immediately visible effect—the prompt moderation of the third party's program of economic reform. In the months of careful pre-coalition planning, it was all Marion Butler could do to tone down the more inflammatory rhetoric of his potential hard-money allies. Republican Settle, a staunch defender of the gold standard, scarcely helped matters: in 1893 he delivered a ringing speech against the Sherman Silver Purchase Act on the floor of the Congress. The Populist chairman gently admonished his goldbug associate:

> I was surprised I must confess at the report of your speech with reference to silver. In view of the coming events in North Carolina it would be best not to go out of your way to express sentiments on issues about which there might be some differences of opinion between us. Excuse the suggestion but you will readily see the force of it.

With proper coalition spirit, Butler promised "to keep mum" on the subject until the two men could confer.[27]

The precise effect of such an inherently compromised position was not an easy matter to measure, but the broad implications were unmistakable. Though it was clear that fusion had produced some surprising and urgently needed reforms, it was equally clear that the electoral weakness of Populism in North Carolina had inevitably contributed to a corresponding decline in commitment to the Populist program itself. Indeed, the essential conditions of fusion demanded such moderating shifts of emphasis. For without fusion, Butler's relatively small third party had virtually no political meaning.

6

By any standard, the most adventurous third-party experiment of the Gilded Age was the popular front of Fabian Socialists and Populists jointly engineered in Illinois by a patrician intellectual, an Iowa farm boy, and their following of single taxers, Bellamy nationalists, farmer radicals, labor socialists, and trade union progressives. The end product was a Labor-Populist Alliance. The intellectual was Henry Demarest Lloyd, author of the provocative, left-wing, non-Marxist analysis of American capitalism, *Wealth Against Commonwealth*. The Iowa farm boy was Henry Vincent, last seen in these pages as the enthusiastic promoter of the Farmers Alliance in Cowley County, Kansas. Their saga had no parallel in Populism.

Without question, Henry Vincent has been the most overlooked and underrated warrior of the agrarian revolt. William Lamb, because of his role in triggering the Cleburne Demands and devising the politics of the sub-treasury to bring the South to Populism, might well deserve this distinction—but for the remarkable tenacity and diversity that characterized Henry Vincent's Populist career. Vincent's achievements seem to have been the product of a very simple personal decision about the nature of his own life: he gave himself permission not only to live a life of ideas, and not only to act politically on the basis of those ideas, but also, and crucially, to alter the structure of his life in whatever ways necessary to ensure that his conclusions were painted on the broadest possible national canvas. With a persistence that no other Populist quite managed, Henry Vincent personally attempted to address every aspect of the Populist political goal of creating a multi-sec-

411

tional, black-white, urban-rural, farmer-labor coalition of democratic reform. His private definition of the "plain people" was not confined by any of the reigning cultural limitations of Gilded Age American life, and his willingness to apply his definitions knew no bounds, not even in his own personal life.

His participation in the Labor-Populist alliance in Chicago logically rounded out his earlier third party experience in Kansas from 1886 to 1891* The Vincent brothers not only helped nurse the Alliance to full growth in Kansas and endured the notoriety flowing from the Republican-sponsored "Coffeyville Anarchist Bomb Plot," of which they were ultimately vindicated; they also touted the general concept of a "newspaper alliance" of reform editors and then assisted in the creation of the National Reform Press Association at Ocala in 1890. Subsequently the Vincents, as the best known journalists of reform in the West, did all they could, both editorially and through personal speaking and organizing tours, to energize the Southern Alliances toward independent political action. Scarcely a Southern state was spared periodic injections of radical Vincentism in the volatile months of 1890–91.[28]

When the creation of the third party seemed imminent, Henry decided that the new institution would require a national journalistic voice possessing somewhat more verve than Macune's *National Economist.* Surveying the new party's political prospects in national terms, he seems to have fixed its probable eastern limit of penetration somewhere near the Ohio-Pennsylvania state line. Therefore, in 1891, in order to give the party a proper anchor in the heartland of Republican orthodoxy, he moved his newspaper to Indianapolis. From that unlikely base of operations the *American Nonconformist* spread the gospel of Populism for the entire period of the third party revolt. The 1892 elections, however, bared the critical weakness of the People's Party in metropolitan centers. That burden, which too many agrarian radicals had cheerfully assigned to the Knights of Labor, proved far too heavy for the

* See Chapters IV, VII, VIII, and IX.

labor order to shoulder, particularly after its rapid decline in the late 1880's and its near-dissolution in 1891–92. Under the circumstances, bold initiatives seemed to be required. Detecting little competition for the assignment, Henry Vincent, characteristically, determined to do the job himself. In 1893, he selected as the most promising target the largest urban center in the West. Leaving the *Nonconformist* in good hands in Indianapolis, he migrated to Chicago, where he established a new Populist newspaper. The Chicago *Searchlight* soon became widely known in Chicago labor and reform circles, and the editor from Iowa acquired a number of new associates. Most prominent among them was Henry Demarest Lloyd.[29]

Lloyd, like Vincent, had a remarkably broad approach to the cause of reform. An 1863 graduate of Columbia University, Lloyd had gone west in 1873 to become an editorial writer for the Chicago *Tribune.* He soon met and married the daughter of one of the newspaper's conservative owners, William Bross. The intellectual quality of Lloyd's journalistic campaigns for railroad regulation in the late 1870's established him, in the words of his biographer, as "a pioneer Gilded Age critic of the doctrinaire formalism of American economic theory." His editorials also made the *Tribune* one of the nation's foremost champions of antimonopolism and the new liberal thought. His national reputation began building with the 1881 publication of "The Story of a Great Monopoly" in William Dean Howells's *Atlantic Monthly.* This well-written and carefully researched attack on the Standard Oil Company was widely reprinted, as was his later study of the corruption underlying Jay Gould's railroad empire.[30]

The social upheavals of 1886 in Chicago, culminating in the Haymarket Affair, brought the reformer into his first intimate contact with laboring men. The "Lloyd Circle," which for years had gathered at his spacious home in Winnetka, expanded to include impoverished Knights of Labor leaders from Chicago. Deeply moved and angered by the death sentences meted out by the vindictive Judge Gary in the Haymarket Affair, Lloyd wrote "Labor and Monopoly," a searing indictment of Gary and of industrial capitalism. When the *Tribune* refused to print the piece, even as a Letter to the Editor, the intellectual break between Lloyd and his father-in-law became complete. Lloyd's plea for clemency for the Haymarket "anarchists" won him a wide following in trade union circles at a time, in the words of one English Fabian, when "the whole press of America was howling for these men's blood." The Trades and Labor Assembly of Chicago circulated 50,000 copies of "Labor and Monopoly," and Lloyd received a letter of praise for the article from a young, liberal attorney who had just arrived in Chicago and whose own career was soon to intersect with Populism—Clarence Darrow. In 1888, a year that saw William Lamb and Samuel Evans of Texas meet with the Vincent brothers and others in Cincinnati to fashion the Union Labor Party's first presidential ticket, Lloyd began calling for a national farmer-labor coalition to bring economic justice to capitalism.[31]

In the early 1890's, as agrarian unrest seeped into the nation's consciousness, the Lloyd Circle expanded. Labor leaders Eugene Debs, Bert Stewart, and Thomas Morgan; academic progressives Richard T. Ely, Edward Bemis, and John R. Commons; liberal attorneys Clarence Darrow and John Peter Altgelt; and greenback anti-monopolists Ignatius Donnelly and James Baird Weaver all came to Winnetka. Lloyd regarded the People's Party as a hopeful sign, and he wrote to Samuel Gompers, urging that the American Federation of Labor support the movement. His letter went unanswered, as did many similar appeals by other reformers to the conservative craft unionist.[32]

Undaunted, Lloyd broadened his efforts to humanize capitalism, avoided sectarian disputes among progressives, and worked to bring the scattered theorists of reform into workable coalition. His own outlook harmonized fairly easily with those of the agrarian radicals who had created the new third party. Starting as an eclectic Emersonian, he formulated his influential social philosophy without insisting upon, or achieving, a systematic theory. His *Wealth Against Commonwealth,* published in 1894, was simply a brilliantly written analysis of the corruption of democracy by large-scale business combinations. In the judgment of one modern cultural historian, it was "the most powerful indictment of monopoly ever written." After studying the legislative origins of the Sherman Anti-Trust Act in the course of early research for the book, Lloyd had predicted—correctly—that the antitrust statutes would be used most effectively against the labor movement. The book was full of such analytical breakthroughs, ideas which, in essence, reflected his underlying purpose. In an effort to reshape the emerging industrial culture toward his own ethical standards, Lloyd wrote not for popular consumption, as Henry George did, nor for a frustrated middle class, as Bellamy did, but for the nation's intellectual elite in behalf of its working poor and unemployed poor. By the depression year of 1894, Henry Demarest Lloyd had become a uniquely American brand of Fabian Socialist, disenchanted with the social complacency of the institutional church, the timidity of academic traditionalists, and the corrosive changes in the structure of power in America. He had also become an associate of the editor of the Chicago *Searchlight,* Henry Vincent.[33]

The drifting years of the Northwestern Farmers Alliance had left a very fragile agrarian base for political reform in Illinois. The People's Party won only 2 per cent of the vote in the state in 1892. The depression of 1893 served as a catalyst for renewed effort, however, and in October of that year the Illinois State Federation of Labor issued a declaration specifying the "necessity for independent political action on the part of producers." A meeting of farm and labor elements the following spring yielded "harmony beyond all hopes," and the labor delegates called a conclave for July to complete organizational plans. The downstate People's Party's cautious leadership promptly called a May meeting at Springfield to ensure a moderate platform. But Vincent and Lloyd had been at work. Among the participants at this convention were twenty-two Populist delegates from Chicago. It was a singularly broad-based coalition, embracing single taxers, orthodox Populists, trade unionists expounding various degrees of moderation and militancy, and urban radicals. The convention adopted the Omaha Platform and nine of the ten planks of the proposed political platform of the state A. F. of L.[34]

The Chicago delegation was headed by Thomas Morgan, a socialist who has been described as "one of the most capable, honest and best read leaders in the American labor movement." Morgan pressed for "plank ten," which demanded "the collective ownership by the people of all means of production and distribution." Populist National Chairman H. E. Taubeneck, one of the delegates, was appalled by plank ten. He quickly mobilized a sizable opposition, and it was roundly defeated by a vote of 76 to 17. Two months later the same issue threatened to split the state labor federation, which also met at Springfield. Lloyd, anticipating difficulties over the issue, obtained credentials as a delegate of the Typographical Union and attended the second Springfield conference. He was determined to forge the farmer-labor alliance. Morgan again pressed plank ten, and he promptly encountered heated opposition from single taxers, Catholic unionists, building trades unions, and the pliant followers of William C. Pomeroy, a notorious labor corruptionist who operated close to Chicago's City Hall. Though Pomeroy's forces were obviously present merely to sabotage the Labor-Populist alliance, the opposition of many others to plank ten was sincere. Populist chairman Maxwell escaped from Vincent's influence long enough to bring the conference to the brink of physical disruption on several occasions before plank ten was finally voted down, 53 to 49. At this point Lloyd rose and spoke for an hour, concluding with a compromise proposal pledging all participants to "vote for those candidates of the People's party at the coming election who will pledge themselves to the principle of the collective ownership by the people of all such means of production and distribution as the people elect to operate for the commonwealth." The deftly worded compromise passed by a single vote. On this basis, Labor Populism prepared to assault the Byzantine world of Chicago politics in 1894 on a platform "broad enough for all the diverse schools of radical thought in the state to stand upon." It was at least that.[35]

The ensuing campaign indeed proved broadly gauged. Down-state agrarians campaigned for the Omaha Platform, some of them emphasizing free silver almost to the exclusion of everything else, while urban radicals campaigned for socialism in the name of the People's party. Pomeroy's labor henchmen, the Catholic Church, and the city Democratic machine, the latter allied with streetcar magnates, all worked to divert as many trade unionists as possible from the new coalition. The right wing of the single tax movement drew back from an alliance with socialists, and the left wing of the socialist movement drew back from alliance with Populists. Meanwhile, thousands of workers listened with interest to the message of the new party of reform. The third party generated a surprisingly vibrant and aggressive campaign among the working poor of the great Midwestern metropolis. Henry Vincent's *Searchlight* became the party organ and the editor enthusiastically declared that "every loyal Populist" could "cheerfully roll up his sleeves and enter into the work." Vincent toured the city at night and wrote moving accounts of the anguish of the urban unemployed: hundreds of men sleeping under the open sky on North pier, other hundreds crowding the floors of a building on the waterfront, still others sleeping on the docks themselves, or in alleys, vacant lots, and hallways. For miles under the viaducts, wrote Vincent, "honest toilers suffering from intolerable legislative and monopolistic wrongs" slept in the open because they could not afford even the five cents that would have provided them a night in "noisome cellars amid vermin and foul air." Vincent's prose was augmented in the *Searchlight* by that of Professor Bemis, who offered his skills of persuasion to the Populist cause.[36]

Behind the scenes, organizers of the new political alliance labored to hold their disparate ranks together. The strongly antisocialist single taxers were especially restless within the coalition; Vincent responded by opening the pages of the *Searchlight* to columns on the George panacea. He balanced this with a column of "Labor Notes" sprinkled with socialist material. Lloyd meanwhile worked to hold the equally restless socialists of Tommy Morgan within the ranks through his intimate personal friendship with Morgan himself. Hard-lining Daniel De Leon and his Socialist Labor Party ridiculed Morgan for his cooperation with Lloyd, Vincent, and the "bourgeois" Populists and predicted the agrarians would sell them all out. Though these diverse pressures from left and right inevitably took their toll, urban Populism continued to exhibit resiliency through the late summer and fall of 1894. A huge ratification

meeting at the Brick Layers Hall attracted 2500 trade unionists in August to ratify the Springfield compact. Maxwell of
the state Populist committee mounted another assault on the
modified plank ten, but Morgan led the defense; Maxwell was
decisively repulsed amid "wild cheering from the socialist section." The Cook County People's Party passed into the hands
of the labor movement and their allies among urban radicals,
the latter comprising a number of Populists of the Henry Vincent stripe. The socialists were not by any means in a majority,
though they contributed a great many precinct workers to the
third party effort.[37]

The new party plunged into the enormous task of building
ward organizations to compete against the entrenched machines of the two old parties. Previously organized "Industrial
Legions" served as a base for some Populist precinct organizations, while Populist clubs elsewhere were built from scratch.
The indefatigable Lyman Trumbull, now eighty-three years
old and as dedicated an antimonopolist as he had been in his
earlier days as one of the nation's foremost anti-Grant Liberal
Republicans, threw his enduring energies into the campaign.
He immediately became the Grand Old Man of Chicago Populism. Weekly downtown meetings drew "thousands" to hear
Lloyd, Trumbull, Clarence Darrow, Tommy Morgan, and
Eugene Debs. The campaign of the People's Party of Chicago
could also draw on a coterie of intellectuals. No less than 140
speakers were eventually mobilized to bear the Populist message through the teeming precincts of the city. In the words of
a Populist handbill, "the great popular demonstrations continue"—and so they did, as the campaign increased in enthusiasm through the final weeks. The third party cause even managed an unofficial union of reform editors. Debs's *Railway
Times* and a second labor paper, the Chicago *Workman,* plus
S. F. Norton's Chicago *Express* and Lester Hubbard's *Vanguard*
joined the *Searchlight* in support of the reform party. Vincent's
paper, its thin exchequer periodically buttressed by contributions from Lloyd, appeared twice, sometimes three times a
week, and it grew with each issue. It reached a peak circulation of 20,000 on election day. For a time the third party augmented its journalistic phalanx with a truly formidable pa-

Two Famous Reformers

Henry Demarest Lloyd, left, and Clarence Darrow, right, helped lead the Populist-Labor Alliance in the colorful campaign of 1894.

per, the Chicago *Times*. Edited by Willis J. Abbot, a well-known Chicago liberal and a friend both of Vincent and Lloyd, the *Times* brought the powerful voice of a daily newspaper to the new cause. The paper's owners gave Abbot free rein because they were desperate to place the paper in an improved financial position so they could sell it. After Abbot threw the paper's editorial support to Debs's union and other embattled strikers, circulation doubled to over 100,000 in the summer of 1894, enough to overcome the effects of an advertising boycott by State Street merchants. The strategy, however, succeeded a bit too well for Populist partisans, for the paper was sold in mid-October and the new owners promptly retreated to a more orthodox position. This development was a body blow to the third party cause, coming as it did just when the campaign was moving into its final and decisive phase.[38]

Nevertheless, the third party pressed on against steadily consolidating opposition. The influential Democratic newspaper, the Chicago *Herald,* worked tirelessly to detach non-

419

Opponents of Populism, from left and right

Daniel DeLeon	Henry George
Revolutionary Socialist	Single Taxer

socialist trade unionists from the third party movement, and Pomeroy's labor minions added their tactics to the same end. With Henry George's help, they were largely successful; all but the most radical single taxers dropped away from the new party crusade. Predictably, the Populist campaign ran out of money, despite generous help from Lloyd. Yet in October 3000 people packed the Central Music Hall as Darrow presided over a Populist mass meeting gathered to hear addresses by Lloyd and Lyman Trumbull. Darrow had become a popular hero because of his action in resigning as counsel for the Chicago & North Western Railroad to defend Debs after the labor champion had been indicted for the Pullman boycott. Darrow added luster to Chicago Populism. But the high point of the evening was Lloyd's quiet, sweeping address, later widely reprinted by the reform press in the Midwest. Lloyd hailed the "revolution of 1894" as the lineal descendant of the revolution of 1776, and defended Populist "calamity howlers" with flair: "when strong, shrewd, grasping, covetous men devote themselves to creating calamities, fortunate are the peo-

ple who are awakened by faithful 'calamity howlers.' . . .
There are thirty-two paragraphs in the Declaration of
Independence; twenty-nine of the thirty-two are calamity
howls. . . ." [39]

The campaign climaxed with a torchlight parade through
the Loop. Seven thousand marchers from Debs's American
Railway Union, Knights of Labor assemblies, trade unions,
and scattered single tax clubs carried flags and banners of
"every imaginable description." Tommy Morgan's socialists
brought red ribbons and carried burning flares along the
route of march. The procession ended at Tattersall's, on the
South Side, where some 15,000 packed into the great amphi-
theater and another 5000 milled outside the building. [40]

But though Populist orators painted their vision of a
future society of the just, an exceptionally well-financed Republican campaign keyed to a "full dinner pail" in the here
and now won a sweeping victory over the other old party as
well as the new party. The Populists polled between 34,000
and 40,000 votes in Cook County. It was described as a "creditable but not a remarkable showing." Darrow confessed that
the results were "wholly disappointing." Reformers offered as
many reasons for defeat as there were factions in the reform
movement—the opposition of Henry George to Populism,
which drew thousands of the more conservative single taxers
away from the ticket, the reluctance of Catholic workers to associate politically with the socialists, and the subversive tactics
of Pomeroy and of a Democratic machine that could use
promises of part-time jobs and other patronage to play upon
the workers' pressing needs in the trough of a depression.
Whatever the causes, the Labor-Socialist alliance had proved
considerably less than an immediate blueprint for the needed
breakthrough in behalf of "the coming revolution." In the aftermath, neither Lloyd nor Vincent appeared downcast, however. Lloyd held to the opinion that the old party managers
had been severely shaken; Vincent readied plans to convert
the Chicago *Searchlight* into a daily to fill the void left by the
departure of the *Times* from the ranks of reform. As with
Populists elsewhere across the nation, their eyes were on the
future. [41]

8

The elections of 1894 proved difficult for Populists to analyze. People's Party strategists discovered in that year that while the reform movement had made sizable gains in the South, it had taken unexpected losses in the West.

In Georgia, Tom Watson, though again robbed of election, led a still growing third party to win 45 per cent of the total state vote—and this in the face of returns even Democrats conceded to be fraudulent. Populists counted over a dozen contested elections from Texas, Alabama, Georgia, and Louisiana as testament to both the strength of reform and corruption of the opposition. Yet the resurgence of the Republican Party in the North and West was shocking, even though it testified to the intense voter dissatisfaction with Grover Cleveland's administration in time of depression. While many voters, particularly in the South, had turned to the third party, even more voters in the West seemed to have turned to the Republican Party. The electorate behaved in strangely volatile ways, Populists told themselves, avoiding speculation that the sizable shifts of 1894 might indicate a different kind of party realignment than the one reformers anticipated.[42]

Whatever the long-term implications, Populists were of at least two minds about what to do. In Kansas, Jerry Simpson nursed the bruises from his unexpected defeat and decided that Populists needed to cooperate more with Democrats. In Colorado, where both the third party and the Democrats had been roundly defeated, other Populists began to consider the same possibility. In the Republican-dominated West, fusion would necessarily be with Democrats, of course, and it could be achieved on the issue of free silver. The idea of a Populist-Democratic coalition, institutionalized since 1890 in Nebraska, thus acquired growing support in 1895 in a number of places in the West. However, the suggested tactic appalled greenback reformers, especially in the South, where elections had become a tense, bitter, and even violent battleground between Democrats and Populists. Tom Watson thought the silver issue to be shallow, and dangerous to the reform party as well. Tom Nugent, in the Southwest, reached the same conclusion, as did other prominent Texas Populists. The reform press, both in the West and South, overwhelmingly shared their opinion, as did Ignatius Donnelly in Minnesota, Davis Waite in Colorado, and George Washburn, one of the party's few prominent spokesmen in the East.[43]

A month after the 1894 general election had brought proof of the party's losses in the West, national party chairman, Herman Taubeneck of Illinois, declared himself: the People's Party had to jettison the Omaha Platform and "unite the reform forces of the nation" behind a platform of free silver. The *Southern Mercury* reacted promptly and violently: the Omaha Platform was the basis of Populism and could not be jettisoned without abandoning all that the reform movement meant. Trade the "coming revolution" for a silverized currency of ultimate redemption? The idea was "disappointing and disgusting," said the paper. Such a course would not only betray the Omaha Platform, it would scuttle every Alliance declaration all the way back to the Cleburne Demands.[44]

But the party's chairman and a number of its prominent politicians—Allen of Nebraska, Simpson and Lewelling of Kansas, and the new coalition Senator from North Carolina, Marion Butler—all seemed to be quite serious. In response, the party's rank and file, centered in the old Alliance movement and buttressed by an overwhelming majority of the editors of the reform press, rallied to defend their cause. Suddenly, and with considerable passion, the People's Party moved headlong into its final crusade—one in which Populism encountered its shadow movement in a tense struggle to define the meaning of American reform.

4

The Triumph of American Finance Capitalism

My object is not to patronize the radicals by patting them on the head as "in advance of their time"—that tired cliché of the lazy historian. In some ways they are in advance of ours. But their insights, their poetic insights, are what seem to me to make them worth studying today.

Christopher Hill, The World Turned Upside Down

The truth of the matter is Taubeneck has been flim-flammed.

Henry Demarest Lloyd

CHAPTER XIV

The Last Agrarian Crusade:
The Movement vs. the Silver Lobby

"We propose to stand by the demands of the industrial people!"

It would be much too facile to portray the fierce internal struggle within the People's Party in 1895–96 as a simple clash between conservative "fusionists" on the one hand and radical "mid-roaders" * on the other. For one thing, the decisive ingredient in the struggle did not emerge from within the ranks of Populism at all, but rather from economic and political groups completely outside the People's Party.

Fusionists had a common characteristic. Almost all of them held office, had once held office, or sought to hold office. They saw the future of the third party in immediate terms. Some, like Senators William Allen and Marion Butler exhib-

---

* The term "mid-road" derived from the 1892 campaign, in which Populists saw their new party as charting a new multi-sectional course between the Republican Party of the North and the Democratic Party of the South. The path of third party radicalism was thus "in the middle of the road" between the sectional agitators in the two old parties. In both the South and West the phrase was widely used by Populists in 1892 to describe their intention to "fight it straight" by opposing both major parties. The term could not, of course, be used to describe the politics of the shadow movement in Nebraska—not even in 1892.

ited no visible qualms over dispensing with virtually the entire Omaha Platform; others, like James Weaver and Jerry
Simpson had greenback pasts. All wanted to win—and at the
next election.

For their part, mid-roaders tended to have a more recogniz-
ably common past, derived from an early identification with
the Alliance movement. They also tended to be from states
that possessed strong third parties or growing third parties.
Tom Watson of Georgia, Thomas Nugent of Texas, and E. M.
Wardell of California were rather typical of this group.

Still other streams of reform thought fed the gathering debate on third-party strategy for 1896. While a handful of students of the experiment in Labor-Populism in Chicago saw
Henry Demarest Lloyd's blueprint of urban radicalism as the
obvious formula for the future, Populism also embraced such
disgruntled Southern Democrats as Claude Kitchin, a North
Carolina pro-silver spokesman. Indeed, whatever ideological
consistency marked the progression of agrarian politics from
1886 to 1896, the scope of the reform movement had been
broadened by the practical needs of the various state parties.
The ideological conflict of 1895–96 took place within this
broadened spectrum but, as events were to show, mostly
beyond it.[1]

Yet there was a far simpler explanation of the third party's
internal struggle. At bottom, it was a contest between a co-
operating group of political office-seekers on the one hand
and the Populist movement on the other. The politicians had
short-run objectives—winning the next election. In contrast,
the agrarian movement, both as shaped by the Alliance organizers who had recruited the party's mass base of partisans
and as shaped by the recruits themselves, had long-term goals,
fashioned during the years of cooperative struggle and expressed politically in the planks of the Omaha Platform

While the movement itself had a mass base, the only popular support that the office-seekers could muster within the
third party itself was centered in those regions of the country
which the cooperative crusade had never been able to penetrate successfully. In some of these regions, notably the indus-

trial East and the upper Midwest, the third party had only a tiny following. In others, especially in the mining states of the West, Populism had drawn its adherents not through the experience of the cooperative crusade, but because, simply enough, one of the elements of monetary reform advocated by the third party concerned the free coinage of silver. Miners wanted free silver not because it meant a "new day for the plain people," but because it meant jobs for themselves. Finally, in one state—Nebraska—the third party following was neither tiny nor organically silverite. Rather, as a shadow movement essentially created outside the framework of the cooperative crusade, the Nebraska Party was not organically anything. Therefore, that state, like the non-Populistic states of the East and upper Midwest and the mining states of the West, was ripe for the kind of third party strategy harmonious to the short-run needs of the party's office-seekers. In sum, where the agrarian movement was strong and growing, the politics of the movement was intact; but where the movement had never sunk genuine roots, or had become stagnant, the third party's political stance was co-optable. Essentially therefore, the contest between Populism and its shadow form in 1896 arrayed the politics of a people's movement against conventional electoral politics.

The precipitating cause of the internal struggle to redefine Populism was the abrupt setback of the third party in the West in the 1894 elections. Even in those instances where coalition had been achieved on the basis of the Omaha Platform, the fusion-based victories of 1892 concealed a frustrating weakness underlying all the Western third parties. After the 1894 elections, the fact had become inescapable that the People's Party, standing alone, had not obtained a majority status in a single state in the West, not even for as much as one election. In such Southern states as Alabama and Georgia where the third party seemed to have won a clear-cut majority, fraud and terrorism deprived the reformers of the fruits of their triumph. In many locales in both sections of the country where the election results of 1894 confirmed Populist weakness—or created new fears of future weakness—the party's candidates searched desperately for a way to pump saving life into their embattled institution of reform. They sought an issue that would attract Democrats or Republicans who had previously resisted all Populist blandishments.

But Populists were not the only ones driven to serious reflection by the turbulent politics of the Gilded Age. Democrats were also pressed toward wholesale reevaluations by the fury of the agrarian revolt. The old party had taken massive losses in 1892 in the West, and the defections in the South reached such tidal proportions in 1894 as to imperil the very future of the party in its "Solid South" heartland. In both regions, Democratic regulars found Grover Cleveland's dedication to "sound money" to be an expensive obsession, one that threatened the destruction of the party as a national institution. The estrangement of frightened Democratic conservatives from their conservative party leader reached an angry dimension in 1894. Looming defeat honed a sharp edge to criticism. Even so traditional a member of the Southern business-planter elite as Alabama's John T. Morgan was heard to remark of Cleveland, "I hate the ground that man walks on."

Cleveland replied in kind, cutting off all patronage to those who fell into the category of "former supporters." This policy, of course, hardened the lines. Congressman Joe Bailey, forced to give up his support of the gold standard by the growing populistic inclinations of his constituents, and embittered because of Cleveland's cold response to his change of front, complained that he "could not name even the post-master of the lowliest village in North Texas." The harassed Bailey broke publicly with Cleveland and made as much capital of it as he could back home. Ben Tillman privately swallowed his pride and wrote the President, asking to be consulted on patronage for South Carolina. Cleveland released the letter publicly without answering it and turned the patronage over to Tillman's enemies. The affair made Tillman an extreme anti-Cleveland Democrat, and, given his style, the most raucous one in the country. After the ominous Southern vote for the People's Party in 1894, defection of Southern Democrats from Cleveland became wholesale in state after state. Those who survived in 1894 without the aid of fraud did so largely because they were able to campaign as individuals and invoke local loyalties, racial phobias, and other ancient shibboleths. The prospect of seeking re-election in the presidential year of 1896 while yoked to a ticket headed by a "Gold Democrat" terrified Democrats from the Ohio River to the Gulf of Mexico. A very real prospect existed that the entire South might fall to Populism and wreck long-standing Democratic political careers by the hundreds.[2]

Similarly, almost everywhere west of the Mississippi River the Democratic Party had virtually ceased to exist as a credible institution. The old party ran a distant third to Republicans and Populists from Kansas to the state of Washington. In Kansas the Democrats polled less than 30,000 votes out of 300,000 in the general elections of 1894. In Nebraska the party mustered less than 20,000 supporters in a voting population of 200,000. In Minnesota, the Dakotas, Colorado, Montana, and Oregon the story was the same—the doctrines of the gold standard had eaten away the very roots of the Democratic Party. To anguished Democratic regulars the evidence was overwhelming: unless something were done to alter traditional Democratic politics, the basic party realignment radicals dreamed of would be confirmed in 1896—at the expense of the party of Jefferson and Jackson! [3]

2

Among the Populists, this state of affairs generated two diametrically opposed analyses. The first appealed to third party politicians with immediate short-run objectives. It went substantially as follows: The absence of a potential Populist plurality in the West, confirmed by the elections of 1894, made fusion with Democrats a necessity if the reform cause were to have a firm basis upon which to challenge Republican hegemony in 1896. The discomfiture of Democrats was a blessing, for it created "Silver Democrats" by the wagonload. All the People's Party had to do, therefore, was to concentrate on the silver issue, unite all dissident forces, and thus bring the "coming revolution" to a solidly contending position in 1896. From North Dakota to Texas, neither of the old parties any longer polled as much as 50 per cent of the electorate. By fusing with the rapidly increasing tribe of silverites in each party, and particularly in the Democratic Party, the Populist cause might well make a quantum leap to power in 1896. A "coalition of the reform forces" could not be made on the basis of the Omaha Platform, of course, as the prospective "catch" of disillusioned Democrats and the lesser number of "Silver Republicans" would not take the bait of so radical a program. But a one-plank Populist platform of unlimited silver coinage would create a winning national coalition. People had memories of silver from the days preceding demonetization. They were used to silver. The white metal was not "radical." It was a vote-getter. It would bring the reform movement to power. Such was the case for Populist-Democratic fusion.

A small but prominent group of Populist politicians desperately seized the silver issue and argued for its immediate adoption as third party policy. As they saw the practical options, the People's Party had done its best to convince American voters of the need for the Omaha Platform. After four years the party had gained a following of anywhere from 25 to 45 per cent of the electorate in twenty-odd states. These facts could be summarized in one word—defeat. Politically, the mathematics of the situation were fatal. Reformers who cannot count to 51 per cent of the vote should not engage in politics. The People's Party needed to broaden its base or see the cause of reform die completely. One did not have to be a Populist politician to accept the reality that reformers had to be in office in order to enact reforms. The whole matter thus constituted an open and shut case of recognizing political reality. To the group of political aspirants who asserted these arguments, the fusionist cause also added large numbers of rank-and-file party members in the Western mining states. Miners in the West did not know or care about chattel mortgages, crop lien systems, land loans, commodity credit, or the relevance of explanations about the commodity value of debts in a contracting currency. Free silver meant full employment in the Western mining centers. Unlimited coinage meant the opening of marginal mines. It meant Western business expansion. It meant prosperity. Indeed, as far as these Westerners were concerned, the silver solution had provided the essential motive for joining the People's Party in the first place. The very planks of the Omaha Platform sounded strange and irrelevant to them.

3

As veteran Populists viewed matters, three things were wrong with this assessment, and they all pointed to one conclusive reality: it would destroy the people's movement. First, in terms of its long-range political effect, one-plank free silverism threw away one of the third party's basic goals at the very moment it was coming within reach. Party realignment was an important objective in itself, because it was a precursor of larger objectives. Since both old parties were in harmony with monopoly, it was necessary to restructure the party system in order to restructure the nation's financial and economic system. That was why the People's Party had to navigate between the sectional barriers of the two old parties and recruit voters from both by hewing to "the middle of the road" and "fighting it straight." Indeed, that was what the Omaha Platform was all about. Even granting the highly debatable proposition that a free silver platform might achieve permanent party realignment, no thoughtful person had any illusion that it would address the underlying economic objective. In fact, by so sharply defining the limits of reform, a victory on the basis of a silver coalition would actually preclude the possibility of attaining significant alterations in the prevailing forms of the American monetary system. Nor could such a victory address the growing, related power of corporate privilege generally. Populists who had spent years trying to mobilize the people in behalf of the greenback and cooperative movements had few illusions about the difficulty of winning converts to serious reform. Their entire effort, agonizing as it had been and still was, would have no meaning if the promised results were given away in the interim. To old-time Alliancemen, silver was an ephemeral issue, and the silverites' capacity for political analysis was just as ephemeral. By any standard, one-plank silverism just did not make political sense in terms of the agreed-upon purposes of the People's Party. It took care of everybody but the people.

The second objection to the stated politics of silver followed ideologically from the first. As a matter of simple monetary analysis, free silver failed to address the existing power relationships that so disfigured the nation's currency and imposed such grinding hardships on the "laboring masses." Free silver did not alter the existing banking system, nor did it end the destructive privilege national bankers enjoyed through their power to issue their own bank notes on which they gathered interest. Mid-roaders regarded this post-Civil War folkway as a veritable license to steal. Silver coinage elevated the folkway into a system; worse, by deflecting debate from the banking system itself as the proper object of reform, free silver actually undermined the greenback cause. What did silver coinage have to do with a flexible currency, for example? While "unlimited coinage at the ratio of sixteen to one" might end the contraction of the currency—if the silver mines held out long enough—it did not provide a flexible monetary system keyed to population expansion and industrial growth. Indeed, it did not even alter the metallic basis of the currency—for silver at a ratio of sixteen to one or at any other ratio was a coin of ultimate redemption.

Though silverites seemed unable to ponder the monetary system long enough to think the matter through, hard-money inflation that left the banking system undisturbed utterly failed to address the real needs of the nation's producing classes—and the reform movement itself had materialized only because these needs had become unbearably magnified by a hard currency that left them in servitude to private moneylenders. In addition to legal tender treasury notes issued by the government, the Omaha Platform called for a postal banking system to serve as the People's Bank and thus reduce to endurable levels the impact of private manipulators on the small mortgage market. As for the needs of farmers, free silver provided neither land loans nor commodity loans. Anyone who grasped the full implications could see that silver coinage was an eccentric device that tied the nation's monetary system to the fluctuating output of Western silver mines; in so doing, it represented a permanent retreat from the doctrines implicit in the sub-treasury plan, a plan which would bring stability to farmer cooperatives and end the servitude that accompanied chattel mortgages and the crop lien system. Veteran Alliancemen and reform editors summarized their financial critique by reminding fusion-oriented party politicians that the Omaha Platform constituted the political culmination of greenback monetary theory; that under the promising new political conditions Populists had helped to engender across the nation, free silver was less an adjunct of greenback doctrines than a palliative to ward off the liberating triumph of a fiat currency. In terms of a decisive monetary breakthrough under capitalism, free silver had therefore become a step backward.

The third objection to Populist-Democratic fusion was also ideological. Silver coinage blandly ignored the ultimate third party objective of rescuing the democratic process from the permanent corruption that was rooted not only in the monetary system, but also in the power of large-scale capital to shape the substance of American politics. In not the slightest way did silver address the accelerating movement toward industrial combination. As John D. Rockefeller had conclusively demonstrated in the course of creating the Standard Oil Trust, railroad networks were a central ingredient both in the combination movement itself and in the political corruption that grew out of monopoly. Silver coinage utterly sidestepped the whole matter of government ownership of the railroads. What were silverites proposing—that railroad lobbyists begin buying state legislatures with silver coin instead of gold? Would that noticeably improve the level of public ethics in the United States Senate? Mid-roaders could summarize all their arguments by asserting that the ultimate monopoly was the "money trust," a banking system of private plunder anchored in a metallic currency and assured of power because it owned both "sound money" parties. "Free silver" was irrelevant to all of these realities.[4]

On intellectual as well as political grounds, then, both the cooperative and the greenback heritages of the People's Party stood in the way of the ambitions of one-plank free silverites. Allied with Alliancemen and greenbackers—the two terms had tended to become synonymous as the agrarian revolt matured—was the overwhelming majority of the editors of the reform press. Their commitment to the reform movement had been an intellectual one, engendered by the modern sweep and practicality of the Omaha Platform. Because of the personal hardships they had endured, including economic hardships, reform editors scarcely looked upon the ambitions of fusionist politicians with tolerance. To the editors, fusionists seemed to be little more than a claque of self-interested opportunists who would sell out the cause of the people for another term in office.

These Populist "mid-roaders" offered a "practical" case, too. They believed the People's Party merely needed to keep its eye on basic reform purposes. In long-run terms, the third party cause had come along in fine shape. Greenback doctrines were no longer confined to a narrow tier of frontier counties in the West; now they permeated a great mass movement which in turn had created a national third party. The party had deep and still spreading roots, all the way from the tenth district of Georgia on the Atlantic coast to the working-class precincts of San Francisco. The crucial political reality lay in the fact that the national Democratic Party had been fatally undermined by the politics of Populism. As constituted, the Democratic Party had all but disappeared from the plains states westward to the Pacific Coast, and it was tottering toward collapse across the South. The Southern colonels could not steal enough votes to hide their own increasing demoralization. To mid-roaders, the new political reality was plain; one only needed to consider the changing public stance of embattled Southern Democratic congressmen. Their mad rush to embrace free silver as a way of appearing responsive to the needs of their impoverished constituents merely verified the power of Populism. Under the circumstances, all reformers had to do was to steer a steady course and hold to it. The clinching argument to mid-roaders was the self-evident fact that Democrats had no saving expedient. Granted that numbers of Democratic politicians might grasp the silver issue in a frantic effort to clothe themselves in some appearance of concern for the people; the fact remained that the silver panacea patently could not address the underlying causes of despair among the "industrial millions." Conceivably, a little silver inflation might return the economy to an 1890 level, but that condition itself was sufficiently unjust to have generated the reform movement in the first place.

Most reassuring of all to veteran Populists was the fact that Democrats could not go beyond free silver to something of more substance without toppling over into the People's Party. If they did they would be welcomed, of course, for on that basis political realignment would have been structurally achieved in the name of authentic monetary reform. Consequently, all the third party had to do was to continue its patient program of education. The revolution of the plain people simply required sufficient poise to hold on and see the matter through. Silver fusionists who called themselves Populists were clearly as politically innocent, or as greedy for office, as the obsequious mossbacks they had been denouncing all these years. Let the silverites have their innocent day or their demagogic day, however one wished to view free coinage propagandists. Their solution could not save the people, and that fact would soon become evident. When it did, the People's Party would be in a position to inaugurate the real solutions of the Omaha Platform.

4

The contesting positions of the advocates of Populism and those of silver fusion manifestly were not compromisable. One reflected the political purposes that had created the third party; the other reflected the political adversities the party had encountered. The Omaha Platform codified the goals of the Alliance cooperative movement and the greenback heritage and attracted the loyalty of the farmers and agrarian radicals they had rallied. The issue of "free silver" was designed to win a crucial marginal increment of additional voters, but at the cost of surrendering that same platform and risking the future of the reform party organized around it. As such, it appealed to the reform party's politicians. Both ideologically and organizationally, therefore, the differences between Populism and silver fusion were fundamental. It is thus not surprising that the debate began on a high level of contention and rapidly became even more acrimonious. If nothing else, the final, climactic trauma of the People's Party constituted a fitting expression of the passionate hopes and expectations that had characterized the agrarian revolt from its inception.

The party's national chairman, H. E. Taubeneck of Illinois, fired the first salvo of the battle in November 1894, when he issued a public statement that the third party had "outgrown many of the 'isms' that [had] characterized its birth and early growth" and would "take a stand on the financial question" to attract all those repelled by the "wild theories" of the Omaha Platform. This pronouncement, coming from out of the blue, stunned reform editors. Warnings flashed angrily in the editorial columns of the third party press throughout the nation. No reform editor was more strategically placed to observe the internal politics of the shadow movement than Thomas Byron, the editor of General Weaver's old paper in Iowa, the *Farmer's Tribune.* His warnings had remarkable precision:

> We are credibly informed that, as a step in this desired change of front, they will attempt to depose W. S. Morgan from the editorship of the Reform Press ready-print mat service, which they think in his hands smacks too much of the despised Omaha Platform and elect Dunning of the *National Watchman,* which is their special organ, in his place.
>
> We are getting very tired of these vexatious self-seekers, these mouthing men at Washington and elsewhere who have no visible means of support except scheming in questionable politics, and we would have exposed them by name and scheme long ago, had we not had a perfect confidence in their inability to do the party any harm. . . . We have felt all along that the men alluded to, while imagining that they are running the party, or that, they may succeed in swinging it around to suit their schemes, are really only flies on the plow-beam, neither drawing the plow nor guiding it. . . . The People's Party is now too intelligent, too determined, too large and too well self-governed for self-seeking, would-be bosses either to harm it or control it.[5]

The confidence of the reform editors grew out of their settled belief that a move to emasculate the Omaha Platform had no chance of being taken seriously by the great mass of third party adherents. This stance was valid enough as far as it

437

went, for the Populist platform authentically represented the entire political experience of both the cooperative and the political phases of the reform movement. Asking them to renounce the planks of the Omaha document constituted a request that they renounce their own political identity and the mass movement that had shaped that identity. Taubeneck's apparent belief that Populists thought their platform consisted of "wild theories" represented a bad misreading of the third party constituency, and reform editors knew it.

But as the debate moved into 1895, the editors began to lose their complacency, and Thomas Byron himself betrayed the reason with his elliptical reference to "these self-seekers . . . who have no visible means of support." With that phrase Byron revealed the detection by Populists of the arrival of a new element in American politics—the growing participation of silver-mining interests and the involvement of some Populist spokesmen. As Byron well knew, one of the "self-seekers," no less a personage than General James Weaver, was a part-owner of Byron's *Farmer's Tribune*. By 1895 the growth of silver lobbying was scarcely a continent-wide secret. On the contrary, the proliferation of "bimetallic" leagues and other front groups for silver coinage was one of the new folkways of national politics. But at first most Populists saw this development for what it seemed to be—an attempt to sell the single-shot legislative idea to both major parties. Yet the sheer effectiveness of the silver lobby in penetrating certain leadership ranks of the People's Party became a growing concern. The Eastern silver publication, the *Silver Knight*, was edited by a Republican, Nevada's Senator Stewart, and reform editors belatedly discovered that the new business manager of the journal was J. H. Turner, a member of the national executive committee of the People's Party. The spectacle of third party functionaries on the public payroll of the silver lobby was unsettling, to say the least. Staff members of such silver journals soon added their labor to that of lobbyists for the American Bimetallic League in developing a cordial correspondence with Populist politicians. They gently emphasized the primacy of the silver issue as the essential prerequisite for silverite-Populist cooperation.[6]

Soon after the 1894 elections the attention of the mine-owners focused upon the disrupted ranks of the Democratic Party. The American Bimetallic League began sponsoring scores of "conferences" at which little business was carried on beyond mass celebrations of the virtues of silver coinage. Democratic politicians found it surprisingly easy to attend these conferences. Senators, Congressmen, and would-be gubernatorial candidates flocked to meetings in Birmingham, Atlanta, New Orleans, and Dallas—and in Chicago, Topeka, Lincoln, and Salt Lake City. Silver clubs and bimetallic leagues began to be organized down to the county and even the precinct level under Democratic auspices. In June 1895 an enormous spectacle was held at Memphis as a South-wide demonstration of strength. Ben Tillman showed up with an entourage of earnest new "Silver Democrats" from South Carolina, and he was amply supported by scores of Congressmen, Senators, and local politicians from Georgia, Alabama, Tennessee, Mississippi, Arkansas, Louisiana and Texas. Attendance was variously reported at anywhere from 2000 to 2700 civic-minded participants, and though no particular program seems to have been formulated, the air was filled with silver oratory. Press coverage might be described as outstanding. The Memphis *Commercial-Appeal* simply turned over its entire front page to a near-verbatim report of every syllable that emanated from the platform. William Jennings Bryan was especially visible, moving easily among the Southerners. His address, though a bit weak on coherent monetary theory even by the loose standards of silverites, nevertheless earned the deeply respectful attention of *Commercial-Appeal* reporters. Any sagacious political observer surveying the local and regional political influence of the participants could have properly concluded that the Gold Democracy of Grover Cleveland had fallen into serious trouble throughout the Old Confederacy. Populist voting strength in 1894, more than silver money, accounted for this new trend of 1895.[7]

The violently white supremacist, staunchly Democratic Memphis *Commercial-Appeal* was much too partisan to play the politics of silver with sophistication. While publications like the *Silver Knight* and the *National Bimetallist* made a special attempt at bipartisan generosity in their praise of all silver advocates, be they Democrats, Populists, or Republicans, the *Commercial-Appeal* beat its drums almost wholly for Democratic silverites. The paper could find room only for one paragraph on the remarks made at Memphis by the most prominent Populist in attendance, the newly elected Senator from North Carolina, Marion Butler. That one paragraph, however, contained a surprising summation of Butler's dedication to the silver cause. The paper quoted the Populist spokesman to the effect that he "loved the cause better than his party and was willing to unite with any party to promote it." Moreover, he was "willing to sacrifice for the time being all other policies of the Populist platform." Allowing for the very real possibility that the newspaper was putting its own construction on Butler's remarks, it remained incontestable that Butler had placed himself in strange company in joining the Democratic silver rally. Though such a clean break with the Populist past constituted the views of only a tiny minority of third party men, they were a potentially influential minority. Joining Butler in such associations—in addition to Taubeneck and Weaver—were Senators Allen of Nebraska and Kyle of South Dakota and Congressmen Kem and McKeighan of Nebraska. A common political fact connected the mutual devotion of these political figures to silver coinage: they all owed their seats in Washington to the politics of Populist-Democratic cooperation in their own states.[8]

Populists with good greenback memories could see that James Weaver's love affair with the cause of reform had produced a very inconstant marriage. Though Weaver gave voice to radical ideas, he manifested a decided distaste for the weakness of radical third parties. This penchant of Weaver's reached all the way back to the days of the Union Labor Party of 1888. Populists belatedly recalled that Weaver owed his 1880's election to Congress as a greenbacker to an early fusion arrangement with Iowa Democrats. One disgusted Iowa reform editor told L. H. "Calamity" Weller in 1888 that "the office-seekers are a greater curse to labor than all the monopolists this side of Hades." The most arrogant office-seeker of them all, said the editor, was Weaver. "Jim

Weaver has killed some seven labor papers in this district. . . .
Fusion has played hell in the sixth district and all labor papers
are blotted out except those that are willing to assist old rotten
bourbon democracy." [9]

After his own presidential defeat in 1892, Weaver mapped
plans for a congressional campaign on a fusion ticket in Iowa
in 1894 and, in the interim, joined fully in Taubeneck's continuing but largely unsuccessful effort to tap the campaign
funds of Western mining interests. Weaver played an active
role in preparations for an 1893 convention of the American
Bimetallic League orchestrated by the lobbyist, William Harvey, and he was rewarded by being allowed to preside over the
three-day mass meeting. A pro-silver Colorado newspaper
owner, Democrat Thomas Patterson of the *Rocky Mountain
News,* worked closely with Weaver and with General A. J. Warner. The latter, as "president" of the American Bimetallic
League, was the nation's most visible silver lobbyist. Further
evidence of silver penetration into the top ranks of the People's Party came with the election of a Boston Populist, George
Washburn, as secretary of the Chicago silver convention.
Washburn, like J. H. Turner of the staff of *The Silver Knight* in
Washington, was a member of the national executive committee of the People's Party. Taubeneck himself accepted a position
as a member of a special silver committee to serve as a Washington lobby for the white metal. Still another prominent Populist who played an active role in the Chicago silver conclave
was Ignatius Donnelly. Shaken by the crushing defeat of his
Minnesota Populists in 1892, Donnelly lost his poise the following year. He not only served on the convention's resolutions committee, but he once again permitted his vanity to get
the better of him. He actually took over the resolution committee and wrote the anticipated free silver declaration himself. Among those impressed by Donnelly's performance in
behalf of the cause of silver was William Jennings Bryan. The
Donnelly resolutions were so narrowly focused on the silver
issue, in fact, that a number of Populists present, led by an
outspoken delegation from Kansas, tried to broaden the declaration to include the basic doctrines of greenback monetary
analysis. The silver lobbyists (who, after all, had controlled the

guest list) had the authenticity of their planning verified by an avalanche of "no" votes that promptly buried the greenback amendments. The embarrassed Donnelly, himself a green-backer, never made such a clumsy public mistake again in the course of his flirtations with silver lobbyists.[10]

Nebraskan William Allen had no such ideological problems. Early on he had made a name for himself as a silverite by con-ducting a fifteen-hour filibuster in the United States Senate in 1893 against the repeal of the Sherman Silver Purchase Act. Allen worked closely with Bryan on this effort as well as on subsequent maneuvers to lure other states into forming sil-verite coalitions of Populists and Democrats modeled after the amiable union in Nebraska. James Kyle of South Dakota, who, like Allen, owed his Senate seat to Democratic votes in his state legislature, also joined in the small circle of Populist office-holders and ex-officeholders pledged to cooperation with the Warner-Weaver-Taubeneck plan of silver fusion.[11]

None of the coterie of Populist political aspirants asserted the fusion argument on such a grandiose scale as North Caro-lina's Marion Butler. Butler's monumentally complex political career, in fact, had no counterpart in third party annals. Among men who attained high status in the People's Party, Butler deserves recognition as the most reluctant Populist of them all, narrowly but definitely surpassing even Nebraska's William Allen in this respect. As mentioned previously, But-ler's sundry political strategies prior to and following L. L. Polk's untimely death in 1892 had massively disfigured the in-augural campaign of the third party in North Carolina. More to the point in terms of Populist tactics in 1896, the relevant details of Butler's white supremacy politics in 1892 provide the essential background to his subsequent brand of fusion politics at the climax of the struggle with mid-roaders.

Throughout the volatile months when Tom Watson, L. L. Polk, and the Texans were carefully shepherding the South-ern Alliances toward independent political action in the winter and spring of 1891–92, Marion Butler maintained strong ties to the party of white supremacy and publicly denounced third party activity in his newspaper, *The Caucasian*. After the Cin-cinnati convention of 1891 Butler all but broke completely with Polk by denouncing the Alliance national president as a would-be "political Moses" and a "demagogue and superlative failure." [12]

By the spring of 1892, the two men had charted separate courses of action. Though Polk predicted "squalls in North Carolina" as a result of his determination to overcome Butler's policies, they never came. Polk's sudden death in June, three weeks before the Omaha convention, left Butler to find his own way. Butler's immediate decision was to man the barricades against the People's Party. He wrote in *The Caucasian:*

> We very much fear that the People's Party will put a State ticket in the field and possibly tickets in every county. Such action, if taken, would be greatly to be regretted and should be prevented if possible. Whatever differences may exist among North Carolinians over questions of national policy, there should be none in the state where Anglo-Saxon rule and good government is the paramount issue.

It was an editorial that could have appeared—and, in substance, did appear—in such orthodox Bourbon journals as the Montgomery *Advertiser,* the Augusta *Chronicle,* and the Dallas *News.* [13]

Three weeks later a delegation of Alliancemen dropped by Butler's office in Sampson County, North Carolina, to inform him of their intention to organize, that day, the "People's Party of Sampson County." Subsequent events were recorded by a contemporary. "Marion," they said, "the convention will meet at twelve o'clock in the court house upon the ringing of the bell. We invite you to come over and preside over the meeting and lead the movement. If you come, there is a great future ahead of you. If you stay out, we are going ahead anyhow and your enemies in Clinton and the town will destroy you." "At noon" on August 6, 1892, as the story goes, "upon the ringing of the bell," Marion Butler joined the People's Party.[14]

Whatever the agony of Butler's belated conversion, his prior public endorsement of the Democratic ticket provided effective campaign ammunition for the opponents of Populism in the autumn campaign. Divided and confused, the

North Carolina Alliance came apart in the fall of 1892, and the Populist ticket gave its presidential candidate only 16 per cent of the state vote.[15]

The striking fact about Butler's subsequent adventure in coalition politics in North Carolina lies in a statistic: of the three parties in the field in North Carolina, the People's Party was always the smallest. The Populist-Republican fusion victory engineered by Butler in 1894 was comprised of approximately 45,000 Populist and 80,000 Republican votes. A form of negative cooperation provided the adhesive for fusion in the state. In white Republican counties of the western mountains and black Republican counties along the eastern shore, Populists generally declined to enter separate slates. In the central piedmont, where the third party was strongest, Republicans returned the favor. The combination proved too much for Democrats, who generally ran second across the entire state. The paucity of contested statewide races in the off-year of 1894 clearly helped the fusionist cause by lessening chances of disagreement over apportioning the spoils of office. On the one obvious source of potential difficulty, vacancies on the state supreme court, Butler adroitly worked out a "nonpartisan" ticket comprised of Republicans, silver Democrats, and Populists. Fusion worked on this basis in 1894, creating a legislative minority of Democrats who were unable to prevent the selection of Marion Butler for the United States Senate seat.[16]

With such a "Populist" experience behind him, Butler found it quite natural in 1895–96 to propose another "nonpartisan ticket" at the national level—one that would include Republicans, Populists, Silver Democrats, and, perhaps, a new national "silver party" to house them all. He moved to create just such a coalition on the state level in 1895 by holding what he was pleased to call the "North Carolina Silver Convention." Butler's old Democratic ties of 1892 were resurrected in the new grand coalition, and the slatemaker even broadened his base to include conservative Democrats who had become disenchanted with Grover Cleveland. Amid such negotiations, the reform doctrines of Populism understandably fell into a rather comatose state. Marion Butler believed in free silver, tariff protection, white supremacy, and good government.

Fundamental Alliance-greenback concepts of permanent national party realignment were as foreign to his thinking as they were to the mind of William Allen in Nebraska. Indeed, a rather complex new plan emerged in Butler's thought: coalition with Democrats became possible on the national level on the silver issue; coalition with goldbug Republicans was possible on the state level if philosophical disputes over silver were played down and the emphasis placed on "election reform." Though it was all a bit confusing, as well as somewhat unrelated to the Omaha Platform, Butler's multifaceted politics seemed quite plausible to one for whom the Populist bell had not tolled until August of 1892. If, in most parts of the South and West, Democratic Bimetallic Leagues seemed to be the pursuers and the Populist faithful the pursued, the opposite was true in North Carolina. Butler's "Non-Partisan Silver Convention" in 1895 was followed by the organization of local "Honest Money Clubs." As subsequent events were to confirm, the idea of a great free silver coalition had no more faithful servant than the third party Senator from North Carolina.[17]

5

Despite Herman Taubeneck's stentorian pronouncement against the "wild theories" of the Omaha Platform, the national chairman's cause was a desperate one. What the silverites had in big names, they sorely lacked in numbers. Most Populists did not run for office, and their respect for the Omaha Platform proved most galling to the party revisionists. Indeed, Taubeneck's thirteen-month campaign that began immediately after the 1894 elections developed into an educational adventure, one in which he discovered the ideological shape of the national agrarian movement of which he was the titular head. His need for such elementary information was a curious product of his own career as a reformer—one that matured in an organizational and ideological environment just outside the mainstream of the agrarian revolt. Perhaps the most telling irony in all of Populism was the third party's selection of a national chairman who had absolutely no knowledge of the long struggle of the Farmers Alliance in the South and West.

Herman Taubeneck had originally made contact with the farmers' movement through the Illinois-based Farmers Mutual Benefit Association, and he became one of three aspiring politicians elected to the 1891 Illinois legislature with FMBA help. Through bizarre circumstances, Taubeneck promptly emerged as a hero to radicals throughout the nation. The 1890 election in both South Dakota and Illinois had created a minority of Republicans in both state legislatures that were to choose United States Senators, and while the long years of agrarian helplessness under Milton George in Illinois had produced a radical presence of precisely three legislators in the Illinois House (all allied with the FMBA), the South Dakota legislature was full of agrarian reformers. Needless to say, Democrats in neither state wanted to see a Republican elected. Gradually, an elaborate two-state plan of cooperation was worked out. The three agrarians in Illinois—who held the balance of power between the two major parties—were to vote for a Gold Democrat for Senator; in exchange, the Democrats in South Dakota would vote for an agrarian, a man named James Kyle. Both Democrats and Populists would get a Senator and the Republicans would get nothing. The bargain was carried out by the Democrats in South Dakota, sending a surprised and delighted Kyle to Washington. But Taubeneck proved recalcitrant in Illinois. To the delight of radical Alliancemen across the nation, he took the rather candid and persuasive position that he had not run for office in order to dispatch goldbugs to Washington. A deadlock raged for weeks before Taubeneck's two associates buckled under the pressure. Apparently, according to an historian of these events, they were well paid for their change of heart. In any case, the Gold Democrat went to Washington by a margin of one vote, and Taubeneck, though defeated, earned a reputation as an incorruptible reformer. These events took place during the very weeks when plans for the Cincinnati convention of 1891 were occupying the attention of Alliancemen. Herman Taubeneck not only attended, he left the city as the provisional national chairman of the People's Party, a position confirmed by convention action of 1892. The new chairman thus had grown up neither with the Alliance movement nor with its Reform Press Association. In his fight for free silver, he learned a great deal about both.[18]

It turned out that Taubeneck did not see the nation's monetary system through the eyes of either angry farmers or greenback theoreticians. He voted against Gold Democrats because he thought the currency should be expanded and that the easiest way to do that was through silver coinage! With such a political background, fashioned wholly outside the experience of the cooperative struggle that had created the Omaha Platform, Herman Taubeneck quite easily came to an early conclusion that Populism might gain armies of recruits if it jettisoned its platform and focused on free silver. Believing that all Populists shared what looked to him to be an obvious conclusion, Taubeneck, in December 1894, sent out several hundred notices inviting Populists to St. Louis to attend "the most important meeting since the Omaha convention." The simultaneous press statement, outlining the impending abandonment of "wild theories," ensured that the naïve party chairman would enjoy a full attendance of those he invited. They came—and they ran over him. Instead of being narrowed to a single silver plank, the Omaha Platform was broadened slightly to include declarations for municipal ownership of utilities. This effort to generate a concrete Populist appeal in the cities was led by Henry Demarest Lloyd, a circumstance that gave Taubeneck a new, though still shaky, insight into the makeup of his own party. Taubeneck announced through the *National Watchman* that the People's Party was imperiled by a socialist takeover. Assuming Lloyd could mold his schismatic Chicago coalition together, the analysis might hold true for Illinois, since Populism had so few agrarians in Taubeneck's home state. But charges of socialism had absolutely no application through the broad heartland of the third party in the South and West. The crucial element of the opposition to a single silver plank that Taubeneck encountered in the ill-fated conference came instead from the members of the reform press. The editors essentially had two reactions to Taubeneck's posturing: either the chairman had lost his mind or he was on

447

the payroll of silver mineowners. The latter charge, often voiced, accurately measured the disbelief of reform editors in the political stance of their party's chairman.[19]

Bruised, Taubeneck decided that the next time he would take steps to mobilize the full force of his own narrow base within the party while holding attendance of all other Populists to an absolute minimum. The conference in December 1894 thus became the first and last mass meeting of Populists that Herman Taubeneck ever called.

Taubeneck's disappointing conference was but one of three critical Populist meetings in the months after the 1894 elections. In February, 1895 the National Reform Press Association convened in Kansas City. The attendance of over one hundred and fifty editors from throughout the nation signaled the degree of indignation they felt at the unexpected new course of the party's national leadership. Taubeneck was without defenders at Kansas City. Seemingly oblivious to that fact, he dispatched a highly indiscreet letter instructing the editors to cease and desist in their propagation of the Omaha Platform. A threat to withhold all advertising placed in the reform press through the national office punctuated this rather imperial edict. The editors were duly outraged and most of them wanted to vote to censure Taubeneck and make the resolution public, but the move was narrowly held in abeyance after it was argued that the metropolitan press would capitalize upon the dispute in ways that might seriously hurt the reform movement. The editors nevertheless showed their disdain for free silver by resoundingly reaffirming their confidence in W. S. Morgan and George Ward, who managed the Populist ready-print and boiler plate services for small weeklies. Both in-house services of the press association clashed frontally with Taubeneck's ambitions, since Morgan and Ward had a habit of writing about all the planks in the Omaha Platform. There was, therefore, very little Taubeneck could do—except possibly carry out his threat to withhold the relatively small amount of advertising he controlled. In any case, it consisted mostly of advertising for free silver tracts, which was purchased through various "Bimetallic Leagues," most notably "Coin" Harvey's lobbying center in Chicago. The editors decided they could

Herman E. Taubeneck
Taubeneck's announcement following the 1894 elections that the People's Party should renounce the
"wild theories" of the Omaha Platform and strive for a "union of the
reform forces" inaugurated the
silver drive that culminated in 1896.

risk the loss of that revenue readily enough. They repri-
manded Taubeneck for his reliance on silver coinage and
praised Morgan and Ward as "Populists in good standing."
And they concluded their meeting with mutual resolves to
defend the Omaha Platform against any and all threats, and
underlined their intention with a press statement to the same
effect.[20]

But the editors went a step further, sending a delegation to
Washington to confront Taubeneck. The party chairman was
induced to sign a statement that the Omaha Platform could
not be altered except by a national convention of duly certified
delegates. For good measure, the editors extracted similar
pledges from the party's silver minded congressmen.
Taubeneck's bid had failed: the party's politicians temporarily
fashioned a lowered silhouette and the national chairman again
retreated.

The National Farmers Alliance also met early in 1895, and
it delivered a final blow to the party chairman. The order
pointedly reaffirmed all elements of its broad-gauged greenback stand on monetary issues by listing them once again in
first place on the agenda of Alliance "demands." Alliance
leaders also signaled a possible interest in broadening the
Omaha Platform by recommending, "as subjects for discussion
and education," a graduated property tax and the initiative

and referendum. It was clear that the National Alliance, too, stood firmly by the Omaha Platform.[21]

The silver balloon had failed to soar: the party's rank and file, and its editors, had spoken and the Omaha Platform remained intact. The People's Party had too many Populists.[22]

As Taubeneck belatedly came to understand, he had assaulted the greenback heritage of the People's Party. The political tenacity and patience of greenbackers proved surprising to him. Few illustrated that characteristic better than Thomas Byron of Iowa. From his embattled outpost on General Weaver's old newspaper, the *Farmer's Tribune,* Byron wrote an article on the politics of the money issue that seemed squarely aimed at bringing both Weaver and Taubeneck to their senses:

> Free silver men in the old party ranks profess to be unable to understand why the People's Party do not jump at the chance to attract their votes and thus possibly assure the new party immediate success by just dropping the rest of the Omaha Platform. . . . Their inability to understand the Populist position is due entirely to their ignorance of the money question . . . Thoughtful men . . . not afflicted with the itch for immediate office-seeking but . . . actuated mainly by love of country . . . deem it best . . . that . . . the party do not grow too quickly, lest the people come into it faster than they can be educated . . . and the party get out of control of its friends, and reforms enacted prove in the new hands only superficial. . . . Hence we had rather not be overrun at this critical juncture by the Silver Goths from the forests of the two old parties. . . . When they can come into the movement understandingly they shall be welcomed as brothers.[23]

Nor was Byron alone. In Kansas, where the Populist tent had begun to flap in the breeze, Stephen McLallin of *The Advocate* hammered in some greenback stakes. When a Populist state senator rallied to the support of the Taubeneck declaration, *The Advocate* called the one-plank idea "the height of absurdity." As Taubeneck discovered, greenback doctrines constituted a fundamental intellectual barrier to the politics of the silver crusade.[24]

450

In the aftermath of these setbacks, the nature of Taube-neck's proprietary chairmanship became even more visible. He re-oiled the ideological weaponry he had first tested the preceding December and once again declared that the People's Party was in danger of a socialist takeover. Citing the actions of the reform editors in Kansas City in support of his charge, he included as additional evidence the barrage of editorials in behalf of the Omaha Platform that had appeared in leading Populist journals. He then publicly called the roll of the offenders who had "gone over to the Socialists"—the leading journals of the agrarian revolt. The reply of the *Nonconformist* was typical of the responses evoked by Taubeneck's ukase:

> Everybody who reads the *Nonconformist* knows very well that it has never swerved an inch from the Omaha Platform or the principles of the Populist Party. . . . We insist that all the misunderstanding arose from the chairman's effort to assume an authority which did not belong to him. . . . [T]he Populist newspapers have always done their duty and have never rendered more substantial service to the party than by refusing to allow the platform to be emasculated and a side show set up in its place at the dictation of a small coterie who imagine they know it all because they have spent a few months in Washington. . . . If supporting the Omaha platform makes a man a Socialist, we are all Socialists. If it was not Socialistic to support the platform for two years up to last December it was not Socialistic to support it after that date.[25]

In the *Farmer's Tribune,* Byron ceased his defense of the party platform and went over to the attack. He informed his readers that he saw more sinister forces at work—"silver barons and certain idle politicians." Worse, said Byron, while the reform press defended the platform, Taubeneck and Weaver were lobbying where it really counted—among the party leaders who would be organizing delegations to the Populist national convention of 1896. The Michigan state convention was said to have declared for the new one-plank policy only after "General Weaver traveled to the state for that especial purpose." Weaver had been the "arch-conspirator in this persistent at-

tack upon the Omaha platform from the first" and had lobbied heavily with the Populist Congressmen in Washington.
His conduct, said Byron, was "animated by an overwhelming
desire to be the fusion candidate of the old party silverites and
the People's Party for president in '96." [26]

Taubeneck and Weaver were not without defenses against
such attacks. Weaver persuaded the principal owner of the
Farmer's Tribune to take editorial control out of Byron's hands.
Rather than submit, Byron resigned, in May 1895. And in
Lincoln, Nebraska, the *Wealth Makers,* another outspoken critic
of William Jennings Bryan and William Allen, failed to survive
the hostile climate of the shadow movement and ceased publication early in 1896.[27]

On the whole, however, reform editors reflected the perspectives of their readers. Manning and Whitehead in Alabama, Burkitt in Mississippi, Watson in Georgia, Norton in Illinois, McLallin in Kansas, and Park in Texas were only
among the most visible of hundreds of reform editors who
closed ranks to defend the party's basic policy through the
period of increasing silver agitation in 1895–96.[28]

Meanwhile, Taubeneck's cry of "socialism" was blunted by
the socialists themselves. In the late spring of 1895, the Chicago coalition completely fell apart and suffered a crushing
defeat in off-year municipal elections. Though the *National
Watchman* chortled in triumph, the matter had become purely
academic. The real battle to define Populism remained in the
larger national arena that involved the monetary politics of all
three parties and the respective instruments of persuasion for
Republican gold, Democratic silver, and Populist greenbacks.[29]

6

The lobbying laurels it turned out, were won by the silverites.
In the winter of 1894–95 they struck a bonanza when the
third pamphlet published by William H. Harvey out of the
Chicago office of the American Bimetallic League became a
national best seller. "Coin" Harvey had produced *Coin's Financial School.* At twenty-five cents a copy, this cleverly written and
profusely illustrated pamphlet of 155 pages enjoyed a surprisingly large sale. As soon as they discovered they had a hit, the

silver lobby purchased and distributed hundreds of thousands of copies of the book in numerous and varied editions. Millions suffering from the maladies of depression and a contracted currency read Harvey's appealing, if wildly inaccurate, analysis of the monetary system and of various gold conspiracies by international bankers. "Coin" Harvey not only re-created much of the atmosphere of hysteria and conspiracy that had accompanied the furor over the "Crime of '73" a generation earlier,* he even paraphrased the very arguments put forward in support of the first silver drive. The goldbug response—again recapitulating the debates in the 1870's over redemption—were scarcely on a higher intellectual plane. The argument that "money was only as good as the gold that is in it" was just as erroneous in 1895 as it had been after the Civil War. But it did have the effect of keeping the silver proponents off balance. Pro-silver arguments in behalf of "bimetallism" necessarily involved elaborate explanations of coinage ratios and the relative weights and availabilities of the two metals. Most silverites, in fact, were not up to this intellectual challenge—certainly William Jennings Bryan was not. His well-publicized silver speech at Memphis in 1895 was a potpourri of evasion and sloganeering.[30]

But slogans, particularly when enhanced by the conspiratorial reasoning of "Coin" Harvey, were, for the time being, sufficient for many thousands of the Democratic faithful, hard-pressed as they were by the deepening depression. By April 1895 a Mississippi Congressman was writing to one of Cleveland's cabinet members of the sudden fame of the new silver propaganda book: "A little free silver book called "Coin's Financial School" is being sold on every railroad train by the newsboys and at every cigar store. . . . It is being read by almost everybody." Kenesaw Landis reported the same phenomenon from Illinois: "The God's truth is the Democratic Party in Indiana and Illinois is wildly insane on this subject. . . . The farmers are especially unruly . . . utterly wild on the money question. You can't do anything with them—just got to let them go." [31]

The struggle for the soul of the People's Party increased in

* See Chapter I.

HOW SILVER WAS ASSASSINATED.

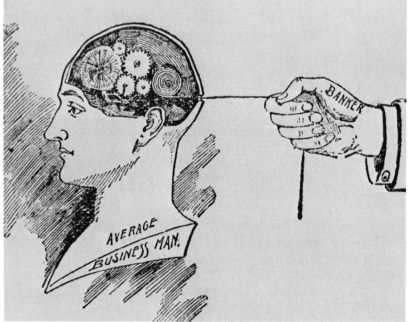

WHAT IT COSTS A FARMER TO DINE AT A FIRST-CLASS CHICAGO RESTAURANT.

The Mass Appeal of "Coin's" Financial School

One of the nation's more successful lobbyists, W. H. "Coin" Harvey

The Silver Captains

A. J. Warner, left, was the nation's chief lobbyist for silver, serving as president of the American Bimetallic League. Marcus Daly, right, a leading western mining king. His contributions helped finance "Coin" Harvey's Chicago lobbying office and other aspects of the campaign for silver.

intensity throughout 1895 as Populist politicians seeking coalition with Democrats wavered, reaffirmed the Omaha Platform, then appeared to embrace the silver solution.

The progress of silver lobbying—indeed, the very popularity of *Coin's Financial School*—added to the determination of the most committed silverites in Populist ranks. For three of the fusionists, Butler of North Carolina, Allen of Nebraska, and Taubeneck, the monetary planks of the Populist platform had never been central to their political advocacy, Butler having established a record in behalf of election reform, silver, the protective tariff, and railroad regulation, while Allen wanted legislative purification, and Taubeneck focused solely on the white metal. All of these positions were consistent with their own unique "Populist" pasts. But James Baird Weaver had spent much of his adult life asserting and defending greenback doctrines. For him, the needs of fusion required special concessions to expediency. His route to a workable fusionist posture was a tortured one. He responded to Thomas Byron's *Farmer's Tribune* with a statement emphasiz-

William Stewart, left, the "Silver Senator" from Nevada, editor of the *Silver Knight,* and a leading Republican exponent of the white metal. William A. Clark, right, one of the principal "Silver Democrats" in the West. Clark served as U.S. Senator from Montana.

ing the primacy of the financial question, "not on the silver issue alone" but also "legal tender government paper, with neither bonds nor banks of issue." Yet less than a month later, Weaver urged Ignatius Donnelly to join in a silver declaration signed by leading fusionists. And, privately, Weaver wrote, "I am a middle-of-the-road man, but I don't propose to lie down across it so no one can get over me. Nothing grows in the middle of the road." [32]

Weaver's elusiveness stirred deep doubts in Davis Waite, the leader of Colorado Populism. "I hardly know what to think of Weaver," he wrote in confidence to Ignatius Donnelly. Weaver was "in sympathy with Bland and Bryan . . . a Democratic movement." Weaver had assured Waite that he had lost confidence in the American Bimetallic League and was prepared to stand firm on the Omaha Platform, but, said Waite, "He came into Colorado in the pay of that outfit and undertook to stampede the Colorado Populists on the single issue of silver." [33]

Others were less disingenuous. A Populist state senator who

survived the general slaughter of reform candidates in Kansas in 1894 placed his advocacy of the silver solution on a basis of naked expediency: "Why a single issue—free coinage? Not because it is the most important question; not because it would benefit the people more than any other reform measure, but because it is the only question that the great majority of the people are really interested in." The anti-fusion Kansas Populist League, weakened in prestige by the defeat of 1894, fought the spread of such sentiments among party politicians through 1895. So did the *Advocate*. But signs emerged of widening cracks in Populist defenses in the West. In the *Advocate*, McLallin himself conceded that "If free coinage of silver will relieve the industrial people of the country until they learn more about the science of money, let's have free coinage." McLallin apparently had no stomach for the coming struggle. Late in the year he announced his imminent retirement and the sale of the paper to Senator Peffer. For the time being, policy remained unchanged. John Willits, the third party gubernatorial candidate of 1890 and once again the president of the Kansas State Alliance, held firmly to the Omaha Platform, but the defeat of 1894 seemed to have sapped the will of many of his fellow candidates who had run on Populist state and local tickets. An increasing number of Kansas politicians said they wanted the Omaha Platform, but they wanted victory, too. The simple fact of the matter was that the silver lobby was making silver popular.[34]

To faithful Populists, however, the vague and conspiratorial talk about "free silver" was as maddeningly irrelevant in the 1890's as it had been to old-time greenbackers in the 1870's. But from the orthodox Populist standpoint, the principal difficulty in making an effective case was that the staunchest anti-Democratic politicians were from the South; though a respectable number had waged successful campaigns, they had been systematically denied office because of Democratic frauds. As spokesmen of the party, they had never achieved national exposure in Washington and were virtually unknown outside their own states. The Southern Populist who was best known nationally was Georgia's Tom Watson, a man who had made his reputation before vote frauds became the way of life in the South. Watson's admonitions to "fight it straight boys . . . some victories cost so much that the army that won them can never fight again" were fondly reprinted in scores of reform papers. And, as it soon developed, these efforts were not without success. For while the fusionists had much the advantage in "big names," they had a weak case to present to a party constituency that had been mobilized from the beginning on greenback doctrines. Despite all the lobbying efforts, the silver cause made only inconclusive progress inside third party ranks. However, there was an unmistakable growth of silver sentiment inside Democratic ranks. This political development had irresistible appeal to Populist office-seekers looking for a formula for victory in 1896.[35]

7

After twelve months of active but frustrating campaigning for "a union of reform forces," Weaver, Taubeneck, and their associates decided at year's end to take authoritarian steps to control the excess of democracy in the People's Party. On the final day of 1895, Weaver confided the results of fusionist planning to William Jennings Bryan. "We have had quite enough middle of the road nonsense, and some of us at least think it about time for the exhibition of a little synthetic force." The first "exhibition" of the new policy came with considerable clarity two weeks later. At a mid-January meeting Taubeneck and Weaver implemented a shameless plan to stack the Populist national convention. After a year of cajolery and hints of imminent silver campaign money, Taubeneck had made headway in diminishing the presumed importance of the Omaha Platform to many members of the Populist natioal committee. That body was, of course, easier to manage than the Populist national convention itself, as the national committee had three representatives from each state irrespective of Populist strength; at the national convention, where state delegations were apportioned on the basis of Populist voting totals in state elections, fusionists would have had to cope with huge Populistic delegations from states like Texas and Georgia. In his pre-convention planning, Taubeneck's increased influence on the national committee came principally

459

from states having little or no Populist presence—New England; the mid-Atlantic states; parts of the upper Midwest; and such border states as Kentucky, Maryland, and Virginia. Adding these to the mining regions of the West that had always been preoccupied with silver, Taubeneck had acquired what he believed to be a majority for silver on the national committee. By inviting some fifteen Populist officeholders in Congress to meet with the committee early in 1896, he apparently put the matter beyond doubt. Populist protests about the structure of this assemblage were well taken, it turned out, for Taubeneck got approval for a surprising plan—an apportionment of delegates to the Populist national convention that markedly under-represented the South. In contrast, the industrial East and selected states with known pro-silver leaders were to be substantially over-represented.[36]

The 90,000 Populist votes cast in Georgia earned 61 delegates, while New York and Pennsylvania, with a combined third party following of less than half of the Georgia total, together received 83 delegates. Mid-road Mississippi's 20,000 Populist votes cast in congressional races in 1894 brought the state 15 delegates under Taubeneck's system, while roughly the same number of votes in Michigan earned 29 delegates. From Maine to Maryland, the third party received a grand total of only 110,000 votes in 1894, yet the eleven states of the Northeast received 179 delegates, more than enough to offset Texas and Georgia with their combined Populist electorate of over 250,000. The reform press predictably raged about such boss tactics, and mid-road forces promised to bring the entire matter up for review at the national convention itself.[37]

But the Taubeneck-Weaver plan to dispense with "middle of the road nonsense" was only partially implemented by this move. Indeed, the very date of the special meeting called by Taubeneck was a function of a much more subtle tactical move that had its ultimate purpose in the careful timing of the Populist national convention in mid-summer 1896. By following Taubeneck's moves carefully—which third party men did with great interest and suspicion—Populists discovered in January 1896 that some of their silver-minded leaders intended to push fusion even if such a course threatened the institutional death of the People's Party itself.

The fusionist plan to "unite the reform forces" had meaning only on the presumption that both major parties cooperated fully by nominating gold-standard candidates in 1896. Free silver then could theoretically "unite" bolting silver Republicans and silver Democrats under the Populist banner in 1896. But the spread of silver sentiment within Democratic ranks in both the Souh and West was verified by the size of every "mass meeting" engineered by the silver lobby throughout the months of 1895. Whatever strategy Taubeneck presumed he and his colleagues were following, the silver mineowners—and William Jennings Bryan—were clearly proceeding toward another objective. Their plan manifestly called for capturing the Democratic Party so the "reform forces" could unite under that somewhat broader umbrella. After nominating a silver ticket, the Democrats would, in effect, confront the Populists with the choice of supporting the major party or ignoring the claims of its own fusionist wing to be working to "harmonize all reformers."

Under these circumstances, midroaders concluded that the raw practical politics of silver promised to bring unity in a way that would destroy the People's Party as an institution of reform. The only way to avoid such an ominous dilemma, directly traceable to Taubeneck's maneuverings, was to hold the Populist convention first, nominate a sound third party reformer for President, and leave to the Democrats any onus attached to dividing the "reform" forces—granting that such a multi-party entity existed in the first place. While the advice of the *Southern Mercury* to this effect was brusquely ignored by Taubeneck, the implementation of an alternate strategy required delicate coordination with both Democrats and the silver lobby. A flurry of correspondence between Taubeneck, Weaver, Butler, Allen, Donnelly, Bryan, and silver lobbyists revealed that the Democratic National Committee planned to meet on January 16, 1896, to select a date for the Democratic convention. Taubeneck thereupon called his own national committee together on January 17, and Weaver privately assured Bryan that the People's Party committee not only would vote to meet after the Democratic convention, but that Populist leaders would even postpone the decision on time and place until they could consult with the chief silver lobbyists in Washington.[38]

When the Democrats selected July 7 in Chicago for their convention, Taubeneck affirmed his control over the Populist national committee—and the committee's subservience to the silver strategists—by postponing for a week the decision on the date of the Populist convention. With plenary powers to act for the People's Party, the fusion leaders promptly entrained for Washington to meet with the lobbyists of the American Bimetallic League. With the silverites' permission, or acquiescence, as the case may be, Taubeneck announced from Washington on January 24 that the Populist national convention would be held on July 22 in St. Louis, two weeks *after* the near-by Democratic convention. In terms of the survival of the People's Party, the magnitude of Taubeneck's action may be seen in the fact that the American Bimetallic League officially launched a new fourth party known as the National Silver Party at the same meeting. The July 22 date selected for the Populist National Convention coincided in both time and place with the projected nominating convention of the new Silver Party. It was as if every move were calculated to prove that the People's Party itself had become superfluous.[39]

Thereafter, the silverite strategy unfolded in a way that must have brought great satisfaction to the American Bimetallic League and to a new organization called the "Democratic National Bimetallic Committee," which suddenly materialized with an adequate treasury. The cause of silver became a visible force in the spring months of 1896, as silverites won control of the Democratic party in state after state across the South and West. The functionaries of the silver lobby kept the Populist fusion leaders off balance during the entire period by alternately providing assurances that goldbugs would control both major parties and by dangling silver money to finance "the approaching campaign." Gerrymandered and slandered by their own party's leadership, Populists watched these developments with growing alarm. The "little synthetic force" that

James Baird Weaver had promised to squelch the Omaha Platform had indeed materialized. Through "Coin" Harvey, the cause of silver was penetrating Democratic ranks from below; through Herman Taubeneck and his small circle of friends, it was penetrating the ranks of the People's Party from above. Silver mineowners directly financed both efforts.[40]

8

The aspirations that had produced the agrarian revolt proved too strong, however, to subside passively in the face of the campaign of the silver lobby. A driving energy persisted in the People's Party, one that merged ideological assertion with a remarkable degree of collective purpose. As much as anything else, this unique circumstance was traceable to the existence of shared memories that, in 1896, stretched back over almost a full generation of hope and effort. And no one, it turned out, was more committed to the Omaha Platform than the Alliance founders in Texas.

The radicalism of the Texas third party often achieved an intensity that in retrospect is not easy to describe. It combined the soft admonitions of Judge Thomas Nugent; the skillful greenback arguments of J. M. Perdue and Harry Tracy; the tactical radicalism of William Lamb and Evan Jones; the oratorical thunder of "Cyclone" Davis, "Stump" Ashby, and John Rayner; and an astonishing degree of rank-and-file militance on the part of farmer-veterans of the Alliance movement. When the American Bimetallic League first suggested the possible need for a new national silver party, Nugent wrote a reply that was characteristically quiet in tone and radical in content. Silver coinage, he said, would "leave undisturbed all the conditions which give rise to the undue concentration of wealth. The so-called silver party may prove a veritable trojan horse if we are not careful." Other Texans expressed similar views with considerably less reserve. A North Texas farmer, for instance, wrote to the *Southern Mercury* in language that scarcely paid lip-service to the parliamentary process:

> I can't see any way out of our troubles except by revolution!
> War to the knife and knife to the hilt. I am in for settling the

question even if it takes blood to do it. The old party following here is small and disorganized. Keep on pouring the hot
shot into them! [41]

The *Mercury* itself occasionally viewed matters in apocalyptic
terms. "With Debs in jail, no American is a freeman," was one
not untypical *Mercury* one-liner. Full-scale editorials produced
phrases about the "bitter and irrepressible conflict between the
capitalist and the laborer," a circumstance requiring "every
wage earner to combine and march shoulder to shoulder to
the ballot box and by their suffrage overthrow the capitalistic
class." These were special moments in the *Mercury*'s editorial
career, however. More often the paper controlled its radical
ardor sufficiently to combine humor with Populism, as when
the paper catalogued the plethora of Populist candidates who
wanted fusion and concluded that the "free silver party is like
a Kentucky militia regiment. It consists of all colonels and no
privates." [42]

As the most authoritative voice of the Reform Press Association in the South, the *Mercury* possessed the credentials and its
editor the temperament for a showdown encounter with the
fusionists. That editor, Milton Park, had the security of knowing that his Alliance readers had for years proclaimed the
ephemeral nature of the free silver panacea. One of the original Alliance organizers, W. H. Davis, wrote in his dual capacity
as president of the Comanche County Farmers Alliance and
chairman of the Comanche County People's Party:

> There are many sidetracks now being built to switch off the
> incoming tide from the old parties. The free silver side track
> is considered the most popular to catch the Populists, but it
> is too weak to hold a heavyweight Populist. He has been
> pinched in more places than one and a one-plank concern
> won't hold him.

Substituting the proper name for the appropriate Alliance
platform, *Mercury* editorials could easily have applied to any
year from 1888 to 1896: "To trim the Omaha platform will be
fatal to the party. It would alienate the Farmers Alliance element and without the Farmers Alliance, the People's Party is
as sounding brass and a tinkling cymbal of discordant ele-

ments. What is the object of these trimmers? To gain votes, doubtless, but where a cowardly policy will gain one raw recruit, it will lose five veterans." [43]

The *Mercury* counseled, prodded, praised, admonished. When some Georgia Populists flirted with fusion, the rebuke was prompt and, with Watson's help, effective. The same counsel had been extended to Taubeneck in 1894, to Simpson and Weaver in 1895, and to Butler in 1896. Radical journals like the *American Nonconformist* and the *People's Party Paper* were praised, while Dunning's *National Watchman* was roundly condemned. The labor movement received a mixed review. Eugene Debs's *Railway Times* was "an earnest, fearless, and honest friend to labor," and the Knights of Labor journal in Chicago was similarly blessed for being "beyond the reach of politicians and the money gang." But Samuel Gompers and much of the rest of labor got low marks in steadfastness, a fact which kept "organized labor disorganized." The Kansas brand of Populism, intermittently beset by fusionist tendencies since 1892 (though usually on the basis of the Omaha Platform), had lost the *Mercury*'s approval quite early, and the paper fairly chortled in triumph when the 1894 returns showed the Texas party, all radical banners unfurled, had outpolled the Kansans in the November elections. As for the Nebraska fusionists, the *Mercury* could scarcely conceal its contempt. The newspaper carefully followed the public speeches of Populist politicians and consigned them, one by one, to seats of dishonor as they caved in to the silverites.[44]

The memory of the long years of organizing that had carried the Alliance from a handful of quarreling frontier farmers to a national political force armed the founders with an evangelical sense of mission to save the People's Party from betrayal by some of its own spokesmen. No single Populist had a longer and more intense memory of the agrarian revolt than the pioneer "Traveling Lecturer" who had carried the order's cooperative message from the original frontier counties in Texas back in the winter of 1883–84. If Herman Taubeneck had come to the People's Party from outside the Alliance experience, S. O. Daws of Parker County, Texas, came as close as any man to being the symbol of that experience. When

Daws heard of Taubeneck's plan to convene a joint meeting of Populist politicians and the national committee to set a late convention date, his indignation at this slur on "the plain people" knew no bounds:

> Why did not the populist national committee invite the Farmers Alliance to meet with them at St. Louis? Why did they not invite other industrial organizations? Don't deceive yourselves gentlemen. . . . The farmers will be on hand at St. Louis to give their views in no uncertain sound. . . . The laboring people are tired of modern party politics. They want a new programme of pure, true principles that mean something for the people. Their diagnosis of the case may seem absurd to modern demagogues, and their remedies may seem visionary, but they are honest and desperately in earnest. We propose to stand by the demands of the industrial people! [45]

Six weeks before the convention the *Mercury* sifted the Populist leadership ranks and selected its presidential candidate. "The way to discourage these trimmers and wreckers is to place in nomination candidates of whom there is not a shadow of a doubt as to their honesty of purpose and adherence to the people's cause, candidates who can stand squarely upon the Omaha Platform without spending their time hiding in some obscure corner of it." The *Mercury* advised the various state parties to send delegates to St. Louis "who are honest and sincere, pledging them to support the Omaha Platform in its entirety, and instructing them to vote for the most broadminded statesman and patriot of the century, Eugene V. Debs, for president." [46]

The mid-road crusade activated all the resources of the reform movement that were free of the influence of Herman Taubeneck and the national silver lobby. Across the nation, these resources were imposing. In employing them, Populists made a conscious effort to strew in the path of the silverites as many practical and symbolic roadblocks as possible. The Reform Press Association, for example, delivered the clearest message it could to the fusionists by electing Milton Park as its national president in 1895. In 1896, the association renewed its long support for W. Scott Morgan's Populist ready-print service and mobilized its internal machinery to disseminate to all reform weeklies throughout the nation the necessary facts, figures, and arguments in support of the party's platform. In the same weeks the National Farmers Alliance issued a ringing challenge to the "platform wreckers" in the form of a new preamble to the famous Alliance demands. The statement climaxed the insurgent heritage of the Farmers Alliance with the most radical declaration of its entire history:

> We hold therefore that to restore and preserve these rights under a republican form of government, private monopoly of public necessities for speculative purposes, whether of the means of production, distribution or exchange, should be prohibited, and whenever any such public necessity or utility becomes a monopoly in private hands, the people of the municipality, state or nation, as the case may be, shall appropriate the same by right of eminent domain, paying a just value therefor, and operate them for, and in the interest of, the whole people.[47]

With this new peg anchoring their left flank, the defenders of the Omaha Platform entered a final pre-convention phase of practical politics. The chairman of the Texas People's Party, H. S. P. "Stump" Ashby, the "famous agitator and humorist," embarked on a convention-organizing tour through the South. One of the most effective orators of the agrarian revolt—and certainly one of the most experienced—Ashby moved to offset Taubeneck's gerrymandering scheme by cementing the Southern convention delegations firmly to "the middle of the road." If his years of management of Populist campaigns in Texas gave him credentials to deflect silverite arguments about "practical politics," his radical greenbackism also provided more than an adequate counterweight to the vague interpretations of the silverites.[48]

As the time approached for the various party conventions, silver advocates in the Democratic Party consolidated their hold on state delegations throughout the South and West. But within the People's Party the tactical position of silverites began to deteriorate, and the mid-road campaign began to bear fruit. The steady pounding by Alliance-greenbackers and by reform editors produced sudden cracks in supposedly solid fusionist state delegations. Taubeneck reported gloomily to Donnelly that "something is out of joint in Indiana," and a Missouri Populist fired off a warning to Marion Butler that silver was a trap set by Democrats who "simply run with the stampeding cattle until they circle them back into camp." Alliance leaders occupying prominent positions in the California People's Party had long defended the Omaha platform against silver politicians, and they stepped up their criticism of fusion tactics as the convention approached. Willits of the Kansas Alliance, supported by such party luminaries as William Peffer, Annie Diggs, and G. C. Clemens, did the same. Mississippi and Arkansas rallied to the Omaha Platform, and Joseph Manning in Alabama defended the Populist cause against the decamping Reuben Kolb. The latter, having never quite made the break with the party of the fathers, had a shorter return distance than most other Populist leaders throughout the South. The Arkansas thirty party, well-honed for years by the educational program of the Wheel, the Alliance, and W. Scott Morgan, was united against the silver panacea in all its forms. Though the Alliance in Nebraska had long since deteriorated, John Powers and a handful of radicals from the Kearney County cooperative movement manfully raised the Populist flag in the very citadel of Democratic-Populist coalition. Even in fusion-steeped North Carolina, one of the state's best known agrarian spokesmen, Cyrus Thompson, who had become highly suspicious of Marion Butler's motives, defended the cause of broad-based reform and otherwise complicated Butler's arduous and self-imposed task of three-party fusion. On the eve of the 1896 Populist national convention, the leader of the Georgia delegation, raised on years of Watsonian teachings, wired that the Georgians were coming to St. Louis "in the middle of the road." Similarly, the old editorial flagship of the North Carolina Alliance, L. L. Polk's *Progressive Farmer,* warned the Populist faithful that the fusionists were attempting "to deliver the entire People's Party into the lap of the Wall Street Democracy at one time." [49]

A pattern was clear: where the roots of the agrarian revolt sank deepest, the Populist dream of broad-based reform had its strongest support. Old Alliancemen were, indeed, "heavy-weight Populists" who, along with one of the oldest of them all, S. O. Daws, proposed "to stand by the demands of the industrial people." By June 1896, some of them had been at the work of reform for almost twenty years. They went to St. Louis in anxiety, but not without some confidence. After all, Populism was, as they told themselves, their movement.

CHAPTER XV

A Cross of Silver

"The Populist convention will not be run by Democrats!"

In the final weeks before the onset of the summer presidential nominating conventions, third party Chairman Herman Taubeneck confidently surveyed the results of his eighteen-month campaign for silver and pronounced his pleasure with the product. "At no time since our party was organized," he wrote Ignatius Donnelly, "have the prospects for a great victory been so flattering as today." [1]

He could hardly have been more mistaken. In a series of quick, rude jolts, Taubeneck's fusion strategy came apart completely. Inexorably, the idea of Populism as a silver crusade became starkly revealed as the contradiction it was. For the Populist national chairman, the result was a nightmare. Imprisoned within narrow options carved by his own previous analysis, he maneuvered frantically in an effort to implement a last-minute ultimatium that became the final repository of his political integrity. In a climax of utter chaos, he retreated abruptly into the background before being invited to endorse a political result he had earlier worked to avoid. He bravely accepted the offer and thus brought an organic logic to his tenure in office, though only by defining structural collapse as a victory for reform. His party torn asunder, he thus claimed credit for his failure. It was a humiliating moment, and he knew it. After the St. Louis convention of the People's Party in 1896, Herman Taubeneck quickly faded from the stage of national politics, never to return.

Taubeneck's troubles were a direct product of his own prior ambivalence as to who was a Populist and who was not. While the theoretical debate of 1895–96 over monetary policy was waged within the ranks of the People's Party, where the Omaha Platform was considered the essence of reform, the real debate, thanks to Taubeneck's previous maneuvers, took place within a larger political arena that extended to those Populists and Democrats who shared the short-run political objective of fusion in 1896. This environment had been artificially shaped by the silver lobby. The various newspapers and periodicals devoted to silver were subsidized, sometimes directly, as in the case of Democrat William Jennings Bryan's Omaha *World* or Republican Senator William Stewart's *Silver Knight,* sometimes indirectly, as in the case of Nelson Dunning's *National Watchman,* and sometimes without any help at all from the mineowners—as with a number of Democratic dailies in the Western states. But of all their experiments in mass persuasion, the silver magnates received their most effective dollar value from the funds allocated to the Chicago lobbying office of William Hope "Coin" Harvey. That investment had yielded the enormously influential *Coin's Financial School.* Coordinate with the efforts of Western and Southern Democrats like Bryan, Richard Bland of Missouri, Ben Tillman of South Carolina, and James Hogg of Texas, and augmented by the close cooperation of such Populist politicians as Taubeneck, Weaver, Allen, and Butler, the campaign of the silver lobby made noticeable, though uneven, headway in the final year before the 1896 convention. Though mid-roaders successfully mobilized both the reform press and the Farmers Alliance in a successful defense of the Omaha Platform—an ideological victory won wholly within the ranks of the People's Party—the silverites won the larger battle for the attention of masses of Democratic Party voters in the South and West. The strength of the fusion position in 1896 was the simple fact that "free silver" was on the minds of hundreds of thousands of non-Populists who earlier had evinced little interest in the intricacies of monetary reform. According to Taubeneck's projected agenda, the Republicans were to nominate a doctrinaire apostle of "sound money," thus alienating "silver Republicans" rallied behind Colorado's Senator Edward Teller, while the Democrats were to follow suit and thereby estrange their own silverites. The Populists were then to gather up the disaffected of both parties in what Taubeneck called "a grand union of the reform forces." [2]

But while the Republicans lived up to expectations by nominating William McKinley on a gold standard platform, the Democrats declined to provide a corresponding degree of cooperation. Indeed, though that party's transformation had taken place right before his eyes, Taubeneck seemed unaware that the Democratic Party of 1896 bore little resemblance to the conservative coalition of Southern states' righters and Tammany-style Northern politicians that had provided the sinew of the Gold Democracy of Grover Cleveland. The agrarian revolt had shaken the very foundations of the post-Civil War Democracy, and the conservative supporters of New York's David B. Hill—a nice blend of Irish politicians and Yankee entrepreneurs—were no longer able to broker the regional desires of their party associates from the South and West. The latter, reeling from six years of the Populist onslaught, were determined to refurbish the party's appearance by writing a silver platform and nominating any one of a half-dozen silver politicians as its presidential candidate.[3]

As the advance guard of Democrats began arriving in Chicago for their convention, Taubeneck at last perceived the new balance of forces within the old party. He immediately abandoned his long-announced objective of "uniting the reform forces of the nation." In a desperate effort to stem the silver tide, he warned the Democrats that the People's Party would nominate its own ticket even if the Democrats should select a candidate friendly to silver. The Populist chairman thereupon discovered how his years of propagandizing for silver had weakened the third party's political leverage. The

Democrats—and their friends in the silver lobby—simply ignored him. They were secure in the knowledge that a number of Populist politicians in the West, encouraged by Taubeneck, had labored to bring silver to the fore as the central campaign issue and that many Populist voters would find it much more difficult to distinguish between two "silver" parties than they had before. Both the Democrats and the silver lobby had looked after their own interests; if Taubeneck had not, the problem was his, not theirs.[4]

Shaken, the Populist chairman anxiously advised his party's spokesmen that Populists "must take a firm stand that we will not endorse the nominee of the Chicago convention if he should be a straight out Democrat." That language heralded Taubeneck's last desperate expedient: if the Populists were to be asked to sacrifice their party for the cause of silver, said Taubeneck, the Democrats should nominate for President on the Democratic ticket the silver Republican from Colorado, Edward Teller![5]

Innocently, if fervently, Taubeneck issued an ultimatum to the effect that the Democrats "must take Teller or be responsible for a division of the silver forces at the polls next November." The third party chairman was able to induce Mary Elizabeth Lease of Kansas to offer public support for the Teller candidacy, a move which promptly earned her the forceful disapproval of Henry Vincent. In Wisconsin, Robert Schilling, the labor greenbacker, refused to sign a Taubeneck-sponsored Populist "petition" for Teller and summarized his feelings about the fusionist leadership in a letter to Ignatius Donnelly: "These fellows run off after strange gods at every opportunity." The Texans, of course, agreed, as did Peffer in Kansas, Watson in Georgia, Donnelly in Minnesota, Manning in Alabama, Wardell in California, and hundreds of reform editors.[6]

The Democratic convention confirmed Taubeneck's worst fears. Though Missouri's "Silver Dick" Bland was the early favorite to win the nomination, William Jennings Bryan's "Cross of Gold" speech transported the delegates. Bland stepped aside and eased the way for the nomination of Bryan; Teller, who was never a real factor at the Democratic convention, endorsed Bryan also. As if to emphasize their Democratic orthodoxy, even at the moment of apparent party schism, the delegates, including whole state delegations pledged to Bryan, supported the vice presidential candidacy of Arthur Sewall, a conservative banker and shipping magnate from Maine. In both of its standard bearers the silver crusade thus possessed spokesmen who were intellectually and politically committed to a hard money, redeemable currency. Greenback principles were anathema to the new crusade—as they had been during the first silver agitation over "the Crime of '73," more than a generation previously. In the immediate aftermath of Bryan's nomination, one political fact was clear: if the "reform forces" of the nation were to be united, the merger would take place on a basis far removed from the Omaha Platform.[7]

Dedicated as Herman Taubeneck was to the cause of silver, the intellectual implications of the situation did not trouble him. The truly distressing product of the Democratic convention lay in a simple political reality: the People's Party, he now saw, was not only trapped, it was threatened with the loss of its own identity. His strategy in ruins, the distraught fusionist leader fell silent. He made his way to the Populist convention city of St. Louis immediately following the Chicago debacle and "sullenly refused to be interviewed."[8]

The hyperactive days of Herman Taubeneck had come to an end. He would not head a grand "union of forces," and the thought stripped him of his political will. On the eve of the third party's most important convention, the Populist national chairman declared his "neutrality" and receded from view. Shorn of any illusion that he was a moulder of events, he consoled himself by reacting as best he could to the initiatives of others. Almost from the moment of Bryan's nomination in Chicago, he became, in every practical sense, an ex-politician.

2

The men whom Herman Taubeneck had rallied to his fusionist cause could not, however, afford such a passive response. They were politicians all—and politicians facing a most critical election. Simpson and Harris of Kansas, Kyle of South Dakota, and Butler of North Carolina all had to find a way to put the best possible face on embarrassing events. William Allen of

Nebraska had no such problem; Bryan was a close friend, not an embarrassment.

For a brief moment, however, some of the party's politicians were almost as shaken by the Democratic coup as was Taubeneck himself. Marion Butler was the most visible. Up until the very moment of Bryan's nomination, Butler had clung to the belief that the Democrats would join the Republicans in nominating an orthodox goldbug. After Chicago, Butler toyed with the thought that the Democrats, in refusing to nominate Teller, had stamped themselves as traitors to the silver cause. Since Teller had himself endorsed Bryan, however, the argument lacked persuasiveness, and an alternative one possessing Populistic substance—that "free silver" undercut greenback monetary reform—was not a part of Butler's political thought.[9]

The North Carolinian reluctantly concluded that Bryan's nomination had created grave problems for the third party: "It would seem that their real underlying purpose in stealing the people's party platform and in nominating Mr. Bryan for the president . . . was done more with a view of crippling the People's Party than with a view to uniting the silver forces to win a great victory." The Democrats, of course, had scarcely stolen the Omaha Platform; they had merely adopted the truncated version that Butler himself held aloft in North Carolina. But for fusionists, Butler's emphasis on platform theft served the useful purpose of minimizing the difference between the Bryan Democracy and Populism, and signaled Butler's intention, soon confirmed by his own actions, to work for a third party endorsement of Bryan.[10]

Other Populist politicians in the West promptly agreed that the unexpected action of the Democrats had left the third party with no other alternative but to nominate Bryan. Kansas' Jerry Simpson, out of office for two years, easily swallowed the Democratic medicine: "We should adopt our own platform and nominate Bryan. That would unite the Democrats and Populists on the silver issue." In a vague straddle, Simpson said he favored the Omaha Platform "with a few elisions." Lewelling and many others among the office-seekers in the Kansas party agreed with Simpson. With considerably less strain, so did almost the whole of the Nebraska third party which had been created in cooperation with Bryan.

Less predictable, however, was the sudden abandonment of the party platform by such prominent Populist luminaries as Colorado's former Populist Governor, Davis Waite. As late as the spring of 1896 Waite had warned against any merger with silverites "unless the Omaha Platform was accepted." In the months that followed, the silver lobby completely captured the organizational structures of the "Silver Democrats" and "Silver Populists" in the mining state. After the Democrats nominated Bryan, Waite announced his "utter surprise" that the Democrats had returned to the old doctrines of Jefferson and Jackson. They had "nominated a good and true man on the platform," Waite said. "Of course, I support him." Ignatius Donnelly, the old greenbacker, also appeared to be wavering. "Narrow Populism to free-silver alone," he wrote in 1895, "and it will disappear in a rat hole." But after the Democratic convention the Sage of Nininger wrote in his diary: "Exciting times these. Shall we or shall we not endorse Bryan, but I do not feel that we can safely accept the Democratic candidate. I fear it will be the end of our party." [11]

Kansas Senator Peffer moved from a mid-road to a fusion position with even greater rapidity. On June 25 he reacted negatively to the Taubeneck campaign for Teller: "I regard the integrity and perpetuity of the populist party as essential to carrying out the plan of reform we have espoused . . . all that remains is for the Populist party to maintain its integrity by nominating its own candidates on its own platform." But two weeks later, on the eve of the Populist convention, Peffer's newspaper, *The Advocate,* editorialized:

> Let our National convention reaffirm the Omaha Platform, revised and brought up to date, and then, if it is deemed best not to name a ticket now, appoint a national committee to perform the usual duties of such committees and to aid in carrying on the work of the campaign. . . . There is so little now between Populists and the Democracy that it does not seem unreasonable to expect that little will disappear through conferences in the future, if we maintain our party organization and platform of principles.[12]

476

A sober political reality underlay this lack of fixed purpose on the part of so many Populist politicians in the West. Such men as Allen of Nebraska, Kyle of South Dakota, Waite of Colorado, and the Kansas Congressmen all owed their offices to the joint support of Populists and Democrats in their own states. The simple fact was that Populism had never attained majority status in any state; throughout the 1890's the third party's margins of victory in the West had been provided through fusion with Democrats. Whether these mergers were achieved on the basis of the Omaha Platform, as in Kansas, or on terms harmonizing with those of Western Democrats, as in Nebraska, victory had been a product of Populist-Democratic coalition. If the People's Party nominated a Populist ticket against both Bryan and McKinley, Populist officeholders in the West were doomed to defeat by a division of their electorate, and they knew it. Taubeneck's strategy had helped create the dynamics that led to Bryan's nomination, but the nomination itself now had a political meaning all its own—and one that had no bearing on the existence of such political ideas as were embedded in the Omaha Platform.[13]

3

Populists thus arrived in St. Louis for their convention to discover that the fusion strategists, far from retreating, had advanced to new ground: the third party should nominate the Democratic ticket of Bryan and Arthur Sewall. To block this strategy—which frankly appalled them—mid-roaders deployed their forces on a number of fronts. They opened a campaign on the most vulnerable portion of the fusionist master plan, the distasteful necessity of nominating Sewall, the conservative Eastern financier, as their vice presidential candidate. Details of Sewall's career as a national banker and transportation magnate were circulated to all delegates. Additionally, the underlying ideological tension was brought to the surface by Harry Tracy, publisher of the *Southern Mercury*, who dispatched a telegram to Bryan inquiring about his attitude toward the Omaha Platform. Whatever form Bryan's answer took, it could scarcely be drafted in a manner to improve the fusionists' maneuvering room within the Populist conven-

Harry Tracy
Publisher of the *Southern Mercury*.
Tracy's telegram to William Jennings Bryan from the St. Louis convention hall figured in the confused nominating process.

tion. Finally, to forestall fusionist attempts to weaken the third party platform, mid-roaders called a mass meeting of delegates at the Texas headquarters in the Southern Hotel in St. Louis. The object, in keeping with earlier pronouncements by the National Reform Press Association and the National Farmers Alliance, was to map plans to retain the substance of the Omaha Platform—or, as the strongly pro-Bryan St. Louis *Post-Dispatch* put it, to shape the party's principles in terms "so radical that Mr. Bryan, if he were nominated, could not accept the platform." [14]

Delegates from twenty-three states attended the mid-road caucus. The ramifications of fusion were endlessly spelled out to wavering delegates variously influenced by the public statements of prominent party spokesmen. Southern third party men circulated among the delegates and indignantly reviewed the fraudulent practices, wholesale intimidation, and election day violence that had characterized the conduct of the Democratic Party in the South. How could reformers in the North and West ask their Southern comrades to embrace their most hated foes? "Free silver" did not purge the Southern Democracy of its inherited style. Even Jerome Kearby, the most renowned trial lawyer in Texas and perhaps Populism's most urbane speaker in the state, was moved to emotional language in describing the brazen vote frauds and violence of the silverite Democracy of Jim Hogg: "Do you expect us to run now with the creatures who heaped these insults on us? . . . So help me God, I will never march with you into the Democratic Party. Now let us see what we can do towards keeping out of that cesspool of hell." Georgia and Alabama mid-roaders added amplifying details about wholesale election thefts in their states. The message was clear: fusion with the Democratic Party would destroy the morale of Southern Populism.[15]

That reality instilled in the Southerners a sense of proprietary interest within the family of reform that kept the 1896 convention in turmoil for four days and reached its climax under almost riotous conditions. Throughout the tumult, those who had learned the greenback lessons of the cooperative movement most fully—the Texans—proved the most tenacious Populists, while those who had not learned them at all—the Nebraskans—spoke for the shadow movement. But the movement for fusion, financed by silver interests, orchestrated by Herman Taubeneck, and massively heightened in meaning by the Democratic Party's nomination of William Jennings Bryan belatedly and abruptly changed the dynamics between Populism and its derived form. The fusionists no longer had to win the battle over the Omaha Platform (fortunately for them, as they did not have the strength to win it); they merely had to nominate Bryan and trust him to ignore the platform in the name of "free silver." The intra-party contest in 1896 took place, therefore, less on the level of political heritage where mid-roaders held a commanding position than on the tactical matter of finding a way out of the political cul-de-sac resulting from Taubeneck's long flirtation with the silver lobby. It was here—on a basis of "what else can we do but nominate Bryan?"—that the struggle took place.

4

Early in the convention proceedings, during balloting over credential contests between rival delegations in various states, the strength of mid-road sentiment became evident. The contests culminated in a successful campaign led by "Stump" Ashby of Texas to seat as part of the Illinois delegation a

Chicago socialist contingent affiliated with Eugene Debs and Henry Demarest Lloyd. On such a highly controversial issue as a public endorsement of socialists, the margin of the convention's decision was narrow, 665 to 642, but the mid-roaders were jubilant.[16]

They suffered from a critical shortcoming, however—their continuing absence of "big names." This circumstance, essentially traceable to Democratic frauds that had deprived Populist candidates in the South of election to statehouses and to Congress, became crucial when the convention made ready to fill the important position of permanent chairman. The only mid-road Populist of genuine national reputation was Georgia's Tom Watson who had originally been elected to Congress as an "Alliance Democrat" in 1890 before vote frauds became a way of life in the South. But Watson was not in attendance in St. Louis. The fusionists, on the other hand, could call on both of the party's 1892 standard bearers, James Weaver of Iowa and James Field of Virginia, as well as Simpson, Lease, Allen, and Butler, and, possibly, Waite, Donnelly, and Taubeneck. The fusionists selected Nebraska's William Allen, who, as a Populist Senator, possessed a name familiar to the delegates. The mid-roaders finally settled upon an obscure Maine radical named James E. Campion. Allen won by a vote of 758 to 564. It was no minor defeat for the mid-roaders: with the election of Allen, any part of the nominating process that turned on rulings from the chair passed firmly into the hands of the fusionists.[17]

In his address to the delegates Allen offered two themes that persisted as the substance of fusionist argument throughout the convention: The convention contained delegates "who desire to promulgate a wild platform that will be the subject of ridicule," and Populists calling for a straight third party candidate were "the minions of Wall Street." Concluded Allen: "I do not want them to say to me that the Populists have been advocates of reforms when they could not be accomplished, but when the first ray of light appeared and the people were looking with expectancy and with anxiety for relief, the party was not equal to the occasion; . . . it was stupid; it was blind; it kept in 'the middle of the road' and missed the golden oppor-

William Allen
U.S. Senator from Nebraska and chairman of the People's Party National Convention of 1896.

tunity." Delegates who would advocate such a course, said the Nebraska coalitionist, "are our enemies, not our friends." In view of Allen's unique path to the People's Party, his intuitions about what constituted a "wild platform" were consistent with his entire history as a participant in two-party coalition politics. Reformers who respected the Omaha Platform—that is to say, Populists—were indeed Allen's "enemies," for their ideas aggravated the difficulty of achieving the kind of fusion with Democrats that had gotten Allen elected in the first place. The Nebraska Senator had no understanding of why anyone would oppose a silverite "union of forces," and it was thus quite natural for him to conclude that such deviants were "minions of Wall Street." They helped the goldbugs by insisting on policies that made winning elections much too difficult. William Allen was not a greenbacker.[18]

In whatever form their arguments were crafted, the fusionist leaders would have to fight to achieve the Populist nomination of a Democrat. However much they had done to gerrymander and stack the covention, they were asking a great deal—not only that the delegates water down their basic platform and accept Bryan, but also that they accept as their vice presidential nominee a financier and businessman with known anti-labor proclivities. Bryan continued to maintain an ominous silence on such basic targets of Populist reform as the national banking system and land and railroad monopolies, which was bad enough; Sewall's nomination constituted a positive repudiation of virtually the entire political history of Populism.

On the morning of the convention's third day, mid-roaders circulated through the hall, telling the delegates that Populist capitulation to Sewall was too high a price to pay for fusion. Their efforts were not wasted: in a definite blow to the fusion agenda, the convention voted 738 to 638 to nominate a vice presidential candidate first—a move that mid-roaders confidently expected would place a Populist on the ticket and make it impossible for Bryan to accept the Populist nomination.[19]

Despite herculean efforts, the fusionists also lost the battle on the platform. The task of shepherding the platform committee through a wholesale ideological retreat from the party's basic principles was entrusted to James Weaver. Though he had some minor successes, he failed on all the principal issues. He did sidetrack mid-road attempts to broaden the platform by adopting woman suffrage and advocating specific programs for government hiring of the unemployed on public works projects. In other ways, however, the platform was broadened. The recommendation of the Farmers Alliance convention for direct legislation by initiative and referendum was added to it. The new document also added some new language specifying the employment of "idle labor" in times of depression on public works "as far as practical." Most important of all, the essential monetary planks of the greenback heritage were all reaffirmed: the abolition of the national banking system and national bank notes; the substitution of "a national money, safe and sound, issued by the general Government only, without the intervention of banks of issue, to be a full legal tender for all debts, public and private"; per capita circulation sufficient to meet the demands of commerce and population growth; free coinage of silver, and the establishment of postal savings banks to reduce the commercial power of private banks and to provide an alternative means for small mortgage loans to the people. The need for government ownership of the means of transportation and communication was also reaffirmed, as were the land planks derived from the Alliance experience and codified in the original Omaha document. Thus, on the great triumvirate of Populist issues—land, finance, and transportation—the tenets of the Omaha Platform were reincorporated in the new "St. Louis Platform." [20]

5

Newspaper reporters were at a loss to locate the prevailing balance of power in the Populist convention. The first day had gone to the mid-roaders with the seating of the Chicago socialist contingent, the second to the fusionists with the election of Allen, and the third again to the mid-roaders with the crucial decisions on the platform and the order of nomination to the vice presidency. For some journalists, the outcome confirmed what they had always suspected—Populists were an unstable lot. Actually, however, a clear pattern persisted; there was a "sense of the convention." On issues where fusionist "big names" were placed in nomination against unknown mid-roaders, fusionists prevailed, as in the election of Allen; where fusionist "big names" contested basic greenback tenets of Populism, the fusionists were defeated, as when Weaver lost the platform fight; when the candidacy of Bryan was counterpointed against the preservation of the People's Party, the fusionists again lost, as in the decision to nominate the vice presidential candidate first. But with all this, a decisive number of delegates—centered in the over-represented states of the East and upper Midwest, where the third party was weak—felt that the various forces in the nation arrayed against "the gold power" should not be divided." Since the Democrats had named Bryan, clearly an "anti-gold" candidate, they felt the Populists should follow suit—as long as such an act would not destroy the People's party. The difficulty of the fusionist position lay in this latter qualification, for the circumstances essential to the preservation of a Populist presence were unacceptable to the Democratic Party. This soon became clear to all.

After the Populists had decided to nominate a vice presidential candidate first, the principle Democratic representative at the convention, Senator James K. Jones of Arkansas, the party's national chairman, wired Bryan of the need for him to state his position to the convention should it select anyone but Sewall for the vice presidency. Bryan forthwith telegraphed a reply to Jones: he said that he could not accept the Populist presidential nomination unless Sewall was his running mate. Jones, overestimating fusionist strength in the convention, thereupon began showing the reply to delegates in the expectation that such information would ensure the nomination of Sewall.[21]

But the very presence of Sewall on the Bryan ticket was the reason for the convention's decision to clarify the Populist vice presidential nomination first. At issue was the simple preservation of a Populist presence nationally. Acceptance of the conservative, hard money Eastern banker was simply too abject a surrender of Populism. Despite Jones's efforts, and despite frenzied organizing attempts by die-hard fusionists centered in the Nebraska and Kansas delegations, Sewall lost heavily to Georgia's Tom Watson, the candidate of the mid-roaders. Notified of his nomination as the Populist vice presidential candidate, Watson, in the belief that Sewall was to be withdrawn by the Democrats, telegraphed his acceptance from Georgia.[22]

Victorious on all crucial issues concerning the platform and the vice presidential nomination, the mid-roaders retired from the third day of deliberations with renewed hope. The Populist delegates awoke the next morning to find Bryan's reply to Jones spread across the pages of the St. Louis newspapers. The Democratic nominee was explicit: Jones was to "withdraw my name if Sewall is not nominated." Each session of the Populist convention had been awash in rumors, and the substance of the Bryan telegram had been communicated to scores of delegates the day before in the course of the Sewall-Watson contest. But seeing Bryan's stark reply in the newspapers lifted the subject out of the category of rumor. They could not have Bryan if they did not take Sewall, and they had not taken Sewall. The delegates may have preserved their party's identity, but now, on the morning of the fourth day of their convention, they had to nominate a candidate for President. What were they to do? [23]

6

As the delegates gathered on the final day, the convention hall filled with a new rash of rumors. The Democratic representatives at the convention were known to have wired Bryan for clarification now that Watson had actually been nominated. New answers were being awaited, or had been received, or would be announced shortly. Mid-roaders wired to inquire if Bryan had formally withdrawn his name, or if he had officially notified the convention of such a course. Democrat Jones and Populist Allen issued cautious statements that revealed nothing and stirred a new tide of rumors. Meanwhile, nominations for President on the ticket of the People's Party were in order.

General Weaver, the 1892 Populist standard-bearer and now a much embattled fusionist, arose to deliver the nominating address for Bryan. In a speech that was adroitly vague on essential issues, Weaver confronted the immediate problem of Bryan's availability by making no direct reference to the telegram, addressing instead the political implications emanating from the unavoidable fact that the morning newspapers had carried its contents. Weaver told the convention that he regarded Bryan's message as "a manly dispatch." "No man could have done less," he said, "and remain a man." He added that "the question has reached a point whether neither Mr. Bryan nor his personal friends have any right whatever to say what the action of this convention shall be. This is a greater question than the personality of its candidates." Whatever this meant, it assuaged few of the delegates' qualms, though it did serve the tactically decisive function of preventing a complete collapse of the fusion plan. The delegates might be uneasy, but they had little choice as long as the route to the nomination of Bryan remained open to the fusionist managers. Bryan could not be prevented from receiving the nomination—if only his name could logically be *placed* in nomination. The politics of the convention came to hinge on this point. Mid-road strategy, therefore, turned on maintaining circumstances that would prevent Bryan from being nominated, while fusion strategy focused on avoiding just such circumstances. Bryan's telegram in effect meant tactical victory for the mid-roaders; Allen, as convention chairman, attempted to outflank the mid-roaders by blandly denying he had received any such telegram.[24]

The delegates grew increasingly restless, and the mid-roaders more vocal. At the conclusion of Weaver's nominating speech, fusionists began marching in demonstration for their candidate. As the procession neared a sprawling mid-road banner which had been erected in the midst of the large Texas delegation—seated, appropriately, on the extreme left of the hall—the fusionists attempted to include the Texas banner in the Bryan procession, and a struggle ensued. Mid-roaders sequestered the Texas and Arkansas standards near their mid-road banner, "around which," according to the St. Louis *Post-Dispatch,* "the radicals formed a hollow square. . . ." A number of the older Texans were crying, and one of them, paraphrasing Bryan's "Cross of Gold" speech, shouted, "we will not crucify the People's Party on the cross of the Democracy!" Mid-roaders from a number of state delegations made their way across the convention hall to gather around the mid-road standard. For tense moments, the two wings of the party confronted one another physically. Fights broke out. "It was a howling mob," decided the *Post-Dispatch.* That newspaper was unsympathetic, but the substance of its report was scarcely exaggerated. Toward the end, the chairman of the Texas delegation, Ashby, somehow got to the convention podium and, in a pointed sally, announced that "Texas was ready to endorse Bryan if Bryan would endorse the platform adopted." The remark brought forth a new surge of contention and applause. The suggestion was "not well received" by fusionists, who were suddenly worried by the volatile mood of the convention. The nomination of Bryan would be assured if the convention could somehow be kept under control, but that prospect seemed increasingly uncertain. The roll call needed to be speeded up and the proceedings brought to a close.

As fast as fusionist managers could achieve it, the Bryan demonstration was quieted. The fusionists attempted to regain momentum by mobilizing an impressive array of Populist luminaries for short speeches seconding Bryan's nomination. Jerry Simpson and Mary Lease spoke for Kansas, Davis Waite for Colorado, and Reuben Kolb for Alabama. Herman Taubeneck was called upon, and dutifully responded, thus endorsing a result he had belatedly worked to avoid. So, after much hesitation, did Ignatius Donnelly, the old greenbacker. When they had finished, Chairman Allen promptly recognized Weaver's 1892 vice presidential running mate, James Field of Virginia, for a motion from the floor. In a step that caught mid-roaders by surprise, Field moved that the rules be suspended so that nominations could cease. The action had the merit of providing a means of overcoming the excess of democracy in the Populist convention by permitting Bryan's nomination to be achieved not only speedily, but by voice vote. Allen quickly called for a voice vote on the Field proposal and declared that the motion to suspend the rules had carried.

The convention erupted in pandemonium. Milford Howard, the Populist Congressman from Alabama, forced his way through protecting fusionists, creating a wild disturbance in the rear of the rostrum, even as the entire 103-man Texas delegation stormed to the very edge of Allen's podium. The Nebraskan hesitated, aware, perhaps, that a raw power play from the chair might endanger its occupant. He decided to let the roll call continue. Robert Schilling of Wisconsin tried to get a recess until Bryan could be heard from, but he was ignored by Allen and howled down by anxious fusionists, now visibly alarmed by the sudden threat of a mass rebellion from below. The roll call proceeded, but when Colorado's name was called the chairman of that state's delegation suddenly cast forty-five votes for the Field motion to nominate Bryan by acclamation. Hundreds of delegates stood on chairs and demanded recognition as Allen, gaveling for order, magisterially prepared once again for a voice vote that would settle the matter once and for all. "The question," he announced, "is on the motion to suspend the rules and nominate Mr. Bryan by acclamation."

"By God, we won't stand it," shouted a delegate from Washington.

"Doesn't it require a two-thirds vote to carry that motion?" screamed an irate Arkansas Populist.

Allen replied that it did not.

A Californian shouted that such a proceeding was unprecedented. "The quintessence of Populism," he said, "is fair play."

Allen then announced that when the roll was called, delegates could vote for Bryan or for anyone else. This ruling provoked another storm of protest and, in the words of a fascinated reporter, "only confounded the confusion." Fights broke out in the Missouri and Indiana delegations. Angry protests from the California contingent kept the right side of the hall in turmoil, while at the opposite side of the building the Arkansas and Texas delegations alternated between loud shouting and hurried conferences. A Georgia Populist kept shouting slogans of protest from the back row, and Milford Howard and an accompanying platoon of Alabamians stormed around the podium, carrying on a conversation with Allen at the top of their lungs. The convention hovered on the edge of a riot. Finally, "as the only way of restoring order," General Field withdrew his motion, and Allen permitted the roll call of states to proceed. Populists were to be permitted to nominate a candidate.[25]

The decisive point was not that such a candidate could, under the circumstances, defeat Bryan, but rather that the mechanics of the balloting process took time. Delay endangered the success of the fusionist requirement to suppress details of Bryan's attitude toward the Populist platform and toward the candidacy of Watson.

Ironically, the shaky position of Chairman Allen was almost demolished by Democratic representatives of William Jennings Bryan. Bryan's message to the convention had been addressed not only to Democratic Senator Jones, but also to Populist Chairman Allen. Bryan sent Allen precisely the information he had dispatched to Jones: "I shall not be a can-

Thomas Patterson
Publisher of the *Rocky Mountain News* and prominent Colorado silver advocate, Patterson failed in his attempt to induce Senator Allen to acknowledge receipt of William Jennings Bryan's telegram declining the Populist nomination.

didate before the Populist convention unless Sewall is nominated." Jones, together with two other fusionist representatives, Democratic Governor Stone of Missouri and Thomas Patterson of Colorado, were fully aware that Allen had Bryan's telegram in his possession at the moment the Populist Senator had made his first denials to the mid-roaders. Both Patterson and Stone grew visibly uneasy at the deception being practiced by Allen. (For his part, Jones had practiced a bit of deception himself, announcing to the press on one day that Bryan would withdraw unless Sewall were nominated, then denying the statement the next day, after Sewall's defeat.) Apparently feeling that their own personal ethics were impeached by Allen's conduct, Stone and Patterson implored the Populist Senator to be candid to his own delegates. Allen refused, for the plain reason that candor would have been fatal to the fusionist cause. When the Democratic onlookers finally insisted on disclosure, Allen continued his public denials and privately took refuge in demagoguery: "the Populist convention," he said to them, "will not to be run by Democrats!" That Allen's own purpose was to implement Democratic fusion strategy, while Patterson and Stone also wished to do so, but on a somewhat more honorable basis, underscored Allen's ethical bankruptcy. As a man who had once confided that "a political party has no charms for me," the spokesman for the shadow movement in Nebraska thus made explicit his determination to deceive the People's Party into a nomination of Bryan, even at the cost of destroying the party's separate identity in American politics.[26]

In a last desperate expedient, fusionists attempted to calm delegate fears about the party's loss of autonomy by circulating rumors that Sewall had agreed to remove himself from the joint Populist-Democratic ticket so that Georgia's Tom Watson could be Bryan's running mate. The departure of Sewall would have preserved a measure of the structural integrity of the third party organization, and the rumor had great influence with wavering delegates. But it was not true.[27]

As fusion planners anxiously tried to quiet wavering delegates by recourse both to silence and to helpful speculations, Ashby of the Texas delegation renewed his efforts to force Allen to acknowledge the contents of Bryan's telegram. The question, "Have you or have you not received a telegram?" had the effect of rekindling the delegates' doubts. Many Populists, reluctantly pro-Bryan, debated urgently with one another as to whether the party organization could survive a campaign such as seemed in the process of being organized.[28]

The mid-roaders, unable to find a "name" candidate after Eugene Debs decided to decline their presidential offer and Ignatius Donnelly, wavering to the last instant, was unable to win the full support of his own Minnesota delegation, settled upon an old-time Chicago greenbacker and reform editor named S. F. Norton. The relatively obscure Norton stirred little enthusiasm, even among those delegates desperately searching for a solution that was both honorable and practical. The Texans, now frantic in their effort to puncture one final and decisive hole in a leaking ship of fusion that appeared to be making port while sinking, caucaused to discuss plans to bolt the convention if the Bryan effort were to prove successful. This threat has some power, for it was certain to generate post-convention publicity that would cast doubt over the propriety and, perhaps, the integrity of the entire proceedings.

The Texans debated whether they should bolt the convention or remain and make one last effort to sidetrack the Bryan steamroller. Which would be more effective? They finally decided on the latter course. Ashby and others renewed the public interrogation of Allen. Fusionists sighed: if only the Texans could somehow be induced to give up the struggle, the Populist convention could end in peace.[29]

But the Texans had too many memories. Even a casual review of the names included in that state's delegation explained the emotional intensity that manifested itself in angry shouts of denunciation, in tears, and, eventually, in total alienation from those they felt were burying the years of labor for reform. Among them were S. O. Daws, who had found a way to instill new life in a group of frontier farmers in 1884; J. A. Perdue, who had written the Cleburne Demands in 1886; R. M. Humphrey, who had founded the Colored National Alliance in 1886; J. B. "Buck" Barry, who had plucked North Carolina farmers "like ripe fruit" in the organizing campaign of 1887; W. E. Farmer, who had helped lead the Great Southwest Strike and had emerged from that struggle a political radical; Jerome Kearby, who had defended the strike leaders in court; Sam Evans, who had helped form the Union Labor Party and had been offered its vice presidential nomination in 1888; Harry Tracy, who had invited bankruptcy by trying to keep the *Southern Mercury* afloat; R. J. Sledge, who had poured his modest savings into the *National Economist;* Evan Jones; John Rayner; and William Lamb. Whatever happened, they could not accept fusion with silver Democrats: as they knew only too well, Jim Hogg, their old nemesis, was a close political ally of William Jennings Bryan!

Three times during the long roll call that followed, Ashby—his own voice augmented by the organized shouts of his delegation—halted the balloting by formally inquiring of the convention chairman if he had received a communication from Bryan. Each time, Allen denied that he had. The Texans, though powerless to do anything about it, did not believe him. Nor were they alone; many delegates, anxious for days, remained deeply uneasy. Groups of mid-roaders from around the hall left their delegations and gathered around the Texas standard. The men of Populism and of its shadow movement glared at each other, both sides visibly troubled. No one wanted to destroy the People's Party. They merely wanted to nominate Bryan with honor, if a way to do so could be found. The mid-roaders, if they did not prove that party suicide was the price of a Bryan nomination, at least stirred numbing doubts in most delegates. The roll call droned on toward its conclusion in an atmosphere muted by irresolution. Finally, Senator Allen announced that the People's Party had nominated the Democratic Party's standard-bearer, William Jennings Bryan, as its own candidate for President.[30]

It no longer made any difference what Bryan thought of the Populist platform; it no longer mattered whether he would accept Tom Watson as a running mate. He was nominated. In a convention wracked by chaos and haltingly stabilized only by the disingenuous statements of the convention chairman representing the shadow movement in Nebraska, the strategy of the silverites had prevailed.

The convention was quickly adjourned. Knots of mid-roaders gathered in an effort to discover a course of action that would save the Populist cause. They discussed the few options remaining open to them and made a few desperate plans. Then, disheartened and defeated, they left the hall.[31]

The Populist agenda of reform embedded in the Omaha Platform had shrunk to the candidacy of a Democrat named Bryan. The cause of free silver was intact. The agrarian revolt was over.

CHAPTER XVI

The Collapse of Populist Morale

"Now we are all at sea. . . ."

Though political movements, like armies, die slowly, a soldier at a time, in skirmishes, battles and campaigns, the terminal moment really comes before the field of conflict is completely surrendered, and is signaled by the loss of faith of the individual rank-and-file recruit. While generals call this phenomenon "declining morale," and reformers of various stripes refer to it as "failure of commitment," it actually encompasses a human emotion that is both more elemental and more precise: a loss of personal participation in a shared hope. Others in the ranks may continue to nurse the hope, and it may thus linger a while longer in those who are so desperate, or so romantic, or so innocent that they do not see the steady desertions of individuals that presage the death of the group.

In much this fashion, the dream of a great national party of "the industrial millions" vanished from the American scene in the autumn of 1896. Between the decision for fusion at the Populist national convention in July and McKinley's impressive victory in November, the driving energy behind the People's Party quietly died. As Tom Watson interpreted the situa-

493

tion a week after the defeat: "Our Party, as a party, does not exist any more. . . . The sentiment is still there, the votes are still there, but confidence is gone, and the party organization is almost gone." [1]

For the men and women of the reform press, even the "sentiment" was no longer present. Ostracized by the business community, the reform press was kept alive by the faith of its editors and their willingness to work at a level of bare subsistence. When that faith was crushed by fusion, they simply closed their papers. Some editors locked their doors on the day of Bryan's nomination in St. Louis and never published another edition. Others fired one final editorial volley at Weaver, Taubeneck, Butler, and Allen before retiring from the field. Long before William McKinley was inaugurated as the nation's twenty-first President, the 1000-member National Reform Press Association—an institution unique in American history—had, for all practical purposes, ceased to exist. The disappearance of the reform editors signaled the terminal bleeding of the agrarian army. [2]

But the People's Party was too sizable to expire in a moment, or in a single place. Populism had its share of desperate adherents: its radical "old guard," who persisted long after hope had vanished everywhere else; its romantics, men like Clarence Darrow in Chicago, who embraced the silver movement not because they shared the politics of its practitioners, but because they elected to see the Bryan campaign as having permanent symbolic meaning; its wishful-thinkers, men like Taubeneck, Allen, and Butler, who saw the silver issue for what it never had been and could never be—a valid basis for structural reform of the American monetary system. It even had its reluctant enthusiasts, men like Ignatius Donnelly, who knew the ephemerality of the silver issue but got caught up in the drama of another campaign against an old and familiar enemy. For these varied participants, the People's Party died at different moments and at the hands of different conquerors. They could reach agreement only on a more general conclusion: the spring of 1896 was the last time of shared hope and expectation; after the Populist convention at St.

Louis, all was confusion, disappointment, recrimination, and national disintegration.

2

The confusion began immediately. Against Bryan's stated announcement that his name be withdrawn, the People's Party had "fused," but only by saddling the Democratic nominee with an extra vice presidential running mate. For fusion to become politically workable, joint electoral tickets of the two parties would have to be created—a gruesome prospect in the South, given the hostility between Populists and Democrats there. But before this obstacle could be approached, another matter threatened to undo all the desperate work of the fusionists at St. Louis: the very real prospect that Bryan would refuse the nomination. A number of Democrats who knew the circumstances under which Bryan's nomination had been engineered at St. Louis advised the Nebraskan to decline the nomination publicly, even before it was formally proffered. Furthermore, tentative inquiries by fusionists as to the possibility of replacing Sewall with Watson had met with emphatic rebuffs from the Bryan camp. The managers of fusion faced a dilemma. How could they get Sewall off the ticket if they were afraid to notify Bryan officially of his nomination? [3]

The new national chairman of the People's Party, named to replace Taubeneck at St. Louis, was Marion Butler of North Carolina. He was a young man on the threshold of a profound political education. Butler's initial post-convention consultations with the Democratic national chairman, Senator Jones, and with such other of Butler's long-time silverite allies as Nevada's Senator William Stewart, provided the North Carolinian with some unwanted and unexpected insights into the underlying politics of the silver lobby. In nominating Bryan the Populists had destroyed their own influence as a separate political entity, and the silverites knew it. The silver men wanted the two million Populist votes; they had no desire to be associated with the People's Party in the process. Now that the Populist fusion leadership had achieved the nomination of Bryan and the Populist rank and file had nowhere else to go, the silver men could get those two million votes without saddling themselves with the Populist image. Silver spokesmen acquainted Butler with these political realities. Nevada's Stewart "gaily announced" that the Democrats would have gunmen stationed along the road to shoot the first Populist who attempted to notify Bryan. Jones, the Arkansas Democrat, bluntly told newsmen that Southern Populists "were not a creditable class" and should "go with the Negroes where they belong." The Democratic chairman added firmly that Sewall would "of course" remain on the ticket and that "Mr. Watson can do what he likes." [4]

It was a somewhat chastened Marion Butler who confronted the task of notifying Bryan of his official nomination by the third party. The young Populist Senator decided to resolve the matter by not notifying the nominees at all. This decision, of course, raised agonizing internal problems within the People's Party's ranks, for it debased the party publicly. After mulling the matter for a full month following the Populist convention, Butler wrote a careful letter to the members of his official Populist notification committee:

> We are situated where we can look over the entire field, and for the good of the party we ask you as a member of the Notification Committee to take no action for the present. The course of wisdom and moderation always proves the best in the end. In due time such action will be taken in this matter as will be satisfactory to all and leave the party in a dignified and honorable position. . . .
>
> Sentiment is now rapidly changing to Watson, not only among Western Populists, but also among Southern Democrats, in a most gratifying way. We should do nothing of doubtful propriety while matters are thus happily shaping themselves in our favor.[5]

Butler's reference to the "gratifying" change in sentiment toward Watson among Western Populists constituted an elliptical public acknowledgment of still another unsettling development—the post-convention refusal of Western fusionists to honor the nomination of the Georgia Populist leader. Indeed, even as Butler wrote his soothing letter, Populists and Democrats in Kansas were putting the final touches on an elaborate agreement in which the leaders of the tiny Democratic party in the state pledged their support to the entire Populist state ticket in exchange for third party support of Bryan and Sewall electors in the presidential contest. Jerry Simpson and his colleagues were to realize their hope of receiving the united support of both parties in their bid to recapture their congressional seats, though they would have to sacrifice Watson and the autonomy of the People's Party in the process. This they found surprisingly easy to do. As Simpson himself had put it in St. Louis, "I care not for party names, it is the substance we are after, and we have it in William Jennings Bryan." Clearly, the loss of his congressional seat had tempered the monetary beliefs of "the rabid fiat greenbacker with communistic proclivities." [6]

Fusion proceeded with ease in Nebraska, of course, as such long-time friends as Allen and Bryan had no essential ideological differences between them. Though the third party in Nebraska outpolled the Democrats four to one in 1894, agreement was speedily reached on a united "Fusion" state and national ticket. Third party candidates received a majority of the places on the state ticket, while, as in Kansas, the Democratic national ticket of Bryan and Sewall was selected to occupy the presidential and vice presidential spaces on the Nebraska ballot. In Colorado, also, exclusive Bryan and Sewall electors were chosen to balance a state ticket comprised of silverites in both parties. Such developments, of course, were hardly in accord with the assurances fusionists had offered anxious Populist delegates on the convention floor weeks earlier in St. Louis. As a result, the national political presence of the People's Party began to disappear with remarkable speed. A corresponding uncertainty spread through the ranks of the third party in state after state.[7]

Mid-roaders were appalled and disheartened by such speedy confirmation of the very results they had feared and predicted. As "fusion" magnified differences between the Populist and Democratic parties in California, a prominent Populist named C. H. Castle could only reflect wryly on the advice he had given to party leaders on the eve of the Populist convention: "indorsement of the democratic ticket . . . would be political hari kari. . . . Look rather to the future effect, than to present success. A victory without practical reform following it will be like the victories of Pyrrhus, barren of result." [8]

Ironically, on the same day this advice was originally offered, J. A. Wayland, the influential editor of *Appeal to Reason,* had calmly pronounced his judgment on place-hunting fusionists within the Kansas third party. "Education is needed more than offices now. When education has done its necessary work, the offices will follow to enforce the wishes of the people. Offices without education will do more harm than good." Prescient though they were, these judgments by reform editors, and by Populists recruited by the mature Alliance movement, could hardly be expected to lift the deep foreboding of the oldest veterans of Alliance-greenbackism. Of those who endured the trauma in 1896, the Populist Old Guard suffered the most. [9]

Few men had labored longer and more centrally for the agrarian cause than the intellectual leader of Arkansas Populism, W. Scott Morgan. Author of one of the official histories of the reform movement, a work grandly entitled *History of the Wheel and Alliance and the Impending Revolution,* Morgan had for more than a decade tended all manner of seedlings in the vineyards of reform. As the original national secretary of the reform press association and editor of its national "ready-print" service for the Populist press, Morgan occupied a position which in many respects was, next to Taubeneck's chairmanship itself, the most crucial in the entire Populist hierarchy. [10]

A week following the Populist convention, Morgan composed an anguished letter to the party's new national chairman in which he confessed he had come home from the convention "much discouraged" and that subsequent developments had "only added to my depression." After reviewing the rejected alternatives at St. Louis, Morgan presented the remaining desperate options:

> The question now arises as what is best to be done? It would please the Bourbons of the South to see the destruction of our party. I think many of them would rather encompass

that object and hold their states intact than to elect Bryan. I fear our brethren of the North first are going to crucify Watson on the altar of their own personal ambitions. You will perhaps remember what I said to you about their purpose during the convention. . . . In Kansas, Nebraska, Colorado, South Dakota and other northwestern states is a wild rush to the hog trough to see who gets the most swill. We are passing through a crucial test. Most of our people are loyal, brave and true, if only they have wise and courageous leadership. The reform press stands ready to hold up the hands of patriotic leadership. God grant that we may have it. We are surrounded by a sea of difficulty. Can we not take the bull by the horns and persuade Mr. Sewall to "rise above party"? . . . [If not,] better by far to choose a man to head the ticket with [Watson] even though we had to suffer four more years of financial despotism, if by doing so we save the iron brigade around which to rally the broken forces now gone wild after false gods. . . ." [11]

In his letter Morgan unconsciously expressed the intellectual agony thrust upon American Populism by the machinations of Taubeneck, Allen, and the silver lobby. If the organizers of Populism, the "iron brigade" in Morgan's emotional but apt phrase, were in such despair, how long could such newly appointed agrarian captains as Marion Butler keep the legions of rank-and-file Populist voters moving in the direction of reform? Indeed, even to party leaders, the proper direction was itself no longer clear. [12]

As a prestigious spokesman of the reform press association, Morgan, of course, had credentials that gave special import to his analysis. But from the most remote latitudes of rural America the party's new national chairman received dozens of other letters echoing Morgan's fears. The deferential message of one rank-and-file Populist correspondent, a farmer from Alabama, touched upon most of the themes that suffused Butler's troubled correspondence. The poignancy of the farmer's plea was, if anything, heightened by the fact that he did not know that the man he was writing to had been one of the national architects of fusion. The farmer's anxiety dated back to Taubeneck's early, pre-convention maneuvers with the silver lobby: "since the first announcement of the date of the national convention of our party, lurking fear took hold upon my mind that something in the nature of what has taken place would . . . destroy us as a party and give to others the . . . fruit of years of thought, hard toil and self-sacrifice." The heart of the letter was an unendurable irony: the two old parties had "by the most needless disregard for the interest of the people, brought oppression and distress to the country and shamefully neglected and abused every opportunity for relief" until the people, "rising in the majesty of their rights," had brought reform within their grasp. "And lo, one of their ancient enemies and oppressors . . . deploying our leaders, captured our forces, [and] took charge of our munitions of warfare." The letter betrayed a crisis of morale. "Even now, the unscrupulous, arrogant and intolerant democracy are beginning to taunt us in humiliating terms with our return as misguided weaklings to the fold." The farmer's solution was one earnestly coveted by thousands of Populists who found themselves ridiculed in their homeland by Democrats who had defrauded them of elections: "the expedient and manliest way out is for those in control to call at once a convention and place a regular Populist ticket in the field and go to work for it. We may not win, having already lost ground, but we'll maintain our identity and independence and be prepared for future usefulness." [13]

The disarray he described in Alabama was corroborated by letters to the Populist national chairman from every Southern state, including Butler's own North Carolina. Democratic fraud having been newly supplemented by taunts, the catalogue of woe did not come only from such veterans as W. Scott Morgan and from rank-and-file Populists. It also came from the official leadership of the movement. John Buchanan, the former Alliance Governor and Tennessee third party chairman, reported the status of Populist-Democratic cooperation by informing Butler that "all negotiations are declared off" and confessed "considerable trouble" in terms of organizing a coherent campaign. Louisiana party leaders reported "we are in a dilemma here," as did the third party hierarchy in Kentucky. Florida Populists were "discouraged and demoralized" and—even more ominously—passed along the information that "we have lost apparently almost our entire later converts, those made during the interval since the last campaign." The death cries of Southern Populism literally rattled through the pages of incoming mail to the party's national chairman.[14]

But though "fusion" was a special emotional burden for Populists in the South, third party men in every region found themselves adrift in the bewildering political climate. The state chairman of the Colorado Farmers Alliance insisted that Sewall be taken off the ticket. "Our people have been fooled so many times that they are determined that they will not be fooled again." The national lecturer of the Alliance and former third party candidate for the governorship of Kansas, J. F. Willits, reported that the fusionists who had dumped Watson from the Kansas ticket were engaged in "wholesale slaughter of the party." Willits notified Butler of the existence of some Populists "who will not be delivered over in this disgraceful manner." To the Kansas Alliance leader, the entire issue came down to a fact and a question: "We have no Populist electors in Kansas. What are we to do about it?" [15]

Discontent broke out in Iowa when the Populists there found the assurances given to delegates by the fusion planners at St. Louis being disproved by events. An Iowa party leader complained that members of his delegation had voted for Bryan "on the assurance that he would accept and on the probability that Sewall would withdraw. Now we are all at sea." The Iowan "did not endorse" the Butler plan of non-notification of the party's candidates. "Our self respect and the perpetuity of our party demands that he be notified at once." [16]

The complaints sent up from the Populist ranks to the party's national chairman contained a central theme: the threatened destruction of the People's Party. Specific grievances about the non-notification of candidates, the collapse of fusion electoral tickets, and the plight of Thomas Watson all were functions of the larger fear that concerned the life of the party itself. "We are all at sea" was the recurring phrase—it appeared in correspondence from a half-dozen states in both the South and West. John Dore, a leader of California Populism, confessed his bewilderment: "So many things have oc-

Davis H. Waite
Populist Governor of Colorado.
Though a committed greenbacker,
Waite wavered at a critical moment
in 1896. He renounced the fusion
ticket in the fall campaign.

curred, so many unexpected, too, since we left St. Louis. It still
seems we are nearly as much at sea as at the close of the convention. I came home believing that Mr. Sewell would be
taken down and Mr. Watson put in his place and that we
would be recognized and treated at least with civility and ordinary courtesy. . . . In all this I have been disappointed." [17]

From the Midwest L. H. "Calamity" Weller, the old greenback Congressman, informed Butler that the price of Sewall
was "the absolute disintegration and destruction of the People's Party organization." Milford Howard, the Populist Congressman from Alabama who served as a member of the
party's notification committee, responded bluntly to Butler's
plan of non-notification: "For a great party with almost two
million votes, we occupy a most humiliating attitude as we bow
the knee before the Democratic throne. I think that we are
treating Mr. Watson wrong and . . . I feel inclined to join in
some sort of movement to relieve ourselves of our present
humiliating attitude. . . . We are all at sea, not knowing
whether our presidential candidate will accept, afraid to
breathe for fear he will not." And from Louisiana J. A. Tetts
reported the consequences of the prevailing mood of doubt:

"The trouble we are going to have is in getting our Populists to go to the polls where they see no hope for Watson." [18]

3

If fusion vastly complicated the life of the party's national chairman, it put unbearable pressure on its vice presidential candidate. The personal relationship of the two Southern Populist captains shattered under the conflicting demands of their respective duties. The tension between them was heightened by their vastly differing personal styles.

Mercurial in temperament and capable at times of an almost evangelical righteousness, Tom Watson also possessed a sober understanding of how power functioned and creative intuitions about how a reform movement had to be mobilized. As a scion of landed wealth and inheritor of the Jeffersonian tradition that sometimes accompanied that circumstance in the South, Watson possessed both Cavalier concepts of honor and Leveller instincts for the folk. Though the Alliance founders in Texas had done much to bring the cooperative movement to the nation's agricultural districts and the ideology of greenbackism to the American South, no single man had served so successfully and so persistently as spokesman, party organizer, political tactician, reform propagandist, candidate, and symbol of Populism as Georgia's Tom Watson.

People loved him, or feared him, or hated him, but he had his own visions, and few, if any, intimate friends. The brazen vote frauds employed by conservative Democrats to twice deny him his seat in Congress stirred some dark human longing in him. He wanted to be honored by the leading members of American society and he wanted at the same moment to achieve vast changes in that society. He was a complex man.[19]

Marion Butler came from less favored circumstances. He worked his way through the University of North Carolina and cultivated friends who, like himself, tended to be business-minded, "forward-looking," and provincially urbane, a political type rather more in evidence in the Progressive era than during the Populist revolt. Though he, too, wrestled with the social contradictions of wealth and poverty, Butler was not an original thinker inclined to question inherited cultural values

Marion Butler
U.S. Senator from North Carolina
and successor to Herman Taubeneck as the Populist national chairman. Butler presided over the disintegration of the third party during
the 1896 presidential campaign.

or to ponder the broader prerequisites of social change. A handsome man, he was courteous, ambitious, phlegmatic, and conciliatory, attributes which served him admirably as a tactician of coalition politics.[20]

Politically, the two men had little in common. Watson had announced his distrust of Herman Taubeneck as early as December 1892, while Butler began working intimately with the fusionist spokesman in 1893. Watson was a relatively sophisticated greenbacker, while Butler did not, and perhaps could not, write or speak coherently on the money question. Watson had derided the silver crusade as a shallow panacea, "a mere drop in the bucket to what we must have if we are ever to save our people from financial ruin"; Butler, in contrast, attempted to erect a "nonpartisan" coalition in North Carolina around the very issue of free silver. Butler cooperated with Republicans on the state level and Democrats on the national level, while Watson advised his Georgia delegation to go to St. Louis and "fight it straight, boys." Cold political realities underlay these differing postures. Watson found it easier to fight his Populist battles "straight" because his regional politics rested upon a large and growing Populist movement that counted almost half of Georgia's voters, even on the basis of fraudulent returns; Butler, burdened by the massive schism within the North Carolina Alliance, had attempted to gain political relevance by forming a legislative coalition with Republicans in state politics and a tactical coalition with silver Democrats in Washington. The two men saw the options open to the third party in 1896 in fundamentally different terms.[21]

In his inaugural campaign speech in Atlanta early in August, Watson began actively pressuring the Democratic Party to remove Sewall from the ticket: "You cannot fight the national banks with any sincerity with a national banker as your leader." Butler reacted negatively to the speech, not because he wanted Sewall to remain, but because he had been intimidated and out-maneuvered by the Demoratic national chairman and by the silver lobby and, as a result, had lost a sense of his own prerogatives and those of the party he headed. Butler's course—to "do nothing of doubtful propriety while matters are happily shaping themselves in our favor"— was more than a passive form of whistling in the dark; it betrayed a fatal lack of political self-confidence.[22]

In one month's time, the practicalities of fusion had imposed upon the fusion leadership a steady and accelerating retreat. The Populist national committee, Butler now acknowledged, would not even insist on straight Bryan-Watson tickets by each state Populist Party. In fusion states, the recognition of Watson would be achieved not by the presence of his name, but "by a just and equitable division of electors." The People's Party thus officially acquiesced in Populist support for Sewall rather than Watson. The mid-road "victory" in nominating Watson had thus been circumvented. Meanwhile, Butler offered a public explanation of the continuing non-notification of the Populist nominees. The party, he said, had not notified Weaver and Field in 1892 because it was the "mission of the Populists to depart from many of the useless practices and customs followed by the old parties." [23]

This was all too much for Tom Watson. He fired off a letter to Butler, correcting him on his statement about the 1892 candidates (they had been notified) and reminding him of what political observers throughout the nation already knew—that the People's Party had publicly acknowledged "it fears to notify Mr. Bryan, lest he should repudiate the nomination." Said Watson, "Every one of these 'fusions' stultifies the Populist who votes the fusion ticket." The storm of complaints from Watson, Howard, and literally scores of other leading Populists protesting the notification delay elicited from Butler only the bland reply that it was "very probable" that the candidates would be notified in "due time." Watson thereupon took a remarkable step that betrayed the extent of his mistrust of fusion leaders. In interviews with the New York press, he attacked them publicly.

> If the National Convention at St Louis did not mean that Messrs. Bryan and Watson should be notified, why was a committee appointed to notify them? Why does Senator Allen, the chairman of the Committee, refuse to do what the convention instructed him to do? Is he afraid Mr. Bryan will repudiate our support? If so, our party has a right to know that fact. If Mr. Bryan is ashamed of the votes which are necessary to elect him, we ought to know it.[24]

By the standards of any self-respecting political party, these observations were eminently reasonable. They also were judged by the Republican press of the East to be highly newsworthy, as the intra-party quarrel among Populists had the effect of complicating Bryan's position as well. Though Butler was dismayed by the "exhibitions through the press" that Watson had created, the party chairman informed a Watson intimate that he did not yet see any merit in notification and added, in a curious statement, that he was "inclined to have nothing further to do with it." [25]

In every region of the nation, reform editors wrung their hands not only over the humiliating notification issue, but also over the multiplying confusions of joint electoral tickets. As might have been expected, the *Southern Mercury* assembled a truly imposing list of suggestions topped by a call for an authentic Populist ticket "even at this stage of the game." That sentiment was now held by increasing thousands of Populists.[26]

One month after the Populist convention, it was unclear

whether the immobilization of the third party's national chairman was a product of his own declining autonomy and will or a simple verification of the relative powerlessness that had descended upon every echelon of the party as a result of fusion. Matters had proceeded to the point that Butler could do nothing about the Sewall-Watson impasse, beyond that which Watson himself was doing—using the public press to put pressure upon the Bryan Democracy. Because of the new balance of power between the two parties that had been created by the circumstances of fusion in St. Louis, the real decision on notification was up to the Democrats. On the more important issues still unresolved, Butler could only continue to be what he had in fact already become, a mere supplicant of his silver allies in the Democratic Party. Populism had lost the one continuing ingredient essential to any political institution—a sense of control over its own destiny.

The Democrats, it developed, were definitely affected by Watson's public pressure, which forcefully applied the sole remaining bargaining lever the People's Party had—the massive bloc of two million votes that had been the fruit of the long years of agrarian protest. The ink had hardly dried on the widespread newspaper publicity attending Watson's public protest before the Democratic leaders suddenly expressed interest in conferring with their Populist counterparts. In a meeting in Washington, Democrat Jones speedily agreed with Butler on a plan whereby Bryan's old associate, William Allen, would notify the Democratic nominee while Butler would compose a letter of notification to the uncontrollable Watson. On September 14 the documents were dispatched and their contents released to the press. With studied casualness, Bryan delayed for two weeks and then accepted on October 3 in a letter that emphasized his fidelity to the decidedly non-Populist platform adopted by the Democratic Party in Chicago. Under the altered power relationships between the two parties, this denouement surprised no one, though it did reveal the irrelevance of another major mid-road victory at the Populist convention—namely, the successful defense of the doctrines of the Omaha Platform. Under such decisive limitations, the Democrats thus permitted the Populists to have public acknowledgment of the two-party association in the nomination of the Democratic presidential candidate. Whatever Herman Taubeneck may have thought, the silver lobby had never been interested in Populism, and the principles of the third party were to have no bearing on the crusade for silver. As "the Battle of the Standards" began to move into high gear, the Populist presence in American politics had all but vanished.[27]

4

Watson, nevertheless, was not wholly isolated. All political movements that are informed with a central passion produce a core of true believers. The true believers of the agrarian revolt were its founders. The 1896 convention of the Texas People's Party at Galveston, held three weeks after the debacle in St. Louis, exhibited a strange combination of reaffirmed radicalism and provincial romanticism. Over 1000 delegates representing the organizational heart of the old Alliance lecturing system cheered their 103 representatives who had "stood squarely by the Omaha platform." Again and again, delegates, reform editors, and lecturers recalled the early Alliance days when the strategy they had followed had uncontestably been their own, as if the exercise would somehow restore the hopes that had flowered in "the morning sunlight of labor's freedom." The *Southern Mercury* set the tone of the proceedings in its last issue before the convention. "The reform movement is a child of Texas," said editor Milton Park, "and the Texans stood by the youth at the St. Louis convention." The year 1884, when the Alliance burst from its frontier base and began its sweep across Texas, was a favorite object of reflection. "Stump" Ashby recalled the emergence of radicalism in Fort Worth "when they laughed at the young preacher." Musing on his long years of agitation, he added, "I am not a politician and never have been. I have always made my way with the one-gallused poor of this country." The shadow of the Christian socialist, Tom Nugent, dead some eight months, also hung over the convention. Ashby remembered, "The last words he ever spoke to me were, 'Stand firm for the principles of Populism and turn neither to the right nor left. You will win at last.' "[28]

The uses of nostalgia have their political limits, and in one final assertion of the energy that had informed their crusade for more than a decade, the Populist delegates decided to go before the electorate of Texas with two symbols of Alliance radicalism heading the ticket. For their gubernatorial nominee they chose Jerome Kearby, the gifted Dallas lawyer who had defended the leaders of the Great Southwest Strike in the 1886 trials and who had been elected as a Populist Congressman in 1894 only to have the election stolen from him. For Lieutenant Governor they picked "Stump" Ashby. As if to prove their point to the fusionist "trimmers," the Texans held aloft the full Populist platform throughout the campaign and attracted enormous crowds to third party rallies. One of the first of these, held early in September, created national attention as the result of an almost predictable development: out of their deep frustration, the most embattled elements of the surviving Populist presence in America coalesced when Tom Watson accepted the invitation of the Alliance founders to open the autumn campaign of Texas Populism.[29]

Though Marion Butler, understandably, had cooled to the idea of a highly visible Watsonian presence in the fall campaign, the Georgian nevertheless embarked on a trip to Texas and Kansas early in September. The political atmosphere Watson found in Texas was hardly conducive to the kind of "patience and moderation" for which Butler had labored. A Watson intimate reported to Butler from Dallas that "Texas we find ripe for revolt. . . . The Pops are solid here against Bryan and Sewall." Indeed, a substantial number of the Texas third party leaders regarded the Bryan candidacy as a positive evil. Not only were they concerned that Populist support of Bryan would destroy the identity of the third party, but they also believed that the campaign's emphasis on free silver would undermine the basic monetary reforms of Populism. The Texans were so disturbed that they seriously considered the endorsement of McKinley as the "least of evils" in the 1896 campaign. When black Republican leaders in Texas offered to support the Populist state ticket in return for third party support of the Republican presidential ticket, the Texas mid-roaders took the matter under close advisement. Rumors of these discussions were in the air when Watson arrived in the state. Little that Watson saw or heard in Dallas was calculated to ease his sense of personal humiliation. Watson responded warmly to the convivial Populist environment. "You must burn the bridges if you follow me," he asserted. To wild cheering, he announced his belief in "Straight Populism," for he did "not propose to be carried to one side of the road or the other." The campaign, he added, was "a movement of the masses. Let Bryan speak for the masses and let Watson speak for the masses and let Sewall talk for the banks and the railroads." Sewall was "a wart on the party. He is a knot on a log. He is a dead weight on the ticket." For good measure, Watson brought Butler and the national fusion leadership of the third party into his line of fire. The Texans, who shared most of these opinions and had a few others of their own, roared their approval.[30]

So did the Republican press of the country. *The New York Times* and the Chicago *Tribune* provided careful coverage of Watson's Texas address. Fully aware of the opportunity for mischief-making implicit in the Populist-Democratic imbroglio, Republican editorialists viewed Watson's humiliating plight with great sympathy, found him far more "forthright" than Sewall, and altogether a man badly served by his party's national chairman and by his supposed Democratic allies.[31]

If Watson's address added immeasurably to the burdens of Marion Butler, the rumors of a Populist-Republican deal for McKinley horrified the party chairman. Truly, the young North Carolina Senator was a man beset on all sides: the Democrats rebuffed him on the Sewall matter, the Kansans were sabotaging what remained of his national efforts for joint electoral tickets across the country, a hundred Populist editors found fault with his every move, Watson was giving excessively candid interviews to the New York press and making inflammatory speeches in the West, and the Texans were apparently trying to undermine Bryan and the entire silver crusade. Virtually every letter he opened, from any part of the nation and from Populists of every rank and station in the party, added something new to his burdens. He alone, in the center of his party but also in the center of the maelstrom of fusion, was forced to bear the brunt of his party's accelerating collapse. Summoning up his strongest personal trait—patience—Butler composed an adroit letter to Watson.

> Allow me to suggest that you be careful to say nothing . . . which can be construed either directly or indirectly as a threat that Bryan shall be defeated and McKinley elected if the Democratic managers should fail to take down Sewall. It would put us in a false light, and besides, put us on the defensive. . . . I beg you in the interests of our party, and in the interest of suffering humanity, to consider well these matters, and have them in view with every public utterance that you make.[32]

5

But while this diplomatic admonition was still in the mails Tom Watson's itinerary took him to Kansas. There the Populist vice presidential candidate walked into Populist state headquarters under streaming banners that proclaimed, "Bryan and Sewall." As if to heighten the insult, Watson found that the very front of the Populist campaign office was decorated with huge portraits of the two Democrats whom the Kansas party took to be its national standard-bearers. Watson's reaction to the portrait of the Maine shipping magnate in place of his own on the Populist headquarters was not recorded. But in any event, a revealing set of circumstances lay behind the Populist display of banners and portraits for the entire national Democratic ticket. The action in St. Louis by the politician-led Kansas party—one of full public support for Bryan and Sewall over the candidacy of Watson—had not met with universal favor among the Populist rank and file when the Kansas delegation returned home. At an acrimonious state convention held in August, the delegates from the towns, hamlets, and crossroads of Kansas had carried the day with a resolution for a straight Bryan-Watson ticket. This, of course, threatened to undercut the very premise of the entire fusionist effort in St. Louis. A "union of the reform forces" would mean nothing if a ticket could not be arranged in such a way that Democrats could vote for Populists in the state races. The fusion planners, led by the party's state chairman, John Breidenthal, countered the convention's action by consummating with Kansas Democrats the instantly famous and infamous ar-

Lorenzo Lewelling
Populist Governor of Kansas from
1893 to 1895 and a leading participant in the fusion politics of 1896.

rangement that exchanged Populist support of Sewall electors
for Democratic support of the Populist state ticket. In speaking in Kansas, Watson was addressing party leaders who had
sacrificed him in the name of their own local and state campaigns. The atmosphere was, to say the least, tense. Nevertheless, at that point the Kansas fusion strategists had no alternative but to try to induce Watson not to stir up a local rebellion
against their bargain.[33]

But Watson had heard the rationale for fusion before, and
he was adamant. "We are willing to fuse," he told the Kansans,
"but we are not willing to be swallowed." Watson's traveling
companion and fellow Georgian, H. W. Reed, a man who had
achieved the rare feat of earning the confidence of both Watson and Butler, conceded to reporters that the Kansas arrangement had "done more to stir up bitterness in the South
and to intensify the demand that Mr. Watson shall have fair
treatment than any other act." Words like "betray" and "mis-
lead" were used to describe the actions of the place-hungry
fusion leaders in Kansas.[34]

Fusion had created an impossible situation, and no one felt
its destructive impact more personally than Tom Watson. In

the words of his biographer, "It is doubtful if any candidate ever to appear on a presidential ticket found himself in quite the humiliating position that Tom Watson occupied in 1896." As much as any man in America who responded to the call of reform launched by the Alliance movement, Watson had labored tirelessly in the people's movement. In Kansas in 1896 he gave his answer to the idea of fusion:

> Someone else must be asked to kill that Party; I will not. I sat by its cradle; I have fought its battles; I have supported its principles since organization . . . and don't ask me after all my service with the People's Party to kill it now. I am going to stand by it till it dies, and I want no man to say that I was the man who stabbed it to the heart. . . .
>
> No; Sewall has got to come down. He brings no votes to Bryan. He drives votes away from Bryan. . . .
>
> My friends, I took my political life in my hands when I extended the hand of fellowship to your Simpsons, your Peffers, your Davises in Georgia. The Georgia Democrats murdered me politically for that act. I stood by your men in Congress when others failed. I have some rights at the hands of Kansas. I have counted on your support. Can I get it? [35]

The Populist audience responded with enthusiasm, pressed around the rostrum, and surrounded his carriage as he prepared to leave. Touched, Watson wrote his wife, "it is quite apparent that the rank and file of our party in Kansas are all right and will vote against their leaders if they get the chance." [36]

6

The Kansas Populists who swarmed around Watson's carriage, like Watson himself, like the old Texas Alliancemen, had too many memories to acquiesce comfortably in the fusion politics of 1896. The spirit of Populism possessed meaning because of these memories. Indeed, collectively, they constituted the essence of the agrarian revolt: memories of farmers on the crop lien bringing food to striking railroad workers; of 2000 men marching silently down a rural courthouse street behind a banner proclaiming "The Southern Exchange Shall Stand"; of Alliancemen wearing suits of cotton-bagging during the long war against the jute trust in the South; of the great lecturing campaigns to organize the South in 1887–89 and the nation in 1890–91; of mile-long Alliance wagon trains and sprigs of evergreen symbolizing the "living issues" in Kansas; of the formation of the "Alliance Aid" association to bring the Dakota plan of self-help insurance to the full agrarian movement; of Leonidas Polk, the Southern Unionist, announcing the end of American sectionalism to the cheers of Michigan farmers; of a day in Florida, "under the orange and banana trees," when a new institution called the National Reform Press Association was created; of the time in South Carolina, so brief in that state, when impoverished farmers rebuked Ben Tillman to his face and tried to set a course different from his; of boys carrying torches in country parades for Tom Watson and girls knitting socks for "Sockless" Jerry Simpson; of the sprawling summer encampments that somehow seemed to give substance to the strange, inspiring, ethical vision of Tom Nugent; of John Rayner's lieutenants speaking quietly and earnestly in the houses of black tenants in the piney woods of East Texas; and, perhaps most symbolic of all, of men and women "who stood on chairs and marched back and forth cheering and crying" in response to the initial public reading of the "Second Declaration of American Independence" on a summer day in 1892 in the city of Omaha. It was this spirit—a collective hope for a better future, it seems—that animated American Populism, and it was these vibrant moments of shared effort that provided the evidence of its vitality, its aspirations, and its defeats.

And finding no coherent way to express itself in fusion, it was this spirit that expired in the autumn of 1896. Tom Watson unconsciously signaled the passing of the People's Party through his September promise on the Kansas plains to "stand by it till it dies." His impulse to speak the phrase at all was an acknowledgment that the moment he feared had already arrived.

CHAPTER XVII

The Irony of Populism

"The People" vs. "The Progressive Society"

The foundations of modern America were constructed out of the cultural materials fashioned in the Gilded Age. The economic, political, and moral authority that "concentrated capital" was able to mobilize in 1896 generated a cultural momentum that gathered in intensity until it created new political guidelines for the entire society in twentieth-century America. Not only was previously unconsolidated high ground captured in behalf of the temporary needs of the election of 1896, but the cultural tactics tested and polished during the course of the campaign for "honest money" set in place patterns of political conduct that proved to be enduring. After McKinley's impressive victory in 1896, these patterns became fully consolidated within the next generation of the Progressive era and proved adequate during a brief time of further testing during the succeeding generation of the New Deal. They have remained substantially unquestioned since, and broadly describe the limits of national politics in the second half of the twentieth century. The third party movement of the Populists became, within mainstream politics, the last substantial effort at structural alteration of organic democratic forms in modern America. * Accordingly, twentieth-century American reform has in a great many ways proven to be tangential to matters the Populists considered the essence of politics. This reality points to the continuing cultural power exerted by the political and economic values which prevailed in the Gilded Age and which today serve to rationalize contemporary life and politics to modern Americans.

The narrowed boundaries of modern politics that date from the 1896 campaign encircle such influential areas of American life as the relationship of corporate power to civil prerogative, the political language legitimized to define and settle public issues within a mass society yoked to mass communications and to privately financed elections, and even the style through which the reality of the American experience—the culture itself—is conveyed to each new generation in the public and private school systems of the nation. In the aggregate, these boundaries outline a clear retreat from the democratic vistas of either the eighteenth-century Jeffersonians or the nineteenth-century Populists.

2

Understandably, during such a moment of cultural consolidation priorities were not quickly isolated or identified; it took awhile for the full implications of the era to become evident. But the power of the hegemony achieved in 1896 was perhaps most clearly illustrated through the banishment of the one clear issue that animated Populism throughout its history—the greenback critique of American finance capitalism. The "money question" passed out of American politics essentially through self-censorship. This result, quite simply, was a product of cultural intimidation. In its broader implications, however, the silencing of debate about "concentrated capital" betrayed a fatal loss of nerve on the part of those who, during Populism, dared to speak in the name of a people's move-

---

* The point, here, of course, is that the socialist alternative, discussed subsequently in this concluding chapter, was culturally isolated, and outside the mainstream of American political dialogue.

ment. Since the implications were so huge, a brief recital of some relevant specific details seems in order.

The enormous success of *Coin's Financial School* induced goldbugs to counterattack in 1895–96 through the writings of a University of Chicago economist named J. Laurence Laughlin. Laughlin not only produced theoretical works, but also books, articles, and pamphlets for popular consumption. His widely syndicated newspaper column imparted an aura of scholarly prestige to the sound money cause, though his journalistic efforts, like his other writings, were almost as conceptually flawed as "Coin" Harvey's efforts. Yet Laughlin's campaign in behalf of the gold standard drew no critics outside the ranks of Populism, for the nation's university faculties were solidly "goldbug." Among respectable elements of American society, greenback doctrines were culturally inadmissable.[1]

However, in 1896 a young Harvard economist, Willard Fischer, decided he personally had endured enough of the currency theories of both "Coin" Harvey and Professor Laughlin. One of the nation's better-informed students of monetary systems, Fischer penned a biting attack on the two competing advocates of metallic-based currencies. Entitled " 'Coin' and His Critics," Fischer's article appeared in the *Quarterly Journal of Economics* in January 1896. Fischer treated with gentle tolerance "Coin" Harvey, whose writings, while badly "flawed," nevertheless produced a number of insights that were "intelligent." He reserved his harsher adjectives for goldbugs, and particularly for his academic colleague, Professor Laughlin. The latter, among other things, was "wrong." In the aggregate, the sheer momentum of Fischer's critique of the arguments of goldbugs and silverites carried him dangerously close to an inferential endorsement of the greenback heresy. No academic *enfant terrible,* Fischer cautiously stepped around this pitfall with an oblique reference to an alternative to metallic-based currencies—one he euphemistically described as "the familiar tabular system." The reference was cordial, but ultimately noncommittal. Beyond such obscurantism, the young professor dared not venture. Though a metallic currency was not an intelligent system of money, Fischer declined to say what was. The word "greenback" did not appear in his article. Coupled with the routine orthodoxy that ruled elsewhere in the academic world, the extreme circumspection of the young Harvard economist tellingly measured the power of the cultural consolidation at that moment being fashioned in America. Certain ideas about the economy, no matter how buttressed with evidence and interpretive skill, had become dangerous.[2]

Though the gold standard was formally legislated into law in 1901 over scattered and desultory opposition, the financial panic of 1907 convinced the Eastern banking community of the need for a more flexible currency. J. Laurence Laughlin, having proved his mettle during the "Battle of the Standards" in 1896, received the blessings of large commercial bankers and was once again pressed into service, this time as the nation's foremost spokesman for "banking reform." Laughlin and two associates wrote the Federal Reserve Act, which was enacted into law in 1913. The measure not only centralized and rationalized the nation's financial system in ways harmonious with the preferences of the New York banking community, its method of functioning also removed the bankers themselves from the harsh glare of public view. Popular attention thenceforth was to focus upon "the Fed," not upon the actions of New York commercial bankers. The creation and subsequent development of the Federal Reserve System represented the culminating political triumph of the "sound money" crusade of the 1890's.[3]

These developments abounded in irony. The panic of 1907 corroborated an essential feature of the analysis behind Charles Macune's sub-treasury system, for the crisis partly materialized out of the inability of a contracted currency to provide adequate capital markets during the autumn agricultural harvest. Throughout the last quarter of the nineteenth century and into the twentieth, calls on Eastern banks by Western banks for funds to move the autumn crops had created stringent shortages within the entire monetary system. While this condition worked to depress agricultural prices—and was not without its benefits to bankers in the matter of interest rates—the banking system itself broke down under these and other burdens in 1907. The demand for a more flexible currency that issued from the banking community following the panic of 1907 was oriented not to the needs of agriculture, however, but rather to the requirements of the banking community itself. Thus, while the 1912 report of the blue-ribbon National Monetary Commission recommended new legislation establishing adequate credit for the nation's farmers, the Federal Reserve Act written by Laughlin and his associates failed to follow through. Though proponents of the Federal Reserve System often described the twelve regional banks established by the act as "cooperative banks" specifically designed to meet the impasse in agricultural credit—a description particularly prominent during public discussion of the enacting legislation—they were not, in fact, so designed. The Act provided easier access to funds only for the nation's most affluent farming interests.[4]

The Federal Reserve System worked well enough for bankers in the ensuing years, but its failure to address the underlying problems of agricultural credit became obvious to all during its first decade of operation. The severe agricultural depression of 1920–21 once again focused public attention on the problem, leading to a marginal expansion of government policies through the establishment in 1923 of federal intermediate credit banks. But the 1923 amendments effectively extended the aid only to the agricultural middle class. In no sense were the credit problems of the "whole class" touched upon in ways that Charles Macune and other Populist greenbackers would have respected. Not until the farm loan acts of the New Deal did the nation directly address the credit requirements of the family farmer. Unfortunately, unlike the Macunite plan of making direct, low-cost government loans not only to aid farmers but as a competitive pressure on bank interest rates generally, the system of New Deal government loans operated wholly through commercial banks. It thus served as an artificial prop for the prevailing financial system. In any event, by the time of the New Deal legislation, literally half the farmers in the cotton belt and the western granary had long since been forced into landless peonage and were effectively beyond help.[5]

A final irony was implicit in these developments—and had they lived to see it, it was one that might have proved too much for old-time greenbackers to bear. The collective effect of twentieth-century agricultural legislation—from the Federal Reserve Act of 1913 to the abrupt ending of the Farm Security Administration's land relocation program in 1943—was to assist in the centralization of American agriculture at the expense of the great mass of the nation's farmers. The process of extending credit, first to the nation's most affluent large-scale farming interests, and then in the 1920's to sectors of the agricultural middle class—while at the same time denying it to "the whole class" of Americans who worked the land—had the effect of assisting large-unit farming interests to acquire title to still more land at the expense of smallholders. Purely in terms of land-ownership patterns, "agri-business" began to emerge in rural America as early as the 1920's, not, as some have suggested, because large-scale corporate farming proved its "efficiency" in the period 1940 to 1970. In essence, "agri-business" came into existence before it even had the opportunity to prove or disprove its "efficiency." In many ways, land centralization in American agriculture was a decades-long product of farm credit policies acceptable to the American banking community. The victory won by goldbugs in the 1890's thus was consolidated by the New Deal reforms. These policies had the twin effects of sanctioning peonage and penalizing family farmers. The end result was a loss of autonomy by millions of Americans on the land.*

In a gesture that was symbolic of the business-endorsed reforms of the Progressive era, William Jennings Bryan hailed the passage of the Federal Reserve Act in 1913 as a "triumph for the people." His response provided a measure of the intellectual achievements of reformers in the Progressive period. Of longer cultural significance, it also illustrated how completely the idea of "reform" had become incorporated within the new political boundaries established in Bryan's own lifetime. The reformers of the Progressive era fit snugly within these boundaries—in Bryan's case, without his even knowing it.

* See Appendix A.

Meanwhile, the idea of substantial democratic influence over the structure of the nation's financial system, a principle that had been the operative political objective of greenbackers, quietly passed out of American political dialogue.[6]

The manner in which the citizens of a democratic society become culturally intimidated, so that some matters of public discussion pass out of public discussion, is not the work of a single political moment. It did not happen all at once, nor was it part of a concerted program of repression. Martial law was not declared, no dissenting editors were exiled, and no newspapers censored. It happened to the whole society in much the same way it happened to young Willard Fischer at Harvard, silently, through a kind of acquiescence that matured into settled resignation. In such a way, a seminal feature of the democratic idea quietly passed out of American culture. This rather fateful process was inaugurated during the climatic political contest of 1896.

3

Popularly known as the "Battle of the Standards" between gold and silver, the presidential campaign between Bryan and McKinley witnessed the unveiling for the first time in America of the broad new techniques of corporate politics. Under the driving supervision of Ohio industrialist Mark Hanna, unprecedented sums of money were raised and spent in a massive Republican campaign of coordinated political salesmanship. The nation's metropolitan newspapers, themselves in the midst of corporate centralization, rallied overwhelmingly to the defense of the gold standard. Their efforts were coordinated through a "press bureau" established by the Republican leadership. The power of the church added itself to that of the editorial room and the counting house, and the morality of "sound money" and the "nation's honor" temporarily replaced more traditional themes emanating from the nation's pulpits. Cultural intuitions about respectability, civic order, and the sanctity of commerce, augmented by large-scale campaign organizing, coordinated newspaper and publishing efforts, and refurbished memories of Civil War loyalties combined to create a kind of electoral politics never previously demonstrated on so vast a scale. Though individual pieces of this political mosaic had been well tested in previous elections, the sum of the whole constituted a new political form: aggressive corporate politics in a mass society.

The Democrats responded with something new of their own—a national barnstorming tour by the youthful and energetic Bryan. Though such undignified conduct was considered by many partisans to be a disgrace to the office of the presidency, the silver candidate spoke before enormous crowds from Minneapolis to New York City. The effort seemed merely to spur the Republican hierarchy to ever-higher plateaus of fund-raising, spending, and organization. The nation had never seen a political campaign like it, and, for one heady moment at least, Bryan thought the electorate would react heavily against such self-evident displays of political propagandizing. But Republicans were able to generate such intense feeling against the "anarchistic" teachings of William Jennings Bryan that many modest church-goers as well as industrial captains felt that no sum of money was too great to ensure the defense of the Republic from the ravages of the silverites. Indeed, one of the striking features of the 1896 campaign was the depth to which many millions of Americans came to believe that the very foundations of the capitalist system were being threatened by the "boy orator of the Platte." That was hardly the case, of course—particularly when it came to the nation's currency. A monetary system responsive to the perspectives of commercial bankers was not at issue in 1896; the relationship of the government to bankers on the matter of currency volume and interest rates was not at issue either. In view of the shared faith of both Bryan and McKinley in a redeemable currency, the entire monetary debate turned on a modest measure of hard-money inflation through silver coinage. The narrowness of the issues involved in the "Battle of the Standards" should have put strong emotional responses beyond possibility—yet the autumn air fairly bristled with apocalyptic moral terminology. Indeed, the fervor of the campaign, for both sides, was authentic: the true issues at stake went far beyond questions of currency volume, to a contest over the underlying cultural values and symbols that would govern political dialogue in the years to come.

4

A great testing was in process, centering on the relative political influence of two competing concepts—that of "the people" on the one hand and of "the progressive society" on the other. Those phrases were by no means habitually employed in 1896, either as informal appeals or in the capitalized versions of political sloganeering destined to become common in the twentieth century. But the values underlying the concepts authentically guided the campaigns of 1896 in ways that imparted enduring meaning to the outcome of their competition.

When he was not talking specifically about silver coinage, Bryan actually used the idea of "the people" as a centerpiece of many of his political speeches. When in Chicago, he said:

> As I look into the faces of these people and remember that our enemies call them a mob, and say they are a menace to free government, I ask: Who shall save the people from themselves? I am proud to have on my side in this campaign the support of those who call themselves the common people. If I had behind me the great trusts and combinations, I know that I would no sooner take my seat than they would demand that I use my power to rob the people in their behalf.[7]

To many Americans, the idea of "the people" represented the very foundation of democratic politics, and many thousands believed it had genuine meaning in the context of the Bryan campaign. But in 1896, the idea was even more specific and more compelling for it described not just "the people" in the abstract but a specific "people's movement" that had pressed itself upon the national consciousness, energized the silverites, and generated the necessary preconditions for agrarian influence in the Democratic Party. Because it was not clear to the nation that the people's movement itself had been destroyed—its cooperatives crushed and its political party co-opted—Bryan came to symbolize its enduring life. This explained why Clarence Darrow, Eugene Debs, and many other Populists who had no illusions about the healing powers of the silver crusade ultimately came to join the "Great Commoner." They hoped he could rally the people to a new sense of their own prerogative and stimulate them, in L. L. Polk's old phrase, to "march to the ballot box and take possession of the government." To the extent that the silver crusade made much sense at all, it was in this symbolic context. The stirring rhythms of Bryan's "Cross of Gold" speech had energized the delegates at the Democratic convention—perhaps he could stir the American people as well. In the autumn of 1896, the hope was there, and this hope gave the Bryan campaign the deepest meaning it possessed.[8]

Given the ballot box potentiality of "the people" as against "the great trusts and combinations," Republicans obviously could not afford to have the campaign decided on that basis. The countervailing idea of the "progressive society" materialized slowly out of the symbolic values embedded in the gold standard. The "sanctity of contracts" and "the national honor," it soon became apparent, were foremost among them. But, gradually, and with the vast distributional range afforded by the Republican campaign treasury, broader themes of "peace, progress, patriotism, and prosperity," came to characterize the campaign for William McKinley. The "progressive society" advanced by Mark Hanna in the name of the corporate community was inherently a well-dressed, churchgoing society. The various slogans employed were not mere expressions of a cynical politics, but rather the authentic assertions of an emerging American world view.[9]

From a Populist perspective, the contest between "the people" and "the progressive society" was, in a practical sense, wholly irrelevant to the real purposes of the reform movement. Indeed, the narrow controversy over the "intrinsic value" of two competing metallic currencies was an affront to greenbackers. Not that they could do much about it; Populism had ceased to be an active force in American politics from the moment the third party had sacrificed its independent presence at the July convention.

The People's Party was therefore not a causative agent of anything significant that occurred during the frenzied campaign between the goldbugs and the silverites. From Marion Butler to Tom Watson, from Nebraska fusionists to Texas mid-roaders, the People's Party had become a reactive agent, responding as best it could to the initiatives of others. After his fiery speeches in Texas and his confrontations with the Kansans, Tom Watson sojourned briefly in the citadel of fusion in Nebraska and then, utterly demoralized, went home to Georgia for the remainder of the campaign. As the sole surviving symbol of a national Populist presence, he had become an anachronism. No one knew this more deeply than Watson or understood more fully what it meant for the future of the third party. The 1896 campaign had to do with the mobilization of new customs that were to live much more securely in American politics than the dreams of the Populists. That many of those customs were precisely the ones that so deeply disturbed the agrarian reformers constituted one of the more enduring ironies of the Populist experience.[10]

The most visible difference in the efforts of the three parties in 1896 turned on money—not as a function of currency, but rather as the essential ingredient of modern electioneering. The Populist national treasurer, Martin Rankin, wrote despairingly to Marion Butler that he was receiving less than a dozen letters a day containing "twenty-five cents to a dollar" from the demoralized Populist faithful throughout the nation. The Populist national campaign was literally almost penniless, and Butler found it necessary to establish his Washington headquarters in a building housing the political arm of the silver lobby, the National Silver Party. Only a belated, if humiliating, subsidy of $1000 from the Democratic national committee enabled the Populists to keep going until election day. Butler's principal achievement in the autumn campaign was, in the words of one writer, "to animate the corpse of his party with some semblance of vitality until the ballots had been cast in November." [11]

The Democratic campaign, although elaborately financed by Populist standards, was also run on a shoestring. The Republican press made great capital out of a supposed massive flow of funds from Western silver mineowners cascading into Democratic coffers. But the relatively modest sums that actually materialized went to the lobbying institutions previously created by the mineowners—the National Silver Party and sundry bimetallic leagues. These funds purchased substantial quantities

Above left: Marcus Hanna, the grey eminence behind the brilliantly managed and elaborately financed Republican campaign for "sound money" and William McKinley. Above right: William Jennings Bryan.

of literature on the money question, including additional new printings of *Coin's Financial School*. Democrats worked desperately to place speakers in the field, but the shortage of money gradually channeled this effort toward the recruiting of self-supporting volunteers. The best educational force for the Democratic cause was Bryan himself. He waged an exhaustive campaign, touring the South and West and invading the Eastern heartland of gold orthodoxy in a campaign swing that climaxed in a rousing rally at Madison Square Garden. Wherever he went, Bryan stirred great enthusiasm. He had a natural gift for oratory, and if his discussions of the monetary system left something to be desired in terms of coherent analysis, few of his listeners seemed to think so. The goldbug attacks on the silver crusade were equally deficient in economic logic. Through the early part of the campaign Bryan was forced to travel by commercial carrier, a circumstance that placed the entire presidential campaign at the mercy of local railroad timetables and earned the "boy orator" considerable ridicule in the goldbug press. The Democratic national committee was ultimately able to provide Bryan with a special train for the closing weeks of the campaign, but the silver crusade never quite lost the ad hoc character that had marked its inception.[12]

In contrast, the massive national campaign for "honest money" engineered by Mark Hanna set a model for twentieth-century American politics. While the Democrats struggled to find volunteer speakers to tour the crucial states of the Midwest, the Republican campaign placed hundreds of speakers in the field. Individual contributions from wealthy partisans sometimes exceeded the entire amount the Democrats raised in their national subscription drive. Offerings from corporations, especially railroad corporations, reached even larger sums. Receipts and expenditures soared into the millions.[13]

Mark Hanna presided over both the Chicago and New York campaign operations, coordinating an elaborate system of printing and distribution that involved many millions of pamphlets, broadsides, and booklets. So controlled and centralized was the Republican effort that the Chicago managers also took it upon themselves to assist in the supervision of state and local campaigns. To add a certain heft to their admonitions, the Chicago office dispatched almost a million dollars to various state organizations. The New York headquarters, focusing on the Eastern states, reported expenses of an additional $1,600,000.[14]

The nation's new business combinations headquartered in New York largely financed the effort. Standard Oil contributed $250,000, a figure matched by J. P. Morgan. Hanna and railroad king James J. Hill were seen in a carriage "day after day," going from Wall Street to the office of the New York Central and the Pennsylvania railroads. Hanna repeatedly importuned the president of New York Life, who just as frequently responded. The corporate contributions mobilized in behalf of the 1896 Republican campaign for McKinley financed America's first concentrated mass advertising campaign aimed at organizing the minds of the American people on the subject of political power, who should have it, and why.[15]

So supported logistically, the cultural politics of 1896 soon unfolded in behalf of the "progressive society." Republican references to the national honor extended to the party's role in the Civil War. The bloody shirt waved in 1896; the fading rhythms of Civil War loyalty were evoked with a measure of subtlety, but evoked nevertheless. From his front porch in

527

Canton, William McKinley framed the larger issues in cultural terms that looked to the past.

> Let us settle once for all that this government is one of honor and of law and that neither the seeds of repudiation nor lawlessness can find root in our soil or live beneath our flag. That represents all our aims, all our policies, all our purposes. It is the banner of every patroit, it is, thank God, today the flag of every section of our common country. No flag ever triumphed over it. It was never degraded or defeated and will not now be when more patriotic men are guarding it than ever before in our history.[16]

In such a manner, the Republican Party first and foremost moved to guard its basic constituency—one that had been created by the war and had been solidified by repeated reminders of the patriotism implicit in that initial allegiance. The politics of sectionalism had always served this primary objective—to ensure the party's organic constituency against anything that might hint at wholesale apostasy. But in 1896, with the war receding in time and with elections more and more depending on the votes of people who had grown to maturity since Appomattox, the appeal of the bloody shirt was boldly employed toward an even more lasting objective—to merge the Republican Party's past defense of the nation with contemporary emotions of patriotism itself. Such an approach promised to elevate sectional memories to national ones, forging a blend of the American flag and the Grand Old Party that might conceivably cement a political bond of enduring civic vitality.

While William Jennings Bryan talked with passion and imprecision about the free coinage of silver, American flags—literally millions of them—became the symbols of the struggle to preserve the gold standard. McKinley himself became the nation's "patriotic leader." The Republican campaign committee purchased and distributed carloads of flags throughout the country and Hanna conceived the idea of a public "flag day" in the nation's leading cities—a day specifically in honor of William McKinley. "Sound Money clubs" of New York and San Francisco were put in charge of enormous flag day spectacles and supporting organizational work was carried forward with unprecedented attention to detail. When no less than 750,000 people paraded in New York City, the *New-York Tribune* soberly reported—thirty-one years after Appomattox— that "many of those who marched yesterday have known what it is to march in war under the same flag that covered the city in its folds yesterday all day long." In the critical Midwestern states, Civil War veterans known as the "Patriotic Heroes" toured with buglers and a cannon mounted on a flatcar. Slogans on the train proclaimed "1896 is as vitally important as 1861." So pervasive was the Republican campaign that frustrated Democrats found it difficult to show proper respect for the national emblem without participating in some kind of public endorsement of McKinley. Inevitably, some Democrats tore down Republican banners—the American flag. Such actions did not hurt the Republican cause.[17]

McKinley adroitly yoked "free trade" to "free silver" as twin fallacies threatening the orderly foundations of commerce as well as the morality of the Republic. These threats were all "Bryanisms" and collectively they added up to "anarchy." The Republican antidotes thus consisted not merely of "sound money" which protected both the sanctity of contracts and the nation's honor, but equally symbolic appeals to the hope of industrial workers for relief in the midst of a depression. To drive this thought home, only one more slogan had to be added to the litany marshaled by the Republicans. The phrase duly materialized and was affixed to McKinley himself. He became "the advance agent of prosperity." Hanna's New York money and Dawes' Chicago printing presses ensured exposure of the slogan throughout the nation. It often appeared emblazoned on huge banners flanked by phalanxes of American flags, the entire panoply carried high in the air by uniformed Civil War veterans wearing "sound money" buttons. Such broadly gauged cultural politics completely overwhelmed the vague call for free silver carried to the country by one barnstorming presidential candidate and a few platoons of volunteer Democratic speakers. In sheer depth, the advertising campaign organized by Mark Hanna in behalf of William McKinley was without parallel in American history. It set a creative standard for the twentieth century.[18]

5

The election itself had an unusual continuity. Some students of the 1896 campaign have concluded that the enthusiasm for Bryan following his "Cross of Gold" speech was such that he would have swept to victory had the election been held in August. After that initial alarm the Republican organization quickly set in place the foundations for the mass campaign that followed, and by October the organizational apparatus assembled by Mark Hanna had clearly swung the balance to the Republicans. Yet the election results appeared fairly close, McKinley receiving 7,035,000 votes to Bryan's 6,467,000. But the Republicans had swept the North. While their margin in the Midwest was not overwhelming, it was a region Cleveland had carried for the Democrats four years before and one Bryan had been supremely confident of winning only a month before the election. Indeed, the results in the Midwest destroyed the party balance that had persisted since the Civil War, thus vastly changing national politics for the forseeable future. In fact, a cataclysm had befallen the Northern Democratic Party. Its progressive symbol in the Midwest, Governor John Peter Altgelt of Illinois, had suffered a surprising defeat, and state party tickets elsewhere in the North had been thrashed. Altgelt himself was utterly disconsolate. The political appeal supposedly implicit in the idea of "the people" had received a powerful defeat.[19]

It took awhile for the full implications to become apparent. The cultural consolidation set in motion in 1896 did not prove during the ensuing eighty years to be any more arbitrary than most other political systems that evolved in advanced industrial societies. The twin heritages of the English common law and the British parliamentary tradition, augmented by the diffusion of power within the three branches of government established under the Constitution, imposed certain limits on the triumphant corporate political culture that became the new American orthodoxy of the twentieth century. These safeguards were, perhaps, easily exaggerated, if for no other reason than it was so reassuring for those who benefited from the "progressive society" to do so. But in the immediate aftermath of 1896, those who extolled the doctrines of progress through business enterprise acquired a greater confidence, while those who labored in behalf of "the people" suffered a profound cultural shock. A number of the influential supporters of William McKinley, newly secure in their prerogatives after the election, advanced from confidence to arrogance; not only the nation, but the very forms of its economic folkways had become theirs to define. In contrast, a number of the followers of William Jennings Bryan, their idea of America rebuked by the electorate, became deferential, either consciously or unconsciously. The idea that serious structural reform of the democratic process was "inevitable" no longer seemed persuasive to reasonable reformers. Rather, it was evident that political innovations had to be advanced cautiously, if at all, and be directed toward lesser objectives that did not directly challenge the basic prerogatives of those who ruled. The thought became the inherited wisdom of the American reform tradition, passed from one generation to another. A consensus thus came to be silently ratified: reform politics need not concern itself with structural alteration of the economic customs of the society. This conclusion, of course, had the effect of removing from mainstream reform politics the idea of people in an industrial society gaining significant degrees of autonomy in the structure of their own lives. The reform tradition of the twentieth century unconsciously defined itself within the framework of inherited power relationships. The range of political possibility was decisively narrowed—not by repression, or exile, or guns, but by the simple power of the reigning new culture itself.[20]

Though it was not immediately noticed, the mature and victorious party of business had muted almost completely the egalitarian ideas that had fortified the party's early abolitionist impulses; the party of "peace, progress, patriotism and prosperity" had become not only anti-Irish, but anti-Catholic and anti-foreign generally. Its prior political abandonment of black Americans had quietly become internalized into a conscious white supremacy that manifested itself through a decreasing mention of the antislavery crusade as part of Republican services to the nation during the Civil War. The assertive party of business that consolidated itself in the process of repelling "Bryanism" in 1896 was, in a cultural sense, the most self-consciously exclusive party the nation had ever experienced. It was white, Protestant, and Yankee. It solicited the votes of all non-white, non-Protestant, or non-Yankee voters who willingly acquiesced in the new cultural norms that described gentility within the emerging progressive society. The word "patriotic" had come to suggest those things that white, Protestant Yankees possessed. This intensely nationalistic and racially exclusive self-definition took specific forms in 1896. The Democratic Party was repeatedly charged with being "too friendly" to foreigners, immigrants, and "anarchists." Indeed, the enduring implications echoed beyond the given tactics of a single campaign to define the restricted range of the progressive society itself. But for many of those who spoke for "the people," and for even great numbers of the people themselves, no amount of fidelity to the new cultural values could provide entry to that society. While black Americans were to learn this truth most profoundly, its dimensions extended to many other kinds of "ethnic" Americans as well as to a number of economic groups and to women generally. The wall erected by the progressive society against "the people" signaled more than McKinley's victory over Bryan, more even than the sanctioning of massive corporate concentration; it marked out the permissible limits of the democratic culture itself. The bloody shirt could at last be laid away: the party of business had created in the larger society the cultural values that were to sustain it on its own terms in the twentieth century.[21]

In the election aftermath, William Jennings Bryan placed the blame for his defeat on the weakness of the silver issue. In the next four years he was to search desperately for a new issue around which to rally "the people" against "the plutocracy." But the decisive shift of voters to the Republican Party that had first occurred in 1894 represented considerably more than a temporary reaction to the depression of 1893. Not only had the new Republican majority been convincingly reaffirmed in 1896, it was to prove one of the most enduring majorities in American political history. Only the temporary split in the Republican Party in 1912 was to flaw the national dominance that began in 1894 and persisted until the Great Depression of the 1930's. In the narrowed political world of the new century, the "Great Commoner" was never to locate his saving issue.[22]

Meanwhile, the unraveling of the fabric of the People's Party between July and November, while fulfilling the predictions of mid-roaders, left little residue other than the bruised feelings and recriminations that Populists inflicted upon one another. Though the Kansas fusionists were rewarded for their efforts by achieving re-election on the joint Democratic-Populist ticket of 1896, it was only at the cost of the deterioration of the third party organization. Even before they could mount another campaign in 1898, Populist spokesmen in Kansas were conceding "the passing of the People's Party" and acknowledging that the agrarian crusade was over. That crusade, of course, had never really come to Nebraska. The stance of the Nebraska third party in 1896—essentially indistinguishable from that of the Nebraska Democratic Party—made the final passing of the vestiges of the Nebraska movement difficult to fix in time. The Nebraska fusion ticket of both 1897 and 1898 was, in any case, dominated by Democrats. In North Carolina, the election reforms passed by the Populist-Republican legislature of 1895 led to the election of a number of black Republicans in 1896, setting the stage for a violent Democratic campaign of white supremacy in 1898. Almost total black disfranchisment resulted as the Democratic Party swept triumphantly back into power. In Texas, Populism polled almost a quarter of a million votes in November 1896—indicating that the third party was still growing at the moment its ideological and organizational roots were severed. The margin of Democratic victory was provided through the intimidation of Mexican-American voters and the terrorism of black voters. Armed horsemen rode through the ranks of Negroes in Populist John B. Rayner's home county in East Texas and destroyed with force the years of organizing work of the black political evangelist. Elsewhere in the South, fusion obliterated the third party. As Watson put it, "Our party, as a party, does not exist any more. Fusion has well nigh killed it." [23]

Pressed to its extremities, the Southern Democracy, "Bryanized" or not, revealed once again that one of its most enduring tenets was white supremacy. It was the one unarguable reality that had existed before, during, and after the Populist revolt. Whatever their individual styles as dissenters from the Southern Way, Mann Page in Virginia, Marion Butler in North Carolina, Tom Watson in Georgia, Reuben Kolb in Alabama, Frank Burkitt in Mississippi, Hardy Brian in Louisiana, W. Scott Morgan in Arkansas, and "Stump" Ashby in Texas all learned this lesson—as their "scalawag" predecessors had learned it before them. But, as black Americans knew, white supremacy was a national, not just a Southern, phenomenon. The progressive society was to be a limited one.

6

North and South, Republican and Democratic, the triumphant new politics of business had established similar patterns of public conduct. Central to the new ethos was a profound sense of prerogative, a certainty that in the progressive society only certain kinds of people had a right to rule. Other kinds of people, perforce, could be intimidated or manipulated or disfranchised. Students of the 1896 campaign have agreed on the fact of overt employer intimidation of pro-Bryan factory workers into casting ballots for McKinley. The pattern was especially visible in the pivotal states of the Midwest. But the fact that the same customs flourished on an even grander scale in the South, where they were applied by Democrats to defraud Populists and Republicans, pointed to some of the more ominous dimensions of the emerging political exclusiveness. Both major parties were capable of participating in the same political folkways of election intimidation because they were both influenced by the same sense of prerogative at the center of the emerging system of corporate values.[24]

The world of centralized business had thus not only fashioned the tools for a powerful brand of mass politics, but the new industrial society was also to be narrower in the styles of permissible social relations. Even the Populists were not exempt from its reach, as James Baird Weaver adequately demonstrated in January 1896 when he advised Bryan that fusionists were planning a "little synthetic force" to ensure the ascendancy within the People's Party of the politics of the silver lobby. And, in 1896, the old Alliance radical, William Lamb, an increasingly successful trader in town lots in his

North Texas town of Bowie, got so carried away with the business possibilities in near-by Oklahoma that one of the items on his agenda at the Populist convention in St. Louis—besides defeating the fusionists—was to seek third party endorsement of new legislation opening up the Oklahoma reservation lands. In ways that he, perhaps, did not fully grasp, Indians, for him, were not part of "the people" either.[25]

For increasing numbers of Americans, the triumph of the business credo was matched, if not exceeded, by a conscious or unconscious internalization of white supremacist presumptions. Coupled with the new sense of prerogative encased in the idea of progress, the new ethos meant that Republican businessmen could intimidate Democratic employees in the North, Democratic businessmen could intimidate Populists and Republicans in the South, businessmen everywhere could buy state legislators, and whites everywhere could intimidate blacks and Indians. The picture was not pretty, and it was one the nation did not reflect upon. In the shadow it cast over the idea of democracy itself, however, this mode of settling political disputes, or of making money, embedded within the soul of public life new patterns of contempt for alternative views and alternative ways of life. The cost of running for office, coupled with the available sources of campaign contributions and the increasing centralization of news gathering and news reporting, all pointed to the massive homogenization of business politics.

In addition to the banishment of the "financial question" as a political issue, two other developments soon materialized in the wake of the 1896 election to establish enduring patterns for the twentieth century—the rapid acceleration of the merger movement in American industry and the decline of public participation in the democratic process itself. Corporate America underwent periodic waves of heightened consolidation, from 1897 to 1903, 1926 to 1931, and 1945 to 1947. Building upon prior levels of achievement, the process accelerated once again in the 1960's. The "trusts and combinations" that the Populists believed were "inherently despotic" rode out the brief popular clamor for anti-trust legislation before World War I. Such largely marginal reforms as were able to run the lobbying gantlet within the United States

Congress were vitiated by subsequent Supreme Court decisions. To the despair of anti-trust lawyers in the Department
of Justice, the combination movement became a historical constant of twentieth-century American life as a structure of
oligopoly was fashioned in every major industry. However
powerful those industries seemed in themselves, they were losing, at the center of capitalism, their monetary battle with the
nation's banking system. In 1974, nearly forty cents of every
dollar of gross earnings by American business—compared to
about fifteen cents as recently as the early 1960's—was committed to interest payments, which were running at the rate of
almost $50 billion a year. At the same time, "bank holding
companies" had fashioned networks of corporate consolidation scarcely imagined by Populist "calamity howlers."
Within the narrowed range of political options available to
twentieth-century advocates of reform, however, this seminal
development within the structure of finance capitalism was not
a matter of sustained public debate.[26]

The passing of the People's Party left the Southern Democracy securely in the hands of conservative traditionalists in
every state of the region. There, "election reform" proved to
have as many dimensions as "banking reform" did nationally.
The process began with the disfranchisement of blacks in Mississippi in 1890 and accelerated after 1896 as state after state
across the South legalized disfranchisement for blacks and
made voting more difficult for poorer whites. The movement
for election reform was accompanied by a marked decline in
the relationship of public issues to the economic realities of
Southern agriculture, a persistent twentieth-century folkway
that contributed to a sharp drop in popular interest in politics
among Southerners. In the twentieth century, the voting per-
centages in the South remained far below the peaks of the
Populist decade. Indeed, throughout the nation the massive
voter participation that had characterized politics in pre-Civil
War America became a thing of the past. Within the narrower
permissible limits of public disputation, more and more Americans felt increasingly distant from their government and concluded that there was little they could do to affect "politics."
The sense of personal participation that Evan Jones felt in

1888 when he summoned 250,000 Alliancemen to meet in more than 175 separate courthouses—without notifying anyone in the courthouses—pointed to a kind of intimacy between ordinary citizens and their government that became less evident in twentieth-century America. To Alliancemen, it was *their* courthouse and *their* government.[27]

Collectively, these patterns of public life, buttressed by the supporting faith in the inevitability of economic progress, ensured that substantive democratic political ideas in twentieth-century America would have great difficulty in gaining access to the progressive society in a way that approached even the marginal legitimacy achieved by Populist "calamity howlers." The American populace was induced to accept as its enduring leadership a corporate elite whose influence was to permeate every state legislature in the land, and the national Congress as well. The Nebraska "oil rooms" of the pre-Populist days were to become more sophisticated, but hardly less self-serving in their domestic lobbying purposes or in their influence on American foreign policy. A new style of democratic politics had become institutionalized, and its cultural boundaries were so adequately fortified that the new forms gradually described the Democratic Party of opposition as well as the Republican Party of power. A decisive cultural battle had been lost by those who cherished the democratic ethos. The departure of a culturally sanctioned tradition of serious democratic reform thought created self-negating options: reformers could ignore the need for cultural credentials, insist on serious analysis, and accept their political irrelevance as "socialists"; or they could forsake the pursuit of serious structural reform, and acquire mainstream credentials as "progressives" and "liberals." In either case, they could not hope to achieve what Populists had dared to pursue—cultural acceptance of a democratic politics open to serious structural evolution of the society. The collapse of Populism meant, in effect, that the cultural values of the corporate state were politically unassailable in twentieth-century America.

7

The socialists who followed the Populists did not really understand this new reality of American culture any more than most Populists did in the 1890's. To whatever extent socialists might speak to the real needs of "the people"—as they intermittently did for two generations—and however they might analyze the destructive impact of the progressive society upon the social relations and self-respect of the citizenry—as they often did during the same period—the advocates of popular democracy who spoke out of the socialist faith were never able to grapple successfully with the theoretical problem at the heart of their own creed. While the progressive society was demonstrably authoritarian beyond those ways that Thomas Jefferson had originally feared, and while it sheltered a party system that was intellectually in homage to the hierarchical values of the corporate state itself—cultural insights that provided an authentic connecting link between Populism and socialism—the political power centered in "concentrated capital" could not be effectively brought under democratic control in the absence of some correspondingly effective source of non-corporate power. While the Populists committed themselves to a people's movement of "the industrial millions" as the instrument of reform, the history of successful socialist accessions to power in the twentieth century has had a common thread—victory through a red army directed by a central political committee. No socialist citizenry has been able to bring the post-revolutionary army or central party apparatus under democratic control, any more than any non-socialist popular movement has been able to make the corporate state responsive to the mass aspirations for human dignity that mock the pretentions of modern culture. Rather, our numerous progressive societies have created, or are busily creating, overpowering cultural orthodoxies through which the citizenry is persuaded to accept the system as "democratic"—even as the private lives of millions become more deferential, anxiety-ridden and (no other phrase will serve) less free.

Increasingly, the modern condition of "the people" is illustrated by their general acquiescence in their own political inability to affect their governments in substantive ways. Collective political resignation is a constant of public life in the technological societies of the twentieth century. The folkway knows no national boundary, though it does, of course, vary in intensity in significant ways from nation to nation. In the absence of alternatives, millions have concentrated on trying to find private modes of escape, often through material acquisition. Indeed, the operative standard of progress in both ideological worlds of socialism and capitalism focuses increasingly upon economic indexes. Older aspirations—dreams of achieving a civic culture grounded in generous social relations and in a celebration of the vitality of human cooperation and the diversity of human aspiration itself—have come to seem so out of place in the twentieth-century societies of progress that the mere recitation of such longings, however authentic they have always been, now constitutes a social embarrassment.

But while the doctrines of socialism have not solved the problem of hierarchical power in advanced industrial society, its American adherents can scarcely be blamed for having failed to build a mass popular following in the United States. While they never quite achieved either a mass movement or a movement culture that matched the size, richness, and creativeness of the agrarian cooperative crusade, they were, in the aftermath of the cultural consolidation that accompanied the Populist defeat, far more politically isolated than their agrarian predecessors had been. To an extent that was not true of many other societies, the cultural high ground in America had been successfully consolidated by the corporate creed a decade before American socialists, led by Eugene Debs, began their abortive effort to create a mass popular base. The triumphant new American orthodoxy of the Gilded Age, sheltering the two-party system in a dialogue substantially unrelated to democratic structural reform of the inherited economic and social system, consigned the advocates of such ideas to permanent marginality. The Populists were thus the last American reformers with authentic cultural credentials to solicit mass support for the idea of achieving the democratic organization of an industrialized society.

But while American socialists, for reasons they themselves did not cause, can be seen in retrospect as never having had a chance, they can be severely faulted for the dull dogmatism and political adolescence of their response to this circumstance. Though their primary recruiting problem turned on their lack of domestic cultural credentials—the working poor wanted justice, but they wanted it as loyal Americans—socialists reacted to continued cultural isolation by celebrating the purity of their "radicalism." Thus, individual righteousness and endless sectarian warfare over ideology came to characterize the politics of a creed rigidified in the prose of nineteenth-century prophets. As a body of political ideas, socialism in America—as in so many other countries—never developed a capacity for self-generating creativity. It remained in intellectual servitude to sundry "correct" interpretations by sundry theorists—mostly dead theorists—even as the unfolding history of the twentieth century raised compelling new questions about the most difficult political problem facing mankind: the centralization of power in highly technological societies. If it requires an army responsive to a central political committee to domesticate the corporate state, socialism has overwhelmingly failed to deal with the question of who, in the name of democratic values, would domesticate the party and the army. In the face of such a central impasse, it requires a rather grand failure of imagination to sustain the traditional socialist faith.

8

As a political culture, Populism fared somewhat better during its brief moment. Third party advocates understood politics as a cultural struggle to describe the nature of man and to create humane models for his social relations. In the context of the American ethos, Populists therefore instinctively and habitually resisted all opposition attempts to deflect new ideas from serious consideration through the demagogic expedient of labeling their authors as "radicals." As Populists countered this ploy, they defended the third party platform as "manly and conservative." This Populist custom extended especially to the movement's hard core of lecturers and theorists, who understood the Omaha Platform as a series of threshold demands, to be promptly augmented upon enactment, as the successful popular movement advanced to implement its ultimate goal of a "new day for the industrial millions." In articulating their own social theory, their cause of "education" could advance in step with each stage of democratic implementation, as the "plain people" gained more self-respect from the supportive culture of their own movement and as they gained confidence in their rights as citizens of a demonstratively functioning democracy.[28]

Populism in America was not the sub-treasury plan, not the greenback heritage, not the Omaha Platform. It was not, at bottom, even the People's Party. The meaning of the agrarian revolt was its cultural assertion as a people's movement of mass democratic aspiration. Its animating essence pulsed at every level of the ambitious structure of cooperation: in the earnest probings of people bent on discovering a way to free themselves from the killing grip of the credit system ("The suballiance is a schoolroom"); in the joint-notes of the landed, given in the name of themselves and the landless ("The brotherhood stands united"); in the pride of discovery of their own legitimacy ("The merchants are listening when the County Trade Committee talks"); and in the massive and emotional effort to save the cooperative dream itself ("The Southern Exchange Shall Stand"). The democratic core of Populism was visible in the mile-long Alliance wagon trains ("The Fourth of July is Alliance Day"); in the sprawling summer encampments ("A pentecost of politics") and, perhaps most tellingly, in the latent generosity unlocked by the culture of the movement itself, revealed in the capacity of those who had little, to empathize with those who had less ("We extend to the Knights of Labor our hearty sympathy in their manly struggle against monopolistic oppression," and "The Negro people are part of the people and must be treated as such").

While each of these moments occurred in the 1890's, and have practical and symbolic meaning because they did occur, Populism in America was not an egalitarian achievement. Rather, it was an egalitarian attempt, a beginning. If it stimulated human generosity, it did not, before the movement itself was destroyed, create a settled culture of generosity. Though Populists attempted to break out of the received heritage of white supremacy, they necessarily, as white Americans, did so within the very ethos of white supremacy. At both a psychological and political level, some Populists were more successful than others in coping with the pervasive impact of the inherited caste system. Many were not successful at all. This reality extended to a number of pivotal social and political questions beside race—sectional and party loyalties, the intricacies of power relationships embedded in the monetary system, and the ways of achieving a politics supportive of popular democracy itself. In their struggle, Populists learned a great truth: cultures are hard to change. Their attempt to do so, however, provides a measure of the seriousness of their movement.

Populism thus cannot be seen as a moment of triumph, but as a moment of democratic promise. It was a spirit of egalitarian hope, expressed in the actions of two million beings—not in the prose of a platform, however creative, and not, ultimately, even in the third party, but in a self-generated culture of collective dignity and individual longing. As a movement of people, it was expansive, passionate, flawed, creative—above all, enhancing in its assertion of human striving. That was Populism in the nineteenth century.

But the agrarian revolt was more than a nineteenth-century experience. It was a demonstration of how people of a society containing a number of democratic forms could labor in pursuit of freedom, of how people could generate their own culture of democratic aspiration in order to challenge the received culture of democratic hierarchy. The agrarian revolt demonstrated how intimidated people could create for themselves the psychological space to dare to aspire grandly—and to dare to be autonomous in the presence of powerful new institutions of economic concentration and cultural regimentation. The Omaha Platform gave political and symbolic substance to the people's movement, but it was the idea animating the movement itself that represents the Populist achievement. That idea was a profoundly simple one: the Populists believed they could work together to be free individually. In their institutions of self-help, Populists developed and acted upon a crucial democratic insight: to be encouraged to surmount rigid cultural inheritances and to act with autonomy and self-confidence, individual people need the psychological support of other people. The people need to "see themselves" experimenting in new democratic forms.

542

In their struggle to build their cooperative commonwealth, in their "joint notes of the brotherhood," in their mass encampments, their rallies, their long wagon trains, their meals for thousands, the people of Populism saw themselves. In their earnest suballiance meetings—those "unsteepled places of worship"—they saw themselves. From these places of their own came "the spirit that permeates this great reform movement." In the world they created, they fulfilled the democratic promise—in the only way it can be fulfilled—by people acting in democratic ways in their daily lives. Temporary victory or defeat was never the central element, but simple human striving always was, as three epic moments of Populism vividly demonstrated in the summers of 1888, 1889, 1890. These moments were, respectively, the day to save the exchange in Texas, Alliance Day in Atlanta, when 20,000 farmers massed in solidarity against the jute trust, and Alliance Day in Winfield, Kansas. Though L. L. Polk made a stirring speech to the Kansans on July 4, 1890 in Winfield, what he said was far less important than what his listeners were seeing. The farmers had assembled in their wagons at their suballiances and the trains of wagons from different suballiances merged at the county line enroute to Winfield. As they neared the city, these trains fell in with similar ones from other county alliances. The caravan entering Cowley County from one direction alone stretched for miles. One can well imagine what this spectacle must have brought home to the participants. The Alliance was the people. And the people were together. On such days in Kansas, in Texas, and in Georgia, the people saw themselves. Because this happened, the substance of American Populism went beyond the political creed embedded in the People's Party, beyond the evocative images of Alliance lecturers and reform editors, beyond even the idea of freedom itself. The Populist essence was less abstract: it was an assertion of how people can *act* in the name of the idea of freedom. At root, American Populism was a demonstration of what authentic political life is in a functioning democracy. The "brotherhood of the Alliance" addressed the question of how to live. That is the Populist legacy to the twentieth century.

9

Social energy is an elusive human phenomenon, difficult either to isolate or to describe. Yet in every society a time comes when some of its members—a sectional group, a class, an occupational or racial group—could rally to collective self-assertion. For American farmers, that moment came in the late 1880's. They built their cooperatives, sang their songs, marched, and dreamed of a day of dignity for the "plain people."

But their movement was defeated, and the moment passed. Following the collapse of the People's Party, farm tenancy increased steadily and consistently, decade after decade, from 25 per cent in 1880, to 28 per cent in 1890, to 36 per cent in 1900, and to 38 per cent in 1910. The 180 counties in the South where at least half the farms had been tenant-operated in 1880 increased to 890 counties by 1935. Tenantry also spread over the fertile parts of the corn belt as an increasing amount of Midwestern farmland came to be held by mortgage companies. Some 49 per cent of Iowa farms were tenant-operated in 1935 and the land so organized amounted to 60 per cent of the farm acreage in the state. In 1940, 48 per cent of Kansas farms were tenant-operated. The comparable figure for all Southern farms was 46 per cent. But in the South, those who had avoided tenantry were scarcely in better condition than the sharecroppers. An authoritative report written by a distinguished Southern sociologist in the 1930's included the information that over half of all landowners had "short-term debts to meet current expenses on the crop." The total for both tenants and landowners shackled to the furnishing merchant reached 70 per cent of all farmers in the South. As one historian put it, the crop lien had "blanketed" the entire region. As in the Gilded Age, the system operated in a way that kept millions living at a level of bare subsistence. The amount advanced to whole families by furnishing merchants averaged $12.80 per month for all food, clothing, and medical needs. The average income for sharecroppers ran from a minimum of 10 cents per day per person to a maximum of 25 cents per day—literally the wages of peonage.[29]

By the time of the New Deal, when the Commodity Credit Corporation was formed and a bank for cooperatives was created, the farmers, crushed by two additional generations under the crop lien and the chattel mortgage, did not have the energy to rally to their own cause. Instead, students of twentieth-century agricultural cooperatives have complained of the "apathy" of the farmers, of plans that seem adequately capitalized and buttressed by adequate government credit—plans that would work—if only the farmers themselves would learn the principles of cooperation and would stick with them. In the day of "the big store of the Alliance." the farmers had been ready.[30]

Considerable evidence suggests that the "apathy" of white and black tenant farmers through the first half of the twentieth century was partly a product of their physical condition. Anguished reports by public health doctors and by the Medical Association of Georgia, among others, chronicle a decades-long fight against malaria, hookworm, and pellagra. In some rural counties upward of 70 per cent of the population was affected by one or more of these diseases. One former president of the Georgia Medical Association, looking back over a lifetime of urban and rural medicine, wrote in 1974 that "much poverty, laziness and lack of ambition in the South, especially in the rural areas, could be attributed to chronic malaria, hookworm infestation, typhoid fever. Once these laid hold of them," he added, "then many would succumb to pellagra because of inadequate diet." Decades of diets on the crop lien had taken an inevitable toll.[31]

As determinants of political involvement or political apathy, the precise relationships between organizational intensity, ideology, health conditions, and economic processes are not easily sorted out. It does seem reasonable to suggest, however, that the traditional explanation of the collapse of Populism— that "prosperity returned"—does not fully describe the underlying causes for the passing of organized expressions of agrarian discontent. The period from the end of the Civil War to the outbreak of World War II was one of uninterrupted poverty for large sectors of agricultural America. For the millions of the Alliance, prosperity never returned. The ubiqui-

545

tous spread of tenantry for over half a century does not testify to the presence of a responsive democratic culture.

In the years of hope, the sense of community engendered within the Farmers Alliance and the People's Party involved a feeling of sharing that, years after the movement had run its course, inspired in more than one participant wistful memories of the meals for thousands, of the "cheers for the Alliance and the speaker," and "cheers for the Pops"—human yearnings made larger by the sheer dimension of their collective striving. And it was this very ingredient of hope that dissolved when their movement surrendered its identity in 1896. They had lost more than their party, they had lost the community they had created. They had lost more than their battle on the money question, they had lost their chance for a measure of autonomy. They had lost more than their people's movement, they had lost the hopeful, embryonic culture of generosity that their movement represented.

10

If the farmers of the Alliance suffered severely, what of the agrarian crusade itself? What of the National Farmers Alliance and Industrial Union, that earnest aggregation of men and women who strove for a "cooperative commonwealth"? And what of the People's Party?

As agrarian spokesmen were forever endeavoring to make clear to Americans—indeed, in S. O. Daws's early "history," published in 1887—the cooperative movement taught the farmers "who and where the enemies of their interests were." [32]

The Alliancemen who learned this lesson first were the men who had been sent out by the cooperatives to make contact with the surrounding commercial world, men like Daws, Lamb and Macune in Texas and Loucks and Wardall in Dakota. Though they possessed different political views and different sectional memories, they were altered in much the same way by the searing experience of participating in, and leading, a thwarted hope. They became desperate, defensively aggressive, angry, and creative. They reacted with boycotts, with plans for mutual self-help insurance societies, with the world's

546

first large-scale cooperatives, and with the sub-treasury plan. The marketing and purchasing agents who learned the lessons of cooperation became both movement politicians and ideological men.

They built their cooperatives, developed new political ideas, and fashioned a democratic agenda for the nation. The destruction of the cooperatives by the American banking system was a decisive blow, for it weakened the interior structure of democracy that was the heart of the cooperative movement itself. Though, in one final burst of creativity, the agrarian radicals were able to fashion their third party, that moment in Omaha in the summer of 1892 was the movement's high tide. There was no way a political institution—a mere party—could sustain the day-to-day democratic ethos at the heart of the Alliance cooperative. In the absence of the kind of hope and momentum engendered by the cooperation vision, the driving democratic energy that was the essence of the agrarian revolt gradually began to wear out. The third party might win elections, it might even intermittently sponsor mass rallies of the people, but it found no way to sustain the democratic ethos itself. The People's Party was many things, even many democratic things, but it was not an unsteepled chapel of mass democracy—its own functionaries saw to that. Beyond this, each stolen election and act of terrorism in the South and each "practical" coalition in the West served to chip away the morale and sap the energy of the movement. It took the strongest kind of parallel communities and the steadiest kind of movement leadership to keep the democratic idea alive in the presence of the sustained hierarchical cultural attacks to which the reform movement was subjected. After the defeat of the cooperatives, the pressure was too great for the People's Party, alone, to bear. The movement lost its animating reality and, in the end, became like its shadow and succumbed to hierarchical politics.

Long before that moment of self-destruction in 1896, the movement's organizational source, the National Farmers Alliance, having rendered its final service to farmers by creating the new party of reform in 1892, had moved into the wings of the agrarian revolt.

In so doing, the Alliance transferred to the political arena the broad aims it had failed to accomplish through its cooperative crusade. The organizational boundaries of the People's Party were largely described by the previous limits of the Alliance. The greenback doctrines of the Alliance were imbibed by those who participated in the cooperative crusade, but by very few other Americans. Though several Western mining states that were not deeply affected by Alliance organizers achieved a measure of one-plank silverism, and Nebraska produced its uniquely issueless shadow movement, no American state not organized by the Alliance developed a strong Populist presence. The fate of the parent institution and its political offspring were inextricably linked and confirmed, as the organic reality of American Populism, the centrality of the cooperative crusade that built both the Alliance and the People's Party.[33]

The largest citizen institution of nineteenth-century America, the National Farmers Alliance and Industrial Union persisted through the 1890's, defending the core doctrines of greenbackism within the People's Party and keeping to the fore the dream of a "new day for the industrial millions." Its mass roots severed by the cooperative failure at the very moment its hopes were carried forward by the People's Party, the Alliance passed from view at the end of the century. Its sole material legacy was the "Alliance warehouse" weathering in a thousand towns scattered across the American South and West. In folklore, it came to be remembered that the Alliance had been "a great movement" and that it had killed itself because it had "gone into politics." But at its zenith, it reached into forty-three states and territories and, for a moment, changed the lives and the consciousness of millions of Americans. As a mass democratic institution, the saga of the Alliance is unique in American history.

11

In contrast the silver crusade may be retrospectively judged to be trivial as a political faith. It nevertheless possessed considerable cultural significance for what it revealed of the values and horizons of those millions of Americans who did not respond to the Omaha Platform but who did embrace the free coinage panacea. The silver Democratic Party of William Jennings Bryan, like the Gold Democracy of Grover Cleveland and the "sound money" Republican Party of William McKinley, was, intellectually, an anachronism. As negative reactions to the Omaha Platform, neither the politics of silver nor the politics of gold shed much light on the democratic values of Populism in America. They do, however, provide evidence of the narrowing political range of the corporate society that was then emerging. In monetary analysis, Gold Democrats were neither better nor worse than Silver Democrats, merely their equals in hyperbole and in their misunderstanding of how monetary systems worked.[34]

In statesmanship, the Bryanites, not achieving office, left no record; the Cleveland Democracy, however, repeatedly proved its inability to perceive the world around it and demonstrated rather forcefully its resulting incapacity to govern. Frozen in a philosophy of laissez faire, Cleveland was virtually immobilized by the depression of the 1890's, and was unable to respond either to the needs of the unemployed or to the imperatives of the inevitable financial crisis. The ultimate effect of his frantic gold bond issues was to transfer sizable portions of the government's reserve from the United States Treasury to the Eastern financial community.[35]

On the other hand, the Republican Party, an increasingly narrow-gauged but powerful engine, made a determined show of running both the nation and its economy. Thanks to the energy of the American industrial system, a demanding and ruthless contrivance, but, relatively speaking, an efficient one, the Republicans were able to do just that. They liked the contrivance, even celebrated it with a self-serving and narrow insularity that blinded them to the costs it exacted in both human and natural resources, in the beauty of the land itself, and in the vigor and range of the national culture. But they did all these things with a public display of confidence and were able to escape relatively unscathed. The Republicans did not respond to the depression with any more verve than Cleveland had managed, but the cutting edge of hard times was marginally blunted by minor economic developments occurring beyond the reach of politicians or monetary policy makers. With its newly consolidated majority position, the Republican Party—except for the Wilsonian interlude—ruled the nation for two generations. During this period America added to its material wealth because of the absence of feudal restraints upon the imaginativeness of its people, because of the energy of both its entrepreneurs and their employees, and because of the great bounty nature had bestowed upon the American continent. The political institutions of the nation were vastly overshadowed in importance by these deeper rhythms that propelled an unbalanced and provincial democracy toward the crises that awaited it in the twentieth century.

12

When those crises came, twentieth-century America found itself still firmly bound to many of the nineteenth-century orthodoxies against which the Populists had rebelled—presumptions that outlined the proper limits of democratic debate, the prerogatives of corporate money in shaping political decision-making, and the meaning of progress itself. Though the first decades of new era were no longer called the "Age of Excess"—they were, in fact, called the "Progressive era"—the acceptable political boundaries for participants in both parties received their definition from the economic values that triumphed politically in the Gilded Age. When the long Republican reign came to an end in 1932, the alternatives envisioned by the Democrats of the New Deal unconsciously reflected the shrunken vistas that remained culturally permissible. Aspirations for financial reform on a scale imagined by greenbackers had expired, even among those who thought of themselves as reformers. Inevitably, such reformers had lost the possibility of understanding how the system worked. Restructuring of American banking was not something about which New Dealers or New Frontiersmen could think with sustained attention. Structural reform of American banking no longer existed as an issue in America. The ultimate cultural victory being not merely to win an argument but to remove the subject from the agenda of future contention, the consolidation of values that so successfully sub-

merged the "financial question" beyond the purview of succeeding generations was self-sustaining and largely invisible.

The complacency of the nation's intellectual elite of the
Gilded Age, it turned out, ranged beyond the dull monometallism of academic economists such as J. Laurence Laughlin or
the superficial satire of E. L. Godkin; it enveloped even those
enlightened literary arbiters who considered themselves in the
vanguard of the new realism. When a sympathetic William
Dean Howells could unwittingly and patronizingly describe
the farmers of the Alliance as "grim, sordid, pathetic, fero-
cious figures" and characterize the cooperative crusade, about
which he almost certainly knew little or nothing, as "blind
groping for fairer conditions," the cultural barriers to analytical clarity were manifestly settling into hardening concrete.[36]

The political sensibility that followed William Dean Howells
in the twentieth century found itself too rigid—and too
dangerously condescending—to support truly expansive vistas
of democratic possibility—such as those afforded by the continuing aspirations of the millions of "the people" who, because of manners, occupation, or skin color, could not gain
access to the benefits of the progressive society. As objects of
study, the Populists themselves were to fall victim to the inability of twentieth-century humanists of various ideological persuasions to conceive that authentic political substance might
originate outside such acceptable intellectual sources as the
progressive, capitalist, middle classes or the European socialist
heritage. Since both traditions continued to employ encrusted
political terms rooted in outdated nineteenth-century languages of prophecy, the antiquarian nature of modern politics
became difficult to overstate. From all quarters, Populists were
denied authentic historical association with their own movement. Accordingly, their chief legacy—a capacity to have
significant democratic aspirations, a simple matter of scale of
thought—faded from American political culture. The reform
tradition that materialized in the twentieth century was intimidated and, therefore, unimaginative. Harry Tracy and
other Populist theoreticians had called for 300 per cent
inflation, on the sole and valid ground that the sub-treasury
system was intelligent and would provide an immediate rem-

edy for a central and long-neglected flaw at the heart of American capitalism. The capacity to think politically on such a scale was Populistic; it passed from the American reform tradition with the defeat of Populism.*

By this process, the relatively expansive pre-industrial sensibilities that had animated Thomas Jefferson, George Mason, and the original Anti-Federalists gradually lost that strand of democratic continuity and legitimacy which, in fact, connected their time and their possibility to our own through the actions of Americans who lived in the interim: the Populist connecting link was lost to the heritage. The egalitarian current that was part of the nation's wellspring became not a constantly active source of ideas, but a curious backwater, eddying somewhere outside both the conveyed historical heritage and the mainstream of modern political thought that necessarily built upon that heritage.[37]

The result is a self-insulated culture, one in which the agrarian movements of the "third world" in the twentieth century have easily become as threatening to modern Americans as the revolt of their own farmers were to goldbugs eighty years earlier. Under such constraints, the ultimate political price that Americans may be forced to pay for their narrowed cultural range in the twentieth century has emerged as a question of sobering dimension.

13

However they were subsequently characterized, Populists in their own time derived their most incisive power from the simple fact that they declined to participate adequately in a central element of the emerging American faith. In an age of progress and forward motion, they had come to suspect that Horatio Alger was not real. The realities of their daily lives made them think about the nation in a new way—less complacently than their fellows. As commercial victims of the financial policies of the emerging industrialized state, they also saw the machine age in a new way. Like everyone else, they wanted the railroads to come to their towns, but they literally

* See Appendix A.

could not bear the price the railroads exacted for coming. Their dilemma made them brood about the shape of the future. In due course, they came to possess a cultural flaw that armed them with considerable critical power. Heretics in a land of true believers and recent converts, they saw the coming society and they did not like it. It was perhaps inevitable that since they lost their struggle to deflect that society from its determined path of corporate celebration, they were among the last of the heretics. Once defeated, they lost what cultural autonomy they had amassed and surrendered their progeny to the training camps of the conquering army. All Americans, including the children of Populists, were exposed to the new dogmas of progress confidently conveyed in the public school system and in the nation's history texts. As the twentieth-century recipients of this instruction, we have found it difficult to listen with sustained attention to the words of those who dissented at the moment a transcendent cultural norm was being fashioned.

But in their own way, the men and women who generated the broad visions of the Alliance cooperative created a community of democratic expectation that attempted to reach out to the whole of America. They knew they were asking a great deal, but they believed in the idea of the larger community that was the American nation. We know this because the Populists said as much. Leonidas Polk of North Carolina, president of the National Farmers Alliance and Industrial Union, died three weeks before the Omaha convention that was to have nominated him as the first presidential candidate of the People's Party. He thus did not see the unveiling of the Omaha Platform, the ideological legacy of the Farmers Alliance to the People's Party. That document, carved out of the agrarian cooperative experience and already fully in place, expressed in political terms the hopes of the men and women who composed the agrarian revolt. But the faith embodied in that platform was expressed by Leonidas Polk himself, long before the agrarian faithful gathered at Omaha. In a speech to the crop-mortgaged farmers of the South, he said:

> I know you are asking today, "How long will it take?" I come to say to you this afternoon however difficult the moment,

553

however frustrating the hour, it will not be long because truth pressed to the earth will rise again. How long? Not long, because no lie can live forever. How long? . . . Not long because the arm of the moral universe is long, but it bends toward justice.[38]

Polk's words reflected the underlying faith of American Populism and the style of those who dared to have large aspirations and to strive democratically for their attainment. The faith itself, and much in the style of its presentation, represents the cultural legacy the Populists left to their descendants of the twentieth century. To a world moving into a strange new age of competing technologies, they offered new ideas about the possibilities of community.

Nevertheless, for their own era, the agrarian spokesmen who talked of the "coming revolution" turned out to be much too hopeful. Though in the months of Populist collapse and for successive decades thereafter, prosperity eluded those the reformers called the "producing classes," the new industrial society preserved the narrowed boundaries of political dialogue substantially intact, as roughly one-third of America's urban workers moved slowly into the middle class. The mystique of progress itself helped to hold in muted resignation the millions who continued in poverty and other millions who, for reasons of the exclusiveness and white supremacy of the progressive society, were not permitted to live their lives in dignity.

As the first beneficiary of the cultural consolidation of the 1890's, the new Republican orthodoxy, grounded in the revolutionary (and decidedly anti-Jeffersonian) political methods of Mark Hanna, provided the mores for the twentieth century without ever having to endure a serious debate about the possibility of structural change in the American forms of finance capitalism or the impact of corporate money on the American political process itself. Political conservatives nevertheless endured intermittent periods of extreme nervousness—such as was produced in 1933 by the nation's sudden and enforced departure from the gold standard. Given the presumed centrality of a metallic currency, it took a while for cultural traditionalists, including bankers, to realize that the influence of the banking community had not suffered organic disturbances—J. Laurence Laughlin to the contrary, notwithstanding. Though the pattern of interest rates during and after World War II continued to transfer measurable portions of the national income from both entrepreneurs and wage-earners to bankers—in the process burdening the structure of prices with an added increment of cost as well as changing the very structure of industrial capitalism—disputes over the distribution of income within the whole society did not precipitate serious social contentions as long as America maintained a favorable international trade and investment balance. It remained clear, however, that unresolved questions about the inherited financial system might well make a sudden and unexpected reappearance if, at any time in the second half of the twentieth century, shifts in world trade and the cost of imported raw materials placed severe forms of competitive pressure on the American economy and on the international monetary system. At such a moment the cultural consolidation fashioned in the Gilded Age would undergo its first sustained re-evaluation, as the "financial question" once again intruded into the nation's politics and the issues of Populism again penetrated the American consciousness. That time, while pending, has not yet come.

For their part, Gilded Age traditionalists did not view the conclusive triumph of the corporate ethos as a foregone conclusion. Themselves insecure in an era of real and apparent change, they were unable to distinguish between authentic signs of economic dislocation and the political threat represented by those who called attention to those signs. On this rather primitive level the politics of the era resolved itself, and the progressive society was born. As an outgrowth of its insularity and complacency, industrializing America wanted uncritical voices of celebration. The agrarian radicals instead delivered the warning that all was not well with the democracy. They were not thanked.

Afterword

What became of the radicals—the earnest advocates who spawned the agrarian revolt? The subsequent careers of the people who have filled these pages merely testified to the diversity of American life. Some Populists adjusted to the collapse of their movement with what others in the ranks regarded as entirely too much poise and equanimity. Others looked desperately for a new political home, and a few, finding none and unable to bear the consequences, committed suicide.

In Kansas, Senator William Peffer recoiled from his brief sojourn into fusion in 1896, publicly described it as a decisive error, and was defeated for re-election. He dallied briefly as a third party Prohibition candidate and thereafter returned to the Republican Party. The fusion-minded chairman of the Kansas party, John Breidenthal, whose political career extended back through the Union Labor Party to the original Greenback Party, flirted with socialism and then grudgingly became a Republican. One of his mid-road opponents in Kansas, G. C. Clemens, became the Social Democratic candidate for Governor in 1900. At Clemens's opening campaign meeting, he was introduced by another convert to socialism, Lorenzo Lewelling, the ex-Governor and former ardent fusionist. Jerry Simpsom went to New Mexico, where he became a land agent for the Santa Fe Railroad.[1]

Frank Doster, the socialist judge, became the Populist Chief Justice of the Kansas Supreme Court after being attacked as a "shabby, wild-eyed, rattle-brained fanatic" by William Allen White, the Emporia editor. Doster's evenhanded decisions and eloquent written opinions won the grudging respect and, eventually, the freely acknowledged admiration of the Kansas bar. In the new century, the courtly jurist had the satisfaction of watching the slow evolution of William Allen White into a Progressive, gracefully accepted White's public apologies, and remained an unreconstructed critic of many features of American capitalism throughout his long life. Doster worked actively for women's suffrage in Kansas, considered the election of Franklin D. Roosevelt a hopeful sign, and died in 1933 while drafting agrarian reform legislation to help the increasing number of tenant farmers in Kansas.[2]

Julius Wayland developed the *Appeal to Reason* into the nation's foremost socialist newspaper. One famed special edition of a million copies required the labor of most of the citizens of Girard, Kansas, to mail. Though a successful businessman as well as an ardent socialist, Wayland ultimately lapsed into despondency and committed suicide.[3]

Marion Butler became a greenbacker and William Allen became a mid-roader—at least fleetingly. After Allen's retirement from the Senate, he ultimately decided the policy of fusion had been a mistake. He attended one of the final, desperate "reorganizing" meetings of mid-road Populists in Denver in 1903 and then focused on his law practice. Marion Butler declared his conversion to a fiat currency in one of his last public addresses in the United States Senate. At the time, 1901, Butler knew he was a lame-duck Senator because Populist-Republican fusion in North Carolina had fallen victim to Democratic terrorism in 1898. In a massive campaign of white supremacy, punctuated by gunfire and arson, the party of the fathers had been swept back into office that year. During Populism's last stand in North Carolina in 1900, two of Butler's old opponents, Harry Tracy and "Stump" Ashby, came into the state in a vain effort to help him combat the organized politics of white supremacy. Butler was at that time one of the last surviving Populist officeholders in the South, and his conversion to the greenback cause apparently was the fruit of his belated association with Tracy, the third party's foremost monetary theorist. Butler's break with the Democratic Party, which followed hard on the heels of the lessons he learned in the fusion campaign of 1896, was permanent. He gradually became more liberal on the race issue. Butler passed into the Southern Republican Party in the new century and never thereafter came to terms with the party of the fathers.[4]

Tom Watson did. The frustration of his Populist years dogged Watson through a hopeless 1908 campaign in which he served as the last presidential candidate of the die-hard Populist remnant. After more than a decade of stolen elections and what he regarded as fusionist betrayals, Watson became deeply embittered. He eventually blamed Blacks, Catholics, and Jews for his own, and the nation's, political difficulties. He became a violently outspoken white supremacist. In the twilight of a life steeped in personal tragedy and blunted dreams, and flawed at its end by the political malice he had developed as a battered campaigner, Watson in 1920 won a surprising victory and became a United States Senator from Georgia. He died in office in 1922. One other prominent Southern Populist, James "Cyclone" Davis, had an almost identical political career. Alienated from most of his fellow Populists in Texas because he was not sufficiently alienated from the Democratic Party, Davis, a covert Texas fusionist in 1896 and an overt one in 1898, made the full return to the party of the fathers as the new century opened. He became a prohibitionist and white supremacist, worked for the Ku Klux Klan, and won election for one term as a Congressman in 1916, taking the old seat that had been denied him by "Harrison County methods" in 1894. As late as 1939, the white-bearded Davis could be heard on the streetcorners of Dallas, making flamboyant speeches on the need to control Wall Street and the necessity for white supremacy.[5]

Reuben Kolb in Alabama and James Weaver in Iowa both remained Bryan Democrats after 1896. Weaver became the Mayor of Colfax, Iowa, and died in that office in 1912. Minnesota's Ignatius Donnelly enjoyed a minor career as a literary figure. Mann Page, the Virginia Populist, became one of the last presidents of the National Farmers Alliance and gradually and reluctantly returned to the Democratic Party of Virginia. The editorial spokesman of Virginia Populism, Charles Pierson, the Oxfordian who edited the Virginia *Sun,* became a Debsian socialist.[6]

Many of the most renowned radical organizers of the Alliance, relatively young men in the early cooperative days in the 1880's, lived well into the twentieth century. South Dakota's Henry Loucks was still writing antimonopoly pamphlets that extolled the virtues of farmer cooperatives as late as 1919. J. F. Willits, leader of the Kansas Alliance, became a socialist. W. Scott Morgan of Arkansas penned a brooding attack on the racial demagoguery of the Southern Democracy and saw it published as a novel in 1904. (It must be said that Morgan's political instincts surpassed his literary gifts.) Joseph Manning, Alabama's relentlessly energetic Populist, fought fusion to the bitter end in 1896 and then joined the rapidly shrinking Alabama Republican Party in the midst of the politics of disfranchisement. He eventually moved to New York, where on one occasion he was honored by a black organization with whom he shared progressive political sympathies. Like Morgan of Arkansas, Manning tried to energize other white Americans to do something about the party of white supremacy in the South. If Manning's politics coalesced easily with Morgan's, his book, *The Fadeout of Populism,* published in 1922, unfortunately also confirmed him as Morgan's equal as a writer.[7]

Henry Vincent spent his life as a printer, editor, and reformer. In the 1920's he received the support of a number of American intellectuals and progressives, including John Dewey and Arthur Garfield Hays, in a new venture called *The Liberal Magazine.* His brother Leopold, whose lyrics found their way into the *Alliance Songster* during the hopeful days of the Alliance national organizing campaign in 1890–91, married a young woman of progressive views and settled in Oklahoma. "Stump" Ashby, the "famous agitator and humorist" and perhaps Populism's most eligible bachelor, also migrated to Oklahoma. He married a daughter of the Comanche Indian nation, and sired a large family. Along with his old radical colleague, S. O. Daws, the original "traveling lecturer" of the Alliance, Ashby helped organize the Oklahoma Farmers Union in the new century. A rangy patriarch of the left whose oratorical powers and humor brought him friends wherever he went, Ashby died in Octavia, Oklahoma, in 1923.[8]

William Lamb became one of the most prosperous of all the old radical organizers. Much of the land he acquired for his Montague County farm became the site of the town of Bowie. Though the early Montague cooperative gin and mill that he and thirteen other Alliancemen helped underwrite in 1886 collapsed because of lack of access to credit, eventually Lamb was able to build a similar enterprise out of the proceeds of the sale of town lots. "Lamb and Hulme, millers and ginners," established a modified "sub-treasury" warehouse of their own by permitting farmers to store their cotton without charge while awaiting higher prices. The firm did one of the largest businesses in the North Texas farming country until it was destroyed by fire in the middle 1890's. In 1906, Lamb's hybrid fruits won prizes at the Fort Worth Exposition—though the aging boycotter did not quite fulfill the role of a gentleman farmer. Among other things, he remained politically radical. Many small American towns before World War II could claim one old iconoclast whose political views had been shaped by bygone struggles. In Topeka, Kansas, his name was Frank Doster; in Bowie, Texas, his name was William Lamb.[9]

2

Irony is the handmaiden of American radicalism, and the sharpest ironies were reserved for Charles W. Macune. As the *Southern Mercury* observed at the time, Macune, having no heart for a radical third party, simply withdrew from the ranks of the reformers in 1892. He never returned. He lived in the East for a while and eventually went back to Waco, the scene of his first great triumph in 1887 and his tactically decisive defeat at the hands of William Lamb in 1891. He lived out his life in Texas as a Methodist pastor, aided by his son in his final endeavor—ministering to the agrarian poor. In 1920, Macune deposited his reminiscences of the Alliance years in the University of Texas library in Austin. The fifty-nine page manuscript, as enigmatic as Macune's own career, raised more questions than it answered. He understood the nation's economy better than most Gilded Age economists, and he understood the limits of the cooperative movement better than other Alliance leaders. But he never understood the radical political world of which he was a part, or how he lost influence in the organization he had done so much to build. Yet, more broadly than anyone else, he lived the entire range of the massive agrarian attempt at self-help and he experienced in a most personal way the traumatic implications of the political movement that grew out of that effort.

In his own time, Macune's sub-treasury system was attacked relentlessly, generally without intelligence, and almost always without grace. His patient explanations were rarely printed and almost never given a fair hearing. Among historians, Macune's political traditionalism, his economic radicalism, and his recurrent opportunism have combined to leave him with few admirers. His cooperative methods have won a too-easy condemnation from those who have not confronted the realities of the financial system that both energized and defeated the cooperative movement in America.[10]

By 1889, those who understood the options best—and Macune certainly more clearly than anyone else—knew that the Alliance dream of a national federation of regional cooperatives was untenable, because of the power and hostility of the American financial community. The sub-treasury promised to save the situation, and it did so as long as it remained merely the source of economic possibility rather than the inspiration for a radical third party. The operative life of the National Alliance, on its own terms, extended over a period of less than five years, from the announcement of the cooperative goal in the spring of 1887, through the shift to reliance upon a government-supported sub-treasury system in 1890, to the cooperative failures across the nation in 1890–92, and to its final service to farmers—as a tactical aid in the creation of the People's Party. This core economic experience of the National Alliance was Macune's experience more than any other man's.

Macune's own political weakness was the general weakness of the Southern Democracy and reflected the environment in which both he and his conservative rivals matured. He had some narrow horizons. Though his ambition for himself and the Alliance encouraged him to lofty nationwide organizing strategies, he never understood the political drives of urban workers, Western farmers, or black Americans. The men he gathered around him in Washington—Terrell, Tracy, Sledge, Tillman, and Turner—were all Southerners, three from Texas, one from Tennessee, and one from Georgia. Obsessed by the challenge of freeing the Southern farmer from the crop lien, Macune performed with unusual creativity. But he did not habitually think in political terms beyond those of his own immediate environment, nor, as his actions in 1892 revealed, did he have the political courage of his economic convictions.[11]

Yet Macune's sub-treasury system for the "whole class" was one of the boldest and most imaginative economic ideas suggested in nineteenth-century America. More significantly for the long run, the sub-treasury plan rested upon a broad theoretical foundation regarding the use of the nation's resources for the benefit of the entire society. Macune's plan was not a completely flawless solution to the rigidity of a metallic currency, but it not only was workable with simple modifications, it was clearly superior to the rigid doctrines of either goldbugs or silverites. Indeed, its potential impact was both widespread and economically healthy. Macune's proposal to put the capital assets of the nation to work for a large sector of its laboring poor had the merit of providing a specific example of how such a concept could be approached in practical terms. He repeatedly explained that the core of the sub-treasury plan was a flexible national currency freed from the dominant influence of a self-interested banking community. The warehouse provisions, though helpful in providing orderly machinery, were secondary. But the substance of the plan, beyond its conceptual basis, was its response to the financial realities of an industrializing state and the new power relationships between bankers and non-bankers that those realities enshrined. On this highly relevant topic, Macune was less rigid, or less culturally confined, than almost all Gilded Age politicians and an overwhelming majority of the nation's academic economists. Indeed, whether in behalf of entrepreneurs seeking capital for expansion, for working Americans seeking a home of their own, or in the context of the health and flexibility of the national economy itself, the country has never found a way to confront the enormous implications of financial relationships structurally geared to the self-interest of private, commercial bankers. It is only just to concede to Charles Macune the significance of his aims, while detailing his failings. He was the boldest single theorist of the agrarian revolt. He was also, in economic terms, one of the most creative public men of Gilded Age America. But in 1892 he vitiated the meaning of much of his own work when, as a white supremacist, he could not bring himself to break with the party of the fathers. He had a great deal of company, North and South.[12]

Origins and Legacy
of a Culturally Inadmissible Idea:
The Sub-Treasury Land and Loan System

"a matter of power, ideology, and culture . . ."

The sub-treasury system proposed by Charles Macune to the National Alliance in 1889 is discussed in the text primarily in terms of its political implications for the Gilded Age. Ironically, while the short-run political utility to the agrarian movement of the sub-treasury system has been seriously underestimated—considering its fundamental role in the successful creation of a Southern-Western third party coalition—the question of its theoretical origin has generated considerable disputation. Unfortunately, the debate has been quite disjointed because the entire subject of communitarian and soft-money cooperative utopianism is one that has not fitted neatly into the categories of political description sanctioned within the capitalist and socialist traditions. In America, the matter has never been treated in both its labor and agrarian contexts. Most important of all, not only have the egalitarian realities of the sub-treasury plan been quietly ignored but the modern implications of the undemocratic land and monetary systems that evolved in America after the rejection of Populist reforms have also been ignored.

While the debate has been narrow and cursory, the merits of cooperative experimentation and its relationship to nineteenth-century labor theory have nevertheless received radically different appraisals. The polarity extends at least from Irvin Unger, *The Greenback Era,* which presents a dim view of the whole proceedings, to Philip Foner, *History of the Labor Movement in the United States,* which treats the subject seriously as part of early labor experimentation in strategies of self-defense, before the author rejects cooperation as ultimately tangential to his interest in the struggle for socialism. The Lassallean origins of labor-cooperatives in America are, however, cogently treated by David Montgomery in his excellent study, *Beyond Equality* (165–67, 178). As the present study strives to affirm, the agrarian contribution to the rather germane role of cooperation as an integral part of nineteenth-century social theory—both in the potential politicizing impact of cooperation on its participants and as a source of democratic theory itself—has really never been treated at all. In the modern world, the implications of this neglect seem to be quite large.

Macune's contribution is central. Surprisingly, even his authorship of the sub-treasury system has been disputed. John Hicks points to the claims of a North Carolina Allianceman named Harry Skinner who, four days before the St. Louis meeting in 1889, published an article about the tariff that contained some ideas suggestive of a portion of the sub-treasury plan.[1] Chester McA. Destler advances the claims of Edward Kellogg as a progenitor.[2] James C. Malin probes European antecedents.[3]

Aside from the detailed analysis written by economist William Yohe (see Appendix B), the best description of the contemporary meaning of Macune's work, other than by Macune himself or by his comrade-in-cooperation, Harry Tracy, may be found in Fred Shannon, "C. W. Macune and the Farmer's Alliance," *Current History*, XXVIII (June 1955), 330–35. Shannon demonstrates the relationship between Macune's 1888 treasury-note proposal and the 1889 sub-treasury plan. Tracy's defense—the most lucid theoretical description of greenback monetary analysis I have found in nineteenth-century literature—is contained in "The Sub-Treasury Plan," in James H. Davis, *A Political Revelation* (Dallas, 1894), 293–399. After his 1888 treasury-note proposal, Macune moved from Texas to Washington early in 1889 to establish the *National Economist*. The impact of the environment of the federal city on his final product is, perhaps, self-evident. The pattern of these modifications, as they evolved in Macune's thought, are visible in issues of the *National Economist* throughout the summer and fall of 1889.[4] The crucial intellectual breakthrough—that the credit to defeat the crop lien system must come from the federal government—was in place by early October 1889, two months before Skinner set forth his own, less-integrated idea.[5]

The claim for Skinner is, therefore, untenable. The sub-treasury plan directly reflected Macune's intense cooperative experience as manager of the Texas Exchange, and he could both explain and defend it in creative detail, two qualifications not so ably demonstrated by Mr. Skinner—even after he had the benefit of Macune's prior writings in the *National Economist*.

As for Edward Kellogg's influence, Macune's problem was that he did not respond to this soft-money advocate as much as he should have. Macune concentrated with such single-mindedness upon commodity loans (the only negotiable asset Southern farmers possessed) that he failed to see the merit of land loans until Kansas Alliancemen pointed it out to him. Land loans were a Kelloggian emphasis, rather more appreciated by Macune's radical rivals in Texas than by Macune himself. The third party convention called

by H. S. P. Ashby in Texas in May 1888—eighteen months before the unveiling of the sub-treasury system—proposed the elimination of the national
banking system and national bank notes "and in lieu therefore we advocate a
legal tender money and a direct loan of the same to the people at a low rate
of interest *on real estate security.*" [6] At the time completely absorbed in the
elaborate preliminaries to June 9, 1888—"the day to save the exchange"—
Macune was so offended by the radical political implications of Ashby's
Waco meeting that he spared time from his cooperative struggle to write a
long letter to the brotherhood warning against independent political action.[7]
It is quite possible that Macune was so put off by the action of the radicals
that he did not read their platform. He should have. The immediate incor-
poration of land loans in his system might have made his plan more persuasive to the hesitant spokesmen of the Nebraska Alliance, thus speeding
up by two years the eventual absorption of the Nebraskans into the organized agrarian movement, and, conceivably, fatally undermining the development of the shadow movement of Populism.

The French precedent cited by Malin—a warehouse storage plan of
1848—is germane; Macune himself cited it in his *Report of the Committee on
the Monetary System* that outlined the sub-treasury system to the 1889 convention.[8]

The observers of nineteenth-century working class America who have
been most responsive to the pioneering contributions of Charles Macune
have not been historians, generally, but trained economists who served as independent specialists in farmer cooperatives. One of the best analyses in
print of the meaning of the sub-treasury system is by Joseph Knapp, *The
Rise of American Cooperative Enterprise* (Danville, Ill., 1969), 65–69, 438. Macune tended to see social problems as a function of class—broadly defined—
and his sub-treasury system was a specific product of that belief. In his
words, the sub-treasury was "calculated to benefit the whole class." This specifically included landless tenants, a group left untouched by land loans. It
was this larger objective—to free "the whole class" from furnishing merchants—that underlay the bold effort to establish a large-scale marketing
and purchasing structure through a centralized statewide cooperative. The
Texas Alliance Exchange was the first such comprehensive effort by any
working-class institution in the world. It can fairly, if unfortunately, be said
that the Texas cooperative was destroyed by the American banking system.
The fullness of this reality was perceived by no one more than Macune himself; his certainty that cooperatives for "the whole class" could not survive in
the absence of fundamental democratic reform of the American banking
system led him to the theoretical basis of the sub-treasury system.

In terms of his contributions in fashioning practical applications of democratic monetary theory, and in terms of theory itself, it would seem that
Charles Macune merits considerable reappraisal. He was America's foremost
agrarian monetary theorist of the nineteenth century, the father of large-
scale cooperation, commodity credit, delayed commodity marketing, and,
thus, of a number of the eventual doctrines of farm parity. Additionally his

sub-treasury system achieved something the Federal Reserve Act of 1913 utterly failed to achieve—a system whereby the government could serve as the lender of last resort as a means of maintaining a flexible and workable monetary system. Above all, Macune's plan brought the nation's monetary system under democratic control and gave millions of citizens access to capital at low interest—an achievement that promised to expand the human possibilities of the entire society. (See Appendix B.) The sub-treasury system was the ideological culmination both of nineteenth-century greenback theory and of the cooperative crusade of the National Alliance. It offered "the whole class" of farmers a way out of peonage, something the "reforms" of the twentieth century did not do.

But the sub-treasury was a culturally inadmissible idea—in the 1890's, as today. Any system involving the termination of the gold standard was unthinkable to the nation's financial and political elites of the 1890's, just as a commodity-based international monetary system and a treasury-based central bank to replace the Federal Reserve System is unthinkable to the same elites today. Indeed, the very idea of democratic influence over interest rates through a central bank of sufficient capital and currency issuing power is one that points toward an important loss of economic privilege by those very financial elites who consolidated their political and cultural power in the 1890's and retain it with augmented authority today. The distortion of Macuneite ideas, both through the Federal Reserve Act of 1913 and through various administrative applications of New Deal farm legislation, contributed directly to the demise of the American system of family farming. This causal relationship is, of course, completely outside the received intellectual traditions dominant in American graduate schools in both history and economics. In a phrase, such a causal relationship violates our idea of progress. The evidence, however, is clear enough.

While the Aldrich Commission's recommendations on the currency in 1912 recognized the compelling need for a new system of agricultural credit, the framers of the Federal Reserve Act, goldbugs all, moved very slowly to incorporate broadly gauged credit features into the nation's basic monetary structure. The original act of 1913 failed utterly to provide the six to nine months of economical credit needed by farmers, and though the 1923 amendments establishing intermediate banks extended credit features to sectors of the agricultural middle class, even modest attempts to reach "the whole class" were not forthcoming until the New Deal. By that time, landless tenantry had engulfed not only the old cotton belt but also the corn belt.[9] Indeed, by providing credit to large-scale farming interests years before it was even partially extended to "the whole class," the effect of this legislation was to help land-owning mortgage companies in the West and furnishing merchants in the South to acquire title to more land. In essence, twentieth-century agricultural "reform" led to centralization of land-ownership in America.[10]

In the modern culture of the progressive society, it has long been fashionable to attribute the centralization of land ownership in agricultural America to the competitive "efficiency" of economies of scale by "agri-business," as compared to the presumed limitations inherent in the operations of family farms. However, evidence exists that the real economies of scale are not technical but artificial, produced by the actions of suppliers, purchasers, and federal tax and subsidy policies.[11]

While the concept of "economies of scale" in agriculture remains debatable, in itself, the more germane historical reality is that centralization of American farmland had occurred *even before* corporate farming could prove or disprove its relative "efficiency." [12] It was simply a matter of capital and the power of those having capital to prevent remedial democratic legislation. The failure to provide credit for seventy years would seem to be the operative ingredient in these dynamics which has been rather overlooked. Culturally, it has not been considered good manners in the American academy to draw critical attention to bankers.

Similarly, the centralization of land in socialist countries has uniformly occurred before the "efficiency" of that mode of organization could prove or disprove itself. Such "proof" as has subsequently materialized can scarcely console the proponents of centralization. Cultural constraints, however, operate to reduce independent opinion in socialist societies also. In both capitalist and socialist worlds in the twentieth century, "efficiency" has become a *post facto* justification of what essentially has been an assertion of raw political or economic control. Land centralization has to do with power, ideology, and culture, not with what is actually taking place on the land.

The one agricultural adventure of the New Deal that most nearly approached Macune's objective of benefiting "the whole class" was the Resettlement Program of the Farm Security Administration, designed to provide land loans at low interest to enable black and white tenants to become owners of family farms. The program was initiated on a small scale in isolated pockets of the South in the 1930s and 1940s. Though the program was successful, land acquisition was halted in 1943 and the process of centralization has since continued, especially affecting black land-owners in the South.[13]

In the absence of significant literature on the subject, land centralization is a process that remains obscure to most Americans, but one they may feel no right to inquire into—given the fact that land centralization is sanctioned by the culture itself. Indeed, the remarkable cultural hegemony prevailing throughout American society mitigates against serious inquiry into the underlying economic health of the democracy itself. Quite literally, Americans no longer feel they have the right to know the central economic facts about the society they live in, so those facts are (1) not available (2) their nonavailability is not a subject of public interest. Large-scale property ownership in America is a legal secret secluded in "trusts," "street names," and "nominees" beyond the reach of any democratic institution in the society.[14]

Be that as it may, the entire subject of large-scale agriculture in the modern state, both under capitalist and communist systems of organization, needs thorough re-evaluation. Such an evaluation should extend to alternatives available as part of the legacy of the National Farmers Alliance and Industrial Union—principally, the example of family farms, united for purchasing and marketing through large-scale and small-scale cooperatives and functionally assisted through modernized "sub-treasury" systems. Such systems of agricultural organization would seem to be particularly suitable for certain national cultures in the "third world"—though certainly not for all of them. Coordinate with the achievement of a commodity-based international monetary system—a sizable alteration in itself—the implications of such democratic innovations could be large, both in terms of international hunger and, conceivably, international peace. To implement such a plan, however, its political supporters in the capitalist world would have to overcome the received culture of mass deference to bankers and the lobbying power of the bankers themselves, both in America and in Europe. Similarly, the plan's proponents in the communist world would have to overcome equally powerful forces—the received culture of socialist dogma and the bureaucratic rigidities of high-level state functionaries. As matters now stand, the peasantry and yeomanry of the third world may expect no coherent help from either party. The last politically active theorists who were culturally autonomous enough to grapple, as an intellectual challenge, directly with organic monetary problems and theory, were politically defeated and culturally isolated eighty years ago.

Their names were Charles Macune and Harry Tracy.[15]

An Economic Appraisal of the Sub-Treasury Plan

BY WILLIAM P. YOHE *

"brave army of heretics . . ."

The very term "sub-treasury" suggests, of course, the widely used alternative name for the Independent Treasury System in effect from 1846 to 1921, under which the Treasury maintained a number of branch subtreasuries to act as depositories and disbursing agents in place of banks.[1] The aura of respectability, as well as the depository analogue, doubtless led to the use of the term. Because of Charles Macune's role in the formulation of the sub-treasury plan immediately after his ill-fated experience with private cooperatives in Texas, the subtreasuries may easily be seen as the solution to the problems of inadequate capital and short-term borrowing opportunities that led to the experiment's failure. In place of private cooperatives would be a nationwide network of public depositories with unlimited capacity for the creation of money and low-cost credit. From 1890 onward, land loans were proposed as one of the leading activities of the sub-treasuries.[2]

Several versions of the plan appeared in National Alliance and People's Party platforms, bills introduced in Congress, and in writings by currency reformers over the 1889–94 period.[3] The most comprehensive plan, incor-

* The author, a specialist in monetary policy, is professor of economics at Duke University and author of many articles on the subjects of money, banking, and the Federal Reserve System. Professor Yohe wishes to acknowledge the assistance of Professor Anna J. Schwartz of the National Bureau of Economic Research, for graciously making available previously unpublished annual estimates of the U.S. net national product, and of Professors Joseph H. Spengler and Lawrence Goodwyn, for bibliographical materials.

porating responses to a number of criticisms of earlier ones, was probably that put forth by Harry Tracy, and his work will receive the greatest attention here.[4]

Later versions of the sub-treasury plan contained, to use Tracy's term, two "planks," the land loan plank and the warehouse and elevator plank.[5] Both were to be administered through sub-treasuries of the U.S. Treasury located in each county whose average annual production of selected commodities in the preceding two years exceeded (in most versions) $500,000. Eighty per cent land loans on 200 acres or less were to be paid to farmers in legal tender up to a ceiling of $3000; loans were to carry maximum maturities of 50 years and maximum interest rates of 2 per cent. Based on various lists of standardized, storable commodities,[6] farmers could obtain 80 per cent loans, payable in legal tender notes, at 1 per cent interest (in most versions) for a maximum maturity of twelve months. Grain was to be deposited in elevators, and cotton in warehouses; farmers were to receive negotiable certificates of deposit specifying the amounts of loans and the margin between the cash value of crops deposited and loans made against them.[7] The certificates had to be redeemed within a year, the loans repaid, and interest, storage charges, insurance, and (later versions) pro-rated shares of other operating expenses paid to the sub-treasuries. Depositors could sell the certificates to commodity buyers (manufacturers or dealers), redeem them themselves, or (later versions) have them called by the sub-treasuries, who could sell directly to buyers.

The basic purpose of the land loans was "to increase the permanent and stable volume of money in circulation" to not less than $50 per capita, while commodity loans were "to facilitate the even distribution of money, prevent its congestion in cities and make the volume of money adjust itself to the demands of business at all times and places." [8] The $50 per capita goal for currency, first advocated in the Ocala Platform of the National Alliance in 1890,[9] was meant to return the per capita stock of currency to nearly that prevailing at the end of the Civil War and to provide for the automatic increase of currency with population.[10] Sub-treasury loans to commodity producers, on the other hand, were designed to stabilize short-run commodity prices, i.e., to remove the strong seasonal movements in such prices caused by the timing of harvests vis-à-vis intertemporally stable demands for commodities.

The rate of interest to be charged on commodity loans in most versions of the sub-treasury plan was 1 per cent or, as some called it, "money at cost." [11] What this referred to was the 1 per cent interest that national banks had to pay the Treasury annually for national bank notes issued to them, which were then lent, not at "cost," but at usurious rates of interest.[12] The sub-treasuries were supposed to eliminate the middleman. Furthermore, the 80 per cent loan value for havested crops was, ironically, related to the collateral requirement for national bank notes, which could be issued up to 90 per cent of the value of U.S. Government securities deposited with the Treasury.[13]

Tracy cleverly avoided many controversial ancillary features of early plans, especially those contained in bills introduced in Congress.[14] Thus, he did not suggest that all currency used to repay commodity loans be destroyed, that the use of banks as U.S. Treasury depositories be abolished and somehow be replaced by sub-treasuries, that sub-treasury agents be appointed and paid by the Treasury, that anyone other than farmers could secure commodity loans from a sub-treasury,[15] or that sub-treasury districts necessarily had to follow single-county boundaries, confining the earlier plans to an estimated richest fourth of all counties and relegating farmers in poor counties to long hauls.[16]

The avowed intent of subtreasury commodity loans was seasonal stabilization of cotton and grain prices and, as a concomitant, the elimination of unnecessary components of wholesale commodity prices paid by manufacturers: "useless shipping, extravagant handling, useless and demoralizing speculation, and useless and demoralizing usury." [17] Every commodity in the warehouses and elevators was supposed to turn over in twelve months or less. Had the plan been implemented, problems would have arisen with stabilizing inter-year commodity prices and marketings, since, because of the vagaries of the weather, some years bring bumper crops and others, poor crops. Pressures would doubtless have arisen for carryover of stocks from surplus years and the extension of loan maturities. Depending on how one looks at it, there is the seed for the agricultural stabilization programs of the 1930s or even for multiple-commodity reserve proposals, which received considerable attention in the 1930s and early 1940s, although of ancient origin. According to one of the leading proponents, Benjamin Graham:

> . . . the world can use its basic, durable commodities as monetary reserves. By so doing it can contribute mightily, and at a single stroke, to solving a host of major post-war problems: the promotion of wide expansion [in economic activity]; the attainment of reasonable price-level stability; the establishing of useful and nondisruptive stockpiles; the creation of more adequate purchasing power in the hands of farmers and of raw-materials nations; and the faciliating of foreign trade, of trade-balance settlements, and of stable currency values.[18]

All of which brings us to the causes and consequences of implementing the sub-treasury system. Populists bemoaned the low prices received by farmers relative to the prices farmers had to pay for living and operating expenses and relative to prices manufacturers and processors had to pay for commodities (so-called wholesale prices). They also bemoaned low prices in general, which they correctly blamed on the currency shortage. Table 1 contains price indices for the cost of living and for wheat and cotton, using the average of 1910–14 prices as the base (100, i.e., 100 per cent, where the per cent is understood). 1910–14 was an extremely prosperous period in U.S. agriculture, and the federal farm price support program has always been based on the prices that prevailed over this period.

Paul Douglas's cost of living index applies to urban wage earners, but, in the absence of any index of prices paid by farmers in the 1890s, it may serve

Table 1. Selected Price Indices, 1890–1900
(1910–14 = 100)

| | Wholesale prices | | | Prices received by farmers | |
	Cost of Living	Wheat	Raw Cotton	Wheat	Raw Cotton
1890	78	90	86	96	78
1891	76	97	67	95	66
1892	76	80	60	72	76
1893	75	68	64	61	64
1894	73	57	54	56	42
1895	73	61	57	58	69
1896	75	65	61	83	61
1897	75	80	56	93	61
1898	75	89	47	66	52
1899	77	72	51	68	64
1900	79	71	74	71	83
1910–14 Average [a]	100	$.989	$.129	$.871	$.110

[a] Prices per bushel of wheat and per pound of cotton.

Sources: cost of living index—Paul H. Douglas, *Real Wages in the United States, 1890–1926* (New York, 1930), p. 60; wholesale prices—U.S. Bureau of the Census, *Historical Statistics of the United States, Colonial Times to 1957* (Washington, D.C., 1960), pp. 116–17; prices received by farmers—*ibid.*, pp. 297, 301–2.

as a proxy for, at least, farmers' living costs. The cost of living was quite stable over the decade, not even falling very much in the severe 1893–94 recession. The prices of wheat and cotton, components of every version of the sub-treasury plan, may be taken as indicators of movements in the prices of storable commodities generally. The volatility of wholesale prices and the even greater volatitlity of prices received by farmers are apparent in the price indices. In the face of stable living costs, cotton and wheat prices were depressed most of the time. In most cases, wholesale prices lagged a year behind movements in farmers' prices.

In Table 2, estimates of implementing the land loan system for increasing currency outside banks to $50 per capita from 1890 to 1900 are presented with respect to the effect on two leading measures of the money stock and the monetary base (vault cash reserves of banks behind deposits plus currency outside banks) supporting the money stock. To see what currency outside banks would have to be to reach $50 per capita, it was necessary merely to multiply Bureau of the Census population estimates for each year by $50. Actual currency per capita over the period varied from a low of $12 in 1896 to a high of $16 in 1900, with $14–15 in most years. The plan would have caused currency in the hands of the non-bank public to be multiplied by three to four times and would have stabilized the amount.

From a modern perspective, one of the most serious defects of the plan did not bear on any of the reasons for which it was attacked in the 1890s,

Table 2. Implementation of $50 Per Capita in Currency
Outside Banks (in Billions of Dollars)

| | Currency outside banks | | Monetary aggregates with $50 per capita | | |
| | | | Money stock [a] | | Monetary base [b] |
	Actual	$50/capita	M-1	M-2	
1890	$0.9	$3.2	—	$13.9	$4.8
1891	0.9	3.2	—	14.1	5.0
1892	0.9	3.3	$12.6	15.8	5.4
1893	1.0	3.3	11.9	14.3	5.1
1894	0.9	3.4	13.3	16.3	6.1
1895	0.9	3.5	14.1	17.7	5.9
1896	0.8	3.5	13.9	18.2	6.0
1897	0.9	3.6	13.8	18.5	6.3
1898	1.0	3.7	14.6	18.6	6.2
1899	1.1	3.7	16.9	21.1	6.3
1900	1.2	3.8	16.5	21.7	6.4

[a] M-1 is currency outside banks plus demand deposits of the non-bank public (individuals, businesses, state and local governments); M-2 is M-1 plus time and savings deposits of the non-bank public.

[b] Vault cash of commercial banks plus currency outside banks; called "currency in circulation" at the time.

Source: Historical Statistics of the U.S., p. 7; Friedman & Schwartz, *Monetary Statistics,* pp. 341; Board of Governors of the Federal Reserve System, *Banking and Monetary Statistics,* p. 34. All columns except actual currency outside banks computed.

but rather the fact that its advocates apparently did not relate the sub-treasury system either to the public's demands for checking accounts (demand deposits) and savings deposits vis-à-vis currency or to banks' demands for vault cash reserves vis-à-vis their deposits.[19] By the 1890s the principal medium of payment had already become checking accounts in banks, and currency constituted only about a fourth of the (now) conventional measure of the money stock (currency outside banks and demand deposits of the non-bank public).[20] Thus, for example, if in 1892 currency had suddenly been increased from $0.9 billion to $3.3 billion in hopes of raising currency per capita to $50 and if (1) the public's demand for currency relative to the money stock remained at the actual level of 26 per cent and (2) banks continued to absorb currency into vault cash reserves behind their deposits at the actual rate of 17 per cent, the volume of currency that ultimately remained outside banks would be only $2.0 billion, as $1.3 billion of the initial currency increase would end up in bank vaults as reserve behind increased demand and savings deposits.[21] As a result, actual currency per capita would be only about $30.

There is no practical way to avoid the result just mentioned. No matter whether the currency was dropped from airplanes (an anachronism in the 1890s) or paid as the proceeds of land loans at a sub-treasury, as soon as it was spent for goods and services or to repay debts, the liquid asset preferences of the non-bank public and the conventional and legal requirements for bank reserves would prevail.[22] As a result, assuming these ratios would be the same in each year with $50 per capita as with the actual state (the ratios were all reasonably stable over the entire period.[23]), the estimates of the corresponding measures of the two leading money stock concepts and of the requisite bank vault cash and currency of $50 per capita are given in the three right-hand columns of Table 2. Thus, to have currency outside banks of $50 per capita in 1892 or a total of $3.3 billion would necessitate total currency issues of $5.4 billion (actual bank vault cash plus currency outside banks in 1892 was $1.5 billion). That is a lot of (mostly) greenbacks! If, as some versions of the sub-treasury plan demanded, national bank notes be eliminated,[24] that is a lot of greenbacks, indeed! Currency outside banks actually reached $3.3 billion in 1918, but currency per capita did not pass $50 until 1940.[25]

The conventional money stock (M-1) in 1892 would have been $12.6 billion with a $3.3 billion currency component, the balance ($9.3 billion) being demand deposits, while the broad money stock (M-2) would have been $15.8 billion, with $3.2 billion in savings accounts. By contrast, the actual M-1 in 1892 was $3.9 billion ($59 per capita), and M-2 was $4.5 billion ($68 per capita).[26]

It is interesting to speculate on the impact such large money stock changes might have had on total spending, price levels, and output in the 1890s. In Table 3, actual net national product according to the Gallman-Friedman and Schwartz estimates [27] is given in the first column. The series hit cyclical

Table 3. Net National Produce, 1890–1900: Actual, Full Employment, and with $50 Currency Per Capita

Net national product [a] *(billions of current dollars)*

	Actual	Full Employment	With $50 per capita
1890	$11.8	$11.5	$40.7
1891	12.1	12.1	41.3
1892	12.7	12.7	44.4
1893	12.5	13.3	40.9
1894	11.0	14.0	41.7
1895	12.1	14.7	47.9
1896	11.4	15.4	48.5
1897	12.6	16.2	52.0
1898	13.2	17.0	47.3
1899	15.1	17.9	52.4
1900	16.4	18.8	55.0

[a] Personal consumption expenditures, net private domestic investment (net of replacement investment), government purchases of goods and services, and net exports.

Source: worksheets supplied by Anna J. Schwartz (based on estimates by Robert E. Gallman).

peaks in 1892 and 1907 (not shown).[28] Taking these peaks as "full employment," the "linked peaks" method may be used to determine full employment levels of net national product in intervening years.[29] In this case, the compound annual growth rate from the 1892 to 1907 peaks was 5.0 per cent, which was then applied to the 1892 figure to obtain the 1893 figure; the 1893 figure was multiplied by 1.05 to get the 1894 full employment figure, etc.[30]

One of the most venerable tools of an economist is the equation of exchange, which states simply that the average amount of money to spend times the average number of times each dollar was spent (called "velocity") equals the total value of goods sold, i.e., price times quantity. Underlying the velocity with which money is spent are complex reasons for wanting to hold money, both institutional and behavioral.[31] Under the drastic simplifying assumption that velocity with the money stock consistent with $50 per capita in currency outside banks would be the same as actual velocity in each year, the last column in Table 3 was generated (velocity would probably be considerably higher, hence so also would be total spending or its obverse, money income). Thus, in every year from 1890 to 1900 the money stock with the subtreasury plan would have caused total spending to be three or more times the basic full employment level. The obvious spillover effect would have been on prices, with powerful real income redistribution in favor of debtors and against creditors and fixed income groups.[32]

How severe the inflation would have been is a difficult question, but some rough estimates may be made. There are really two questions: what would happen to the price level when the land loan plan was originally implemented and what would subsequently happen to prices as the plan was continuously maintained in response to the growth of population and changes in the banks' and the public's demands for liquid assets? Table 4 contains the estimates. Several assumptions lie behind them: (1) the price level at continuously full employment would have grown at the constant compound annual rate obtained by linking the 1892 and 1907 peaks (i.e., 1.1 per cent per year); (2) total spending with a money stock consistent with $50 currency per capita consists of full employment real output (i.e., deflated by actual prices) multiplied by the index of prices that would result relative to actual prices;[33] and (3) the plan would be implemented in 1890 or earlier, so that 1890 spending and prices fully reflect the adjustment to the increased money stock.

While the price level under the land loan plan would be over three times as high as actual prices, subsequent changes in prices after the shock of the initial adjustment would have been relatively small, with year-to-year price level decreases more frequent than and more than offsetting price increases.

As already mentioned, the much higher level of prices would redistribute income from creditors to debtors, since the real value of existing debt (e.g., loan) contracts would fall substantially.[34] People living on fixed incomes or whose incomes lag behind prices would suffer, at least initially. The real value of accumulated savings that were fixed in nominal terms (e.g., bank

Table 4. Price Indices, for the Net National Product, 1890–1900: Actual, Full Employment, and with $50 Currency Per Capita

(Average of Actual 1890–99 Prices = 100)

	Actual	Full Employment	With $50 Per Capita	Annual rate of inflation (percent)
1890	107	100	380	+247
1891	106	101	363	−4
1892	102	102	357	−2
1893	105	103	321	−10
1894	98	104	292	−9
1895	97	106	315	+8
1896	94	107	295	−6
1897	94	108	303	+3
1898	97	109	270	−11
1899	100	110	292	+8
1900	105	111	308	+5

Source: worksheets on net national product from Anna J. Schwartz, *Monetary Statistics,* Table 2 above.

deposits) would fall precipitously, inducing their holders to alter spending plans. To the extent that commodity loans removed seasonal movements in the prices of basic agricultural products and removed or reduced resource costs associated with transportation and speculation, prices received by farmers could be relatively higher, while those paid by producers (and, ultimately, consumers) could be relatively lower—on balance, another important aspect of real income redistribution under the sub-treasury plan.

Market determined interest rates simultaneously are the resultant of several sets of forces: the supply and demand for capital reflecting expected real returns to saving and productive investment, shocks caused by money stock changes and/or government surpluses or deficits, and lenders and investors' expectations about future movements in the price level.[35] In the period of adjustment to the plan's implementation, interest rates would probably first have fallen, then risen above beginning rates because of the effect of rising prices, and then returned to earlier levels. With low and fixed interest rates, borrowers from sub-treasuries would have enjoyed negative real costs of borrowing during the initial inflation. Thereafter they would have enjoyed a subsidy equal to the difference between their one or two per cent loans and either what they would have had to pay private lenders or what the government forewent by not lending to other borrowers at market rates of interest.

A fact that has long puzzled scholars is why, at least before World War I, the note issue power of national banks, even when most profitable, was so little used, being only about 20 per cent of what it could have been in 1890 and 28 per cent in 1900.[36] In other words, national bank notes could, based on the market value of government bonds eligible for deposit in order to issue notes, have been over $700 million greater in 1890 than they actually were ($182 million) and nearly $800 million greater than in 1900 ($300 million).[37] This was more than enough excess capacity to have expanded the monetary base (currency outside banks and bank vault cash) to full employment levels. For example, in the severe recession year of 1894, the actual monetary base was $1.6 billion, while the full employment monetary base is estimated at $2.0 billion. In 1900, the gap is even smaller ($250 million).[38] In 1894 the actual money stock (M-2) was $4.2 billion, while the full employment M-2 is estimated to have been $5.5 billion; in 1900, the figures are $6.4 billion and $7.4 billion, respectively. The paucity of national banking offices in rural areas and restrictions on their mortgage and agricultural lending would, however, have made it complicated to have tapped this excess capacity.

What effect would the sub-treasury plan have had on the gold standard and the highly venerated automatic specie-flow mechanism? On first thought, one might think that U.S. gold reserves would all simply disappear in a gigantic "Gresham's Law" ("bad money drives out good money") cataclysm.[39] On second thought, however, what probably would have happened is quite similar to what did happen from 1861 to 1879, when the U.S. was on a dual monetary standard.[40] Greenbacks and gold were not legally interchangeable at a fixed rate, so the greenback price of gold (and the gold price of greenbacks) was market determined. For Gresham's Law to operate, there would have had to be a fixed official rate of exchange between gold and greenbacks that differed from the market price of gold in greenbacks. Lacking that, the greenback price of gold coin and bullion would have risen along with all other prices, and gold would have remained in circulation.[41]

Where international trade and the balance of payments are concerned, the same line of reasoning applies. As it was, the U.S. experienced chronic trade deficits from 1790 to 1895, which were financed by capital inflows and gold outflows; after 1895, all of this, generally speaking, was reversed, with chronic trade surpluses financed by capital outflows and gold inflows.[42] With official exchange rates fixed by the gold content of standard monetary units of trading countries and with a dual monetary standard in effect, implementation of the sub-treasury plan and the resulting inflation would initially stimulate imports and depress exports, causing the rest of the world to accumulate U.S. currency, deposits in U.S. banks, and unpaid bills. The dual monetary standard would have led to dual exchange rates. Just as the price of gold coin, bullion, and certificates would have risen in terms of bank deposits and other currency, so, also would the prices of foreign exchange in terms of deposits and currency. The rise in exchange rates (also known as "exchange depreciation") would stimulate exports and dampen imports, thus reversing the initial effects of inflation. Some of the foreign holdings of deposits and currency would be used to buy gold, as well, which, under a pure gold standard, would reduce money, credit, and prices and thus stimulate exports and reduce imports; the effect of the automatic gold flows under the dual monetary standard would probably have been negligible.

If the preceding scenario had actually begun to unfold, it is possible that Congress—even a Populist-dominated Congress—would have been under considerable pressure to enact trade restrictions, e.g., import quotas and tariffs and export subsidies. This would have maximized the extent of the inflation resulting from the implementation of the sub-treasury plan.

> Money, Money, quite contrary,
> Where do your links all go—
> Through interest rates, or goods that sell,
> Or assets all in a row? [43]

This verse is a very cryptic summary of the major issues, past and present, in monetary theory. Populists believed in the money-spending link for alleviating the debt and income problems of farmers, as well as deficient aggregate demand for the whole economy. The sub-treasury plan they advocated would quantitatively have been the largest government program, excepting wars, until the 1930s. The mechanism for making land and commodity loans was a very subtle one, which simultaneously would have contended with the problems of financing cooperatives, the seasonal volatility of basic commodity prices, the scarcity of banking offices in rural areas, the lack of a "lender of last resort" for agriculture, inefficient storage and cross-shipping, the downward stickiness of prices paid by farmers vis-à-vis prices received for crops, and the effects of the secular deflation on farmers' debt burdens, all of which, in a far less comprehensive fashion, were the objects of legislation in the next five decades.

The chief shortcoming of the plan is the excessive inflation its literal implementation would have produced. It would have quickly produced as large an increase in the price level as actually took from 1890 to 1947 to attain.[44] The magnitude of the "overkill" proposed was probably due both to the lack of statistics and the lack of understanding of the importance of banks' demand for vault cash reserves and the public's demand for bank deposits, in addition to currency.[45] Theoretically sound as it was, however, the sub-treasury concept constituted a workable basis for the monetary system, even considering the unnecessary margin of inflation its advocates were willing to tolerate. It would have achieved what its supporters claimed—real income redistribution in favor of "the producing classes."

In their replies to critics, advocates of the sub-treasury plan were quite correct that it was not "class" legislation that would benefit only farmers. They foresaw some of the ideas in the revolution in economic thinking that occurred in the 1930s: the "multiplier effect" on total spending throughout the economy that results from any sustained increase in domestic government spending.[46] The Populists quite properly belong to, in the words of Lord Keynes, "the brave army of heretics . . . who, following their intuitions, have preferred to see the truth obscurely and imperfectly rather than to maintain error, reached indeed with clearness and consistency and by easy logic, but on hypotheses inappropriate to the facts." [47] Herein doubtless lies the reason they were ignored by contemporary intellectuals. It is interesting to observe, however, that one of the few scholars deeply sympathetic to the Populists in the 1890s was Richard T. Ely, the founder of the American Economics Association.

The Northwestern Farmers Alliance:
Opponent of Populism

"Organizationally derivative, intellectually without purpose . . ."

Populism's shadow movement of "silver-fusion" was an organic product of a small agrarian group that institutionally opposed the formation of the People's Party in the first place. The history of this institution, including its failure to merge with the National Alliance in 1889, makes clear its relationship to the eventual shadow movement of Populism.

1. A Brief History

The agrarian organization officially calling itself the National Farmers Alliance but more commonly known as the Northwestern Alliance was the creation of a Chicago magazine editor named Milton George. While quite traditional politically and strongly anti-labor, George, in common with most Americans of his era, nursed certain anti-monopoly sympathies. Specifically, he felt something ought to be done about railroad abuses. From his editorial base on a farm journal called the *Western Rural,* George decided in 1880 to organize local "farmers alliances" to induce Congress to regulate public carriers. He thereupon created and published in his magazine a model constitution for his alliance and called upon farmers to organize local affiliates. But, according to one observer, "nothing was accomplished because no one could be induced to form the first local." The first unit was formed in the office of the *Western Rural* and christened the Cook County Alliance.[1]

The ice broken, George continued to promote his idea in the magazine and soon reported he was sending out ten local charters a week. After seven months, he determined that enough interest had been created to hold a national convention. Using the magazine to publicize the event, and inviting a number of Midwestern governors, George attracted several hundred farmers and representatives of the agricultural press to the meeting. Some thirteen states were said to be represented; they passed a half-dozen anti-railroad resolutions and an additional one that encouraged farmers to forgo subscribing to agricultural journals not in sympathy with the new movement. The resolutions completed, half of the participants went home. The remainder organized the National Farmers Alliance. Dominated by George and one of his editorial writers, the group adopted a constitution that called for national, state, and local units. Though quite vague in organizational specifics and silent in terms of a continuing program, the document gave the national office great power, for it alone could charter local affiliates. As the *Western Rural* had wide circulation and grievances against railroads were rampant, the order grew to several hundred units in the first year. But there was no structure for unified action. Members got what guidance they could by reading the *Western Rural*. Despite constitutional authorization for state chapters to be formed as soon as twenty-five locals had been established, the unseen members on their farms found this a difficult task to complete since they did not know one another. The organization generated no income at any level—apparently not even for George, as he later asserted he had been forced to subsidize his Alliance throughout his long association with it. The order did, however, produce magazine subscriptions. Local units were conceived as—and in fact became—"discussion" groups. George's rivals in the field of agricultural journalism derided his effort, one of them jeering at "titular agriculturalists who plow with a lead pencil and reap with the instrument used by Samson against the Philistines." However ungenerous this sentiment may have been, George's exclusive control of the organization, coupled with what was apparently an enduring incapacity to think in terms of organizational needs, dissipated whatever energies may have existed among farmer members seeking a vehicle for their grievances.[2]

The lone meeting of 1881 confirmed the business manager of the *Western Rural* as the order's "national secretary" and the following year a writer on the publication became "national lecturer." On this basis, the "farmer" organization endured, ostensibly at least, for four more years. In fact, it died the next year. Having nothing to do within the organization, local farmers apparently decided they could talk to one another without benefit of an alliance charter. With all authority vested in the Chicago magazine office, the powerless "national president" did not bother to put in an appearance at the 1883 meeting, and the unproductive ritual of national meetings was thereupon abandoned. The editor attempted to bridge the hierarchical difficulty by creating "honorary memberships" so that individuals could join free of charge without the added burden of rallying a sufficient number of neighbors to form a local lodge. The innovation did not seem to galvanize the membership noticeably. Judging by the columns of the *Western Rural,* George himself seems to have abandoned the project. Other than occasional "discussion topics" that George offered to his readers, the name of the magazine editor's group all but disappeared from the pages of the magazine. In response to various grievances and sudden economic shocks, spasmodic local initiatives—of a kind which sometimes produce vital institutions—developed over the years, but they received no coherent reaction or guidance from the magazine office.[3]

Finally, in 1886, perhaps as a result of reading about the growth of the Dakota Alliance, the Arkansas Wheel, or the Texas Alliance, George decided to resurrect his group. He called another "national convention" in his magazine office. After receiving a telegram of good wishes from Charles Macune on behalf of 185,000 Texas farmers, George promptly extended his organizational net to the Southwest and announced to his convention guests that his alliance numbered 500,000 members in sixteen states. The figure presumably meant the group had acquired—during its period of dormancy—in addition to the farmers of Texas some 300,000 members in the other fifteen states. Unfortunately, state level reports that might have confirmed this sudden infusion were unavailable, a folkway that persisted throughout George's seven-year stewardship. Actively functioning state chapters, in truth, did not exist—at least none that felt they could profit by an association with the magazine editor. In Dakota Territory, Henry Loucks's cooperative movement flowered in splendid isolation. Aside from Milton George's creative promotional claims, his 1886 national convention was silent in terms of organizational policy. The session consisted wholly of speeches that reflected an affinity for agrarian platitudes—a benign contest in which the rather conservative founder participated on an equal footing with his members. A measure of thinly veiled hostility toward the Knights of Labor intruded, but otherwise the gathering was devoid either of intellectual expression or programmatic content. Nevertheless, George seems to have become convinced that the times were ripe for alliance-building. Though the curious structural shell remained unreformed and the first organizational goal had yet to be fashioned, the magazine editor resumed the promotion of the order in his publication and reinstituted the ritual of dispatching charters to unseen subscribers who indicated an interest. The idea was occasionally voiced by a reader that the alliance might name weekly newspapers in each state to support the cause. But this somehow did not materialize; the *Western Rural* alone spoke for the order.[4]

One distinct innovation, however, was the site of the 1887 meeting, Minneapolis, the first held outside the magazine office. The meeting, unfortunately, was a failure. Only sixteen farmers appeared from out of state for the "national" convention, and they were barely outnumbered by a thin host delegation drawn largely from the city of Minneapolis. The attendance revealed that the Northwestern Alliance was in reality merely a caucus of aspiring spokesmen. A. J. Streeter, the presiding officer, stressed two themes in his brief address, nostalgic remembrances of the order's first eighteen months at the beginning of the decade and wistful references to Texas, where "farmers are organized all over the state and mean business." Actually, Streeter, one of only two radical greenbackers who bothered to participate in George's group, did so because he aspired to be the presidential candidate of whatever third party Western agrarians fielded in 1888. To this end, Streeter not only rode the agrarian hustings in the West but also toured the South in 1887. The journey from Georgia through Texas brought him in contact with the spreading cooperative movement of the National Alliance, and he mentioned this phenomenon to his listeners at the Minneapolis gathering. Unfortunately, he was unable to explain precisely what it was the Southerners were doing. Apparently, no one present in Minneapolis had much feel for the topic either, as the constitution they adopted devoted only one highly generalized sentence to the subject of cooperation. The other speeches at the meeting were couched in agrarian homilies that reflected the social tradition of the Grange. The group did achieve a breakthrough of sorts, however. In writing the constitution, they pirated the organization away from the editorial clacque of national officers in Chicago. This had the effect of placing authority in the hands of new officials named at Minneapolis. None of the latter seemed to find the new situation a liberating one, however, for the Northwestern order struggled into 1888 still lacking a defined sense of purpose. Its entire national membership at the time numbered less than 10,000.[5]

The new president, Jay Burrows of Nebraska, soon confirmed that he had no more grasp of the principles of marketing and purchasing cooperatives than did the magazine editor or the outgoing president. Actually, it was with Burrows that the full legacy of the George regime became institutionalized. Burrows represented the other half of the two-man radical contingent in the Northwestern leadership group, and he also shared Streeter's tendency to look upon farmers as voters above all else. His personal political ambition seems to have been the central ingredient of his stewardship and may have reflected his determination to recover a measure of dignity after an ignominious defeat in 1886 when he ran for governor of Nebraska. Burrows had received only 1 per cent of the vote on an anti-monopoly ticket. Conceivably, the experience might have concentrated his attention on achieving certain preliminary organizational plateaus prior to attempting political insurgency in the future, but throughout 1888–89, as the cooperative crusade of the National Alliance swirled around him in neighboring Kansas and Missouri, Burrows remained almost wholly oblivious. He eventually learned to refer to the topic in generalities, but he was unable to implement a specific approach. Under his tutelage the leadership caucus continued to flounder. Quite simply, the Northwestern Alliance developed no internal lecturing system because it continued to have nothing to lecture about. Despite these liabilities, the group had climbed to one undeniable plateau by escaping Milton George. The possibility existed, at least theoretically, that any ideas generated from below—or from outside—might no longer terminate in a magazine office. The main problem continued to be that the group had no way to keep active anyone who might join. The Burrows group, like the George group before, desperately needed to develop something for its participants to do.[6]

After the failure of the Northerners to put in a promised appearance at the 1888 Alliance conclave at Meridian, Macune dispatched his national lecturer, Ben Terrell, to the annual meeting of the Northwestern Alliance in Des Moines early in 1889. In view of the extravagant membership claims George had reported for years in the *Western Rural,* Macune and Terrell could hardly have been prepared for the organizational disarray that had become characteristic of the get-togethers of the magazine editor's leadership group. Terrell's subsequent report must have proved difficult for most Texans to believe, because Evan Jones, in his capacity as the order's new national president, returned to the midwest later in the spring to have a second look. Startled by the skeletal organizational structure he found—one still unencumbered by a lecturing system—and alerted by the absence of a cooperative effort to the further fact that the order could not have many permanent members aside from its officers, Jones returned home considerably sobered. Publicly, he said of the Northwestern group, "I find their principal efforts are toward political cooperation but with little doing in financial cooperation." In fact, any purported goals of "political cooperation" in the Northwestern group could have been little more than a cover for general inactivity. Jones filled in enough details in his report to make it clear he felt the Northerners had not yet started organizing. A leader of the Nebraska Alliance, John Powers, agreed. Soon after Jones's departure, he confided that he had detected in Nebraska farmers "a feeling of discouragement and despondency, a want of faith in the possibility of any efforts of their own resulting in their relief." [7]

Meanwhile, Milton George, despite his fall from leadership, was not through playing a stifling role in his home territory of Illinois. In 1889, Northern manufacturers of binder twine, perhaps taking a hint from the jute combine in the South, abruptly announced a 50 per cent price increase. Illinois farmers promptly organized a statewide mass meeting. The "Farmers Defensive Movement," lacking the kind of structural integrity an authentic agrarian institution could have provided, never met again, so the brief uprising carried no long term implications, but the initial outburst was enough to convince startled manufacturers to set aside the price increase for the time being. The success convinced some farmers of the value of a state organization and they moved, somewhat inexpertly, toward fashioning one. A controversy between George and Burrows, however, greatly complicated the farmers' efforts. In common with other states of the Northwest, the original Illinois state Alliance had been dormant since 1882, so Burrows, acting under the new constitution, tried to exercise his right to issue new charters in unorganized states. Chafing over his loss of power at Minneapolis, George contended that the Illinois state body still existed and that only its state secretary—his own editorial assistant—could issue charters. Cranking up the charter mill in his magazine office once again, George issued credentials freely, without much care whether the recipients were farmers or not. The resulting controversy became too petty to warrant recounting, but it postponed any statewide organization in Illinois until late in 1889 and effective organization until December 1890. By the latter date the struggling order, numbering perhaps no more than a thousand active members, had been overwhelmed by aggressive cooperative campaigns generated by the Farmers Mutual Benefit Association and the National Farmers Alliance. The Northern order, having never fashioned organizational goals, simply had no program and was helpless in the face of organizations that did.[8]

Had the George group merged with the National Alliance at Meridian in 1888, and thus acquired the kind of cooperative foundation that W. P. Brush carried to Kansas from the same meeting, the entire history of the agrarian revolt might well have been altered. Both Milton George and Jay Burrows stand as examples of spokesmen impeding organizational growth from within.[9]

Though, as described in the text (pp. 201–11), the cooperative movement eventually penetrated Nebraska in the spring of 1890, the Northwestern Alliance as a whole remained opposed to the third party to the end. In January, 1892, the order voted down a proposal to send delegates to the founding meeting of the People's Party due to take place the following month in St. Louis. Three of the four most prominent Northwestern spokesmen through the 1880s—Milton George of Illinois, and August Post and N. B. Ashby of Iowa—remained aloof from Populism throughout the 1890s. In 1896, they all voted for McKinley. (The subsequent career of the fourth, Burrows, is treated below as part of the history of Populism's shadow movement.) [10]

The Northwestern Farmers Alliance never at any time achieved a stable national membership of as many as 50,000 in all the states in its claimed jurisdiction; only those farmers belatedly recruited in Nebraska in the spring and summer of 1890 participated in the political phase of the agrarian revolt. Even in the case of the Nebraskans, the price to the agrarian movement of that participation was high.

2. *The Merger Failure*

The controversy among Populist historians over the failure to achieve a national coalition in St. Louis in 1889 may be viewed as a part of a more central question concerning the origin, development, and ultimate nature of the agrarian revolt. The viewpoint of the Northwestern Alliance was offered by N. B. Ashby in his book, *Riddle of the Sphinx* (Des Moines, 1890), which named as the causes of the merger failure: sectional differences— specifically, the racial exclusiveness of the Southern order; disagreement over secrecy between the "Open Alliance" of the North and the "secret Alliance" of the South; Northern opposition to and Southern support of the sub-treasury plan; the presumed centralization of authority in the Southern order, as contrasted with the more democratically organized Northwestern Alliance; and economic rivalry, resulting from a new process of manufacturing compound lard from cottonseed oil. This last hurt Northern hog producers, aided Southern cotton growers, and fashioned their contrasting positions on pending legislation known as the Conger bill. For the perspective of the National Farmers Alliance, Nelson A. Dunning, Macune's editorial assistant and ardent disciple, offered a single reason in his book, *The Farmers' Alliance History and Agricultural Digest* (Washington, 1891): "A careful analysis . . . discloses the fact that sectionalism, that old enemy of national organized labor, was the controlling factor." [11]

The topic has been addressed in some detail by three historians: Herman Nixon, "The Cleavage in the Farmers Alliance Movement," *Mississippi Valley Historical Review*, XV, No. 1 (June 1928), 22–23; Hicks, *Populist Revolt*, 119–124; and Theodore Saloutos, *Farmer Movements in the South*, 81–82. With the exception of Ashby's implications on the race issue, which Hicks and Nixon reject and Saloutos ignores, all three scholars generally accept Ashby's list as a working basis for analysis. Nixon additionally discounts the secrecy issue; his emphasis is upon the Conger bill. He added still another reason—Northern fear of third party action by the radical Southerners. Hicks reverses this judgment: "Already the idea of a third party had appeared, and in the North it was receiving serious thought. But apparently, the South was irretrievable wedded to the one-party system." (Hicks, 122). Hicks also endorsed the one Ashby point that Professor Nixon had avoided: "The Open Alliance," said Hicks, "felt that secrecy, which had rarely had a part in (its) work . . . should be left optional with each state." For his part, Saloutos, following Hicks, accepted Ashby's view of the sub-treasury issue: whereas Southern Alliance leaders "enthusiastically endorsed" the sub-treasury, many rank and file members opposed it, as most of their brethern in the West also did. It is clear from this evidence that Ashby has been far more successful than his rival, Dunning, in setting the terms of post-Populist scholarly analysis. Within the environment of the agrarian movement, N. B. Ashby, though influenced at times by Bellamy Nationalism, shared with others in the conservative leadership of the Iowa Alliance a persistent opposition to the idea of a radical third party. [12]

Ashby had little understanding of the cooperative movement in 1888 when he first came in contact with the National Farmers Alliance and he clearly had learned very little more about the subject by the time he came to write *The Riddle of the Sphinx*. In thirty-four pages devoted to cooperation, culled almost totally from other sources, Ashby was able to produce only one vaguely generalized paragraph on the program of the Iowa Alliance. Ashby's 1889 article in the *National Economist* on the agrarian movement in Iowa also contained one paragraph on cooperation; it was so primitively innocent that it must have caused snickers among the Alliance business agents throughout the nation. [13]

Ashby's singular lack of organizing success as the national lecturer of the Northwestern group merely confirmed that he had no program to offer farmers. He wrote not with the authority of an informed participant in the agrarian movement, but as a discredited and injured victim of its democratic momentum.

The following thoughts are offered on the affair at St. Louis. The dispute involving the Conger bill did not become a visible issue, even among the informed elite of the agrarian movement until 1890, was not a central issue then, and certainly was not germane to the events of 1889. It was offered after the fact by an embattled Northwestern spokesman at a time when his organization was bearing the onus for the merger failure, had become stridently defensive because its territory was being organized by the National Farmers Alliance and—not least—because it was in a state of incipient collapse.[14]

In the summer and fall of 1891, the National Farmers Alliance had approximately 1,500,000 members in forty-three states and territories; at the same time, the Northwestern group counted less than 40,000 members in three states—Nebraska, Iowa and Minnesota—and less than 2,000 others in Illinois and Wisconsin. Roughly half this number was in Nebraska and they were about to decamp to the National Farmers Alliance. In 1890–91, Iowa spokesmen for the Northwestern group were employing the Conger bill as a desperate expedient to hold back the organizing drive of the National Farmers Alliance, then beginning its delayed attempt to spread through Illinois, Wisconsin, Indiana, Ohio and Michigan, as well as Iowa.[15]

Similarly, the sub-treasury plan was not an issue at St. Louis; it, too, was seized upon by Ashby after the fact. It may be said, in passing, that Ashby's *post facto* indictment of the sub-treasury, and Hicks' acceptance of his analysis, has apparently contributed to the almost universal opinion among students of the agrarian revolt that the Macune plan had little appeal in the West. The evidence to the contrary is considerable. Without exception the Western states that developed a strong Populist presence voted unanimously to endorse the sub-treasury at Ocala and, with the exception of Nebraska, the Alliances of the Northern plains also organized extensive lecturing systems on the sub-treasury.[16]

Secrecy, too, was a transparent issue. The "Open Alliance" of the Northwest became "secret" at its next annual meeting when the national body met in secret and then formally adopted a secret ritual as part of its organic constitution. As has been pointed out elsewhere in this study, and as was true of almost all voluntary agricultural institutions, the adoption of "secrecy" generally signaled an attempt to gear up for a programmatic effort at cooperation. The Grange, the FMBA and the Agricultural Wheel all were cooperative, and secret, organizations. Secrecy, of course, was merely a preliminary step: to attain a cooperative program one had to have organizational structure. Unfortunately, as the halting cooperative effort of 1891 soon revealed, this was the one ingredient the Northwestern group never at any time was able to attain.[17]

Finally, Ashby's implication of greater "democracy" in the Northwestern group, as compared to the "centralization" in the National Alliance, was also specious. The true distinction was not that the National Alliance had too many layers of leadership, but that the Northwestern group had no infrastructure at all—indeed, not even enough to permit a minimum of democracy to work from the bottom up, as the history of the order from 1880 to 1890 convincingly illustrated. On the one occasion when genuine cohesion was developed unilaterally from below—Omar Kem's 1889 county-level cooperative movement in Nebraska—local alliancemen had great difficulty finding anyone competent at the top with whom they could share their successful blueprint for economic organization and political insurgency.

Ironically, in raising this latter issue, Ashby inadvertantly isolated the decisive distinction between the two organizations: the National Farmers Alliance had a program which produced both internal structure and external purpose, while the Northwestern group did not. As for the status of democracy within the National Farmers Alliance, the events of 1890–92 demonstrated rather dramatically the intense interplay of opinion at every level of the organization. No one was more discomfited by the democratic thrust of the National Alliance than its founding president, Charles Macune, unless it was the loyal Democrat who headed the Georgia Alliance, Lon Livingston.[18]

N. B. Ashby, a minor and tangential participant in the politics leading to the People's Party, enjoys the power of being one of the two most readily available historical sources of the internal life of the ill-fated Northwestern Alliance. The other is Milton George, the magazine editor. The two men are valuable guides to the inner dynamics of the agrarian movement in only one sense—they accurately reflect the political purpose of their leadership caucus, one that on its own terms had no intention of participating in an organized revolt against the structure of Gilded Age politics and did not do so. The comments of Ashby and George on those who did participate in the politics of protest were not only inherently self-serving—a mild enough hazard for the historian—but they were also seriously misinformed and sometimes disingenuous about what was actually taking place.

3. The Silver Drive

The sometimes formless, sometimes silverite expression that historically has been regarded as "American Populism"—and which has appeared in these pages as the "shadow movement"—was a natural outgrowth of the intellectual and programmatic aimlessness of the Northwestern Farmers Alliance. As such, the shadow movement has historical meaning only in the context of the actual agrarian movement mounted by the National Farmers Alliance and Industrial Union.

Since movements of democratic reform require a flag to follow, a set of beliefs given civic and symbolic meaning by the candidacy of a person who represents those beliefs, a movement following the leader of some other movement, holding some other beliefs, has clearly ceased to function in significant ways. Institutionally, the People's Party died in St. Louis on the evening of June 25, 1896, when Populist Senator William Allen of Nebraska deceived his own delegates for six hours and then declared a Democrat named William Jennings Bryan to be the nominee of the People's Party. The funeral was ritually played out in the autumn campaign itself, when the autonomy and organization of the People's Party were revealed to be either nonexistent or irrelevant and the morale of its adherents was consequently destroyed. Self-respect is crucial to the shared hope that animates political movements, and Populists had lost theirs; they were taunted in the South by their Democratic "allies" and they were denounced in the West by their Populist compatriots from the South. In both regions, the Populist rank and file lost the essential emotional ingredient of collective action—faith in their own movement.

The administrators of fusion at the Populist convention and in the autumn campaign—William Allen and Marion Butler—did not understand this psychological ingredient of democratic reform politics. Both men participated in a reform movement whose sources they did not grasp and whose interior energy did not become a part of their own political consciousness. The politics of Senators Allen and Butler—which initially had been the politics of the silver lobby and which later became the politics of William Jennings Bryan and the silver Democratic Party of 1896—was the politics of grand coalition, the merger of whole parties. While such a method of procedure is a perfectly acceptable form of conventional political conduct, it was not Populism. Coalition politics involves the brokering of the needs—and the ideas, if there are any—of disparate groups. Needs being easier to broker, politically, than ideas, coalition politicians quickly learn to dislike ideas, for they impede the consummation of the kinds of agreements that facilitate victory at the polls. Assertive coalition politicians like William Allen and Marion Butler—and like William Jennings Bryan—are essentially men without ideas.

But the political movement that was Populism grew out of an idea. In one sense, of course, Populism was a doctrine of belief about the prevailing structure of American finance capitalism, a doctrine codified in the Cleburne, Dallas, St. Louis, Ocala, and Omaha Platforms and given specific definition by the sequential cooperative and political experiences of the Alliance movement that created those platforms. But the heart of Populism was the hope and self-confidence embedded in the democratic idea animating the movement itself. The achievements of this movement, the human experiences within it, and the resulting political forms that took shape in the Omaha Platform of the People's Party collectively represented the cultural statement generated by the agrarian revolt. Participants in this experience were Populists, and the political ideas they advanced in the their platform describe "Populism." Similarly, the incomplete achievements of the ambitious national lecturing campaign that the creators of the agrarian movement assigned themselves in the period 1887–92 pointed to the hazards faced by Populism.[19]

As political assertion, the shadow movement is patently less interesting than Populism, being little more than an imitative reprise on the superficial agitation over the "Crime of '73" that had helped to sidetrack greenback reform a generation earlier.* The second silver drive proved no more coherent than the first. The shadow movement as it triumphed in 1896 in Kansas, in 1894 in North Carolina, and in 1890 in Nebraska had common

* See Chapter I.

characteristics: it was led by politicians, its tactics were defined by them, and the usefulness of such tactics depended upon the successful avoidance of the intellectual content embedded in the Populist platform. Some fusionist politicians, like Senator Peffer of Kansas, gave up the Populist faith reluctantly and only temporarily; others, like Allen in Nebraska, had never known it; but in embracing the silver expedient, they all identified themselves with a cause that originated outside the People's Party and was financed by mining interests whose goals were inimical to the objectives of Populism. Indeed, the silver drive gained its greatest number of followers in a rival political institution, the Democratic Party. In confronting William Allen, Marion Butler, or the silver politics of 1896, one deals, therefore, not with Populism, but with a derived form that developed in places where Populism could not, or ultimately did not, live. The second silver drive of 1896 is rather easily described as a mutation of Populism that developed in those regions of the nation where the agrarian organizational base was deemed insufficiently broad to support the purpose of the third party movement as it defined itself.

The symbolic spokesman of both the Northwestern Alliance and the shadow movement was Jay Burrows of Nebraska who, having never grasped the meaning of the cooperative crusade, and never having experienced its political lessons, could write in 1896 that William Jennings Bryan was "practically a Populist except in name." [20]

Organizationally derivative, intellectually without purpose, the shadow movement never fashioned its own political premise; inevitably, its sole criterion became the process of politics itself—the desire of office-seekers to prevail at the next election. In attempting to address their own short-run electoral needs, the tacticians of fusion adopted as their own the political purposes of the silver mineowners. But having no political or cultural base independent of others, the fusionists had no hope of surviving on the goals of others. Their moment of tactical triumph, lasting a few hours at the Populist convention in 1896, was inherently ironic: in achieving the nomination of William Jennings Bryan, they not only ensured their own organizational extinction, they also provided a way for farmers to submerge themselves in the new, two-party, corporate politics of modern America.

Ideological Origins of the Omaha Platform

"The radical momentum of the cooperative movement . . ."

The three major subjects addressed in the Omaha Platform concerned transportation, land, and monetary policy.

The transportation plank reflected the experience of Alliancemen, during the period 1886–1892, in observing the evolving attempts by government to regulate railroads in the public interest. The 1886 Cleburne Demands of the Texas Alliance called for the passage of an interstate commerce law to equalize freight rates and to halt rebates and pooling. After the Congress established a relatively powerless Interstate Commerce Commission in 1887, the 1888 Dallas Demands of the Texas Alliance called for the act to be amended "to secure to the whole people the benefits of railway transportation at just rates, and rigidly enforced by a railroad commission." No railroad commissions having materialized by 1889, the St. Louis Demands of that year called for government ownership. After such states as Kansas, North Carolina and Texas began to acquire state railroad commissions in 1890–91—all of them created with high hopes that they would provide the solution of the regulatory problem—the Ocala Demands of 1890 temporized on the question of government ownership: "We demand the most rigid, honest and just state and national government control and supervision of the means of public communication and transportation, and if this control and supervision does not remove the abuse now existing, we demand the government ownership of such means of communication and transportation." This phraseology was repeated in the Cincinnati platform of 1891,

593

but by February 1892, the farmers had seen enough of the abortive experiment in railroad regulation. Both the St. Louis and Omaha Platforms of 1892 renewed the 1889 call for government ownership.

The land plank dated from the Cleburne Demands of 1886 and required only slight modification in the 1888 Dallas Demands and the St. Louis Platform of 1889 before reaching its final Cleburne-like form at the founding convention of the People's Party in 1892. The Cleburne document called for prohibition of alien land ownership and added that "large bodies of land held by private individuals or corporations for speculative purposes shall be rendered for taxation at such rates as they are offered to purchasers, on credit of one, two, or three years." The 1888 Dallas Demands, drawing from the Texas Union Labor Party platform of the same year, produced a modified solution to the speculative problem, specifying that "corporations holding grants of public lands from State or National government be required to alienate to *bona fide* settlers in small bodies . . . all lands within a period of twelve years from date of grant, or forfeit of title." (Italics in the original). This specific solution was made more general at St. Louis in 1889, calling on Congress to devise "some plan" to reclaim the speculative landholdings of railroad and other corporations. The Omaha Platform did not further define what "some plan" should be: "All land now held by railroads and other corporations in excess of their actual needs, and all lands now owned by aliens, should be reclaimed by the government and held for actual settlers only." Since the solution was stated in such general terms, it can be seen that the specific measures offered at Cleburne in 1886 (for rendering speculation unprofitable through taxation) and at Dallas in 1888 (reversion within twelve years of all unsold lands) were not subsequently expanded upon.

The monetary plank, though both the most important and the most complex in its provisions, had an even simpler evolution. The essential greenback planks calling for a flexible currency keyed to industrial and population growth, the elimination of national bank notes, the substitution of legal tender treasury notes, and unlimited coinage of silver, were contained in the Cleburne Demands. The Dallas Demands of 1888 added a key provision "prohibiting forever hereafter the issuing of interest-bearing bonds or the chartering of banks with the power to issue notes that shall circulate as money." In terms of political consciousness, the central development was the elevation of the greenback plank from its position as the eleventh "demand" of the 1886 document to the first three places in the Dallas Demands of 1888.

The radical momentum of the cooperative movement is clearly visible in this progression: though discreetly buried in the seventeen demands at Cleburne, greenback doctrines split the 1886 Alliance; the unanimous support of the 1888 demands measured the impact upon the political consciousness of farmers of their cooperative struggle with bankers for credit. Through this process, the monetary theory that was to undergird the Omaha Platform of 1892 became Alliance doctrine in Texas in 1888 and in the National Alliance in 1889.

Since the Texans were able to transmit their own radical evolution to the agrarian movement as a whole, the greenback heritage upon which the Cleburne monetary plank was based, and the ascendancy of its ideological importance made explicit by the Dallas Demands of 1888, provide the necessary basis for interpreting the evolution of Populist monetary theory. Though rooted in the document at Cleburne, the August 1888 Dallas Demands of the Texas Alliance drew directly from a platform promulgated six weeks earlier in July of 1888 by the Texas "Nonpartisan Convention" chaired by William Lamb. (See Chapter V, pp. 141–42). The latter document, in turn, closely tracked the platform of a "Convention of Farmers, Laborers and Stock Raisers" called by H.S.P. Ashby in Waco, Texas, in May 1888 (See Chapter V, pp. 140–41) while Lamb was in Cincinnati for the organizational meeting of the national Union Labor Party. Both the Lamb and Ashby meetings were preliminary organizational components of the creation of the Texas Union Labor Party—which event followed by one day the meeting of Lamb's "non-partisans" in the same city, Fort Worth. (See Chapter V, p. 141). These declarations in Waco, Fort Worth and Dallas from May through August 1888 called for a flexible currency accruing from abolition of the national banking system and national bank notes and the substitution of legal tender treasury notes, plus the free coinage of silver, government ownership of the railroads, a graduated income tax, and prohibition of alien and corporate land ownership for speculation—in short, the entire substance, save the sub-treasury plan itself, of the St. Louis and Ocala Demands of the National Alliance and the Omaha Platform of the People's Party.

The orderly refinement of these land, transportation, and monetary issues in successive documents from 1886 through 1888 is at least partly explained by the fact that the radical Texas minister, J. M. Perdue, was the single most influential participant in the process of their evolution. Perdue had had some practice—in the early 1880s, he had helped write the platform of the Greenback Party.

It was Perdue who explicitly conveyed the greenback heritage to the Farmers Alliance: he was the principal author of the Cleburne Demands and the immediate public defender of the document when it came under attack from Alliance conservatives and the metropolitan press in 1886. After the Ashby and Lamb conventions of May and July 1888 had drafted radical planks beyond those formulated at Cleburne in 1886, Perdue began the process of integrating these advances into the evolving Alliance political platform. This was done immediately; Perdue was chairman of the "Committee on the Industrial Depression" that wrote the Dallas Demands in August 1888. (See Chapter V, p. 142). Those radical planks of 1888 not incorporated in the Dallas Demands were integrated into the National Alliance platform at St. Louis the following year.

Yet it would be too much to designate J. M. Perdue—or any one of the other Texas agrarians—as the "father" of the Omaha Platform. Perdue's ideas essentially reflected and synthesized the greenback heritage that supplied much of the ideological substance of the agrarian revolt. And greenback doctrines had a hundred "fathers," including Robert Owen, Francois Fourier, Karl Marx, Pierre Proudhon, Edward Kellogg, Alexander Campbell, General S. F. Cary and, as Professor William Yohe shows in Appendix B, back to the time of Plato. Indeed, if a bit of irony is needed, the 1892 Omaha Platform of the People's Party contained only one genuinely new innovation not contained in the Texas platforms of 1888—the sub-treasury plan of Perdue's old rival, Charles Macune. The irony here, of course, falls upon Macune: though he was tactically opposed to the political activists among the Alliance founders led by Lamb, Perdue, Daws, Jones, and Ashby, he shared their theoretical interpretation of the ills of the American version of capitalism. Indeed, Macune's report on the monetary system at St. Louis in 1889 specifically and repeatedly denounced the power that bankers exercised as a "class." Macune's tactical difficulty was that, in the deepest psychological dimension of his personal autonomy, he could not bear where his economic analysis carried him in political and social terms. Macune would fit well, it may be seen, into the culturally confined politics of the twentieth century.

Sources

Winkler, *Platforms of Political Parties in Texas,* 223–229; 234–237; 256–257; 260–263; 268–271; 278–279; 293–299; Dallas *News,* August 8–9, 1886; May 15–18, July 3–7, August 20–25, 1888; *Southern Mercury,* November 12, 19, 26, December 5, 12, 1886; April 19, 31, July 24, August 7, 28, November 4, 1888; August 22, 1889; Fort Worth *Gazette,* June 6–9, July 2–5, 1888; "Report of the Committee on the Monetary System," in Dunning, *Farmers Alliance History and Agricultural Digest,* 124–30, and in Tindall, *A Populist Reader,* 80–87. For the impact on Kansas radicals of the 1888 platforms of the Texas Alliance and the Texas Union Labor Party, see Rightmire, "Alliance Movement in Kansas—Origins of the People's Party," (p. 3).

A Kansas Proclamation: "The Tramp Circular"

". . . or even in obedience of a mere whim. . . ."

(*In December 1893, the Populist governor of Kansas, Lorenzo D. Lewelling, issued an executive proclamation that was essentially a defense of "the crime of being poor." The proclamation contained advice to local police authorities in Kansas on the proper treatment of the "standing army of the unemployed." In Republican circles, the document came to be known as "The Tramp Circular." The proclamation, properly symbolic of the democratic legacy of Populism, follows*).

In the region of Elizabeth, the highways were filled with the throngs of the unemployed poor, who were made to "move on," and were sometimes brutally whipped, sometimes summarily hanged, as "sturdy vagrants" or "incorrigible vagabonds." In France, just previous to the revolution, the punishment of being poor and out of work was, for the first offense, a term of years in the galleys, for the second offense, the galleys for life. In this country, the monopoly of labor saving machinery and its devotion to selfish instead of social use, have rendered more and more human beings superfluous, until we have a standing army of the unemployed numbering even in the most prosperous times not less than one million able bodied men; yet, until recently it was the prevailing notion, as it is yet the notion of all but the work-people themselves and those of other classes given to thinking, and whosoever, being able bodied and willing to work can always find work to do, and section 571 of the general statutes of 1889 is a disgraceful reminder how savage even in Kansas has been our treatment of the most unhappy of our human brothers.

The man out of work and penniless is, by this legislation, classed with "confidence men." Under this statute and city ordinances of similar import, thousands of men, guilty of no crime but poverty, intent upon no crime but that of seeking employment, have languished in the city prisons of Kansas or performed unrequited toil on "rock piles" as municipal slaves, because ignorance of economic conditions had made us cruel. The victims have been the poor and humble for whom police courts are courts of last resort—they can not give bond and appeal. They have been unheeded and uncared for by the busy world which wastes no time visiting prisoners in jail. They have been too poor to litigate with their oppressors, and thus no voice from this underworld of human woe has ever reached the ear of the appellate court, because it was nobody's business to be his brother's keeper.

But those who sit in the seats of power are bound by the highest obligation to especially regard the cause of the oppressed and helpless poor. The first duty of the government is to the weak . . . It is my duty "to see that the laws are faithfully executed," and among those laws is the constitutional provision that no instrumentality of the state "shall deny to any person within its jurisdiction the equal protection of the laws." And who needs to be told that equal protection of the laws does not prevail where this inhuman vagrancy law is enforced? It separates men into two distinct classes, differentiated as those who are penniless and those who are not, and declare the former criminals. Only the latter are entitled to the liberty guaranteed by the constitution. To be found in a city "without some visible means of support or some legitimate business," is the involuntary condition of some millions at this moment, and we proceed to punish them for being victims of conditions which we, as a people, have forced upon them.

I have noticed in police court reports that "sleeping in a box car" is among the varieties of this heinous crime of being poor. Some police judges have usurped a sovereign power not permitted the highest functionaries of the states or of the nation, and victims of the industrial conditions have been peremptorily "ordered to leave town."

The right to go freely from place to place in search of employment, or even in obedience of a mere whim, is part of that personal liberty guaranteed by the Constitution of the United States to every human being on American soil. If voluntary idleness is not forbidden; if a Diogenes prefer poverty; if a Columbus choose hunger and the discovery of a new race, rather than seek personal comfort by engaging in "some legitimate business," I am aware of no power in the legislature or in city councils to deny him the right to seek happiness in his own way, so long as he harms no other, rich or poor; but let simple poverty cease to be a crime.

In some cities it is provided by ordinance that if police court fines are not paid or secured the culprit shall be compelled to work out the amount as a municipal slave; and "rock piles" and "bull pens" are provided for the enforcement of these ordinances. And so it appears that this slavery is not imposed as a punishment, but solely as a means of collecting a debt.

Such city ordinances are in flagrant violation of constitutional prohibition . . . Let the dawn of Christmas day find the "rock pile," the "bull pen" and the crime of being homeless and poor, obsolete in all the cities of Kansas governed by the metropolitan police act.

It is confidently expected that their own regard for constitutional liberty and their human impulses will induce police commissioners to carry out the spirit as well as the letter of the foregoing suggestions.

L. D. LEWELLING
GOVERNOR

A CRITICAL ESSAY ON AUTHORITIES

Since the National Farmers Alliance and the People's Party were sequential expressions of the same popular movement and the same democratic culture, the gradual evolution of the cooperative crusade that generated both was the central component of the agrarian revolt. This understanding came largely from primary sources: early Alliance newspapers such as the *Rural Citizen* (Jacksboro), *Southern Mercury, American Nonconformist, Kansas Farmer, Progressive Farmer, The Advocate* and the *National Economist;* later, the journals of the reform press association throughout the South and West, together with the surviving private papers, organizing pamphlets, and books of such agrarian spokesmen as L. H. Weller, A. P. Hungate, S. O. Daws, Henry Vincent, Charles Macune, W. Scott Morgan, Nelson Dunning, L. L. Polk, S. M. Scott, John B. Rayner, Charles Pierson, Thomas Cater, and Gasper C. Clemens, among others; papers of key opponents of the agrarian organizing drive: A. J. Rose, Pitchfork Ben Tillman, and James Hogg; manuscript collections bearing on silver lobbying: William Jennings Bryan, William Allen, Marion Butler, Ignatius Donnelly, Davis Waite, and William Stewart; and, lastly, national, state, and local organization records of the National Farmers Alliance and Industrial Union. The response of the larger society to the farmers' movement was visible in the nation's metropolitan press: the Dallas *News* was particularly useful in the early years, and, as the agrarian movement expanded, so were the Atlanta *Constitution,* Cincinnati *Enquirer,* Topeka *Capital,* Chicago *Tribune,* Montgomery *Advertiser,* the Nebraska *Jour-*

nal, the *Post-Dispatch, Republic,* and *Globe-Democrat* of St. Louis, the *Journal* and *Sentinel* of Indianapolis, the *Chronicle* and *Examiner* of San Francisco, the Memphis *Appeal-Avalanche* and the New York *Times.* These sources, along with rural weeklies and other primary materials cited throughout the footnotes, unavoidably create a completely restructured picture of the democratic dynamics of Alliance-Populism. Such a restructuring inevitably leads to a drastic reappraisal of the secondary literature of the agrarian revolt.

Adherents of the two political traditions that have acquired cultural sanction in twentieth-century thought, capitalism and socialism, have reached agreement about the specific events of the agrarian revolt. Drawing freely from one another in such a way as to produce a general consensus about "what happened" in the Gilded Age, they have proceeded in confidence that each could "see through" the doctrinal narrowness of the other concerning what it all meant. In these endeavors, scholars of both persuasions have relied on formal categories of political description that have been sanctioned as part of their respective intellectual traditions. With an apparent assurance so far unsubstantiated by the results achieved, socialist historians have applied class analysis to the national politics of the agrarian revolt. Capitalist historians, while borrowing a number of interpretative techniques from Marxist theory, have generally been content with less tightly organized modes of analysis; interestingly, their approaches to the politics, economics, and culture have often been based on assumptions about mass movements and capitalist economics that are even more remote from the realities of life than the class assumptions of their ideological competitors.

While these diverse efforts have produced a number of verdicts about the relative rigidity or flexibility of American capitalism, they have not generated much that is revealing about Populism. No one, it seems, has regarded the agrarian revolt as a mass democratic movement that was organically shaped by its own internal dynamics and by its own evolving popular culture of democratic thought.* Rather, Populism has emerged as some sort of spontaneous bourgeois or interest group protest, one that was either too radical to be accepted by the larger society or too conservative and insular to have historic meaning beyond its own moment in time.

At least five writers variously responsive to Marxist perspectives have written about the agrarian revolt—Norman Pollack, William Appelman Williams, Anna Rochester, Matthew Josephson, and Chester McArthur Destler. Understandably, in America, a much larger group of scholars—several hundred in fact—have written about Populism from a capitalist perspective. Clearly, the liberals and conservatives of the capitalist school have been far more influential in shaping both our perception of what happened and our

---

* For discussions of the effect of the prevailing categories of political description upon historical interpretations of the dynamics of popular democratic movements, see p. 623, n. 4; pp. 625–26, n. 49; p. 627, n. 51; p. 629, n. 18; p. 632, n. 14; p. 634, n. 32 and 39; pp. 638–39, n. 9; pp. 640–41, n. 15; pp. 649–50, n. 34 and 36; pp. 651–53, n. 39; p. 656, n. 4; p. 660, n. 6; pp. 666–67, n. 35; pp. 674–75, n. 44; pp. 676–77, n. 10; p. 679, n. 40; p. 683, n. 30; p. 685, n. 23; pp. 688–89, n. 26 and 28; p. 691, n. 34 and 35; p. 692, n. 10; p. 694, n. 15; and p. 701, n. 7.

sense of its social meaning. Indeed, inasmuch as John Hicks's description of the movement has been taken as a general guide to what happened, his pioneering work, *The Populist Revolt,* has strongly influenced all subsequent interpretations irrespective of point of view. Unfortunately, since the Alliance cooperative movement was not seen by Hicks as the core experience of the agrarian revolt, his lengthy work on the shadow movement of free silver has had a crippling influence on subsequent scholarship.*

The idea of the shadow movement as the crux of the agrarian revolt governs both the most influential attack on Populism, Richard Hofstadter's *The Age of Reform,* and its most ardent defense, Norman Pollack's *The Populist Response to Industrial America.* Of the two, Hofstadter's study has been far more pervasive in its impact. Correctly finding the free-silver arguments of William Jennings Bryan and "Coin" Harvey to be superficial, Hofstadter persuasively indicts what he takes, on Hicksian terms, to be "Populism." He fortifies his analysis through the creation of an elaborately crafted cultural category, which he styled "The Agrarian Myth." Through this device, Hofstadter imputes to Populists a number of modes of self-analysis and national political analysis that were wholly alien to the actual interpretations American farmers achieved as a result of their cooperative struggle. While Hofstadter's misreading has a quality of grandeur, the source of his difficulty is not hard to locate: he managed to frame his interpretation of the intellectual content of Populism without recourse to a single reference to the planks of the Omaha Platform of the People's Party or to any of the economic, political, or cultural experiences that led to the creation of those goals. Indeed, there is no indication in his text that he was aware of these experiences.

Populists are not "intransigents," as they are to Hicks; to Hofstadter, they are scarcely present at all. A Populist indictment of corporate concentration, for example, "reads like a Jacksonian polemic." The dismay of Populists at the practices of American railroad land syndicates and English and Scottish land companies reveals the "anti-foreign" proclivities of people who viewed themselves as "innocent pastoral victims of a conspiracy hatched in the distance." Given the large-scale centralization of land ownership in America in the decades immediately following the agrarian revolt, one is persuaded that the land problems besetting Populists originated a bit closer to home. (See Appendix A.) Similarly, agrarian reservations about the practices of "the town clique"—doubts arising from banker and merchant hostility to the cooperative movement—are seen as providing evidence for Hofstadter's conclusion that Populists suffered from misplaced "anti-urban" manias. In the same vein, "the curiously ambiguous" disenchantment of Populists with the cause of international bimetallism is taken to signify a "nativist" hostility to "cooperation with European governments for any ends at all." Skepticism about the monetary rigidity and inadequacy of bimetallism—a Populistic premise widely shared by modern economists—seems an ambiguity to Hofstadter for the rather elementary reason that the greenback critique at the

---

* Hicks's role in denying Populists close association with their own movement is discussed at greater length on pp. 638–40, n. 8, 9, 10; and pp. 670–71, n. 15.

heart of Populism is far from the heart of his analysis. For venturesome and creative students of intellectual history such as Richard Hofstadter, the shadow movement of free silver provided a shaky perspective, indeed, from which to interpret Populism.[1]

Similarly, Norman Pollack begins from premises laid down by Hicks and defends the silver crusade as "the last assertion of Populist radicalism." Since Populists were appalled by this particular assertion, Pollack cannot conveniently focus upon their understanding of agrarian purposes. And he does not.[2] While Hofstadter attacks Populism by emphasizing the ephemeral politics of William Jennings Bryan, Pollack defends the movement by defending the same man. Though Hofstadter easily has the best of this discussion, it seems prudent to remember that Bryan was not a Populist. As well as any other, this fact may suggest how far afield the whole matter has been carried. The cooperative dynamics that shaped the Omaha Platform and created the democratic ethos of Populism are not organic to either study.

There is, however, a noteworthy difference in the cultural implications each author draws from the agrarian revolt. On those occasions when Pollack focuses solely on the ideas of Populism, as distinct from specific political and cultural developments presumed to be associated with those ideas, his analysis of the constructive and egalitarian nature of the third party crusade, including its greenback premise, seems unarguable. At such times in *The Populist Response to Industrial America* the shadow movement recedes into the background and Populism emerges.[3] If, on the other hand, in all pertinent interpretive passages concerning "Populism" in *The Age of Reform,* one substitutes the words "proponents of a metallic currency" for the word "Populist," the critique drawn by Richard Hofstadter of the provincialism of Gilded Age America becomes much more precise and persuasive. Such a substitution, of course, alters the meaning of the book at the level of its premise, for *The Age of Reform* then becomes a sweeping criticism of the culture of the corporate state rather than a sweeping criticism of Populism. The democratic rationality of both major parties would then necessarily fall prey to Hofstadterian skepticism. Unfortunately, the rather confined categories of political description available to Hofstadter within his culturally sanctioned intellectual tradition apparently made such an analysis very difficult to achieve.[4]

The narrow limits of Populism that materialize from the work of Hicks, Hofstadter, and Pollack have inevitably exerted a constraining influence on the scores of studies that have subsequently materialized on various aspects of the agrarian crusade. Because the centrality of the cooperative movement has not been understood, another relevant political dynamic has been missing—the pivotal role of what I have called "the politics of the sub-treasury" in combating sectionalism and turning rank and file Alliance farmers into rank and file third party radicals. Historians have found other causes for the presence or absence of Populism in the various regions of America. A kind of fragile economic determinism has prevailed, in the absence of handier explanations. Where strong third parties emerged, the cause has most frequently been seen to have been "hard times." Where they did not, the weakness of reform was traceable to diversified farming leading to "good harvests" or, conversely, to temporary improvements in commodity prices resulting from "poor harvests." In the great mass of Populist literature, in short, the third party, like the Alliance, just "happened." As one author described the agrarian revolt, "Like Topsy, it just grew." [5] Populism has simply not been seen as a political movement containing its own evolving democratic culture in which people could "see themselves" and, therefore, could dare to aspire for the kind of society conductive to mass human dignity.

When creative historians err, they err grandly; in sustaining a major book-length misreading of agrarian radicalism, the only serious rival to John Hicks and Richard Hofstadter is William Appleman Williams. While Hicks and Hofstadter mistook radical greenback anti-monopolists for pragmatic or nostalgic silverites, Williams chose to regard all farmers as a petit-bourgeois class. This view enabled him to link affluent Grangers, landless Alliancemen, place-hunting silverite politicians, and agrarian radicals in one massive potpourri of reaction. Indeed, in his study of foreign policy, *The Roots of the Modern American Empire* (1970), this farm "class" was more reactionary than an unsuspecting Gilded Age business community which, in Williams's view, was unwittingly pulled by the farmers into imperialist adventures overseas! The influential farmer spokesman who achieved this impressive feat included L. L. Polk and Charles Macune of the Alliance, Oliver H. Kelly of the National Grange, and William Jennings Bryan of the Democratic Party. Here again, the rigidities of certain sanctioned categories of political description, Marxist in this case, have simply overwhelmed the raw evidence of historical events. Yet, Williams is eclectic in his utilization of interpretive categories. In finding agrarians more threatening than he takes captains of finance and industry to be, Williams—once past his class analysis—seems to have been even more heavily influenced by Richard Hofstadter than he was by Karl Marx.

The Populist Movement in the United States by Anna Rochester (1943) broadly follows Hicks's description of the events of the agrarian revolt. To this foundation, Rochester ritualistically affixes a Leninist framework of analysis. The resulting edifice necessarily will not bear much weight. While Rochester's analysis is more or less ideologically consistent on its own terms, the People's Party she condescendingly portrays does not remotely resemble the one that existed. Another socialist, Matthew Josephson, analyzed Populism in the course of his broad study of the Gilded Age, *The Politicos* (1938). Considerably more enamored of democratic ideas than Rochester, Josephson was also much less patronizing toward the farmers. But, he, too, was unable to go much beyond Hicks and, therefore, failed to grasp the interior reality of the democratic mass movement that was Populism. Josephson, however, was not so beguiled that he failed to see the nomination of Bryan in 1896 as fatal to the agrarian cause. On balance, his account is better than most. In *American Radicalism, 1865–1901* (1946) Chester McArthur Destler's colorful portrait of the Populist-Socialist alliance in Chicago in 1894 is marred only by the author's assumption, encouraged by Hick's portrait, that the Lloyd-Vincent-Darrow-Morgan coalition was a rare Populist specimen of popular democracy in action. For all its passion, the brief Chicago movement cannot be said to have surpassed in forethought or constancy either the far-flung cooperative crusade or scores of Populist campaigns across the South and West in the 1890s. But when dealing with the specific subject at hand, Destler's vivid account of urban Populism in Chicago is the finest local treatment of the movement in all of Populist literature.

Like their socialist counterparts, capitalist historians have tracked the findings of John Hicks, sometimes embellishing their accounts of the shadow movement with Hofstadterian flourishes and sometimes defending the silver episode in the style of Pollack. Stanley B. Parsons subjects the Nebraska silverites to quantification techniques in a recent work that is entitled, with unwitting irony, *The Populist Context* (1973). In *From Populism to Progressivism in Alabama* (1969), Sheldon Hackney imposes upon rather imprecise and sometimes almost opaque legislative documents a heavy burden of ideological and political interpretation in the course of reaching conclusions in harmony with Hofstadter's. *The Climax of Populism* by Robert F. Durden (1966) is a sympathetic treatment of Marion Butler's harried tenure as third party custodian of the campaign for silver in 1896. Those of his conclusions that concern the efficacy of the silver drive accordingly coincide with Pollack's. In *Populist Vanguard* (1975), a study that emphasizes religious influences more than monetary analysis, Robert McMath finds a significant ingredient of agrarian organizing to be the "congenial social settings" in which the farmers met. In *Farmer Movements in the South* (1960), Theodore Saloutos intermittently observes the cooperative movement of the Alliance but does not see its defeat as a central event. Rather, the Farmers Alliance is "undermined" by the People's Party.

The intensely democratic "movement culture" of self-respect and aspiration generated by the cooperative crusade, a way of thinking that created the radical new third party of Populism, is not visible in any of these portraits.

In a theoretical sense, there is no absolutely compelling reason why either capitalist or socialist historians in America should be blocked off from perceiving a mass desire for social change as incubating in the particular way it did within the agrarian movement—even given the narrowness of the categories of political description dominant in both modes of analysis. Rather the problem has to do with what might be called the separate habits of thought undergirding the two intellectual traditions. In this operative sense, the idea of mass cultures of democracy being created as parallel institutions of self-respect and aspiration—or as "unsteepled places of worship" in E. P. Thompson's evocative phrase—is one that remains generally foreign to the traditions of either capitalist or socialist historical analysis, as these traditions have evolved in America.

Capitalist historians, generally starting from the unconscious premise that the country has always been a fairly effective democracy, have not imagined a need for any of its citizens to establish parallel institutions where people could experiment in democratic forms.* So they have not inquired into the interior life of the cooperative crusade where, in thousands of suballiances, the political culture of American Populism came into being.

On the other hand, socialist historians, apparently overwhelmed psychologically by the near totality of their intellectual isolation in America, have seemingly been unable to imagine a mass popular movement in this country containing a decidedly anti-corporate center. So they have not looked either.

In both instances the initial failure of interpretation seems to have been more an absence of cultural poise and critical imagination than an organic insufficiency of theoretical weaponry that might be brought to bear. The narrowness of the inherited categories of political description, of course, has not helped either. In general, the works of capitalist historians seem to have suffered at least as much from their doctrinal complacency about capitalism as a synonym for democracy as the works of socialist historians have suffered from their cultural isolation. But socialists have demonstrated a complacent reliance on doctrine, too, as attested by the works of Williams, Rochester, and, to a lesser extent, Pollack.

Because the political basis of the national Populist movement has proven such a universal pitfall, several of the most interesting and substantial studies of Populism have been produced by cultural historians who were not primarily dealing with the third party's structural and political evolution. In relating what Populists said to what they did, such writers as O. Eugene Clanton and Walter T. K. Nugent, for example, have provided a much clearer picture of the third party movement in Kansas. Clanton's *Kansas Populism: Ideas and Men* (1969) concludes that Populists were broadly progressive. Nugent, in his more sharply focused study, *The Tolerant Populists* (1963), investigates the day-to-day realities in the life of the third party in Kansas, tests all of Hofstadter's major findings, and finds them inapplicable. Nugent was doubtless aided in his inquiry by his familiarity with monetary issues. His study of post-Civil War financial struggles, *Money and American Society, 1865–1880* (1967), probes a number of the differences between greenbackers, silverites, and goldbugs. Robert Sharkey, is even more authoritative on financial matters in *Money, Class, and Party* (1959), but Irvin Unger's *The Greenback Era* (1964), proceeding from Hofstadterian premises, is much narrower and less useful in its description of greenback doctrines. Allan Weinstein's *Prelude to Populism* (1970) is a careful study of the first

---

* Indeed, among behaviorists who seem to take as their starting point the received presumptions of the prevailing culture, such popular democratic actions, should they somehow occur, are seen as "dysfunctional" to the social order and point to some neurotic affliction on the part of the participants. (See Neil J. Smelser, *Theory of Collective Behavior*, 1963). It is impossible to take this fragile and culturally confined school of analysis seriously, though, one observes, a considerable number of American psychologists, sociologists, and political scientists seem earnestly to be trying to do so. Its most beguiling and artful practitioner, however, has been a historian—Richard Hofstadter. As they have traditionally written, the disciples of the behaviorist school may be counted on to survive and prosper because their efforts tend to provide a comforting rationalization for things as they are. They thus can be expected to continue to enjoy powerful cultural sanction.

silver drive of the 1870s, but the author unfortunately relates money to late nineteenth-century politics in ways reflecting the influence of John Hicks. This impediment vitiates a good deal of the political meaning of his study.

Given the mass democratic movement at the heart of the agrarian revolt, Populism offers a fertile field for future inquiries by social and political historians. Much can be learned about the social realities and political power relationships within nineteenth-century American society through studies of the day-to-day life of the cooperative crusade in each of the states touched by the Alliance lecturing campaigns of 1887–91. Such inquiries will also tell us much more about the Alliance movement in each state than we now know. The particulars through which the ideological culmination of the cooperative effort—the "politics of the sub-treasury"—either were or were not orchestrated through the lecturing system of each state Alliance should illuminate the specific organizational dynamics leading both to strong and to weak state-level third parties across America in 1892. Such particulars will tell us much more about the People's Party in each state than we now know. Though the existing monographic literature is vast, it does not address these matters.

Beyond these political questions about the Alliance and the People's Party lie deeper questions for the social historian. How did the first fragile efforts toward cooperation at the local level—election of suballiance business agents and the creation of county trade committees to bargain with merchants—affect the average farmer caught in the crop lien or the chattel mortgage? If the cooperative crusade raised political consciousness to a level seldom since attained by large numbers of Americans, how, precisely, did this occur? What raised the sights of people more—cooperative success or cooperative defeat? Was the acceptance of the sub-treasury solution, and of greenback doctrines generally, largely a matter of faith and shared allegiance to one's cooperative brothers and sisters in the Alliance, and to one's lecturers, or was it more than this? To summarize, in ways that are more precise than those elaborated in this study, how did the people of Populism acquire the self-confidence to create a new party to challenge the received political culture? One has only to ponder the difficulty facing would-be third party organizers in modern America to perceive the full meaning of the Alliance political achievement in fashioning the People's Party of the 1890s. In one way, at least, the task facing the agrarian reformers was even more arduous, for they had to generate enormous popular momentum in order to break the sectional bonds of Civil War loyalties.

In addition to these questions about the Populists are larger ones that go to the structure of power and privilege in America. Among the higher priorities, the economic, political, and social ramifications of American banking practices, in both the nineteenth and twentieth centuries, stand as a singularly neglected area of investigation, one affecting hundreds of millions of Americans, past and present. The long-standard works on the origins and development of the Federal Reserve System have emanated from the pens of gold-standard apostles who wrote the Federal Reserve Act—J. Laurence

607

Laughlin, H. Parker Willis, and Paul Warburg. (See p. 686, n. 3); Similarly, the most comprehensive studies of American banking in historical literature are by Bray Hammond, an employee of "The Fed." This material can scarcely be said to constitute a probing or balanced body of evidence. *A Monetary History of the United States, 1867–1960* by economists Milton Friedman and Anna Schwartz (1963) approaches the politics of money with extreme circumspection, leaving many central issues untouched. *Money* by John Kenneth Galbraith (1975) is urbanely skeptical of a number of sanctioned assumptions and institutions—from the values and intelligence of American bankers to the economic utility of the Federal Reserve System—but the author makes no sustained effort to formulate broadly applicable alternatives. The subjects of money and banking, in their meaning as social and political realities as well as arcane financial topics, do not seem to be in immediate danger of being overworked by American scholars. Since Populism, serious and full-scale appraisals of the monetary system have not been attempted. A beginning, however, has been made with respect to the helplessness of Congress. *The Money Committees* by Lester Salamon (1975) probes the adverse impact of the banking system and banker lobbying on, among other things, the housing aspirations of millions of Americans.

Biographers could profitably supplement the five worthy studies of Populist leaders now available: C. Vann Woodward's *Tom Watson: Agrarian Rebel* (*2nd edition*, 1973); Chester McArthur Destler's *Henry Demarest Lloyd and the Empire of Reform* (1963); Martin Ridge's *Ignatius Donnelly: The Portrait of a Politician* (1962); Stuart Noblin's *Leonidas Lafayette Polk: Agrarian Crusader* (1949), and Michael J. Brodhead's *Persevering Populist: The Life of Frank Doster* (1969). Charles Macune of Texas and Henry Vincent of Kansas are the most obvious subjects for investigation. The known historical sources may be too thin for well-rounded biographies of other Populists who come to mind, Henry Loucks of South Dakota, William Lamb and John Rayner of Texas, and W. Scott Morgan of Arkansas, but this may not be the case for L. H. Weller of Iowa, Milford Howard of Alabama, Stephen McLallin of Kansas, Frank Burkitt of Mississippi, and Tom Nugent of Texas. Most of these men, in addition to their other roles, were reform editors. The Reform Press was to the People's Party what the lecturing system was to the National Alliance—the critical internal communications network within the movement culture. A most remarkable group of Americans, the reform editors stand in need of full-scale scholarly investigation. In the meantime, one regional study, "The Reform Editors and Their Press," by Seymour Lutzky, a long-unpublished dissertation on the Populist editors in the West, merits publication.

Finally, one senses that women played a more prominent role in the agrarian revolt than the present study suggests. The evidence is both tantalizing in implication and difficult to gather. Suggested points of entry: the careers of Annie Diggs of Kansas, Sophronia Lewelling of Oregon, Bettie Gay of Texas, Luna Kellie of Nebraska, Ella Knowles of Montana, Sophia Harden of South Dakota, and of course, the author of the famous injunction to farmers to "raise less corn and more hell," Mary Elizabeth Lease of Kansas. Luna Kellie's epitaph for Populism suggests the depth of her personal involvement: "I dared not even think of all the hopes we used to have and their bitter ending . . . and so I never vote."

Of the existing monographic literature, the best single state study of Populism remains A. M. Arnett's *The Populist Movement in Georgia* (1922), written before later interpretive constraints were fashioned. Four recent studies are also of merit. In *One-Gallused Rebellion: Agrarianism in Alabama, 1865–1896,* by William Warren Rogers (1970), a work based on extensive use of primary sources, Alliance-Populism emerges as authentic human striving; and in *Bourbonism and Agrarian Protest* by William Ivy Hair (1969), the third party's checkered struggle against the inheritance of white supremacy in Louisiana is delineated. *Urban Populism and Free Silver in Montana,* by Thomas Clinch (1970), is a careful study in a state where Populism was a labor movement. The grab-bag nature of the silver crusade is clearly visible in Mary Ellen Glass's *Silver and Politics in Nevada: 1892–1902* (1969). An older study by a political scientist, Roscoe Martin's *The People's Party in Texas* (1933), is also useful, though Martin appears unaware of the national organizing role played by the same reformers whose efforts he so aptly describes on the state level—a circumstance perhaps evolving from the author's decision to take the fading months of 1891 as the starting point for his research. *Populism and Politics,* by Peter H. Argesinger (1974) is excellent on the machinations of the fusionists in Kansas but less so when the author, basing his work primarily on Kansas sources, attempts to interpret the movement beyond that state's borders.

Overall, the best guides to the national Populist experience remain the Populists themselves. Two thoughtful collections of agrarian thought are available: *The Populist Mind* by Norman Pollack (1967), and *A Populist Reader* by George Tindall (1966). Also useful is "The Rhetoric of Southern Populists: Metaphor and Imagery in the Language of Reform," by Bruce Palmer, a recently completed and as yet unpublished dissertation. For those who want more of the Populists in unvarnished form, the depression year of 1894 brought forth Henry Demarest Lloyd's anti-monopoly classic, *Wealth Against Commonwealth;* Henry Vincent's deeply sympathetic account of the plight of the unemployed, *The Story of the Commonweal,* and, for those who can take a combination of full-blown Populist rhetoric blended with a thoughtful investigation of the monetary system, there is James H. "Cyclone" Davis's *A Political Revelation,* containing a lengthy supplement on the Sub-Treasury System by Harry Tracy (see Appendix B).

Some excellent works by specialists bear directly on the issues of Populism. Hans Birger Thorelli, explores the rise of oligopoly in his monumental study, *The Federal Anti-trust Policy: Organization of an American Tradition* (1955). With the essential legal flanks safeguarded, the movement toward corporate concentration continued unimpeded into the modern era, as Ralph L. Nelson shows in *The Merger Movement in American Industry, 1895–1956* (1957). While the Justice Department was losing its battle to cope with the combination movement, the Interstate Commerce Commission met a corresponding fate at the hands of American railroads, a process detailed in Gabriel Kolko's *Railroads and Regulation, 1877–1916* (1965). *Triumph of Conservatism* (1963), by the same author, traces the similar accommodations to large-scale manufacturers, merchandisers, and processors by the Federal Trade Commission and to Eastern commercial banks by the Federal Reserve System. The social impact of the emerging corporate state is brilliantly interpreted in *Work, Culture, and Society in 19th Century America,* by Herbert Gutman (1975).

In the presence of consolidating corporate power, the fragility of the American labor movement is visible in Norman J. Ware's old but still useful study of the Knights of Labor, *The Labor Movement in the United States, 1860–1895* (1929). The analogous plight of Southern farmers under the crop lien system is effectively portrayed by Harold Woodman in *King Cotton and His Retainers: Financing and Marketing the Cotton Crop of the South, 1800–1925* (1968). However, in a work that treats the problem of agricultural credit in the Western granary, *Money at Interest* (1955), Allan Bogue engages in a somewhat strained defense of the policies of mortgage companies. The matter of tenancy and land centralization in the plains states in both the nineteenth and twentieth centuries can bear some more attention. A relevant body of evidence is available in Fred A. Shannon, "The Status of the Midwestern Farmer in 1900," *Mississippi Valley Historical Review* (December 1950), 491–510. In a recent study, *The Shadow of Slavery: Peonage in the South, 1901–1969* (1972), Pete Daniel has provided a valuable example of what can be achieved on a most relevant and long-neglected subject. The conservative rationale for rural poverty—that farmers brought their troubles on themselves through "overproduction"—is effectively debunked by two economists, an economic historian and a historian, respectively: Roger Ransom and Richard Sutch, "The 'Lock-in' Mechanism and Cotton Overproduction in the Postbellum South," *Agricultural History* (April 1973), 405–22; Stephen DeCanio, "Cotton 'Overproduction' in Late Nineteenth Century Southern Agriculture," *Journal of Economic History* (Sept. 1973), 608–33; and Thomas D. Clark, "The Furnishing and Supply System in Southern Agriculture since 1865," *Journal of Southern History* (Feb. 1946), 24–44. The historical record of the cooperative idea is presented in *The Rise of American Cooperative Enterprise* (1969) by Joseph Knapp.

The passing of the People's Party in America left the way clear in the South for the achievement of political hegemony by businessmen. *In the Shaping of Southern Politics* (1974), an effectively documented work that probes the process by which a white supremacist, business-dominated "Solid South" was constructed, J. Morgan Kousser traces the near-total disfranchisement of blacks and the partial disfranchisement of low income whites. The new edifice of politics was fully completed by 1910. The same forces were at work nationally, a process that is often visible in *The American Party Systems,* edited by William N. Chambers and Walter Dean Burnham. Should any future historian harbor Hofstadterian doubts that the grievances of

Populists and the objectives of the Omaha Platform were real, the work of these specialists may give him pause.

Finally, the unique contribution of C. Vann Woodward merits special mention. While concerned with a larger topic, Woodward's classic study of the post-Reconstruction South, *Origins of the New South* (1951), is laden with insights about the political evolution and cultural implications of Southern Populism. The chief limitation of Woodward's analysis is traceable to the regional scope that was a product of his larger purpose—which was not to write about the agrarian revolt in the nation but to write about the American South in the Gilded Age. Woodward's essential cultural statement about Southern Populism, that it was demonstrably more humanistic than its political rivals, applies to American Populism. His essential political statement about Southern Populists, that they were "midroaders," also, of course, applies to the national movement. Despite a number of impediments in the secondary literature relating to the origins of the cooperative movement and the evolution of Alliance monetary theory, Woodward, while not locating the centrality of cooperation or the movement culture it created, drew attention to the Alliance lecturing system and the National Reform Press Association developed by agrarian strategists as necessary educational corollaries of their organizing campaign. Accordingly, he had little difficulty in outlining the structure of Populist economic reform and the corresponding ephemerality of the silver issue. In short, in economic as well as political terms, Woodward wrote about Populism as Populism, rather than as the fusion politics of free silver. And, of course, Woodward's magnificent biography of the tortured life of Tom Watson is one of the enduring triumphs of American historical literature and, indeed, of American letters.

After over a half-century of research on America's largest mass movement of the nineteenth century, the original question remains: what does the Populist experience reveal about the evolution of political and economic power in industrial America?

One is persuaded that it reveals a great deal. As for the style of the nation's emerging financial elite, one cannot easily find a political doctrine narrower and more self-serving than the fixation of the American banking hierarchy upon "sound money." Leaving aside the piety about "the sanctity of contracts" and "the nation's honor," the artificially contracted currency of the gold standard had three undeniable and linked products: it curtailed the nation's economic growth; it helped measurably to concentrate the capital assets of the nation in the pockets of the nation's bankers; * and it helped measurably to consign generation after generation of non-banker Americans to lives of hardship and dependence. Beyond this, the triumph of the

---

* Though—because of the prevailing legalities of the situation—it is impossible to construct an accurate picture of bank ownership in America, there is some evidence to suggest that many and perhaps most Southern banks chartered in the period 1880–1940 were capitalized by furnishing merchants. But in general, serious scholarly work in this area has not yet begun—and cannot—until the disclosure laws are reformed (see Appendix A).

political and cultural values embedded in the gold standard provided the economic foundation for the hierarchical corporate state of twentieth century America. In turn, the values and the sheer power of corporate America today pinch in the horizons of millions of obsequious corporate employees, tower over every American legislature, state and national, determine the modes and style of mass communications and mass education, fashion American foreign policy around the globe, and shape the rules of the American political process itself. The scope of intimidation extends deep into the American academy and into the very core of American intellectual life. Perhaps nothing illustrates the subtle power of the received culture more tellingly than the paucity of serious inquiry—by economists, historians, and political scientists—into the economic and political substance of that central component of American capitalism—commercial banking. Self-evidently, corporate values define modern American culture.

It was the corporate state that the People's Party attempted to bring under democratic control. The sheer scope of that goal measures the intensity of the parallel culture of mass self-respect and human aspiration generated by the agrarian revolt. At bottom, that culture expressed the democratic promise that was the ultimate meaning of Populism in America.

The long inability of Americans encased in "the progressive society" to comprehend the agrarian revolt may be taken as a fairly instructive index of the social relevance of modern political thought, sadly confined as it is by the ubiquitous ethos of the corporate state. The victims of modern culture have tried to view their personal resignation and intellectual submission as a form of sophistication and have attempted to sustain their morale by teaching the young not to aspire too grandly for too much democracy. In America the two political names for this narrowed despair are liberalism and conservatism. The language of one is grounded in civic illusion, the other in self-interested complacency. The Gilded Age silverites and goldbugs were the immediate progenitors of each; indeed, their tangential "Battle of the Standards" in 1896 turned out to be a foretaste of much of electoral politics in twentieth-century America.

But the Omaha Platform was generated by other Americans who were not so culturally organized or so politically cowed. It may be that the Populists have never been made a seminal part of the national heritage because to do so would diminish the present, and the people who live in it, too profoundly. It would be difficult, indeed, for the implicit comparison to coexist easily with the sundry ideas of progress so necessary to the political morale of twentieth-century people. Today, a loyal but disenchanted citizenry, aware that it can do little to affect "politics," endeavors to take what solace it can from the pursuit of material goods.

But, though Americans consume more products today, they are less free than they used to be; and in the privacy of their minds, they suspect it. It is essentially a matter of scale of thought, or more precisely, of scale of aspiration. Our hopes have become cramped; our achievements necessarily have also. It is not, however, a uniquely American phenomenon. The modern cultures of mass resignation and privatism verify this unhappy truth—in the United States, in the Soviet Union, in the industrial world. Though the distinctions from country to country in the degree of relative resignation and relative liberty are quite important, everywhere the self-perpetuating structures of capitalism and communism have placed themselves beyond effective democratic change. In both camps the citizenry does not seem to be able to alter significantly the essential patterns of power and privilege. It is the one political reality that binds the people of the "advanced industrial world."

In the singularly uncreative political environment of the twentieth century, an environment that locks billions of people into rigid theoretical categories conceived by capitalist and socialist prophets now long dead, men and women are in danger of unconsciously relinquishing the broad democratic dreams that quickened mankind's speculative energies through the preceding 400 years. Individually diminished by the social demands of large-scale technology and the constricting cultures it has nurtured, the peoples of the industrial world find it increasingly difficult to develop genuinely democratic ways to cooperate with each other. To do so, they need to participate in self-generated democratic forms, but we seem to have few contemporary suballiances where individual political self-confidence can be encouraged and where collective democratic hopes can take life. The intense psychological isolation of the great mass of people in industrialized societies may be seen to constitute the essential rigidifying factor in twentieth century political regimes. With the political self-confidence of individual people and the collective idea of "the rights of the people" varyingly curtailed by large-scale corporate cultures and by large-scale state cultures, both ideologically sanctified, it has become increasingly difficult for the citizenry to find a coherent way to aspire for greater human freedom. This development would be much more widely understood were it not for the fact that—for reasons most members of modern societies have chosen not to ponder too much—the people of the industrial world are losing their capacity to think in germane ways about their own personal autonomy or their own political self-respect.

In America, part of the difficulty lies in our complacent understanding of our own heritage. It is by no means a heritage of utter failure, but it is also in no sense one of uninterrupted democratic triumph. Once we find the national poise to cease our culturally undifferentiated celebration of the American past, the poise, therefore, to confront the sources both of white resignation and of black anguish, the promise of democracy will once again become a possibility in the lives of Americans. At such a moment, and one believes it may come, the Populist heritage will be useful. For above all else, the men and women who filled the Alliance wagon trains and the Populist summer encampments, and those who set out on arduous journeys to talk to black sharecroppers and to white tenants—such people believed in the promise of the democratic idea. They dared to aspire grandly in behalf of their vision of human possibility.

When Americans can generate the individual sense of self and an ethos of collective hope necessary to understand them, the words of Populism can, for the first time, become part of the democratic poetry of the common heritage. But for this to happen, the narrowly focused and defensive sophistication of modern culture must give way to self-respect. Though the people's culture created by the agrarian revolt was deeply embattled and too new ever to be more than fragile, the Americans who participated in it came to possess, for a time, that very quality—unintimidated self-respect. It is the one essential ingredient of an authentic mass democracy. No industrial society in the world has yet attained it.

The agrarian revolt therefore is something more than a democratic memory; from the moment of its conception, it concerned the future. The prophetic words of S. O. Daws in 1886 describe the legacy of the agrarian reformers and suggest the challenge facing those who live in the twentieth century: "If the Alliance is destroyed, it will be some time before the people have confidence in themselves, and one another, to revive it, or organize anything new."

Notes

CHAPTER I

1. Geoffrey Blodgett, *The Gentle Reformers: Massachusetts Democrats in the Cleveland Era* (Cambridge, Mass., 1964). With a fine feel for the humor that could be extracted from the situation, Blodgett records the unease of patrician Mugwumps as they settled into the Irish Catholic world of the Massachusetts Democratic Party, and he notes the "gulf of distrust which then as now divided the New England populace into native Yankee and immigrant stock." The Protestant motivation was not always defensive, as the emergence of the aggressively anti-Catholic American Protective Association illustrates. John Higham, *Strangers in the Land* (New Brunswick, N.J., 1955). See also Paul Kleppner, *The Cross of Culture: A Social Analysis of Midwestern Politics, 1875–1900* (New York, 1970), 251–56; Henry J. Browne, *The Catholic Church and the Knights of Labor* (Washington, D.C., 1949).

2. As the example of wartime "copperheads" indicates, the entire subject of sectionalism is more complex than this short review can suggest; nevertheless, conceding all exceptions, the broader point is the significant one: in terms of the basic constituencies of the two parties, sectionalism was the most important postwar political reality. "Rotten borough of republicanism" is Blodgett's phrase and refers to New England. It may be applied much more broadly. David Montgomery, speaking of postwar voting patterns of rural areas from Pennsylvania westward to Missouri, summarizes: "These largely rural and rapidly developing areas dominated by farmers and small entrepreneurs, whether their past was Whig or Democrat, were now Radical bastions. . . ." *Beyond Equality* (New York, 1967), 76–77 See also Robert P. Sharkey, *Money, Class, and Party: An Economic Study of Civil War and Reconstruction* (Baltimore, 1959).

3 Abolitionism within the postwar Republican Party has received sophisticated scholarly attention since 1960. James M. McPherson, *The Struggle for Equality: Abolitionists and the Negro in the Civil War* (Princeton, 1964), and by the same author,
"Grant or Greeley? The Abolitionist Dilemma in the Election of 1872," *American
Historical Review*, LXXI (Oct. 1965), 43–61; and "Coercion or Conciliation? Abolitionists Debate President Hayes's Southern Policy," *New England Quarterly*, XL
(1966), 474–97; Eric McKitrick, *Andrew Johnson and Reconstruction* (Chicago, 1960);
Kenneth Stampp, *The Era of Reconstruction, 1865–1877* (New York, 1965); John
and LaWanda Cox, *Politics, Principal and Prejudice, 1865–1866* (New York, 1963);
Stanley Hirshson, *Farewell to the Bloody Shirt: Northern Republicans and the Southern
Negro* (Bloomington, 1962); Vincent DeSantis, *Republicans Face the Southern Question: The New Departure Years, 1887–1897* (Baltimore, 1959).
4. Walter T. K. Nugent, *Money and American Society* (New York, 1967), 205–18, 267–
69; Allan Weinstein, *Prelude to Populism* (New Haven, 1970), 365. Weinstein places
the attainment of hegemony later in the century than Nugent does. The essential point, in political terms, however, is the gradual but unmistakable ascendancy
of enterpriser ideology in both parties after the war. See also Montgomery,
Beyond Equality, 446–47. An excellent study of Republican ideology before the war
is Eric Foner, *Free Soil, Free Labor, Free Men* (New York, 1970).
5. C. Vann Woodward, *Origins of the New South* (Baton Rouge, 1951),1–73, 142–74.
6. Vincent DeSantis, "Negro Dissatisfaction with Republican Policy in the South,
1882–1884," *Journal of Negro History*, XXXVI (1951), 148–59; "Benjamin Harrison and the Republican Party in the South, 1889–1893," *Indiana Magazine of
History*, LI (1955), 279–302; and "The Republican Party and the Southern Negro,
1877–1897," *Journal of Negro History*, XLV (1960), 71–87.
7. Though the marginal realignment of Northern and Western Gold Democrats
into coalition with hard-money Republicans awaited the politics of 1896, the basic
postwar restructuring of the mass constituencies of the two parties had been
largely completed much earlier. Subsequent adjustments, including the important
shift of 1894, took place within this matured realignment. In a phrase that seems
both broad and flexible enough, Montgomery, in describing matters at the end of
Reconstruction, speaks of the "resiliency of the social equilibrium that was emerging" (*Beyond Equality*, 446).
8. Indeed, as this study attempts to demonstrate throughout, sectionalism in the late
1880s and early 1890s persisted as an enormous political barrier to reformers
bent on creating a multi-sectional third party. The emphasis here is specifically on
the whole constituency of the parties rather than on marginal increments of
voters whose movement from one party to the other was often critical in determining elections during this period of party equilibrium. Marginally, issues, such
as the tariff, could be intermittently relevant, but in defining the underlying
reasons most Americans regarded themselves as Democrats or Republicans in this
period, sectional loyalty was transcendently more important than the domestic effects of international trade—or anything else. The Catholic exception has been
noted.

The basic stability of the Republican constituency from 1868 to 1888 continued
to indicate that as a vote-getter, the bloody shirt—whether waved aggressively or
not—was worth any number of tariff bills. Local issues, particularly those touching religious values, as did the Bennett Law in Wisconsin in 1890, could produce
important temporary shifts, but such examples merely emphasized the stability of
party constituencies that prevailed normally. From the standpoint of a third party

seeking an entire new constituency—as distinct from a marginal new increment of voters—the decisive importance of war-related sectionalism, when compared with the numerically insignificant utility of the tariff issue, was clear. This explained why Populists were to talk so much about ending sectionalism—its persistence was their albatross.

The tariff issue most coherently provided a rational party choice to one group of Americans—hard-money businessmen who were not too rigid in their social conservatism. As long as the Eastern Democracy remained orthodox on the financial and labor questions, shippers, jobbers, and other Yankee businessmen who favored low tariffs for reasons of commercial self-interest could find a home of sorts in the immigrant-filled Northern Democratic Party, while their high-tariff business associates remained Republican. The tariff issue thus could "explain" the political choices of such businessmen—again, as long as both parties remained orthodox on other pertinent economic questions. But even this example must be qualified. Many businessmen who preferred lower tariffs remained Republican out of their individual responses to the sectional legacy of the war, and others did so for social or class reasons. Indeed, self-interested maneuvering between low and high tariff Republican businessmen imparted a bit of factional flavor to congressional lobbying without in any way affecting the loyalty of the participants to the G.O.P. (For a more sweeping judgment of the importance of the tariff in rationalizing the constituencies of the parties, see Morgan, *Hayes to McKinley,* 120, 538, 541, passim.)

9. Sharkey, *Money, Class, and Party,* 3–140.
10. Nugent, *Money and American Society,,* 4–5; Irwin Unger, *The Greenback Era* (Princeton, 1964), 3–28, 120–62.
11. Nugent, *The Money Question During Reconstruction,* 23–33, 58–64; Unger, *Greenback Era,* 163–94. The sardonic goldbug view of the new currency, contributing to the name, was that they "had nothing behind them but the green ink on their back side."
12. The "morality" of the gold standard has received due attention in Unger, *The Greenback Era.* "Given the heritage of Geneva and the conservative financial tradition of the American puritan clergy . . . the[ir] financial views . . . would be a powerful force for hard money" (p. 28). Nugent, *Money and American Society,* adds, "the question of what the proper standard of money ought to be . . . was very close to saying what the proper moral standard ought to be" (p. 4). For the more germane economic considerations involved, see Sharkey, *Money, Class, and Party,* esp. 31–32, 42, 49–53, 59–67, 83–84, 221–311; and Nugent, *Money and American Society,* 14–64, 92–95, 175–78. The corroborating view of a modern economist is available in George G. Sause, *Money, Banking and Economic Activity* (Boston, 1964), esp. 58–60.
13. Sause, *Money, Banking and Economic Activity,* 58–60.
14. *Ibid.*
15. In this example, of course, stable currency velocity is assumed.
16. Sause, *Money, Banking and Economic Activity,* 60–64.
17. *Workingman's Advocate* (Chicago), April 21, 1866, quoted in Nugent, *Money and American Society,* 5.
18. "The Influence of Edward Kellogg upon American Radicalism," in Chester M. Destler, *American Radicalism, 1865–1901* (New London, Conn., 1946), 50–77; Sharkey, *Money, Class, and Party,* 187–91; Unger, *Greenback Era,* 94–100. This discussion concerns American origins. The intellectual sources of greenback think-

ing can be traced to eighteenth-century works by such "anti-metallists" and inflationists in England and France as Sir James Stewart, John Law, and Bishop
Berkeley. See Joseph Schumpeter, *History of Economic Analysis* (New York, 1954),
and Douglas Vickers, *Studies in the Theory of Money, 1690–1776* (Philadelphia,
1959); and Appendix B.

19. Destler, *American Radicalism*, 56; Unger, *Greenback Era*, 50–60, 97–101; Nugent,
    Money and American Society, 28–32. The conservative Henry Carey ran a rather
    poor last in this contest of early soft-money theorists. Schumpeter concluded a
    discussion of "Careyism" with the observation that "there was an element of
    greatness in his errors." See also Foner, *Free Soil, Free Labor, Free Men*, 19–20,
    36–37; Sharkey, *Money, Class, and Party*, 153–56.

20. Nathan Fine, *Labor and Farmer Parties in the United States* (New York, 1961), 63–70;
    Unger, *Greenback Era*, 110, 286–321; Nugent, *Money and American Society*, 229–42;
    Sharkey, *Money, Class, and Party*, 308.

    In focusing on both the ideological substance and the broad interest-group
    divisions arising from the resumption debate, Unger, Nugent, Sharkey, and
    Weinstein have corrected earlier accounts that, in viewing the silver issue of the
    '70s from the perspective of the Populist era, portrayed soft-money ideology as a
    product of Western discontent. The point is particularly relevant to this study,
    which draws attention to the central role that indigenous agrarian greenbackism
    played in the creation and subsequent life of the People's Party. Nevertheless, the
    whole matter can easily be treated too finely as an intellectual exercise. In strictly
    political terms, it is still necessary to say that while the principal early theoreticians
    of a fiat currency were, as these scholars have shown, not Western agrarians, a
    great many of its supporters on election day were—even before the 1890s.

21. Nugent, *Money and American Society*, 229–42; Unger, *Greenback Era*, 286–321.
    Nugent refers to the political plight of early greenbackers as "far from the arena
    of power, fighting a frustrating guerilla battle against an overwhelming ortho-
    doxy" (Nugent, 43). Despite its title, Unger's *The Greenback Era* is concerned much
    more with silver inflation than with the threat posed by full-scale greenbackism.
    Properly so—for the 1870s. Unger's book is strongest on its principal topic, silver
    and inflationist sentiment among some business groups; his grasp is less sure in
    his interpretation of greenback doctrines, either as a theory of monetary systems
    or as a popular movement. See Chaps. V, VI, VII, VIII, IX, XII, XIV, XVII,
    and Appendix A.

22. The severity of the depression is treated in Milton Friedman and Anna Schwartz,
    A Monetary History of the United States, 1867–1960, (Princeton, 1963); See also
    Nugent, *Money and American Society*, 92–95, 175–78; Unger, *Greenback Era*, 43,
    374–407.

23. Paul M. O'Leary, "The Scene of the Crime of 1873 Revisited: A Note," *Journal of
    Political Economy*, LXVII (Aug. 1960); Weinstein, *Prelude to Populism*, 6–32; Nu-
    gent, *Money in American Society*, 140–61.

24. Nugent, *Money and American Society*, 177–84; Unger, *Greenback Era*, 222.

25. Weinstein, *Prelude to Populism*, 354–68.

26. Unger asserts that "once past their initial prejudice against coin, the paper money
    men almost universally embraced the new panacea." In support of this rather
    large contention, he cites two moderate Indiana newspaper editors and adds two
    labor papers which offered a qualified support for silver as a temporary infla-
    tionist expedient (*Greenback Era*, 332). Weinstein, on the other hand, concludes
    that "only a few agrarian inflationist leaders participated meaningfully in the

silver drive and most greenbackers provided only tepid support for remonetization" (*Prelude to Populism,* 356). As a matter of fact, silverites were sometimes moved to anger at the overt greenback disdain for their cause. Populism would test these harmonies and dissonances rather thoroughly.

27. For careful discussions of the problem of greenback vs. silver inflation, a central one to Gilded Age reform politics, see Sharkey, *Money, Class, and Party,* 15–55; 81–140; 211–311 Nugent, *Money and American Society,* esp. 202–4.

28. Morgan, *From Hayes to McKinley,* 232.

29. Henry D. Wilson to Luhman H. Weller, May 27, 1885, Weller Papers, Wisconsin State Historical Society. Other early examples are J. B. Weaver and E. H. Gillette to Weller, May 29, 1885; W. H. Shaw to Weller, July 9, 1885. Gillette was chairman of the national executive committee of the Greenback Party and Weaver its 1884 Presidential candidate. The quotation in the text is from W. S. Wilcox to Weller, Jan. 4, 1889.

CHAPTER II

1. James E. Sellers, "The Economic Incidence of the Civil War in the South," *Mississippi Valley Historical Review,* XIV (1928–29), 188–91; William E. Laird and James R. Rinehart, "Post-Civil War South and the Great Depression: A Suggested Parallel," *Mid-America,* XLVIII (July 1966), 206–10; Robert P. Sharkey, "Commerical Banking," in David T. Gilchrist and W. David Lewis (eds.), *Economic Change in the Civil War Era* (Greenville, Del., 1965), 28–31; William E. Laird and James R. Rinehart, "Deflation, Agriculture and Southern Development," *Journal of Agricultural History* (April 1968), 116–17; Alex M. Arnett, *The Populist Movement in Georgia* (New York, 1922), esp. chap. III, "The Basis of Agrarian Discontent," 49–75.

2. Thomas D. Clark, "Imperfect Competition in the Southern Retail Trade after 1865," *Journal of Economic History,* III (Supplement, Dec. 1943), 39–40; Thomas D. Clark, "The Furnishing and Supply System in Southern Agriculture Since 1865," *Journal of Southern History,* XII (1946), 28–31. Detailed discussions of the crop lien may be found in Charles H. Otken, *The Ills of the South* (New York, 1894), 12–247; Matthew B. Hammond, *The Cotton Industry* (Ithaca, N.Y., 1897), 141–65; and Woodward, *Origins of the New South,* 175–88.

3. Hammond, *The Cotton Industry,* 141–65; Margaret Pace Farmer, "Furnishing Merchants and Sharecroppers in Pike County, Alabama," *The Alabama Review,* XXIII (April 1970), 147.

4. Clark, "Furnishing and Supply System," 38; T. G. Patrick & Company Journals, quoted in Clark, 42.

5. Ike Jones Ledger, 1884–1901, personal account of Matt Brown, quoted in Clark, "Furnishing and Supply System," 41–42.

6. Dallas *News,* Aug. 24, 1890; Hallie Farmer, "The Economic Background of Southern Populism," *South Atlantic Quarterly,* XXIX (Jan. 1930), 81. American journalists who thought that farmers "bought too much" doubtless had little idea of the realities of life facing people like Matt Brown, who were able to spend only $8.42 for food for an entire year. Reporters who covered the "Alliance beat" seemed to be continuously trying to remind their readers, and perhaps their editors, that the farmers were "earnest" and "sober"—that is to say, that their strivings deserved to be taken seriously.

7. Clark, "Furnishing and Supply System," 36.
8. Hammond, *Cotton Industry*, 150–51; M. Farmer, "Furnishing Merchants and Sharecroppers in Pike County, Alabama," 149–50.
9. Ulrich B. Phillips, "Conservation and Progress in the Cotton Belt," *South Atlantic Quarterly*, III (1904), 5–6, quoted in Woodward, *Origins*, 182.
10. *Tenth Census*, 1880, I (Texas), 4.
11. Government data for agricultural uses were quite misleading during the last half of the nineteenth century, not only in regard to prices but also concerning more "scientific" data such as meteorological information. See, for example, *Tenth Census*, 1880, V, "Physico-Geographic and Agricultural Features" (Texas), 16.
12. Rupert N. Richardson, Texas, *The Lone Star State* (Englewood Cliffs, N.J., 1958), 233; William Curry Holden, *Alkali Trails: Social and Economic Movements of the Texas Frontier, 1846–1900* (Dallas, 1930), 44–46, 72, 127–47.
13. *Tenth Census*, 1880, I, 79. For example, listing 1880 population figures in parentheses, the figures for 1870 were: Comanche County 1001 (8608); Erath County 1801 (11,796); Montague County 890 (11,257). Parker County actually declined during the decade of the Civil War from 4213 to 4186 only to rise to 15,870 by 1880. All of the above-named counties became strongholds of the Farmers Alliance by 1885. See also Walter P. Webb, *The Great Plains* (Waltham, Mass., 1931), 17–26, 334.
14. For assistance in reconstructing the details of the early Lampasas Alliance, the author is indebted to Mrs. Pearrie Allen Stevenson of Austin, Texas, daughter of J. R. Allen, at whose farm the first Alliance was organized; Mrs. L. H. Baldwin of the Lampasas County Historical Society; the officers and employees of the Texas Historical Survey Commission; and, particularly, Mr. James P. Cole of Austin. Mr. Cole, author of "The History of the Lampasas County" (Unpublished M.A. thesis, Sam Houston State College, 1969), made available the fascinating memoirs of one of the Lampasas founders, A. P. Hungate.

   "Lecture to the Donaldson Creek Alliance," Jan. 9, 1895, Hungate Memoir-Notebook, Part II, 8–26. Hungate's evidence was confirmed by a special Alliance committee on origins (*Southern Mercury*, Oct. 8, 1891) and further supported by the Diary of D. C. Thomas, privately held by Mrs. Thomas B. Huling, a former Lampasas resident, as well as by the Report of the Secretary of State, *Election Returns, 1880*, and by Cole, "History of Lampasas County," 18–21. See also John R. Allen, quoted in the Galveston *News*, Sept. 13, 1891, and *The People's Journal* (Lampasas), Aug. 16, 1895. The tradition that the National Farmers Alliance originated in 1874–75 or that it had connecting antecedents in other regions apparently cannot be sustained in the presence of this varied and mutually supporting evidence. Cf. Nelson A. Dunning, *The Farmers' Alliance History and Agricultural Digest* (Washington, D.C., 1891); Fred G. Blood, ed., *Hand Book and History of the National Farmers' Alliance and Industrial Union* (Washington, D.C., 1893); W. L. Garvin and S. O. Daws, *History of the National Farmers Alliance and Co-operative Union of America* (Jacksboro, Tex., 1887), hereafter cited as Garvin and Daws, *Alliance History;* Hicks, *Populist Revolt*. Both Dunning, who cited Texas and New York origins "in 1874 or 1875," and Blood, who cited Kansas origins, wrote after the Alliance had become a multi-sectional organization with internal needs for many "origins." The needs of both publicists were not conducive to accuracy, either in terms of geography or the calendar.
15. As Solon Buck has noted, the influence of the Grange on the Alliance is apparent in the declaration of purposes of the Texas Alliance in 1880, paraphrasing earlier

Grange rituals and literary ideas. Solon Buck, *The Agrarian Crusade* (New Haven, 1920), 112.

16. The founder whose memoirs have survived, A. P. Hungate, was not immune to the events that served to radicalize farmers at the end of the century. After Populism, he became a socialist. Hungate Memoir-Notebook, XII, especially a poem by Hungate entitled, "The Red Flag."

17. Garvin and Daws, *Alliance History,* 35–37. The earliest Alliance history, published two years before the Garvin and Daws history, is an 84-page pamphlet by Garvin, entitled, *History of the Grand State Farmers Alliance of Texas* (Jacksboro, Tex., 1885).

18. Garvin and Daws, *Alliance History,* 36–37; Morgan, *Wheel and Alliance,* 289.

19. As a measure of the relative importance of the two men in the early agrarian movement, see Morgan, *Wheel and Alliance,* 365–66, for a biographical sketch of Daws; pp. 367–68 for a sketch of Garvin.

20. Garvin and Daws, *Alliance History,* 38. The "joint stock" store followed the "Rochdale plan" of cooperation, originally developed in England. It involved a cash store, capitalized by member contributions. Stockholders got special consideration and shared in the profits, if any.

21. G. W. Hill (ed.), *Yearbook of the United States Department of Agriculture, 1899* (Washington, D.C., 1900), 764. The December quotations for each of these years was: 17.9 cents in 1871; 9.0 cents in 1883; 4.6 cents in 1894. Throughout the period of the agrarian revolt, the statistical practice of the U.S. Department of Agriculture in using December prices artificially inflated the percentage of the national income annually received by farmers. See John S. Spratt, *The Road to Spindletop* (Dallas, 1955), xii. The topic of farm costs and farm prices is complex and remains a subject of dispute. See Fred A. Shannon, *The Farmer's Last Frontier* (New York, 1945), 291–92, and graphs on 293–94; Samuel P. Hays, *The Response to Industrialism* (Chicago, 1957), 31; Harold Woodman, *King Cotton and His Retainers* (Lexington, Ky., 1968), 270–317.

22. Laird and Rinehart, "Deflation, Agriculture and Southern Development," 116–18; Woodward, *Origins,* 111–12. For an example of Daws's style, see the *Rural Citizen* (Jacksboro, Tex.), May 20, 1886. See also Garvin, *History,* 66–67.

23. Garvin and Daws, *Alliance History,* 38–40, 50. Of the mysteries of the credit system, a future national president of the Alliance said, "It was a new kind of slavery they did not understand," C. W. Macune, "Farmers Alliance," typed manuscript, 1920 (University of Texas), Austin.

24. B. B. Paddock (ed.), *Twentieth Century History and Biographical Record of North and West Texas* (Chicago, 1906), 631–33; Weatherford *Times,* March 27, 1886; *Rural Citizen* (Jacksboro, Tex.) March 25, 1886. Russell G. Pepperell, private interview in Houston, Texas, July 16, 1970. Mr. Pepperell is the step-grandson of William Lamb. Renne Allred, private interview in Bowie, Texas, July 12, 1968. Dunning, *Alliance and Digest,* 39. The 1884 meeting created a cooperative marketing committee for both cotton and produce. Lamb was one of eight named to it (Garvin, *History,* 72).

25. Ruth A. Allen, *Chapters in the History of Organized Labor in Texas* (Austin, 1941), 20–21; *Rural Citizen,* Aug. 6, Oct. 15, Nov. 19, 1885, and Feb. 4, 25, 1886.

26. In addition to the biography in Morgan, *Wheel and Alliance,* 363–66, a sketch of Daws may be found in (no author), *History of Texas together with Biographical History of Tarrant and Parker Counties* (Chicago, 1895), 452–53. See also Dunning, *Alliance and Digest,* 39.

27. Spratt, *Road to Spindletop,* 191–93; Garvin and Daws, *Alliance History,* 37–39.

28. *Rural Citizen*, Aug. 13, Sept. 17, 1885; Morgan, *Wheel and Alliance*, 290, 365; Spratt, *Road to Spindletop*, 192–93; Dunning, *Alliance and Digest*, 39; Garvin and Daws, *Alliance History*, 39.

29. *Rural Citizen*, Aug. 20, 1885, Sept. 17, 1885. After the first Knights of Labor assembly had been organized in Texas in 1882, growth had been rapid (Allen, *Chapters in Labor History*, 20–21).

30. *Whitesboro News*, quoted in *Rural Citizen*, Oct. 29, 1885.

31. H. J. Gooch to A. J. Rose, Oct. 29, 1885, A. J. Rose Papers, University of Texas.

32. *Rural Citizen*, Nov. 12, 1885.

33. Garvin and Daws, *Alliance History*, 36; Andrew Dunlap to A. J. Rose, Oct. 12, 1885 and J. T. W. Loe to Rose, Sept. 14, 1885.

34. The concept of a cash cooperative store, known as the Rochdale method, had been developed in Yorkshire, England, in the 1840s by workers who were active supporters of Owenism and Chartism (Philip Foner, *History of the Labor Movement in the United States*, II (New York, 1955), 418). The plan was imported to America by the National Grange after the Civil War. As was the case for Chartism itself, the Rochdale system attempted to achieve greater economic equity without disturbing the basic exploitive features imbedded in the monetary systems of western industrial-capitalism. It could not, therefore, provide an adequate basis for the organizing principle that began to germinate in the Farmers Alliance in the middle 1880s—large-scale cooperation. The latter challenged these exploitive features directly.

35. "The Purpose of the Grange," *National Grange Bulletin* (1874). The document reflected the "Declaration of Purposes of the National Grange," adopted at the order's 1874 national convention; *Patron of Husbandry* (Columbus, Miss.), quoted in Robert Calvert, "The Southern Grange" (Unpublished Ph.D. dissertation, University of Texas, 1968), 46; emphasis in the original. The newspaper claimed to represent members of the order in Alabama, Arkansas, Louisiana, and Texas, as well as Mississippi. The Grange was floundering in each state—and for the same reason. See also Solon Buck, *The Granger Movement* (Cambridge, Mass., 1913), 63–65, 70–75, 80–122.

36. Spratt, *Road to Spindletop*, 190–93; Dallas *News*, Oct. 10, 1885; *Rural Citizen*, Feb. 11, 1886.

37. Dallas *Mercury*, quoted in *Rural Citizen*, Nov. 11, 1885.

38. *Rural Citizen*, Nov. 19, 1885.

39. *Rural Citizen*, Feb. 4, 1886.

CHAPTER III

1 Allen, *Southwest Strike*, 24. The account that follows is largely taken from the work of this scholar. Of the national total of 906 Knights of Labor locals in 1886, 128 were in Texas. Nathan J. Ware, *The Labor Movement in the United States, 1860–1895* (New York, 1929), 159. The St. Louis *Post-Dispatch*, which closely followed the strike, asserted that since wages on the Gould lines permitted workers to support their families only at a level of bare survival, deferment of paychecks was "simply practicing upon the weakness of the poor." St. Louis *Post-Dispatch*, May 13, 1882. Among metropolitan U.S. dailies, the *Post-Dispatch's* opinion was an uncommon one.

2. Allen, *Southwest Strike*, 44, 50, 69; Fort Worth *Gazette*, March 1, 2, 1886; Dallas *News*, March 2, 1886.

3. Allen, *Southwest Strike,* 55, 63–64.
4. Allen, *Southwest Strike,* 71, 76–77, 81. Spratt, *Road to Spindletop,* 241–44, Richardson, *Texas,* 236, and Philip Foner, *History of the Labor Movement in the United States,* II, 83–86, present brief accounts of the strike. All three authors generally accept the view, presented at length in Allen, that Gould precipitated the strike in order to destroy the Knights of Labor. Though the violence of the strike and newspaper interpretations of the circumstances surrounding violent incidents did much to array public opinion against the Knights, a large number of local Alliances supported the strikers throughout. The important point, perhaps not understood by the farmers themselves, in 1886, was that the internal communications network of the Alliance lecturing system was creating a new democratic culture that insulated the participants from the hierarchical culture of the larger society. Farmer support of striking workers says much about the class orientation that developed among many Alliancemen during the order's first large-scale organizing campaign in 1886. The second campaign, that was to recruit some one million Southern farmers, began the following year.
5. Austin *Statesman,* March 25, 1886; Allen, *Southwest Strike,* 78–79.
6. Allen, *Southwest Strike,* 72–73, 76; Austin *Statesman,* March 18, 1886. The Palestine Texas terminal of the Texas Pacific Railroad contained 37 useless engines. Two had been derailed, 8 were "held" by strikers, and 27 had been "killed." The first newspaper reports concerning the recalcitrant strike-breakers said thirty men were involved. The figures used in the text (nine) is from Allen.
7. Galveston *News,* March 14, 17, 24, April 4, 1886; Fort Worth *Gazette,* March 20, April 6, 1886.
8. Dallas *News,* March 21, 1886.
9. Austin *Statesman,* March 18, 1886.
10. Waco *Examiner,* March 8, 15, 1886. One exception was the San Antonio *Light* which was outraged by the appointment of the gunman as marshal: "It is a criminal act to place a man of his known antecedents in the lead when the peace of society is threatened" (April 10, 1886).
11. *Rural Citizen,* Nov. 24, 1881; July 30, 1885; Roscoe Martin, "The Greenback Party in Texas," 161–78; Roscoe Martin, *People's Party in Texas* (Austin, 2nd, ed., 1971), 31–32; *Comanche Chief,* July 17, 1936.
12. *Rural Citizen,* Feb. 25, 1886.
13. Ruth A. Allen, *The Great Southwest Strike* (Austin, 1942), 24. *Rural Citizen,* Feb. 25, March 25, 1886; Weatherford *Times,* March 27, 1886; Fort Worth *Gazette,* March 14, Jan. 31, 1886.
14. *Rural Citizen,* Feb. 25, 1886.
15. *Rural Citizen,* March 4, 1886.
16. Richardson, *Texas,* 236; Fort Worth *Gazette,* March 1, 1886.
17. *Rural Citizen,* March 4, 1886.
18. *Rural Citizen,* March 11, 1886; Weatherford *Times,* March 27, 1886.
19. For examples of journalistic attitudes toward the strikers, Galveston *News,* March 14, 17, 24, 1886; Dallas *News,* March 12, 14, April 2, 4, 1886; Fort Worth *Gazette,* March 20, April 6, 1886.
20. *Rural Citizen,* March 18, 25, April 1, 22, May 6, 1886; Dallas *News,* March 6, 1886.
21. The longest account of the Lamb-Dunlap controversy, apparently the complete file as assembled by Dunlap, appeared in the Weatherford *Times,* March 27, 1886. The *Citizen* printed the story on March 25, 1886.
22. The Labor Movement in Texas, *Papers, 1845–1943,* Folders No. 5, 14, University of Texas; Allen, *Southwest Strike,* 86–87; Dallas *News,* May 24, 30, 31, 1886.

23. Waco *Examiner*, April 3, 1886; Dallas *Mercury*, April 16, 1891; Austin *Statesman*, April 8, 1886; Galveston *News*, April 6, 1886.
24. Fort Worth *Gazette*, April 7, 1886; Galveston *News*, April 8, 1886.
25. *Rural Citizen*, March 25, 1886; Dallas *Mercury*, March 26, 1886.
26. *Rural Citizen*, March 25, April 1, 1886.
27. *Rural Citizen*, April 22, 1886; Bonham *News*, April 23, 1886. A measure of agrarian poverty was the fact that many individual members of the Alliance read the state journal at Alliance meetings, the subscription being held by the suballiance and paid out of dues. When an Alliance canceled its lone subscription, as this Alliance did, it was severing the entire relationship that existed between many of its members and the official state journal.
28. *Rural Citizen*, Feb. 11, March 18, 1886. Something over 50 per cent of the Knights membership were not re-employed by the Gould line, (Allen, *Southwest Strike*, 90–91). See also Ware, *The Labor Movement in the United States, 1860–1895*, 66, 145–49. Ware lists four causes for the destruction of the union: the Haymarket bomb of May 4, 1886; the failure of the Southwest Strike; the opposition of the Catholic Church; and hostility of trade unions to the "One Big Union" philosophy attributed to the Knights (Ware, 316). Foner, on the other hand, details critical weaknesses in the Powderly regime (*History of the Labor Movement*, II, 40–91).

    After the carnage, the Knights national president, Terence V. Powderly, penned these afterthoughts. "Martin Irons (the Texas strike leader) and I knew where the weak places were in our organization . . . The truth was that we had no strong points of vantage in our favor outside of a fickle public opinion inclined to opposition to corporate power rather than friendship for the cause of striking workmen . . . Martin Irons was a student and an educated man. To educate a few to go out and teach the many was his hope, but the needs of the men were pressing; Irons could not extend his vision to them and they could not wait, they could not wait. Perhaps it had to be that way" (Terence Powderly, *The Path I Trod* (New York, 1940), 133, 139).

    The strategic, tactical, and administrative incompetencies of the Knights are detailed at length by both Allen and Foner. However, given the balance of forces then existing between the Gould lines and their employees, it was apparent the union had no chance to prevail in the contest—with or without the help of the Farmers Alliance.
29. *Rural Citizen*, May 5, 1886.
30. Fort Worth *Gazette*, May 13, 1886; Austin *Statesman*, May 28, 1886. Also see Galveston *News*, May 15, 22, 29, 30, 1886; Fort Worth *Gazette*, May 30, 31, 1886.
31. Dallas *News*, May 15, 30, 31, 1886; Dallas County Alliance, quoted in the Ft. Worth *Gazette* May 30, 31, 1886.
32. *Rural Citizen*, May 20, 1886.
33. Dunlap's endorsement was printed in the same issue of the *Citizen* (May 20, 1886) that carried Daws's views. It is possible that Dunlap did, indeed, understand the long-term implications of the policy outlined by Daws. But he also knew that his own county Alliance, among others, was rampant with political independency and that as president he needed to placate the insurgents or see his organization sundered. The significant point, of course, is that the emerging radicalism of the Texas Alliance was an insurgency from below, rather than one force-fed from the top by radical leaders. By May 1886, Andrew Dunlap represented the right wing of the organization; while he had allies, they were becoming a minority faction. As a result of the experiences they were to have in the cooperative movement, however, almost all of them would become Populists in the 1890s.

34. *Rural Citizen,* July 30, 1885; May 20, 1886.
35. The Alliance counted 555 sub-alliances in August 1885, over 800 by mid-October, 1300 at year's end and 1700 at the time of the Great Southwest Strike in the spring of 1886 (*Rural Citizen,* Aug. 13, Oct. 20, 1885; Dallas *News,* Jan. 3, July 6, 1886; Ralph Smith, "The Farmers Alliance, in Texas, 1875–1900," *Southwestern Historical Quarterly,* xxxviii (Jan. 1945) 354; Dallas *Mercury,* March 26, April 30, 1886).
36. Dallas *News,* May 19, 30, 31, 1886; *Rural Citizen,* June 3, 17, 1886.
37. Dunning, *Alliance and Digest,* 43; Winkler, *Platform of Political Parties in Texas,* 235.
38. Weatherford *Times,* June 5, 26, 1886.
39. Dallas *News,* July 16, 1886.
40. *Rural Citizen,* July 22, 1886.
41. Fort Worth *Gazette,* May 24, 1886. For the longevity of such endorsements in the "Solid South," see Chap. IX.
42. *Rural Citizen,* July 22, 1886. This was the last issue of the *Citizen* published under the imprimatur of the Texas Alliance. See below, n. 46.

   The Daws formula for political action was applied with creative variety: virtually every weekly newspaper and city daily in North and Northwest Texas carried stories of these "Citizens," Anti-Monopoly," "People's," "Non-Partisan," and "Farmer and Laborers" conventions. The Dallas *News,* July 5–22, reported a dozen such assemblages in its immediate circulation area. These reports were balanced by *News* accounts of meetings of various county Alliances that concluded the order was not "going into politics." It is possible the *News,* which certainly amassed sufficient evidence, read the signs but preferred not to say so. See also the Austin *Statesman,* July 21, 1886; McKinney *Gazette,* June 3, July 22, 1886; Bonham *News,* July 16, 1886; Austin *Weekly Statesman,* July 7, 1886; Dallas *News,* July 4, 5, 6, 7, 11, 16, 1886; Dallas *Mercury,* July 2, 9, 16, 23, 30, 1886; Hamilton *Herald,* quoted in Dallas *News,* Aug. 14, 1886; Waco *Examiner,* July 5, 1886; Fort Worth *Evening Mail,* July 2, 1886; Comanche *Town and Country,* March 8, 1886; Gatesville *Advance-Sun,* quoted in Comanche *Town and Country,* May 1886; Beeville *Bee,* June 17, 1886; Austin *Record,* June 5, 1886.
43. Dallas *News,* Aug. 4, 1886.
44. Winkler, *Platforms of Political Parties,* 235.
45. Garvin and Daws, *Alliance History,* 45.
46. Dallas *Mercury,* Aug. 13, 1886. In a story headlined "We are Rewarded," the *Mercury* proudly referred to itself as the Alliance's "herald" and "trumpet" and announced that its "language shall be such as all can understand." In the era of the People's Party, as the *Southern Mercury,* the paper became the leading editorial voice of Populism in the South.
47. The Cleburne Demands are contained in Winkler, *Platforms of Political Parties,* 235–237, and Dunning, *Alliance and Digest,* 41–43.
48. Viewed in context, these pleas for "alien land laws" seem no more "nativist" than the protective tariff.
49. It is an interesting historical sidelight that the stormy events of 1886 leading to the Cleburne Demands were not recorded in the official Alliance history and have subsequently been overlooked—with rather profound consequences for the reconstruction of the national Populist experience. Left unrecorded were the boycott proclamation of William Lamb, the steps toward political coalition with the Knights of Labor, the fashioning by S. O. Daws of the new Alliance approach to the political process, and the internal revolution in tactics and ideology signaled by the Cleburne Demands. Since the ultimate culmination of these events was the

export of the Alliance movement to the South and West and the development of the Omaha Platform of the People's Party, the omission has had the effect of suppressing the central causal link that brought American farmers to Populism. (See Appendix D)

From a broad political standpoint, the omission of the emergence of Alliance radicalism in Texas in 1886 has also obscured the internal dynamics that actually produced the People's Party—for the radicals who led the Texas Alliance to the Cleburne Demands also played a strategically decisive role in leading the National Alliance to the People's Party (Chapter VIII). The omission in turn, has caused historians to minimize the underlying values of Alliance radicalism—the greenback interpretation of the American monetary system—both before and after 1886. Thus, the Populist schism a decade later between "midroaders" and "fusionists" has been seen largely in terms of short-run tactics pertinent to the 1896 election (Chapters XIV, XV, and XVI). Considerably more was at issue than that—namely, the objectives of broad-based structural reform of the American monetary and party systems and a fundamental readjustment of the economic relationship between "concentrated capital" on the one hand and the "industrial millions" on the other (Chap. XVII). Arrayed alongside these goals, the issues of 1896—the candidacy of William Jennings Bryan and the cause of "free silver"— were minor elements in the ideological struggle, not the formula of the struggle. This distinction follows from the fact that "Populism" *was* Alliance radicalism, as both the third party's basic document, the Omaha Platform, and the entire history of the agrarian revolt from Cleburne in 1886 to St. Louis in 1896 amply demonstrates. In short, the fundamental historiographical error in interpreting American Populism begins here.

The primary historical source for the events of 1886 is *The History of the National Farmers Alliance and Co-operative Union of America* (1887), written by two Alliance organizers, W. L. Garvin and S. O. Daws, and published by the order's ex-editor, J. N. Rogers of the *Rural Citizen*. The latter fact is the pertinent one. The contract for the book had apparently been signed prior to Rogers's ouster at Cleburne. Thus, a full rendition of the controversial events of 1886 by Garvin and Daws would have involved asking Rogers to publish the full details of his own defeat at the hands of William Lamb. They either did not write it, or wrote it and had it deleted by Rogers prior to publication. The text itself seems to indicate the latter occurred for the transition from 1885 to 1886 is extremely abrupt and noticeably out of keeping with the detailed chronology existing to that point in the narrative. The principal result was that the name of William Lamb—the man who reminded Rogers at the height of the boycott controversy that "one suballiance killed a weekly newspaper some time ago and we are looking forward to men that will advocate our interest"—does not appear in the Alliance history. Nor, it should be reiterated, does any reference appear to the boycott, to farmer-labor cooperation, or to the resulting movement toward independent political action. In short, the emergence of Alliance radicalism was deleted from the history of the agrarian revolt. Since Alliance radicalism *was* "populism," the interpretive ramifications in historical literature that could have resulted—and, in fact, have resulted—from this omission are large. See Critical Essay on Authorities.

50. Dallas *News*, Aug. 14, 1886. The Galveston *News*, Dallas *News*, Austin *Statesman* and Fort Worth *Gazette* were among the dailies carrying lengthy reports on the Cleburne meeting. See also Woodward, *Origins*, 190. In Jacksboro, J. N. Rogers, beginning a new career of bitter opposition to the Alliance, agreed with the Dallas *News* criticism of August 14.

51. The statement of the conservative "non-partisans," attacking the Cleburne Demands as a greenback document, appeared in the Dallas *News,* Aug. 8, 1886, and the counter-statement by the radicals the following day. The latter was written by J. M. Perdue, a rising figure in the Alliance and a greenbacker of considerable prominence in Texas. Replying to an Alliance "non-partisan" who had said he would willingly support all of the Cleburne Demands "in a Democratic Party convention," Perdue offered the thought that such a stance could scarcely be described as "non-partisan." The substance of this intra-Alliance dispute was to resound across the South in 1891–92 as the Alliance moved toward the formation of the People's Party.

   Both William Lamb and J. M. Perdue were to play central roles in creating the specific tactics of greenbackism—namely, the political use of what would come to be known as "the sub-treasury plan." These tactics became the radical prerequisite to the creation of the People's Party as a multi-sectional institution of reform. See Chap. VIII and Appendix D, "The Ideological Origins of the Omaha Platform."

52. Biographical sketches of Macune appear in Morgan, *Wheel and Alliance,* 354–56; Annie L. Diggs, "The Farmers' Alliance and Some of Its Leaders," *Arena,* V (April 1892), 598–99; and Theodore Saloutos, "Charles W. Macune—Large-Scale Cooperative Advocate," in Joseph G. Knapp and Associates (eds.), *Great American Cooperators* (Washington, D.C., 1967), 10–12. See also C. W. Macune, "Farmers Alliance." A biography of Jones, second president of the National Alliance, appears in Morgan, 357–60; see also Martin, *People's Party in Texas,* 31–32.

53. Garvin and Daws, *Alliance History,* 40; Morgan, *Wheel and Alliance,* 292–93.

54. William Ivy Hair, *Bourbonism and Agrarian Protest, Louisiana Politics, 1877–1900* (Baton Rouge, 1969), 150; Morgan, *Wheel and Alliance,* 292, 358; Macune, "Farmers Alliance," 17.

55. This was the verdict of a Granger. Ralph Smith, "Grange Movement in Texas, 1873–1900," *Southwestern Historical Quarterly,* XLII, 303. The Alliance state secretary said in September that the order was adding "50 to 75" sub-alliances per week. Jacksboro *Gazette,* Sept. 16, 1886.

56. E. C. Matthews to A. J. Rose, Sept. 17,1886, Rose Papers; Smith, "Farmers Alliance," 356–57. The Alliance had 87 "organizing officers" by Aug. 1885 (Garvin, *History,* 82). Included among the defectors to the Alliance in 1886 was the state secretary of the Grange.

CHAPTER IV

1. One carefully composed view of the political reactions to the Cleburne Demands came from Charles Macune who, as events were to demonstrate, was both a radical greenbacker, ideologically, and a loyal Democrat, culturally. From Macune's cautiously articulated viewpoint, objections were raised to the Cleburne Demands "not because of opposition to their substance, but because many felt it was a political move" (Macune, "Farmers Alliance," 14). Whatever this meant, Macune was ultimately to be forced into a choice between his deeply held beliefs in the greenback monetary interpretation of American capitalism, on the one hand, and his loyalty to the party of white supremacy on the other. At Cleburne in 1886, he still had six years in which to try to resolve this dilemma.

2. Macune, "Farmers Alliance," 16–18. An edited version of the speech appears in Dunning, *Alliance and Digest,* 49–53.

3. The secretary of the state Alliance reported in September 1886 that three orga-

nizers had been dispatched out of the state and added, "there are calls for them from Kansas, Missouri, Louisiana, Alabama, and Georgia." Actually, individual Alliancemen, during the course of trips "back home" in 1886, had organized some suballiances as far away as Kentucky and Alabama as well as the nearby states of Arkansas, Louisiana, and Oklahoma Territory.

As for the implications of the Waco meeting itself, Macune offered the opinion that the "adoption of these measures was so interesting and inspiring that the difference about smaller matters rapidly melted away" (Macune, "Farmers Alliance," 17). A somewhat less partisan source, the staunchly Democratic Waco *Examiner,* largely confirmed the effect Macune says his proposals had on the delegates. The *Examiner* reported that "dissensions are all healed and the order is stronger than ever." The paper added that "the Cleburne . . . minority faction suffered Waterloo defeat and appears to be reconciled" (Waco *Examiner,* Jan. 22, 1887). See also Waco *Day,* Jan. 18, 19, 20, 1887; Garvin and Daws, *Alliance History,* 46; Dunning, *Alliance and Digest,* 46–55; Morgan, *Wheel and Alliance,* 293.

4. National Farmers Alliance and Cooperative Union of America, *Proceedings* (Shreveport, La., Oct. 12–14, 1887), 14; Garvin and Daws, *Alliance History,* 47–48; Morgan, *Wheel and Alliance,* 294. The figures listed in the text are a combination of these three sources plus additional organizers mentioned in monographic studies of the agrarian movement in the South. Though higher than those listed by the Alliance official histories, the figures are probably low. It seems reasonable to estimate that the Texas Alliance dispatched something approaching 100 organizers to the South and West in 1887–88. As for the expectations of the organizers, the *Mercury* confidently predicted 500,000 new members within six months. (Dallas *Mercury,* Feb. 24, 1887).

5. Garvin and Daws, *Alliance History,* 49–50; John D. Hicks, "Farmers Alliance in North Carolina," *North Carolina Historical Review,* II (April 1925), 170. As a state settled largely by immigrants from other Southern states, Texas was ideal as an organizing base; many Texas Alliance lecturers proceeded to organize their home states. J. B. Barry, for example, had originally emigrated to Texas from North Carolina.

6. For the entrance of Daws into Mississippi, see Morgan, *Wheel and Alliance,* 294; James S. Ferguson, "Agrarianism in Mississippi, 1871–1900" (Unpublished Ph.D. dissertation, University of North Carolina, 1952), 90–91.

7. *Southern Mercury,* April 29, 1887; William W. Rogers, *One-Gallused Rebellion: Agrarianism in Alabama* (Baton Rouge, 1970), 131–34; Theodore Saloutos, *Farmer Movements in the South* (Los Angeles and Berkeley, 1960), 185.

8. Alex M. Arnett, *The Populist Movement in Georgia* (New York, 1922), 77–79; James A. Sharp, "The Entrance of the Farmers Alliance into Tennessee Politics," *East Tennessee Historical Society's Publications* (Knoxville, 1937), 77–92; C. Vann Woodward, *Tom Watson, Agrarian Rebel* (2nd ed., Savannah, 1973), 115–16; A. R. Venable to Charles H. Pierson, June 17, 1891, quoted in Woodward, *Origins,* 197.

9. Putnam Darden to A. J. Rose, June 25, 1888, Rose Papers; *Proceedings,* Twenty-third Session of the National Grange (1889), 54, 66.

10. *Proceedings,* National Farmers Alliance and Co-operative Union of America (Shreveport, Oct. 12–14, 1887).

11. *Barber County Index,* Oct. 23, 1889, quoted in Raymond C. Miller, "The Populist Party in Kansas" (Unpublished Ph.D. dissertation, University of Chicago, 1928), 64.

12. *The Alliance Bulletin* (Harper, Kan.), Sept. 26, 1890, quoted in Donald H. Ecroyd,

"An Analysis and Evaluation of Populist Political Campaign Speech Making in Kansas, 1890–1894," (Unpublished Ph.D. dissertation, State University of Iowa, 1949), 377.

13. Raymond C. Miller, "The Background of Populism in Kansas," *Mississippi Valley Historical Review*, XI (March 1925), 481; Hallie Farmer, "Economic Background of Frontier Populism," *Mississippi Valley Historical Review*, X (March 1924), 421; O. Eugene Clanton, *Kansas Populism: Ideas and Men* (Lawrence, Kan., 1967), 19.

14. Clanton, *Kansas Populism*, 27–28.

15. Glenn H. Miller, "Financing the Boom in Kansas, 1879–1888, with Special Reference to Municipal Indebtedness and to Real Estate Mortgages," (Unpublished M.A. thesis, University of Kansas 1954), 202; Farmer, "Economic Background of Frontier Populism," 411–15; Edward C. Kirkland, *A History of American Economic Life* (New York, rev. ed., 1940), 507; Miller, "Populist Party in Kansas," 27.

16. The professoriate had begun to participate in the boomer psychology of the emerging corporate culture. See F. H. Snow, "Is the Rainfall of Kansas Increasing?", *Kansas City Review of Science and Industry*, VIII (Dec. 1884), 457–60; John Barnhart, "Rainfall and the Populist Party in Nebraska," *The American Political Science Review*, XIX (Aug. 1925), 236–38, 527–40; Samuel Aughey, *Sketches to the Physical Geography and Geology of Nebraska* (Omaha, 1880), 34–52; Samuel Aughey and C. D. Wilber, *Agriculture Beyond the 100th Meridian* (Lincoln, 1880).

17. Miller, "Financing the Boom in Kansas," 105–6, 204. Allan Bogue, *Money at Interest* (Ithaca, 1955), based on very limited sources, presents a sanguine view of the mortgage business in Kansas which has not been corroborated by Kansas historians, before or since its publication. See Clanton, *Kansas Populism*, 259.

18. Walter T. K. Nugent, *The Tolerant Populists* (Chicago, 1963), 53. In short, agrarian hardship in Kansas in 1888 did not translate into third party insurgency. As this chapter and the succeeding five chapters seek to demonstrate, significant political protest—as differentiated from assertions of temporary mass irritation—cannot emerge simply from "hard times." Populism was not a "spontaneous uprising" nor was it a "religious" movement; it cannot be explained either through recourse to class analysis or various modes of economic determinism. Coherent reform movements—and Populism was one—require an organizational framework that can provide a schoolroom for political interpretation, self-identity, and self-confidence. See Chaps. V, VII, VIII, XVII, Appendix A, and Critical Essay on Authorities.

19. H. L. Loucks, "Our Daily Bread Must Be Freed from the Greed of Private Monopoly" (Watertown, S.D., 1919), 9–10 (Minnesota Historical Society); Kenneth E. Hendrickson, Jr., "The Populist Movement in South Dakota" (Unpublished M.A. thesis, University of South Dakota, 1959), 224–25; Henderickson, "Some Aspects of the Populist Movement in South Dakota," *North Dakota History*, XXXIV, No. 1 (Winter 1967), 77–80; Glenn L. Brudvig, "The Farmers Alliance and Populist Movement in North Dakota" (Unpublished M.A. thesis, University of North Dakota, 1956, 39–46.

20. The *American Nonconformist and Kansas Industrial Liberator* (Winfield, Kan.), Oct. 7, 1886. The maiden issue of the *Nonconformist* also contained what it called "Gould's Prayer." It began: "Our father who art in England, Rothschild be they name, thy financial kingdom come to America, thy will be done in the United States as it is in England. Give us this day bonds in gold, but not in silver; give us plenty of laboring men's votes to keep monopoly in power and its friends in office . . ."

21. *American Nonconformist*, Oct. 21, 1886; March 3, July 14, Aug. 18, 25, Sept. 8, 15,

1887; *History of the Farmers and Laborers Union, Farmers Alliance, Agricultural Wheel, Farmers Mutual Benefit Association and the Grange* (St. Louis, 1890), 41; Richard Dean Prankrantz, "A Study of the Continuity in Leadership and Platforms Between the Kansas Alliance and the People's Party" (Unpublished M.A. thesis, Kansas State Teachers College, Pittsburgh, 1968), 4; Elizabeth Barr, "The Populist Uprising," William E. Connelly (ed.), *A Standard History of Kansas and Kansans,* II (Chicago, 1918), 1115–95; Homer Clevenger, "The Farmers Alliance in Missouri," *Missouri History Review,* XXXIX (Oct. 1944), 28.

22. The Vincents had made contact with the Lamb-Evans group in Texas at least as early as August 1887 (*American Nonconformist,* Aug. 18, 1887). See also Cincinnati *Enquirer,* May 15–18, 1888; Chicago *Tribune,* May 16–18, 1888; *American Nonconformist,* May 17, 1888; Fort Worth *Gazette,* Oct. 6, 29, 1888.

The Videttes provide one of the more intriguing sidelights of the formative years of the agrarian revolt. The organization existed most visibly in Kansas, Arkansas, and Texas and seems to have originated in Texas. The order had a politically radical secret ritual (pledging members "never" to support either major party) which had an unfortunate tendency toward being "exposed" in opposition newspapers a week or so before elections. Somewhat battered, not to say slandered, the Videttes seem to have been abandoned, at least as a secret order, before the People's Party was formed. However, to replace the Alliance organizational base in the Populist years, the third party undertook to form local Populist clubs, called "Industrial Legions," that were to a large extent led by ex-Videttes. For a public defense of the Videttes by General B. J. Chambers, editor of the Cleburne (Texas) *Tribune,* see *American Nonconformist,* Dec. 20, 1888. Chambers the 1880 vice-presidential candidate of the Greenback Party and an old and respected Texas reformer, was probably one of the founders of the Videttes. He had proposed a similar organization, "The Greenback Guard" years earlier (clipping in the Shilling Papers, Wisconsin State History Society). One of the announced purposes of the Videttes was to protect the sanctity of the ballot box—no small task as the experience of the People's Party in the South was to confirm. That the Videttes were influential in the shaping of the Union Labor Party and platform there can be no doubt. See Chaps. VI and VII. For the Agricultural Wheel, see Chap. V.

23. Chicago *Tribune,* May 18, 1888; Cincinnati *Enquirer,* May 17–18, 1888. In Texas, the Democratic press had come to regard Evans, along with Lamb, as a leading symbol of much that was threatening about the Farmers Alliance. See, especially, Fort Worth *Gazette,* Oct. 29, 1888. William Lamb was reported to be "Chief" of the Videttes. For an account of the failure to achieve an agrarian-labor third party coalition at Cincinnati in 1888, as viewed from the perspective of eastern labor socialists, see Nathan Fine, *Labor and Farmer Parties in the United States, 1828–1928* (New York, 1928), 51.

24. *Kansas Farmer,* July 19, 26, Aug. 2, 1888. Barr records that Henry, Leopold, and Cuthbert Vincent made the trip (Barr, "The Populist Uprising," 1140). W. F. Rightmire credits himself, John Rogers, and Cuthbert Vincent (W. F. Rightmire, "The Alliance Movement in Kansas—Origins of the People's Party," *Transactions of the Kansas State Historical Society, 1905–1906,* IX (1960), 1–8. The Rightmire account, written years after the event, contains numerous factual errors, all of a self-serving character that maximize his own role. His version does not indicate he was aware of the Vincent brothers' familiarity with the Texas Alliance prior to the pilgrimage, the fact that several Texans and, later, a Kansan named W. P.

Brush had organized a number of suballiances months earlier or that Brush, as lecturer for the Kansas Alliance, had participated in the National Alliance convention in Meridian. The Vincents were much better informed. For example, the *Nonconformist* of Aug. 23, 1888, months before the Texas pilgrimage, carried a news account of a Cowley County Alliance meeting of delegates from six suballiances—a meeting called by Brush and presided over by Ben Clover. In any event, it is quite possible that journeys to Texas were made by several Kansas groups, it being little more than a half day's train ride from southern Kansas to Alliance headquarters in Dallas in northern Texas. The subject is discussed in Pankrantz, "Continuity in Leadership and Platforms," 3–4. See also W. W. Graves, *History of Neosho County.* (St. Paul, Kansas, 1951), 580. Concerning Peffer's belated participation in the Alliance movement, as late as February, 1889 when he addressed a small gathering of the Northwestern Alliance (see Chap. VI), Peffer revealed his uncertain grasp of the doctrines of cooperation. While he listed "seven chief objects of the order," none related either to cooperative marketing or cooperative purchasing by farmers (*Capital-Commonwealth* (Topeka) Feb. 7, 1889).

25. *American Nonconformist*, Jan. 10, 1889. The new Alliance state president, Ben Clover, was from Cowley County, appropriately enough, as was Louis B. King, soon to become treasurer of the state cooperative in Kansas. Ft. Scott Weekly *Tribune*, April 4, May 23, 1889; Pankrantz, "Continuity in Leadership and Platforms, 30. Fred Shannon, *The Farmers Last Frontier* (New York, 1961), 313, places farm foreclosures in Kansas at 11,000 for the period 1889–93.

26. Ft. Scott *Weekly Tribune*, Aug. 22, 1889; Pankrantz, Continuity in Leadership and Platforms, 3–4; *Kansas Farmer*. Dec. 11, 1889.

27. W. P. Harrington, "Populist Party in Kansas," *Collections of the Kansas State Historical Society*, Vol. XVI (1924), 408.

28. *Election Returns, 1888–1889,* Cowley County, Winfield, Kansas.

29. *The Daily Visitor* (Winfield), Jan. 27, 30, 1889.

30. The rapid four-month development of the cooperative movement in Cowley County is revealed by the following news stories in the *Nonconformist:*

Jan. 10, 1889—the Ben Clover statement: "extensive movements are on foot."

Jan. 17, 1889—a report that the Union Labor Party is without funds.

Jan. 24, 1889—the announcement of the formation of a national newspaper for the Farmers Alliance, *The National Economist.*

Jan. 31, 1889—the announcement of plans for a cooperative store in Winfield; Alliancemen of Silverdale are reported to be shipping cattle on a cooperative basis.

Feb. 7, 1889—a story carrying details of cooperative planning: "Cooperation, when carefully managed is a hard competitor to buck; but the men who compose this company are not looking after the downfall of others, but simply going to patronize themselves awhile."

March 14, 1889—the Cowley County Alliance numbers 2,000; suballiance representatives meet to form a County Alliance Exchange; a new column begins, entitled "Alliance and Labor."

March 21, 1889—of eighteen items in "Alliance and Labor" column, eighteen concern Alliance activities.

March 28, 1889—the column is renamed "County Alliance Notes." All farmers are urged to subscribe to *The National Economist*, published by the National Farmers Alliance in Washington, D.C.

April 11, 1889—the Cowley County Alliance is reported as numbering 2500 members. Front page story appears on cooperation.

May 2, 1889—*Nonconformist* prints a letter from a reader suggesting that the county buying cooperative be augmented by a selling cooperative.

May 9, 1889—"Farmers Alliance Notes" begins appearing on the front page.

CHAPTER V

1. G. W. Hall (ed.), *Yearbook of the United States Department of Agriculture, 1900* (Washington, D.C., 1901), 699, 709.
2. Shannon, *The Farmers Last Frontier*, 95–115; 291–94.
3. Miller, "Background of Populism in Kansas," 469–98; Hicks, *Populist Revolt*, 60–64.
4. Cochran and Miller, *Age of Enterprise*, 193–224, 356; Unger, *Greenback Era*, 115.
5. Everett Dick, *The Sod-House Frontier* (Lincoln, Neb., 1954), 125, 167–68, 302–14.
6. Farmer, "Economic Background of Frontier Populism," 406–27; Farmer, "The Railroads and Frontier Populism," *Mississippi Valley Historical Review*, XIII (1926), 387–97; Hicks, *Populist Revolt*, 67.
7. Barr, "Populist Uprising," 1141; Evan Jones, Presidential address to the Farmers and Laborers Union of America, *Proceedings* (1889), 5–11.
8. Hammond, *Cotton Industry*, 135–36; Woodward, *Origins*, 177–86.
9. Arnett, *Populist Movement in Georgia*, 63–64; Hammond, *Cotton Industry*, 164–65.
10. M. P. Farmer, "Furnishing Merchants and Sharecroppers," 143, 150; Otken, Ills of the South, 24–25, 57, 165–86; *Tenth Census* (1880), II, 520; Shannon, *Farmers' Last Frontier*, 92, 95–115; John McMatthews, "Studies in Race Relations in Georgia, 1890–1930" (Unpublished Ph.D. dissertation, Duke University, 1970), 189; George K. Holmes, "Peons of the South," American Academy of Political and Social Sciences, *Annals*, IV, no. 2 (Sept. 1893), 265–74; 'Furnishing and Supply System," 26, 29, 31, 37.
11. Ben Robertson, *Red Hills and Cotton* (New York, 1942), 84; M. P. Farmer, "Furnishing Merchants and Sharecroppers," 146–50; Arthur Raper and Ira DeA. Reid, *Sharecroppers All* (Chapel Hill, 1941), 19–22; Woodman, *King Cotton and His Retainers*, 295, 318; Leo Alilunas, "Statutory Means of Impeding Emigration of the Negro," *Journal of Negro History,* XXII (1937), 148–62; Oscar Zeichner, "The Legal Status of the Agricultural Laborer in the South," *Political Science Quarterly*, LV (1940), 412–28; Rupert Vance, *Human Factors in Cotton Culture* (Chapel Hill, 1929).
12. James Agee and Walker Evans, *Let Us All Praise Famous Men* (Boston, 1960), 268.
13. *Tenth Census*, II, pt. II, 62–63, 156.
14. The question of whether most of the farmers of the Alliance were landowners or tenants is not central. The operative fact concerned the accumulation of land in the hands of furnishing merchants in the South and railroads and mortgage syndicates in the West. Some tenants had lost their land, others had never owned any; hundreds of thousands of landowners were en route to becoming tenants. Under the circumstances, a case can be made that a landowner threatened with a furnishing debt rising inexorably to meet the value of his land—making foreclosure imminent—might be more "radical" than a tenant. Under these circumstances, "class" categories, as interpretive devices, need to be handled with some precision. The matter is discussed further in the Critical Essay on Authorities, 601, 605, 612 and in n. 39, pp. 651–53.

15. *Proceedings,* Twenty-third Session of the National Grange (1889), 54, 66.

16. From 1889 to 1892, the pages of Macune's *National Economist* repeatedly stressed the fundamental difference between the cooperative effort of the Alliance and the inherited tradition of joint-stock stores derived from the English Rochdale plan and embodied in the approach of the Grange. An outline of Macune's general approach, as offered by him to the Texas Alliance may be found in Morgan, *Wheel and Alliance,* 312–13. Field reports from Texas lecturers on their experiences in the Southern organizing campaign are contained in the *Southern Mercury,* April 22, 29, May 6, 1887.

17. *Southern Mercury,* June 7, 1888; T. Ivey to L. L. Polk, July 1, 1887, Polk Papers (University of North Carolina); Noblin, *Polk,* 149, 157, 204–10; L. L. Polk to Elias Carr, July 2, 1887, Polk Papers.

18. James O. Knauss, "The Farmers Alliance in Florida," *South Atlantic Quarterly,* XXV (July 1926), 301–5; Lloyd W. Cary, "The Florida Farmers Alliance" (Unpublished M.A. thesis, Florida State University, 1963), 30–35.

19. William W. Rogers, "The Agricultural Wheel in Alabama," *Alabama Review,* XX (Jan. 1967), 5; Rogers, *One-Gallused Rebellion,* 152–53.

20. Arnett, *Populist Movement in Georgia,* 79–80; Robert P. Brooks, *The Agrarian Revolution in Georgia* (Madison, 1914), 102, 127.

21. William Dubose Sheldon, *Populism in the Old Dominion* (Princeton, 1935), 24–25, 33; Woodward, *Origins,* 245.

22. Ferguson, "Agrarianism in Mississippi," 90–99; James A. Sharp, "The Entrance of the Farmers Alliance into Tennessee Politics," East Tennessee Historical Society's *Publications* (Knoxville, 1937), 77–92; Francis B. Simpkins, *Pitchfork Ben Tillman, South Carolinian* (Baton Rouge, 1944).

23. Newton *Messenger,* March 2, 1889, quoted in William Warren Rogers, "Farmers Alliance in Alabama," *Alabama Review,* XV (Jan. 1962), 9; Ferguson, "Agrarianism in Mississippi," 144–45. Ferguson refers to the "nationwide prestige" of the Texas Exchange and adds that Mississippians "planned to follow the Texas arrangement very closely." The Arkansas Wheel pursued the same course. Morgan, *Wheel and Alliance,* 102–10.

24. Macune, "Farmers Alliance," 18; Ralph Smith, "Macuneism: The Farmers of Texas in Business," *Journal of Southern History,* XIII (May 1947), 229; Fred A. Shannon, "C. W. Macune and the Farmers Alliance," *Current History* (June 1955), 333; Clarence Ousley, "A Lesson in Cooperation" *The Popular Science Monthly,* XXXVI (April 1890), 822.

25. Dunning, *Alliance and Digest,* 364–67; Smith, "Macuneism," 228; Macune, "Farmers Alliance," 17.

26. Macune, "Farmers Alliance," 20–22; Smith, "Macuneism," 230–31.

27. For a review of the benefits achieved for farmers through the Texas Exchange, as recounted by Macune, see Morgan, *Wheel and Alliance,* 306–25.

28. Ousley, "A Lesson in Cooperation," 824. The joint-note plan was attributed by the minutes to "one of the directors" though Ousley, who was present in Texas at the time, thought "it probably owes its origin to the manager (Macune) who was the controlling spirit of the exchange enterprise." If the joint note plan was not Macune's, it probably came from Harry Tracy, then rising to prominence in the Texas Alliance and destined to play a strategic role in the development of Southern Populism. (For Tracy's tactical and theoretical role in Alliance-Populism, see Chap. VIII and Appendix B.) For an indication of Tracy's knowledge of the exchange operation, and his deep emotional commitment to making it a success, see Morgan, *Wheel and Alliance,* 338–43.

29. Smith, "Macuneism," 232; Macune, "Farmers Alliance," 23–24.
30. Subscriptions to the *Mercury* rose steadily in conjunction with the campaign to explain the exchange operation to the Alliance membership. By June 1888 the *Southern Mercury* had a circulation of over 35,000 in twenty-three states, making it one of the larger agricultural weeklies in the nation at that time (*Southern Mercury,* June 7, 1888.)
31. Fort Worth *Gazette,* June 6, 1888; Ousley, "A Lesson in Cooperation," 824.
32. Fort Worth *Gazette,* June 6, 1888; Smith, "Macuneism," 234; Ousley, "A Lesson in Cooperation," 825.

   Some have suggested that the American banking system was simply not equal to the demands placed upon it by farmers engaged in large-scale cooperation. Aside from the fact that such an argument tends to justify the greenback critique of the American monetary system and further justifies the need for government commodity credit, the argument in technical terms is seriously flawed. Macune went to the provincial bankers at the very time in the year when their capital assets, however large or small they may have been, were most liquid. "Through the late spring and summer, in particular, when only the corn was stirring in the great farm areas, unused assets piled up on the books of the country banks. These were often transferred to New York where they found an interest-paying outlet. Unfortunately, they did not serve the general New York business community well since they had to be kept liquid for instant return if needed by the Western banks. This restricted their use to call loans, which could be employed only by brokers and stock market speculators. During the summer then with call loan funds available, the stock market and the speculative exchanges boomed. In the fall, when rural banks withdrew their funds to help finance crop movements, an annual stringency occurred in New York which often approached panic proportions" (Unger, *Greenback Era,* 115). It seems the bankers must have had some other reason for rebuffing the Texas farmers in the late spring of 1888.
33. *Southern Mercury,* May 31, 1888; Ousley, "A Lesson in Cooperation," 825.
34. Ibid.
35. *Gillespie County Alliance Minutes, 1886–1896* (Univ. of Texas), 71.
36. Austin *Weekly Statesman,* June 14, 1888; Dallas *News,* June 10, 1888.
37. Fort Worth *Gazette,* June 10, 1888. Rusk *Standard Enterprise,* June 13, 1888; Austin *Weekly Statesman,* June 14, 1888; Dallas *News,* June 10–12, 1888; Clarksville *Standard,* June 21, 1888; Galveston *News,* June 10–12, 1888; *Southern Mercury,* June 14, 1888. The *Mercury* received telegrams from twenty-five county presidents, reporting contributions totaling $13,000. In many locales, Alliancemen blamed much of the exchange's troubles on rumors spread by the metropolitan press and refused to admit reporters to the June 9 meeting or to reveal the results afterward. This is evident from the reports contained in general summaries prepared both by the Dallas *News* and the Austin *Weekly Statesman.*
38. Dallas *News,* June 10, 1888; *Southern Mercury,* April 19, 1888.
39. *Southern Mercury,* Sept. 4, 11, 1888; Morgan, *Wheel and Alliance,* 338; As a measure of the relative economic resources available to Southwestern merchants, as compared to farmers, businessmen in the city of Austin raised $100,000 in May 1888, as a subsidy to induce the San Antonio and Aransas Pass Railroad to extend its line eighty miles from San Antonio to Austin. The businessmen possessing this capital served a trade area population of less than 20,000 (Austin *Weekly Statesman,* May 10, 1888). After farmers had been energized by the Alliance cooperative, such news stories tended to make them think in a new way about how "the

system" operated. Inevitably, cooperation, especially large-scale cooperation that promised significant results, had a radicalizing impact on its participants. Large-scale cooperation was the source of Populism.

40. Dallas *News*, Aug. 23, 1888; *Southern Mercury*, Aug. 28, 1888.

41. An excellent summary of the treasury-note plan is contained in Fred A. Shannon, "C. W. Macune and the Farmers Alliance," 330–35. See also Smith, "Macuneism," 240–41.

42. Morgan, *Wheel and Alliance*, 312–13.

43. Dallas *News*, Aug. 24, 25, 1888.

44. *Southern Mercury*, Sept. 4, 1888.

45. Dunning, *Alliance and Digest*, 84. Italics added. See Appendix A.

46. Harry Tracy to L. L. Polk, Dec. 14, 1888, quoted in Morgan, *Wheel and Alliance*, 341. Polk, recoiling from the burdens imposed by a central exchange, basically adhered to Rockdale methods in North Carolina; by 1889 he had begun receiving cricism from North Carolina Alliancemen because of the inadequacy of the cooperative effort in the state. See n. 62 below and Chap. XI.

47. Winkler, *Platforms of Political Parties in Texas*, 256–57.

48. *Southern Mercury*, April 19, May 17, 31, June 7, July 24, Aug. 7, 1888; Fort Worth *Gazette*, July 3–6, 1888; Winkler, *Platforms*, 257, 260–63, 268–71. The "non-partisans" who met in Fort Worth were the Videttes. See p. 630, n. 22–3, for the history of this self-selected radical elite group. Jones publicly supported the third party ticket in 1888. The radicals who met at Waco put up $20,000 in farm land for the Exchange. Their effort to borrow $10,000 on this security was rebuffed by Texas bankers, however (Fort Worth *Gazette*, June 5, 1888).

Some Texas radicals were bitter at Macune for his persistent and damaging opposition to third party planning. In their wrath, two of them, A. L. Kessler, director of the order's Cooperative Manufacturing Alliance, and J. R. Bennett, editor of the *Southern Mercury*, turned against Macune during the controversy over the management of the Texas Exchange. As chairman of a specially appointed investigative "committee of five" within the Exchange, Kessler wrote, and the *Mercury* published, a report sharply critical of Macune's stewardship (*Southern Mercury*, Oct. 2, 1888). Similar editorial judgments by Bennett in the *Mercury* further impaired Alliance efforts to maintain farmer confidence in the centralized cooperative program.

It is difficult to render a judgment on this controversy, but its effect was to sap the strength both of the Union Labor Party and of the state cooperative. A second effect was the resignation of Bennett as *Mercury* editor and Macune as business manager (*Southern Mercury*, Oct. 9, 23, 1888).

The direct relationship of the cooperative struggle, the ascendancy of radical greenbackism, and the creation of the People's Party is further developed in Chap. VIII and Appendices A and D.

49. *Southern Mercury*, Aug. 28, 1888.

50. *Kansas Commoner*, March 29, 1889; *American Nonconformist*, March 14, 1889. See also the *Kansas Farmers Alliance and Industrial Union*, April 1893, People's Party Clippings (Kansas State Historical Society).

51. H. L. Loucks, *Our Daily Bread* (Watertown, S.D., 1919), 23–24; Kenneth E. Hendrickson, Jr., "The Populist Movement in South Dakota," 226–27; Glenn L. Brudvig, "The Farmers Alliance and Populist Movement in North Dakota," 44–46, 63–64, 77–80; Taylor, *Farmers' Movement*, 234–43; Dunning, *Alliance and Digest*, 238–39.

52. Ferguson, "Agrarianism in Mississippi," 44–45; Woodward, *Origins,* 197; Saloutos, *Farmer Movements in the South,* 99.

53. Rogers, *One-Gallused Rebellion,* 158–64; Spratt, *Road to Spindletop,* 203; Woodward, *Origins,* 198; *Southern Cultivator and Dixie Farmer* (Atlanta), July 1890, 457; Macune, "Farmers Alliance," 26–29; Cary, "Florida Farmers Alliance," 43; Woodward, *Watson,* 120–21.

54. *Kansas Commoner,* April 5, 1889; Edwin G. Nourse and Joseph G. Knapp, *The Co-operative Marketing of Livestock* (Washington, D.C., 1931), 103–5; Harrington, *Populist Party in Kansas,* 407; Barnhart, "Alliance in Nebraska," 144.

55. *Southern Mercury,* Aug. 28, Dec. 20, 27, 1888. Saloutos, *Farmer Movement in the South,* 84–94; Smith, "Macuneism," 242–43.

56. The details of Macune's departure from the Exchange are contained in n. 48, p. 635. Woodward, *Origins,* 194; *Proceedings,* National Farmers Alliance and Cooperative Union (Shreveport, La.), Oct. 12–14, 1887, 9. The *National Economist* replaced the *Southern Mercury* as the national Alliance journal in the summer of 1889. *Southern Mercury,* July 11, 1889.

57. *Proceedings,* National Farmers Alliance and Cooperative Union (Meridian, Miss., Dec. 5–6, 1888), 5–6.

58. Morgan, *Wheel and Alliance,* 125.

59. Clifton Paisley, "Political Wheelers and the Arkansas Election of 1888, *Arkansas Historical Quarterly,* XXV (Spring 1966), No. 1, 3–21; Rogers, "Agricultural Wheel in Alabama," 5. The Agricultural Wheel awaits its historian. While the order's militance landed it in more controversy, per capita, than even the Alliance managed, the Wheel must be regarded as the second most important institution of the agrarian revolt. Considered in the context of its time, both the national and subordinate state leaders of the Wheel were impressively egalitarian on the race issue. After a promising start in 1887, the Wheel in Alabama suffered internal dissension over the racial liberalism and Union Labor proclivities of its leaders, fell upon hard times and, by 1888, had been overwhelmed by the Alliance. Formal merger between the Alliance and the Wheel was consummated in Sept. 1889 (*National Economist,* Sept. 28, 1889). See also Francis C. Elkins, "The Agricultural Wheel in Arkansas" (Unpublished Ph.D. dissertation, University of Syracuse, 1953), 126–56.

60. Morgan, *Wheel and Alliance,* 83–117. As of the Meridan meeting, approximations of Wheel membership by state (with the somewhat enthusiastic claims of its spokesmen listed in parentheses) are: Arkansas 60,000 (75,000); Tennessee 30,000 (42,000); Missouri 40,000 (67,000); Alabama 10,000 (75,000); Kentucky 7000; Texas 2000; Mississippi 500; Indian Territory, 500. Though the various state organizations had a total membership—by their own generous estimates—of 270,000 in 1888, W. Scott Morgan, the Wheel historian, placed membership early in 1889 at 500,000. Morgan, *Wheel and Alliance,* 69.

61. For the political implications of the sub-treasury plan, and the tactical delicacy of the setting in which it was presented, see Chap. VI.

62. *Proceedings,* Farmers and Laborers Union of America (St. Louis, Dec., 3–7, 1889), 5–11. While Evans Jones described the Alliance cooperative as "the foundation that underlies the whole superstructure," L. L. Polk of North Carolina said that "the Subordinate Alliances are the foundation stone of the whole superstructure" (*Progressive Farmer* (Raleigh) July 17, 1888). Since farmers joined the suballiance to participate in the cooperative, the two statements are not as incompatible as they might otherwise seem. Actually, the phraseology selected by the two Alliance

presidents was a product of their relative radicalism, in a general sense, as well as in the context of cooperation. Polk did not undertake a central state exchange in North Carolina, despite importunings by both Macune and Harry Tracy that he do so. The organizational cohesion of the North Carolina Alliance was weakened as a result, as the events of 1892 were to reveal. Yet—lest these ideological, economic, and political connections seem too pat—Polk arrived at political insurgency before Macune, though not, predictably, before the old greenbacker, Jones.

63. Proceedings, *Farmers and Laborers Union of America*, 5–11.
64. *Proceedings*, Farmers and Laborers Union of America, 15–32; Joseph G. Knapp, *The Rise of American Cooperative Enterprise*, 1620–1920 (Danville, Ill., 1969), 438. The explanation and defense of the sub-treeasury plan is contained in the "Report of the Committee on the Monetary System" submitted to the Alliance convention of 1889 and printed as *The Sub-Treasury System as Proposed by the Farmers Alliance*, Library of National Economist Extras (Washington, D.C., 1891), 9–14. The report is conveniently available in George Tindall, *A Populist Reader* (New York, 1966), 80–87. A discussion of the ideological origins and legacy of the sub-treasury system is contained in Appendix A and its economic implications, in terms of real income redistribution, are analyzed in Appendix B.

CHAPTER VI

1. Roy V. Scott, *The Agrarian Movement in Illinois* (Urbana, 1962), 45–52, and "The Rise of the Farmers Mutual Benefit Association, 1883–1891," *Agricultural History* (Jan. 1958), 44–55; Taylor, *The Farmers' Movement*, 218–19; 255.
2. Loucks, "Our Daily Bread," 23–24; Hendrickson, "Populist Movement in South Dakota," 44–46; *National Economist*, March 14, 1889, and many subsequent issues.
3. N. B. Asby, *The Riddle of the Sphinx* (Des Moines, 1890), 363.
4. Martin Ridge, *Ignatius Donnelly: The Portrait of a Politician* (Chicago, 1962), 245–60.
5. Brudvig, "Farmers Alliance and Populist Movement in North Dakota," 44, 94–99; Ridge, *Donnelly*, 267–71.
6. Ignatius Donnelly to Theodore M. Nelson, Nov. 28, 1889; Donnelly to Robert Eckford, Dec. 1, 1889; Donnelly to G. A. Thayer, April 23, 1890, Donnelly Papers. Ridge, *Donnelly*, 270–71.
7. *The New York Times* placed Alliance membership in Kansas at 70,000 in 1200 suballiances at the time of the St. Louis meeting (*Times*, Dec. 14, 1889). For the organizing campaign itself, see S. M. Scott, *The Champion Organizer of the Northwest* (McPherson, Kans., 1890), 7–66, 129–40, 160. Though Allianceman Scott's broader claims as an organizer need to be placed in a somewhat less enthusiastic perspective, his account of the central role of the cooperative movement in the organizing process corroborates previous testimony of Alliance lecturers in the South in 1887–89. See also *Daily Monitor* (Fort Scott, Kan.), March 14, 1890; *American Nonconformist*, April 5, 1888, Jan. 31, Feb. 7, March 14, 21, 28, April 11, May 16, 1889; Topeka *Daily Capital*, March 28, 1890; *Kansas Commoner*, Jan. 25, March 1, 29, April 5, 1889; *The Advocate* (Meriden), Aug. 17, Oct. 12, 1889; March 6, 1890; *Capital-Commonwealth* (Topeka), Feb. 7, 1889; William Peffer, *The Way Out* (Topeka, 1890); Pankrantz, "Continuity of Leadership and Platforms Between the Kansas Alliance and the People's Party," 4; Annie Laporte Diggs, typescript, Kansas State Historical Society, 1; Martha A. Warner, "Kansas Populism: A Socio-

logical Analysis (Unpublished M.A. thesis, Kansas State Teachers College, Pittsburg, 1956), 97; Paul Dean Harper, "The Speechmaking of Jerry Simpson" (Unpublished M.A. thesis, Kansas State College of Pittsburg, 1967), 33; Clanton,
Kansas Populism, 54.

8. The source of this reputation is Hicks, *Populist Revolt,* 96–103. Hicks writes that
the Northwestern Alliance in 1887 "was growing with considerable rapidity. . . .
Only seven states of perhaps twice that number entitled to representation had
delegates at the Minneapolis meeting but the interest apparently was great and
hope for future was high. . . . Within the next few years, the Farmers Alliance
increased enormously in membership and became a power to be reckoned with in
the whole Northwest" (102–3). Also "Among the various rural organizations to
gain prominence in the United States after the Civil War, none had a greater
record of achievement than the national farmers alliance (Northern Alliance)
which appeared in the northwest as early as 1880 and continued active until well
toward the close of the century" (Hicks, "The Origin and Early History of the
Farmers Alliance in Minnesota," *Mississippi Valley Historical Review,* IX (Dec. 1922),
203–6). Cf. App. C "The Northwestern Farmers Alliance: Opponent of Populism."

For the status of the Northwestern affiliate in Kansas in 1888, see Lyons *Republican* (Lyons, Kan.), Aug. 9, 1888. This Republican journal expressed pleasure at
the conservatism of the delegates, though it was disappointed by the small attendance. A Kansas historian adds: "The careful provision made by this body for the
organization of local and county Alliances would imply that there were no such
subordinate bodies then in existence, and certainly the delegates at Lyons were
not representative" (Miller, "Populist Party in Kansas," 82); see also *Kansas Commoner,* Aug. 16, 1889. Actually, a few subordinate lodges existed at the time,
though they had no means of communication with one another and were in a
state of chronic disorganization because the national body had no program. In
the months following the organization of a state unit, the Kansas affiliate of the
Northwestern Alliance was unable to fashion any program for farmers and gave
up the struggle in 1889, some of its few members abandoning the agrarian movement and others joining the National Farmers Alliance. The latter, at that point
near year's end, numbered in the vicinity of 60,000 to 75,000 in Kansas (*Kansas
Farmer,* Dec. 11, 1889; Pankrantz, "Continuity of Leadership and Platforms," 3–4;
New York Times, Dec. 14, 1889).

For the status of the Nebraska Alliance in 1888, see "Ledger, Accounts with
Local Alliances," *Nebraska Farmers Alliance Papers* (Nebraska State Historical Society), 6–132. A Nebraska scholar places total suballiances chartered in Nebraska in
the two-year period, 1887–88, at ninety (John D. Barnhart, "A History of the
Farmers Alliance and of the People's Party in Nebraska" (Unpublished Ph.D. dissertation, Harvard, 1929), 174; hereinafter cited as "Alliance in Nebraska"). Receipts for 1888 indicate almost no growth in Nebraska, 1887; $382.10 in 1887;
and $395.00 in 1888 ("Ledger, Accounts with Local Alliances," *Nebraska Farmers
Alliance Papers,* 23, 31). Active statewide membership may be placed at approximately 2000 for both years. The only period of real growth in the order came in
the first six months of 1890. For 1888–89 in Kansas and Nebraska, see Barnhart,
173–75, 428, passim.

9. It seems that the relevance to Populism of the Northwestern Farmers Alliance has
been exaggerated. A detailed history of the group has no place in an account of
the agrarian revolt. Those interested in the historiographical details are referred
to Appendix C: "The Northwestern Farmers Alliance: Opponent of Populism."

For other views, see, in addition to Hicks, *Populist Revolt*, 96–103, Milton George (ed.), *Western Rural Yearbook, A Cyclopedia of Reference* (Chicago, 1886), 130–43; *Western Rural*, Nov. 20, 1886; Roy V. Scott, "Milton George and the Farmers Alliance Movement," *Mississippi Valley Historical Review*, XLV (June 1958), 90–99; Saloutos, *Farmer Movements in the South*, 77; Bryan, *Farmers Alliance*, 57–58; Clanton, *Kansas Populism*, 50; Taylor, *The Farmers' Movement*, 214–16. Saloutos is not beguiled.

The organizational potential in the Midwest is evident from a comparative figure: the cooperatively organized FMBA recruited some 75,000 or so members, primarily in Illinois and Indiana, by 1890–91. George's group had no more than 1000 constantly changing members in the same region.

Traditional views that agrarian protest in the Midwest did not exist because of the relatively "prosperous" condition of the farmers need to be assessed against such organizational realities. "Protest" required an organizational forum; organization required a program of sufficient vitality to recruit farmers. The failure of insurgency in parts of the midwest was less an outgrowth of "prosperity" (the facts simply will not support such a conclusion) than it was the prior failure of organization. The matter is relevant in that the absence of protest has frequently been taken as a positive measure of the degree of democracy inherent in the American economic system. The topic is discussed in the concluding chapter, in Appendix A, and in Critical Essay on Authorities.

10. *Proceedings,* National Farmers Alliance (Minneapolis, Oct. 6–7, 1886); Barnhart, "Alliance in Nebraska," 22–30; Dallas *Mercury,* Nov. 19, 1886; *Western Rural,* Nov. 20, 1886; *Southern Mercury,* Dec. 18, 1886. The FMBA total is based on 942 lodges reported in Scott, *Agrarian Revolt in Illinois.*

Approximations of Northwestern Alliance membership at the time of the Meridian meeting in 1888; Kansas, 500; Nebraska, 2000; Minnesota, 1500; Iowa, 2000; Illinois and Wisconsin, less than 500 each; Dakota Territory, 20,000.

For Iowa, see *Proceedings,* Iowa State Farmers Alliance, Oct. 29–31, 1890, 22–23. The Iowa Alliance was dormant as late as 1886 and what growth it was to attain materialized briefly in 1890. For Minnesota, St. Paul *Pioneer Press,* Feb. 12, 1890, placed active Alliances as of Sept. 1889 at eighty for the entire state. Hicks, *Populist Revolt,* inferentially shows the numerical weakness of the Minnesota Alliance in 1888 (p. 223). See also Ridge, *Donnelly,* 267; Carl Henry Chrislock, "Politics of Protest in Minnesota, 1890–1901" (Unpublished Ph.D. dissertation, University of Minnesota, 1955), 104; Donald F. Warner, "Prelude to Populism," *Minnesota History,* (Sept. 1951), 134.

The estimate for Illinois, unorganized at the time at the state level, is based on the delegate turnout to a meeting in June 1889 that had as its purpose the organization of a state body. Twelve persons participated. Scott, *Agrarian Movement in Illinois,* 41, 44.

At the time, Milton George claimed "140 locals" in the state, which figure may well have been accurate since he issued charters to individuals. It was, in fact, organizationally dangerous for the George group to go beyond individual members and develop local lodges. Discovering no program in their own organization, serious farmers tended to decamp to the FMBA or, later, to the National Farmers Alliance.

Wisconsin, also claimed by George as a participant in the Northwestern group, counted only sixteen suballiances in January, 1889 after an attempt had been made in 1888 to activate the dormant state body (Barnhart, 34). For the move of

Wardall to Kansas, see Douglas A. Bakken, "Luna Kellie and the Farmers Alliance," *Nebraska History*, Vol. 50, No. 2 (Summer 1969), p. 204, n. 19.

In the summer of 1889, six months before the merger attempt, the "Alliance Aid Association," chartered on the lines of the Dakota cooperative insurance program and headed by Wardall, was officially sanctioned by Macune and the National Alliance. For the increasingly close relationship of the National Alliance and the cooperative program of the Dakotas, see *National Economist*, March 14, April 13, June 1, 8, 15, 22, 29, July 6, 13, 20, Oct. 19, 1889. For the Wheel, see Morgan, *Wheel and Alliance*, 80–112, 184–85, and Rogers, *Rebellion*, 121–32.

11. The cause of the merger failure has been a matter of considerable speculation and dispute among historians. The question is treated in Appendix C.

12. The perspective of Stelle and the FMBA is contained in Scott, *Agrarian Movement in Illinois*, 52.

13. The separate declaration of the Northwestern Alliance, considerably in advance of anything the order had achieved in preceding policy statements over the years, may be found in Hicks, *Populist Revolt*, 428–30. The subsequent political conduct of the Northwesterners proved conclusively, however, that they did not take the 1889 document seriously. It may have been written by Henry Loucks, whose views it did reflect, or, alternatively, the Northwesterners may have been temporarily influenced by the more radical statement issued at St. Louis by the National Alliance. In 1891, the Northwestern group rejected the Ocala Platform of the National Alliance, which tracked the 1889 Demands. See Appendix C.

14. John R. Commons and associates, *History of Labor in the United States*, II, 40: "The list of demands speaks volumes for the mental subjection of the Knights of Labor to the farmers' movement." See also Ware, *Labor Movement in the United States*, 67, 366–68.

The Knights had never recovered from the twin blows of the Southwest Strike of 1886 and the propaganda battering the organization received in the aftermath of the Haymarket affair of the same year. Actually, the central experience of the Knights of Labor, as a national organization, had taken place in less than two years. After achieving what it chose to regard as tacit recognition from the Gould lines in 1885, the order utilized this unprecedented achievement as its basic organizing tool. The claim that "we made Jay Gould recognize us!" was impressive and the Knights used it to multiply their membership from 100,000 to 700,000 in the space of a single year. More locals were formed in the twelve months ending July 1, 1886, than in the preceding sixteen years of the Knights' existence. In 1886, however, Gould crushed the union, not only destroying its membership cohesion in the Southwest, but its morale across the nation. The "anarchistic" reputation improperly affixed upon the order by the nation's press after the Haymarket incident completed the cultural isolation of the Knights. Thereafter, the order's "Grand Master Workman," Terence Powderly, proceeded with great caution, and by 1887 had begun to experience mounting opposition from an increasingly restless left wing. This opposition from below came to be centered in the West after the great national trade assemblies of the industrial states withered under the twin pressures of aggressively anti-union employers and passive retreat by Powderly in 1888–89. The most succinct account of the Knights' decline under Powderly is in Foner, *History of the Labor Movement*, II, 157–70.

15. St. Louis *Globe Democrat*, Dec. 7, 1889; Noblin, *Polk*, 213; Taylor, *Farmers' Movement*, 260–61.

Macune's description of the relationship between currency volume and prices has been derided by some as a simplistic "quantity theory of money." Such comments are inappropriate. While it is true that very few people in the Gilded Age understood that the velocity with which money circulated had a bearing on the serviceability to the whole society of a given amount of currency in circulation, the fact does not destroy the prior relevance of the direct relationship between the quantity of currency in circulation at a given rate of velocity and general price levels. In this sense, Macune was far closer to modern monetary theory than orthodox goldbugs.

Beyond this comparison, Macune and his colleague, Harry Tracy, publisher of the *Southern Mercury,* and Cuthbert Vincent in Kansas were among the few political theorists in the nation who *did* comprehend the relevance of currency velocity. Macune understood fully the implications for the nation's currency and banking system of the sub-treasury system; indeed this was precisely why he insisted it was "the most essential thing."

Macune could be criticized, on the other hand, for being too deferential. His almost unconscious faith—in the speech quoted in the text—in the good will of "the authorities" was the kind of remark that caused Alliance radicals to blink. But he was far less vulnerable on grounds of simple political analysis when the issue was reduced to an intelligent management of currency. Indeed, in the currency debate of the Gilded Age, he had few rivals—and none outside the ranks of the agrarian movement.

With respect to the broader political, financial, and cultural issues at stake in the monetary confrontation of the 1890s, perhaps American historians would not be acting too precipitously if they accepted the long-settled judgment of economists, including quite conservative economists, that greenbackers had much the better of the debate on the currency question. For the traditional view see Hicks, *Populist Revolt,* Unger, *The Greenback Era,* and Hofstadter, *The Age of Reform.*

16. The sub-treasury system, was presented at St. Louis in the Alliance "Report of the Committee on the Monetary System."

17. *National Economist,* Dec. 14, 21, 1889. Various favorable contemporary appraisals of the sub-treasury plan are available in Dunning, *Alliance and Digest,* 124–30 (Macune); 336–54 (Tracy); C. C. Post, "The Sub-Treasury Plan," *Arena,* V (Feb. 1892), 342–52; William Peffer, *The Farmers' Side* (New York, 1892); 244–47; Harry Tracy, "The Sub-Treasury Plan," in James H. Davis, *A Political Revelation* (Dallas, 1894), 292–399; S. M. Scott, *The Sub-Treasury Plan and the Land and Loan System* (Topeka, 1891); J. E. Bryan, *Farmers Alliance,* 86–109; Thomas E. Watson, *People's Party Handbook,* 199–205. For critical appraisals, see House Ways and Means Committee, *Report No. 2143,* 52nd Cong., 1st sess. (1892); N. B. Ashby, *Riddle of the Sphinx,* 314–15, 419; John D. Hicks, "The Sub-Treasury: A Forgotten Plan for the Relief of Agriculture," *Mississippi Valley Historical Review,* XV (Dec. 1928), 355–73. For a modern evaluation, see Appendix B.

18. The promising interstate cooperative for the marketing of livestock was destroyed in Kansas after its success had aroused the determined animosity of Midwestern commission houses. They refused to grant to the cooperative membership in the commission association and voted to bar their own members from any dealings ·with farmer members of the cooperative. The reason announced was that the cooperative, in its profit sharing approach, was "operating contrary to the anti-rebate rule of the livestock exchanges" (Nourse and Knapp. *The Cooperative Marketing of Livestock,* 105).

For the introduction of Western leadership into the National Alliance hierarchy, see *Proceedings, Farmers and Laborers Union* (1889). Alonzo Wardall was named to the three-man national executive committee and the Kansas State president, Benjamin Clover, was made vice-president of the order. The permanent staff at the Washington headquarters, however, remained almost exclusively Southern in this period.

19. Technically, the farmers suffered, in the selling of their products, from "monopsony," the presence of few buyers and many sellers, rather than from "monopoly," the presence of few sellers and many buyers.

20. The Texas Alliance and the *Southern Mercury* began avoiding references to membership totals after the collapse of the Texas Exchange late in 1889. *Appleton's Annual Cyclopaedia* (1890) placed the Texas total at 150, 000 for 1890 (p. 301). As a rough estimate, the figure serves, though the temporary loss of membership may even have been greater.

21. *National Economist,* Dec. 14, 1889.

22. Nablin, *Polk,* 213; Taylor, *Farmers' Movement,* 260–61.

23. L. L. Polk, presidential address to National Farmers Alliance and Industrial Union, Dec. 2, 1890, Ocala, Fla., *Proceedings;* Evan Jones, presidential address to Farmers State Alliance of Texas, Aug. 21, 1888, Dallas, Tex., *Proceedings;* John Willits, president of the Jefferson (Kan.) County Alliance, Nov. 22, 1889, in *The Advocate* (Meriden, Kan.), quoted in Clanton, *Kansas Populism,* 46; W. Scott Morgan, in *Wheel and Alliance,* 15.

24. *Progressive Farmer,* Aug. 16, Nov. 4, 1890. For the expansion of the Alliance, see *Proceedings . . . Ocala* (1890), 3–41; Ernest D. Stewart. "The Populist Party of Indiana," *Indiana Magazine of History,* XIV (Dec. 1918), 332–67. Schilling Papers (Wisconsin State Historical Society); Blood, *Handbook and History of the National Farmers Alliance and Industrial Union* (*Southern Mercury,* Nov. 27, 1890).

See also Morgan, *Wheel and Alliance,* 239–48; Thomas A. Clinch, *Urban Populism and Free Silver in Montana* (University of Montana Press, 1970), 16; William J. Gaboury, "The Beginning of the Populist Party in Idaho" (Unpublished M.A. thesis, University of Idaho, 1960), 27–28; Thomas Kruger, "Populism in Wyoming" (Unpublished M.A. thesis, University of Wyoming, 1960). For the planting of the Alliance in New Mexico, see Morgan, 245, the *Southern Mercury,* Sept. 18, 1890, and Robert W. Larson, *New Mexico Populism* (Boulder, 1974). For the Far West: Gordon B. Ridgeway, "Populism in Washington," *Pacific Northwest Quarterly,* XXXIX (Oct., 1948), 285–311; Carroll H. Woody, "Populism in Washington," *Washington Historical Quarterly,* XXI (1930), 103–19; Thomas C. McClintock, "Seth Lewelling, William S. U'Ren and the Birth of the Oregon Progressive Movement," *Oregon Historical Quarterly* (Sept. 1967), 201–5; Walter Schumacher, "Thirty Years of the People's Rule in Oregon: An Analysis," *Political Science Quarterly,* XLVII (June 1932), 242; R. Hal Williams, "Politics and Reform, The California Democrats in the Cleveland Years" (Unpublished Ph.D. dissertation, Yale University, 1968), 207–12; Tom G. Hall, "California Populism at the Grass-Roots: The Case of Tulare County, 1892," *Southern California Quarterly,* XLIX (June 1967) 193–95; Marion Cannon, president of the California Farmers Alliance, to Thomas V. Cator, Dec. 30, 1891, Cator Papers (University of California, Berkeley).

On Jan. 1, 1891, the *Southern Mercury* claimed 43,000 suballiances in the nation. Each had its "lecturer."

25. Harper, "The Speechmaking of Jerry Simpson, 34–40; James L. Ranchino, "The

Work and Thought of a Jeffersonian in the Populist Movement, James Harvey 'Cyclone' Davis" (Unpublished M.A. thesis, Texas Christian University, 1964), 9–10.

26. An excellent brief summary of the educational campaign of the Alliance in 1890–91 may be found in Woodward, *Origins*, 194–95. In 1888, Henry Vincent had organized an "Independent Newspaper Union" as a chartered corporation in Kansas and established a "Union Labor Ready Print Service" to carry the greenback message of radicalism to participating newspapers. (*American Nonconformist*, April 5, 1888). Charles Macune proposed a "newspaper alliance" linking the state and national journals of the order in his presidential address at St. Louis in 1889 (*Proceedings*, Farmers and Laborers Union of America (St. Louis, Dec. 3–7, 1889), 29; see also C. W. Macune to Jay Burrows, *Farmers Alliance* (Lincoln, Neb.), Sept. 28, 1889.

27. Presuming that the order meant what it said in the document, the St. Louis Platform ideologically committed the Alliance to political insurgency. (See Appendix D.)

As editor of the order's national journal, Macune became president of the National Reform Press Association. It is difficult to imagine that he felt politically at ease among his fellow officers of the newspaper alliance. The executive board was composed of Cuthbert Vincent of Kansas, William Lamb of Texas, and Ralph Beaumont of the Knights of Labor. The Secretary was W. Scott Morgan of Arkansas (W. Scott Morgan to L. H. Weller, March 23, 1891, Weller Papers). As the politics of 1890–92 revealed, this was an enormously influential group—in terms of radical policy perhaps *the* most influential single group in agrarian circles. For the roles played by Beaumont, Lamb, Morgan, and the Vincent brothers in creating a multi-sectional third party, see Chaps. VIII and IX. It is probable that Morgan's shift from Arkansas to St. Louis, coupled with the establishment of an avowedly third-party newspaper there, was designed as a radical counterweight to the relatively moderate politics of Macune. The name of Morgan's new journal, *The National Reformer*, contra Macune's *The National Economist*, suggests such a probability. For Morgan's role after the third party was formed, see Chaps. XIV and XVI. An example of the view of Macune from the larger society—as a "wild" radical—may be found in the *New York Times*, Dec. 12, 1890.

CHAPTER VII

1. Evan Jones to Percy Daniels, in Percy Daniels, *A Crisis for the Husbandman* (Girard, Kan., 1889), unnumbered page between p. 4 and p. 5, People's Party Pamphlets (Kansas State Historical Society).

2. St. Louis *Republic*, Dec. 1–8, 1889; *Farmers Alliance* (Lincoln, Neb.), Jan. 4, 18, 1890; Henry Loucks to L. H. Weller, April 27, 1891 (Weller Papers); Brudvig, "Farmers Alliance and Populist Movement in North Dakota," 44; Hendrickson, "The Populist Movement in South Dakot," 226.

3. *Farmers Alliance* (Lincoln), Jan. 4, 18, 1890; *Proceedings*, Nebraska State Farmers Alliance (Grand Island, Neb.), Jan. 7–8, 1890; Quarterly Reports, Nebraska Farmers Alliance Papers (Nebraska State Historical Society).

4. Harrington, "Populist Party in Kansas," 407, Peter H. Argersinger, "Road to a Republican Waterloo: The Farmers Alliance and the Election of 1890 in Kansas," *Kansas Historical Quarterly*, XXXIII (Winter 1967), 448; W. W. Graves, *History of Neosho County*, II (St. Paul, Kan., 1951), 580; Pankrantz, "Continuity of Leader-

ship and Platforms," 7; Scott, *Champion Organizer of the Northwest*, 118–19; R. C. Miller, "Economic Basis of Populism in Kansas," 35.

5. Scott, *The Sub-Treasury Plan and the Land and Loan System*, 97; Clanton, *Kansas Populism*, 48, 54; Harrington, *Populist Party in Kansas*, 407; Miller, "Economic Basis of Populism in Kansas," 48.

6. Argersinger, "Road to a Republican Waterloo," 450; Harrington, *Populist Party in Kansas*, 406–7.

7. Topeka *Daily Capital*, March 19, 28, 1890; Rightmire, "The Alliance Movement in Kansas," 5; Clanton, *Kansas Populism*, 55.

8. Harrington, *Populist Party in Kansas*, 410; Rightmire, "The Aliance Movement in Kansas," 5.

9. Topeka *Daily Capital*, March 28, 1890; Harrington, "Populist Party in Kansas," 410.

10. Barr, "Populist Uprising," 1147; Argersinger, "Road to a Republican Waterloo," 454–55.

11. *Ibid.*, 453.

12. Clanton, *Kansas Populism*, 57, 82, 260.

13. The most detailed account of the "Coffeyville plot" is contained in Charles Richard .Denton, "The American Nonconformist and Kansas Industrial Liberator: A Kansas Union Labor-Populist Newspaper, 1886–1891" (Unpublished M.A. thesis, Kansas State College at Pittsburg, 1961), 1–98; see also, Seymour Lutzky, "The Reform Editors and Their Press" (Unpublished Ph.D. dissertation, University of Iowa, 1951), 157–61; Miller, "Populist Party in Kansas," 60.

14. Topeka *Daily Capital*, July 24, Sept. 18, Oct. 16, 18, 30, 1890; *Weekly Kansas Chief* (Troy, Kan.), June 19, 1890.

15. Harrington, *Populist Party in Kansas*, 413, 414.

16. Noblin, *L. L. Polk: Agrarian Crusader*, 40–45, 50–71.

17. *Ibid.*, 94–95, 103–8, 150, 156–62, 166–82.

18. *Ibid.*, 223.

19. Rightmire, "The Alliance in Kansas," 6.

20. Noblin, *Polk*, 10–12.

21. *Ibid., Polk*, 15–18. The idea that farmers had a "right" to go into politics was by no means a recent conclusion of Polk's. He was saying the same thing as early as Feb. 1888. See Woodward, *Watson*, 117.

22. Noblin, *Polk*, 19.

23. Harper, "Speechmaking of Jerry Simpson," 101; Rightmire, "The Alliance in Kansas," 6.

24. Barr, "Populist Uprising," 1148–49; *American Nonconformist*, Sept. 25, 1890; Ecroyd, "Populist Campaign Speech Making," 142–47, 160.

25. Quoted in Eric F. Goldman, *Rendezvous with Destiny* (New York, 1953), 37–38; Nugent, *Tolerant Populists*, 55. Harper, "The Speechmaking of Jerry Simpson," 37–38. Annie L. Diggs, *The Story of Jerry Simpson* (Wichita, 1908), 110.

26. Barr, "Populist Uprising," 1160; Clanton, *Kansas Populism*, 59, 80–82.

27. *Ibid.*

28. William Allen White, *An Autobiography* (New York, 1946), 217–18; Harper, "The Speechmaking of Jerry Simpson," 31, 37; Clanton, *Kansas Populism*, 82; Hamlin Garland, "The Alliance Wedge in Congress," *Arena*, V (March 1891), 451.

29. Topeka *Weekly Capital*, July 24, Sept. 18, Oct. 16, 30, Nov. 20, 1890; Jan. 8, Sept. 17, Oct. 29, 1891, quoted in Noblin, *Polk*, 225–26. Also see Clanton, *Kansas Popu-*

lism, 87–88. Actually, Polk's newspaper in Raleigh had one of the largest circulations of any newspaper in North Carolina.

30. *Ibid.*

31. Clanton, *Kansas Populism,* 87.

32. Harrison, quoted in William Appleman Williams, *The Roots of the Modern American Empire* (New York, 1969), 337; Bureau of the Census, *Historical Statistics of the United States: Colonial Times to 1957* (Washington, D.C., 1960), 691.

33. Anabel L. Beal, "The Populist Party in Custer County, Nebraska: Its Role in Local, State and Nebraska Politics, 1889–1906" (Unpublished Ph.D. dissertation, University of Nebraska, 1965), 29–37; *Nebraska Agriculture Statistics, 1866–1954,* Nebraska Department of Agriculture and United States Department of Agriculture, 12–18; *Farmers Alliance,* July 10, 24, Sept. 29, 1889. Burrows offered his congratulations to the Custer Alliance after the November victory but he failed to see the connection between a well-populated local cooperative movement and a successful local political ticket. It was not until a year later that he suggested in his newspaper that all Nebraska Alliances should have some kind of "cooperative store" (*Farmers Alliance* (Lincoln), Nov. 8, 1890). Earlier in 1889, would-be organizers in Nebraska were still writing their state president about their attempts to win merchant cooperation—a very preliminary stage of any cooperative effort. Tom Wheedon to Jay Burrows, May 25, 1889 (*Nebraska Farmers Alliance Papers*).

34. Henry Vincent to Jay Burrows, *Farmers Alliance,* July 24, 31, 1889.

35. Beal, "Populist Party in Custer County," 37–39; *Proceedings,* Farmers and Laborers Union of America (St. Louis, Dec. 3–7, 1889); Barnhart, "Alliance in Nebraska," 143. The national association of state business agents of the National Alliance was formed by Macune in New Orleans in 1888. The Nebraskans had named a state "business agent" in 1889, but his subsequent public pronouncements, prior to the St. Louis meeting, merely revealed the shallowness of his grasp of the assignment he faced. (*Farmers Alliance,* July 24, Dec. 21, 1889; Jan. 4, 11, 18, 1890).

36. Edwin G. Nourse and Joseph G. Knapp, *The Cooperative Marketing of Livestock* (Washington, D.C., 1933), 103–5; Barnhart, "Alliance in Nebraska," 143–45; *Farmers Alliance,* Jan. 18, March 29, 1890; May 7, 14, 1891.

37. Barnhart, "Alliance in Nebraska," 189.

38. Marie U. Harmer and James L. Sellers, "Charles Van Wyck, Soldier and Statesman," *Nebraska History,* XI (July–Sept. 1929), "Contest for Re-election and Retirement to Private Life," 344; and XII (Oct.–Dec. 1929) "Populist Days," 349.

39. At the time of the Custer County victory, the Nebraska Alliance, after nine years of existence, had penetrated into only one-third of the state's counties (*Farmers Alliance,* Nov. 16, 1889). For the spread of the Alliance, see Barnhart, "Alliance in Nebraska," 199–201. For Burrows on cooperation, see *Farmers Alliance,* Feb. 8, April 22, and May 10, 1890; Barnhart, "Alliance in Nebraska," 135, 140–43, 170–74, 200, 207. Of the issues enumerated by the Nebraska State Alliance platform of 1890, none related to cooperation. Platform of Farmers Alliance Convention, July 29, 1890 (*Nebraska Farmers Alliance Papers*).

40. Stanley B. Parsons, *The Populist Context: Rural versus Urban Power on a Great Plains Frontier* (Westport, Conn., 1973), 78.

41. Harmer and Sellers, "Charles Van Wyck," 349, 354.

42. J. M. Thompson, "The Farmers Alliance in Nebraska, Something of Its Growth and Influence," *Proceedings and Collections of the Nebraska State Historical Society,* 2nd

Series (Lincoln, 1902) V, 203; Parsons, *Populist Context*, 78. Harmer and Sellers, "Charles Van Wyck," 354; Beal, "Custer County," 42–44; Barnhart, "Alliance in Nebraska" 201–3.

43. Beal, "Custer County," 47; Barnhart, "Alliance in Nebraska," 208–9. The belated "call" by state Alliance officials was issued on June 28. On June 13, Hamilton County farmers had voted 413–83 for an independent ticket. Parsons, *Populist Context*, 80–81.

44. Barnhart, "Alliance in Nebraska," concludes that a total Alliance membership figure for Nebraska of 50,000 "is probably liberal" (p. 42). The Nebraska state secretary's report on the year complained that the growth of 1890 had been "imperfectly done so that the largest part of the labor of the year had to be spent in strengthening and building up the Alliances already organized." The report for 1891 put the best possible face on a deteriorating situation: "The past season has been one of unusual stress of work on the part of farmers of our state, and the apparent lack of interest in local Alliance work was largely due to this cause." Neither report contained a single reference to cooperation. Such an innovation in the secretary's report came only after the Nebraskans joined the National Farmers Alliance and Industrial Union in 1892. A political assessment of Alliance growth is available in Parsons, *The Populist Context*, 198–99.

45. For the passage of Nebraska into the National Farmers Alliance in 1892, see Barnhart, "Alliance in Nebraska," 423–24.

46. The election of 1890 and the failure of the reform legislature are treated in Barnhart, 240–47 and 252–77.

47. For reasons that are self-describing, the only regions of Nebraska producing a political movement genuinely resembling Populism were the handful of counties—none too far from Custer County—which had generated at least the beginnings of a cooperative movement. From such counties came authentic greenbackers, such as Mrs. Luna Kellie, a tireless reform editor, and—a sure sign of the culture of Populism—movement songs. See Douglas A. Baaken, "Luna Kellie and the Farmers Alliance," *Nebraska History* (Summer 1969).

48. Noblin, *Polk*, 227–28.

49. Jacksonville (Florida) *Times-Union*, Nov. 30, 1890.

CHAPTER VIII

1. The phrase "Alliance ticket" was employed in Kansas in 1890, though many have subsequently used "Populist ticket" to describe the politics of that campaign. The quotation in the text is from the *Atlanta Constitution*, June 6, July 4, 7, 1890.

2. Arnett, *Populist Movement in Georgia*, 105, 116; Sharp, "Entrance of the Farmers Alliance in Tennessee Politics," 82–83; Woodward, *Origins*, 204.

3. William DuBose Sheldon, *Populism in the Old Dominion* (Princeton, 1935), 65; Saloutos, *Farmer Movements*, 116.

4. Rogers, *One-Gallused Rebellion*, 183; Sharp, "Alliance in Tennessee," 84–87.

5. *National Economist*, V (1891), 322; *Southern Mercury*, May 19, 1892; Francis B. Simkins, *Pitchfork Ben Tillman* (Baton Rouge, 1944), 90–91, 147–48; Saloutos, *Farmer Movements*, 106–9; Woodward, *Origins*, 237–38; Arnett, *Populist Movement in Georgia*, 107.

6. *Rural Citizen* (Jacksboro, Tex.), Nov. 12, 1885; *Proceedings* Farmers and Laborers Union of America (St. Louis), Dec. 1889.

7. Harrison Sterling Price Ashby Biographical Folder (University of Texas); *Indianapolis Sentinel*, Nov. 20, 1891; Martin, *People's Party in Texas*, 123, 132; Fort Worth *Mail*, July 2, 1886; Dallas *Herald*, Oct. 6, 1886; Fort Worth *Gazette*, Oct. 127, 1886; Dallas *News*, July 3, 1888, Aug. 18, 1891, June 25, 1892, Sept. 16, 1894.

8. Ernest Winkler, Platforms of Political Parties in Texas (Austin, 1916), 234–37, 262–63; Cincinnati *Enquirer*, May 17, 1888; Chicago *Tribune*, May 17–18, 1888; Dunning, *Alliance and Digest*, 58, 63; Dallas *News*, Aug. 8, 1886, July 4–6, 1888, Feb. 2, 1891; *Southern Mercury*, March 27, 1890; Morgan, *Wheel and Alliance*, 305; *Proceedings*, Farmers State Alliance of Texas (Dallas), Aug. 21–23, 1890; *Proceedings*, Supreme Council of the National Farmers Alliance and Industrial Union (Ocala, Fla.), Dec. 2–8, 1890, 25. For Perdue's role in the development of the Omaha Platform of the People's Party, see Appendix D.

9. Ellis A. Davis and Edwin H. Grobe (eds.), *Encyclopedia of Texas* (Dallas, n.d.), 648; Jack Abramowitz, "The Negro in the Populist Movement," *Journal of Negro History*, XXXVIII (July 1953), 262; *Southern Mercury*, Oct. 23, 1888; Frank Drew, "The Present Farmers' Movement," *Political Science Quarterly*, VI (June 1891), 287; R. M. Humphrey, "History of the Colored Farmers' National Alliance and Cooperative Union," in Dunning, *Alliance and Digest*, 288–92; Saloutos, *Farmers Movements*, 79–80. Macune printed five columns of Humphrey's address to the National Alliance convention of 1890 (*National Economist*, Dec. 27, 1890).

10. For Tracy's views on large-scale cooperatives, see Morgan, *Wheel and Alliance*, 338–43; on the sub-treasury plan and greenback interpretation of the American monetary system, the perspectives of Tracy may be found in Dunning, *Alliance and Digest*, 338–54, Davis, *A Political Revelation*, 293–399 and in Appendix B.

11. "William R. Lamb," a biographical sketch, in typescript, in possession of Russell G. Pepperell, Houston, Tex. See also Cincinnati *Enquirer*, May 16, 1888; Chicago *Tribune*, May 15–18, 1888. Lamb's paper underwent several name changes: *The Labor Sunbeam* (1888), *The Bowie Independent* (1889); *The Montague County Independent* (1890) and the *Texas Independent* (1891); see the *Montague County Independent*, Jan. 21, 1890, and *Texas Independent*, Aug. 12, 1891. For various aspects of Lamb's career as a radical organizer prior to the formation of the People's Party, see the Dallas *News*, July 3–6, 1888; Aug. 23–25, 1890; April 24, July 2, 5, 12, Aug. 17–18, 1891; Winkler, *Platforms of Political Parties in Texas*, 260–63; *Southern Mercury*, Aug. 28, 1890. Macune blocked his rival out of columns of the *National Economist* but upon Lamb's accession to the executive board of the National Reform Press Association in 1890, Macune had no choice but to print his name (*National Economist*, Dec. 27, 1890.)

12. Macune tenaciously opposed these efforts. See the *Southern Mercury*, April 19, May 18, 31, 1888. For the efforts themselves, see Winkler, *Platforms of Political Parties*, 257, 260–63; Cincinnati *Enquirer* and Chicago *Tribune*, May 15–18, 1888, Dallas *News*, July 3–6, 1888; Austin *Weekly Statesman*, July 12, 1888; Martin, *People's Party in Texas*, 35; *Southern Mercury*, Aug. 7, 14, 21, 28, Oct. 2, 1888.

13. Winkler, *Platforms of Political Parties*, 288; Martin, *People's Party in Texas*, 26; Dallas *News*, Aug. 20, 1890. In conservative circles, Hogg was considered "safe" (Dallas *News*, Nov. 4, 1890, quoted in Cotner, *Hogg*, 250).

14. Dallas *News*, August 20, 1890. The injunction by the Texas Democratic Party against the idea of government credit was general: "We oppose the collection and distribution, by the federal government, of any money . . . or loan to any citizen or class, upon any sort of security, whether government or commercial bonds,

farm or other products" Winkler, *Platforms of Political Parties*, 288. The wording is interesting in that leading Democrats in the state proposed lending state school trust funds to railroads.

15. Dallas *News*, Aug. 22, 23, 1890; *Southern Mercury*, Aug. 28, 1890. It should be emphasized that, in a given State Alliance, the context of a vote on the subtreasury described its political meaning. In Texas in 1890, a vote for the subtreasury—after the state Democratic Party had rejected the proposal—had serious third-party implications which, under other conditions, it might not have had. By the summer of 1891, the sub-treasury issue tended to carry third party connotations in all states. See below.

16. *Southern Mercury*, Aug. 28, Sept. 4, 18, 25, Nov. 20, 27, Dec. 4, 1890; Dallas *News*, Feb. 2, 1891. Alliance radicals also used the August state meeting to regain control of the *Southern Mercury*, which had temporarily fallen into the hands of a Hoggite. The effort involved no power struggle; since the editor had followed Hogg into opposition to the sub-treasury, both Macune's admirers and the radicals opposed him. As events soon revealed, these two factions, both committed to the sub-treasury, constituted something over 95 per cent of the Texas agrarian leadership.

17. *Proceedings*, Supreme Council of the National Farmers Alliance and Industrial Union (Ocala), Dec. 2–8, 1890, 5. A number of states that did not have delegates at Ocala had been organized at the state level earlier in 1890. See Morgan, *Wheel and Alliance*, 239–48. A compromise worked out at Cleburne in 1886 continued to permit, while ostensibly preventing, political education within the order. The first paragraph of the Alliance declaration of purposes read: "To labor for the education of the agricultural classes in the science of economical government, in a strictly non-partisan spirit, and to bring about a more perfect union of said classes." In practical effect, this was a restatement of the Daws formula that evolved in Texas in 1886. The wording was reaffirmed at Ocala—along with the highly political "Ocala Demands." Dunning, *Alliance and Digest*, 163–68.

18. Hamlin Garland, "Alliance Wedge in Congress," *Arena*, V (March 1892), 447–67.

19. *Proceedings*, Supreme Council of the National Farmers Alliance and Industrial Union (Ocala), 9–11, 36. Sheldon, *Populism in the Old Dominion*, 73. Of the thirteen non-Southern votes against the Lodge bill, eleven came from the border states of West Virginia, Kentucky, Maryland and Missouri. The other two were from California.

20. The wording is significant. Having become alarmed by the spread of third party talk among the Alliance leadership, Macune placed his emphasis upon the political influence of rank and file farmers. Lamb, of course, had already moved to accept battle on precisely these terms. Both radical and moderate Alliance leaders thus demonstrated their confidence that their personal political beliefs reflected the deepest instincts of their common constituency. But Lamb was in touch with that constituency more frequently and more intimately than Macune.

21. *New York Times*, Dec. 5, 25, 1890; Taylor, *Farmers Movement*, 264; Rightmire, "Alliance in Kansas," 1–8; Martin Michael La Godna, "Kansas and the Ocala Connection of 1890" (Unpublished M.A. thesis, Florida State University, 1962), 35.

22. *Proceedings*, Supreme Council of the National Farmers Alliance and Industrial Union, 1890 (Ocala, Dec. 4–8, 1890), 1–32.

23. *National Economist*, Dec. 20, 27, 1890; W. Scott Morgan to L. H. Weller, March 23, 1891 (Weller Papers). The National Reform Press Association was created at a meeting of reform editors "beneath the banana and orange trees" at Ocala on Dec. 8, 1891. The Vincent brothers of the *American Nonconformist* and Dr. Ste-

phen McLallin of *The Advocate* played leading roles in this event (*American Nonconformist,* Dec. 18, 1890; La Godna, "Kansas and the Ocala Convention," 43).

24. The Citizens Alliance was designed to appeal to potential third party voters who lived in cities. Though its origins were in Kansas, a national structure was fashioned at Ocala, with James D. Holden, a Kansas greenbacker as President. Fearing that Holden was too moderate, W. F. Rightmire promptly formed a second "national" organization, known as the "National Citizens Industrial Alliance." Both organizations became third party vehicles and both were accorded delegate representation at the 1892 founding convention of the People's Party at St. Louis in 1892. La Godna, "Kansas and the Ocala Convention," 49–50; Declaration of Principles Platform, Constitution and By-Laws of the National Citizens Industrial Alliance, *Proceedings of the National Assembly,* Jan. 13–17, 1891 (Topeka, 1891); Rightmire, "Alliance Movement in Kansas," 6; *National Economist,* Jan. 31, 1891; *American Nonconformist,* Dec. 11, 1890; Jan. 22, Feb. 5, 1891.

25. In 1891, the Citizens Alliance opened a newspaper in Washington dedicated to independent political action. Its editor, Ralph Beaumont, was the national lecturer of the Knights of Labor. Delegates of the Knights had voted 53 to 12 in favor of independent political action at a meeting of the Knights' General Assembly in Denver one month before Ocala (*Journal of Knights of Labor* (Chicago), Nov. 27, 1890). The political purpose of the Confederation of Industrial Organization was carried to its conclusion by Macune and Terrell at the February 1892 meeting. In a last ditch effort to ward off the third party, Terrell ran for permanent chairman of the 1892 conference. See Chap. IX.

26. Peter H. Argesinger, *Populism and Politics: William Alfred Peffer and the People's Party* (Lexington, Ky., 1974), 80–82; Dallas *News,* April 22, 1891; Feb. 11; April 23, 1892.

27. Dunning, *Alliance and Digest,* 165; *Proceedings* (Ocala), 16–17. One member of the executive board, U. S. Hall of the Missouri Alliance, voted against the inclusion of the sub-treasury plan in Ocala Demands. Among all delegates, four votes were recorded against (Dunning, 165).

28. Martin, *People's Party in Texas,* 27, 36; *Southern Mercury,* Feb. 24, March 3, 10, 1891. One of the Governor's suggestions was a plan to lend public school trust funds to railroads whose securities passed muster with the Hogg-appointed railroad commission (Cotner, *Hogg,* 251). This proposal imparted a somewhat different thrust to the commission's duties than Texas voters had perhaps been led to expect.

29. Austin *Statesman,* March 6, 1891; Martin, *People's Party in Texas,* 27, 128.

30. Dallas *News,* March 8, 1891.

31. Dallas *News,* April 12, 19, 1891.

32. Dallas *News,* April 22, 1891; Austin *Statesman,* April 20, 1891; Dallas *Herald,* April 21, 1891.

33. Waco *News,* April 22, 1891; Dallas *News,* April 22–24, 1891; *Austin Statesman,* April 25, 1891; Fort Worth *Daily Mail,* April 26, 1891.

34. Kansas Alliancemen, deeply fearful of being isolated in insurgency, invested a remarkable amount of organizational energy in the sub-treasury campaign across the South in 1891–92. (Rogers, *One-Gallused Rebellion,* 194; Hair, *Bourbonism and Agrarian Protest,* 204–205; Ferguson, "Agrarianism in Mississippi," 392–494; Robert C. McMath, *Populist Vanguard,* (Chapel Hill, 1975), 115; Peter H. Argesinger, *Populism and Politics* (Lexington, 1974), 80–109. However, in the broad organizational sense of reaching the great mass of Southern Alliancemen, there were dis-

tinct limits to what outsiders could do. The decisive factor proved to be the degree to which the entire Alliance lecturing system was mobilized.

Insights into the politics of the sub-treasury at work in 1891 at the local level are available in Webbie Jackson Lever, "The Agrarian Movement in Noxubee County (Mississippi)," (Unpublished MA thesis, Mississippi State University, 1952), 59; and Willliam B. Gregg, "The Agrarian Movement in Granada County (Mississippi)," (Unpublished M.A. thesis, Mississippi State University, 1953), 67–70. Though the necessary relationships are not always explicit spelled out by the authors cited, Lamb's lecturing campaign on the sub-treasury is visible in Populist literature: for Alabama, Rogers, *One-Gallused Rebellion*, 115, 177, 190; for Georgia, Woodward, *Watson*, 150, 175–76, 180; for Minnesota, Ridge, *Donnelly*, 283–84; for North Carolina, McMath, *Populist Vanguard*, 124. The practical politics of the sub-treasury (as distinct from the sub-treasury plan itself) is traced in the following chapter and, for some states, in Chap. XI. The subject is summarized in the concluding chapter and is one of the interpretive elements discussed in the Critical Essay on Authorities. See also Chap. XIV, "The Last Agrarian Crusade: The Movement vs. The Silver Lobby."

For some of the forms of the sub-treasury lecturing campaign in the West, see S. M. Scott, "The Sub-Treasury Plan and the Land and Loan System" (Topeka, 1891), 1–97. Scott was assistant state lecturer of the Kansas Alliance and the organizing pamphlet he wrote in 1891 was designed to serve—and did serve—as the basis of a coordinated lecturing campaign. A second model, entitled "A Lecture on the Sub-Treasury Plan," was prepared and printed by J. M. Ritchie, the lecturer for Montgomery County, Kansas. The North Dakota Alliance endorsed the sub-treasury at the state level in 1890 while the South Dakota Alliance mobilized an extensive lecturing system on the subject in 1891. The membership in the Dakotas and the reform editors in the West supported the sub-treasury "wholeheartedly" (Hendrickson, "Some Aspects of the Populist Movement in South Dakota," 85–86; Hendrickson, "The Populist Movement in South Dakota," 230); Brudvig, "The Farmers Alliance and Populist Movement in North Dakota," 137; Seymour Lutzky, "Reform Editors and Their Press" (Unpublished Ph.D. dissertation, University of Iowa, 1951), 168.

35. Dallas *News*, April 23, 25, 26, 1891.

36. Dallas *News*, April 23, 24, 1891. Again, the swiftness with which controversial issues could be transformed into an agreed-upon policy, when properly explained, is striking. Six months before unanimity was achieved at Waco in April 1891, delegates from twenty-three counties had voted against formal endorsement of the sub-treasury, while sixteen other county delegations had abstained. The controversial Cleburne Demands of 1886 had undergone a similar transformation five years earlier. However, the qualification "when properly explained" is an important one. In all the Southern states, time was the critical element in judicious management of the politics of the sub-treasury to bring on the third party. The creation of a third party in the South depended on the rapid mobilization of the Alliance lecturing system, and on the willingness of Alliance leaders in a given state to deploy it. See fn. 39, below, and "Critical Essay on Authorities," p. 607.

37. Waco *News*, April 25, 1891; Dallas *News*, 24, 25, 1891. Also joining the executive board of the Reform Press Association was the prominent Macunite, Harry Tracy. Tracy's near commitment to independent political action signaled that relatively "moderate" Texas Alliance leaders had begun to coalesce with the order's

radicals—over the objections of Macune. By this time, all, of course, were green-backers.

38. Waco *News,* April 25, 1891.

39. On the basis of the history of the agrarian movement through the spring of 1891, it is possible at this juncture to summarize the process that brought the People's Party into American politics.

The necessary starting point, for reformers, was the unhappy fact that the central political reality of post-Civil War politics reposed in the sectional memories of the American people, memories that, along geographical lines, divided millions of farmers and laborers into two parties whose policies were responsive to the self-interest of businessmen. Though, to greenbackers, the result was an exploitive economic organization of the whole society, the party loyalties of millions were shaped by noneconomic impulses. For a new party to bring Northerners and Southerners together on the basis of new ideas about economic and political democracy, these sectional memories had to be overcome.

This the Alliance began to do in 1884–85 through the day-to-day realities of its cooperative struggle. The meaning of these experiences, in which literally two million people eventually participated, were discussed by the farmers and by the 40,000 suballiance lecturers who made up the Alliance lecturing system. Macune's newspaper, the *National Economist,* provided the theoretical model of monetary interpretation—one that was vastly augmented by the flood of books, pamphlets, and, most of all, suggested outlines for suballiance lecturers, that were printed by the National Economist Publishing Company in Washington and by state and county alliances. The effect of all this was to cause ordinary Northerners and Southerners to ask themselves questions about their old political habits—in short, to question their received cultural heritage. Given the power of culture, this was scary business. If things were as out of joint as the sad results of the cooperative movement seemed to indicate they were, the one party that waved the bloody shirt and the other that called itself the party of the fathers, far from being worthy vessels for one's loyalty, were really instruments of deception.

The issue that forced these unwanted facts upon the farmers with dramatic clarity was the sub-treasury plan. Its appeal to farmers was not hard to grasp, North or South—it promised to free people from a usurious credit system that bound them to frustration and hard times. When both the Democratic and Republican parties pronounced against the sub-treasury, the way was left open for a new kind of mass democratic politics in America. The critical issue of 1890–91, an issue of transforming cultural dimension, was whether American farmers were sufficiently informed as to the implications of the sub-treasury as an antidote to the American banking system to cause them to renounce their received political heritage.

To those comfortably at home in the emerging corporate politics of industrial America, such as Republican Senator John J. Ingalls in Kansas and Democratic Governor James Hogg in Texas, these new political possibilities seemed quite remote. The political environment of Jim Hogg was as far removed from the crop lien world that defined the daily lives of millions of Southerners as John Ingalls was from the ethical world of Henry Vincent in Kansas. Neither showed they could be responsive to the humiliating conditions pervading American agriculture; while Ingalls saw the Alliance as something to be loftily ignored, Hogg, in common with such other ambitious Southern politicians as South Carolina's Ben Tillman and Georgia's W. J. Northen, viewed the farmer organization as something to be exploited or managed and, ultimately, as something to be destroyed. In the era of the agrarian revolt, self-described "reform Democrats" in the South and orthodox Republicans in the North were sufficiently distant from the realities that guided the Farmers Alliance that they consistently misread both the anguish of organized farmers and the genuineness of their longings. Neither Ben Tillman in South Carolina nor Hogg in Texas ever understood, for example, that in attacking Macune, they were assaulting the one national Alliance spokesman most committed to the Democratic Party. Macune appeared so radical to them all that they could not conceive he had come to represent, in 1890–91, the conservative wing of the agrarian movement (for Tillman, see Chap. XI). A prominent Southern "silver Democrat," U.S. Senator John Reagan, wrote Hogg that the sub-treasury was "the dangerous question." He went on to say: "They ought to throw Macune and his set overboard. If he is not being paid to break up the Democratic party he is doing that work as effectively as if he was; and for the good of the country, he ought to be squelched" (Reagan to Hogg, Nov. 16, 1890, Hogg Papers). These relationships—which were present throughout the South in 1891–92, as they were in Texas in 1890–91 and in Kansas in 1890—revealed the extent to which even so-called "reform" politicians of the major parties had become alienated from the roots of reform. Depending upon how one wished to view the dynamics involved, their complacency in the presence of mass suffering among Alliance farmers and their ignorance of the maturing political sentiments of Alliance leaders, precipitated the third party revolt; or such ignorance and complacency, by proving how far removed the American political system was from the world of ordinary Americans, justified the revolt.

But in terms of the political prerequisites to the formation of a radical new third party, the failure of "reform through the Democrats" in the South in 1891 was not, in itself, an adequate cause for the development of strong state third parties across the region. "Reform through the Democrats" did not occur in any Southern state in 1891–92—any more than "reform" had occurred in most American states at any time since Reconstruction. Yet, as events were to demonstrate, the emotional hold of sectional loyalties to the "party of the fathers" was sufficiently powerful that strong Southern third parties developed *only* in those states in which the large Alliance constituencies were exposed to education on greenback monetary principles through the coordinated effort of state leaders and the Alliance internal lecturing system specifically mobilized on the sub-treasury issue. Only through this process was it possible to develop sufficient political self-consciousness among farmers to overcome sectional loyalties and transfer large portions of the Alliance constituencies to the new third party. In essence, one had to grasp something of the sweep of the sub-treasury system to fully understand the promise of "the new day for the industrial millions." In the absence of this understanding, it was simpler to stay with one's "old party."

The fact is fundamental in isolating the origins and subsequent meaning of American Populism. The sub-treasury system, as conceived by Charles Macune, represented the ideological culmination both of the cooperative crusade and of greenback monetary theory; as such, it merits study on its own terms. But it was the *politics* of the sub-treasury, as orchestrated by William Lamb, that was essential to the creation of a strong Populist presence in any Southern state. There were no exceptions: in the South, where the state Alliance lecturing system was mobilized on the sub-treasury issue, a strong People's Party emerged; where it was not, as in Tennessee, the third party was marginal. While the dynamics were slightly different in the West, even there strong Populist parties developed only in states which organized their lecturing systems on the sub-treasury. Where this was not done, as in Nebraska, a shadow movement, uninstructed by greenback doctrines, emerged.

In sum, the People's Party was a product of the Alliance cooperative movement and the culture it generated; politically, Populism was radical greenbackism, practically symbolized by the sub-treasury monetary system. Macune's system threatened to change the relationship between bankers and non-bankers, between "concentrated capital" and the American "producer," between corporate politics and citizen politics. That was what Populism was about.

CHAPTER IX

1. Cincinnati *Enquirer,* May 19, 1891.
2. Clanton, *Kansas Populism,* 98–103; Taylor, *Farmers' Movement,* 264–67.
3. Chicago *Tribune,* May 18, 19, 20, 1891; *New York Times,* May 18, 21, 1891; Cincinnati *Enquirer,* May 19, 20, 1891.
4. Cincinnati *Enquirer,* May 19, 1891; Dallas *News,* April 20, 22, 1891.
5. Woodward, *Origins,* 242; *National Economist,* May 4, 16, 30, 1891.
6. Noblin, *Polk,* 269–70. Cincinnati *Enquirer,* May 20, 1891. The political background of Herman Taubeneck, the third party's new chairman, is treated on pp. 445–49.
7. Woodward, *Origins,* 236–41. The struggle between the Alliance and Ben Tillman in South Carolina is treated on pp. 337–39.
8. Arnett, *Populist Movement in Georgia,* 150–51; Woodward, *Watson* (2nd edition), 118–19.
9. Woodward, *Watson,* 112–15, 119.
10. Woodward, *Watson,* 146.
11. Woodward, *Watson,* 150–51.
12. Arnett, *Populist Movement in Georgia,* 103–5; Woodward, *Watson,* 154–55.
13. Arnett, *Populist Movement in Georgia,* 129–31; Woodward, *Watson,* 155–60; Hicks, *Populist Revolt,* 222.
14. *Progressive Farmer* (Raleigh), Jan. 19, 1892; *Farmers Advocate* (Tarboro), Sept. 2, 1891, quoted in Bruce Palmer, "The Rhetoric of Southern Populists: Metaphor and Imagery in the Language of Reform" (Unpublished Ph.D. dissertation, Yale University, 1972), 335.
15. Rogers, *One-Gallused Rebellion,* 115, 177, 190, 263; *Southern Alliance Farmer,* quoted in Palmer, "Rhetoric of Southern Populists," 230; *Proceedings,* North Carolina Farmers State Alliance (Raleigh, 1890), 24; Church, "Farmers Alliance in South Carolina," 52. For Tillman, see pp. 337–39.
16. The vote in Florida for the sub-treasury was 71 to 5 (Knauss, "Farmers Alliance in Florida," 313). For Tennessee, see Sharp, "Entrance of Farmers Alliance in Tennessee Politics," 84, 88.
17. Albert D. Kirwan, *Revolt of the Rednecks* (Lexington, Ky., 1951), 86–89; Ferguson, "Agrarianism in Mississippi," 103–6.
18. Woodward, *Origins,* 198. The candidates originally held joint debates but, according to one writer, the campaign "became so intense" and the contenders "so overwrought" that they were discontinued by mutual consent (Cecil Johnson, "The Agrarian Crusade with Special Reference to Mississippi" Unpublished M.A. thesis, University of Virginia, 1924, 14).

19. Kirwan, *Revolt of the Rednecks*, 89–102. Alliancemen helped Burkitt rebuild his printing office (Ferguson, "Agrarianism in Mississippi," 239).

   The precise relationship of the election, the race issue, and violence to Burkitt is difficult to reconstruct. In 1890, a Mississippi constitutional convention effectively disfranchised most of the state's Negroes. Burkitt was the leader of the minority faction opposing the suffrage code and the only one of either faction to refuse to sign it. Burkitt said the law would disfranchise "50,000 of the state's best voters," a reference, presumably, to upland white farmers. The conservative George faction, however, certainly possessed no monopoly on supporters inclined toward white supremacy. In any event the sub-treasury issue engendered heights of contention in Mississippi unmatched anywhere else in the South or West. Some of Barksdale's "closest friends" were moved to take the stump against him (Kirwan, 86). See also McCain, "Populist Party in Mississippi," 20–21, and Ferguson, "Agrarianism in Mississippi," passim.

20. Morgan, *Wheel and Alliance*, 259–60. Paisley, "Political Wheelers," 17.

21. Paisley, "Political Wheelers," 17–20.

22. L. L. Polk to James W. Denmark, May 27, 1891, quoted in Noblin, *Polk,* 270.

23. *Proceedings,* Supreme Council of the National Farmers Alliance and Industrial Union (Indianapolis), November 15–19, 1891, 30–31; Taylor, *Farmers' Movement,* 270–73.

24. Indianapolis *Journal,* Nov. 16, 23, 1891; Indianapolis *Sentinel,* Nov. 15, 20, 1891.

25. Louck's election embittered Livingston. He predicted "the third party movement will wreck the Alliance in Georgia" (Indianapolis *Sentinel,* Nov. 20, 1891). Woodward, *Watson,* 160.

   The American press continued to encounter difficulties in analyzing the internal politics of the agrarian movement. The Indianapolis *Sentinel* saw the dominance of third party sentiment as "Dr. Macune's great victory." It was hardly that, of course. Though Macune remained almost as cautious on the third party question at Indianapolis as he had been at Waco, Texas, seven months earlier, the *Economist* editor, together with the entire coterie of Alliance functionaries he had gathered around him over the years in Washington, remained opposed to independent political action. The secretary of the order's national executive committee, J. F. Tillman of Tennessee, said as much, as did Ben Terrell of Texas, the national lecturer (Indianapolis *Sentinel,* Nov. 14, 1891).

26. Brudvig, "Alliance in Dakota," 90–91; Ridge, *Donnelly,* 264, 276; Carl Henry Chrislock, "The Politics of Protest in Minnesota" (Unpublished Ph.D. dissertation, University of Minnesota, 1955), 129–39. The 1000 active chapters of early 1891 had fallen to 373 by January 1892 (Ridge, 292–93).

27. The basic histories of the agrarian movement in Iowa are Frederick E. Haynes, *Third Party Movements with Special Reference to Iowa* (Iowa City, 1916), and Herman C. Nixon, "The Populist Movement in Iowa," *Iowa Journal of History and Politics,* XXIV, 1, Jan. 1926, 3–107. These need to be placed in the context of the national cooperative movement and should be supplemented by the internal records of the Iowa Farmers Alliance and the papers of L. H. Weller, both in the Wisconsin State Historical Society.

28. Supreme Council of the National Farmers Alliance and Industrial Union, *Proceedings,* 1890, 48; August Post to L. H. Weller, Jan. 27, 1891; Jonathon Shearer to Weller, April 20, 1891; Will Sargent to Weller, April 2, 1891. Post retired from the organizing effort in June (August Post to Weller, June 19, 1891, Weller Papers). He seemingly did not want to oppose farmers to businessmen. See Appendix C.

29. *Proceedings,* Iowa Farmers Alliance, Annual Meetings, 1890, 1891, 1892; Presidential Letter No. 2, Iowa Farmers Alliance, J. H. Sanders, Dec. 1, 1890 (Weller Papers). Attempts by veteran greenbackers to secure organizing posts in the Iowa Alliance were turned down. Post to Weller, Loucks to Weller, April 27, 1891, Weller Papers. The Iowa suballiances that bolted to the National Alliance were located in the northwestern part of the state. They organized cooperatives and found a radical political spokesman in a middle-class farmer named A. J. Westfall. In 1892, Westfall became People's Party national committeeman for Iowa (Haynes, *Third Party Movements,* 313).

   Weller, as might have been expected given his radical past, threw his support behind the National Alliance attempt to organize Iowa in 1891–92. See Haynes, *Third Party Movements,* 318; Sargent to Weller, April 30, 1891; Post to Weller, June 19, 1891; Ignatius Donnelly to Weller, June 10, 1891, Weller Papers.

30. Barnhart, "Alliance in Nebraska," 423–24; *Farmers Alliance* (Lincoln), Jan. 28, Feb. 4, 18, 25, 1892.

31. *Farmers Alliance,* Feb. 4, 18, 25.

32. Chicago *Tribune,* Jan. 27, 28, 1892; Haynes, *Third Party Movements,* 310, 313–14. The order had not learned anything in the six years since its reactivation by Milton George in 1886. The 1892 meeting was as filled with agrarian platitudes as the reorganization meeting of 1886 in Minneapolis. (See Appendix C.) The Iowa Alliance, numbering under 10,000, lingered into the mid-1890s, successfully avoiding third parties (Nixon, "Cleavage in the Farmers Alliance Movement," 32). For all practical purposes, the order had ceased to exist elsewhere. It had never developed either an economic or political purpose.

33. *St. Louis Republic,* Feb. 21, 22, 1891; Haynes, *Third Party Movements,* 257. At St. Louis, the Southern Alliance had 246 delegates, Colored Farmers National Alliance had 97, Knights of Labor 82, F.M.B.A. 53, National Citizens Alliance 52, plus a scattering of small delegations representing various reform urges. Taylor, *Farmer Movements,* 160; Noblin, *Polk,* 273; Haynes, *Third Party Movements* 258; Hicks, *Populist Revolt,* 226. The Northwestern Alliance was awarded 49 votes, despite its formal decision not to participate in the formation of the People's Party. The relatively conservative Patrons of Industry, based in Michigan, was awarded 75 votes, though it, too, brought few recruits to the new party. (Sidney Glazer, "Labor and Agrarian Movements in Michigan," Unpublished Ph.D. dissertation, Univ. of Michigan, 159).

34. Noblin, *Polk,* 274.

35. St. Louis *Globe Democrat,* Feb. 23, 1892.

36. Ridge, *Donnelly,* 287, 295–96.

37. The platform of the People's Party was essentially a restatement of the Ocala Demands with the wording on government ownership of the railroads following the language of the St. Louis Platform of 1889. See Appendix D, "The Ideological Origins of the Omaha Platform."

38. Haynes, *Third Party Movements,* 258–60; St. Louis *Republic,* Feb. 24, 1892. Macune's reference to the provisional national committee of the People's Party headed by Taubeneck was—under the circumstances of his own prior opposition—necessarily somewhat vague. The rise of Herman Taubeneck to national party chairman, and the consequences therefrom, are discussed in the context of the silver campaign of 1895–96 in Populist ranks. See Chaps. XIV and XV, esp. pp. 445–47. Other accounts of the St. Louis convention may be found in Taylor, *Farmers' Movement,* 275–78 and Hicks, *Populist Revolt,* 223–30.

39. S. M. McLallin to L. L. Polk, April 26, 1892, Polk Papers.

40. Montgomery *Advertiser,* May 4–5, 1892.
41. H. H. Boyce to L. L. Polk, April 13, 1892, Polk Papers.
42. Noblin, *Polk,* 226; Woodward, *Origins,* 243–44.
43. Frank Tracy, "Menacing Socialism in the Western States," *Forum,* XV (May 1893), 332.

CHAPTER X

1. *Arena,* XXV (Dec. 1891), 95–96.
2. Sterling Stuckey, in the *New York Times,* Feb. 13, 1971.
3. Dallas *Mercury,* Oct. 22, 1886; *National Economist,* Jan. 25, 1890; Robert M. Humphrey, "History of the Colored Farmers National Alliance and Cooperative Union," in Dunning (ed.), *Farmers Alliance History and Agricultural Digest,* 288–[89].
4. *National Economist,* Sept. 7, Dec. 14, 1889; Dec. 17, 1890. Humphrey's claims were wildly inflated. The figure of 1,200,000 included 55,000 in North Carolina and 50,000 in Virginia, but six months earlier the superintendent for those states had reported memberships of 15,000 and 8000 respectively (Robert McMath, "The Farmers Alliance in the South: The Career of An Agrarian Institution" Unpublished Ph.D. dissertation, University of North Carolina, 1972, 249).

  The figure of 250,000 would seem to be a fair rough estimate of the size of the Colored National Alliance. Even this number is impressive, given the impediments to recruiting then existing. The organizing problem of the Colored National Alliance was crushingly simple: because of American white supremacy, black farmers were not permitted to "see themselves" experimenting in democratic forms. See pp. 542–44.
5. Jack Abramowitz, "The Negro in the Agrarian Revolt," *Agricultural History,* XXIV (April 1950), 94; Herbert Aptheker, *A Documentary History of the Negro People in the United States,* II, 808; Helen M. Blackburn, "The Populist Party in the South, 1890–1898" (Unpublished M.A. thesis, Howard University, 1941), 38; LaGodna, "Kansas and the Ocala Convention," 70; James Lawson Reddick, "The Negro and the Populist Movement in Georgia" (Unpublished M.A. thesis, University of Georgia, 1937), 35; William Alexander Mabry, *The Negro in North Carolina Politics since Reconstruction* (Durham, 1940), 28; *Southern Mercury,* Oct. 23, 1888; *National Economist,* Nov. 1, Dec. 20, 1890; March 7, 21, April 11, 1891.
6. William Chafe, "The Negro and Populism: A Kansas Case Study," *Journal of Southern History,* XXXIV (Aug. 1968), 404.
7. Quoted in Rogers, *One-Gallused Rebellion,* 143.
8. Mabry, *Negro in North Carolina Politics;* Sheldon, *Populism in the Old Dominion,* 36; William Warren Rogers, "The Negro Alliance in Alabama," *Journal of Negro History* (Jan. 1960), 38–44; George B. Tindall, *South Carolina Negroes, 1877–1900* (Columbia, S.C., 1952), 118. Lawrence D. Rice, *The Negro in Texas* (Baton Rouge, 1971), 72.
9. News reports on the activities of the Colored Farmers National Alliance occasionally surfaced in the metropolitcan press of the South. See, for example, the Atlantic *Constitution,* Sept. 11, 1889; Sept. 7, 1891; Mobile *Daily Register,* Sept. 12, 1891; New Orleans *Picayune,* Sept. 13, 29, 1891. See Martin Dann, "Black Populism: A Study of the Colored Farmers Alliance Through 1891," *Journal of Negro History* (Oct. 1972).
10. Rogers, "The Negro Alliance in Alabama," 40; Aptheker, *Negro People,* II, 808;

National Economist, Oct. 5, 1889, Dec. 20, 1890; March 7, 1891; April 11, 1891; Saloutos, *Farmer Movements,* 79.

11. Winkler, *Platforms of Political Parties,* 275; Dallas *News,* July 5, 1889; Allen, *Great Southwest Strike,* passim.

12. The following account is taken from detailed stories in the Dallas *News,* Aug. 18, 19, 1891, and the Fort Worth *Gazette,* Aug. 18–20, 1891.

13. William Holmes, "The Arkansas Cotton Pickers Strike of 1891 and the Demise of the Colored Farmers Alliance," *Arkansas Historical Quarterly* XXXII (Summer 1973), 107–19; *Progressive Farmer* (Raleigh, Sept. 19, 1891; *National Economist,* Sept. 26, 1891.

14. Holmes, "Cotton Pickers Strike," 107–19. Blacks in South Carolina may have also walked out of the fields briefly (Tindall, *South Carolina Negroes,* 118–19).

15. Holmes, "Cotton Pickers Strike," 107–19. For a chilling account of the murder of Colored Farmers Alliancemen in one Mississippi county, see William Holmes, "The Leflore County Massacre and the Demise of the Colored Farmers' Alliance," *Phylon* (Sept. 1973), 267–74.

16. At Ocala, all but one of the delegates from the Colored Alliance endorsed the call for the formation of a third party. The dissenter, E. S. Richardson of Georgia, was closely allied with the anti-third party president of the white Alliance in Georgia, Lon Livingston. Humphrey and Richardson clashed at St. Louis in 1892 over the third party issue. The meaning of this latter event, in terms of Humphrey's "white supremacy" has been variously interpreted by historians, but its political meaning in terms of radical politics is not hard to fathom. See Charles Crowe, "Tom Watson, Populists and Blacks Reconsidered," *Journal of Negro History,* LX (April 1970), 117; Helen M. Blackburn, "The Populist Party in the South," 8–22; Atlanta *Constitution,* Feb. 23–26, 1892; Florida *Times-Union* (Jacksonville), Dec. 6, 1890, quoted in Cary, "Farmers Alliance in Florida," 101. The somewhat partisan (and errant) accounts in the Atlantia *Constitution* have played a role in the historiographical dispute. Richardson had earlier opposed the cotton pickers' strike.

17. Rogers, *One-Gallused Rebellion,* 313–14, 214.

18. Rogers, *One-Gallused Rebellion,* 219.

19. William Alexander Mabry, "Negro Suffrage and Fusion Rule in North Carolina," *North Carolina Historical Review,* XII (April 1935), 83; Noblin, *Polk,* 253; Francis Emeline Smith, "The Populist Movement and Its Influence in North Carolina," 78, passim; Helen Grey Edmonds, *The Negro and Fusion Politics in North Carolina* (Chapel Hill, 1951), 136; Donna Jean Paoli, "Marion Butler's View of the Negro, 1889–1901" (Unpublished M.A. thesis, University of North Carolina, 1969).

20. Woodward, *Watson,* 190–207, 320–29, and *Strange Career of Jim Crow,* 61; Robert Saunders, "Southern Populism and the Negro, 1893–1895," *Journal of Negro History,* LIV (July 1969), 240–61; Charles Crowe, "Tom Watson, Populists and Blacks Reconsidered," 99–116; Clarence Bacote, "The Negro in Georgia Politics, 1880–1908" (Unpublished Ph.D. dissertation, University of Chicago, 1958), 165–66, 199. See also Thomas E. Watson, "The Negro Question in the South," *Arena,* VI (Sept. 1892), 550.

21. For examples of pro-black comments in the *Southern Mercury,* see issues of Feb. 3, Nov. 14, 1889; June 30, Aug. 11, Oct. 13, 1892; July 19, 1894; June 11, July 23, Oct. 8, 1896. For anti-black comments, Oct. 13, Dec. 29, 1892; Oct. 19, 1893; Aug. 16, Dec. 6, 1894. For friendly "advice," Nov. 15, 1894. For the Texas third party at its worst, see "Cyclone" Davis in the Dallas *News,* July 31, 1892; at its best,

A. W. Warren on the "Force Bill" in the *Southern Mercury,* April 7, 1892, and Harry Tracy on political coalition with the Colored National Alliance, in the Kansas City *Times,* Dec. 5, 1890, quoted in Girard Thompson Bryant, "The Populist Movement and the Negro" (Unpublished M.A. thesis, University of Kansas, 1938), 30. See also Chap. XII.

22. Winkler, *Platforms of Political Parties,* 333. Two years later, the third party added to this language, "and each race shall have its own pro rata portion of the school fund" and "we further demand that where the law provides that scholastic trustees shall be appointed to take the census, that white trustees shall be appointed to take the census of white children and colored trustees shall be appointed to take the census of colored children (Winkler, 382–83, 399). The Democratic-controlled legislature of the state had passed a law banning blacks from becoming school trustees.

23. Thomas, *Arkansas and Its People,* 239; Francis C. Elkins, "The Agricultural Wheel in Arkansas," 190–91. Cf, the *Arkansas Gazette:* "A vote for either the Populists or Republicans is a vote for Negro supremacy and bayonet rule" (July 22, 1892).

24. Charles G. Summersell, "The Alabama Governor's Race in 1892," *The Alabama Review,* VIII (Jan. 1955), 12; Kirwan, *Revolt of the Rednecks,* 63–64; Ferguson, "Agrarianism in Mississippi," 464–65; Stine, "Ben Tillman and the Farmers Alliance," 23–24; and Richard Gergel, "Wade Hampton and the Myth of Moderation" (Unpublished seminar paper, Duke University, 1974), 5–47; *National Economist,* Aug. 27, 1891.

25. Sharp, "Farmers Alliance and People's Party in Tennessee," 105; J. Eugene Lewis, "Tennessee Gubernatorial Campaign and Election of 1892," *Tennessee Historical Quarterly,* VIII (June 1954), No. 2, 118–25.

26. The *Progressive Farmer* under L. L. Polk generally avoided racial commentary in an effort to keep matters focused on economic issues. Polk had definite white supremacist tendencies, though he generally kept them in check in the interests of the overall agrarian cause. For example, *Progressive Farmer,* Aug. 26, 1890, and Noblin, *Polk,* 92–93, 253. See also Edmonds, *Negro and Fusion Politics,* 136. Virginia Populists urged repeal of restrictive franchise legislation passed by Democrats, as did both Tennessee and Alabama Populists. The latter, under Reuben Kolb, became quite interested in an "honest ballot and a fair count" after the enormous vote frauds of 1892 and 1894 but his "Jeffersonians" were not as advanced on Negro rights as the straight Populist faction led by Joseph Manning. See Chap. XI and Saunders, "Southern Populists and the Negro," 124–25; Joseph Manning, *Fadeout of Populism* (New York, 1928), 133–46; *Southern Mercury,* July 26, 1894. Mississippi Populists, under Frank Burkitt, had faced an uphill fight from the time the Mississippi Alliance had attempted to articulate the politics of the sub-treasury during the tumultuous George-Barksdale contest in 1891, one year after black disfranchisement had come to the state (see Chap. IX). Burkitt had opposed black disfranchisement, and subsequently, as a Populist, advocated additional funds for black schools. J. Morgan Kousser, *The Shaping of Southern Politics: Suffrage Restriction and the Establishment of the One-Party South, 1880–1910* (New Haven, 1974), 139–45. See also Kirwan, *Revolt of the Rednecks,* 63–64; McCain, "Populist Party in Mississippi," 48; Johnson, "Agrarian Crusade in Mississippi," 24; Ferguson, "Agrarianism in Mississippi," 464–65.

For advocacy of Negro rights in Watson's *People's Party Paper,* see Dec. 2, 23, 1892; March 31, 1893; May 25, Sept. 21, Oct. 5, 26, 1894. But in 1895, Watson retreated. See *People's Party Paper,* March 29, April 12, 1895, quoted in Saunders, "Southern Populists and the Negro," 240–61.

It is perhaps helpful to set a firm limit on these breaches of tradition. I have found no politician, in the People's Party or in the two major parties, who advocated "social equality" in the 1890s.

The wavering Populist stance should be compared to that of Democratic "moderates" such as William J. Northen of Georgia, who advocated "control" and "management" of black labor in language that went a bit beyond the limits of paternalism: "requirements (of labor) should be adhered to and strictly enforced . . . If our labor were not so restive under restraint, so lacking in judgement, idle, wasteful and destructive, more might be trusted to their control and management" (quoted in McMath, "Farmers Alliance in the South," 253). On another occasion, Northen said, in language that completely skirted the realities of the crop lien system, "We have not diversified our crops because the Negro has not been willing to diversify . . . Because he is unwilling to handle heavy plows, we have permitted him to scratch the land with his scooter just deep enough for all the soil to be washed to the surface" (quoted in Rupert B. Vance, *Human Geography of the South*, Chapel Hill, 1932, 192).

27. Martin, *People's Party in Texas*, 133; Woodward, *Watson*, 206–7; Rogers, *One-Gallused Rebellion*, 144.

28. *Southern Mercury*, July 19, 1894; Mabry, *Negro in North Carolina Politics*, 28.

29. *Southern Mercury*, June 13, 1895; Martin, *People's Party in Texas*, 126–27.

30. John B. Rayner to Col. Edward House, April 14, 1914, John B. Rayner Papers (University of Texas); Clippings in the Rayner papers.

31. Private interviews with Mrs. Susie Roligan, Calvert, Tex., May 20, 1967 and with Ahmed Rayner, Austin, Tex., July 1, 1971. Mrs. Roligan is the daughter and Mr. Rayner the grandson of John B. Rayner. The quotation is from an undated note in the Rayner Papers.

32. Northern black newspapers, overwhelmingly Republican, almost without exception opposed the third party movement from the outset. See, for example, *The Freeman* (Indianapolis), March 12, June 25, July 9, July 16, 1892. For the third party's stance on the race issue in Kansas, see William Chafe, "Populism and the Negro in Kansas" (Unpublished M.A. thesis, Columbia University, 1967).

33. Kousser, *The Shaping of Southern Politics* is an authoritative study of the entire process of disfranchisement. See also Frederick C. Douglass, "Lynch Law in the South," *North American Review*, CLV (July 1892), 21–24.

34. John McMatthews, "Studies in Race Relations," 189–91. See also Leo Alilunas, "Statutory Means of Impeding Emigration of the Negro," *Journal of Negro History*, XXII (1937), 148–62; Oscar Zeichnar, "The Legal Status of the Agricultural Laborer in the South," *Political Science Quarterly*, LV (1940), 412–28; Pete Daniel, *Shadow of Slavery: Peonage in the South, 1901–1969* (Lexington, Ky., 1973).

35. William F. Holmes, "Whitecapping: Agrarian Violence in Mississippi, 1902–1906," *Journal of Southern History*, XXXV (1969), 165–85.

CHAPTER XI

1. Ray Ginger, *The Bending Cross: A Biography of Eugene Debs* (New Brunswick, N.J., 1949), 64–84.

2. Foner, *History of the Labor Movement in the United States*, II, 154, 166–67, 323; Gerald N. Grob, *Workers and Utopia* (Evanston, Ill., 1916), 93–97, 167; Nathan Fine, *Labor and Farmer Parties in the United States, 1828–1928* (New York, 1961), 36–44; Ware, *The Labor Movement in the United States*, 364–67. Daniel De Leon of the Socialist Labor Party dissented from the left and formally barred members

from entering Populist coalitions. So many did anyway that by 1894, De Leon's executive committee suspended party sections flaunting the rule. David Herreshoff, *American Disciples of Marx* (Detroit, 1967), 117–20.

3. *The New Nation*, March 5, 1892, July 9, 1892, quoted in J. Martin Klotsche, "The 'United Front' Populists," *Wisconsin Magazine of History*, XX (June 1937), 377. Nationalism "lost its identity" in the People's Party (Destler, *American Radicalism*, 14.)

4. In the light of the furious struggles that were to come in 1895–96 over the actions of Taubeneck and the national executive committee, the lack of comment about Taubeneck's rise to party leadership in the Populist press in 1892 is indicative of widespread third party preoccupation, above all other considerations, with the sudden immediacy of the "coming great contest." Alliance radicals clearly had not pondered the perils of maintaining an effective reform posture within the party of reform itself.

5. The official name of the organization was "National Citizen's Industrial Alliance." National Citizens Industrial Alliance, *Proceedings of the National Assembly* (Topeka, Kan., Jan. 13–17, 1891). For a brief time two "Citizens Alliances" appeared, both led by Kansas third party men.

6. Once the third party had been formally created in 1892—and the rank and file of the Alliance had been fully, partially, or marginally conveyed to the new institution—the practical organizational value of the sub-treasury plan sharply diminished. To voters who understood it, the sub-treasury was liberating: it helped them to overcome inherited party loyalties and become workaday Populists; but to those who did not understand, Macune's scheme was much "too radical." To the millions of non-Alliance members that the People's Party wished to recruit after 1892, the sub-treasury could only have continuing recruiting value if it could survive the barrage of cultural attacks from the goldbug metropolitan press to which it was fated to be subjected. As matters developed, these assaults were sufficiently effective in shaping American public opinion that by 1895 a number of Populists concluded that while greenback doctrines—grounded as they were in a democratic conception of money and commerce—continued to be organic to the idea of economic fairness, they nevertheless could no longer effectively be advocated through specific examples drawn from the sub-treasury system. The simple political reality was that the power of the corporate culture had overwhelmed the credibility of a new, effective, but deeply threatening, idea.

7. *Farmers Alliance* (Lincoln), Jan. 14, 21, 28, 1892. The Nebraskans had gathered 200 lecturers for a meeting the preceding August but the Secretary's report contained not a single reference to the cooperative movement. The exodus of the curious, and the needy, did not stop. *Annual Report of State Secretary*, 1891 (Nebraska Farmers Alliance Papers).

8. Barnhart, "Nebraska," 325–26; Merrill, *Bourbon Democracy in the Middle West*, 222–25; Paolo E. Coletta, "William Jennings Bryan's Second Congressional Campaign," *Nebraska History*, XXXX (Dec. 1959), 275–91. Some inferences have been drawn that were not explicit in these sources.

9. Clanton, *Kansas Populism*, 112, 116–23. See also Dawn Daniels, "Lorenzo D. Lewelling, a leader of the Kansas Populists" (Unpublished M.A. thesis, Northwestern University, 1931), and Dew, "Kansas Fusion Movements."

10. Harrington, "Populist Party in Kansas," 421–25; Clanton, *Kansas, Populism*, 128.

11. Herbert S. Schell, "History of the Farmers Alliance and the People's Party," in *History of South Dakota* (Lincoln, Nebr., 1961), 223–32; Hendrickson, "Populist Movement in South Dakota," 87–88; Brudvig, "Farmers Alliance and Populist Movement in North Dakota," 172–66.

12. Leon W. Fuller, "Colorado's Revolt Against Capitalism," *Mississippi Valley Historical Review* (Dec. 1934), 343–60; Leonard Peter Fox, "Origins and Early Development of Populism in Colorado" (unpublished Ph.D. dissertation, University of Pennsylvania, 1916), Chap. 6, pp. 11–35; Hicks, *Populist Revolt*, 298–99. James Edward Wright, *The Politics of Populism* (New Haven, 1974), 147: "The Populist movement in Colorado existed within the context of a consensual tripartisan demand for the free coinage of silver."

13. Mary Ellen Glass, *Silver and Politics in Nevada, 1892–1902* (Reno, 1969), 41–90; William J. Gaboury, "The Beginnings of the Populist Party in Idaho" (Unpublished M.A. thesis, University of Idaho, 1960), 30–60.

14. Louis L. Gould, *Wyoming, A Political History, 1868–1896* (New Haven, 1968), 137–92; see also Thomas Krueger, "Populism in Wyoming" (Unpublished M.A. thesis, University of Wyoming, 1960).

15. Thomas A. Clinch, *Urban Populism and Free Silver in Montana* (Helena, 1970), 41–64; James McClellan Hamilton, *From Wilderness to Statehood, 1805–1900* (Portland, 1957), 580–82.

16. Gordon B. Ridgeway, "Populism in Washington," *Pacific Northwest Quarterly*, XXXIX (Oct. 1948), 285–311; Carroll H. Woody, "Populism in Washington," *Washington Historical Quarterly*, XXI (1930), 103–19; Russell Blankenship, "The Political Thought of John R. Rogers," *Pacific Northwest Quarterly*, XXVII (Jan. 1946).

17. Walter Schumacher, "Thirty Years of the People's Rule in Oregon: An Analysis," *Political Science Quarterly*, XLVII (June 1932), 242; Thomas C. McClintock, "Seth Lewelling, William S. U'Ren and the Birth of the Oregon Progressive Movement," *Oregon Historical Quarterly*, XXXII (1940), 283–96; Marion Harrington, "The Populist Movement In Oregon, 1889–1896" (Unpublished M.A. thesis, University of Oregon, 1935), 29–42. R. Hal Williams, "Politics and Reform: The California Democrats in the Cleveland Years" (Unpublished Ph.D. dissertation, Yale, 1968), 207–12. The militance of Populism in California is visible in the papers of a moderate California party leader, Thomas Cator (University of California at Berkeley). It became more public in the Labor-Populist Alliance in San Francisco and in the national intra-party struggle in 1896.

18. Circular to "Loyal Alliances of Wisconsin," Farmers Alliance Papers (Wisconsin State Historical Society).

19. Ridge, *Donnelly*, 293–309; Warner, "Prelude to Populism," 141–45; Chrislock, "The Alliance Party," 302; and "The Politics of Protest in Minnesota," 114–15, 148–51.

20. For the third party's aborted crusade in this region, see Richard Henry Barton, "The Agrarian Revolt in Michigan 1865–1900" (Unpublished Ph.D. dissertation, Michigan State University, 1958); Nixon, "The Populist Movement in Iowa"; Gerald L. Prescott, "Yeomen, Entrepreneurs and Gentry: A Comparative Study of Three Wisconsin Agricultural Organizations, 1873–1893" (Unpublished Ph.D. dissertation, University of Wisconsin, 1968); Stewart, "Populist Movement in Indiana"; Max L. Shipley, "The Populist Party in Illinois" (Unpublished M.A. thesis, University of Illinois, 1927).

21. Rogers, *One-Gallused Rebellion*, 176, 189–91, 201–5.

22. Woodward, *Origins*, 262; Rogers, *Rebellion*, 221–26, 289; John B. Clark, *Populism in Alabama* (Auburn, 1927), 133–37.

23. Joseph C. Manning, *Politics of Alabama* (Birmingham, 1893), 19; Rogers, *Rebellion*, 268; Clark, *Populism in Alabama*, 140; Albert B. Moore, *A History of Alabama* (University of Alabama, 1934), 624.

24. Arnett, *Populist Movement in Georgia,* 143–44, 150–52.

25. Woodward, *Watson,* 205.

26. Woodward, *Waston,* 206–8; Arnett, *Georgia,* 153–55. The fraud surrounding the Watson-Black campaign of 1892 in Augusta is vividly portrayed by William B. Hamilton in "Political Control in a Southern City: Augusta, Georgia in the 1890's" (Senior Honors thesis, Harvard, 1972).

27. Dewey Grantham, "Georgia Politics and the Disfranchisement of the Negro," *Georgia Historical Quarterly,* XXXII (March 1948), 2; Arnett, *Georgia,* 154; Woodward, *Watson,* 203–9.

28. Richardson, *Texas,* 259–72; Cotner, *Hogg,* 215.

29. Martin, *People's Party in Texas,* 93–99; Lawrence D. Rice, *The Negro in Texas, 1874–1900,* 69–77.

30. Wayne Alvord, "T. L. Nugent, Texas Populist," *Southwestern Historical Quarterly,* LVIII (July 1953), 65–81; Dallas *News,* June 25, 1892, quoted in Woodward, *Origins,* 246.

31. Catherine Nugent, *Life Work of Thomas L. Nugent* (Stephenville, Tex., 1896), 167–69; Dallas *News,* July 22, 1893; Alvord, "Nugent," 66–67.

32. Martin, *People's Party in Texas,* 93–102; Cotner, *Hogg,* 315.

33. Martin, *People's Party in Texas,* 168–72; Cotner, *Hogg,* 396–398.

34. *Southern Mercury,* Sept. 16, 1894, March 2, 23, June 13, July 18, 1895; April 9, June 16, Oct. 15, 22, 1896; Martin, *People's Party in Texas,* 68, 74, 95, 126–32, 138, 171–72, 184–85; Galveston *News,* April 20, 1894, Aug. 6, 1896; Dallas *News,* June 22, 1894, Feb. 9, 1895; Cotner, *Hogg,* 392–406; Rice, *Negro in Texas,* 78–80.

35. Two generations later, Professor Martin interviewed over a score of prominent political leaders of the region and found "not one Populist" who failed to charge fraud in Harrison County "nor one Democrat" who was unwilling to admit it had taken place. Martin, *People's Party in Texas,* 183, n.; Dallas *News,* Jan. 7, 1895. See also Ranchino, "Davis," 87–88.

36. Martin, *People's Party in Texas,* 158.

37. Henry C. Dethloff, "The Alliance and the Lottery," *Louisiana History,* VI (Winter 1965); Lucia E. Daniel, "The Louisiana People's Party," *Louisiana Historical Quarterly,* XXVI (1943), 1055–1149; Hair, *Bourbonism and Agrarian Protest,* 142–69, 204–5, 212. All students of race relations in late nineteenth-century America are indebted to Professor Hair for his fine monograph on Gilded Age Louisiana.

38. Hair, *Bourbonism and Agrarian Protest,* 217, 246–61.

39. Hair, *Bourbonism and Agrarian Protest,* 260–62.

40. Hair, *Bourbonism and Agrarian Protest,* 237, 264–67, 279.

41. Charleston *Weekly News and Courier,* June 17, 1891.

42. Columbia *Daily Register,* July 25, 1891; Benjamin Tillman to J. B. Morrison, July 31, 1891; Tillman to Charles Crosland, Aug. 26, 1891, "Notes on Tillman Manuscripts," Frances Butler Simkins Papers (University of North Carolina).

43. Tillman to John L. M. Irley, April 19, 1892, Simkins Papers; *The State* (Columbia), May 19, June 30, 1892. A careful analysis of the Tillman-Alliance confrontation in South Carolina is contained in Harold E. Stine, "The Agrarian Revolt in South Carolina: Ben Tillman and the Farmers Alliance" (Senior Honors thesis, Duke University, 1974). Another view is available in Francis B. Simkins, *Pitchfork Ben Tillman, South Carolinian* (Baton Rouge, 1944) and, by the same author, *The Tillman Movement in South Carolina* (Durham, 1926). See also Church, "The Farmers Alliance in South Carolina," 51–57.

44. Joseph A. Sharp, "The Farmers Alliance and the People's Party in Tennessee,"

The East Tennessee Society's *Publications,* X (1938), 91–113; Robison, *Bob Taylor and the Agrarian Revolt in Tennessee,* 147, 166, 176–77; Lloyd Walter Cory, "The Florida Farmers Alliance, 1887–1892" (Unpublished M.S. thesis, Florida State University, 1963), 78–104; Knauss, "Farmers Alliance in Florida," 300–315.

45. Woodward, *Origins,* 88–105; Sheldon, *Populism in the Old Dominion,* 53; Charles E. Wynes, *Race Relations in Virginia, 1870–1902* (Charlottesville, 1961), 17, 38, 48.

For examples of limitations in the lecturing system and the cooperative movement of the Virginia Alliance, see J. H. C. Beverley to C. H. Pierson, Oct. 20, 1890; A. R. Venable to Pierson, Nov. 4, 22, 1890; J. H. C. Beverley to Pierson, Nov. 4, 1890; J. J. Silvey to Pierson, June 27, 1891; William Deering and Co. to Pierson, Nov. 29, 1890. Pierson Papers (University of Virginia).

On the lack of understanding of the sub-treasury, see J. W. Porter to Pierson, Sept. 15, 1890; Robert Beverley, Jr., to Pierson, Nov. 14, 1890; J. Thompson Brown to Pierson, Dec. 23, 1890.

For bloody shirt attacks on Virginia Populists, see John Hammond Moore, "The Life of James Gaven Field, Virginia Populist" (unpublished M.A. thesis, University of Virginia, 1953), 175–85, 196–202; Allen W. Moger, *Virginia, Bourbonism to Byrd, 1870–1925* (Charlottesville, 1968), 108.

For Democratic vote frauds, see Sheldon, 90–92; Moore, 204–5; Woodward, 261.

46. Paisley, "Political Wheelers," 3–21. Thomas, *Arkansas,* 202–52.

47. Noblin, *Polk,* 278–81; Elias Carr to L. L. Polk, March 28, 1892; L. L. Polk to J. W. Denmark, Feb. 8, 1892, May 10, 29, 1892; J. H. Gilbreath to Polk, April 6, 1892, Polk Papers; H. Larry Ingle, "A Southern Democrat at Large: William Hodge Kitchin and the Populist Party," *North Carolina Historical Review,* XL (April 1968), 185–90. See also Adolph J. Honeycutt, "The Farmers Alliance in North Carolina" (Unpublished M.A. thesis, North Carolina State College of Agriculture and Engineering, 1925); John Hicks, "Farmers Alliance in North Carolina," 162–87.

48. Edmonds, *The Negro and Fusion Politics in North Carolina;* William A. Mabry, *Negro in North Carolina Politics since Reconstruction,* Historical Papers, Trinity College Historical Society, Ser. XXIII (Durham, 1940), 34–36; Steelman, "Progressive Era in North Carolina," 32–33, 36, 126–36.

49. Hicks, *Populist Revolt,* 272–73.

50. Memphis *Appeal-Avalanche,* Nov. 14–16, 1892.

51. *The Texas Independent* (Bowie), Aug. 12, 1891.

52. Dallas *News,* Aug. 17–18, 1891.

CHAPTER XII

1. By any reasonably prudent historical standard, the specific characterizations of "Populist language" in this chapter are unprovable. Obviously, Populists and their opponents wrote millions of words in the 1890s; any attempt to bring either cultural meaning or thematic order to such a limitless cornucopia must inherently require a highly selective process. The wildly divergent interpretations of Hofstadter and Pollack illustrate the point well enough. I have attempted to be representative in the following ways: the various parts of the Populist constituency are represented—the campaigning politician of reform, certainly, but also the admonishing reform press, the Alliancemen who built the movement, and the farmers and other "plain people" who gave it electoral meaning. Within these

various sections, relative impact is considered: such journals as *The Advocate,* the *Southern Mercury, American Nonconformist* and *Progressive Farmer* are quoted because they had an editorial presence for longer periods of time and had more to do with defining and reflecting the specific shape of Populism than such sudden literary happenings, created by outsiders, as *Poverty and Progress,* by Henry George, *Looking Backwards,* by Edward Bellamy, or *Coin's Financial School* by W. H. Harvey (the last-named tract being treated in Chap. XIV for what it was—a propaganda document paid for by silver mineowners); among third party politicians, Donnelly, Watson, Lewelling, Peffer, Butler, and Davis are quoted because they were both representative and influential. Yet, the "representativeness" of a given spokesman's words must be weighed in the context both of what he said and his credentials to say it. Thus, Ignatius Donnelly's ideas in the Omaha preamble were clearly more "representative" than his beliefs about the task of an agrarian organizer—another way of saying, merely, that Donnelly proves a better guide to the popular expression of the agrarian revolt than he does to its underlying organizational dynamics. For the same reasons, Populist monetary ideas are presented in the words of the party's leading theorist, Harry Tracy, as well as in the language of its editors and politicians. Finally, an effort has been made to place quotations in some sort of fathomable political context so that the circumstances under which words were uttered are included with the words themselves.

2. Paolo E. Coletta, "Greenbackers, Goldbugs and Silverites," in H. Wayne Morgan (ed.), *The Gilded Age: A Reappraisal* (Syracuse, 1963), 118; Cuthbert Vincent, "Bimetallic Parity under a Gold Standard," *Arena,* VIII (1893), 156.

3. Henry Vincent, *The Story of the Commonweal* (Chicago, 1894).

4. The observation about Grover Cleveland is drawn from H. Wayne Morgan, *From Hayes to McKinley* (New York, 1969), 275.

5. The point here is that these Populist views were generic. A sampling, almost literally selected at random:

On the "subsidization" of the press: Milford Howard, *The American Plutocracy* (New York, 1895), 24–25; *Gadsden* (Alabama) *Leader:* "The [Montgomery] *Advertiser* is owned body, soul and breechers by the monopolists," quoted in Rogers, *One-Gallused Rebellion,* 268–69.

On the decline of democracy: "Speech of Governor Lewelling," July 26, 1894 (Kansas State Historical Society); Michael J. Brodhead, *Persevering Populist: The Life of Frank Doster* (Reno, 1968), 88; James B. Weaver, *A Call to Action* (Des Moines, 1892), 27–48; Donnelly's preamble to the Omaha Platform. This view of the corruption of the democratic process was scarcely limited to Populists. A staunch and at times vindictive opponent of the third party, Frank Tracy, described as an "ultra-conservative Nebraska newspaperman," condemned the "bold and unblushing participation of the railways in politics." He added: "At every political convention, their emissaries are present with blandishments and passes and other practical arguments to secure the nomination of their friends. The sessions of these legislatures are disgusting scenes of bribery and debauchery" (Frank Tracy, "Rise and Doom of the Populist Party," *Forum, 16,* Oct. 1893, 242). The characterization of Tracy is by Barnhart, "Alliance in Nebraska," 483.

6. The Watson Papers at the University of North Carolina are primarily business papers, reflecting the strained fiscal condition of the *People's Party Paper.* The story of the travail of the *Southern Alliance* is taken from Rogers, *One-Gallused Rebellion,* 258–59.

7. Woodward, *Origins,* 194, 247–48; Martin, *People's Party in Texas,* 200; Rogers *One-*

Gallused Rebellion, 263–66. The figures on the reform press, by state, are, at best, a compilation of various informed estimates.

8. Lutzky, "Reform Editors and Their Press," 118.

9. Lutzky, "Reform Editors," 201.

10. As a continuing source of greenback commentary on the monetary question, the *National Economist* was unsurpassed in reform ranks up to the time it ceased publication in 1893. Greenback doctrines were thereafter carried forward in the Populist years by Stephen McLallin's *Advocate* and Julius Wayland's *Appeal to Reason* in Kansas, Henty Vincent's *American Nonconformist* and Chicago *Searchlight*, Tom Watson's *People's Party Paper* in Georgia, Ignatius Donnelly's *The Representative* in Minnesota, S. F. Norton's *Chicago Express*, Thomas Gaines's *Texas Advance*, Henry Louck's Dakota *Ruralist*, Harry Tracy's *Southern Mercury*, George Gibson's *Wealth Makers* in Nebraska, W. Scott Morgan's *National Reformer* in Arkansas, and Thomas Byron's *Farmer's Tribune* in Iowa—to name all but one of the more influential third party journals. Curiously, although James Murdock of the *Progressive Farmer* in North Carolina possessed a rather sophisticated understanding of the changing industrial system, and its implications for the organization of society in the twentieth century, he mastered to a far lesser extent the subtleties of the monetary system. *Progressive Farmer* (Raleigh), May 18, 1891; March 20, 1892, quoted in Palmer, "The Rhetoric of Southern Populists: Metaphor and Imagery in the Language of Reform."

11. The triumph of the new creed of progress has had diverse interpretation, including Robert H. Wiebe, *The Search for Order* (New York, 1967); Ray Ginger, *The Age of Excess* (New York, 1965); Hofstadter, *The Age of Reform;* Paul Gaston, *The New South Creed* (New York, 1970); Sidney Fine, *Laissez-faire and the General-Welfare State* (Ann Arbor, 1956).

12. Halvor Harris to Ignatius Donnelly, Jan. 29, 1891, quoted in Norman Pollack, *The Populist Mind* (New York, 1967), 33–34.

13. T. W. Foster to editor, *Southern Mercury*, April 19, 1894; Mrs. Susan Orcutt to Gov. L. D. Lewelling, June 29, 1894, quoted in Gilbert C. Fite, *The Farmers' Frontier, 1865–1900* (New York, 1966), 129.

14. Quoted in Rogers, *One-Gallused Rebellion*, 137; Otken, *Ills of the South*, 21–22; Fite, *The Farmers' Frontier*, 131.

15. Thomas Gaines, editor, *Pioneer Exponent* (Comanche, Tex.) to editor, *Town and Country* (Comanche, Tex.), July 1886; W. T. McCullock to Ignatius Donnelly (1892), quoted in Pollock, *Populist Mind*, 35.

16. Quoted in Barnhart "Farmers Alliance and People's Party in Nebraska," 226–27.

17. Cotner, *Hogg*, 431.

18. Biography of E. L. Godkin by Rolo Ogden in the *Dictionary of American Biography*, VII (New York, 1931) 347–50; *The Nation*, Feb. 5, 1891; Feb. 23, 1893; July 1892. I am indebted to Professor William Russ for his perceptive article, "Godkin Looks at Western Agrarianism: A Case Study," *Agricultural History*, XIX (1945), 233–42. Professor Russ characterizes Godkin's response to farm unrest as one of "superficial satire and ridicule."

19. *The Nation*, May 16, 1889; March 6, 13, 20, April 3, July 31, Nov. 6, 20, 1890; Jan. 15, May 28, Nov. 26, 1891; Oct. 27, 1892, Jan. 19, Feb. 23, March 16, May 4, Dec. 21, 1893 (quoted in Russ, *Godkin*, 233–42).

20. *Public Opinion* (May 31, Dec. 31, 1890), 168; Arnett, *Populism in Georgia*, 97.

21. Moore, "Field," 158, 173; William V. Allen, "Western Feeling toward the East," *North American Review* (May 1896), 588–96.

22. Dallas *Herald*, Aug. 22, 1891; Arnett, *Populism in Georgia*, 150–52; Woodward, *Origins*, 259–60; Brudvig, "Farmers Alliance and People's Party in North Dakota," 162.
23. Harry Tracy, "The Sub-Treasury System," in James H. Davis, *A Political Revelation* (Dallas, 1894), 351.
24. Ibid., 359.
25. Ibid., 372–73.
26. William A. Peffer, *The Farmer's Side* (New York, 1891), 71–72.
      A further sampling of greenback doctrines: N. A. Dunning, *The Philosophy of Price and Its Relation to Domestic Currency*, 2nd ed. (Washington, D.C., 1890); Ignatius Donnelly, *The American People's Money*; C. C. Post, "The Sub-Treasury Plan," *Arena*, V (Feb. 1892), 342–53; J. M. Perdue in the *Southern Mercury*, March 27, 1890; Cuthbert Vincent, "Bimetallic Parity under a Gold Standard," *Arena*, VIII (1893), 156.
27. Clanton, *Kansas Populism*, 79. *Montrose Union*, Oct. 13, 1892, quoted in Kent V. Frank, "An Analysis of the Vote for the Populist Party in South Dakota in 1892" (Unpublished M.A. thesis, University of South Dakota, 1959), 28.
28. *The Advocate*, quoted in *Farmers Alliance* (Lincoln), Feb. 25, 1892; Clanton, *Kansas Populism*, 105.
29. *Texas Advance*, Sept. 16, 1893, quoted in Palmer, "The Rhetoric of Southern Populists: Metaphor and Imagery in the Language of Reform," 183–84; *Southern Mercury*, Sept. 19, 1895.
30. Palmer, "Rhetoric of Southern Populists," 374–75.
31. James H. Davis, *A Political Revelation* (Dallas, 1894), 244–51.
32. James L. Ranchino, "The Work and Thought of a Jeffersonian in the Populist Movement, James Harvey 'Cyclone' Davis" (Unpublished M.A. thesis, Texas Christian University, 1964), 8–10.
33. The Cincinnati *Enquirer* earned the dubious distinction of providing Mr. Davis with his sobriquet.
34. Ranchino, "Davis," 149–50. Another authority points out that Davis, despite his reputation as the third party's "high priest" of Jeffersonianism, "made the most thorough use among the Southern Populists of the commerce clause, the general welfare clause, and a loose construction of the Constitution to argue for the expanded role of government in society" (Palmer, "Rhetoric óf Southern Populists," 159).
35. The simplest way for Populists to frame their democratic but culturally embattled ideas in traditional language was through the use of religious imagery. This was rather easily done inasmuch as great swaths of the New Testament harmonized rather well with the values and objectives of the Omaha Platform. Metaphors that emphasized these relationships brought desperately needed cultural sanction to economic perspectives which, in the constricting public climate of the emerging corporate culture of the 1890s, were being characterized in the metropolitan press as "anarchistic."
      Some historians, by quoting religious metaphors and omitting the economic premise, have emphasized what they take to be Populist "religiosity." This fairly recent scholarly tendency, stimulated by Richard Hofstadter's *Age of Reform*, has produced some ludicrous and unfortunate results. One beguiled artisan has even taken an Alliance organizing pamphlet and managed to overlook virtually its entire contents except the author's use of religious symbols. (This feat was not easily accomplished since the organizing pamphlet, quite naturally, emphasized the co-

operative crusade as the centerpiece of the farmer's movement for self-help.) In the climate of the Gilded Age, the Populists were neither more nor less "godly" than their political opponents—though Populists frequently made interesting analyses of the political implications of class hierarchies within the nation's churches. Indeed, some Populist partisans focused so sharply on those of the nation's religious leaders who allied themselves with financial and industrial magnates that they stimulated rather more controversy than was politically advantageous for the third party cause. In North Carolina Cyrus Thompson, a prominent Populist, created a furor by attacking the Southern Protestant ministry for its "slavishness" to the money power. Similarly, Western Populists, led by a number of reform editors, periodically condemned the political orientation of clergymen serving affluent urban constituencies. But perhaps the most inclusive one-sentence broadside was delivered by Harry Tracy, the publisher of the *Southern Mercury:* "Preachers may preach and exhorters may rave, but just as long as the ministers of the gospel antagonize labor organizations, support the powers that have reduced American wealth-producers to slavery, prefer the smiles of the plutocrat to the prosperity and happiness of the race, refrain from denouncing tyranny in all its forms, and refuse to advocate from the pulpit justice to all and exclusive privileges to none, refusing to align themselves with the great reform sentiment now sweeping over the United States, and clinging to the cause of the rich tax-eaters, they will find their churches traveling further and further from the masses."

36. Marvin Meyers, *The Jacksonian Persuasion: Politics and Belief* (Stanford, 1957).
37. *Caucasian* (Raleigh), May 31, 1894; *Progressive Farmer,* Oct. 13, 1891; Lampasas *People's Journal,* Jan. 20, 1893, quoted in Palmer, "Rhetoric of Southern Populists," 211–12.
38. C. J. Buell, "The Money Question," *Arena,* VIII (1893), 193–94.
39. *People's Party Paper,* (Atlanta), April 24, 1893.
40. Michael J. Brodhead, *Persevering Populist: The Life of Frank Doster* (Reno, 1969), 91; Clanton, *Kansas Populism,* 67, 165; Pollack, *Populist Mind,* 14.
41. Robert David Ward and William Warren Rogers, *Labor Revolt in Alabama: The Great Strike of 1894* (Tuscaloosa, Ala., 1965), 122; Lorenzo D. Lewelling, July 26, 1894 (Kansas State Historical Society). The essential elements of this lengthy and meaty address are conveniently available in George Tindall (ed.), *A Populist Reader* (New York, 1966), 148–59, and in Pollack, *The Populist Mind,* 4–11.
42. Woodward, *Origins,* 234; Milford Howard, *The American Plutocracy* (New York, 1895), 24–25, 112.
43. C. S. White, *Alliance and Labor Songster,* 20; quoted in Hicks, *Populist Revolt,* 168–69.
44. National Farmers Alliance and Industrial Union, *Proceedings,* Ocala, Fla. (Dec. 2–8, 1890), 21.
45. William Allen White, *Autobiography* (New York, 1946), 218.

CHAPTER XIII

1. The precise strength of the third party movement in the South will never be known—not only because of massive terrorism, fraud, and doctored returns, but also, in the case of Georgia, because relevant records were destroyed. In appraising the strength of Georgia Populism, I have followed Woodward, *Origins,* and Arnett, *Populist Movement in Georgia.* In Nevada, although evidence was available as early as 1892, the narrowness of the base of the reform movement became con-

firmed in 1896 when the People's Party declined to fuse with the Silver Party. The Populists were decisively defeated. Glass, *Silver Politics in Nevada*, 114–16.

2. Richard Hofstadter, "William Jennings Bryan: The Democrat as Revivalist," in *The American Political Tradition* (New York, 1948), 186–205; Marian Silveus, "The Antecedents of the Campaign of 1896" (Unpublished Ph.D. dissertation, University of Wisconsin, 1932), 3.

3. Stanley L. Jones, *The Presidential Election of 1896* (Madison, 1964), 19–31; Silveus, "The Antecedents of the Campaign of 1896," 3–4. I have benefitted greatly from Professor Jones's detailed account of the campaign of 1896.

4. Washington *Evening Star*, June 26, July 22, Aug. 1, 1893; Nov. 19, 1894; March 6, 1895; Memphis *Commercial-Appeal*, May 15–17, 31, 1895; Omaha *World-Herald*, July 29, Aug. 1, 5, 12, 1894; Hofstadter, "William Jennings Bryan," in *American Political Tradition*, 196.

5. H. E. Taubeneck to Ignatius Donnelly, July 27, 1892; July 8, Dec. 18, 1893; Jan. 29, 1894, Donnelly Papers. When Populists protested to Taubeneck, they got arrogant and condescending replies (Taubeneck to W. Scott Morgan, Jan. 29, 1895, Davis Waite Papers, Colorado State Archives). See also *National Watchman*, Sept. 28, 1894; Jones, *Presidential Election of 1896*, 21–25; Ridge, *Donnelly*, 321, 328; Destler, *American Radicalism*, 227; W. M. Stewart to Donnelly, Nov. 7, 1895; W. J. Bryan to Donnelly, Nov. 13, 1895; Thomas V. Cator to Donnelly, Nov. 13, 1895; W. H. Harvey to Donnelly, Dec. 10, 1895; Edward R. Light to Donnelly, March 9, 23, 1896, Donnelly Papers.

The switch in the editorial policy of Dunning's *National Watchman* came in the autumn of 1894. Dunning's criticisms of the pro-silver maneuvers of Taubeneck, Weaver, Allen, and Bryan (June 15, 22, July 20, Aug. 3, 10, 1894) abruptly changed to denunciations of proponents of the Omaha Platform as "socialists and world savers!" (Nov. 30, Dec. 7, 1894; Jan. 11, 25, 1895). Though no contemporary observer caught Dunning red-handedly receiving support from the silver magnates, he scarcely concealed from his readers the identity of the beneficiaries of his reoriented solicitude: "Let us be conservative and consistent in order to secure the support of the business men, the professional men, and the well to do" (*National Watchman*, Feb. 22, 1895).

6. Albert Shaw, "William V. Allen: Populist," *Review of Reviews* (July 1894) 34–39. Allen's confusion about the dates of the Ocala meeting and of his own conversion to the third party movement surfaced in an 1894 interview when he attempted to backdate his third party credentials. Though he told the *Review of Reviews* he left the Republican Party "in the summer of 1890," a Nebrasks historian places that important decision for Allen in 1891. The later date corresponds to Allen's statement, made in the same interview, that he converted "after Ocala." (See Addison E. Sheldon, "Nebraskans I Have Known," *Nebraska History*, XIX (1938), 194.) Though Allen did not seem to remember, the latter event occurred in December 1890. The 1894 fusionist gubernatorial candidate, Silas Holcomb, has also been a convert to the third party in 1891. That such late arrivals to the cause of reform as Allen and Holcomb could assume a position of top leadership in the Nebraska movement reveals much about the aimlessness of the third party in the state.

The Allen papers at the Nebraska Hist. Soc., while brief, reveal the narrowness of his political perspective. See Allen to Mrs. Allen, July 7, 1894; Silas Holcomb to Allen, May 22, June 6, 1895; Charles F. Manderson to Allen, Jan. 20, May 8, 1896; and two Allen speeches: "Silver Coinage," Aug. 24, 1893 and "Financial Policy," Jan. 7, 1898. Allen did not abandon the metallists' "intrinsic value" premise until 1903.

7. Shaw, "William V. Allen," 34–39.

8. *Senate Journal of the Legislature of the State of Nebraska, 1893* (York, Neb. 1893), 38–49; Barnhart, "Alliance in Nebraska," 338–46. A measure of Allen's standing, even among the most traditional Nebraska conservatives, was provided by Frank Tracy, the nervous newspaper editor who had perceived the specter of socialism in the Populist demonstration at Omaha in 1892. A year later, Tracy was able to write of Allen: "He is a conservative, pure, incorruptible man, who won renown as an eminent attorney and a just, upright judge." Tracy, "Rise and Doom of the Populist Party," *Forum,* XVI (Oct. 1893), 246–48.

9. Barnhart, "Alliance in Nebraska," 343–46. Railroad rivalry seems to have played an important and perhaps decisive role in Allen's election by the Nebraska legislature. The major railroads of Nebraska, the Union Pacific and Burlington, each had willing servants in the leadership of both major parties, as well as in the metropolitan press. The Union Pacific functioned in the Republican Party through its general counsel and the GOP's most influential figure, John M. Thurston, the 1893 railroad candidate for the U.S. Senate. The Union Pacific's man in the Democratic Party was George Miller, the state's most prominent Democrat, aside from J. Sterling Morton. The spokesmen for the Burlington Railroad were Morton in the Democratic Party and Charles H. Gere, editor of the *Nebraska State Journal,* in the Republican Party. Gere was the most important Republican figure in Nebraska, aside from Thurston. When the five Gold Democrats proposed Morton as the compromise conservative candidate in 1893, they were, in effect, suggesting that a Burlington man take precedence over the Union Pacific's Thurston. The outnumbered Democratic conservatives were bluffing their Republican counterparts and when the latter, immobilized by an absence of unanimity among their railroad backers, hesitated, the Democrats made good the bluff and put Allen in the Senate. The Nebraska Senator thereafter had a justifiable concern about the strength of his reform base. This anxiety may perhaps explain his subsequent passion for moderation and fusion.

10. Omaha *Bee,* Feb. 8, 1893.

11. Barnhart, "Nebraska," 352–59. For a much more alarmed major party response to the 1894 Populist threat in Georgia, Alabama, South Dakota, Texas, and Minnesota, see Arnett, *Georgia,* 182–84; Rogers, *Rebellion,* 245; Hendrickson, "South Dakota," 231; Cotner, *Hogg,* 396–400; and Ridge, *Donnelly,* 336–38.

12. Omaha *World Herald,* July 29, Aug. 3, 5, 8, 11, 16, 1894; Paolo E. Coletta, "William Jennings Bryan's Second Congressional Campaign," *Nebraska History* (Dec. 1959), 288–89; Richard Hofstadter, "William Jennings Bryan: The Democrat as Revivalist," 190–96; For early fusion in Nebraska at the local level, see Lee A. Dew, "Populist Fusion Movements as an Instrument of Political Reform, 1890–1900" (Unpublished M.A. thesis, Kansas State Teachers College, 1957), 28.

13. Omaha *Bee,* Aug. 21, 23, 1894; Omaha *World Herald,* Nov. 5, 1894. The editor of the Omaha *Bee,* Edward Rosewater, told his party: "You have nominated a man for governor who has been branded as an accessory to forgery and perjury by a Republican congressional committee of which Hon. Thomas B. Reed was chairman, a man who stands self-convicted of falsifying official records and procuring the issue of a fraudulent voucher while in the capacity of president of the senate; a man who has consorted with boodlers and jobbers . . . a man who has been the pliant tool of the railroads, in and out of season." Barnhart, "Nebraska," 368–69, 375. See also Farmer, "Economic Background of Frontier Populism," 420.

14. *House Journal of the State of Nebraska, 1895* (Lincoln, 1895), 4–5, 9–11, 50–63.

Statewide fusion candidates trailed Republicans by an average of 8500 votes in five races. In three others where no fusion occurred and the People's Party fielded a "straight" candidate, the third party lost by slightly over 25,000 votes. In raw terms of victory or defeat, the lesson of 1894 was clear: since the third party had proved unable to add to its 32 to 35 per cent performance in the campaigns of 1892, 1893 and 1894, fusion with the Democratic Party had become organizationally tantamount to survival.

15. The correlating ideas of Populism as a synonym for fusion, and advocacy of the Omaha Platform as anomalous extremism, jointly constitute the conceptual basis of Hicks, *The Populist Revolt,* 254–63, 337, 347–372, 385, 395–97, 409. The reference to Livingston as "dubious and shifty" is taken from Woodward, *Watson* (2nd edition), 154.

The Greenback interpretation of the American monetary system, as integrated into the national agrarian movement through the cooperative crusade, is not seen as organic to the ideas and organization of the People's Party. (Hicks, 97–127, 153–79, 186–237). For fusionists as "the genuine Populist," see Hicks, 122, 316–19, 377–78, 402, passim. For Populist greenbackers as "intransigents," 357–58, passim.

Rather than being grounded in the cooperative movement, "the success of the Southern Alliance had always been regarded as due in no small part to the hold that secret work gave the national order over its members. Largely by virtue of this characteristic, the Southern Alliance could act with a unity that the Northern Alliance had never been able to achieve" (p. 120).

The following interpretations of Populism ensued from these perspectives: though the Northwestern Farmers Alliance is described as more radical than the National Farmers Alliance in the 1880s, proponents of the Omaha Platform developed by the latter are depicted as "a motley group" (122, 380–403, passim). When the author focuses upon the need for popular influence over the national banking system, however, these "intransigents" become "old-school Populists" (317, 413), "old-fashioned Populists" (318), and, on one occasion, "orthodox Populists" (345). While the role of the Kansas Alliance is rather consistently understated throughout, "strong Populist states" are taken to be Colorado, Kansas, Minnesota, Nebraska, and North Carolina (448). Actually, the strongest third party movements were in Kansas, Georgia, Texas, and Alabama. See Appendix C, "The Northwestern Farmers Alliance: Opponent of Populism."

Among scholars basing their analysis of Populism on definitions quarried from Hicks, undoubtedly the most influential has been Richard Hofstadter, *The Age of Reform* (New York, 1956), 19–20, 30–35, 62–63, 70–76, 81–85.

Though this subject is discussed at greater length in the Critical Essay on Authorities (602–3), one thought is offered in passing. To those who have managed to see "Bryanism" as the authentic expression of Populism, the reforming drive of silverites has loomed as a subject for serious discussion. Referring to the 1894 Nebraska Democratic platform, a Nebraska historian comments, "Should one eliminate from this platform the principles advocated by the Populists, there would be little left except the tariff plank" (Barnhart, "Farmers Alliance and People's Party in Nebraska," 364). However, should the criteria of Populists be applied to the same comparison, the following appraisal would be self-evident: deducting from the Populist platform every measure advocated by the Nebraska Democrats, "there would be little left" except the central doctrines of the agrarian revolt: the abolition of the national banking system, the substitution of legal tender notes issued by the United States Treasury, a flexible currency keyed to population expansion and industrial growth, regulation of land syndicates and interest rates, and government ownership of the railroads. The distinction is not small. While Hofstadter and Barnhart differ in their critical assessment of silverites, both discuss what they take to be "Populism." The analysis of neither scholar, however, derives from the animating doctrines of the People's Party.

In this connection, Stanley Parsons, in his recent study, *The Populist Context,* notes, without added comment, that Populist "boiler plate material" (of the kind provided by W. Scott Morgan of the ready-print service of the National Reform Press Association) was "considerably more radical than that encountered in locally edited editions" (pp. 66–67). This apparent anomaly, of course, cannot be further pursued in the context of fusionism as Populism.

Fusion in Nebraska, however, did have one consistent and vocal critic in the state capital. A populist newspaper in Lincoln defined Bryan in the following terms: "His hope is to draw the Populists away from their platform [and] the legislation we demand and need, to elect him as a Democrat . . . Mr. Bryan either lacks the disposition of heart, or the grasp of truth, to be a Populist . . . He has conceived the great idea of gathering the people of all parties about himself, his plan, his platform, his person." *Wealth Makers* (Lincoln), Aug. 9, 1894. However, William Allen, not this Lincoln editor, was the authentic voice of Populism, Nebraska style.

16. Charles G. Summersell, "A Life of Reuben F. Kolb" (Unpublished M.A. thesis, University of Alabama, 1930), 9–10, 32–33, 42, 56; Clark, *Populism in Alabama,* 74–75, 90; Rogers, *Rebellion,* 265. Kolb went to some length to reassure Alabama's "Big Mules" that "my election will work no harm to organized capital" (James F. Doster, "Were Populists Against Railroad Corporations?" *Journal of Southern History* (Aug. 1954), 397). The Kolbites even sent a contesting delegation to the 1892 Democratic National Convention (Clark, 132). Only after being rebuffed at this level did Kolb make the decision to support Weaver.

17. Jerrell H. Shofner and William Warren Rogers, "Joseph C. Manning: Militant Agrarian, Enduring Populist," *Alabama Historical Quarterly,* XXIX (Spring-Summer 1967), 21, 28–29; Allen J. Going, "Critical Months in Alabama Politics, 1895–1896," *Alabama Review* (Oct. 1952), 278.

18. In some places in Alabama, cotton apparently fell to four cents. A. B. Moore, *History of Alabama* (Chicago and New York, 1927), 730–31.

19. William Denson's attempted defection did not materialize. He was turned down by Seventh District Populists in favor of Milford Howard. Denson thereupon returned to Democratic ranks and ran against Howard. The latter prevailed by a margin of almost two to one. Daniel Alan Harris, "The Political Career of Milford W. Howard, Populist Congressman from Alabama" (Unpublished M.A. thesis, Alabama Polytechnic Institute, 1957), 36–56. Like the Civil War, the agrarian revolt not only split friends, but families. Philander Morgan, brother of the Democratic Senator, joined the People's Party in 1892 and became prominent in the Alabama third party movement.

For an earlier and considerably more hostile view of the agrarian movement by the Alabama Senator, see John T. Morgan, "The Danger of the Farmers' Alliance," *Forum,* XXI (Nov. 1891), 399–409.

20. Harris, "Howard," 56; Woodward, *Origins,* 277. "Conceded" may be the wrong word. The seating of Populist Albert T. Goodwyn in Congress came only after he had contested the official returns. *Contested Election Case of Albert T. Goodwyn vs. James E. Cobb* (Government Printing Office, Washington, D.C., 1895). The Demo-

cratic frauds were fairly transparent; the congressional vote to seat Goodwyn in the House of Representatives was not close. Louise G. Mustin, "Albert T. Goodwyn" (Unpublished M.A. thesis, University of Alabama, 1946), 60. A Democratic election judge in Lowndes County in Goodwyn's district publicly stated in 1896: "If it is necessary for Lowndes County to cast 4,995 votes against a candidate for governor who is an enemy to her honor, we will do so, if my pulse still beats." Since Goodwyn was the gubernatorial candidate referred to in 1896, the figure of 4,995 apparently represented an upward revision in the requirements of fraud, necessitated by the failure to defeat Goodwyn for Congress in 1894. The "official" Lowndes County vote in 1894 showed 3455 total votes—all but 189 of them Democratic. Going, "Critical Months in Alabama Politics," 279, Mustin, "Goodwyn," 58, and Rogers, *One-Gallused Rebellion*, 313.

The two Alabama Republicans elected in 1894 also had to file formal contests to gain their seats while Howard had to defend himself against a harassing Democratic contest to claim his office.

21. John Sparkman, "The Kolb-Oates Campaign of 1894" (Unpublished M.A. thesis, University of Alabama, 1924), 27–40. Under Alabama law, Kolb, as a candidate for a purely state office, had no tribunal to which to appeal his case. He was twice elected governor by his peers—the second time probably by anywhere from 25,000 to 50,000 votes. A close student of the agrarian revolt in Alabama believes the revolutionary tactics of the conservatives ultimately destroyed the morale of the third party in Alabama (Rogers, *One-Gallused Rebellion*, 316).

"Governor" Oates scarcely allowed himself to be outshone by his election judges (see n. 20, above) in public declarations defending the idea of vote-stealing. In the midst of his campaign against Kolb, Oates announced: "the man who counts a ballot as it is cast every time is no friend to his country" (Going, "Critical Months in Alabama Politics," 279). For other black belt "majorities" in 1894, see Shofner and Rogers, "Manning," 21.

22. From an era that preceded George Gallup, it is virtually impossible to reconstruct the preferences of large numbers of citizens on specific issues as complex as the currency question. Some clues are available through the campaign emphases of candidates seeking popular support. When Milford Howard discussed the monetary system in his 1894 Alabama campaign for Congress, he tended to speak first about free coinage of silver and then followed with greenback issues. Once elected, he reversed the order. Such indications are merely suggestive, of course. In any case, there is evidence from these and other criteria to conclude that Populism in 1894 remained radical in Georgia and Texas, a bit less so in Kansas and Alabama, still less so in North Carolina and Colorado, and not radical at all in Nebraska. See below.

23. Fusion in 1892 had been accomplished at some cost. John Otis, elected third party congressman in 1890, was "sacrificed in 1892 for the fusion nominee from the fourth district" (Clanton, *Kansas Populism*, 159). Such tactics naturally armed midroaders; indeed, the anti-fusion "People's Party League of Kansas," organized in 1894, had John Otis as its state president.

24. Argesinger, *Populism and Politics*, 162–91; Walter T. K. Nugent, "How the Populists Lost in 1894," *Kansas Historical Quarterly*, XXXI (Autumn 1965), 245–55; Dew, "Populist Fusion Movements as an Instrument of Reform," 42; Harrington, "Populist Party in Kansas," 434–35; Clanton, *Kansas Populism*, 168. The disingenuous and sometimes frantic efforts of Populist officeholders in Kansas to achieve some kind—any kind—of fusion with Democrats is thoroughly treated in Arges-

inger, *Populism and Politics*. For the climax of these efforts following the 1894 elections, see Argesinger, 201–32.

25. Marion Butler to Thomas Settle, March 1, 1893. Settle Papers, University of North Carolina.

26. Joseph F. Steelman, "Republican Party Strategists and the Issue of Fusion with Populists in North Carolina, 1893–1894," *North Carolina Historical Review* (July 1970), 244–69; Helen G. Edmonds, *The Negro and Fusion Politics in North Carolina, 1894–1901* (Chapel Hill, 1951), 15–48.

27. Marion Butler to Thomas Settle, Aug. 25, 1893, quoted in Steelman, "Republican Party Strategists and the Issue of Fusion with Populists in North Carolina," 257. The third party polled a smaller percentage of the vote in North Carolina than in seven other Southern states (Kousser, *Shaping of Southern Politics*, 184–86).

28. See Chaps. VIII and IX.

29. The Henry Vincent Papers in the Joseph Labadie Labor Collection at the University of Michigan have suffered unfortunate archival losses in recent years. Biographical material on Henry Vincent is contained in the *American Nonconformist and Kansas Industrial Liberator* (Winfield, Kan.), Oct. 20, 1886; April 5, Aug. 23, Dec. 20, 1888; *American Nonconformist* (Indianapolis), Aug. 20, Sept. 3, 1891; March 16, 1893; Kansas State Historical Society Library *Biographical Circular*, II, M-2. For the Coffeyville affair, see Henry Vincent, *The Plot Unfolding* (Winfield, 1890); *Proceedings of the Joint Committee of the Legislature of the State of Kansas . . . to Investigate the Explosion Which Occurred at Coffeyville, Kansas*, Oct. 18, 1888 (Topeka, 1891); and Denton, "The American Nonconformist and Kansas Industrial Liberator," 29–30, 55, 93. For the Chicago years, see the Chicago *Searchlight*, June 21, 1894; Henry Vincent, *The Story of the Commonweal* (Chicago, 1894): and Lutzky, "Reform Editors and Their Press," 36, 68, 122, 217–18, 290–91. For an insight into his post-Populist progressive politics, see Henry Vincent to Robert Schilling, May 17, 1922 (Schilling Papers).

The *Nonconformist* achieved a circulation of 20,000 in Kansas prior to removal to Indianapolis. In the fall of 1892, Vincent, generally a fairly judicious though somewhat uninterested businessman, accepted too many twenty-five-cent "campaign subscriptions" and burdened the *Nonconformist* with a press run of 100,000 that it could not afford. He sold the paper to a group of understanding Indiana Populists and agreed to stay on as editor, but the constraints of not having an absolutely free hand precipitated his departure. He made his Chicago debut as editor of S. F. Norton's Populist paper, the Chicago *Express*. Vincent's insistence on praising the Coxey movement led to a break with Norton, however, and he was soon using the free time thus acquired to write *The Story of the Commonweal* early in 1894. Proceeds from the book permitted him to launch the Chicago *Searchlight* and thus play a central role in the events described herein.

30. Chester McArthur Destler, *Henry Demarest Lloyd and the Empire of Reform* (Philadelphia, 1963), 15–120.

31. Ibid., 120–70.

32. H. D. Lloyd to Samuel Gompers, July 20, 1892, quoted in Foner, *Labor Movement*, II, 308–9; Stuart B. Kaufman, "Samuel Gompers and the Populist Movement" (Unpublished M.A. thesis, University of Florida, 1964), 4, 44, 50, 81. See also Samuel Gompers, "Organized Labor in the Campaign," *North American Review* (Aug. 1892), 93–95.

33. Henry Demarest Lloyd, *Wealth Against Commonwealth* (Chicago, 1894). The assessment of *Wealth Against Commonwealth* is contained in Harold U. Faulkner, *American*

Political and Social History (New York, 1948), 490. These events are treated in Destler, *Lloyd*, 179–314.

34. Destler, *American Radicalism*, Chap. VIII, "Consummation of a Labor-Populist Alliance in Illinois, 1894," 162–74; Chap.IX, "The Labor-Populist Alliance in Illinois in the Election of 1894," 175–211.

35. Destler, *American Radicalism*, 169–73; Max L. Shipley, "The Populist Party in Illinois" (Unpublished M.A. thesis, University of Illinois, 1927), 57–58. Every student of American Populism is indebted to Professor Destler for his creative and exhaustive research in reconstructing the inner dynamics of the agrarian-labor coalition of 1894–95 in Chicago.

   The fragility of the agrarian movement in Illinois was traceable not only to the Northwestern Alliance but also to the destruction of the political morale of reformers growing out of the bizarre "Palmer episode" in 1891. See 445–47. (Chap. XIV).

36. Destler, *American Radicalism*, 175–87; Foner, *Labor Movement*, II, 303–5; Willis J. Abbot, "The Chicago Populist Campaign," *Arena*, XI (Feb. 1895), 330–31; Chicago *Searchlight*, July 12, 19, 26; Aug. 2, 4, 9, 16, 30, 1894.

37. Foner, *Labor Movement*, II, 310, 323; Abbot, "The Chicago Populist Campaign," 330–36; Destler, *American Radicalism*, 187–92.

38. Destler, *American Radicalism*, 189, 195, 215.

39. In a Chicago speech on Oct. 10, 1894, Henry George attacked the People's Party, the Omaha Platform, and the Springfield Compact and was in turn castigated by Abbot in one of the last issues of the Chicago *Times* before it changed ownership. See also Destler, 200–202; "Mr. George and the People's Party," editorial in the Chicago *Times*, Oct. 12, 1894. Henry George remained a Democrat throughout the agrarian revolt.

40. Destler, *American Radicalism*, 205–11.

41. H. D. Lloyd to Benjamin Andrews, Feb. 19, 1895, quoted in Foner, *Labor Movement*, II, 326. For Vincent's post-election response, see Henry Vincent to H. D. Lloyd, Nov. 7, 28, Dec. 6, 1894; Jan. 8, 1895 (Lloyd Papers, University of Wisconsin).

42. B. O. Flower to Marion Butler, Dec. 14, 1894, Butler Papers.

43. Woodward, *Watson*, 241–45; *Southern Mercury*, June 6, 1895; Davis Waite to Donnelly, Dec. 11, 1894; George Washburn to Donnelly, Dec. 22, 1894, Donnelly Papers; Donnelly to Waite, Dec. 14, 1894, Waite Papers. For the reform press, see next chapter.

44. *Southern Mercury*, Nov. 29, Dec. 6, 20, 1894.

   As organizers of a new political institution seeking recruits from the old parties, People's Party strategists naturally looked for all practicable ways to induce major party regulars to join the cause of reform. As the Populist-Socialist alliance in Chicago indicated, fusion was not necessarily a prima facie indication of opportunism. In terms of the content of reform, the ethical meaning of any coalition move depended on the specific political basis upon which it was achieved. When Populists accepted the modified plank 10 of the socialists (relating to the mode of achieving the government ownership of the means of production), they were manifestly not engaged in "trimming" the Omaha Platform. For the same reason, Populist-Republican fusion could often be achieved in the South on the twin principles of the Omaha Platform and a protected franchise for black Americans. Indeed, if greenback monetary principles were kept intact, Populist-Republican fusion in the South carried racial implications that were heavy with long-term meaning.

But fusion on the basis of jettisoning the Omaha Platform in favor of free silver was quite another matter—whether advocated in the South or in the West, and whether to win Democratic or Republican support.

CHAPTER XIV

1. Perhaps nothing more dramatically illustrates the dangers of appraising a national movement through a narrow local focus than the conclusion about third party prospects drawn in 1895 by the American correspondent of Keir Hardie's London *Labour Leader*. Both Hardie and his American reporter were trade union socialists, and the latter's knowledge of the People's Party did not extend much beyond the world of Tommy Morgan and Henry Demarest Lloyd in Chicago. This somewhat limited view yielded the following appraisal of the fusionist vs. midroad struggle: "The People's Party is becoming Socialistic, and even the Socialists who have hitherto worked on the narrow, jealous lines of [De Leon's] Socialist Labour party are now coming to the People's Party. The effort to narrow down the People's Party to a mere Silver party has utterly failed. Only one People's party paper has declared for the so-called Silver Party. This means the People's party will win the Collectivist city vote and the farmer's currency vote. It means that the People's party ['s] 1,800,000 votes will soon increase to 3,000,000 and be cast for Socialism" (May 4, 1895, quoted in Destler, *American Radicalism*, 243).

   Some fourteen months later, at the 1896 Populist national convention, the socialist presence was restricted to less than twenty delegates out of 1300. This beleagured platoon represented a faction from Chicago that was seated only after a floor fight engineered by the dominant agrarian-based midroad wing of the party (see the following chapter).

2. Woodward, *Origins*, 277–85.
3. *Nebraska House Journal* . . . (1895), 50–56; Clanton, *Kansas Populism*, 287.
4. For the fusionist rationale, see H. E. Taubeneck to W. Scott Morgan, Jan. 29, 1895, Waite Papers; for the midroad appraisal, see Morgan to Davis Waite, Feb. 4, 1895, Waite Papers, and Morgan to Marion Butler, August 5, 1896, Butler papers. In the interest of clarity and economy, I have summarized in this passage the general and specific arguments of both fusionists and midroaders. As the subsequent narrative seeks to make clear, the arguments themselves, though advanced with all the passion common to a heated political controversy, paralleled the foregoing summary, essentially employing the same terminology. See below, this chapter, and Chaps. XV and XVI. See also Chap. XII, "The Language of Populism."
5. Quoted in Lutzky, "Reform Editors and Their Press," 224–25.
6. Penetration of the leadership of the People's Party by the silver lobby is most readily visible in the papers of Ignatius Donnelly, William Jennings Bryan, Marion Butler, Davis Waite, William Stewart, Thomas Cator, and Henry Demarest Lloyd, among others. For the pressure applied to Donnelly, see J. E. Taubeneck to Ignatius Donnelly, July 27, 1892; July 8, Dec. 18, 1893; Jan. 29, 1894; William Stewart to Donnelly, Nov. 7, 1895; William Jennings Bryan to Donnelly, Nov. 13, 1895; Thomas V. Cator to Donnelly, Nov. 13, 1895; William H. Harvey to Donnelly, Dec. 10, 1895; M. C. Rankin to Donnelly, Dec. 16, 1895; Edward R. Light to Donnelly, March 9, 23, 1896, Donnelly Papers. See also Jones, *Presidential Election of 1896*, 21–25; Argesinger, *Populism and Politics*, 192–232; Ridge, *Donnelly*,

321, 328; Destler, *American Radicalism*, 227; *National Watchman*, Sept. 28, Nov. 30, 1894; Jan. 11, 25, Feb. 15, 22, 1895.

7. Woodward, *Origins*, 279–81; Jones, *Presidential Election of 1896*, 49, 61–73; Silveus, "Antecedents of the Campaign of 1896," 4–28; Memphis *Commercial-Appeal*, June 11–17, 1895. The coverage of the *Commercial-Appeal* may be described as both reverent and parliamentarily correct; the paper quite literally printed everything from the opening prayer to the motion to adjourn.

8. Memphis *Commercial-Appeal*, June 14, 1895.

9. E. O. Davis to L. H. Weller, June 16, 1888, Weller Papers. For a similar judgment, based on Weaver's conduct in the Populist years, see George F. Washburn to Ignatius Donnelly, Dec. 22, 1894, Donnelly Papers.

10. Chicago *Tribune*, Aug. 1–4, 1893; Jones, *Presidential Elections of 1896*, 24–25; Ridge, *Donnelly*, 323; William Jennings Bryan, *The First Battle* (Chicago, 1896), 153.

It seems fair to conclude that during his tenure as Populist national chairman, Taubeneck (1) received consulting fees from the most important organization for silver lobbying, the American Bimetallic League and (2) acted in a manner consistent with his own rather narrow and simplistic beliefs, i.e., did not "sell out," as midroaders sometimes charged. However, it is also necessary to add that such close and repeated associations have the effect of circumscribing the options of a political leader, especially a chairman of a national party, in ways that easily produce a distorted view of political reality. There is hardly any other explanation—short of imputing to Taubeneck a massive cynicism—for his strangely narrow belief that he could publicly characterize the planks of the Omaha Platform as "wild theories" without encountering a storm of protest from the party's faithful. Silver lobbyists, of course, thought the Omaha Platform was counter-productive to their cause and rightly so; for Taubeneck to reflect their perspective so closely, however, says much about the isolated political world in which he chose to live while serving as party chairman. His ultimate disarray after being outmaneuvered by the silver forces in 1896 tended to confirm his personal sincerity, while of course, also confirming his political innocence. At the end, he was a badly compromised politician. See below and the chapter following.

James Baird Weaver's conduct is more difficult to explain in terms other than narrow self-interest, in view of his oft-stated greenback beliefs. His association with Gen. A. J. Warner, the nation's chief silver lobbyist, was an intimate one: Weaver, too, received money for speeches made in behalf of the silver cause. (Nixon, "Populist Movement in Iowa," 71; Davis Waite to Ignatius Donnelly, July 10, 1895).

In contrast, the fusionist policies of Nebraska Senator William Allen and North Carolina Senator Marion Butler were consistent with their own earlier actions and with their limited understanding of the sources and purposes of the reform movement. Neither man achieved a serious analysis of the nation's monetary system, prior to 1900, and both, consequently, had little attachment to the doctrines of the Omaha Platform during the intra-party struggle of 1895–96. I have found no reason to believe that Allen or Butler profited financially from the campaign of the silver lobby. Their conduct was traceable to other causes. For a discussion of the shadow movement, see Appendix C.

As politicians, therefore, Taubeneck, Allen, and Butler seem to belong in one category—"inexperienced political pragmatists" is a workable definition—while Weaver and most of the Kansas fusionists fit another. The latter group, greenbackers all, were ethically trapped by the tactical demands of the politics of the silver drive. Taubeneck's gerrymandering scheme of 1896 and Allen's conduct at the 1896 Populist convention were, however, ultimately to place them nearer the ethical posture of Weaver than the more candid stance of Marion Butler. Butler seems to have been the only leading fusionist figure who was not deeply and personally compromised by the demands of the politics of silver-fusion. He merely failed.

11. Barnhart, "Alliance in Nebraska", Argesinger, *Populism and Politics,* 204.

12. Theodore Saloutos, "Marion Butler," *Dictionary of American Biography* (New York, 1928–58), XXII, 78–79; Joseph Flake Steelman, "The Progressive Era in North Carolina, 1884–1917" (Unpublished Ph.D. dissertation, University of North Carolina, 1955), 27–33. According to Steelman, Polk was "irreconcilably opposed to further cooperation with Democrats in state politics." See also L. L. Polk to John D. Thorne, March 29, 1892, Polk Papers.

13. *Caucasian* (Raleigh), July 14, 1892.

14. Josephus Daniels, *Tar Heel Editor* (Chapel Hill, 1939), 385–87. This source was not invariably a model of accuracy on the subject of Populism. Whatever the details of Butler's transition to the reform movement, his own published reports in the *Caucasian* verify the reluctance of his participation in the third party crusade.

   A delineation of the political struggle between Butler and Polk in 1891–92 would require lengthy treatment. As his subsequent career illustrated, Butler was a consummate negotiator, though burdened with the kind of vision conducive to short-term tactical victories and long-run strategic defeats. Polk possessed a much surer feel for the operative dynamics of Southern Populism than his young rival. Butler's posture, however clever it may have appeared to him in 1891, was utterly untenable in the summer of 1892, as illustrated by his subsequent actions, even in the absence of pressure from Polk. The best account on Polk is Noblin, *Polk,* 239–81.

15. Theron Paul Jones, "The Gubernatorial Election of 1892 in North Carolina" (Unpublished M.A. thesis, University of North Carolina, 1949), 44–69. See also Kousser, *Shaping of Southern Politics,* 184–86.

16. Edmonds, *The Negro and Fusion Politics in North Carolina;* Steelman, "Republican Party Strategists and the Issue of Fusion With Populists," 244–69.

17. G. F. Weaver, "The Politics of Fusion," 18–27; Steelman, "Progressive Era in North Carolina," 124–25; Woodward, *Origins,* 282. For Butler's contradictory positions on monetary policy, see Palmer, "Rhetoric of Southern Populists," 222.

   An extremely critical appraisal of Butlerian politics is contained in Philip Ray Miller, "New South Populism, 1884–1900" (Unpublished Ph.D. dissertation, University of North Carolina, 1971), 43–72. The author locates a conservative "New South" ideology in Butler and in his protectionist-minded Populist associate, Harry Skinner. Miller successfully removes any lingering doubt that Butler ever at any time harbored a deep interest in the doctrines of the Omaha Platform. Actually, Marion Butler was neither a radical agrarian nor a New South boomer, but rather a gambling pragmatist plagued by an inadequate political base—the latter partly a product of his own insularity, his inhibiting social ties to North Carolina's conservative elite, and an emotional identification with white supremacy that he was never quite able to overcome, even when it was in his own political self-interest to do so.

18. Scott, *Agrarian Movement in Illinois,* 104–17; Hendrickson, "Some Aspects of the Populist Movement in South Dakota," 85.

19. *National Watchman,* Nov. 30, 1894; Jan. 11, 25, 1895. Lutzky, "Reform Editors

and Their Press," 219–25. Weaver's disappointment with the December conference is duly recorded in Weaver to Donnelly, Jan. 23, 1895, Donnelly Papers. See also Durden, *Climax of Populism*, 1–7; Destler, *American Radicalism*, 226–30; Argesinger, *Populism and Politics*, 202–6.

20. Lutzky, "Reform Editors," 1, 43–44, 226–28.

21. *Proceedings*, Supreme Council of the National Farmers Alliance and Industrial Union (Raleigh), Feb. 5–8, 1895, pp. 5, 15, 23–26.

22. Silveus, "The Antecedents of the Campaign of 1896," 28; Lutzky, "Reform Editors and Their Press," 229–30. See also the *Advocate, Feb.* 20, March 13, 1895; *Southern Mercury,* Jan. 31, Feb. 7, 14, 21, 1895; *American Nonconformist,* Feb. 21, 28, March 7, 1895; *Farmers Tribune* (Des Moines), Feb. 20, 27, 1895; Woodward, *Watson,* 240–45; Destler, *American Radicalism,* 243. In Alabama, reform editors decided early in February 1895 to organize themselves on a statewide basis. The Alabama Reform Press Association was also heavily committed to the "middle of the road" (Rogers, *One-Gallused Rebellion,* 269, 297). Weaver, now deeply implicated in the campaign of the silver lobby, had followed the December free-silver press statement of Taubeneck with a second manifesto that further alerted reform editors on the eve of their meeting.

23. *Farmers Tribune,* Feb. 27, 1895.

24. *The Advocate,* Dec. 12, 1894, For McLallin's long record of editorial deemphasis of silver, see Clanton, *Kansas Populism,* 104, 174–78.

25. *American Nonconformist* (Indianapolis), March 7, 1895. This defense did not deter the "anti-socialist" propaganda of the silverites. *The National Watchman,* now the unabashed editorial voice both of Taubeneck and of the silver lobby, insinuated in its issue of April 13, 1895 that the editors of the *Nonconformist* (Indianapolis), the *Advocate* (Topeka), the *Farmers Tribune* (Des Moines), and the *Wealth-Makers* (Lincoln) were going to launch a new movement "known as the socialist labor party" (Destler, *American Radicalism,* 251). *The Southern Mercury* replied acidly, "this bugaboo of socialism was never heard of until this one-plank silver party came into existence" (April 11, 18, 1895).

26. *Farmers Tribune,* Feb. 27, March 6, 1895.

27. Lutzky, "Reform Editors," 136, 230–31.

28. For a brief moment, Watson expressed alarm at the reports by Taubeneck and Dunning of a socialist presence in the third party. But he soon isolated the party's tactical difficulties as originating with the silver crusade and resumed his defense of the Omaha Platform.

29. Destler, *Empire of Reform,* 273, and *American Radicalism,* 248–52.

30. William H. Harvey, *Coin's Financial School* (Chicago, 1894). For Bryan, see the Memphis *Commercial Appeal,* June 15–17, 1895.

31. Hofstadter, in introduction to reprinted edition of William H. Harvey's *Coin's Financial School* (Cambridge, Mass., 1963), 4–8.

32. *Farmers Tribune* (Des Moines), Feb. 27, 1895; Haynes, *Weaver,* 357–59. In February 1896, Butler convened a small gathering of Democrats, silver Republicans, and Populists in Washington to agree on "unequivocal support" of free silver and "Anglo-Saxon Supremacy" (Steelman, "Progressive Era in North Carolina," 127).

33. Davis Waite to Ignatius Donnelly, July 10, 1895, Donnelly Papers; Ridge, *Donnelly,* 347; *Farmers Tribune* (Des Moines), Feb. 27, 1895. A prominent California Populist shared Waite's opinion: "Weaver, Taubeneck, Dunning, and Turner have lost in party esteem all over the nation by their connubiating with silver men to aid in forming a new party. The most intelligent men in our party, or those who have been placed in the lead and are by that fact recognized as exponents of

populist principles, seem to have been more obtuse than the least informed members of our party. It is a cause for rejoicing that our party still keeps step to music of Omaha principles and that this exhibition of weakness has shown itself this early" (John Dore to Thomas Cator, May 7, 1895, Cator Papers).

34. Clanton, *Kansas Populism,* 176–80.

35. Woodward, *Watson,* 242–52; Watson on fusion, quoted in the *Southern Mercury,* Nov. 29, Dec. 27, 1894.

36. Weaver to Bryan, Dec. 31, 1895, Bryan Papers; *Southern Mercury,* Feb. 20,1896; Saunders, "Ideology of Southern Populists, 176–93.

37. Saunders, "Ideology of Southern Populists," 190, 193; *Southern Mercury, May* 21, 1896. Butler's home state, North Carolina, with only about 55,000 Populist votes in 1894, received 95 convention delegates, while Texas, with some 160,000 votes, also received 95 delegates. This result was achieved by counting as "Populist" the entire Republican vote in North Carolina that had been cast for fusion candidates in 1894. Since most of those candidates, running in areas of strong Republican voting strength, had been committed goldbugs, Taubeneck's method of delegate apportionment added something of a new dimension to American party politics.

38. *Southern Mercury,* Oct. 10, 1895. The *Advocate* followed the *Mercury* on Oct. 30 with the same advice. For fusion planning, see Taubeneck to Donnelly, Dec. 16, 1895; M. C. Rankin (Populist national treasurer) to Donnelly, Dec. 16, 1895; Bryan to Donnelly, Jan. 1, 1896; A. J. Warner (president, American Bimetallic League), H. G. Miller (chairman, National Silver Committee), and R. C. Chambers (president, National Bimetallic Union) to Donnelly, Jan. 4, 1896, Donnelly Papers. Weaver to Bryan, Dec. 31, 1895; Bryan to Weaver, Jan. 3, 1896; Bryan to Marion Butler, Jan. 1, 1896; and Butler to Bryan, Jan. 8,1896, Bryan Papers. Lafe Pence to Davis Waite, March 3, 1894; Bryan to Waite, Dec. 2, 1895, Waite Papers. The silverites gradually began to coopt Donnelly. Despite his well-honed greenback convictions, he acquiesced in the idea of a late convention (Donnelly to Thomas Cator, December 22, 1895, Cator Papers). Veteran Alliancemen, however, were not beguiled (Henry Loucks to Davis Waite, Sept. 20, 1895, Waite Papers).

39. Jones, *Presidential Election of 1896,* 84–87, 185; William Stewart (editor of the *Silver Knight*) to Donnelly, Dec. 20, 1895, Donnelly Papers; Stewart to Taubeneck, Dec. 16, 1895 Stewart Papers; and Stewart to Thomas Cator, Dec. (n.d.) 1895, Cator Papers.

40. Edward R. Light (secretary, American Bimetallic League) to Donnelly, March 9, 1896, Donnelly Papers. Nothing was promised; everything was implied. This letter from the command post of the silverites contained the following carefully phrased intelligence: "A committee of prominent bi-metallists are about to go West with a view of raising necessary funds to assist in conducting the approaching campaign. We do not expect to raise all the money necessary for this campaign in the West, but the people there have been so liberal we have concluded we can raise more money there for immediate use than elsewhere." Two weeks later, the lobbyist provided a further report: "The silver friends in three states subscribed a certain amount of money to conduct this office" (Light to Donnelly, March 9, 23, 1896). See also J. J. Mott (National Silver Party) to Butler, June 21, 1896, and Taubeneck to Donnelly, Feb. 18, 29, 1896. Taubeneck had now become disingenuous by habit: e.g., in his continuing effort to isolate Donnelly, his Feb. 29 letter to the Minnesotan claimed the ascendancy of Taubeneck's policy among reform editors generally and within the Texas People's Party as well.

41. Nugent, in the *Southern Mercury*, June 6, 1895; M. A. Spurgin, in the *Mercury*, June 13, 1895.

42. *Southern Mercury*, May 5, 1892, quoted in Woodward, *Origins*, 251–52; also see *Southern Mercury*, June 20, 1895, March 12, July 9, 1896.

43. *Southern Mercury*, March 12, 1896. It is, perhaps, relevant to the ideological dispute of 1896 that in the first speech ever made from a Populist platform in the South—the keynote address at the founding convention in 1891 in Texas—William Lamb told his colleagues: "I wish to call your attention to the fact that free and unlimited coinage of silver will do us but little good. The tariff issue has [similarly] been used as a stumbling block over which our people have fallen into the hands of monopoly and are today helpless invalids because they have taken that dose from the hands of politicians for the last twenty-five years." Lamb also recommended, "as the most efficient and ready plan for putting money in circulation," that "the national government build at once as many as seven trunk lines of railway and that a full legal tender paper money be issued by the government to pay for the construction and that they be owned and operated by the government. This is better than war, which has been the former plan to remit money to the people when they have been deprived of it as now. There is in my judgment no reason why the federal government should always be a renter and therefore it would be well for all postal buildings to be constructed by the government and paid for by the issue of full legal tender paper money. The money will wear out about as fast as the buildings will" (Fort Worth *Gazette*, Aug. 18, 1891).

44. *Southern Mercury*, April 6, 1893; Aug. 30, Nov. 29, 1894; Jan. 31, 1895, Feb. 7, 14, 21; July 11, Sept. 28, 1895; Jan. 30, March 12, 1896.

45. S. O. Daws, State Lecturer, Farmers Alliance of Texas, quoted in *Southern Mercury*, Feb. 20, 1896.

46. *Southern Mercury*, May 21, 1896. From Woodstock jail, Debs had written Henry Demarest Lloyd in August 1894 a prediction that "The People's Party will come into power with a resistless rush" (Destler, *Empire of Reform*, 272).

47. *Proceedings*, Supreme Council of the National Farmers Alliance and Industrial Union (Washington, D.C.), Feb. 4–6, 1896, 19. To safeguard greenback doctrine, the Texans dispatched Harry Tracy to the Alliance convention, but the precaution proved unnecessary.

48. *Southern Mercury*, March 18, 1896.

49. Taubeneck to Donnelly, May 23, 1896, Donnelly Papers; George Wilson to Marion Butler, May 30, 1896, Butler Papers; E. M. Wardell, chairman of the executive committee, California State Farmers Alliance, to Ignatius Donnelly, June 10, 1896; Clanton, *Kansas Populism*, 179; Argesinger, *Populism and Politics*, 236; *The Advocate* (Topeka), Oct. 2, 1895; May 6, 20, June 17, 24, 1896; Shofner and Rogers, "Joseph C. Manning: Militant Agrarian, Enduring Populist," 28; Barnhart, "Alliance in Nebraska," 366, 369; Steelman, "Progressive Era in North Carolina," 125, 136; Cyrus Thompson to Marion Butler, May 2, 1896, Butler Papers; *People's Party Paper*, June 19, 26, 1896; quoted in Woodward, *Watson*, 253; Arnett, *Populist Movement in Georgia*, 197; *Progressive Farmer* (Raleigh), June 30, 1896.

CHAPTER XV

1. H. E. Taubeneck to Ignatius Donnelly, May 15, 1896, Donnelly Papers.

2. Jones, *The Presidential Election of 1896*, 207–8; Ridge, *Donnelly*, 350–51. For details

of fusionist strategy at the opening of the Democratic convention in Chicago, see Thomas Cator to E. M. Wardell, July 8, 1896, Cator Papers.

3. Margaret Leech, *In the Days of McKinley (New York,* 1959), 78–80. George H. Mayer, *The Republican Party* (New York, 1967), 246–50; Paul Glad, *The Trumpet Soundeth* (Lincoln, 1960), 54–55; Jones, *The Presidential Election of 1896,* 86; Ray Ginger, *The Age of Excess,* (New York, 1965), 176–78.

4. "Uniting the reform forces of the nation" was a phrase popularized in the 1890s by the silver lobby. It had logical appeal to the politically unsophisticated. In contrast, an appreciation of the counter-argument of Alliancemen and reform editors necessarily required a certain understanding of the monetary system. Those Populists who asserted that the precipitous decline in popularity of the Gold Democracy of Grover Cleveland signaled the emergence of the opportunity to "unite the producing classes" behind the greenback doctrines of the Omaha Platform had a case that could be persuasive only to those who had studied the monetary system as well as the politics of party realignment. To the average voter in the nation, the previously forthright third party position had become, thanks to the silver drive, simply too sophisticated for an electorate that, then as now, had only a hazy notion about how money and credit functioned.

   But this analysis is Populistic; the non-Populistic shadow movement, led by Taubeneck, was not only a foil, but a willing foil, of the silver lobby. The third party chairman had no better understanding of monetary systems than William Jennings Bryan did. But the "Great Commoner" was to prove more adroit in functioning in his own political self-interest.

5. H. E. Taubeneck to Ignatius Donnelly, June 20, 1896, Donnelly Papers.

6. Henry Vincent to Donnelly, June 16, 1896; Robert Shilling to Donnelly, June 22, 1896; Taubeneck to Donnelly, June 20, 22, 1896, Donnelly Papers; Thomas Cator to E. M. Wardell, July 9, 1896, Cator Papers; Lutzky, "Reform Editors," 44, 117–18, 172, 219, 225–36.

7. Bryan, *The First Battle,* 199–206, 214–19. In ways unrelated to structural reform of the monetary system, the Democrats revealed the modest impact that heavy Populist electoral gains had made on their public political stance. The new silver Democracy opposed court injunctions as a means of preventing strikes, and called for an undefined "enlargement of powers" in the Interstate Commerce Commission to provide a "stricter control" of railroads.

8. The St. Louis *Republic* reported Taubeneck's new public stance on the third party schism he had been instrumental in creating: he was "neutral" (St. Louis *Republic,* June 21, 1896).

9. Although Butler had asserted in 1893 in his newspaper, *The Caucasian,* that "there is no way to prevent the plutocratic power from controlling a currency that is based on gold and silver," his subsequent excursion into coalition politics had necessitated a crucial redefinition of his stance on the monetary system. By 1895, he was calling for a redeemable paper money based on gold and silver (Palmer, "Rhetoric of Southern Populists," 222).

10. Marion Butler to Samuel A. Ashe, quoted in Steelman, "Progressive Era in North Carolina," 139–40.

11. Simpson quoted in the St. Louis *Post-Dispatch,* July 20, 1896, and Atlanta *Constitution,* July 21, 1896; Barnhart, "Nebraska," 399–400; Davis Waite to Ignatius Donnelly, July 12, 1896, Donnelly Papers; Donnelly Diary, July 18, 1896, quoted in Jones, *Presidential Election of 1896,* 246–47.

12. Pittsburg (Kansas) *Headlight,* July 2, 1896; quoted in Dew, "Populist Fusion Move-

ment as an Instrument of Political Reform, 1890–1900," 77; *The Advocate* (Topeka) July 15, 1896; Argesinger, *Populism and Politics,* 254–64.

13. The organizational limitations of the People's Party in Kansas, in the context of the spread of fusion sentiment among office-seekers, are discussed by Nugent, *Tolerant Populists,* 129–31, 151–61, 187–90; by Clanton, *Kansas Populism,* 185–87, 233; and by Argesinger, *Populism and Politics,* 104–275.

14. St. Louis *Post-Dispatch,* July 21, 22, 1896; St. Louis *Republic,* July 20, 21, 1896; St. Louis *Globe-Democrat,* 21, 23, 1896.

15. St. Louis *Globe-Democrat,* July 22, 23, 1896; Woodward, *Watson,* 293–94; Martin, *People's Party in Texas,* 239–40; Arnett, *Populism in Georgia,* 195.

16. *New York Times,* July 23, 24, 1896, St. Louis *Republic,* July 22, 23, 24, 1896; St. Louis *Post-Dispatch,* July 24, 1896; San Francisco *Chronicle,* July 23, 24, 25, 1896.

17. St. Louis *Republic,* July 23, 24, 1896; Durden, *Climax of Populism,* 33–36; Woodward, *Watson,* 299; Hicks, *Populist Revolt,* 357–62.

18. Bryan, *The First Battle,* 264–70; Jones, *Presidential Election of 1896,* 256.

19. The complex role of Butler's North Carolina delegation in this affair is focused upon in Durden, *Climax of Populism,* 35–36. Butler, more attuned than the Westerners to the realities of Populist-Democratic conflict in the South and thus more aware of the political need to preserve a third party identity, even while working for Bryan's nomination, threw his support behind the move to nominate a vice-presidential candidate first. He had another reason—pressure from his own delegation. San Francisco *Chronicle,* July 25, 1896; St. Louis *Republic,* July 24, 1896; Dallas *News,* July 24, 1896; Chicago *Tribune,* July 24, 1896; Atlanta *Constitution,* July 24–25, 1896.

20. The Populist platform of 1896 is reprinted in full in Bryan, *First Battle,* 271–76.

21. St. Louis *Post-Dispatch,* July 25, 1896; Jones, *Presidential Election of 1896,* 258–59; Durden, *Climax of Populism,* 41–42.

22. The precise circumstances surrounding Watson's acceptance is a matter of some dispute. See Woodward, *Watson,* 261–63; Durden, *Climax of Populism,* 38–39; Jones, *Presidential Election of 1896,* 259–60; St. Louis *Republic,* July 25, 26, 1896.

23. St. Louis *Post-Dispatch,* July 25, 1896. Durden, *Climax of Populism,* 41–42; St. Louis *Republic,* July 25, 26, 1896. "So great was the confusion that it was doubtful that there was one man or group of men in St. Louis as the Populist Party made its nominations who could boast any general understanding or control of the convention" (Jones, *Presidential Election of 1896,* 261).

24. Allen's conduct of the convention has been variously construed by Hicks, *Populist Revolt,* 366–67; Matthew Josephson, *The Politicos* (New York, 1938), 681–84; Woodward, *Watson,* 259–60, and *Origins,* 286; Pollack, *Populist Response to Industrial America,* 103–43; Jones, *Presidential Election of 1896,* 261–62; Durden, *Climax of Populism,* 42–43 and "The 'Cow-Bird' Grounded: The Populist Nomination of Bryan and Tom Watson in 1896," *Mississippi Valley Historical Review* Dec. 1963), 397–423; Ridge, *Donnelly,* 355–56. Henry Demarest Lloyd, who was present, offered the earliest interpretation: "The Populists at St. Louis," *Review of Reviews* (Sept. 1896), 301–3.

25. In addition to secondary sources listed in the preceding citation, this summary of the early part of the fourth day of the convention is drawn from: St. Louis *Post-Dispatch,* St. Louis *Republic,* St. Louis *Globe Democrat,* New York *Times,* New York *Herald,* Chicago *Tribune,* San Francisco *Chronicle,* Dallas *News,* and Atlanta *Constitution.* The incident involving Congressman Milford Howard is partly drawn from David Allen Harris, "The Political Career of Milford W. Howard, Populist Con-

gressman from Alabama" (Unpublished M.A. thesis, Alabama Polytechnic Institute, 1957), 95.

26. It may therefore be argued that midroad strategy to preserve the identity of the People's Party by denying the nomination to Bryan actually prevailed at St. Louis in 1896; it was neutralized by the extraordinary deception of William Allen. Henry Demarest Lloyd offered this view: "Curious that the new party, the Reform party, the People's party, should be more boss-ridden, ring-ruled, gang-gangrened than the two old parties of monopoly. The party that makes itself the special champion of the Referendum and Initiative tricked out of its very life and soul by a permanent National Chairman—something no other party has! Our Initiative and Referendum had better begin, like Charity, at home" (Caro Lloyd, *Henry Demarest Lloyd,* Vol. 1, New York, 1933, 259–60).

27. The pro-Bryan St. Louis *Post-Dispatch* put the best possible face on fusionist maneuverings throughout the convention. The *Post-Dispatch* preferred to view the midroad effort as a conspiracy financed by Mark Hanna (St. Louis *Post-Dispatch,* July 21–26, 1896). The misapprehension of delegates about the true nature of Sewall's impending "withdrawal" came forcefully to the surface during the fall campaign (see the chapter following). But the decline in morale was visible at the convention itself. One disheartened reformer wrote to "Calamity" Weller from St. Louis: "I am sick and weary and tired of it all. I sometimes feel like never taking any further part in politics at all, not even to vote . . . Somebody has blundered. Our convention should never have been postponed until after those of the old parties . . . I admire the firmness of those middle of the road men. Their predictions are being fulfilled" (G. W. Everts to L. H. Weller, July 26, 1896, Weller Papers).

28. St. Louis *Globe-Democrat,* July 26, 1896; St. Louis *Republic,* July 26, 1896.

29. Eugene Debs to Henry Demarest Lloyd, July 25, 1896, Lloyd Papers; Ridge, *Donnelly.* The Republican St. Louis *Globe-Democrat* rather enjoyed the various discomforts of the fusionists and reported the ebb and flow of midroad fortunes in a manner that—for that era of journalism—passed for objectivity. A *Globe-Democrat* reporter covered the Texas caucas (St. Louis *Globe-Democrat,* July 26, 1896). Senator Peffer of Kansas also rebuffed the Texans (Argesinger, *Populism and Politics,* 259).

30. Though many in their ranks bowed to the inevitable at the end, some 200 diehard midroaders from other states joined the 103 Texans in voting against Bryan. The final tally was Bryan 1042 and Norton 321. This result has been interpreted by some historians as a valid indication of comparative fusion and midroad strength in the People's Party. Indeed, the presumption that the shadow movement of free silver was the essence of "Populism" may well have its origin in this simple statistic! To achieve this conclusion, however, it is necessary to ignore the history of the agrarian revolt from its inception in 1877 through the Democratic convention of 1896.

31. Durden, *Climax of Populism,* 49.

CHAPTER XVI

1. *People's Party Paper,* Nov. 13, 1896, quoted in Woodward, *Watson,* 285.

2. Lutzky, "Reform Editors and Their Press," 118. Professor Lutzky emphasizes the precipitous decline in morale of the reform editors following the triumph of fusion: "an enormous proportion of the reform press ceased publication."

3. Durden, *Climax of Populism,* 49–50; Woodward, *Watson,* 266–69.
4. Butler had been named to the party chairmanship by the fusionist national executive committee which, in the final hours of the St. Louis convention, had been given plenary powers by the convention to conduct the elaborate and delicate negotiations necessitated by fusion (Durden, *Climax of Populism,* 48). This action by the convention, which "gave further indication of its uncertainty and confusion," was a recognition that fusion had "left many issues in doubt" (Jones, *Presidential Election of 1896,* 262). The disarray of the Populist leadership is treated in Woodward, *Watson,* 261–86, and passim; Jones, 318–31 and passim; and Durden, 50. The quotations by silver leaders in this paragraph are from Woodward, 267–68; Chicago *Tribune,* Aug. 3, 1896. The Democratic chairman, Jones, tried to disavow his remarks about the third party, but the disavowal contained further attacks on Populists in the South by the Arkansas Senator (St. Louis *Post-Dispatch,* Aug. 4, 1896). See also Jones, 298.
5. Marion Butler to People's Party Notification Committee, Aug. 26, 1896, Butler Papers.
6. Argesinger, *Populism and Politics,* 241–43, 266–68; Simpson is quoted in Arnett, *Populist Movement in Georgia,* 197.
7. Barnhart, "Alliance in Nebraska," 403–9; Jones, *Presidential Election of 1896,* 321; Durden, *Climax of Populism,* 78n.
8. C. H. Castle to Thomas Cator, July 18, 1896, Cator Papers.
9. *Appeal to Reason,* July 18, 1896, quoted in Lutzky, *Reform Editors and Their Press,* 138.
10. Morgan's early role is alluded to briefly in Chaps. VIII and XIV.
11. W. Scott Morgan, Hardy, Arkansas, to Marion Butler, Aug. 5, 1896, Butler Papers. Morgan's possessed an intimate knowledge of the internal politics of the People's Party. His warnings about the abandonment of Populist doctrine by state third parties led by office-seekers in Kansas, Nebraska, and Colorado were issued well before the jettisoning of Watson by the fusion leadership in those states.
12. See below, this chapter.
13. T. B. Bickley, Spring Valley, Alabama, to Butler, Aug. 7, 1896, Butler Papers.
14. J. P. Buchanan, Wayside, Tenn., to Butler, Aug. 17, Sept. 10, 1896; T. J. Guice, Grand Cain, La., to Butler, Aug. 11, 1896; J. A. Tetts, state central committee, Louisiana People's Party to Butler, Oct. 3, 1896; Jo A. Parker, Louisville, Ky., Aug. 21, 1896; C. C. Post, Seabreeze, Fla., to Butler, Sept. 7, 1896. In North Carolina: Robert W. Sossaman to Butler, Sept. 30, 1896; W. A. Guthrie to Butler, Oct. 4, 1896; R. W. Osborne to Butler, Oct. 5, 1896; in Kansas, John W. Breidenthal, state party chairman, to Butler, Aug. 2, 1896; and Abe Steinberger, Girard, Kan., to Butler, Aug. 26, 1895.
15. H. C. C. Childs, Provisional Chairman, Colorado State Farmers Alliance, to Butler, Sept. 3, 1896; J. F. Willits, McClouth, Kan., to Butler, Sept. 9, 1896.
16. A. W. C. Weeks, Winterset, Iowa, to Butler, Aug. 2, 1896.
17. John Dore, Fresno, Calif., to Butler, Aug. 30, 1896.
18. L. H. Weller, Independence, Iowa, to Butler, Aug. 15, 1896; Milford Howard, Ft. Paine, Ala., to Butler; J. A. Tetts to Butler, Sept. 10, 1896.
19. See especially Watson's defense of himself in a letter to Theodore Roosevelt, quoted in Woodward, *Watson,* 265.
20. Butler is treated at length in Durden, in *The Climax of Populism;* Steelman, "Progressive Era in North Carolina"; and in Miller, "New South Populism."
21. It perhaps should be emphasized that these different experiences were not

"givens" that materialized beyond the control of either regional Populist leader: the transfer of rank and file Georgia Alliancemen to the Georgia People's Party was partly an outgrowth of Watson's forceful leadership in the year of crucial choice, 1892. On the other hand, the failure of the North Carolina People's Party to recruit much more than one-third of the North Carolina Alliance was traceable in important ways to Butler's resistance to the third party from the spring of 1891 through "the ringing of the bell" in Sampson County in August 1892. The decisive element seems to have been the race issue. Watson was willing to take clear-cut political risks by advocating a black-white coalition of Populist farmers while Butler feared the third party because a division of the white vote on economic issues would, in his words, endanger "Anglo-Saxon rule and good government" in North Carolina (*Caucasian*, July 14, 1892). See Chap XIV, infra, for Butler's role in these relationships. For correlating positions of the Georgia Populist, see Woodward, *Watson*, 110–24, 143–210.

22. The depth to which the "movement culture" of Populism permeated the third party in Georgia is evident in the emotional reception given Watson by the Populist faithful—as described by a reporter for the Atlanta *Constitution*, Aug. 8, 1896, and quoted in Woodward, *Watson*, 270.

23. When Butler first began pondering the options facing the People's Party during the interim between the Democratic and Populist conventions, he had proposed a joint electoral ticket in each state of the nation. Summarily rebuffed by Democratic chairman Jones, Butler fumed at the Democrats for "wanting the Earth!" (Durden, *Climax of Populism*, 29). Despite this fleeting moment of Populistic assertion, Butler quickly rallied to Bryan's candidacy. Similarly, Butler asked Jones to withdraw Sewall following the Populist convention. Jones shrewdly countered by raising the specter of a public repudiation of the Populist nomination by Bryan, a move that would have effectively destroyed the shaken credibility of fusionist spokesmen such as Butler, as well as confirming the validity of the convention posture of midroad delegates. Maneuvered into this corner, Butler had only two options: to lapse into silence, tacitly accepting Sewall, or to press the point, risk Bryan's repudiation, and react by calling a Populist convention to nominate a full third party ticket. The latter was unthinkable to the fusionists, as it doomed silver coalitions to defeat, both in the West and in North Carolina.

24. Watson to Marion Butler, Aug. 24, 1896; Butler to Milford Howard, Aug. 25, 1896; Butler to Watson, Aug. 27, 1896, Butler Papers; Woodward, *Watson*, 272–73; Durden, *Climax of Populism*, 57–58.

25. Butler to H. W. Reed, Aug. 27, 1896; Butler Papers.

26. *Southern Mercury*, Aug. 6, 13, 20, 27, 1896; Woodward, *Watson*, 273–75.

27. Butler to Watson, Sept. 1, 1896, and Allen to Bryan, Sept. 1, 1896; Woodward, *Watson*, 274. Watson delayed even longer, until Oct. 14, and replied in a bristling denunciation of the fusion leadership that reflected developments occurring since his letters to Butler of Aug. 24 and Sept. 1, 1896. See below.

28. *Southern Mercury*, Aug. 7, 13, 20, 1896.

29. *Southern Mercury*, Aug. 13, 20, Sept. 3, 10, 1896.

30. H. W. Reed to Butler, Sept. 7, 1896, Butler Papers; *Southern Mercury*, Sept. 10, 17, 1896; Dallas *News*, Sept. 8, 1896; Martin, *People's Party in Texas*, 241–43; Woodward, *Watson*, 276.

31. Chicago *Tribune*, Sept. 8, 1896; *New York Times*, Sept. 8, 1896, quoted in Jones, *Presidential Election of 1896*, 323–24. The Democratic press, of course, did not share the Republican enthusiasm for Watson's Dallas speech. The strongly pro-

Bryan St. Louis *Post-Dispatch,* which for months had asserted that all mid-road agitation was a direct product of subsidies by Mark Hanna, announced that Watson "had thrown off his mask and declared himself the Judas of this campaign (St. Louis *Post-Dispatch,* Sept. 8, 1896, quoted in Durden, *Climax of Populism,* 90–91).

32. Butler to Watson, Sept. 8, 1896, Butler Papers.
33. Woodward, *Watson,* 276–77; Clanton, *Kansas Populism,* 192–95; Dew, "Populist Fusion Movements," 88. The Kansas fusion leadership, confronting the delegates with the *fait accompli* of the Populist National Convention, kept Watsonian sentiment restricted to resolutions.
34. Woodward, *Watson,* 274–77.
35. *Ibid.*
36. *Ibid.*

CHAPTER XVII

1. J. Laurence Laughlin, *The History of Bimetallism in the United States* (New York, 1889); *Facts About Money* (Chicago, 1896); "Causes of Agricultural Unrest," *Atlantic Monthly* (Nov. 1896), 298–303.
2. Willard Fischer, " 'Coin' and His Critics," *Quarterly Journal of Economics* (Jan. 1896), 187–208.
3. Given the presence of existing disputes and a heritage of mutual suspicion, the most difficult political problem faced by New York commercial bankers in their efforts to establish, simultaneously, a central banking mechanism *and* a more flexible currency, lay in obtaining the support of provincial bankers. The legislative task, winning congressional approval of their product, proved less onerous.

    The New York bankers and the economists they employed to work with Senator Carter Glass on the drafting of the Federal Reserve Act have all written extensively about their own roles. See J. Laurence Lauglin (ed.), *Banking Reform* (Chicago, 1912), and Laughlin, "The Banking and Currency Act of 1913," *Journal of Political Economy,* xxii (1914), and Laughlin, *The Federal Reserve Act: Its Origins and Problems* (New York, 1933); Paul Warburg, "The Owen-Glass Bill as Submitted to the Democratic Caucus," *North American Review* (1913), and Warburg, *The Federal Reserve System: Its Origins and Growth* (New York, 1930); H. Parker Willis, *The Federal Reserve System: Legislation, Organization and Operation* (New York, 1923), and Willis and William H. Steiner, *Federal Reserve Banking Practice* (New York, 1926); A. Barton Hepburn, "Criticisms of the Proposed Federal Reserve Bank Plan," *Proceedings of the Academy of Political Science,* IV (1913), and Hepburn, *A History of Currency in the United States* (New York, 1915); Frank A. Vanderlip, "The Rediscount Function of the Regional Banks," *Proceedings of the Academy of Political Science,* IV (1913), and Vanderlip, "Address Before the Economic Club of New York, Nov. 13, 1912 (New York, 1913).

    Warburg, Hepburn, and Vanderlip were bankers whereas Willis, an economist, was a student of Laughlin's at the University of Chicago. For the technical ramifications, see "Gold Inflation and Banking Reform, 1897–1914," 135–88, in Milton Friedman and Anna Schwartz, *A Monetary History of the United States* (Princeton, 1963). The most detailed historical account is contained in Gabriel Kolko, *The Triumph of Conservatism* (New York, 1963), 182–89, 218–54. See also Appendices A and B.

4. Friedman and Schwartz, "Early Years of the Federal Reserve System, 1914–1928," 189–239, esp. 233, 238, in *Monetary History of the United States;* John Maynard

Keynes, *Tract on Monetary Reform* (New York, 1923), and Keynes, *Treatise on Money* (New York, 1930); Herbert Myrick, *The Federal Farm Loan System* (New York, 1916); A. Clarence Wiprud, *The Federal Farm Loan System in Operation* (New York, 1921). For provisions of the 1912 Monetary Commission Report that were ignored in the writing of the Federal Reserve Act, see *Federal Banking Laws and Reports, 1780–1912*, U.S. Senate Committee on Banking, "Report of the National Monetary Commission" (Washington, D.C., 1963). See also Laurence E. Clark, *Central Banking Under the Federal Reserve System* (New York, 1935).

5. "The Agricultural Crisis and Its Causes," *Report of the Joint Commission of Agricultural Inquiry*, 1921, House Report No. 408, 67 Congress, 1st Session (Washington, D.C., 1921). For the theoretical background of the dispute that progressed through these years between "intrinsic value" monometallists of the Laughlin persuasion and greenback theorists who believed a nation's currency was "based on the entire wealth of the country," two rather dense works and one well-written introductory account are John Maynard Keynes, *A General Theory of Employment, Interest and Money* (New York, 1936), and Joseph Schumpeter, *History of Economic Analysis* (New York, 1954), and Paul A. Samuelson, *Economics, An Introductory Analysis* (New York, 1948). Still useful is Thurman Arnold's *The Folklore of Capitalism* (New Haven, 1937) and John Maurice Clark's *Alternative to Serfdom* (New York, 1948).

6. In American banking circles Bryan's helpful role is regarded as having been "indispensable" (Martin Mayer, *The Bankers*, New York, 1974), 398.

   Actually, such "reforms" of the Progressive Era as the Clayton Anti-Trust Act and the Federal Reserve Act formed the cultural cement of the corporate state by providing the appearance of reform without its substance. As long as no one insisted on looking closely, such gestures quieted the anxious and preserved the illusion of democratic progress. Among twentieth-century American reformers, this mode of conduct has become institutionalized; structural reform is no longer a culturally admissible idea, even among those considering themselves "progressive." In its narrowness, the cultural hegemony that has been achieved is unique among Western industrial societies. See Appendix A.

7. Bryan, *First Battle*, 303–4.

8. Gilbert Fite, Paul Glad, Ray Ginger, Paola Coletta, James A. Barnes, and Stanley Jones, among others, have all alluded to the narrowness of the silver issue as a method of creating a broad interest-group coalition. See Fite, "William Jennings Bryan and the Campaign of 1896: Some Views and Problems," *Nebraska History*, 47 (Sept. 1966), 247–64; and Barnes, "Myths of the Bryan Campaign," *Mississippi Valley Historical Review*, XXXIV (1947), 369.

9. Leech, *In the Days of McKinley*, 87–94. The larger cultural issue raised in this passage is discussed at some length subsequently in this chapter.

10. Butler to Watson, Sept. 22, 30, Oct. 26, 1896; Watson to Butler, Sept. 27, Oct. 14, 28, 1896; Butler to George F. Washburn, Sept. 24, 28, Oct. 1, 5, 6, 8, 24, 1896; Butler Papers; Durden, *Climax of Populism*, 94–124; Woodward, *Watson*, 278–84. After returning to Georgia from his Western trip in September, Watson made one brief trip to Tennessee, returned home—and brooded.

11. Martin C. Rankin to Butler, Sept. 19, 1896; Butler to Rankin, Sept. 11, 17, Oct. 9, 1896, Butler Papers; Durden, *Climax of Populism*, 62–64; Jones, *Presidential Election of 1896*, 319, 329–30 (hereafter cited as Jones, *1896*).

12. Paoli E. Coletta, *William Jennings Bryan*, vol. I: *Political Evangelist, 1860–1908* (Lincoln, 1964), 161–212; Jones, *1896*, 311; Bryan, *First Battle*, 292, 315–37.

13. Glad, *The Trumpet Soundeth*, 56; Hollingsworth, *The Whirligig of Politics*, 99.
14. Jones, *1896*, 279–82.
15. Ginger, *Age of Excess*, 178; Jones, *1896*, 279–82; Herbert Croly, *Marcous Alonzo Hanna* (New York, 1923), 210–27.
16. Quoted in Jones, *1896*, 285. See also Durden, *Climax of Populism*, 130. Donnelly attributed the Republican victory in Minnesota to sectionalism (Donnelly to W. A. Bentley, Dec. 29, 1896, Donnelly Papers).
17. Jones, *1896*, 291–93. In one of his few sorties from his front porch in Canton, Ohio, McKinley, campaigning in Nebraska, opposed the pension policy of the Democrats by telling "a stirring war story" (Barnhart, "Alliance in Nebraska," 372).
18. Hollingsworth, *Whirligig of Politics*, 29; Robert H. Wiebe, *The Search For Order* (New York, 1967), 104; Jones, *1896*, 276–78.
19. *Appleton's Annual Cyclopaedia* (1897), 673, 770; Harry Barnard, *Eagle Forgotten: The Life of John Peter Altgelt* (Indianapolis, 1938).
20. Wiebe, *Search for Order*, 105–6; Hollingsworth, *Whirligig of Politics*, 84–107.
21. Ginger, *Age of Excess*, 178; Wiebe, *Search for Order*, 104–6.
22. Hofstadter, *The American Political Tradition*, 186–205.
23. William Peffer, "The Passing of the People's Party," *North American Review* (Jan. 1898), 12–23. See also Clanton, *Kansas Populism*, 289; Argesinger, *Populism and Politics*, 274–75; Barnhart, "Alliance in Nebraska," 454; Rogers, *One-Gallused Rebellion*, 319; Steelman, "Progressive Era in North Carolina," 123–77; Edmonds, *Negro and Fusion Politics*, 133–45; Mabry, "Disfranchisement of the Negro," 262–63, 280–82; Kousser, *Shaping of Southern Politics*, 182–95; Martin, *People's Party in Texas*, 136–39, 236–37; Woodward, *Watson*, 285.
24. Ginger, *Age of Excess*, 178; Hollingsworth, *Whirligig of Politics*, 93; Durden, *Climax of Populism*, 136–37; Wiebe, *Search for Order*, 103–6; Kousser, *The Shaping of Southern Politics*, 1–265; Jones, *1896*, 335, 341–45.
25. Weaver to Bryan, Jan. 1, 1896, Bryan Papers; St. Louis *Republic*, July 21, 1896.
26. Ralph L. Nelson, *The Merger Movement in American Industry* (Princeton, 1957), 3–37; Hans B. Thorelli, *The Federal Anti-trust Policy* (Baltimore, 1955), "(R)elating anti-trust to the general industrial development of the nation, it is at once apparent that the policy failed utterly to arrest the combination movement" (p. 606). See also Meyer, "Living on the Edge of an Abyss," *The Bankers*, 521–45.

The extent to which the major banking institutions of America participate in the ownership of the nation's industries is not a matter of public record. The practice of using "nominees" and "street names" in reporting ownership of companies as well as claims of confidentiality (under the National Banking Act, administrative rulings of the Comptroller of the Currency, or as a matter of "company policy") effectively prevent public access to such information (U.S. Congress, Senate Committee on Government Operations, *Disclosure of Corporate Ownership*, Staff Report of the Subcommittee on Intergovernmental Relations and Subcommittee on Budgeting, Management and Expenditures, 93d Congress, 2nd session, March 4, 1974 (Washington, D.C., 1974), 4–5, 115, 143–61, 317–34. Some ownership patterns are known, however. For example, eleven banks own 38 per cent of the common stock of CBS (p. 169). See also U.S. Congress, House Committee on Banking and Currency, *Commerical Banks and Their Trust Activities, Emerging Influence on the American Economy*, Staff Report for the Subcommittee on Domestic Finance, 90th Congress, 2nd session, July 8, 1968 (Washington, D.C., 1968); Robert M. Soldofsky, *Institutional Holdings of Common Stock: 1900–2000* (Ann Arbor, 1971); Lee Metcalf, "The Secrecy of Corporate Ownership," *Indiana*

Law Review, VI, no. 4 (1973). See also Sargant P. Florence, *The Logic of British and American Industry* (London, 3rd ed. 1972), 211–41; Edward S. Herman and Carl F. Safanda, "Proxy Voting by Commercial Bank Trust Departments," *Banking Law Journal,* vol. XC (Feb. 1973), 91–115; Andrew Shonfield, *Modern Capitalism: The Changing Balance of Public and Private Power* (London, 1965); Sigmund Timberge, "Corporate Fictions: Logical, Social and International Implications," *Columbia Law Review, XLVI* (July 1946), 533–80; and Thomas C. Cochran and William Miller, *The Age of Enterprise: A Social History of Industrial America* (New York, rev. ed., 1961), 190–91. Also see Appendix A.

27. J. Morgan Kousser, *The Shaping of Southern Politics;* Key, *Southern Politics,* 534, 547, passim; William Nisbet Chambers and Walter Dean Burnham, *The American Party Systems: Stages of Political Development* (New York, 1967).

    In *The Shaping of Southern Politics,* Kousser employs elaborate quantification methods in support of his conclusion that the Southern business-planter elite planned and carried out the disfranchisement of blacks and poor whites. An excellent critical bibliography of the literature of the period of disfranchisement further enhances this important contribution to Southern social and political history. See also Ginger, *Age of Excess,* 178; Hollingsworth, *Whirligig of Politics,* 93; Durden, *Climax of Populism,* 136–37; Wiebe, *Search for Order,* 103–6; Jones, *1896,* 335, 341–45.

28. Though Harry Tracy, the third party's leading monetary theorist, defended the Omaha Platform root and branch and believed the sub-treasury system would "completely revolutionize the industrial system," he formulated his call for radical action in democratic language that was somewhat less than apocalyptic: "Let us inaugurate the system so as to make as few radical changes as possible from present systems. Some of the best reforms ever proposed have failed, not because there was any defect . . . but because the people were not in mental condition to utilize them . . . go slow till the masses understand" (Tracy, in Davis, *A Political Revelation,* 383–87). L. L. Polk employed similar terminology in 1891–92 in attempting to bring moderate-conservative Southerners to Populism. After his ringing third party speech at Indianapolis in 1891, Polk wrote a North Carolina Democrat, "My message was most heartily and warmly received by the level headed and conservative . . ." (Polk to Elias Carr, Nov. 24, 1891, quoted in McMath, *Populist Vanguard,* 129).

29. Rupert Vance, *Farmers Without Land,* Public Affairs Pamphlet No. 12 (Washington, D.C., 1927), 3–18; Roger Ransom and Richard Sutch, "Debt Peonage in the Cotton South after the Civil War," *Journal of Economic History* (Sept. 1972), 641–69. George Tindall, *The Emergence of the New South* (Baton Rouge, 1971), 319–28, 397, passim; Paul K. Conkin, *Tomorrow a New World: The New Deal Community Program* (Ithaca, 1959); Sidney Baldwin, *Poverty and Politics: The Rise and Decline of the Farm Security Administration* (Chapel Hill, 1968); Donald Holley, "The Negro in the New Deal Resettlement Program," *New South* (Winter 1972), 53–65; Charles S. Johnson, Edwin Embree, and Will Alexander, *The Collapse of Cotton Tenancy* (Chapel Hill, 1936). See also William Z. Ripley, *Selected Readings in Rural Economics* (New York, 1916), esp. B.H. Hibbard, "Tenancy in the Southern States," 528; Arthur F. Raper and Ira De A. Reid, *Sharecroppers All* (Chapel Hill, 1941), 3–27; Farmer, "Furnishing Merchants and Sharecroppers in Pike County, Alabama," 143. Those interested in pursuing this topic are advised to start with William C. Murray, "Problems in Using County Records in Farm Mortgage Research," *Journal of Farm Economics,* XIV (Oct. 1932).

30. Norman Ray Huddleston, "Attitudes and Knowledge of Farmers and Urban

Leaders Concerning Farmer Cooperatives in Mississippi" (Unpublished Ph.D. dissertation, Mississippi State College, 1968), 70.

"Farmers simply don't understand the class basis of farmer coops and the relation to middlemen (and) prices. They are afraid. They don't grasp the need for group solidarity" (R. L. Kohls, "Can Cooperative Bargaining Associations Succeed?", paper presented at the National Conference of Fruit and Vegetable Bargaining Cooperatives, Lafayette, Ind., Jan. 1966, pp. 6–7, quoted in Huddleston). See also T. E. Hall, *A Study of the Source of Capital Used by Forty Cooperative Elevators in Southwestern Kansas* (Kansas State College of Agriculture and Applied Science, 1937), 15–19; Harold Frank Doran, "Why Farmers Support Copperatives" (Unpublished M.A. thesis, Pennsylvania State College, 1948); Henry H. Bakkin and Marvin A. Schers, *The Economics of Cooperative Marketing* (New York, 1937); Charles B. Robbins, "Financial Management Analysis of Farmer Cooperatives in Mississippi" (Unpublished M.A. thesis, Mississippi State College, 1956), 6–10; J. K. Stern, *Membership Problems in Farmer Cooperative Purchasing Associations*, Bulletin 261 (Penna. Agricultural Experiment Station, 1931); Jessie E. Pope, "Agriculture Credit in the U.S.," *Quarterly Journal of Economics*, XXVIII (Aug. 1914), 701. For the modern situation, see Ray Marshall and Lamond Godwin, *Cooperatives and Rural Poverty in the South* (Baltimore, 1971).

31. Dr. James McDaniel, Atlanta, to author, Feb. 5, 1974. See also T. F. Abercrombie, *History of Public Health in Georgia, 1733–1950* (Atlanta, 1953), esp. 65–77; "The Relation of the Insanitary Privy to Typhoid Fever, Dysentary, and Hookworm Diseases," *Bulletin*, Georgia State Board of Health, I, no. 3 (Atlanta, 1913). (N.A.), "Malaria Destroys Homes and Stunts Community Growth," *Journal of Medical Association of Georgia*, Vol. XXVII (Atlanta, 1938); T. F. Abercrombie, "Malaria and Its Relation to the Economic Development of Georgia," *The Emory University Quarterly*, X (Oct. 1954), 168–71.

For another aspect of the problem, see Henry A. Bullock, *A History of Negro Education in the South from 1619 to the Present* (Cambridge, Mass., 1967).

32. Daws, in fact, provided the operative dynamics of the agrarian revolt in one paragraph in 1887: "The management of the cotton during the past year, with the unity of the members in the markets and the strong opposition met, fully illustrated the magnitude and importance of the work they had begun . . . These exceptional cases of opposition were a benefit and a great blessing in every way, for they brought the farmers face to face with the evils and wrongs that stand opposed to their interests in marketing their produce. The efforts on the part of the enemies of the Alliance in some of the markets to break the combinations of the farmers have done much good for the Order as any one thing. It taught them who and where the enemies of their interests were" (Garvin and Daws, *History of the National Farmers Alliance and Co-operative Union of America,* 40).

33. All of which is to say that the Alliance was not "undermined" by the People's Party. On the contrary, the cooperative movement having failed, the Alliance had no way to preserve its institutional vitality. The agitation in 1891–92 over the subtreasury to bring on the third party actually prolonged the life of the Alliance briefly.

In some places, however, the organizational endurance of the order was remarkable. The "Pennsylvania State Farmers Alliance and Industrial Union" fashioned a mutual insurance plan and a cooperative store that benefited farmers for years and maintained a relatively healthy farmer organization in a handful of Pennsylvania counties. The order held its fifty-fourth annual meeting in 1944.

The Alliance store did $20,000 business annually and was "owned by the membership" [*Proceedings,* Fifty-fourth Annual Meeting, Pennsylvania State Farmers Alliance and Industrial Union (Coudersport, Pa., Jan. 11–13, 1944), 19].

34. The People's Party failed in the Northeast because it never found an institutional means to break through the barrier of sectionalism and carry its message to urban workers. But there was a deeper reason: the People's Party did not know what to say to urban workers. No concept in the Populist theoretical armory addressed the immediate self-interest of workers with a power matching the appeal the Alliance cooperative crusade had to the nation's farmers. The "money power" was a lifeless abstraction that failed utterly to bridge the various gaps, cultural and otherwise, existing between Protestant agrarian organizers and urban Catholics— or even urban Protestants. The furnishing merchant and the chattel mortgage were no abstractions; hundreds of thousands of men and women responded to the Alliance because the cooperative crusade addressed the central reality of their lives. Not until the concept of the sit-down strike provided the CIO with a similar self-describing value in the 1930s did an American working class institution achieve the internal emotional drive comparable—in scale—to the one that animated the Farmers Alliance during its great organizational sweep of the late 1880s. The People's Party simply had no comparable tool to give strength to the organizing effort among the millions of potential recruits who did not live on farms (see chap. XI, 307–11).

35. If the Bryan Democracy left no concrete political record because it never attained power, the same may be said for all the state-level People's parties throughout the nation. Standing alone, the third party never simultaneously won control of the executive and legislative branches of the government in a single state during the entire course of the agrarian revolt. Legislative roadblocks plagued Populist governors while gubernatorial vetoes thwarted Populist legislatures. In most states, the minority Populist legislative contingent, unable to enact a program of its own, was forced to play brokerage politics by attempting to take advantage of whatever democratic maneuvering room was made available to it by factional splits within the major parties. In terms of *Realpolitik,* therefore, the People's Party left no parliamentary record that could be called its own—anywhere.

36. William Dean Howells, *Preface to Contemporaries, 1892–1920,* George Arms (ed.) (Gainesville, Fla., 1957), 38, quoted in Larger Ziff, *The American 1890s: Life and Times of a Lost Generation* (New York, 1966), 94.

37. The subject is discussed in the Critical Essay on Authorities.

38. Noblin, *Polk,* 271.

AFTERWORD

1. Peffer headed the Prohibitionist ticket in 1898 and returned to the Republican Party in 1900. Clanton, *Kansas Populism,* 219–23, 238; *Gasper Christopher Clemens Note Book,* 1894–1900 (Kansas State Historical Society). Breidenthals's return path to orthodoxy was circuitous. After the defeat of 1898, the fusionist leader proclaimed fusion a mistake and said that the party had to "get back to just principles." Yet, he headed the fusion ticket of 1900. He then flirted with the Kansas Social Democratic Party before returning to the Republican Party (John Breidenthal to Jacob C. Ruppenthal, Jan. 3, 1899, Ruppenthal Papers, Kansas State Historical Society); Karel Denis Biche, "Jerry Simpson, 'Populist Without Principle,'" *Journal of American History* (Sept. 1967), 291–306.

2. Brodhead, *Persevering Populist,* 95–96, 113–51; 169–73.
3. Harold A. Trent, "The History of the Appeal to Reason: A Study of the Radical Press" (Unpublished M.A. thesis, Kansas State Teachers College, 1934), 32–95. Lutzky, "Reform Editors and Their Press," 10, 14, 78; Charles L. Scott, "Appeal to Reason: A Study of the 'Largest Newspaper in the World' " (Unpublished Senior thesis, Kansas State Teachers College, 1947), 18, 26.
4. For details of the 1903 meeting in Denver, see clipping in the James W. Baird Papers, University of Texas; for Butler's conversion to greenbackism, see *Congressional Record,* XXXIII, 1717–18 and 2540–41, 56th Congress, 1st session. For the limits of Butler's racial liberalism, see *Congressional Record,* XXXIII, 1553–54, 56th Congress, 1st session, and Miller, "New South Populism," 131, 138, 159, 166, 187, 190.
5. Woodward, *Watson,* 373–421; James H. Davis Papers, in possession of Mr. Frat Davis, Sulphur Springs, Tex.; private interview with Mrs. Latane Lambert, Dallas, Tex., July 19, 1969.
6. Sheldon, *Populism in the Old Dominion,* 149; Haynes, *Weaver,* 407; Ridge, *Donnelly,* 393–401.
7. Loucks, "Our Daily Bread;" W. Scott Morgan, *The Red Light* (Moravian, N.C. 1904); Rogers, *One Gallused Rebellion,* 318–20; Jerrell H. Shofner and William Warren Rogers, "Joseph C. Manning, Militant Agrarian, Enduring Populist," *Alabama Historical Quarterly,* XXIX (1967), 35–37; Joseph Manning, *Fadeout of Populism* (New York, 1922).
8. Henry Vincent to Robert Schilling, May 17, 1922, Schilling Papers; *Southern Mercury United with Farmers Union Password,* Jan. 11, 1906; Harrison Sterling Price Ashby Autobiographical Folder, University of Texas; Martin, *People's Party in Texas,* 127–29, 191–92.
9. Russell G. Pepperell, private interview, Houston, Tex., June 16, 1970; Paddock, *History of North and West Texas,* 631–33.
10. *Southern Mercury,* Dec. 1, 1892; May 18, 1893. Macune, "Farmers Alliance," 1–59. Critics have habitually shied away from the awkward fact that concepts of smaller dimensions than Macune's failed—in conception—to address the needs of poorer farmers and tenants who were yoked to the furnishing merchant by the crop lien system. This reality simply cannot be passed over as it was the very foundation of agrarian discontent in the South. The Rochdale cash plan of the Grange might have been theoretically sound; it was also conceptually inadequate. The point is not that Macune failed to defeat the credit system through the cooperative movement but that the cooperative movement—in every state—was defeated by the American banking system whenever it was attempted on anything above the smallest scale (see Appendix A).
11. Macune's political maneuverings in 1892 are discussed in Chapters IX and XI. Legitimate questions exist about his integrity as well. He dabbled disastrously in an 1890 Georgia Senatorial election by supporting a Democratic railroad lawyer over more progressive candidates. The affair brought him no end of criticism and further served to diminish his maneuvering room inside the order. The fact that he received money—reputedly $2000—from the candidate who benefited from his support did not help his reputation, though there is some reason to believe he used the money to pay off pressing debts of the *National Economist.* While the acceptance of money seems indefensible, his decision in the election campaign was in keeping with his own political vision. The railroad lawyer was

for the sub-treasury plan, a commitment a number of self-styled "progressive" politicians were unwilling to make. To Macune, whose own self-esteem was intimately involved in the system he had created, the sub-treasury plan was the transcendent political issue. Indeed, his preoccupation with the economic implications of his monetary system—namely, sizable income redistribution from creditors to debtors—blinded him to its political uses in the hands of William Lamb.

12. For an analysis of the economic implications of the sub-treasury system, see Appendix B. For its ideological origins and legacy, see Appendix A.

APPENDIX A

1. *Populist Revolt*, 189.
2. *American Radicalism*, 7–71.
3. "The Farmers Alliance SubTreasury Plan and European Precedents," *Mississippi Valley Historical Review*, XXXI (Sept. 1944), 255–62.
4. Vol. I (June–Aug. 1889), 167, 188–89, 211, 275, 344; Vol. II (Sept.–Dec. 1889), 24, 29, 82, 216, 226–27. This listing is not complete by any means.
5. See Skinner in *Frank Leslie's Illustrated Newspaper*, Nov. 30, 1889, and Macune in the *National Economist*, Mar.–Nov., 1889.
6. Winkler, *Platforms*, 257, emphasis added.
7. *Southern Mercury*, May 31, 1888. For the political setting, see Chap. V.
8. Dunning, *Alliance and Digest*, 128–29. As a harbinger of "Macuneism," a transplanted English chartist named J. F. Bray seems to have a better theoretical claim than Kellogg, Skinner, or, in precise terms, the French of 1848. Bray, a labor greenbacker in Michigan, suggested that the government lend greenbacks to labor cooperatives (Unger, *The Greenback Era*, 106, n. 153). The suggestion apparently got in print only once or twice, in a labor paper in Chicago in 1878.
9. See Chap. XVII, 545–47.
10. For a modern—and oblique—acknowledgment of this historical pattern, see the *Wall Street Journal*, Aug. 26, 1975, p. 1.
11. Ray Marshall and Allen Thompson, "Economies of Size and the Future of Black Farmers," paper presented to the Workshop on the Development Potential of Black Land, Duke University, Dec. 6, 1974. For literature demonstrating the relatively small scale of operation required to optimize efficiency—even in the post-World War II era of mechanized farm operations—see J. Patrick Madden, *Economies of Size in Farming*, U.S. Dept. of Agriculture, Economic Research Service, Agriculture Economic Report No. 107 (Washington, D.C., 1967).
12. See Chap. XVII, 516–21.
13. In 1943 the resettlement program, long under attack from large-unit farming interests within the Department of Agriculture, from large-unit farming interests in the Farm Bureau Federation, and from Congressmen responsive to the lobbying power of large-unit farming interests, was killed. See Lester Salamon, *Land and Minority Enterprise: The Crisis and the Opportunity*, a Report to the Office of Minority Business Enterprise, U.S. Department of Commerce (Washington, D.C., 1976); and Salamon, *The Time Dimension in Policy Evaluation: The Case of the New Deal Land Reform Experiments*, Sage Professional Papers in American Politics (Beverly Hills, Calif., forthcoming in 1977).
14. U.S. Congress, Senate Committee on Government Operations, *Disclosure of Corporate Ownership*, Staff Report of the Subcommittee on Budgeting, Management

and Expenditures, 93rd Congress, 2nd session, March 4, 1974 (Washington, D.C., 1974); U.S. Congress, House Committee on Banking and Currency, *Commercial Banks and Their Trust Activities, Emerging Influence on the American Economy*, Staff Report for the Subcommittee on Domestic Finance, 90th Congress, 2nd session, July 8, 1968 (Washington, D.C., 1968).

While, as a policy matter, it is clear that there were defects, and an antidemocratic bias, in the administration of many democratic land programs of the New Deal, the pattern is historic. For similar defects in the original homestead acts of the nineteenth century, see Paul W. Gates, *History of Public Land Law Development* (Washington, D.C., 1968), 402–15. For additional background on the land and credit problems of the South, see Arthur Raper, *Preface to Peasantry* (Chapel Hill, 1935). For continuing peonage in America, see Pete Daniel, *The Shadow of Slavery* (New York, 1972).

15. See Appendix B. Following the defeat of Populism, the cultural isolation of monetary reformers was sufficiently complete that very little needed to be said to safeguard prevailing customs and institutions. Indeed, since serious interest in structural reform passed out of the mainstream American reform tradition in the 1890s (see Chap. XVII), very few persons in Washington or elsewhere, other than specialists, have had even a perfunctory understanding of the central component of the economy—commercial banking. Thus it was routine for the rare advocate of a more democratic banking system to be dismissed as "a crank" or as a proponent of "funny-money." The most obvious example, of course, is the long and futile career as a banking reformer of the chairman of the House Banking and Currency Committee, the late Congressman Wright Patman. So effective was the banker's cultural campaign against Patman that virtually the only Americans who took him seriously were a handful of reform-minded—and massively outnumbered—monetary specialists.

APPENDIX B

1. See especially Esther R. Taus, *Central Banking Functions of the United States Treasury, 1789–1941* (New York, 1943), 49–50, 135.

2. Government land banks had their origin in England during the debate over the chartering of the Bank of England: "The landed gentlemen in the House of Commons were no more, than were and are any other agrarians, able to see why they should not borrow as easily and cheaply as traders or financiers." Joseph A. Schumpeter, *History of Economics Analysis* (New York, 1954), 295 (hereafter cited as Schumpeter, *Economics Analysis*). On the U.S. history of land loan proposals and their relationship to the greenback movement, see Sidney Fine, *Laissez Faire and the General-Welfare State: A Study of Conflict in American Thought, 1865–1901* (Ann Arbor, 1956), 305–6, 309. Firmly rooted in the antimetallist tradition, the first proposal was made in 1693 and was popularized in John Law's 1705 proposal for a land bank, which was to make loans in legal tender notes (Schumpeter, *Economic Analysis*, 295–96).

Plans for government loans or currency issues in legal tender notes secured by commodities also have a long history. Populists, themselves, were aware of the use of tobacco and turpentine currencies in colonial America, "assignats" issued against confiscated property during the French Revolution, and the apparent success of commodity currency in France during a financial crisis in 1848–49 (Tracy,

325–26, 390–92, 397; Tindall, *Populist Reader*, 85–86). To this list might be added one of the earliest plans for a commodity currency, that of the noted Italian economist, Ferdinando Galiani, in 1751, especially noteworthy because its author was a staunch metallist; Galiani proposed the issue of "living together" money, a community currency consisting of warehouse receipts for commodities. (Schumpeter, *Economic Analysis*, 292; Filippo Cesarano, "Monetary Theory in Ferdinando Galiani's *Della Moneta*," forthcoming in *History of Political Economy*, 1976). As early as 1662, Sir William Petty advocated, as a remedy for "scarcity of money" problems, the establishment of "public-loan banks" to accept deposits, among others of "cloth, wool, silke . . . and other durable commodities" (Douglas Vickers, *Studies in the Theory of Money, 1690–1776* (Philadelphia, 1959), p. 29).

3. The original "Report of the Committee on the Monetary System," introduced at St. Louis in 1889 and included in the Ocala (1890) and Omaha (1892) platforms, is reprinted in George B. Tindall, *A Populist Reader* (New York, 1966), 80–96.

4. For a brief biographical sketch of Tracy, see p. 219.

5. "Appendix: The Sub-Treasury Plan," in James H. (Cyclone) Davis, *A Political Revelation* (Dallas, 1894), 292–399. For Tracy's role in the development of cooperative theory in the National Alliance, see pp. 138–39. Other Populist writings on the sub-treasury included S. M. Scott, *The Sub-Treasury Plan and the Land and Loan System* (Topeka, 1891); and C. C. Post, "The Sub-Treasury Plan," *The Arena*, 1892, 342–53.

6. "Standardized" means they could be graded objectively by quality, while "storable" means they are subject to little or no deterioration while stored. Such are the commodities traded on centralized commodities exchanges and for which there are markets for "futures" (i.e., future delivery).

7. While these have frequently been referred to as "crop loans," that terminology is avoided here to avoid confusion with loans secured by unharvested crops (also called crop-liens), the principal lending activity of furnishing merchants.

8. Tracy, 298.

9. Tindall, *Populist Reader*, 88.

10. Post, *The Sub-Treasury Plan*, 349, and Tracy, 300. The accuracy of the calculation of currency per capita in 1865 is amazing, since, *circa* 1890, there were no comprehensive estimates of either currency outside banks or population in non-census years. Friedman and Schwartz's recent estimate of currency outside banks in mid-1865 is $736.1 million, and the Bureau of the Census estimate for the population is 35.7 million, yielding currency per capita of $48.50. Milton Friedman and Anna J. Schwartz, *Monetary Statistics of the United States* (New York, 1970), 225 and U.S. Bureau of the Census, *Historical Statistics of the United States, Colonial Times to 1957* (Washington, D.C., 1960), 7.

11. R. B. Hassell, "The Independent Party and Money at Cost," *Arena* (1891), 348–49. Other plans called for 2 per cent loans.

12. Post, "The Sub-Treasury Plan," 345–47, 350.

13. John D. Hicks, "The Sub-Treasury: A Forgotten Plan for the Relief of Agriculture," *Mississippi Valley Historical Review* (1928), 360.

14. See especially U.S Congress, House of Representatives. Committee on Ways and Means, *Report, System of Subtreasuries*, Aug. 5, 1892 (Washington, D.C., 1892).

15. The House Ways and Means Committee had observed that, under the 1892 bills, a speculator could buy $100,000 in commodities, use them as collateral for an $80,000 loan at 1 per cent interest, which could then be used to buy commodities qualifying for a $64,000 loan, etc., until a total of $500,000 had been purchased,

$400,000 of which was financed by loans at 1 per cent interest (pp. 3–4; the Committee made arithmetical errors, which have been corrected here).

16. Hicks, "Sub Treasury," 366–67. Tracy proposed that two or more counties could form a single sub-treasury district. (Tracy, 347–48). Further, Tracy provided for direct sales by sub-treasuries to buyers and for an impossible rule for determining the value of a commodity for either loans or redemptions: the current price adjusted by what the price would be if the public's currency holdings were $50 per capita instead of the then prevailing $15 per capita. (Tracy, 349–50). Again, the estimate of $15 per capita is amazing, given the lack of data for population and currency outside banks. For 1893, the year before Tracy's piece was published, currency per capita was $14.93, based on Friedman and Schwartz (p. 341) and Bureau of the Census data (*Historical Statistics*, 7). Writing in the depths of the severe 1894 recession, he evidently would not have had a crude quantity theory interpretation for his pricing rule, in which case it becomes indeterminate except in the context of a complex model of the economy. This kind of problem is dealt with subsequently.

17. Tracy, 380. Tracy estimated the cost savings at about 30 per cent.

18. *World Commodities and World Currency* (New York, 1944), viii. See also his *Storage and Stability: A Modern Ever-normal Granary* (New York, 1937). In the latter he noted (p. viii) that the word "pecuniary" is derived from *pecus*—cattle.

The sub-treasury plan and its underlying arguments have a variety of relationships to the many theoretical positions current in the eighteenth and nineteenth centuries. To wit:

1. Free silver, greenbacks, and national bank notes (see Chap. I). It was largely on political grounds that the Populists became allied with the silver and greenback causes (for greenbacks, see Chap. V; for silver, Chap. XIV). While unlimited purchases of silver, against which silver certificates would be issued or coins struck, is an application of the "depository principle" underlying the sub-treasuries, no loans were involved: the government became the owner of the silver stocks, silver prices were to be set above market prices, and the only charge would be for "brassage" (minting costs). On the other hand, greenbacks and national bank notes were backed only by the general creditworthiness of the government, as opposed to commodity reserves (e.g., Post, *"The Sub-Treasury Plan,"* 350–51; Hicks, "Sub-Treasury Plan," 360–61. See also the discussion above of "money at cost" vis-à-vis national bank notes. To a metallist, the value of greenbacks is supposed to be related to their "image of convertibility," i.e., the prospects for future redemption in specie.). Indeed Tracy suggested that there were three ways to increase currency in circulation: through appropriations, gifts, and loans; taxes and greenbacks are in the first category and sub-treasury issues in the last (Tracy, 303).

2. The "real bills" doctrine and the simple quantity theory of money. These are essentially contradictory views about the ultimate causes of changes in the money stock and in the price level and output. (The standard references on the development of these doctrines in the nineteenth century are Lloyd W. Mints, *A History of Banking Theory in Great Britain and the United States* (Chicago, 1945), and Jacob Viner, *Studies in the Theory of International Trade* (New York, 1937), Chaps. III–V. (For an interesting discussion of the doctrines which relates them to contemporary controversies, see A. B. Cramp, "Two Views on Money," *Lloyds Bank Review* (July 1962), 1–15.) The "real bills" doctrine or, as it is sometimes called, the "commercial loan theory of banking" is the fruit of the English Banking

School and saw its greatest victory in the passage of the original Federal Reserve Act in 1913 (many of the subsequent amendments to the act were necessary to remedy deficiencies in the doctrine). A "real bill" is a loan, the proceeds of which are paid in money to the borrower, which makes possible the production of goods that otherwise could not be produced for lack of working capital financing; when the goods are sold, the proceeds are used to repay the loan, and money and credit then go down. For example, a farmer needs funds to buy seed and fertilizer, to pay or otherwise sustain his hired hands, to rent equipment, and to meet his own living expenses in order to produce a crop to sell; he may finance himself out of the previous year's sales proceeds, he may borrow from a bank, or he may borrow from another lender (e.g., a crop-lien from a furnishing merchant), who, in turn, either draws on his own capital or borrows from a bank. Such a loan is "real" because it is accompanied by real output, and it is "self-liquidating," since it yields output, the sale of which generates the proceeds to repay the loan. To keep the goods moving through manufacturing and wholesale and retail sales requires a chain of subsequent working capital loans until finished goods are sold to consumers. In the "real bills" doctrine, lenders at any stage of production are passive accommodators of the "needs of business," and money, credit, and output go up and down together, so prices are not affected. The trick is for the banking system (directly or indirectly) to satisfy all the "needs of business," or recessions and depressions may result; when these needs are met, the currency is said to be "elastic."

At first glance, the sub-treasury would appear to be consistent with the "real bills" doctrine: sub-treasury agents stand passively ready to store and make loans in legal tender notes on all new produce presented and to withdraw such notes when crops are redeemed (land loans, of course, are not "real bills"). Unfortunately, only one link in the necessary chain of "real bills" is satisfied. The farmer still needs his working capital financing in order to have a crop to deliver. He uses his loan from the sub-treasury to repay his creditors or to finance his crops next season, so it is doubtful that, on balance, any increase in active currency outside banks results. When the crops are redeemed, the sub-treasuries impound the proceeds; for the goods to keep moving requires new money and credit for dealers, manufacturers, etc. (The failure to view the commodity loans in this larger context has resulted in gross miscalculations of what the plan would accomplish—see, for example, Hicks, "Sub-Treasury Plan," 362.) Finally, the purpose of the sub-treasury loans is to stabilize commodity prices seasonally, rather than to stimulate output.

On the other hand, many writers have contended that the Populists were, "for the most part, advocates of the quantity theory of money," the diametric opposite of the "real bills" doctrine (Fine, *Laissez Faire and the General-Welfare State,* 309; see also Hicks, 362 ("the quantity theory of money to which the farmer economists pinned their faith"). The quantity theory is the monetary theory from the English Classical School heritage, more particularly the Currency School. To a quantity theorist, in the 1890s the ultimate source of money stock changes is either outside actions by the Treasury or the central bank or a variety of "shocks" e.g., gold discoveries, legislation, or changes in the balance of payments. (This is the central thread in, *inter alia,* Milton Friedman and Anna Jacobson Schwartz, *A Monetary History of the United States, 1867–1960,* Princeton, 1963). Such actions or shocks are transmitted by "active," profit-maximizing banks into money stock changes, which, while they may have transitory effects on output and employment, eventually affect only nominal (as opposed to "real") variables—e.g., price levels, money incomes, and market interest rates. Output and employment, except in the very short-run, are determined entirely by real forces. Involuntary unemployment and output at less than the economy's capacity are solely due to "market imperfections," i.e., too few or too large buyers and/or sellers in product and labor markets or government interference (e.g., price controls); reductions in the money stock may temporarily have an adverse effect on output and employment, but subsequent downward movements in prices will soon neutralize this effect.

Advocates of the sub-treasury lamented, in the People's Party platform itself, the slow growth of currency and the secular fall in prices over the three decades after the Civil War. The total money stock grew too slowly to offset the decline in income velocity (or increased demand for money), so prices fell. (One can, of course, argue that the increased demand for money was the result of the deflation, since falling prices may induce the holding of money to take advantage of still lower prices in the future.) The remedy for what Macune called the chronic "depressed condition of agriculture" was to reflate through land loans, the proceeds of which were to be paid in legal tender notes. The result was expected to be both higher output and prices. Since the constraints on output may be interpreted as "market imperfections" (e.g., non-competitive private credit sources), then the reasoning is consistent with the simple quantity theory.

3. Underconsumption theories of the business cycle. In response to criticisms that low agricultural prices and the depressed state of agriculture were due to overproduction, the standard Populist response was to blame underconsumption, i.e., insufficient demand for consumption goods because both of the money shortage and the effect of excessive interest and transportation costs on eventual food and cotton prices. (W. Scott Morgan, "Over-Production—The Law of Supply and Demand," in Tindall, *Populist Reader*, 14; Tracy, 363, 377–78, 381, 385, and Chap. VII, herein.) For a survey of underconsumption theories, see Gottfried Haberler, *Prosperity and Depression*, 4th ed. (Cambridge, Mass., 1958), Chap. 5. With the writings of John Maynard Keynes in the 1930's, the underconsumption (or oversaving) theory of recessions and depressions came to enjoy considerable repute, and it would be tempting to call Populists forerunners of the theory. It is, however, probably more accurate to put them either with classical Say's Law ("supply creates its own demand") economists, to whom demand can only be deficient because of market imperfections, or to monetary theories of the business cycle, in which underconsumption is a symptom of deflation (Harberler, *Prosperity and Depression*, 120, 353–54).

4. Cartalists, inflationists, and the antimetallist tradition. Cartalism, which dates back at least to Plato, is the antithesis of metallism, asserting that the value of money is not derived from the commodity value of the metals (or other commodities) into which it is convertible. Inflationists were eighteenth-century cartalists who advocated money stock increases not constrained by gold or silver reserves in order to stimulate output and employment; they were, in fact, early greenbackers. (Vickers, *Studies in the Theory of Money*, Chaps. 7–9; Schumpeter, *Economic Analysis*, 288–99). Advocates of the sub-treasury plan, as some of them were careful to point out, do not belong to this tradition. (As Tracy, pp. 325–26, put it: "Some ignorant or unprincipled people try to compare this plan to the John Law [inflationist] scheme . . . when the facts in the case show unerringly that there is not one feature of similarity between them.") Legal tender notes issued with land

loans and commodity loans were redeemable in land and commodities, not future promises to pay in metals. Basically, buying for and selling from government stockpiles, with money issues directly related thereto, would stabilize prices at full employment and stabilize the intertemporal use of commodities.

19. See n. 45. There was, however, considerable discussion of "money substitutes" (bank deposits), generally to criticize their availability in rural areas (see Hassell, "The Independent Party and Money at Cost," 350–51); Hassell argued that the legal tender notes were similar to certified checks).

20. Computed from Federal Reserve data in *Banking and Monetary Statistics*, (p. 34); from 1892 to 1900 the ratio of currency to the conventional money stock exhibited the secular decline that was to continue well into the twentieth century, the result of the growth of commercial banking.

21. To make the actual computations lurking behind these figures, it is necessary also to know that the ratio of currency to the broad money stock (M-2 in Table 2) was 0.208. The $3.3 billion would all be in the monetary base (currency outside banks and bank vault cash).

22. See Friedman and Schwartz, *A Monetary History*, 51–53. Even restricting the use of legal tender notes to certain kinds of transactions or to certain holders would merely force the adjustments elsewhere by displacing unrestricted liquid assets.

23. 1894 was an exception, when the ratio of bank vault cash to deposits rose substantially—see Friedman and Schwartz, *Monetary History*, 120–23. See also note 20 above. Assuming the ratios were invariant to cyclical factors altered by the implementation of the land loan plan is a drastic oversimplification but one that would be very difficult to improve.

24. For example, the National Alliance platform of 1890 and the People's Party platform of 1892.

25. *Historical Statistics*, 7; Friedman and Schwartz, *Monetary Statistics*, 405, 413. Currency in circulation (bank vault cash plus currency outside banks) passed $5.1 billion also in 1918 (Friedman and Schwartz 405). See n. 45.

26. Friedman and Schwartz, *Monetary Statistics*, 341; *Banking and Monetary Statistics*, 34.

27. *A Monetary History*, 705–74. Friedman and Schwartz have since interpolated Robert E. Gallman's estimates for ten year averages for the net national product (gross national product less capital goods used up in producing GNP) and kindly supplied the author with their data.

28. According to the Douglas-Stinebower estimate of the unemployment rate in manufacturing and transportation, 1892 had the lowest rate (3.7 per cent) in the 1890–1900 period. Paul Douglas, *Real Wages in the United States, 1890–1926* (Boston, 1930), 445.

29. E.g., see L. R. Klein and R. S. Preston, "The Measurement of Capacity Utilization," *American Economic Review* (March 1967), 34–58.

30. Similarly, the figures for 1891 and 1890 are obtained by dividing the succeeding year figures by 1.05.

31. E.g., see David E. W. Laidler, *The Demand for Money: Theories and Evidence* (Scranton, Pa., 1969). An example of institutional influences on the demand for money are the timing and frequency of wage and salary receipts vis a vis bills due. Behavioral influences include the rates of return on money substitutes and non-money assets and the state of confidence in the payments system (chiefly banks).

32. A recent survey is Edward Foster, "Costs and Benefits of Inflation," *Studies in Monetary Economics*, No. 1 (Federal Reserve Bank of Minneapolis, 1972).

33. In the actual computation of the third column in Table 4, the price index with

$50 currency per capita ($P_{50}$) was estimated from net national product with $50 currency ($Y_{50}$), net national product at full employment (Y_f), and the index of actual prices (P_a) as follows:

$$P_{50} = \frac{Y_{50}}{Y_f/P_a}$$

The denominator is full employment income valued at actual prices.

34. In other words, the purchasing power of payments of interest and principal fixed in dollars would fall in inverse proportion to the increase in prices and spending.

35. See, for example, William P. Yohe and Denis S. Karnosky, "Interest Rates and Price Level Changes, 1952–69," *Review,* Federal Reserve Bank of St. Louis (Dec. 1969), 18–38.

36. Friedman and Schwartz, *A Monetary History,* 23.

37. Data are from *Banking and Monetary Statistics,* 408.

38. Actual data were obtained from Friedman and Schwartz, *Monetary Statistics,* 341. Full employment figures were computed from Table 3, Friedman and Schwartz' velocity estimates (*A Monetary History,* 774), and from ratios of actual currency to M-2 and vault cash to deposits (*Monetary Statistics,* 341).

39. Gresham's Law derives from Sir Thomas Gresham's advice to Queen Elizabeth I not to introduce an issue of new full weight coins at par with old worn coins, as the latter would drive the former out of circulation. The law is most frequently applied to bimetallic (gold and silver) standards, as there is generally a discrepancy between the mint and the commodity market ratio of the values of the two metals, which causes one of them (the one undervalued at the mint relative to the market) to be driven from use as money.

40. Friedman and Schwartz, *A Monetary History,* 25–9.

41. It is interesting that in some parts of the country prices were quoted in gold dollars, with payments in greenbacks requiring a premium, while in other sections prices were in greenbacks, with payments in gold commanding a discount (p. 27).

42. *Historical Statistics* 564–65. Beginning about 1958, the trade surpluses were more than offset by long-term capital outflows, causing the U.S. to lose gold and foreigners to pile up short-term capital in the U.S. (e.g., bank deposits).

43. William P. Yohe, Book Review in the *Journal of Finance* (June 1973), 770.

44. *Historical Statistics,* 126–27. The consumer price index for "food at home" is available for the entire period and was used to make this observation.

45. The subtleties in the functioning of a fractional reserve banking system were not widely understood, even by economists, until the 1920s.

46. This was the so-called "Keynesian revolution" associated with J. M. Keynes, *The General Theory of Employment, Interest and Money* (New York and London, 1936). Cf. Tracy, 333–34.

47. Keynes, *op. cit.,* 371. Keynes' praise was specifically directed toward an underworld army of mercantilists and under consumptionists, who were denied academic respectability during the days of economists' preoccupation with the optimality of a competitive market mechanism.

APPENDIX C

1. Milton George (ed.), *Western Rural Yearbook: A Cyclopedia of Reference* (Chicago, 1886), 130–43. Roy V. Scott, "Milton George and the Farmers Alliance Movement," *Mississippi Valley Historical Review*, XLV (June 1958), 90–92.
2. *Western Rural*, Nov. 20, 1886; Scott, "Milton George and the Farmers Alliance Movement," 92–99; Hicks, *Populist Revolt*, 96–101; Saloutos, *Farmer Movements in the South*, 77; Bryan, *Farmers Alliance*, 57–58; Taylor, *The Farmers' Movement*, 214–16.
3. *Western Rural, 1880–1886*; Barnhart, "Alliance in Nebraska," 22–24; Scott, "Milton George," 100–104; Hicks, *Populist Revolt*, 101; Saloutos, *Farmer Movements*, 79.
4. *Dallas Mercury*, Nov. 19, 1886; *Western Rural*, Nov. 20, 1886; Barnhart, "Alliance in Nebraska," 29–30; Saloutos, *Farmer Movements*, 78–82; Scott, *Agrarian Movement in Illinois*, 35; George claimed the Texas Alliance as part of his membership from 1886 until the merger meeting in 1889!
5. *Proceedings*, National Farmers Alliance (Minneapolis), Oct. 6–7, 1886; *Proceedings*, Inter-State Convention of Farmers (Atlanta), Aug. 1887, 32–33; Clarksville (Texas) *Standard*, Sept. 1, 1887. For a review of membership totals, see Chap. VI, n. 8 and n. 10.
6. J. M. Thompson, "The Farmers Alliance in Nebraska," *Proceedings & Collections of the Nebraska State Historical Society*, Second Series, V (Lincoln, 1902), 201; Barnhart, "Alliance in Nebraska," 169.
7. Jones, quoted in *Southern Mercury*, April 4, 1889; John Powers quoted (in June), in Barnhart, "Alliance in Nebraska," 175. The 1889 meeting produced the first political statement by the Northwestern group, a vague and almost plaintive appeal for the Congress to "improve" the Interstate Commerce law and increase the volume of the currency. The brief document did not contain specific suggestions about how the latter was to be done, however (Ashby, *Riddle of the Sphinx*, 414–15). *Kansas Farmer*, Jan. 31, 1889, contains an account of Terrell's speech before the Northwestern Alliance in Jan. 1889. Details of the proceedings reveal the vague manner in which Northwestern Alliance leaders had by this time begun exhorting the membership to "cooperate"—almost as if the topic were being addressed for the first time: "There is a very decided disposition among Alliances to cooperate in the purchase of supplies as well as in the selling of farm products, thus dispensing with, as much as possible, the expensive luxury of middlemen. In some localities an extensive plan of cooperation of Alliances in this direction is in successful operation and is giving satisfaction" (*Proceedings*, National Farmers Alliance (Des Moines), Jan. 10, 11, 1889. Also see *Kansas Farmer*, Feb. 14, 1889 and Barnhart, "Alliance in Nebraska," 31. The officers did not venture into a discussion of county trade committees, cooperatively owned warehouses, suballiance business agents, or, needless to say, central state exchanges or even state agencies for purchasing. That part of Terrell's address that related to the cooperative movement must have mystified everyone, leaders and delegates alike. For Jones's response to the Northwestern group, see *Southern Mercury*, April 4, 1889. Macune had journeyed to the Midwest to confer on merger possibilities as early as January, 1888.
8. The helplessness of the Northwestern Alliance may be detected in Scott, *Agrarian Movement in Illinois*, 41–45.
9. The organizational potential in the Midwest in evident from one comparative figure; the cooperatively organized FMBA recruited 40,000 members in southern Il-

linois and Indiana by 1889; George's group had no more than 1000 in the same region.

10. *Western Rural,* Jan. 16, 1892. The conduct of Milton George is quite consistent, of course, if he is not regarded as an organizer-spokesman for insurgency which, indeed, he was not.

11. Ashby, 417–19; Dunning, 133.

12. J. H. Sanders, Iowa state president, to L. H. Weller, Jan. 19, Aug. 24, 1892, Weller Papers; August Post, in E. A. Allen, *Life and Public Services of James Baird Weaver* (Richmond, 1892), 396–405; Ashby, 4, 400.

13. Ashby, 353–87; *National Economist,* April 27, 1889.

14. *Proceedings,* Iowa State Farmers Alliance, Des Moines, Oct. 29–31, 1890; Oct. 13–15, 1891; Oct. 11–12, 1892; Henry Loucks to L. H. Weller, April 27, 1891; Jonathan Shearer to Weller, April 29, 1891; August Post to Weller, June 19, 1891; *National Economist,* Feb. 14, 1891; Ashby, 400, 417–19; Lyons (Kansas) Republican, Aug. 9, 1888; Barnhart, "Alliance in Nebraska," 173–75, 428; St. Paul (Minnesota) Pioneer Press, Feb. 12, 1890; *Proceedings,* Nebraska State Farmers Alliance (Grand Island, Neb.), Jan. 7–8, 1890.

15. Will Sargent to L. H. Weller, April 16, 1891; J. H. Sanders to Weller, Dec. 8, 1891; Ashby, 393. For a sample of the rather severe intellectual and political limitations of the Northwestern leadership, see Will Sargent to L. H. Weller, Feb. 16, 1891. Sargent was the state lecturer of the Iowa Alliance.

16. See p. 650, n. 34, and pp. 263, 315.

17. *Proceedings.* . . . Omaha, Jan. 27–29, 1891.

18. Chaps. VII, VIII, and IX.

19. See Chap. VIII, n. 39, pp. 651–53.

20. Jay Burrows to James Baird Weaver, May (n.d.) 1896, quoted in Silvers, "Antecedents of the Campaign of 1896," 211–12.

CRITICAL ESSAY ON AUTHORITIES

1. Richard Hofstadter, *The Age of Reform: From Bryan to F.D.R.* (New York, 1956), 19–20, 30–35, 62–63, 70–76, 81–85.

2. Norman Pollack, *The Populist Response to Industrial America* (New York, 1962), 85–143.

3. Pollack, 13–84. But, for an author who defends the extreme right wing of the movement, Populism "emerges" in curious raiments—as a crypto-Marxist institution (11–12, 85–102).

4. For the Pollack-Hofstadter controversy at its inception, see Norman Pollack, "Hofstadter on Populism: A Critique of 'The Age of Reform,' " *Journal of Southern History,* XXVI (1960), 478–500.

5. Arnett, *Populist Movement in Georgia,* 76.

Acknowledgments

In the course of nine years of research and writing, one acquires a number of substantial debts to colleagues, archivists, and friends. It is a pleasure to acknowledge this assistance publicly, though in my case such a modest display of gratitude in no way constitutes fair reciprocity for the help I have received.

If a national mass movement can be said to have had one moment in time that was symbolic of a decade of passionate striving, that moment for the agrarian revolt surely came on June 9, 1888, "the day to save the exchange." Nell Goodwyn searched for and discovered every extant source bearing on that frantic summer of effort when the dream of the cooperative commonwealth met its first critical test in Gilded Age America. It was but one of her many intuitions about the dynamics of democratic movements that went into the shaping of this inquiry. This study of American Populism has, from its inception, been a joint enterprise of the two of us.

My colleague at Duke, Peter Wood, has been an understanding and creative critic over many months. His suggestions are strewn through the manuscript and my debt to him is a special one. This is also true of William Chafe, who not only helped me to fathom the Populists, but from time to time, as my preoccupation with the Gilded Age impinged, good naturedly shouldered more than his share of the burdens of our joint Oral History Program at Duke.

This work would not have been possible without the initial encouragement, now so many years past, of William Goodman of New York, Roger Shattuck of the University of Virginia, and—especially—John Silber of Boston University. I thank each of them.

Bruce Palmer, Harry Boyte, John Cell, and Robert Durden each read most or all of the manuscript and made suggestions that materially enhanced the narrative, including parts they did not agree with. Carey Goodwyn, B. T. Bonner, and Robert Calvert have been encouraging in ways only close friends can be. My indebtedness to another friend, Elizabeth Airth, is very great. She freely volunteered her time, her rich archival expertise, and her democratic sympathies. Two young but now quite experienced researchers, Wade and Laurie Goodwyn, gave up many hours of their time going through card catalogues, xeroxing Gilded Age documents, and—since this endeavor lasted long enough for them to become teenagers—offering political advice. Helen Goodwyn and Bill and Jo De Reese have also been understanding and supportive.

While it would be a challenge to acknowledge adequately the assistance I have received from library staffs in a number of places, especially in the states of the West and South, I particularly wish to express my gratitude to Emerson Ford of Perkins Library at Duke University for his five years of meticulous and good-hearted assistance. He is a man of Populistic generosity. Similarly, Thelma Kithcart, when not transcribing oral interviews, found the time, poise, and good humor to decipher my handwriting and type the entire manuscript. She is a woman of Populistic tenacity. My editors at Oxford University Press, Caroline Taylor and Sheldon Meyer, both put their stamp on this effort, Caroline in the text and Sheldon in the title. I am much appreciative of the sense of personal engagement they brought to our joint undertaking.

The unattributed sentence in the frontispiece is a paraphrase from E. P. Thompson, and was suggested by his book, *The Making of the English Working Class.* Material from the Ignatius Donnelly Papers is quoted by permission of the Minnesota State Historical Society and material from the Marion Butler Papers and the Leonidas Lafayette Polk Papers by permission of the Southern Historical Collection at the University of North Carolina. It is also a pleasure to acknowledge the special efforts of the Wisconsin State Historical Society, the Kansas State Historical Society, the staffs of the newspaper collections at the libraries of the University of California at Berkeley and the University of Texas at Austin, the Oral History Collection at Columbia University, and the Shomberg Collection of the New York Public Library.

Finally, I wish to express my deep gratitude to Mrs. Susie Roligan of Calvert, Texas, for the manuscript material and personal information that she graciously provided on her father, perhaps the most intrepid Populist of them all, John B. Rayner.

April 12, 1976   L.G.
Durham, N.C.

Index